# ISSUES IN CHILD PSYCHOLOGY

Second Edition

# ISSUES IN CHILD PSYCHOLOGY

## Second Edition

Edited by

## Dorothy Rogers

**State University of New York
College at Oswego**

**BROOKS/COLE PUBLISHING COMPANY**
**Monterey, California**

A Division of Wadsworth Publishing Company, Inc.

Printed in the United States of America

10 9 8 7 6 5 4 3 2 1

Library of Congress Cataloging in Publication Data

Rogers, Dorothy, 1914–        comp.
    Issues in child psychology.

    Includes bibliographical references and index.
    1.    Child psychology—Addresses, essays, lectures.
I. Title.
BF721.R633      1977      155.4′08      76–28503
ISBN 0–8185–0193–6

Manuscript Editor: *Margaret Tropp*
Production Editor: *Joan Marsh*
Interior and Cover Design: *John Edeen*
Photographs: *Jim Pinckney*

# Preface

This volume is organized around 19 important issues in child psychology, with two or more selections relating to each. The introduction to each issue contains a brief statement of its significance and current status. The student who wishes to explore any topic in greater depth should refer to the references accompanying the articles and to the editor's suggested readings.

Several criteria were used in choosing the articles. When an issue is polarized into two relatively distinct positions, in most cases the articles represent these two points of view. When an issue is more complex, embracing a variety of intertwined, only roughly differentiated aspects of the same general issue, articles have been chosen that portray the overall picture, indicating where the controversial pieces fit into place. In general, the authors included in the book either have been parties to a controversy or have covered an issue in an especially lucid manner.

The second edition of this book has been completely revised and updated. Only the general outline and a few comments in introductions to issues remain of the first edition. Every reading has been written within the past half-dozen years. Several new topics have been added, including alternatives in child education, concepts of work and play, children's rights, alternative families, and systems of child rearing.

Unfortunately, space limitations have required omitting many excellent articles altogether and abridging some of those retained.

However, every effort has been made to preserve intact the author's main thesis and ideas. In a few cases, only a specific section of a longer article has been used, because of its special relevance to the question.

Books of readings in general, and readings about issues in particular, have certain special merits. Although textbooks may provide excellent summaries, space limitations prohibit the inclusion of primary-source materials, except for brief excerpts. By contrast, a book of readings exposes students to a broad range of the authentic, undiluted ideas of outstanding experts and researchers in the field. The limited resources of many small libraries preclude access to certain of these important articles. Even the larger libraries lack the multiple copies that permit large numbers of students to study the same articles within a sufficiently compressed period to permit group discussion.

A book of readings about issues has additional merits. When students are presented only one point of view in a textbook, they may succumb to the notion that anything is true because it is in print or because "the author says so." But when they read opposing views on the same issue, each by an acknowledge authority, they come to realize that topics can be viewed in several ways, perhaps none completely right or wrong. Moreover, in a fast-changing world of shifting values and relativism, students must learn to deal with points of view in the process of formation.

Hopefully, students will be helped to think about issues critically and to perceive knowl- **V** edge as dynamic, not static. By choosing certain issues for further study and utilizing the references and suggested readings, they learn to dig deep into specific questions. Finally, the acquisition of knowledge via the issues approach is inherently more exciting to students than is a mere survey of noncontroversial subject matter.

It is not expected, intended, nor even desired that students will assume a position after reading the brief excerpts provided. Since only a sampling of views is given, students should guard against accepting any of these views as definitive. The very fact that a topic is still at issue indicates that it is not yet fully resolved. Certainly, the articles presented here do not contain all possible ways of viewing each question. However, students will have been provided a sound basis for further reading and discussion about the subject, as directed by the instructor. In fact, they should come to view their positions as permanently tentative, in the sense that they should remain open-minded to evidence.

This book is the companion to another book, *Child Psychology*, by the same author and publisher. That book contains chapters concerning 14 areas of child psychology. Each book can of course stand alone, but the two together provide a thorough and up-to-date coverage of the issues and major concerns of child psychology.

I would like to acknowledge the helpful suggestions given at the manuscript stage by Professors Ethel Adams of Glassboro State College, Gregory Fouts of the University of Calgary, and Jeanene Pratt of Oregon State University. I would also like to thank Cherie Blanchard and Ann Hoefer for their typing help and Margaret Tropp for editing the manuscript.

*Dorothy Rogers*

# Contents

Contents

# 1

# Heredity versus Environment

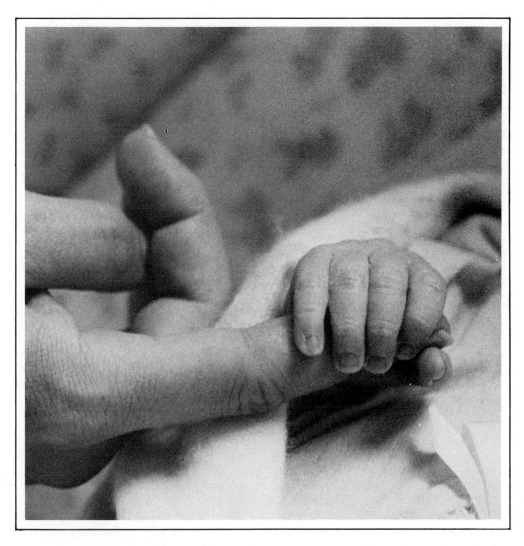

Notions about the relative impact of heredity and environment are part of our popular folklore and professional heritage. Traditionally, the hereditarian has been a sort of genetic determinist, who believes that heredity writes the script enacted by the individual over a lifetime, whereas the environmentalist has claimed almost limitless modifications of heredity by environment. The hereditarian position is implicit in such expressions as "Blood will tell," the environmentalist's in the saying "As the twig is bent, the tree's inclined."

A characteristic of child psychology has been the tendency for the pendulum to swing from one extreme to the other. Thus we tend to think of heredity or environment as primarily responsible for human behaviors. After publication of Darwin's *Origin of Species* (1859), great emphasis was placed on heredity. However, with the advent of the behaviorists, and thereafter until about mid-century—in fact, with diminishing emphasis, until now—the environmentalists have reigned supreme.

Efforts to estimate the heritability of behavioral characteristics often involve comparing same-sexed dizygotic (DZ), or fraternal, twins and monozygotic (MZ), or identical, twins (Beck & Rosenblith, 1972). The most striking findings from such studies have been in the medical and psychiatric fields. Identical twins are much more similar than are fraternals with regard to several mental diseases and length of life (Kallman, 1961). Since MZ twins have the same genetic makeup, variations between members of a pair of MZ twins may be attributed to environmental causes. By contrast, variations between members of DZ pairs include both environmental and genetic factors. Hence, if the variation between MZ twins is less than that between DZ twins, the difference can be attributed to differences in genetic factors. However, the data on such studies do not explain how genes operate or what genes are operating. They only indicate whether genetic factors are operating and roughly how much of the total variation is genetically caused.

## ENVIRONMENTAL INFLUENCES

Several factors have contributed to the environmental emphasis, one being the anthropological studies that demonstrated what great variations human behaviors may assume. Animals, the environmentalists admit, are the victims of their instincts; but humans have relatively few stereotyped responses and possess great capacity to learn. Another factor has been the need—derived from a broad spectrum of social, political, and historical influences—to conceive of all persons as one big happy family, identical genetically except for the genes determining appearance; anyone who suggests the existence of other differences, however innocuous, is branded a racist.

Further impetus to environmentalism has come from perinatal research, primarily with animals. It has confirmed the fact that the appearance of a trait at birth is no proof of its genetic origin. Instead, it may have resulted from some prenatal influence. For instance, an infant's emotionality at birth may be due to tranquilizers given the mother during pregnancy. Research with animals has also shown how prenatal environmental factors may permanently and dramatically modify the organism. On the other hand, among humans it has been shown that certain congenital defects, supposedly incurable, are susceptible to treatment.

Other characteristics commonly accepted as genetic may derive, to some extent, from environment. For example, Provence (1970) rejects the common view that maturation is simply the unfolding of prestructured, internally programmed, genetic capacities. Instead she believes that certain common features in the child's physical and social environment result in many experiences that at least partly account for infants' regular development.

## HEREDITARY INFLUENCES

Despite the continuing dominance of environmentalism, heredity is still a factor to be reckoned with. Each organism, says the hereditarian, contains patterns and outlines of its future. Despite the strongest environmental stresses, children seem to possess a tough essence that often enables them to resist the most stringent environmental pressures (Macfarlane, 1952).

Other research has identified specific traits as especially durable, among them activity level and degree of introversion-extroversion (Willerman, 1973; Schuckit, Goodwin, & Winoker, 1972). The activity levels of identical twins correlate more highly than do those of fraternal twins. In addition, activity level shows some continuity through early infancy and childhood (Willerman & Plomin, 1973). Genetics may also influence dominance. Among pet-reared dogs, terriers prove more dominant than beagles. If dogs are raised in isolation, the same pattern holds. However, when an isolate beagle or an isolate terrier is paired with a pet-reared beagle, the pet-reared beagle then becomes dominant (Fuller, 1970).

Genetics also help to explain and treat clinical syndromes, including propensity to alcoholism. The incidence of alcoholism is higher among individuals who had alcoholic natural parents but were raised by nonalcoholic foster parents than among others who did not have alcoholic natural parents but were raised by alcoholic foster parents (Schuckit et al., 1972). Also heritable are the rate of acquisition, retention, and extinction of conditioned fears. We are much less certain about genetic contributions to normal behavior (Beck & Rosenblith, 1972).

Heredity contributes differently to different roles and functions. Differences in susceptibility to stress and preference for alcohol, as well as in motivation and temperament, are strongly affected by heredity. General intelligence is more heritable than are special abilities and personality traits, although hereditary factors play a part in these, too (Gottesman, 1960). Other factors such as height and aging depend largely on heredity, but may be modified by environment to an unknown extent.

Heredity's relationship to mental disorders is confusing. If one of a pair of identical twins becomes schizophrenic, there is an 86% chance that the other one will develop the disorder, too (Eysenck & Prell, 1951). However, the only neuropsychiatric disorder that is clearly hereditary is Huntington's chorea, which involves a chronic mental deterioration. The part that heredity plays in determining psychoneurosis—a serious incapacitation arising primarily from nonorganic causes—is more indirect and less certain. Perhaps the role of heredity in such disorders is largely one of inherited predisposition. That is, inferior or mutant genes may distort one of the body's biochemical systems, which in turn reduces an individual's resistance to a particular disorder. Thus the individual who gives way under stress may have remained healthy under more benign conditions.

Heredity certainly contributes more to some traits than to others. It plays its greatest part in physical traits, and a lesser, but still important, part in personality. It sets limits on an individual's ultimate development, although those limits are broader, and the potential influence of environment far greater, than once believed.

## STATUS OF CONTROVERSY

For some years the long-standing heredity-environment controversy was muted; many authorities had decided that it was not possible to decide which factor was more important. Development, they said, was a function of both, interacting with each other. However, one prosaic and one more dramatic factor rekindled interest in the controversy. For one thing, discoveries in genetics have proceeded apace, compelling a certain respect for hereditary influence, at least among those who remained abreast of the field. For another, in 1969, Arthur Jensen published a lengthy article in the *Harvard Educational Review* in which he claimed that differences in intelligence by race are largely due to hereditary factors. In America's racially tense environment, Jensen's article kindled a spark that broke into flames of controversy. A few scientists supported Jensen, while the majority condemned his data as unscientific, his attitude as racist, and his conclusions as erroneous and dangerous.

Of late, the dust of conflict has settled again, and most psychologists have reaffirmed the earlier conclusion that pursuing specific ratios of hereditary-environmental influences is futile. According to Hirsch (1970), "the plain facts are that in the study of man a heritability estimate turns out to be a piece of 'knowledge' that is both deceptive and trivial" (p. 98). Perhaps the most broadly accepted hypothesis can be summed up as follows: Heredity and environment do not combine "in a static, additive fashion." Instead, "human and animal behavior [is] a process of constant change in which genes and environment are components of a reciprocal feedback system. Thus, the proportional contribution of heredity to the variance of a given trait varies under different environmental conditions. Similarly, under different hereditary conditions, the relative contributions of various environments will differ" (Elias, 1973, p. 125).

Current behavior geneticists also note that only genes can be inherited. Since their influence on behavior is always indirect, the question to ask is how, rather than how much,

heredity and environment influence behavior. However, many questions remain. For example, exactly what do we mean by *heredity*? What is the functional relationship between constitutional and environmental factors throughout the process of development? What implications does available knowledge in this area have for child rearing?

In the following article, David Krech, Richard Crutchfield, and Norman Livson provide a succinct formulation of the nature-nurture problem, representing the generally accepted view of the topic today. Much evidence relative to the heredity-environment controversy has derived from twin studies; hence, the interpretation of this type of research, with special reference to personality, is especially relevant.

The second article, which reports a conversation with Jerome Kagan, indicates that environment can effect very important modifications in personality. In fact, cross-cultural comparisons, such as those provided here, dramatically demonstrate how malleable the human personality is.

## REFERENCES

Beck, S. L., & Rosenblith, J. F. Constitutional factors in behavior. In J. F. Rosenblith, W. Allinsmith, & J. P. Williams (Eds.), *The causes of behavior: Readings in child development and educational psychology.* Boston: Allyn & Bacon, 1972.

Elias, M. F. Disciplinary barriers to progress in behavior genetics: Defensive reactions to bits and pieces. *Human Development,* 1973, *16*, 119–132.

Eysenck, H. J., & Prell, D. B. The inheritance of neuroticism: An experimental study. *Journal of Mental Science,* 1951, *97*, 441–465.

Fuller, J. L. Genetic influences on socialization. In R. A. Hoppe, G. A. Simmel, & B. C. Milton (Eds.), *Early experiences and the processes of socialization.* New York: Academic Press, 1970.

Gottesman, I. I. *The psychogenetics of personality.* Unpublished doctoral dissertation, University of Minnesota, 1960.

Hirsch, J. Behavior-genetic analysis and its biosocial consequences. *Seminars in Psychiatry,* 1970, *2*, 89–105.

Jensen, A. How much can we boost IQ and school

achievement? *Harvard Educational Review*, 1969, *39*, 111–112.

Kallman, F. J. Psychogenetic studies of twins. In S. Koch (Ed.), *Psychology: A study of a science.* New York: McGraw-Hill, 1961.

Macfarlane, J. *Research findings from a twenty year study of growth from birth to maturity.* Mimeograph, University of California, Institute of Child Welfare, 1952.

Provence, S. The complexity of infant development. *Children,* 1970, *17,* 31–32.

Schuckit, M. A., Goodwin, D. A., & Winoker, G. A study in half siblings. *American Journal of Psychiatry,* 1972, *128,* 1132–1136.

Willerman, L. Activity level and hyperactivity in twins. *Child Development,* 1973, *44,* 288–293.

Willerman, L., & Plomin, R. Activity level in children and their parents. *Child Development,* 1973, *44,* 854–858.

# Formulation of the Nature-Nurture Problem

## David Krech
## Richard S. Crutchfield
## Norman Livson

The recognition that our behavioral traits result from the interaction of heredity and environment has changed the formulation of the nature-nurture problem. We no longer speak of the nature-nurture controversy (heredity *versus* environment). The questions we ask assume, at the outset, that both heredity and environment are involved. The three questions of concern to research workers in the field are: First, what

proportion of variation in any given trait in a group of individuals is determined by heredity and what proportion by environment? Second, what is the specific nature of the genetic mechanism responsible for the inheritance of behavior tendencies or traits? Third, how much difference can variations in the environment make in traits that are partly determined by heredity?

With regard to the first question, the relative importance of heredity and environment is seen in terms of the average contribution of each factor in a population living in a particular environment. Let us elaborate on this point. Within a given individual the relative importance of heredity or environment can be very far from the average value. Thus, whatever we know regarding this value with respect, say, to intelligence, is utterly irrelevant to an individual who is unfortunate enough to possess the single extra chromosome that has been found to be responsible for the severe mental retardation known as "trisomy-21." Here, heredity plays a massive dominant role, and the child is doomed to be intellectually defective. Yet, even aside from such extreme cases, it is clear that hereditary intellectual endowments, as well as intelligence-stimulating environments, vary enormously in the general population, so that, for a given person, we are unable to say to what extent his intellectual attainment is attributable to heredity on one hand and to environment on the other.

Furthermore, rarely can we pinpoint, as in the case of trisomy-21, the exact genetic element that is responsible for a given behavioral outcome, particularly in human beings. Our inability to do so does not preclude experimental investigation of the genetic influence upon various behavioral phenomena, as we shall see in the following discussion of behavior genetics.

The answer to the third question is implicit in the preceding discussion. Again, we must caution that whatever result we obtain can apply only to a certain population of organisms in general. Take the realm of personality as a broad example. Without going into details concerning the influence of heredity upon various personality traits, the potential influence of environmental variation on a given facet of personality depends heavily upon the hereditary base on which this variation impinges. Thus, the interaction between an inherited potential for schizophrenia and the environmental forces that can prevent or promote the emergence of this disorder is crucial. Lacking the supposed hereditary susceptibility, even the worst of psychological environments will not result in a schizophrenic breakdown. But, given the genetic potential, some people will become schizophrenic, and others will not, depending upon the stress present in their environments. Thus, when we speak of genetic influences on behavior, it is critical to remember that, apart from hereditary defects resulting from the presence of trisomy-21 or of specific genes that cause extreme mental deficiency, most hereditary traits are not exhibited in an all-or-none fashion. Generally, genetic factors are predisposing elements; any behavioral outcome is necessarily a varying blend of what was given at conception and the environmental forces that have since operated upon it. The organism's inheritance at times may set limits—often quite broad ones—on how widely a trait can range but only very rarely does its presence determine its precise nature.

This theme of continual interaction between nature and nurture, with its almost inevitable guarantee against a rigid link between genes and behavior, is a fortunate, and even an indispensable, aspect of man's development as an individual and as a species. Most changes that have been observed in the nature of humankind's existence on earth throughout written history are the outcome more of extraordinary environmental modifications than of genetic factors. As the geneticist Dobzhansky (1967) has observed:

> The preponderance of cultural over biological evolution will continue or increase in the foreseeable future. We would not wish this to be otherwise: adaptation to environment by culture is more rapid and efficient than biological adaptation. Moreover, control of the cultural evolution is achievable probably more easily than control of the biological evolution.

This is not to assume that we have ceased to evolve biologically and that all cultural evolution builds upon the same distribution of genotypes as existed at our beginnings. Even if no other factors were operative, the simple fact that each new set of parents throughout time represents a potential for new and unique genetic combinations would ensure continuing biological change. The relation of genetic potential to expressed behavior poses many interesting questions; the field of behavior genetics has undertaken their investigation. . . .

## HEREDITARY FACTORS

There is convincing evidence that genetic constitution plays some role in determining individual differences in intelligence among persons of the same background. The data on genetic determination of the nonintellective aspects of personality are not as clear. For one thing, the available measures of intelligence are better validated and more widely accepted than are the measures of most personality attributes. And, in general, less research work has been done on the inheritance of personality. Nevertheless, the available evidence does seem to indicate that heredity plays a powerful role in influencing certain aspects of personality. Possibly most influenced is "temperament," a term that refers to such facets of personality as mood, reactivity, and energy level. In this general area animal breeders have something of interest to tell us. They have long been aware, for example, of the marked differences in temperamental characteristics of animals of various breeds and strains. Some breeds of dogs are placid, others skittish and easily upset. Carefully controlled studies in behavioral genetics confirm this picture.

### Studies of Kin Resemblance

Similar studies with human beings are understandably lacking, so that we must rely on less direct lines of evidence. Foremost among them are studies of kin resemblance, that is, studies of the degree to which *relatives* of the people we are interested in show similar personality characteristics. The major limitations of these studies is that environmental similarity usually goes along with genetic similarity. Children of the same parents tend to be exposed to the same family atmosphere, so that any resemblance in personality among them may not be regarded as exclusively reflecting hereditary factors. We all know children who take after their parents, but this fact alone, when it is indeed a fact rather than a family myth, can by itself confirm nothing about the extent of genetic influence.

Comparisons of fraternal and identical twins do provide some useful clues, however. For example, Gottesman (1963) finds that identical twins are more alike in personality on several scales of the MMPI and the CPI than are fraternal twins. Other investigators (e.g., Nichols, 1965; Schoenfeldt, 1968) report similar differences for adolescent twins—identicals versus fraternals—on various personality and interest questionnaires, though the computed heritability estimates for such measures are not highly consistent and are considerably lower than for ability measures.

But to interpret these findings as evidence for a hereditary factor assumes that the *environments* of identical twins are no more similar than are those of fraternal twins. When we consider such facts as the custom of dressing identical twins alike and the difficulty that even friends have in telling them apart (being therefore less able to treat them differentially), the assumption of no-more-similar environments is not easily supported. However, under certain circumstances and for certain personality characteristics an exception must be made.

An ingenious way to bypass the problem of possible environmental differences in the rearing of identical and fraternal twins has been indicated by Freedman and Keller (1963), who made monthly assessments of various physical, mental, and emotional characteristics of twins during the first year of life. The critical point of this study is that during the first year of life it is not at all obvious, without special tests, whether a given pair of twins is identical or fraternal. The parents of identical twins therefore could not have been treating them more alike throughout the first year than the parents of fraternal twins were treating their children.

For the same reason, the investigators could not accidentally introduce bias into their observations, bias that might make identical twins spuriously appear more alike than fraternal ones. Only after the year of observation was completed were the identical/fraternal differences diagnosed (by means of blood-group determinations) and only then was the degree of resemblance on various traits calculated, separately, for the now-known sets of identical and fraternal twins. The major finding of this study was that, for *every* characteristic measured, identical twins showed greater similarity than did fraternal twins, indicating at least some degree of hereditary influence throughout a broad sampling of traits.

Of course, if children are raised by other than their own parents, hereditary and environmental factors tend to be separated. If, furthermore, the children are identical twins reared in different families, the experimental situation for evaluating genetic influence is ideal. An effective study employing this design for personality traits was carried out in England by Shields (1962), who, through an appeal on a BBC television program, was able to locate forty-four pairs of identical twins who had been reared apart for a substantial period of time. Most had been separated by the age of six months, and the separation had endured for a minimum of five years. Primarily from this same source, Shields also located an equal number of identical twins whose homes had been the same throughout their childhoods. At the time the twins in both groups were assessed —through interviews, intelligence tests, questionnaires, and physical examinations—they ranged in age from eight to fifty-nine, although most were in their thirties and forties. Great care was taken to assure that the twins were indeed identical, employing such techniques as comparison of blood groupings, fingerprints, tendency to color blindness, and physical characteristics.

The outcome of this investigation strongly supports the influence of hereditary factors in the determination of a number of characteristics. Identical twins, whether raised apart or together, when compared to a third group of thirty-two pairs of fraternal twins, were very much more alike in almost all characteristics measured. For example, identical twins reared apart had an average weight difference of 10.5 pounds, whereas those raised together differed by 10.4 pounds. Contrast this similarity with an average weight difference between fraternal twins of 17.3 pounds. Similar results, that is, minimal differences between both sets of identical twins and substantial ones for fraternal twins, were also found for intelligence and for questionnaire measures of temperament. Even smoking habits showed this same kind of result: 78 percent of the separated twins were both either smokers or nonsmokers; 71 percent of the reared-together twins showed this similarity in smoking habits, but only 50 percent of fraternal twins were thus similar.

But the complexity of analyzing the intricate interplay of hereditary and environmental factors even in such twin studies is well demonstrated by a further and unexpected finding by Shields. It turned out that for certain personality measures, identical twins raised apart were actually *more* similar than were identicals raised together. That is, the effect of a common family environment for those raised together was to render them less, rather than more, similar. The reason for this seemingly paradoxical finding is probably that for those pairs living together the very fact of their twinship had an effect on their personality development. Slight initial differences between the twins in such interpersonal traits as dominance, influenceability, extraversion, etc., may have been magnified as they lived together and interacted. Analogous results were obtained by Wilde (1964), who found that fraternal twins raised apart resembled each other *more* than fraternals raised together with respect to scores for neurotic instability, extraversion, and self-critical versus self-defensive test-taking attitudes.

This general hypothesis, that interaction may lead to discordance between the twins in personality and behavior, seems to have been suggested first in 1883 by Sir Francis Galton,

who observed the tendency of one twin to be a leader. It has been further suggested that a differentiation of personality, or division of labor, occurs between twins, so that one acts as a sort of minister of foreign affairs for the pair, while the other assumes the role of minister of domestic affairs. A number of other publications dealing with twin relations are summarized by Koch (1966). They support the impression that there are traits that, despite a possibly high genetic component, are made discordant as a result of twins being raised together. When they are reared separately the genetic determinant of behavior apparently is given a better opportunity to manifest itself.

## REFERENCES

Dobzhansky, T. Changing man. *Science,* 1967, *155,* 409–414.

Freedman, D. G., & Keller, B. Inheritance of behavior in infants. *Science,* 1963, *140,* 196–198.

Gottesman, I. I. Heritability of personality: A demonstration. *Psychological Monographs,* 1963, *77*(9).

Koch, H. L. *Twins and twin relations.* Chicago: University of Chicago Press, 1966.

Nichols, R. C. The national merit twin study. In S. G. Vandenberg (Ed.), *Methods and goals of human behavior genetics.* New York: Academic Press, 1965.

Schoenfeldt, L. F. The hereditary components of the project TALENT two-day test battery. *Measurement Evaluation Guide,* 1968, *1,* 130–140.

Shields, J. *Monozygotic twins brought up apart and brought up together: An investigation into the genetic and environmental causes of variation in personality.* London: Oxford University Press, 1962.

Wilde, G. J. S. Inheritance of personality traits: An investigation into the hereditary determination of neurotic instability, extraversion, and other personality traits by means of a questionnaire administered to twins. *Acta Psychologica,* 1964, *22,* 37–51.

# Do the First Two Years Matter? A Conversation with Jerome Kagan

The theory that intelligence can be predicted during the first year or two of life—and that early learning deficiencies may be irreversible—has become increasingly popular among educators. Freud, Piaget, the learning theorists, the animal psychologists—all offered seemingly incontrovertible evidence in support of this theory. Jerome Kagan, Harvard University's highly respected human developmentalist, believed it too—until he discovered a tiny village in Guatemala where the children broke all the "rules" of development.

*SR:* What happened in Guatemala to make you reverse your thinking?

*Kagan:* I found myself in a thirteenth-century, pre-Columbian village, located on the shores of Lake Atitlan. I saw 850 Indians, poor, exploited, alienated, bitter, sick. I saw infants in the first years of their lives completely isolated in their homes, because parents believe that sun and dust and air or the gazes of either pregnant women or men fresh with perspiration from the field will cause illness. It's the evil-eye belief. So the infants are kept in the hut. Now these are bamboo huts, and there are no windows, so the light level in this hut at high noon in a perfectly azure sky is what it should be at dusk. Very dark. Although parents love their children—mothers nurse on demand and hold their infants close to their bodies—they don't talk or interact with them. And there are no toys. So at one and one-half years of age, you have a very retarded child.

Reprinted from "A Conversation with Jerome Kagan," *Saturday Review of Education,* April 1973, *1* (3), 41–43. Reprinted by permission.

*SR:* What are the children like?

*Kagan:* Not only are they quiet, somber, motorically passive, and extremely fearful, but on tests of maturational and intellectual development, they are four or five months behind American children.

*SR:* What kinds of tests do you use?

*Kagan:* Here's an example of a maturational test. Take a child nine months of age, cover an object with a cloth, and then, through sleight of hand, remove the object. We know from Piaget's work that if he pulls off the cloth and the object's not there, he shows surprise, indicating that he knows the object should be there. That ability should occur somewhere in the last third of the first year. None of the Guatemalan babies showed this until 18 months of age. We also know that babies in the Western world become frightened of strangers at about eight months. It's called "stranger anxiety." You won't get that [in Guatemala] until the middle of the second year. In the Western world children begin to talk between 12 and 18 months. The Guatemalan kids don't talk until about two and a half to three years. If I had seen infants like the Guatemalans in America prior to my experience, I would have gotten very upset, called the police, had the children removed, and begun to make gloomy statements about the fact that it was all over for these children.

*SR:* But they do recover.

*Kagan:* That's the paradox. The 11-year-olds in this Guatemalan village are beautiful. They're gay, alert, active, affective, just like 11-year-olds in the United States. They're *more* impressive than Americans in a set of "culture-fair" tests—where the words and the materials are familiar. For example, we asked them, "What is brown, hard, and found near the shore of the lake?" And they'd say, "a wharf." They have no problem with this. In reasoning, memory, inference, deduction, and perception, these children at 11—who, we must assume, were "ghosts" as infants—had recovered. Therefore, one must conclude that the first two years of life do not inexorably doom you to retardation and that there's much more potential for recovery than Western psychologists have surmised, including me. I didn't go to Guatemala to prove this; I found it a complete surprise.

*SR:* Don't the experiments that Harry Harlow

[a psychologist at the University of Wisconsin] conducted with monkeys contradict that conclusion?

*Kagan:* They did until last year, when Harlow published a very important report. He took monkeys and put them in isolation for six months, and they emerged with the expected bizarre, abnormal, crazy behavior. But this time he placed them with normal infant female monkeys three months younger than themselves for 26 weeks (seven months). He reports that after seven months they could not be distinguished from normal monkeys. If we can do this in seven months with a creature less complex than we, then certainly it does not require an enormous stretch of imagination to believe that in nine years a human infant, treated less bizarrely, can recover.

*SR:* Any human studies to support your findings?

*Kagan:* Freda Rebelsky spent several years in eastern Holland, where there is a middle-class, stable, nuclear family arrangement. In this small part of this very small country, it's local custom to isolate a child for the first ten months. He's put in a room outside the house; he's tightly bound—no mobiles, no toys, and minimal interaction. Like our Guatemalan children. He emerges at one year absolutely retarded, but at five years of age he's fully recovered.

*SR:* But what about René Spitz's [a professor of psychiatry at the University of Colorado] observations?

*Kagan:* Spitz made his observations on South American children in an orphanage. He saw ghostlike (what he called "marasmic") children much like the ones I saw. They lacked both stimulation and affection, so he made the same mistake many analysts have made and concluded their retardation was due to lack of affection. It's not the affection, because my infants in San Marcos are on their mother's bodies three-quarters of the day, and they get lots of physical holding, lots of skin contact. So it's not the love, but the input, that's important.

*SR:* If you kept the infant or the monkey deprived for a longer period of time, would there be permanent effects?

*Kagan:* We don't know. I am not saying that there is no treatment you can give a child from which he cannot recover. That is obviously too strong. We do have extreme case-history reports: for instance, a mother locked her kid up in a closet for six years. He emerged mute but still managed to learn language later. But I'm trying to be a reasonably cautious person. What I can say with confidence—and had I not had this experience, I would have resisted it—is that an abnormal experience in the first two years of life in no way affects basic intellectual functions or the ability to be affectively normal—to experience gaiety and sadness, guilt and shame.

*SR:* What implications do you see for American schools?

*Kagan:* I think my work suggests we've got to stop the very early, and, I think, premature rank-ordering of children in grades one, two, and three. We decide too soon. Poor children enter the school system (a) with less motivation, because they see less value in intellectual activity, and (b) one or two years behind in the emergence of what I call executive-cognitive functions (what Piaget would call concrete operational thinking). They are going to get there, but they are a year or two behind. We arbitrarily decide that age seven is when the race starts, so you have a larger proportion of poor than of privileged children who are not yet ready for school instruction. And then we classify them, prematurely. Let's use the example of puberty. Suppose we decided that fertility was important in our society and that fertility should occur at age 13. Then if you're not fertile at 13, we conclude that you are never going to be fertile, and we give you a different kind of life. It's illogical, because that 13-year-old who is not fertile now will be next year.

*SR:* In other words, learning does not follow the same pattern in every child.

*Kagan:* Yes. We used to think that all learning was continuous—like a "freight train." There is a series of closely connected cars: you start at car one and do certain things; then you jump to car two, and you carry your baggage with you. But now let me substitute an analogy that makes more sense: development as a series of lily pads. I choose that because lily pads are farther apart, because each child dumps a lot of baggage in traversing the lily pads (he doesn't have to carry everything with him), and because he can skip some of the lily pads. American psychologists have surmised that you could never walk unless you crawled. Now we know that is false. I could prevent a child from crawling—bind him up until he was two and then unbind him—and we know he would walk. He wouldn't have to crawl. Now maybe that analogy holds for a lot more in mental development than we have surmised.

*SR:* How has the public reacted to your rather optimistic conclusions?

*Kagan:* What I say is often misunderstood. When I say kids can catch up, people say that can't be right, because they know that a poor child always remains retarded relative to a middle-class child in the school system. But these people—most Americans—are confusing relative and absolute standards. Absolute retardation refers to a lack of certain fundamental motor, affective, and intellectual skills that are basic to our species. They include crawling, walking, standing, speaking, inference, and reasoning. Now if a child isn't walking by three, he is absolutely retarded. If a child cannot remember four numbers when he is ten years old, he is absolutely retarded.

*SR:* Then what is "relative retardation"?

*Kagan:* If kids don't have certain culturally arbitrary skills—like being able to read—they are retarded relative to some other reference group. When we say a Mexican-American child from a ghetto is retarded, we mean relative to that arbitrary reference which is the middle-class child. The analogy of physical development should make that distinction clearer. There are natural skills like walking or running which you get better at each year; if a child of ten cannot run as fast as a three-year-old, we worry about it. So it makes sense to say that this ten-year-old is physically retarded. But would we ever say that a ten-year-old who can't play hockey is retarded? Well, when it comes to intellectual skills, that's exactly what we do; we say if this child can't multiply, he is retarded. But multiplication is like hockey; no child's going to know how to multiply unless you teach him how to multiply. See the mistake we make? In the physical area we never confuse relative with absolute retardation. But in the mental area we do.

*SR:* Given the vast implications of your study, where do you plan to go from here?

*Kagan:* I want to see schools begin to serve the needs of society. Ancient Sparta needed warriors, Athens needed a sense of the hero, the ancient Hebrews needed knowledge of the Testament, nineteenth-century Americans needed managers and technicians—and the schools responded beautifully in each case by providing the kind of people the society needed. What do we need now? I believe that we need to restore faith, honesty, humanity. And I am suggesting in deep seriousness that we must, in the school, begin to reward these traits as the Spartans rewarded physical fitness. I want children rank-ordered on the basis of humanism as we rank-order on the basis of reading and mathematics. I'm dead serious. When I was a kid, deportment was always a grade. In a funny way, I want that, but instead of deportment, I want him graded on humanism: How kind is he? How nurturant is he?

*SR:* But aren't we getting back then to the same problem of sorting?

*Kagan:* Every society must sort its children according to the traits it values. We will never get away from that. A society needs a set of people whom it can trust in and give responsibility to for the management of its capital and resources, for the health of its people, the legal prerogatives of its people, the wars of its people. The function of the school system is in fact to prepare this class.

# SUGGESTIONS FOR FURTHER READING

Ausubel, F., Beckwith, J., & Janssen, K. The politics of genetic engineering: Who decides who's defective? *Psychology Today,* January 1974, pp. 31–32; 34–43. Genetic screening is discussed in terms of potential advantages and disadvantages against the background of recent findings on the topic.

Bakwin, H. Body-weight regulation in twins. *Developmental Medicine and Child Neurology,* 1973, *15,* 178–183. The genetic factor is often lost sight of in dealing with physical problems of children. For example, among 6- to 12-year-old children differences in body weight between identical twins are much less than between fraternal twins. The birth weight of fraternal twins is greater than that of identical twins. Thus genetic factors become important in controlling the body weight of children.

Elias, M. F. Disciplinary barriers to progress in behavior genetics: Defensive reactions to bits and pieces. *Human Development,* 1973, *16,* 119–

132. In broad perspective, provided by an inter-disciplinary approach to behavior, genetics is interpreted as essential for synthesizing relevant data and applying the resultant generalizations to societal needs. The essential question in the nature-nurture issue is how heredity and environment interact to influence behavior; hence, increasing stress is being placed on the underlying mechanisms of heredity-environment interaction.

Final round in the debate on heredity, race, intelligence, and environment. *Phi Delta Kappan,* 1972, *53*(7), 415–427. Diverse views concerning the heredity-environment issue, as related to IQ, are presented in articles by three well-known authorities: William Shockley, A. R. Jensen, and N. L. Gage.

Furth, H. G. Piaget, IQ and the nature-nurture controversy. *Human Development,* 1973, *16,* 61–73. Certain basic assumptions of IQ tests are analyzed and found incompatible with Piaget's theory. It is concluded that the concepts of heredity and environment cannot be statistically separated and that from Piaget's point of view, the nature-nurture controversy is simply devoid of meaning.

Gewirtz, J. L. Levels of conceptual analysis in environment-infant interaction research. *Merrill-Palmer Quarterly,* 1969, *15,* 7–47. This article concerns ways that theory and research might be improved in the study of environmental impact on child behavior.

Lin-Fu, J. S. New hope for babies of Rh negative mothers. *Children,* 1969, *16,* 23–27. The development of Rh immunoglobulin for the prevention of sensitization to the Rh factor may, within a generation, eliminate deformities in children of Rh-negative women. Related research and its implications are discussed.

Nichols, R. C. Nature and nurture in adolescence. In J. F. Adams (Ed.), *Understanding adolescence: Current developments in adolescent psychology* (2nd ed.). Boston: Allyn & Bacon, 1973. Literature is surveyed concerning the influence of genetic, school, and family factors on individual differences in adolescent intelligence and personality. The data indicate that inherited differences exert greater influence than does education on achievement and intelligence, and that the relative importance of heredity and environment in personality formation has not yet been decided.

Sarason, S. B. Jewishness, blackishness, and the nature-nurture controversy. *American Psychologist,* 1973, *28,* 962–971. The nature-nurture controversy is examined in terms of time perspective, social change, and historically rooted group attitudes.

Sinsheimer, R. L. Genetic engineering: The modification of man. *Impact of Science on Society,* 1970, *20,* 279–291. Sinsheimer predicts that the rapidly progressing field of molecular biology will, in the not so distant future, permit overcoming certain constraints of heredity and, to an extent, permit control of human evolution.

# 2

## Significance and Constancy
of the IQ

During the first years of the 20th century, there were many attempts to measure mental ability; and IQ, as derived from intelligence tests, came to be regarded as a basic human characteristic. Presumably all that was worth evaluating about mental development was subsumed in this measure. Only special talents, such as mechanical and artistic skills, were deemed not included. Counselors used IQ scores as a basis for curricular advice. School administrators used them to determine children's grade placement or to establish homogeneous groupings. Adoption agencies used them as a criterion for matching children with prospective foster parents.

Such applications are generally based on the assumption that a child's IQ, or intellectual potential, is constant. This so-called *constancy hypothesis* presumes the IQ to be stable over the years and not easily modified by experience. If the IQ were completely constant, a child's mental performance relative to that of others of the same age would remain about the same year after year. Constancy would also suggest that intelligence is largely hereditary, so that mental growth proceeds regularly according to some genetically pre-ordained design. Actually, no one argues that a child's IQ scores are completely constant, because all testing is subject to errors and all tests to weaknesses.

## THE CONSTANCY POSITION

Advocates of constancy in IQ point to the consistency of IQ and related mental traits. For example, measures of attentiveness—which test the infant's ability to maintain attention or to switch attention from familiar to new stimuli—taken at age 1 relate closely to IQ scores obtained from the same infants at age 4 (Lewis et al., 1966). Most efforts to raise IQ appear to have ended because impressive gains in IQ rarely last (Kaye, 1973). On the basis of such data, Jensen (1969) claims that compensatory education has failed and that IQ is mostly a matter of heredity.

Advocates of constancy ascribe fluctuations in IQ scores to flaws in intelligence tests, to testing error, or to emotional and motivational factors in the child being tested. Moreover, fluctuations in IQ may reflect differences in functions measured at different ages. Tests for very young children typically measure motor abilities, whereas those for older children involve relatively more verbal factors. Fluctuations may also occur when individuals under consideration are undergoing brief, atypical jogs in otherwise consistent mental-growth patterns. Moreover, say the constancy advocates, test items inevitably measure both innate capacities and those dependent on experience. However, even as presently constructed, tests have demonstrated considerable constancy, at least after infancy.

## THE ANTICONSTANCY POSITION

During the 1950s many researchers began to reassess the constancy hypothesis, and in time, the majority rejected it as invalid. If optimum experience is provided at proper stages, they decided, it can have an almost unlimited effect on an individual's effective mental capacities. Intelligence, they argued, matters only to the extent that it promotes environmental adaptations. And it is futile to debate what proportion of demonstrated abilities are innate.

The anticonstancy advocates can marshal an impressive array of evidence to support their position. According to McCall, Hogarty, and Hurlburt (1972), the relationship between mental status at 8 months and later IQ is not great. In other research (Irwin, 1972) children who attended a day-care preschool center for a year gained an average of 12 IQ points as compared to two points registered by a control group on the outside.

Apparently environmental influences have greatest impact in early years. In an extremely barren institution, or crèche, 28 children adopted before they were age 2 attained a mean IQ of 96; whereas 30 who were adopted between the ages of 2 and 4 never overcame their retardation (Bronfenbrenner, 1974). However, they did make gains in middle childhood, numerically equivalent to the years of adoption, and after a few years in adoptive homes, their average IQ reached 81. While those adopted early in life gained an average of 50 IQ points, experiential deprivation that persists after age 2 tends to limit mental growth permanently. Another 40 foundlings adopted after age 4, even after years of family life, attained an average IQ of only 77.

The apparent constancy sometimes reported can also be explained (Kaye, 1973). The IQ tests themselves were designed so as to focus only on those abilities that are least affected by experience, thereby leading to stable scores. In other words, claims for constancy are made in terms of IQ testing, although the constancy of IQ is built into tests in the process of their construction. Since only those items have been used that are most resistant to experience, IQs naturally show little increase after a program of compensatory education.

Other writers—for example, Bodmer—believe that there is no way, as yet, to determine the heritability or constancy of IQ (Bruner, 1974). On the basis of available data, Bruner believes that there is "a considerable element of hereditability in IQ" (p. 173). Nevertheless, adds Bruner, environmental intervention does improve intellectual performance and IQ. In fact, children's performance can be improved simply by improving mothers' interactions with their children. Where animals are concerned, genetic effects can be shown across many generations—for example, by inbreeding stocks of maze-dull and maze-bright rats. However, experience can make a difference, too: providing rats with early opportunities can make dull animals brighter, "possibly by increasing dendritic density in the cortex and changing conductivity in the central nervous system, by altering the metabolism of the acetylcholine and cholinesterase that conduct nerve impulses across synapses" (p. 173).

Of late the IQ controversy has largely subsided, and most educators today favor the anticonstancy position. For one thing, movements to end the suppression of racial and ethnic minorities have made the IQ concept and IQ testing extremely unpopular. For another, psychologists and educators themselves reflect an era that is dedicated to respecting individual differences and providing the best possible environment for all. Nonetheless, the question of whether or not IQ is constant within the individual over the years remains a matter of some consequence. If intelligence is inconstant, then the fallacy of placing children in tracks on the basis of mental ability would be obvious. Also, if an individual's IQ fluctuates over the years, he or she would have a hard time planning for a career. One might aspire to a career requiring a high order of intelligence for success only to find that one's IQ has diminished over time, and with it one's potential for successful competition. On the other hand, if IQ is relatively constant, one can afford to plan ahead in terms of tasks demanding particular levels of mental endowment.

A closely related issue concerns the heritability of IQ—whether it is determined primarily by heredity or by environment. In general, those who believe that IQ is largely a matter of heredity assume the constancy position, whereas environmentalists and interactionists (see Issue No. 1) believe the IQ modifiable, and hence lacking in constancy.

The readings that follow summarize and

interpret major research on these questions—David Krech, Richard Crutchfield, and Norman Livson on constancy of IQ and David Cohen on heritability of IQ. Cohen discusses uses that are made of IQ-test scores. Since the IQ concept has aroused so much controversy, one might infer that IQ scores play a large part in children's destinies. Such is not the case, concludes Cohen, and complaints by minorities who insist that IQ tests discriminate against them have reduced the tests' impact still further.

## REFERENCES

Bronfenbrenner, U. Developmental research, public potency, and the ecology of childhood. *Child Development,* 1974, *45,* 1–5.

Bruner, J. Book review: Eysenck's inequality of man. *Times Educational Supplement,* February 1974, pp. 170–176.

Irwin, T. How much can a six-month infant learn in school? U.S. Dept. of Health, Education, and Welfare, Office of Child Development, with permission from *Parade,* January 9, 1972.

Jensen, A. How much can we boost I.Q. and scholastic achievement? *Harvard Educational Review,* 1969, *39,* 1–123.

Kaye, K. I.Q.: A conceptual deterrent to revolution in education. *Elementary School Journal,* 1973, *74,* 9–23.

McCall, R. B., Hogarty, P. S., & Hurlburt, N. Transitions in infant sensorimotor development and the prediction of childhood I.Q. *American Psychologist,* 1972, *27,* 728–748.

# The Stability of IQ

## David Krech
## Richard S. Crutchfield
## Norman Livson

The major question that may be asked about the development of intelligence is: "How stable is intelligence over time?" It is known that mental age increases with chronological age, at least up to adolescence. However, there is still the question of whether or not IQ (mental ability *relative* to chronological age) remains the same for a given individual throughout his life. The basic question of stability of intelligence comprises two issues: first, the *average* trend of mental ability from birth to death in the general population; second, the constancy of IQ over time for a given individual. These issues have different theoretical and practical implications.

## AGE AND INTELLIGENCE

We have seen that *absolute* mental ability increases up to adolescence. However, beyond adolescence it is by no means obvious what trend, if any, is to be expected with age. What then is known of the fate of intelligence through the adult years?

### Cross-Sectional Studies

The general picture from *cross-sectional* studies (people of different age groups measured at a single point in time) is that intelligence reaches its peak about age thirty and then begins to fall off ever more rapidly as old age approaches. This observation is true (in Wechsler's terms) of both "verbal" and "performance" intelligence, although the former reaches its peak, for the average person, a few years earlier. In a pioneer report of cross-sectional data of age differences in IQ, Jones and Conrad (1933) anticipated what has proved to be a reliable generalization. They found that performance on tasks involving general information declines very little, if at all, with age; however, tasks in which rapid responses are critical do show a considerable drop. Sheer speed of response seems to figure in many mental-test tasks. Thus, some of the age-related decline may be attributable to a "non-intellectual" slowing down of the general pace of response as we grow older.

Furthermore, the cross-sectional method is susceptible to confounding factors. One has to do with the changing level in educational standards over time. This factor might be especially important for studies conducted before the advent of universal minimum-education standards in the United States. For example, it is known that less-educated people score somewhat lower on intelligence tests than better-educated people. If persons now aged sixty had received less education when they were young than present-day thirty-year-olds when *they* were young, a difference in tested intelligence between these age groups *might* reflect an historical trend in educational standards, rather than age changes per se.

A study by Tuddenham (1948) supports the reasonableness of this argument. He found that World War I and World War II soldiers (the latter with a higher average education) differed considerably in intelligence *when tested at the same age*. The World War II men scored higher, indicating that generational differences in educational standards may account for age differences in mental-test scores in cross-sectional studies.

Both of these studies point to the probability that intelligence, as measured by mental tests, does increase with longer exposure to formal education, and that even traditional schooling is effective in raising IQ. Consider then the distinct possibility that more effective educational techniques and maximum educational opportunities for all children may hold the promise of raising intelligence levels, scholastic success, and consequently occupational achievement.

## Longitudinal Studies

Longitudinal studies bypass this confounding of education level and age-related mental development by testing the intelligence of the *same* individual at two or more points in time. These studies, using representative samples of subjects over a wide range of intelligence, suggest that there is generally an increase in IQ during the adult years. Rigorous data on this came from three extensive longitudinal investigations, which included study of mental development from late adolescence up to age forty to fifty years. Two of these studies have mental test data on the same subjects going back to the earliest ages, some of which shall soon be reported. Honzik (1973), comparing IQ scores for Berkeley (California) Guidance Study subjects at eighteen and forty years, and for Oakland (California) Growth Study subjects at seventeen and forty-eight years, finds at the very least a maintenance of mental ability level, with strong indications that certain facets of intelligence do in fact increase over these age spans. Subtests measuring vocabulary, information, and comprehension showed significant gains into the adult years for both men and women. Another longitudinal study—the Berkeley Growth Study (Bayley, 1968)—showed similar results.

These subtests are all highly verbal and are closely related to academic success in the high school years immediately preceding the eighteen-year mental test. Girls at that age did less well than boys, but their increase to age forty brought them to a par with adult men. Honzik speculates that this earlier "disability" was a product of societal attitudes, which valued social over academic success for girls. As the feminist movement today would predict, women still hold to these values despite the fact that their actual performance has so improved. Typical comments of women at age forty, taking these mental tests about 1970, included "I've slipped" and "I haven't learned a thing since I left school." This led Honzik to note that: "A great deal of reassurance and approval was needed to give these women enough confidence to complete the test." Cultural (and therefore *self-*) expectations regarding mental ability can interfere with valid assessments of mental ability and therefore result in spuriously low estimates of intelligence in any group from which society expects relatively poorer performance.

Other longitudinal studies also indicate increases in mental ability into adulthood. In one instance, both men and women, spanning the average range of IQs, showed significant increases in intelligence between two mental tests given when they were about thirty and forty-two years old (Kangas & Bradway, 1971). They also report that for women, the lower the earlier IQ, the greater the gain in IQ. This once more supports the notion that women's mental-test performance—especially at younger ages—may be depressed by attitudinal factors. In the low IQ range, Charles (1953) followed up people who had been adjudged mentally deficient during their elementary school years. Those available for retesting at about age forty-two achieved an average IQ of 81. This was significantly above the initial mean IQ of 58 for these same people as children. Furthermore, Charles reports that the majority of this sample made social adjustments in their adult life—in marriage, parenthood, economic self-support—that could not have been anticipated from their earlier diagnosis of mental deficiency.

Charles' data of course do not directly demonstrate mental growth in the post-adolescent years, but they do contribute to a suspicion that should be growing in the mind of the alert reader—that IQ is neither a totally stable nor a totally predictable attribute characteristic of any individual.

Recent investigations indicate that the growth of intelligence does level off in later life and that there is some decline in intelligence in old age, although at quite different times for different tests and with enormous individual differences. In one study (Blum, Fosshage, & Jarvik, 1972) verbal abilities, as measured by a variety of mental subtests (vocabulary and information are examples), were found, on the average, to show some slight decline in eighty-year-olds. Even in the nineties the decline was quite moderate. The slight decline in verbal intelligence found in these advanced years refers to *average* scores; some people actually show increases in their eighties and nineties. Nonverbal subtests, especially those that heavily weight speed of response, do decline markedly in this age range.

Some recent research (Jarvik, Eisdorfer, & Blum, 1973) indicates that a certain pattern of change in mental ability may forecast death. Specifically, if there is a rather abrupt decline on three subtests—vocabulary, the ability to identify similarities between words, and speed and accuracy of matching numbers with symbols—then there is a substantial probability of dying within five years. This relation was found for aged subjects who were in reasonable physical health at the time of testing, and it is not at all related to the person's actual age. This pattern of decline may be due to certain brain function changes which presage death. These changes in brain function, or in oxygen supply to the brain, may be so subtle as to remain undetected by the usual physical tests currently available to the doctor. We may have here another instance of the generally valid observation: Behavioral and mental tests are more sensitive in detecting brain malfunctioning than are physical or physiological tests. Of course, to detect this ominous change, careful and repeated testing over a long period is needed; it most certainly cannot be detected by general observations of behavior or even by a single, however careful, mental test administered to the individual at any one age.

In summary, growing old, even very old, by no means brings about any massive intellectual decline. Most mental abilities hold up fairly well, and the abilities necessary to be informed and even wise are the sturdiest of all. The team of investigators from whom we have been citing evidence in this section have a moral to draw. They urge that

> A life-span investigation of intellectual changes should be approached in terms of individual differences in specific abilities and not in terms of "global intelligence." To ignore the individual variations is to fall into the perennial trap of lumping the aged together as having outlived their usefulness—instead of recognizing it is the individual, not the age, that makes the difference. (Blum, Jarvik, & Clark, 1970)

## STABILITY AND PREDICTABILITY OF INTELLIGENCE

Investigation of stability and predictability of intelligence is the exclusive preserve of longitudinal studies because such questions require repeated measurement of the same people over time. Not only do the data from such studies promise eventual understanding of adult changes in intelligence with age, but they also cast into a different light the apparent regularity of intellectual development implied by the average mental-growth curves. The fact that the *average* curve is smooth up through adolescence does not require the inference that all, or even most, children show the same regular progression in intellectual development. Quite the contrary is true; this regularity masks quite substantial changes in tested intelligence for many children during this period.

How stable and predictable is *an individual's* intelligence (as measured by mental tests) from birth to middle age? The answer to this question has been summarized by Honzik (1973) from the results of a number of longitudinal studies of normal individuals in cities all over the world. The findings are that test scores are highly predictive over short periods, but the longer the interval between tests, the less accurate the prediction. Also, the younger the child when given his first test, the less accurate the prediction. Thus, in the Berkeley Guidance Study, the correlation between IQs at age three and IQs at age five (a two-year period) is .54, but for the two-year period from ages twelve to fourteen, the correlation jumps to .90. *Infancy* presents a different situation since it is a period of rapid development of the brain and is marked by an increasing ability to process information from the environment. Mental tests given to infants during the first months of life give stable results for a few months, but gradually changes take place. The rate of such changes varies with the individual baby. This means that prediction from infant test scores to IQs in the preschool years is low, and prediction to IQs in the school years is negligible. The *preschool years,* from age two to five, constitute a period of marked increase in predictive power. A two-year-old's

test score has little predictive value, but the five-year-old's IQ significantly predicts IQs *at all future age periods, even to age forty.* This does not mean that all individuals maintain the same absolute level of functioning from ages five to forty years. Far from it. All it means is that on the average people tend to maintain their position *relative to their peers* from the age of five into middle age. That is, the brightest five-year-old of his group will tend also to be the brightest forty-year-old of the same group.

Even during the relatively stable school years (nine to eighteen), 85 percent of the children in the Berkeley Guidance Study varied ten or more IQ points on the eight tests they were given, and almost 10 percent of the children fluctuated at least thirty points. Although marked changes occur in some individuals, prediction during the mature years is fairly high. Correlations between IQs obtained in the late teens and IQs earned twenty to thirty years later are usually about .70.

Although very early mental tests do not predict later intelligence, the possibility remains that certain items or groups of items *can* predict later intelligence. A report by Cameron, Livson, and Bayley (1967) lends some support to this speculation. They find, for example, that a tendency to vocalize in infant girls substantially predicts later IQ (as late as age thirty-six), whereas the *total* score on infant-intelligence tests has *no* predictive value. Kagan (1971) also finds "unusual stability of infant girls' vocalizations" in his study of change and continuity in infancy. These results confront us once again with a challenge to the common view that intelligence is a unitary trait. In addition, the fluctuation of IQ arouses the suspicion that intelligence may be a heterogeneous assortment of separate abilities developing at different rates.

## REFERENCES

Bayley, N. Cognition and aging. In K. W. Schare (Ed.), *Theory and methods of research on aging.* Morgantown, West Virginia: West Virginia University Press, 1968.

Blum, J. E., Fosshage, J. L., & Jarvik, L. F. Intellectual changes and sex differences in octogenarians: A twenty-year longitudinal study of aging. *Developmental Psychology,* 1972, *7,* 178–187.

Blum, J. E., Jarvik, L. F., & Clark, E. T. Rate of change on selective tests of intelligence: A twenty-year longitudinal study of aging. *Journal of Gerontology,* 1970, *25,* 171–176.

Cameron, J., Livson, N., & Bayley, N. Infant vocalizations and their relationship to mature intelligence. *Science,* 1967, *157,* 331–333.

Charles, D. C. Ability and accomplishment of persons earlier judged mentally deficient. *Genetic Psychology Monographs,* 1953, *47,* 3–71.

Honzik, M. P. Predicting IQ over the first four decades of the life span. Paper presented at the biennial meeting of the Society for Research in Child Development. Philadelphia, 1973.

Jarvik, L. F., Eisdorfer, C., & Blum, J. E. (Eds.). *Intellectual functioning in adults.* New York: Springer, 1973.

Jones, H. E., & Conrad, H. S. The growth and decline of intelligence. *Genetic Psychology Monographs,* 1933, *13,* pp. 34; 192; 756.

Kagan, J. *Change and continuity in infancy.* New York: Wiley, 1971.

Kangas, J., & Bradway, K. Intelligence at middle age: A thirty-eight year follow-up. *Developmental Psychology,* 1971, *5,* 333–337.

Lewis, M. K., Kagan, J., & Kalafat, J. Patterns of fixation in the young infant. *Child Development,* 1966, *37,* 331–341.

Tuddenham, R. D. Soldier intelligence in World Wars I and II. *American Psychologist,* 1948, *3,* 54–56.

# Does IQ Matter?

## David K. Cohen

The last four or five years have not exactly been years of glory for American liberals. Some of the reasons for this—like the war or the President—are ephemeral. At least one other, however—the depressing performance of recent liberal social programs—probably is not. The poor record of the social legislation of the 60's has seriously shaken confidence in traditional liberal reform strategies, and since education has always occupied a favored role in those strategies, it has come in for a good share of the questioning. The apparent failure of programs like Headstart has raised doubts as to whether investment in education for the poor will promote equality.

Most commentators have responded to this development in a characteristically American fashion. The failure of earlier programs has been attributed to inadequate resources, indifferent professionals, or intractable bureaucracies. Reform can proceed, we are told, only when more money is spent, or when educational institutions are made more responsive, or when the professions are made more accountable. In response to apparent failure a whole new generation of optimistic proposals has sprung up.

A few critics of Great Society programs, however, have been less hopeful. Some ask whether education is in fact the mechanism by which the distribution of wealth, power, or status has been affected in America. If schooling has not promoted equality among whites, after all, it would be a little silly to expect it to do so for blacks. Others have asserted that the failure of educational programs owes more to the deficiencies of poor children than to the defects of their schools. If the sources of school failure among the poor are either habits of mind imposed by culture or intellectual barriers im-

Reprinted from *Commentary,* by permission. Copyright © 1972 by the American Jewish Committee.

posed by heredity, they argue, it hardly makes sense to spend money on school-improvement programs that rest on contrary assumptions.

Each of these two major lines of thought raises serious questions about received liberal doctrine, because each suggests that institutions or individuals are not malleable as we have hitherto assumed. But there has been greater fascination with the question of deficiencies in the poor than with the possible limits of schooling as an equalizing strategy. A few years ago, in an essay in the *Harvard Educational Review*, Arthur Jensen reviewed the evidence on group differences in intellectual ability and school achievement; everything showed large and consistent gaps among groups. On the average, children whose families were poor or black did much less well on tests than children whose families were well-to-do, or white. Jensen also pulled together a considerable body of research which suggested that differences in intelligence among individuals seemed to be caused more by heredity than by environment. And finally he ventured the idea that heredity may explain intellectual differences among groups as well as it appears to account for differences among individuals.

More recently H. J. Eysenck, a British psychologist, brought out a book which purported to subject Jensen's work to a critical assessment.* Although there is little indication of such assessment in this pot-boiler, it does support Jensen's appraisal of the research, as well as his speculation concerning the genetic sources of racial differences in IQ. Finally, a few months ago Richard J. Herrnstein, a Harvard psychologist, published an essay in the *Atlantic Monthly* which generated quite a stir. Herrnstein broadened, refined, and defended arguments laid down earlier. He maintained that what IQ tests measure is an important and stable human attribute. He marshaled evidence that IQ differences among individuals are mostly accounted for by genes, not by environment. And he pressed the idea that intelligence is an increasingly powerful influence

*The IQ Argument,* The Library Press, 156 pp. $5.95.

on the allocation of status, wealth, and power in advanced industrial societies. Although Herrnstein did point out the difficulty of generalizing from individual to group differences, his essay questioned the traditional liberal idea that stupidity results from the inheritance of poverty, contending instead that poverty results from the inheritance of stupidity.

These arguments, of course, are nothing new. The heritability of IQ first became a major public fixation in reaction to the turn-of-the-century deluge of poor European immigrants. It bubbled to the surface once again just after the *Brown* decision in 1954, when racial mixing in public schools seemed to loom on the horizon. And not surprisingly it reemerged when the disappointing results of recent school-improvement programs for the poor became known. As this little chronicle may suggest, recent attention to the subject is not wholly the product of scientific interest. While the heritability of IQ holds a constant fascination for psychologists and demographers, most of the time they are the only people who care enough about the matter even to mention it. Only when there are broader issues involving ethnic or racial minorities—in which the character of the culture, or the allocation of public resources, or the composition of society is at stake—does the relationship between genes and IQ reach the front page of anything other than arcane professional journals.

But while this may help us understand the recent interest in the IQ question as a social phenomenon, it doesn't say much about the arguments themselves. *Does* heredity account for most individual differences in IQ? Does it account for class and racial differences in IQ? Is IQ really a good measure of intelligence, or a good predictor of the things that make for success in America?

Of all these issues, the role of heredity in making for differences in individual IQ has been the most thoroughly probed. One way of approaching it has been to compare the intelligences of identical twins who have been raised in different environments. Since identical twins have the same genetic endowment in all respects, any difference in their IQ's that are not due to errors in measurement would presumably be traceable to differences in environment. In general, studies show that only about 20 or 30 per cent of the variation in the IQ's of twins can be attributed to variations in their environment—the rest is presumably due to heredity.

Another approach has been to compare the intelligence of unrelated children reared together. Since their genetic material can safely be assumed to have nothing in common, any relationship between their IQ's would probably be the result of environmental similarity. Studies of this kind have yielded roughly the same results as the research on twins—namely, that only about 20 to 30 per cent of the variation in IQ is attributable to environment.

This evidence is nothing to sneeze at, but it might easily be misinterpreted. For one thing, genes and environment may interact in ways which would lead to overestimates of genetic influence: a child with a low IQ will probably be treated accordingly, while a brighter child would get more stimulation. This could easily enhance the bright child's IQ while depressing the dull child's even further; in studies of the sort summarized here, such effects, which are really environmental, would all be marked down to heredity. The magnitude of effects like these has never been estimated, nor is it clear that it could be.

Another problem with the twin studies has to do with the distribution of environments. Identical twins reared apart are nearly as rare as hen's teeth, and constriction in the range of their environments might overstate the importance of heredity. However, while the environments studied do not fully cover the available extremes in the U.S. or Britain, the range was still pretty considerable. That is, in at least a few cases one twin was sent to Scarsdale to grow up, and the other to Hoboken.

But let us suppose that instead of going to Scarsdale one twin had been placed in some sort of super-enriched environment, absolutely booming and buzzing with the varieties of stimulation that psychologists regard as brain food. We don't know very much about the effects of changing the intensity of environments or of reversing inequalities in their distribution. The few small experiments that have been conducted here and there around the country suggest that certain varieties of stimulation do produce considerable IQ gains in disadvantaged children. Some of them, in fact, have produced gains of roughly the same magnitude as the gap which on the average separates the IQ of blacks and whites. These programs have involved either highly structured pre-schools or home-visiting programs designed to improve effectiveness of parents as teachers. They generally last about nine months or a year. In one experiment now under way in Milwaukee, however, children from poor families have been exposed to far more intense stimulation than usual. Instead of being visited by a teacher once a week, or being placed in a highly structured pre-school in the mornings, children and their families are absolutely bombarded with environmental stimuli. The initial results show quite phenomenal IQ gains—often on the order of thirty or forty points. It is much too soon to tell whether the gains will last. Evidence from other experiments indicates that as the experience recedes into the past so does its effect diminish. Three or four years after most such experiments end, researchers find that the gains have by and large vanished. No one knows what would happen if the experiments were more intense, or if they lasted for nine years instead of nine months. And for the immediate future, at least, these questions will remain unanswered.

One important point about all these studies, then, is that they show the malleability of IQ. But another is that the results are still compatible with the general pattern of findings on the relative influence of heredity and environment on IQ. Thus, to say (by way of example) that genes seem to account for 80 per cent of the variation among the IQ's of individuals is not necessarily to say that only 20 per cent of anyone's IQ is malleable. No one knows whether there is a "ceiling" on environmental effects or not, or what it might be.

All of this should be enough to persuade any sensible reader that the issue will never be resolved in the pages of COMMENTARY. Indeed, it would be astonishing if people ever stopped arguing about the relative influence of heredity and environment on individual IQ differences. Hereditarians will always point to evidence which shows that (things being what they are) more of the variability in IQ is explained by heredity, and environmentalists will always be able to point to evidence which encourages the belief that if environments were radically altered, IQ's might be sharply changed. Since these phenomena are not mutually exclusive and since experiments to test the limits of environmental effects are unlikely to be devised, the argument will probably continue for the next thirty years in much the same terms as it has for the last thirty.

The question of chief interest, of course, is not that of individual but of group differences. The sources of such differences, however, are not nearly so well illuminated by research. That there is a substantial gap in test scores between the races seems clear. What people want to know is whether the gap is a result of differences in heredity or environment, but the answer is hard to get at. The same conditions which make for interest in the question—the existence of large differences in both measured ability and social achievement—make it very difficult to decide where cause ends and effect begins. It is hard to figure out whether poverty causes low IQ or low IQ causes poverty, because they tend to occur in the same persons. The very people who are continually suspected of being genetically underendowed with respect to IQ have also been socially underendowed with respect to environment. This means, for example, that the full range of environmental differences that characterized native Wasps in the 1920's did not characterize immigrant Italians, and as a result it would have been well-nigh impossible to find comparable samples of Italians and Wasps on whom to conduct research.

The same holds for blacks and whites today. One can investigate the relative influence of heredity and environment among blacks, just as in the studies of white children summarized earlier. But such studies of black children would only tell us how much of the IQ variation among blacks themselves is due to heredity; they would not tell us how much of the gap in test scores *between* the races is due to heredity and how much to environment. We can imagine ways to get around this problem: study unrelated black and white children who were raised in the same home; or study a population of black and white adults who have had the same environments; or (as one wag has suggested) find several pairs of identical twins who have been reared apart and each pair of whom consists of one white and one black twin. But simply listing the examples reveals the problem: securing blacks and whites with the same environments is only a little easier than securing blacks and whites with the same natural parents. The environmental differences America has created between blacks and whites are profound and ancient, and they can be expected to endure for some time. Until such differences have become a thing of the past for at least some blacks, it is hard to see how respectable research can be done on the sources of the racial IQ gap. It is likely, however, that by the time such social equality is attained, either the environmentalists will be proved right by the disappearance of the IQ gap, or the very fact of social equality will cause everyone to lose interest in the question. Who now cares whether Italians have lower or higher IQ's than native white Americans?

Oddly enough, in most of the arguments about genes and IQ over the past thirty years much greater attention has been paid to the question of the relative importance of circumstances and heredity than to figuring out exactly what IQ means, or what it is good for. Most people with very high IQ's seem very stupid. But people in between—which is where almost everyone is—are full of surprises. The fact that the tests can distinguish extremes so evident in everyday life inclines one to believe they measure something important. The fact that things get unclear in the middle, however, should make one dubious as to the value of the measuring-stick for most of everyday life.

What do IQ tests measure? Some people naively believe they provide a summary index of a general human ability to cope, but this would appear unlikely: think of the psychologist next door who nearly became unhinged trying to put together a hi-fi kit, or of the university sociologists who lost their shirts running a consulting firm, or of the brilliant computer freak who is incapable of writing an intelligible English sentence.

There are psychologists who believe that IQ tests measure one dimension of some more general and unified underlying intelligence. Perhaps, but at the moment it is hard to know. Psychologists are not in agreement on the elements of this underlying intelligence, and available research shows that sometimes the elements in question are connected only weakly or not at all. In fact, IQ is about the only thing psychologists *have* learned to measure with much validity or consistency, and as a result good research on the relation between IQ and other aspects of intelligence or personality is not plentiful.

Finally, there are people who think that intelligence is simply the ability to perform well at whatever one's social situation seems to require. This is obviously true in some ways, but in extreme form the notion is not really useful at all. Does it make sense to say that Lewis Strauss was smarter than Robert Oppenheimer? Or to argue that a high-school student who flunked out and then became a successful numbers runner is just as smart as the valedictorian of his high school who couldn't get a job after graduation? Intelligence may not be timeless and unitary, but pushed to the extreme the relativist view dissolves in horrible contortions.

No doubt this debate could go on forever—in fact it probably will—but most people would not wish to pursue it. They assume a social definition of intelligence; they care about not what it is as a psychological construct, but how it works as a phenomenon in society. Indeed, many of those who worry about the proper definition of IQ do so chiefly because they think it is becoming the central criterion for distributing the good things of life. People care about IQ because they regard it as the basis on which society's rewards and punishments are allocated; they believe that America is becoming a society in which status and power are now, and will increasingly be, a function of brains.

This view is so widely held that it has become a sort of secular catechism. It certainly is repeated often enough, and in many different connections. Radicals attack America for allocating rewards on the basis of technical talent rather than need or human value; liberals bemoan the fact that discrimination has kept members of minority groups from competing on their own merits; Jews fear the demise of merit standards in employment and education, and blacks attack the standards themselves as racist. Conservatives used to attack merit standards too, on the ground that some things were more important than intelligence, but the fact that this argument no longer has enough credibility to be used in defense of privilege—it is now employed only on behalf of the poor—suggests how widespread is the belief that meritocracy is upon us.

In the light of this concern, the fuss over IQ is indeed as important as Professors Eysenck and Herrnstein believe it to be. However muddy the tests or biased their results, they exist; in a meritocracy of the sort we are said to have, such tests would undoubtedly be a major criterion for the allocation of rewards. The basic question, then, is whether, and how much, IQ counts in America in terms of status and power.

Perhaps the best place to begin is the schools. Schools, after all, are where IQ is supposed to have its greatest impact, because it is in schools that children get routed on the various educational tracks, which are presumed to play a considerable role in their chances for wealth and status later on. Really bright children are supposed to be routed into college preparatory work, and really not-so-bright children into vocational courses. Those in between are assigned to "general," business, or similar curricula. Then everyone graduates and goes to work, or drops out, or goes to college, and moves on to his appointed niche.

This picture is far from being wholly false, but it is by no means as true as most educators make it out to be. Take, for example, what is probably the most critical decision made during a child's school career: the kind of high-school program he will follow. In a perfectly meritocratic system based on IQ this decision would rest exclusively on test scores; in a perfect caste system it would rest exclusively on one's inherited status. In the United States things are much more confused. According to studies of curricula assignments of high-school students, measured ability is only one among several influential factors; others include the social and economic status of a student's family, his own aspirations for a career, and the degree of encouragement his parents have offered to those aspirations. The most comprehensive studies suggest in fact that these latter three influences on placement in high school are only slightly less important than measured ability.

Of course, a good deal happens to children in school before they even reach the point where decisions are made about their high-school curriculum. They are graded and grouped from the very beginning, and all of these classification procedures undoubtedly have some impact—if not on how children regard themselves at least on what the teachers think about them. But the assignment of children to ability groups, like the assignment to curricula, seems to be determined by all sorts of things in addition to IQ. And grades too seem to be influenced as much by the attitudes of the children, their behavior toward authority, and their general demeanor as by their test scores.

But the most important point is that all of these factors together—ability, aspirations, inherited status, etc.—account for less than half of the actual variation in the assignment of students to one high-school track or another. A majority of the differences among students in this respect, in other words, are caused by something other than either status or brains. This is not as odd as it might seem. Some of the differences probably arise from mistakes in assignments—bright children who want to go to college but lose out because of a slip or who are incorrectly assigned because of a perverse teacher. Some of the differences probably are caused by variations in the attitudes and motivation of the family, which seem to have a considerable impact on schooling decisions quite independently of parents' status or children's ability; lots of poor parents push their children very hard, and lots of non-poor parents don't. And some of the differences probably are caused by variations in deportment or motivation, or the encouragement students get

from teachers, or other factors that usually go unmeasured. In short, if we consider only measured intelligence or inherited status, we cannot explain most of the variation in placement of students in high school.

What is the relative importance of IQ and inherited status as far as getting into college is concerned? Here, after all, is one of the great divides in American life. A college degree is regarded increasingly as the only sure way to gain access to the good things in this society, and certainly college entrance is the goal toward which so much of the work of the schools is supposed to be aimed. How great a role does IQ play here?

If we look only at the relative influence of tested ability and inherited social and economic status, the available evidence does not show that college entrance is chiefly determined by academic ability. In fact, the relative importance of these two influences seems to be roughly equal. Consider, for example, a high-school senior whose family is in the lowest fifth of the population with respect to both social status and test scores. Not only is this young person less bright than at least 80 per cent of all high-school seniors, but his family is less affluent than at least 80 per cent of American families. In the early 1960's, he had roughly one chance in ten of entering college the year after high-school graduation.

By way of contrast consider his friend down the street, similarly situated with respect to family circumstances, but in the top fifth of the ability distribution. His family is poorer than over 80 per cent of the population, but he is smarter than over 80 per cent of all high-school seniors. He had roughly six chances in ten of entering college the year after graduating high school.

A comparison of these two seniors reveals that among poor students, when family circumstances are roughly the same, more brains means a much better chance of going to college.

What about more advantaged students—do IQ and status operate in the same way? Consider two seniors who come from families in the upper fifth of the distribution of social advantages and economic status. If one of them fell in the bottom fifth of the ability distribution, he would have roughly four chances in ten of going to college. If the other fell in the top fifth of the ability distribution, he would have nine chances in ten of going to college. This comparison reveals that brains are a help at the top of the social pyramid, just as at the bottom: rich boys and girls with high IQ's go to college more often than rich boys and girls with low IQ's.

But now a comparison of the first pair of students with the second pair reveals that getting rich (moving from the bottom to the top of the social pyramid) is nearly as big a help in increasing a student's chances of going to college as getting smart (moving from the bottom to the top of the IQ distribution). More precise analyses of the data on college-going confirm the impression gained from these examples: measured intelligence is of slightly greater influence on college attendance than inherited status. This is a great deal different from a world in which going to college is wholly determined by family position, but it is far from a world in which going to college is wholly determined by intellectual ability.

Once again, however, these comparisons do not reveal what must be the most important fact—namely, that ability and status combined explain somewhat less than half the actual variation in college attendance. As in the case of curriculum placement, we must turn to other factors—motivation, luck, discrimination, chance, and family encouragement or lack of it—to find likely explanations. Existing research provides support for the idea that these other factors do play a role (although it does not afford comprehensive estimates of their relative importance).*

*It could be argued that the research I have summarized understates the influence of social and economic class, because dropouts were not included in the computations; but when they were included, the results barely changed. It could be argued that the role of intelligence is understated because a single test score can't summarize intelligence; yet when scores in four different tests were included instead of just one, nothing much changed either. And while there are plenty of other difficulties with the studies summarized here, none of them seem important enough to change the general pattern of results I have presented.

Thus, while academic ability or intelligence is important to educational success, other factors, measured and unmeasured, seem to have at least as much weight in determining who gets ahead in the world of American schools. But this in turn raises an absolute swarm of problems. If test scores are only moderately important, should steps be taken to increase their influence? Or would relying more heavily on social inheritance leave less room for people to be selected on other criteria, such as motivation? If the influence of inherited status on selection ought to be reduced, how great should the reduction be? In a perfect meritocracy, after all, the objective would be to remove the effect of any social advantages parents had achieved on the life-chances of their children—but what sort of society would that be? Would it be consistent with a society of nuclear families? Does anyone want a society in which every child has an equal chance to be a clam-digger or a cardiac surgeon, subject only to IQ differences? The idea seems bizarre, for it suggests a social rat-race which would make the Great American Status Scramble look like a party game for retired schoolmarms. And if a perfect meritocracy seems like a perfect neurotic nightmare, then just how much, or how little, of an educational advantage would we want families to be able to pass along to their children?

Anyone who thinks about these questions for more than ten seconds will realize that no easy answers are available. More equality in education would be a good thing, and it is sensible to suppose that this implies some effort to reduce the influence of social and economic inheritance on school success. But the questions reveal that we have no well-formed conception of how much the impact of families ought to be reduced, or how much of a role IQ ought to have in reducing it. Nor, indeed, is it clear that IQ should bear that burden at all. Distributing rewards in accordance with IQ scores, after all, is not the only known device for reducing social and economic differences, even in education.

Of course, one's view on these last issues will depend in part on the role one thinks intelligence actually plays in the allocation of adult status and power. If it turned out that IQ was crucial, it would be hard to maintain that it ought not to be the principal means for discriminating among school children. So before going any further with these questions about meritocracy in schools, it might be wise to find out just how important IQ is once people get out of them. I will deal with occupational status first, because that is what seems to fascinate most writers on the subject.*

One way of looking at this question—as Eysenck and Herrnstein did—is by pointing to the evidence on the average IQ's of people in different occupations. Thus, manual laborers turn out to have much lower IQ's than professors of theology, and this is assumed to mean that IQ is an entry requirement for these occupations. But simply presenting the gross differences begs all the basic questions. First, the averages don't reveal the considerable dispersion of IQ's within occupational groups, which reveals that there are lots of people in working-class jobs whose IQ's are in the same range as those in higher-status occupations, and vice versa. But more significantly, listing IQ differences among occupations only tells us that differences exist; it does not tell us how important IQ was in getting people into those occupations.

A satisfactory account would indeed require that we know the IQ's of people in different occupations, but it would require other information as well. We would need to know, for example, how far people got in school and what social and economic advantages their parents had, because these might have had a real impact on their own occupational status as adults to say nothing of their IQ's. Armed with evidence of this sort—which is hard to come by because it covers almost the entire lifecycle—we could compare the relative importance of IQ and other influences on the sorts of jobs adults wind up with. Now we do in fact have a good deal of research which shows that people who stay in school longer wind up on

the average with higher status jobs, and that on the average people who begin life with more social and economic advantages wind up with more of them as adults. But when researchers try to assess the relative importance of education and social inheritance they begin to part company. Some argue that staying in school is a considerably more important influence on occupational attainment than inherited status; others find the opposite to be true. The former category of researchers also tend to think of America as a relatively open society, in which schooling serves as a vehicle of social mobility from one generation to another. Researchers in the second category tend to think of America as a relatively closed society, in which the schools mostly transmit the same status from parents to children. Since both judgments are manifestly true to some degree, and since the evidence is not entirely adequate to resolve the matter, the argument will continue for some time. But what is important for our purposes is not how much mobility there is, or to what extent schooling contributes to it; rather we want to know whether IQ has an effect on occupational status which is *independent* of these two influences.

The available evidence suggests that it does not. IQ seems to have little or no independent effect on the sorts of jobs people wind up with as adults, all other things being equal. IQ does help moderately and indirectly, because it has a moderate influence on how long people stay in school, and the length of their stay in school affects the sorts of jobs they get. But once the influence of schooling is taken into account, IQ appears to have no independent relation to occupational success. If a meritocracy is a society in which intelligent people do well regardless of their parents or their schooling, America is not such a society.

To make this concrete, consider several adults who differ in every aspect under discussion here—jobs, IQ's, length of stay in school, and social and economic backgrounds. The differences in their inherited status and in the length of time they stayed in school account for a fair proportion (somewhat less than half) of the differences in the status of their jobs. Since those who have higher IQ's will have stayed in school somewhat longer, IQ can be said to have

*Occupational status is a term derived from studies of the prestige in which Americans hold different sorts of jobs. Generally, they think that professional and managerial jobs are very prestigious and that common labor is not. Indices of occupational prestige are very highly correlated with general indices of social and economic status.

a moderate effect on occupational status. But when people with equal amounts of schooling are considered, differences in their IQ's turn out to account for none of the differences in the status of their jobs. Having a higher IQ is no help in getting a higher status job for people who have the same educational attainment and the same social and economic background. In addition, there is an abundance of studies showing that the grades of college students are not related either to their income or to their occupational status once they get out of college; similarly, research on what differentiates good from bad workers (within broad occupational categories) shows that workers who produce more or who are rated highly by their supervisors generally do not have higher test scores, although they do tend to have "better" attitudes, greater "motivation," better "deportment"—in effect, more of the attributes which also seem to make for success in school.

Thus, the process of selection to occupations in America does not appear to be more than mildly dependent on IQ. And here too, as in the case of high-school placement and college entrance, recent research has shown that IQ, schooling, and inherited status together account for less than half of the variation in the occupational attainment of American males. More than half of the differences in the job status of American men is explained neither by their IQ, nor by how long they went to school, nor by the social and economic advantages (or burdens) they inherited. Some of these unexplained differences are undoubtedly due to errors in the ways sociologists measure things, but others are probably due to such imponderables as enterprise, motivation, the luck of the draw, and preferences unrelated either to brains or to economic background.

That, however, is not the end of the matter. Whatever the evidence may suggest about the modest influence IQ presently exerts on occupational selection, the popular mythology is that it is much greater now than it was fifty years ago. America, we are told, is a "knowledge society"; we are moving into a post-industrial age, in which talent will rule. Yet when we turn to historical evidence concerning

the role of IQ in occupational selection, once again we find little support for such claims. If IQ were becoming a more important force in occupational selection we would expect the IQ averages of people in any occupation to have become more similar over time: the IQ's of professional people should have grown more nearly equal as merit selection proceeded, and the same would be true of blue-collar workers. But the fragmentary evidence we have suggests this is not true: the dispersion of IQ's within occupational categories for native American whites seems to have remained pretty stable over the last four or five decades. Similarly, if IQ were becoming more important we might expect the intellectual level of intellectually demanding occupations to rise, and the level of undemanding jobs to fall. But no such development seems to have taken place. Finally, if IQ were becoming more important to adult success, we would imagine that the main instrument by which IQ makes itself felt in America—schooling—would have become more important to getting a job. But according to the historical evidence concerning the effect of schooling on occupational attainment over the past four or five decades, education seems to bear no more powerful relationship to the job one gets today than it did earlier in the century.

Now all of this evidence is partial, and subject to a variety of caveats. But the striking thing is that nowhere can we find any empirical support for the idea that brains are becoming increasingly more important to status in America. Of course, this by itself is not incompatible with the observation that "knowledge" is an increasingly central aspect of life. For one thing, measures of occupational status are based on opinion surveys in which random samples of the American people are asked about the relative prestige of occupations. Thus, the "importance" of intellectual work would appear to change only if people thought its prestige was changing. But in general public attitudes toward the relative prestige of various occupations have changed very little over time, so that paradoxically intellectual work may in fact be becoming more important even though this is not reflected in the measures used by sociologists. No one has ever actually set out to measure how much more important technological and scientific work is now than in 1920, and probably no one ever will.

But even if we assume that brains *are* becoming more important or powerful (a moot point in my view), other things are changing as well. Fifty years ago most Americans never finished high school, and only a tiny percentage went on to college. Now almost everyone finishes high school, and more than one third go on to some form of post-secondary education. This means that lots of ordinary people who would never have had the chance fifty years ago to be doctors or teachers or engineers have the chance today. If brains are becoming more powerful at the same time as schooling becomes more universal (and thereby opens up opportunity through the power of certification), the two tendencies may cancel each other out. Of course I am speculating here, but observed evidence would tend to support this view, and to suggest also how complicated the relationship among intelligence, status, and power can be; some social forces may be acting to intensify the connection at the same time as others are weakening it.

If, then, we measure adult status by way of occupational prestige rankings, and merit by IQ, America does not appear more than mildly meritocratic. Nor is there reason to believe that IQ has grown more important to individual success during the past five or six decades. This does not mean that the symbols of learning—or its apparatus—have not become more important. Indeed, it is clear that the length of time one stays in school is more relevant to occupational attainment than is raw IQ. Rather than a social hierarchy based on intellect, we may be creating a "school-ocracy." But the importance of schooling to occupational status may itself be based on a variety of non-intellectual factors. Employers use the school system as an elaborate behavior-screening mechanism, on the theory that certain kinds of work require certain kinds of personalities. This would explain why schools place so much stress on deportment, and why they screen out youngsters who have a hard time sitting still for long periods of time, or who don't have the right appearance; these tend to get tracked to lower-status school work and to lower-status jobs. Students who have "better" manners, who behave "properly," who accept authority, and who look the way they should, tend to be routed into higher-status school work and occupations. This screening system may or may not accord with the actual behavior which is required in various sorts of occupations, but it does seem to fit what people *think* is appropriate behavior.

Another cause of the connection between schooling and adult success may be that schools are becoming the principal vehicle for "professionalizing" occupations. Especially in the marginal and semi-marginal professions, adding educational requirements for certification and licensing is a way of enhancing the standing and respectability of a given line of work in the eyes of its practitioners and clients. It also is a way of persuading people that the occupation in question is up-to-date, modern, and in touch with the latest wisdom. And it often is a way (as with teachers, for example) of getting a bigger pay-check. But whatever the explanation, the additional educational requirements cannot be said to have much relation to job performance.

When schooling becomes necessary to later occupational standing for essentially non-intellectual reasons, various unhappy consequences can result. One such consequence is the subversion of the legitimate purposes of educational institutions, and the breeding of contempt for what they do; another is the creation of an occupational selection system in which the ability to remain glued to the seat of a chair for long periods of time becomes a prime recommendation for advancement. (The ability to sit still is useful for many purposes, but especially among children it may not be related to the ingenuity, enterprise, and cleverness which any lively society would want to promote.) Under such a system of occupational selection, we are as likely to produce an unhealthy accumulation of boredom and discontent as we are to create a dangerous maldistribution of intellect.

Developments like these are the more distressing because of the greater uniformity they promise, both in what people do and in how they think about it. Such uniformity has not always characterized American society. There is fairly convincing evidence, for example, of ethnic differences in the role that schools have played in promoting occupational mobility. Studies of European ethnic groups show that during this century all of them made substantial increases in occupational status, but that they did so in rather different ways. The children of Russian immigrants (which means Jews for the most part) completed more years of school, on the average, than children from other groups. In addition, educational attainment had a much stronger relationship to the later occupational attainment of these children than it did for children from other groups—which probably means that a disproportionate number of Jews went into occupations which had substantial educational requirements. Not all nationalities had the same experience; Italian and Polish children, for example, tended to complete fewer years of school than those of some other groups. But for Italians and Poles educational differences were not in themselves an important influence as far as later occupational status was concerned.

The history of ethnic variations in the importance of schooling suggests in turn the underlying differences in the avenues that various ethnic groups have taken to achieve higher social and economic status. And these different avenues probably reflect cultural and historical differences from group to group with regard to the sorts of work which were known and esteemed in the parent country. They even may have been indicative of ethnic differences in the "talent for school," for there were very considerable IQ differences among the European immigrant groups which roughly corresponded to their success or failure in school. But the important point is that to the extent that schooling is made an unavoidable requirement for occupational entry or advancement, it may close off genuine cultural differences in occupational values, and irrationally stifle alternatives which might otherwise flourish. To the extent that success in a homogeneous system of schooling becomes the *sine qua non* of entry to occupations, cultural diversity in conceptions of success and worthy work may be diminished. It is

hard to think of any good which could possibly come from that situation.

In a sense, however, all the attention to the relative status of occupations is misleading. It is easy to understand why intellectuals might be obsessed with the question, but it is important in the discussion of meritocracy only because of the assumption that jobs which require brains wield more power than jobs which don't. If it turned out that people with high IQ's did not really have more power than ordinary folks, there wouldn't be very much left for one to argue about.

Normally when intellectuals write about this question they bemoan the fact that people like themselves have *little* power and influence. Indeed, they have mourned this situation for so long that most Americans who read what intellectuals write probably concluded long ago that anyone who has power is either a knave or a fool. As a result, it comes as something of a surprise to hear that intellectuals are in danger of having too much power. But if holding political office, for instance, is an index of power, it is hard to see any cause for alarm, for there certainly is no evidence of an undue concentration of raw IQ among the ranks of government officials. Indeed, it is hard to imagine why anyone would think government officials should have unusually high IQ's. After all, the motives which lead men and women into public life probably have more to do with the desire for power, or money, or recognition, than with the need to exercise a restless and powerful intellect.

Politics, however, is only one of the several sources of power and influence in America; great wealth is another. Here again, it should come as no great surprise to learn that a high IQ is not the main requirement for having lots of money. People with more schooling do tend to have somewhat higher incomes, but the relationship between the two is not even as strong as the relationship between schooling and occupational status. Partly this is due to the fact that lots of jobs with rather high status— preaching, teaching, and the like—don't come with cushy salaries, and lots of jobs with rather low status, like being a plumber or a machinist, do. There also is the fact that spending decades in school is a condition of employment in most of the high-status but low-paying jobs, but not a condition of tenure in the others. And finally, doing well in school is not yet a prerequisite for inheriting money.

Then there are the other ways of attaining power, or at least influence. The people who write for newspapers and talk on television offer one example, and the "experts" who work for Congressional committees and executive agencies offer another. And university professors who spend half their lives traveling to consultations with government officials or corporate managers offer yet another. Still, one is at a loss to imagine why journalists should be either brighter or more influential than they were fifty years ago, and a modest stint of watching television would not lead anyone to conclude that the medium is in peril of being taken over by people with dangerously high IQ's. Finally, anyone who imagines that "experts" with high IQ's have a great future in public life ought to visit his nearest government agency and see how it works. Most important government business turns not on the technical skills that experts do monopolize, but on ethical and political considerations. Experts have had to relearn this lesson every few years since the Progressive era.

Let us try to summarize, in general form, the conclusions of all this. First, America is not a meritocracy, if by that we mean a society in which income, status, or power are heavily determined by IQ. All the evidence suggests that IQ has only moderate impact on adult success, and that this impact is exerted only through the schools.

Second, America seems on balance not to have become more meritocratic in the course of the 20th century. All the evidence suggests that the relationship between IQ and income and status has been perfectly stable. While opportunity has opened up for great segments of the population, the criteria for advancement seem to have involved many things in addition to, and other than, IQ.

Third, something we often incorrectly identify with IQ—namely schooling—seems to be a much more important determinant of adult success than IQ. If getting through school

is a mark of merit, then America is moderately meritocratic. But then, in a society in which education is an increasingly universal experience, such a conception of merit begins to lose its meaning.

And finally, among all the many factors which lead to a situation in which some people are poor or hold low-status jobs, lower intellectual ability is not a terribly important one. Being stupid is not what is responsible for being poor in America.

## SUGGESTIONS FOR FURTHER READING

Baltes, P. B., & Schaie, K. W. Aging and IQ: The myth of the twilight years. *Psychology Today,* October 1974, pp. 35–40. IQ is found as not necessarily declining with age except in the very last years before death. It is suggested that IQ tests are biased against older people. The result is that older people are judged as less intelligent than they actually are.

Bickham, S. The educational implications of Arthur Jensen's research. *Intellect,* 1974, *103,* 161– 164. Arthur Jensen's genetic hypothesis that people are cognitively different in enduring ways is examined and related to Jensen's theory that associative learning is the best remedy for children with underdeveloped intellects.

Burt, S. C. Intelligence and heredity. *New Scientist,* 1969, *42,* 226. A leading authority offers his views on the controversy about heredity versus environment in determining intelligence. Burt perceives mental ability as inherited in much the same way as physical characteristics are inherited.

Eysenck, H. J. Battleground IQ: Race, intelligence, and education. *Phi Delta Kappan,* 1972, *53*(11), 33–34. A well-known psychologist assesses the evidence concerning racial differences in IQ.

Fowler, W. A developmental learning approach to infant care in a group setting. *Merrill-Palmer Quarterly,* 1972, *18*(2), 145–175. In a three-year day-care program designed especially to provide quality day care and education for infants, the infants involved made considerable gains in IQ and in certain special competencies including language, social competence, and comprehension.

Herzig, M. E., & Birch, H. G. Longitudinal course of measured intelligence in pre-school children of different social and ethnic backgrounds. *American Journal of Orthopsychiatry*, 1971, *41*, 416–426. Measured IQ for Puerto Rican working-class and white middle-class children was determined at 3, and again at 6 years of age. The results are related to problems of IQ stability.

Jensen, A. R. *Educability and group differences*. New York: Harper & Row, 1973. A controversial psychologist analyzes extensive evidence concerning differences in learning ability according to race, attempting to support his hypothesis that between half and three-quarters of the average IQ difference between American blacks and whites can be attributed to genetic factors.

Jensen, A. R. Cumulative deficit: A testable hypothesis? *Developmental Psychology*, 1974, *10*, 996–1019. Cumulative deficit is an hypothesis relating to lower mental-test scores made by culturally deprived persons. In this study a significant age decrement occurred in verbal but not in nonverbal IQ among disadvantaged children.

Kagan, J. Continuity in cognitive development during the first year. *Merrill-Palmer Quarterly*, 1969, *15*(1), 101–119. Kagan considers especially sex differences in continuity of early cognitive behaviors and concludes that girls are more stable than boys in infancy as well as later childhood.

Kaye, K. IQ: A conceptual deterrent to revolution in education. *Elementary School Journal*, 1973, *74*(1), 9–23. In this attack on IQ as a concept inimical to the best interest of education, a developmental psychologist at the University of Chicago describes pioneer work concerning intelligence tests, as well as sophisticated recent work and its implications for educational theory and practice. He portrays the IQ concept as having done great damage in education, both past and present. He calls for the discreditation of such practices as ability grouping that have continued to accord IQ an importance he feels it does not deserve.

McCall, R. B., Appelbaum, M. I., & Hogarty, P. S. Developmental changes in mental performance. *Monographs of the Society for Research in Child Development*, 1973, *38* (3, Serial No. 150). The study reported here concerned patterns of IQ change with age, in a population of normal middle-class children, and parental behaviors associated with various developmental profiles.

# 3

## Constancy of Personality

Considerable research has focused on determining the constancy both of personality in general and of specific traits. Underlying the research on individual differences in basic personality is the assumption that such traits are at least moderately constant; and studies designed to test this assumption are multiplying fast. Typically, individuals are rated by trained persons on various traits, and rated again on the same traits at a later age by other investigators using the same set of criteria. Some of these traits have been studied for a brief period, others over a span of many years.

There are several problems inherent in such research. Only extensive, longitudinal research programs, as exemplified by the Berkeley Growth and Fels Institute studies, can supply the answers required. Yet such studies are expensive and difficult to maintain. Quantities of data must be compiled over a span of years. Children involved may move, die, or be withdrawn from observation. Research monies may give out, or leadership for the project may dissolve. Hence, many studies have relied upon already existing data from earlier longitudinal research. However, issues can be sharply defined and records properly maintained only when longitudinal projects are designed with relevant hypotheses in mind.

## SOME FINDINGS CONCERNING CONSTANCY OF PERSONALITY

Research on this topic is still somewhat conflicting and often confusing. After reviewing the literature, Mischel (1968) concluded that attempts to demonstrate persistence of traits have not been altogether successful. Similarly, Block (1968) reported a lack of real empirical evidence for personality consistency. By contrast, other researchers have reported considerable consistency, for certain traits, once they stabilize. In one case, two trained observers spent a minimum of two hours every week observing each of several children from birth until the second birthday. Over this period, two of the children developed totally different and distinct personalities with meaningful and consistent differences. One proved to be simply reactive, the other initiatory in social behaviors, and these patterns proved highly self-consistent over time (Escalona, 1973). Another researacher, Korner (1971), reported enduring tendencies among children either to seek out or to withdraw from new situations; to respond to situations either impulsively or reflexively; and to be primarily reactive, expressive, or retractive-inhibitive. The children also had distinctly different and persistent ways of dealing with stimulation. Moreover, concluded Korner, children's differences in "responsiveness, regulation, and synthesis of strong external and internal stimuli are, in all likelihood, an expression of differences in [their] neurophysiological makeup" (p. 616).

Another research team, including Bell, Weller, and Waldrop (1971), reported less sweeping conclusions. In general, the newborn's behavior repertoire proved a poor source of clues for the child's later behavior. However, some predictive factors were identified. For example, male infants with the highest respiration rate during the newborn period had low scores on intensity of play, assertiveness, and gregariousness during the preschool period. Differences in respiration rate in the newborn period were also associated with variations in attention at preschool age.

Various factors—notably, sex—apparently limit the modifiability of particular characteristics. Parker (1971) reported only five high-stability characteristics for both sexes: alertness, efficiency, initiative, quickness, and thoroughness. Only three low-stability characteristics proved common for the sexes: awkwardness, laziness, and moodiness. Those characteristics that appeared to be most stable were those that were deemed appropriate for the respective sexes.

Characteristics that are symptomatic of behavior pathology—such as immaturity, laziness, moodiness, and sulkiness—generally have low stability, possibly because an individual is motivated to reduce the unfortunate traits (Baumeister & Kellas, 1968). Moreover, Erikson (1968) theorizes that young people who have not attained a stable sense of identity will experience various emotional difficulties. However, it is yet to be determined which types of stability are symptomatic of maladjustment and which are not.

The stability of a characteristic also depends on an individual's age and personality pattern. Certain core traits, once formed, are difficult if not impossible to change; whereas secondary, or peripheral, traits are more susceptible to modification. Most traits stabilize in early childhood, but others crystallize later. An especially significant finding from the Fels study was the so-called "sleeper effect" (Kagan & Moss, 1962). Certain traits would tend to sink and surface again. That is, individuals might seem to change, but later revert to familiar patterns.

Various factors have been thought to account for the relative stability of certain traits. One is body chemistry, which remains basically the same throughout life. Another normally constant factor is quality of experience. The child generally remains in the same sort of social milieu. He has the same parents and the same siblings over the years. He is also accorded a specific role, which tends to organize his traits. As he plays that role, he creates an image in the eyes of others. He reacts to their expectations, further reinforcing the sort of child he already is.

The failure of children to manifest persistent traits may be due partly to inadequacies in research techniques. When a child has had a wide variety of experiences during the period intervening between earlier and later assessment of traits, cause and effect may be entangled. Even where persistent traits exist, their basic quality may have become overlaid with overt, but relatively superficial, behaviors that merely constitute an individual's working relationship with the environment. It is also possible that basic, or core, traits may be more stable than indicated on tests. Later tests may not measure exactly what was measured the first time, because the same test would hardly be appropriate at a later age.

## QUESTIONS RELATING TO CONSTANCY OF PERSONALITY

Even if it is decided that personality, once established, is relatively constant, other important questions remain to be answered. Is constancy primarily due to hereditary, or to prenatal, or to postnatal influences, or to some combination of these? If constancy hinges on hereditary factors, programs of eugenics would seem logical. If constancy is the result of prenatal or early environmental influences, every effort should be made to get children off to a good start.

To whatever extent personality traits can be changed, certain questions seem relevant. Is it possible that imaginative environmental engineering could effect significant personality change? If such changes might, in fact, be achieved, how can such modifications be made consistent with the best interests of the individual and society? If they cannot be made, shouldn't children be helped to become better acquainted with themselves in order to utilize their potential to the fullest? Also, shouldn't schools do a better job of teaching youngsters how to build on what they are?

A related question is this: What hope exists for making long-term predictions for particular children? Thus far, it would appear that some children are far more predictable than others. Perhaps the more predictable children have simply lived in more consistent environments from year to year. Or perhaps such children are somehow endowed with more inflexible traits by their heredity.

The answers to such questions carry important implications. If it is concluded that certain traits are relatively inflexible, a child should be helped to adapt his or her style of life to those traits. But if those factors that cause a trait to "congeal" can be discovered, environmental engineering could conceivably ensure a propitious assortment of factors at successive periods in development.

On the other hand, if core traits can be changed, children should be assisted to modify those traits that prove maladaptive. But who is to judge for a specific child whether a particular trait will or will not prove adaptive? For example, provision for self-determination and active exploration of the environment tends to produce an independent, creative, autonomous type of personality (MacKinnon, 1962). However, such traits could prove maladaptive for a girl, if society dictates that she should play an auxiliary role in life (as our society, to a considerable extent, continues to do).

Still other questions remain to be answered. Are traits more susceptible to alteration at certain periods than others, and does the "critical period" for individuals differ? Which traits, once formed, are almost irreversible? What factors, both in the individual and in the environment, are relevant to such change? How does the modifiability of personality traits relate to such factors as sex role and manner of child rearing? What could, and should, be the role of environmental engineering in this area?

The first reading, by Anneliese Korner, describes behavioral differences among newborns and shows how they relate to the differences in later behaviors, including mother-infant relationships and cognitive styles. The second, by Virginia Crandall, describes the well-known Fels Longitudinal Project and the implications of fetal behavior for later personality development.

## REFERENCES

Baumeister, A. A., & Kellas, G. Intrasubject response variability in relation to intelligence. *Journal of Abnormal Psychology,* 1968, *73,* 421–423.

Bell, R., Weller, G., & Waldrop, M. Newborn and preschooler: Organization of behavior and relations between periods. *Monographs of the Society for Research in Human Development,* 1971, *36,* (1–2, Whole No. 142).

Block, J. Some reasons for the apparent inconsistency of personality. *Psychological Bulletin,* 1968, *70,* 210–212.

Erikson, E. H. *Identity: Youth and crises.* New York: W. W. Norton, 1968.

Escalona, S. K. Basic modes of social interaction: Their emergence and patterning during the first two years of life. *Merrill-Palmer Quarterly,* 1973, *19,* 205–232.

Kagan, J. & Moss, H. A. *Birth to maturity.* New York: Wiley, 1962.

Korner, A. State as variable, as obstacle and as mediator of stimulation in infant research. *Merrill-Palmer Quarterly,* 1972, *18*(2), 77–94.

Mischel, W. *Personality and assessment.* New York: Wiley, 1968.

Parker, G. V. C. Prediction of individual stability. *Educational and Psychological Measurement,* 1971, *31,* 875–886.

# Individual Differences at Birth: Implications for Early Experience and Later Development

## Anneliese F. Korner

In recent years, a growing number of investigators have become interested in infant research. This research has taken three different directions with markedly different goals. One group of investigators has focused on the effect of early sensory stimulation on the infant's cognitive development, another on the impact of the mother-child relationship and still another on the role of individual differences in the unfolding of later development. By far the greatest concern of clinicians has been the importance of the earliest mother-infant relationship on the infant's development. Since the infant in this dyad is frequently viewed as the passive recipient of maternal care, the focus most often has been on the mother, her attitudes, conscious or unconscious, her ministrations and child care practices, and her acceptance of the maternal role. What the infant brings to the mother-infant relationship, what *he* represents right from the very start, is frequently overlooked. (For a discussion of the historical reasons for this one-sided view, see Korner.[13])

Much of the impetus to study individual differences among infants and what these may contribute from the start to the reciprocal exchange between mother and child, came from the field of psychoanalysis. For example, Freud[7] emphatically stated his conviction that "each individual ego is endowed from the beginning with its own peculiar dispositions and

From "Individual Differences at Birth: Implications for Early Experience and Later Development," by Anneliese F. Korner, *American Journal of Orthopsychiatry*, 1971, *41*(4), 608–619. Copyright © 1971 by the American Orthopsychiatric Association, Inc. Reprinted by permission.

tendencies." Hartmann[10] pointed out that variations in the primary ego apparatuses may influence the choice of later defenses. It was mostly after the appearance of a series of psychoanalytic articles that stressed the importance of predispositions in the development of the neuroses that reports of systematic observations of innate differences among young infants began to appear in the literature.[3, 5, 8, 28]

My own interest in the field of individual differences originated from clinical work with adults and children in which I was struck over and over again by the enduring style of an individual's reaction patterns and by the logical cohesion of his adaptive efforts. In taking developmental histories, one can see impressive evidence not only of the impact of historical events and experiential factors, such as the effect of traumatic experiences, pathological parent-child interactions and identifications with parental models, but also of the consistency of a person's life style. Also striking is the logic and cohesion of a person's ways of *resisting* change and of making new adaptations *after* change.

I thus began my neonatal studies with the working hypothesis that, if one wants to understand the earliest phases of development, one must assess not only the mother's mothering but also the infant's characteristics and what these represent as a stimulus to his caretaker. As the work progressed, the following subsidiary hypotheses became useful in conceptualizing the factors involved in individual development:

1. Individual differences at birth, when they *do* contain the rudiments of later characteristics, may affect development in either short-range or long-range terms. The differences that may have long-range effects, and that in all likelihood originate from differences in neurophysiological make-up, may, in conjunction with reinforcing experiential conditions, favor the later adoption of certain modes of impulse management and the choice of later defenses and cognitive and characterological attributes. These are the differences that probably are most contributory to the persistence in the *style* with which each developmental task is approached and mastered. By contrast, other types of innate differences, while probably also

exerting a powerful, though indirect, influence on later development, may be observable in their original form only for a brief period of time in that they become absorbed and transformed in the ever-changing *content* of the developmental sequences. Part of Piaget's[26] developmental theories may help conceptualize this process. Piaget postulated that there exist inborn schemata that are related, though not identical, to their precursors. With this conceptualization one can readily see both the continuity and the diversity of the developmental process in that specific behavior patterns, observable shortly after birth, will exert an influence on subsequent developmental acquisitions but may change radically in their form of expression.

2. Innate differences will not only influence the unfolding of many later functions but will also affect the manner in which different infants will subjectively experience and perceive the world and universal childhood events.[1]

3. Individual differences among infants *should* evoke differences in mothering, if mutuality is to develop between mother and child. Such differences may thus be instrumental in shaping the child's environment.

Added to this is, of course, *what the mother as a person in her own right* brings to this situation, her attitudes, conscious and unconscious, her child rearing philosophy, her aspirations, her cognitive style and mode of impulse management, not to speak of what the father adds in all these dimensions. Added also are the effects of sheer circumstance, such as being born a boy or a girl, first born or one of many siblings, black or white or of a given socioeconomic or ethnic origin. This profusion of interacting variables, both internal and external, highlights how truly difficult it is to make any kind of longitudinal predictions.

## METHODOLOGICAL CONSIDERATIONS

If, nevertheless, one wishes to tackle the problem of assessing innate differences among infants and their influence on short-range or long-range development, one has to take a number of methodological precautions to obtain reliable results. For example, in our neonatal studies, which included both naturalistic observations and a wide variety of experimental procedures, we attempted to assess the differences among babies before differential maternal handling could have materially affected the infants' responses. Thus, the assessments were made when the infants were between two and four days old. This decision was based on the rationale that with an uneventful, normal delivery, the infant will have largely recovered from the birth process, and if given routine nursery care, his experience up to that point will have been fairly uniform. To forestall finding ''individual differences'' among newborns that are merely a reflection of prenatal or postnatal complications, precautions have to be taken to exclude all infants whose behavior might be affected by such complications. We thus developed stringent selection criteria to include for study only healthy, full-term neonates of average weight, delivered vaginally, spontaneously or through low forceps, whose Apgar ratings were eight or above one minute after delivery, and whose physical examinations reflected no abnormalities during the entire lying-in period. Excluded were infants who showed any signs of fetal or postnatal anoxia, whose mothers had excessively long or short labors or large doses of sedative drugs, or whose parents had a history of any kind of metabolic or neurological disease. Since we and others have found differences in arousal levels of first born infants and infants born to multiparae, and of breast and bottle-fed infants, and since the sexes differ, at least in their spontaneous discharge behaviors during sleep,[14] precautions also have to be taken to consider these groups separately, and if compared, matched in numbers.

It should be stressed that when reference is made to individual differences, more is meant than merely the variations of behavior among infants that invariably occur by chance whenever any trait is measured. To obtain reliable individual differences in any behavior, infants have to differ significantly from each other in statistical terms and, on repeated testing, they have to hold their ranks reasonably well relative to the sample. It should also be stressed that it is easy to find individual differences that are totally meaningless if the conditions of observations vary from infant to infant. While it is not possible to present here the many details of the methods used in each of our studies, I shall present in broad outline how we attempted to insure that the infants were observed under identical external conditions and how we tried to control for variations of internal state. All the infants were observed at the same time of day; illumination and temperature were kept constant. In our experimental studies, the sensory stimuli provided were standard in duration and intensity. Since sensory thresholds vary greatly not only with each state the baby happens to be in, but also with hunger and satiation, we controlled for the time elapsed since the last feeding and the infant's state with each type of stimulation.[16] Were one not to control for these factors one would surely observe differences among the infants that are purely the function of their state and not of their individuality. To determine the infants' states, we used Wolff's[30] behavioral criteria with very minor variations to classify the states of regular sleep, REM or paradoxical sleep, irregular sleep, drowse, alert inactivity, waking activity and crying. At the beginning of each study and periodically throughout, we checked observer reliability. Agreements between two observers have ranged from 86% to 100% depending on the behavior categories observed.

In one of our studies,[19] we used film to record the infants' behavior. In fact, we have taken 1000 feet of film on each of thirty-two babies and we have thus accumulated a bank of behavioral data on the neonate that can be used by us and other investigators for any number of investigative purposes. Rather than using movies as is commonly done to illustrate certain points, we used film to record periodic and unselected time samples of the infants' behavior. A timer attached to the camera automatically turned the camera on and off, thus taking behavior samples that were identical in length and in the interval since the last feeding for each child. These time samples provide a permanent and objective record of a multitude of neonatal behaviors which permit both a qualitative and quantitative comparison among the babies in any variable we choose to study.

## FINDINGS

In presenting evidence regarding individual differences among young infants, I shall draw not only upon my own research with newborns, but also upon the findings of other investigators. In dealing with my own research findings, I shall pool our observations from three separate studies[18-20] and discuss them topically. I hope to show not only how much infants differ from each other from the start, but also to elucidate, whenever possible, how these differences may affect short-range or long-range developmental acquisitions, how they *must* affect the infant's early experience, and how they *should* evoke differences in mothering. At the very least I hope our observations will convey that the newborn is neither the unorganized nor the passive receptive organism he is commonly believed to be.

How truly unpassive the infant is was very nicely shown by Moss and Robson[23] in a study of fifty-four mother-infant pairs. In a six-hour home visit of infants one month old, these authors recorded, among other things, the frequency with which either the baby or the mother started an interaction sequence. In roughly four out of five instances, it was the infant who initiated the exchange. Since newborns cry much more than one-month-old infants, this ratio must be even higher during the neonatal period. In my own study, in which I monitored the infants' states continuously over four half-hour periods at predetermined times during two feeding cycles, I found that infants differ significantly from each other both in the frequency and the duration of spontaneous crying (with an analysis of variance, $p < .01$ and $< .05$, respectively). It follows that infants will vary markedly from each other in how much they initiate interaction with their mothers and, as a consequence, how much caretaking they will elicit.

Not only do babies vary in irritability, but they also differ significantly in how readily they are soothed and how long they remain comforted ($p < .01$). These differences must have considerable impact on the mother and her feelings of competence as a caretaker. This should be particularly true if she is inexperienced. Also of interest, incidentally, were the kinds of interventions that proved most soothing to neonates. Contrary to folklore and much of the early stimulation literature, it was *not* body contact that produced the most striking effects. We recently completed an experimental study[20] in which we explored the relative efficacy of body contact and of vestibular stimulation, with and without the upright position, both in soothing babies and producing visual alertness in them. These types of stimulation were given singly and in combination and within the context of common maternal ministrations. In summary, the results showed that vestibular stimulation, the experience of being picked up and moved, had a far greater effect both in soothing the infant and in rendering him alert than did body contact. The findings imply that, at least during the neonatal period, the vestibular stimulation that is part and parcel of almost every caretaking activity may be a far more potent form of stimulation than touch and body contact. Yet, with the prevailing emphasis on the importance of body contact, this hidden form of stimulation is often overlooked.

Returning to individual differences among babies and the effects these differences may have on early experience, we have noted marked variations in the degree to which newborns make postural adjustments or mold to the person holding them. The lack of this quality has often been associated with severe pathology and while this may be true for extreme cases, it is amazing how much normal infants vary in how cuddly they are. Again, it should be pointed out how much this must affect the mother's feelings of relatedness, particularly if her own needs for this kind of closeness happen to be strong. While it is difficult to quantify the degree to which an infant molds to the body, it has been my impression that the restless, highly aroused and active babies are the ones who are the least cuddly. This impression dovetails with the findings of a longitudinal study that highlighted the far-reaching developmental permutations of this simple trait. Schaffer and Emerson[27] closely followed thirty-seven mother-infant pairs over the first eighteen months of life. On the basis of the infants' behavior in a variety of commonly occurring contact situations, the authors classified nine subjects as "non-cuddlers," nineteen subjects as "cuddlers," and the remaining nine infants as an intermediate group. "Non-cuddlers" were so classified if, throughout the eighteen months, the infants responded negatively to cuddling, even when they were tired, frightened or ill. Infants were classified as "cuddlers" if they consistently enjoyed, accepted and actively sought physical contact in all forms. "Non-cuddlers" were found to be more active, more restless and quite intolerant of physical restraint. Their motor development was significantly accelerated as compared with the "cuddlers" and probably as a consequence of this, their developmental quotients were significantly higher. The "cuddlers," on the other hand, were generally more placid, needed significantly more sleep and formed specific attachments to others earlier and with much greater intensity. They also tended more frequently to acquire transitional objects and to engage in autoerotic activities.

In examining their data on the mother-infant interaction, the authors were unable to demonstrate consistent differences among the mothers of "cuddlers" and "non-cuddlers" in handling their infants. From this and other data analyses, the authors concluded that the need for and resistance against close physical contact is not primarily a reactive or social phenomenon but an expression of a general aspect of the infant's personality to be observed above all in the level of his activity drive. They also concluded that deprivation of physical contact may affect some infants more than others, and that it may be primarily the "cuddlers" who require contact comfort for satisfactory developmental progress.

Returning to our own studies, we found from our film analyses that infants differed significantly from each other in how much they engaged in spontaneous oral activity, such as sucking and mouthing, and in the degree to which they sought, persisted and succeeded in self-comforting as expressed in such behaviors as fingersucking and hand-mouth contact. (With an analysis of variance $p$ was $< .01$ with respect to each of these behaviors.[17]) We thus found marked quantitative differences in the manifestations of oral drive and the capacity to deal with this drive. Obviously, these differences should affect early experience both by way of differences in the kind of homeostatic adjustment the infant will make in the earliest weeks of life, and in the degree to which the infant will require his mother to be a mediating, tension-reducing agent. These variations in the strength of the oral drive and the capacity for self-comforting may also influence the intensity with which weaning is experienced, quite apart from what the mother's handling of this situation may contribute to this experience.

So far then, I have presented evidence that babies differ significantly from each other in how much they cry, how soothable they are and how capable they are of self-comforting behavior. Differences in these dimensions should help set the stage for many aspects of the infant's early weeks of life, both in terms of his experience of pleasure and of pain and the memory traces these may leave, and in terms of what is required for optimal mothering. These variations in early behavior suggest that there may exist, from the very start, differences in the degree to which infants avail themselves of others for purposes of seeking comfort. This, in addition to the mother's contribution and reactions, may differentially influence the intensity and depth of the infant's first attachment. I believe that, while these differences exert a subtle though profound influence on later development, these are the types of differences that become part of larger schemata so that they are not necessarily recognizable in their original form at a later time. More specifically, it is probably these types of differences that are contributory to vague feelings of helplessness, omnipotence, dependence, separateness or oneness with the mother and which, in combination with maternal differences, will feed into the kinds of object relations the child will develop.

Next, I will present evidence of individual differences at birth, the derivatives of which are perhaps more directly traceable in later

functioning than the ones described so far. I am referring to qualitative and quantitative differences in the capacity to take in and synthesize sensory stimuli. Optimally, these functions should be reciprocal in strength. When they are widely discrepant, this may constitute a major source of vulnerability.

First, I will present some evidence regarding the neonate's sensory capacities and the variations observed in sensory thresholds. Recent experimental work in many different laboratories has shown that the neonate is a good deal more capable of seeing and hearing than had formerly been assumed. Fantz,[6] for example, demonstrated that infants less than forty-eight hours old show consistent preferences for certain visual stimuli. Interestingly enough it is the picture of a human face they look at significantly longer than at any other patterns. Neonates respond even to soft tones with changes in behavior, in heart rate and respiration. Furthermore, newborns can be made to follow visually a moving object and the source of a sound.[30] In our studies, we took measures of the frequencies and durations of spontaneous visual alertness, levels of alertness in response to maternal types of ministrations, frequency of visual pursuit of a moving object and frequencies of response to a buzzer and to the sound of the camera. We found that infants differ from each other in most of these to a highly significant degree. When, in one of the studies, we inter-correlated the visual measures with each other and with the auditory measures, the correlations were sufficiently high so that one could designate the infants as having high, moderate or low thresholds within the visual modality as well as across the visual and auditory modality[15] (see also Birns[3]).

Differences among infants in sensory sensitivity obviously have major implications for how they will experience the world around them, how much stimulation they require, and how much stimulation they can take. Benjamin,[1] for example, suggested that infants with low sensory thresholds are very prone to develop colic during the third and fourth postnatal week, when all babies go through a maturational spurt in their sensory capacities but when they have not as yet developed an adequate stimulus barrier. Very sensitive babies tend to become overwhelmed with over-stimulation unless a mothering person acts as a shield and tension-reducing agent. Benjamin postulated that the outcome of this "crisis" may even have important implications for the predisposition to anxiety.

Contrasting to this are the infants who have high sensory thresholds to all sensory stimuli. These are the infants who, for optimal development, require a great deal of stimulation. Two of our studies[18,20] shed light on one of the best ways a mother can provide stimulation for her infant in the first weeks of life. Paradoxically, it is by soothing the infant. When a crying baby is picked up and put to the shoulder he not only usually stops crying, but he almost invariably will become bright-eyed and he will scan all over his visual surrounding. Quite apart from whatever effect this soothing experience may have on the infant's *affective* development, this type of comforting will inadvertently provide him with a great deal of visual stimulation. Considering only the opportunities for visual experiences, it will be the infants with high sensory thresholds who will need the experience of being picked up more than infants who are more capable of providing visual experiences for themselves. This also suggests that infants with high sensory thresholds will show the effects of maternal neglect more acutely than infants who, unaided, are more receptive to environmental stimuli.

Judging from the literature, the balance between sensory threshold levels and the individual's integrative functions may exert a major influence both on pathological and normal development. In pathological development (e.g. childhood psychosis, autism) it has as yet not been possible to identify whether excessively low sensory thresholds, a defect in the integrative functions, or a combination of both are contributory factors. That an imbalance of these functions is involved in these major pathologies is strongly suggested by the work of Mednick[21] with high risk children for schizophrenia, by Ornitz and Ritvo's[24] work on perceptual inconstancy in infantile autism and by Bergman and Escalona's[2] retrospective

study, which linked unusual sensory sensitivity in early childhood to later psychosis. Within the sphere of more normal development, it likewise seems plausible that it is the balance between sensory threshold levels and the integrative functions that may be critically contributory to *how* development will proceed. It is in this balance that we may some day find the predispositional core that will influence the choice of later cognitive control and defense structures and preferred and enduring ways of impulse and affect management.

In searching the literature for personal characteristics that persist through development, one finds in different guises and from workers of different persuasions, consistent evidence that the most enduring characteristics of an individual derive from his capacity to take in and to synthesize sensory stimuli. For example, Honzik,[11] in discussing the results of the Berkeley Guidance Study, concluded that the tendency that was most persistent throughout childhood and adolescence was the propensity to be primarily "reactive-expressive" or "retractive-inhibitive." Thomas et al,[28] in longitudinal work with infants aged three months to two years, found strong persistence in the children's tendency to seek out new stimuli or to withdraw from new situations. Kagan,[12] also through longitudinal work, found a consistent and enduring cognitive style that made some children respond quickly and impulsively to any problem situations and made others respond consistently with reflectiveness and caution. Pavlov,[25] in his work with dogs, described temperamental differences in his animals which, when extreme, required totally different handling for conditioning to be effective. Pavlov believed that these dogs had different types of nervous systems. He described one extreme as reacting quickly to every stimulus, vivacious, exuberant, and when meeting new people, becoming demonstrative to the point of annoyance. It was possible to condition this kind of dog only by continuously varying stimulation. The other extreme was a dog who responded to every new and unfamiliar stimulus by cowering to the floor or by inhibiting his movements. This kind of dog was extremely slow in getting used to new surroundings, but, once familiar, he became an excellent subject for conditioning.

Meili-Dworetzki,[22] who studied in great detail the contrasting development of two brothers from birth through the ninth year of life, found that, throughout this span, the hyperkinetic child Hans responded to every stimulus with global action. He had weak boundaries between seeing and moving. He was attracted to strong and to new stimuli and he experienced pleasure with surprises. Fatigue augmented his restlessness. Fantasy was put in the service of wish fulfillment. He perceived the world as a source of total pleasure or total disappointment. By contrast, Max, a moderately active child, showed strong boundaries between seeing and moving. Seeing an object inhibited his motility. Instead of moving or acting, he looked attentively and, as he grew older, he became very persistent in attempting to cope through cognitive mastery. Novel stimuli evoked avoidance, motor inhibition, and rejection. He disliked surprises. Fatigue diminished his restlessness. Fantasy was put in the service of mastering insecurity on the one hand and reality on the other. Life was perceived and experienced as a difficult task. Escalona[4] found very similar behavioral characteristics in the two most and the two least active infants from her Topeka sample. She described the active babies as engaging mostly in forceful, total body activation. Fatigue increased restlessness and evoked loud screaming and often continuous crying. The inactive babies, by contrast, very rarely moved forcefully, relied mostly on gentle, coordinated small body movements and on *looking* instead of acting. Fatigue often decreased activation, usually led to whimpering, sometimes crying, but never to loud screaming. Escalona's description not only highlighted the differences in reaction patterns of these children, but also the differences in stimulus requirements for bringing out their optimal functioning.

These, and other examples in the literature, suggest that the individuals described represent clear-cut and extreme examples of differing ways of dealing with excitation. Such differences in the responsiveness, regulation and synthesis of strong external and internal stimuli are, in all likelihood, an expression of differences in neurophysiological makeup. From the evidence in the literature, I would postulate that there are two basic regulatory principles for dealing with overstimulation, each of which, if excessively relied upon, favors the adoption of broad categories of ego characteristics, ego defenses and cognitive styles. One of these will serve to sift, to diminish or to make manageable incoming stimuli. Focusing, sharpening,[9] a field independent[29] and an analytic and reflective approach[12] come to mind as cognitive control principles; obsessive-compulsive mechanisms, isolation, intellectualization and rationalization as defense mechanisms; and caution or avoidance of novel stimuli or strong excitation as general ego characteristics. The other regulatory principle, if strongly relied upon, would favor the management of strong stimulation through motor or affective discharge, through hypermotility, impulsivity, action rather than reflection, externalization, field-dependence, and/or displacement behavior. Novelty, change and strong excitation would be experienced as ego-syntonic. The choice or heavy reliance on any one type of coping strategy or defense mechanism *within* these two broad categories of reaction are very likely rooted within an experiential and/or maturational matrix. Maturationally, certain defenses may be adopted with the emergence of certain age-specific modes of thought or as a consequence of issues generated by the psychosexual stages. Experientially, this choice may be influenced by the kind or the intensity of the conflict to be defended against, or may be mediated through identification with, or internalization of parental modes of defense.

Obviously, it would be of great interest to identify in the neonate manifestations of the preponderance of either of the two postulated regulatory principles of dealing with overstimulation. In one of our studies, we have made a small beginning in identifying the associations of organismic tendencies in the neonate that resemble the behavioral clusters noted in Meili-Dworetzki's[22] and Escalona's[4] children. We found statistically significant correlations between the infants' tendency toward motor inhibition and the frequency of visual behavior on the one hand and the reliance on small motions on the other. Infants prone toward motor discharge, by contrast, were much less visually exploratory and tended to rely heavily on diffuse motor activity. We are currently getting equipped to test the hypotheses generated by this earlier study with a larger group of babies and through longer observations. We thus will monitor automatically the infants' activity on a 24-hour basis during their entire hospital stay with apparatus that will yield a differential count of large and of small motions. We will also assess the predominance of the infants' tendency to respond to sensory stimulation through motor abreaction or through motor inhibition. This will be done with the help of an instrumental bottle that records changes in rate and amplitude of non-nutritive sucking and that can be used to test the infant's reaction to a wide variety of sensory stimuli, including the strong and stressful ones that usually attend routine medical procedures in the newborn nursery.

## CONCLUSION

The observations presented here have implications both for child rearing and for longitudinal research. The finding that infants differ significantly from each other right from the very start suggests that there is more than one way of providing good child care; that, in fact, the only way to do so is to respond flexibly to the individual requirements of each and every child. It is regrettable that the trend of our times is exactly in the opposite direction. In clinical practice, for example, individual assessment and diagnosis have become devalued skills. The prevailing emphasis is on the fervent advocacy of one treatment method or another, rather than on the importance of a case-specific *choice* of treatment. Certain child care practices and certain forms of early stimulation are considered universally beneficial regardless of a given child's particular needs. We are thus forever looking for *the* method to raise children, to educate, to cure. One aspect of this trend is to see the mother and the care and stimulation she provides as almost solely responsible for the

normality and deviation of her child's development. While this stance feeds into the illusion that with the "correct methods" and the "right attitudes" we are in control of our children's destiny, it also produces a lot of guilt. This, in turn, undercuts parental effectiveness in dealing flexibly with each child's strengths and vulnerabilities. The practical implications of our findings are quite clear: In working with parents, it is important that we stress not only their crucial influence on their children's development but also that we free them to see, to hear, to tune in and to trust their own intuition in dealing differentially with what their children present as *separate* individuals.

The findings presented here also suggest that certain individual characteristics in the newborn will affect short-range adaptations, and others may color much of later development. For longitudinal follow-up of the latter, it would be strategic to follow mostly those infants who show a given tendency with unusual clarity, consistency and strength. This is based on the assumption that the combination of "an average expectable environment"[10] with "an average expectable child" will mostly reflect the successful amalgamation between the child's original tendencies and his environmental influences. This is apt to be less true of infants who are strongly endowed in one direction or another, since the persistence of a trait, or the derivative of a trait, may largely depend on its original strength. In line with this reasoning, it would be strategic to explore the range of responses in a given variable, or a group of variables, in a large sample of neonates, and then to follow longitudinally the extreme or the most clear-cut cases.

## REFERENCES

1. Benjamin, J. 1961. The innate and the experiential in development. *In* Lectures on Experimental Psychiatry, H. Brosin, ed. University of Pittsburgh, Pittsburgh.
2. Bergman, P., & Escalona, S. 1949. Unusual sensitivities in very young children. *In* The Psychoanalytic Study of the Child, vol. 3/4, P. Greenacre et al., eds., International Universities Press, New York.

3. Birns, B. 1965. Individual differences in human neonates' responses to stimulation. Child Developm. 36:249–256.

4. Escalona, S. 1963. Patterns of infantile experience and the developmental process. *In* The Psychoanalytic Study of the Child, vol. 18, R. Eissler, et al. eds., International Universities Press, New York.

5. Escalona, S., et al. 1952. Early phases of personality development: a non-normative study of infant behavior. Monograph of the Society for Research in Child Development 17 (Serial No. 54, No. 1).

6. Fantz, R. 1963. Pattern vision in newborn infants. Science 140:296–297.

7. Freud, S. 1937. Analysis terminable and interminable. *In* Collected Papers, vol. 5. Hogarth Press, London, 1950.

8. Fries, M., & Woolf, P. 1953. Some hypotheses on the role of the congenital activity type in personality development. *In* The Psychoanalytic Study of the Child, vol. 8, R. Eissler et al., eds. International Universities Press, New York.

9. Gardner, R., et al. 1959. Cognitive controls. A study of individual consistencies in cognitive behavior. Psychological Issues 1(4) monograph 4.

10. Hartmann, H. 1958. Ego Psychology and the Problem of Adaptation. International Universities Press, New York.

11. Honzik, M. 1964. Personality consistency and change: some comments on papers by Bayley, Macfarlane, Moss and Kagan, and Murphy. Vita Humana 7:139–142.

12. Kagan, J. 1967. Biological aspects of inhibition systems. Amer. J. Dis. Children 114:507–512.

13. Korner, A. 1965. Mother-child interaction: one- or two-way street? Social Work 10(3):47–51.

14. Korner, A. 1969. Neonatal startles, smiles, erections, and reflex sucks as related to state, sex, and individuality. Child Developm. 40(4):1039–1053.

15. Korner, A. 1970. Visual alertness in neonates: individual differences and their correlates. Perceptual and Motor Skills 31:499–509.

16. Korner, A. 1971. State as variable, as obstacle and as mediator of stimulation in infant research. Merrill-Palmer Quart. In press.

17. Korner, A., & Kraemer, H. 1971. Individual differences of spontaneous oral behavior in neonates. Third Symposium on Oral Sensation and Perception: The Mouth of the Infant, J. Bosma, ed. Charles C Thomas, Springfield, Ill. In press.

18. Korner, A., & Grobstein, R. 1966. Visual alertness as related to soothing in neonates: implications for maternal stimulation and early deprivation. Child Developm. 37:867–876.

19. Korner, A., & Grobstein, R. 1967. Individual differences at birth: implications for mother-infant relationship and later development. J. Amer. Acad. Child Psychiat. 6(4):676–690.

20. Korner, A., & Thoman, E. 1970. Visual alertness in neonates as evoked by maternal care. J. Exper. Child Psychol. 10:67–78.

21. Mednick, S. 1966. A longitudinal study of children with a high risk for schizophrenia. Ment. Hyg. 50(4):522–535.

22. Meili-Dworetzki, G. 1959. Lust und Angst. Regulative Momente in der Persönlichkeitsentwicklung zweier Brüder. Beiträge zur Genetischen Charakterologie, No. 3. Hans Huber, Bern.

23. Moss, H., & Robson, K. 1968. The role of protest behavior in the development of the mother-infant attachment. Paper presented at a symposium on attachment behaviors in humans and animals. 76th Annual Convention of the American Psychological Association, San Francisco.

24. Ornitz, E., & Ritvo, E. 1968. Perceptual inconstancy in early infantile autism. Arch. Gen. Psychiat. 18:76–98.

25. Pavlov, I. 1927. Conditioned Reflexes. Dover Publications, New York, 1960.

26. Piaget, J. 1936. The Origins of Intelligence in Children. International Universities Press, New York, 1952.

27. Schaffer, H., & Emerson, P. 1964. Patterns of response to physical contact in early human development. J. Child Psychol. Psychiat. 5:1–13.

28. Thomas, A., et al. 1963. Behavioral Individuality in Early Childhood. New York Universities Press, New York.

29. Witkin, H. 1965. Psychological differentiation and forms of pathology. J. Abnorm. Psychol. 70(5):317–336.

30. Wolff, P. 1966. The causes, controls, and organization of behavior in the neonate. Psychological Issues 5(1): Monograph 17.

# The Fels Study: Some Contributions to Personality Development and Achievement in Childhood and Adulthood

## Virginia C. Crandall

In view of the active nature-nurture controversy of the 1920s, it is not surprising that a new scientific institute should be charged by its sponsor, Samuel S. Fels, with finding those factors that give rise to differences among individuals as they develop. From this broad directive, the Fels Institute has evolved such that its present scientists are currently engaged in projects dealing with nine areas of basic research: behavioral physiology, biochemistry, dental research, endocrinology, pediatric research, physical growth and genetics, social development, perceptual-cognitive development, and the development of motivated behavior. To achieve a better understanding of the processes in each of these disciplines, researchers have sought the sequelae of naturally occurring genetic, physiologic, and psychologic conditions, and have experimentally created various task, test, and social situations to observe their effects on human responses. Although many of the studies and experiments conducted at Fels draw upon samples from maternity hospitals, nursery schools, summer camps, elementary and high schools, colleges, and senior citizens groups in the surrounding area, those that are devoted to investigating changes in the same individuals over time have obtained their data from a core population of subjects, followed longitudinally.

## FELS LONGITUDINAL PROJECT

### Subject Population

Fels subjects are actually enrolled in the longitudinal project from the fourth to the seventh mo prenatally. The regular psychologic program runs from birth through the 18th yr. From the initiation of the project in 1929 until 1944, six to eight infants were brought into the program each year. A minimum of ten infants have been added each year thereafter. Offspring of the original Fels subjects are included in this core sample if the parents continue to reside in the area. Thus, about 180+ children, ranging from birth to age 18, are actively engaged in the psychologic program at any one time. There are now relatively complete data for the first 18 yr of life on approximately 400 subjects, gathered since the beginning of the project. Less complete data are on file for additional children of Fels subjects who have moved away from the area.

Families from which the core sample has come volunteer for participation in the study, and they live within a 40-mile radius of the Institute in southwestern Ohio. Although about a fourth of them have lived in nearby cities, about half in small towns, and a fourth on farms, the educations, occupations, and life styles of the subjects do not follow usual rural-urban distinctions.

Approximately 15% of the fathers have been major professionals or executives, 35% businessmen and lesser professionals, 35% tradesmen and white collar workers, and 15% skilled and semiskilled laborers. Although the mean occupational level is somewhat above national norms, there is extensive variability around that mean, and it is probably more misleading than helpful to describe it only as "middle class." This is particularly true since the sample includes unusually wide representation of political and social values, levels of sophistication, and "ways of life." However,

Reprinted from *Seminars in Psychiatry*, 1972, 4(4), 383–398. Reprinted by permission of Grune & Stratton, Inc. and the author.

about 60% of both mothers and fathers have attended a year or more of college, 28% more have high school diplomas, and the remaining 12% did not finish high school. Thus, educational levels of the subjects' parents are markedly higher than those of the general American population, and it is probably accurate to conclude that they are relatively homogeneous in the high value they place on academic achievement.

*Psychologic Assessments.* Two to three-hr observations of the behavior of each mother and her child are made in the homes by trained observers at approximately 6-mo intervals. Detailed narrative summaries of these observations are written after each visit, and the mother's behavior is also rated on the Fels Parent Behavior Rating Scales.[1,2] The behaviors which are rated tap dimensions of affection-rejection, autonomy-control, protectiveness and nurturance, training of skills, rational-arbitrary discipline, and punitiveness. The semiannual home visit data have been gathered from birth to 6 yr of age throughout the history of the Institute, and annual observations through age 12 were also made until 1957. Each child is also observed from age 3 through age 5 at the Fels nursery school, which he attends twice yearly for 3-wk sessions. He is then brought for annual 8-day sessions to the Fels Day Camp throughout the elementary school years. Detailed time sampled observations are made on each child throughout each nursery school and day camp session, and he is rated on scales covering aggression, achievement behavior, dependency overtures, imitation, sex-role play, dominance attempts, conformity, sociability, and language use. At the conclusion of the session, a narrative summary is also prepared for each child describing other behaviors not covered in the rating scales.

During adolescence, interviews have been obtained at 2- or 3-yr intervals, and these are currently conducted at ages 11½, 14½, and 17½. An abbreviated Thematic Apperception Test is also administered at those ages. Interviews have been obtained on part of the sample at annual intervals from ages 6–12, and supplementary interviews during adolescence have been carried out on portions of the sample for particular studies underway at the time.

Mothers are also interviewed informally during each home visit. Additional structured interviews with both mothers and fathers have been obtained for portions of the sample to meet the requirements of certain studies.

To track the course of sensory motor and intellectual performance, the Gesell Developmental Schedule and the Merrill-Palmer Test were administered at regular intervals during infancy, the Stanford Binet through childhood, and the Wechsler-Bellevue and Primary Mental Abilities tests during adolescence. Since 1967, however, the series has consisted of the Bayley Infant Scales at 1, 3, 6, 9, 12, and 18 mo of age and the Merrill-Palmer Test at 2½ yr. The Stanford-Binet is given at 3½, 6, and 10 yr, and the newer Wechsler series overlaps the Binets with administrations at 4½, 7, and 9 yr. The Wechsler tests also extend beyond the Binets to ages 11, 13½, 16, and 18 yr. Since the subjects attend a variety of schools in the area, a standardized measure of school achievement, the Metropolitan Achievement Test, is administered at the institute at the end of the first grade yr, the sixth grade yr, and upon graduation from high school.

There are, in addition, biochemical assays and unusually complete data on the physical development of these subjects, covering anthropometric measurements, and dental, bone, muscle, and fat growth throughout the infancy, childhood, and adolescent years and beyond. Heart rate and other autonomic and psychophysical response measures have also been obtained on approximately 100 of the subjects.

## IMPLICATIONS OF FETAL BEHAVIOR AND ENVIRONMENT FOR PERSONALITY DEVELOPMENT

A series of studies by Sontag and his collaborators, designed to explore the behavior of the human fetus, point to a number of factors that exist or occur even before birth and may influence the course of personality development.[3–5]

The early work discovered three different types of fetal movement: (1) the sharp kicking or punching of the extremities, which increases steadily during the last trimester; (2) the slow squirming or writhing movements of the third to fourth mo before birth; and (3) the sharp, convulsive movements that have been described as a fetal hiccup or diaphragmatic spasm. Not only did weekly measurements of these activity levels demonstrate wide differences between the fetuses of various mothers, but also from one fetus to another in successive pregnancies of the same mother. Subsequent measures after birth revealed that high fetal activity levels were predictive of greater activity, restlessness, and resistance to handling during the first yr of life. Furthermore, Richards and Newberry[6] found that the active fetuses showed advanced performance on the Gesell Developmental Schedule at 6 mo and 12 mo of age. There was also a small but significant relationship of this activity level with the body mass of the newborn such that active fetuses were likely to weigh less in proportion to their length. That they should become thinner babies appeared reasonable, since calories used in fetal "exercise" cannot be stored as fat.

Reports by mothers that sudden loud noises that they experience in the course of their normal activities seemed to produce fetal activity, sometimes so pronounced as to be painful, provided the impetus for more controlled studies of the relationship of sound to activity level. When a small block of wood was placed on the mother's abdomen in the vicinity of the fetal head and struck with a clapper, there was an immediate and violent convulsive response on the part of the fetus in about 90 per cent of the cases. This movement appeared to be a sort of startle reflex, comparable to the Moro reflex after birth, and was accompanied by a pronounced increase in heart rate. In addition, fetal heart rate records demonstrated a lesser response to the sound as it was repeated at weekly intervals and the heart rate returned to normal levels more quickly than was the case for control groups of fetuses of the same gestational ages. This habituation or adaptation to repeated auditory stimuli raises the broader question concerned with adaptation that may take place in utero as the result of events that the mother encounters in her normal daily activity. Depending on the frequency and in-

tensity of those stimuli, fetuses may develop decreased levels of sensitivity to similar stimulation. Such "personal filters" may readily affect the impact of comparable environmental events to which the child is later exposed.

During the 10-yr course of these studies, there was by chance a small number of the women to whom sudden and severe emotional trauma occurred (desertion, husbands' psychotic break, husbands' death). Their fetal activity and heart rate records before the trauma provided base lines against which to compare the fetal responses after them. In each instance, the fetal activity rate increased from four- to tenfold, and the fetal heart rate increased by 20–25 beats per min. Furthermore, these elevations persisted for a matter of several weeks and well after the mother's overt manifestations of distress had disappeared. As compared with the others being studied, these fetuses became hyperactive and irritable babies, tended to have more frequent stools, cried more and slept more poorly. Some had severe feeding problems, greater intolerance of food, and tended to spit up more. These infant behaviors have often been shown to affect the parent-child relationship. The maternal solicitousness, protectiveness, overt or covert rejection and hostility that may ensue can have profound effects on the child's developing personality and social adjustment.

## SELECTED ASPECTS OF PERSONALITY DEVELOPMENT FROM BIRTH TO YOUNG ADULTHOOD

From 1957–1960, Kagan and Moss brought back to the institute 71 of the Fels longitudinal subjects, who were at that time 20–29 yr of age. A number of interview and test procedures were used to obtain adulthood data concerned primarily with passivity and dependency, aggression, and achievement. The childhood data for these subjects in the Fels files were divided into four age periods: 0–3 yr, 3–6 yr, 6–10 yr, and 10–14 yr, and the child's own behaviors and those of his mother were rated for each period. These ratings were then related to the data from the special adulthood assessment and the findings are reported in Kagan and Moss.[7]

As one might anticipate, the foundation of many adult behaviors began to be established during the childhood yr. While the child's behaviors during the very first 3 yr of life bore little relationship to those in adulthood, some behaviors began to stabilize during the preschool yr. By 6–10 yr of age most of the dependency, aggression, and achievement behaviors were quite similar to the amount of those behaviors the individuals displayed in young adulthood.

Second, there was greater stability of aggressive behaviors for males than for females; greater stability of passive-dependent behavior for females than for males. The authors have interpreted these differences in stability as a function of cultural pressures for appropriate sex role behavior. Because aggression is considered appropriate for males, it is culturally sanctioned and reinforced and thus maintains its stability. For females, on the other hand, aggression is considered inappropriate. Girls then are likely to develop more conflict about aggression and express it with less consistency. Conversely, dependency and passivity are likely to generate conflict for males, resulting in more fluctuation of those behaviors, while females are allowed to express dependency and thus maintain dependent responses across time. Achievement behaviors were quite stable for both sexes from 6–10 yr onward, presumably because it is culturally approved for both males and females.

The maternal behaviors examined in this study also showed differential stability depending on the sex of the child. Mothers were quite consistent throughout childhood in the degree to which they protected and nurtured their sons and in the degree to which they encouraged and fostered development of the boys' skills. These maternal behaviors showed more change over time for daughters. On the other hand, restriction of the child's freedom and activity, and the degree of hostility mothers evidenced toward their children were more stable for mothers of girls than for mothers of boys.

The maternal behaviors were also found to have differential impact on the child's later behavior, depending on his age at the time they occurred. In general, maternal treatment of the child in the first 3 yr of his life had a greater influence on his behavior at subsequent ages than did that same maternal behavior when it occurred later in development. For instance, maternal protectiveness and nurturance at 0–3 yr had a greater relationship to boys' passivity at 6–10 yr, and to their achievement attempts and their conformity at 6–10 and 10–14 yr, than did the same maternal treatment during the elementary school yr. There were, in fact, a number of instances in which maternal behaviors were correlated *only* with later child and adulthood behavior and showed no particular impact on the offspring at intervening age levels. For example, maternal hostility and lack of protectiveness toward daughters during the first 3 yr were good predictors of their achievement in adulthood, while exactly the reverse maternal treatments (again during infancy) were equally good predictors of sons' achievement in adulthood. In both cases, protection and hostility at later periods of the children's lives had little bearing on their adulthood achievement. This relation between maternal actions in early life and the child's behavior much later in time, when little consequence can be detected in the interim, has been termed a "sleeper effect."

Two possible explanations of this phenomenon were offered by investigators. Maternal behavior in infancy may set up a chain of events which ultimately, though not immediately, leads to a particular behavior on the child's part. For example, the mother's protectiveness during infancy may first lead to a dependency upon her solicitousness and affectionate response. Later, as adults begin to impose standards on the child's behavior and make their responsiveness contingent on his conformity to those standards, he may become more conforming and more achieving to obtain adult approval.

Maternal behavior in the very early years may also be a good indicator of the mother's own needs, attitudes and values. Because her infant is relatively more amorphous as an individual than he becomes in later childhood, her treatment of him in infancy is less likely to reflect his individuality and changes and problems that occur in his behavior. For this reason, maternal practices in the early years of life may be a more sensitive index of the mother's basic attitudes toward her child and, thus, of her long-term effect on his personality and behavior.

# REFERENCES

1. Baldwin, A. L., Kalhorn, J., and Breese, F. H.: Patterns of parent behavior. Psychol. Monogr. 58 (No. 3), 1945.
2. —, —, and —: The appraisal of parent behavior. Psychol. Monogr. 63 (No. 4), 1949.
3. Sontag, L. W.: War and the fetal maternal relationship. Marriage and Family Living 6:3, 1944.
4. —: The possible relationship of prenatal environment to schizophrenia. *In* Etiology of Schizophrenia. Basic Books, 1959, Chap. 7.
5. —: Implications of fetal behavior and environment for adult personalities. N.Y. Acad. Sci. 134:782, 1966.
6. Richards, T. W., and Newberry, H.: Studies in fetal behavior: III. Can performance on test items at six months post-natally be predicted on the basis on fetal activity? Child Develop. 9:79, 1938.
7. Kagan, J., and Moss, H.: Birth to Maturity. New York, Wiley & Sons, 1962.

# SUGGESTIONS FOR FURTHER READING

Bell, R. Q., Weller, G. M., & Waldrop, M. F. Newborn and preschooler: Organization of behavior and relations between periods. *Monographs of the Society for Research in Child Development,* 1971, *36*(1–2 Serial No. 142). Certain characteristics were studied in the same individuals as newborns and later as preschoolers; and in the follow-up sample significant relationships were found between characteristics manifested in the two periods. The study is summarized on pages 129–132.

Butcher, J. N., & Ryan, M. Personality stability and adjustment to an extreme environment. *Journal of Applied Psychology,* 1974, *59,* 107–109. A study of undergraduate explorers and Antarctic explorers, involving tests and retests eight months apart, showed significant differences between the two groups but no changes in personality profiles from the first test to the second.

Carrie, S. F., Holzman, W. H., & Swartz, J. D. Early indicators of personality traits viewed retrospectively. *Journal of School Psychology,* 1974, *12,* 51–59. Longitudinal-research data collected in the first grade and each of the next six years are used to identify personality traits that serve as precursers of later adjustment.

Crandall, V. C. The Fels study: Some contributions to personality development and achievement in childhood and adulthood. *Seminars in Psychiatry,* 1972, *4,* 383–397. A description is given of the Fels Research Institute's longitudinal project that began in 1929, including data on the first 18 years of life of about 400 subjects and their families. Studies of fetal behavior suggest prenatal factors that may influence later personality development. A comparison of behaviors of the same individuals in childhood and adulthood indicate that most of the dependency, aggression, and achievement behaviors displayed at ages 6 to 10 were similar to those displayed in young adulthood.

Davie, R., Butler, N., & Goldstein, H. *From birth to seven: The second report of the National Child Development Study.* New York: Humanities Press, 1972. This report of a longitudinal study of British children, traced from birth to age 7, deals with such factors as the children's education, family and social-class background, emotional problems, and relevant medical and health programs.

Fagot, B. I., & Patterson, G. R. An *in vivo* analysis of reinforcing contingencies for sex-role behaviors in the preschool child. *Developmental Psychology,* 1969, *1,* 563–568. Two nursery-school classes of 3-year-olds were rated on a sex-role behavior checklist intermittently for a year. Sex-appropriate behaviors proved stable over time, and these behaviors were consistently reinforced by teachers.

Haan, N. Personality development from adolescence to adulthood in the Oakland Growth and Guidance Studies. *Seminars in Psychiatry,* 1972, *4,* 399–414. The author presents data from Oakland studies of the Institute of Human Development and reports analyses of data for the adolescent to adult period. The topics considered include the stability of personality variables over time, the validity of stage theory, the increasing and decreasing importance of certain traits, and the individualization of developmental trends.

Jones, M. C., Bayley, N., McFarlane, J. W., & Honzik, M. P. *The course of human development*. Waltham, Mass.: Xerox College Publishing, 1971. This book pulls together from many publications the chief results of three programs of longitudinal study. These studies trace the course of many aspects of development by analyzing the same individuals over a number of years.

Kupfer, D. J., Detre, T. P., & Koral, J. Relationship of certain childhood "traits" to adult psychiatric disorders. *American Journal of Orthopsychiatry*, 1975, *45*, 94–80. This investigation relates adults' psychiatric problems to their childhood difficulties and lifelong personality traits.

Neugarten, D. L. Continuities and discontinuities of psychological issues into adult life. *Human Development*, 1969, *12*, 121–130. The author discusses discontinuities between the psychologies of childhood and adulthood, between those of the investigator and the subject, and between the stances of clinician and pediatrician.

Rosenblith, J. F. Relations between neonatal behaviors and those at 8 months. *Developmental Psychology*, 1974, *10*, 779–792. In this replication of earlier research, newborn behaviors are compared with those at 8 months. Scores on the 8-month examination and performance at 8 months are found to be significantly related to newborn behaviors in many respects.

Smith, A. C., Flick, G. L., Ferris, G. S., & Sellman, A. H. Prediction of developmental outcomes at seven years from prenatal, perinatal, and postnatal events. *Child Development*, 1972, *43*, 495–507. Certain prediction variables have proved useful in long-range prediction of normalcy and deviance.

Thomas, A., & Chess, S. Development in middle childhood. *Seminars in Psychiatry*, 1972, *4*, 331–341. In the longitudinal study described here, which followed the behavioral development of 136 children from early infancy onward, findings indicate that new behavioral characteristics emerge during the middle childhood period. The term *latency* is judged an inappropriate and confusing way to characterize children between the ages of 6 and 12. Instead, the authors suggest the use of simple descriptive designations, such as middle childhood or elementary school age, that connote no assumptions or theories about the dynamics of psychological development.

# 4

# Three Related Concepts: Imprinting, Instinct, and Critical Period

# INSTINCTS

Three closely related concepts in developmental theory are those of instinct, imprinting, and critical period. The first of these terms, *instinct,* has long occupied an important, though now declining, role in psychologists' deliberations. Instinctive behavior is expected to appear the first time an adequate stimulus is presented for which a response has not been learned. Instinctive behavior is relatively complex, and it must continue for a time in the absence of the stimulus that provoked it—unlike a reflex, which operates quickly and is simple by comparison. An instinctive behavior must also be characteristic of the whole species, else its genetic base is in doubt. Earlier, instinctive behaviors were defined as those whose appearance was not dependent on any special environmental stimulus. More recently, they have been defined as behaviors produced by maturation rather than learning.

In the prescientific period, it was generally believed that children were a complex of instincts, which were ready to appear full-blown whenever an adequate stimulus should release them. Thereafter, many psychologists discarded the term *instinct,* perhaps because confusion about what the term meant made it almost useless. Currently, many evade the discussion of human instincts, while conceding that certain animal behaviors, being more closely tied to biology, may be instinctual. Few psychologists today believe instinct of use in explaining human behavior. Nevertheless, many textbooks still deal with the topic, if for no other reason than that most students hold many of the popular but false notions on the topic. Besides, instincts hold an important place historically in psychological theory.

Interpretations of instinct in recent or current textbooks vary considerably. Krech, Crutchfield, and Livson (1974) call instincts *biological motives.* In this sense, all behaviors are portrayed as serving tissue needs, whether directly or indirectly. For example, the motive to acquire social prestige, a second-order drive, may be said to serve the primary first-order sex drive. Sutton-Smith (1973) differentiates between instinctive responses and instinctive behaviors. The child is manifesting an instinctive response who "jumps at the drop of a dish or pan"(p.27). Instinctive reflex actions play a more significant role in animal than in human behavior. For example, after the female cat has her first litter she eats the placenta, kills any deformed kittens, and then nurses the survivors. Such behavior is generally called instinctive rather than learned. However, even among animals much behavior called instinctive has been shown to depend on normalized conditions. For example, Rhesus monkeys reared by machines that dispense food, rather than by other monkeys, later on fail to show a normal range of mating and other social responses that had been considered instinctive (Harlow & Zimmerman, 1959). Sutton-Smith (1973) concludes that human behaviors do not qualify as instinctive behaviors, even in the case of motherhood. He notes that women throughout the world care for their babies in highly varied ways. Some mothers even abandon their children at birth. It is significant that in recent issues of *Psychological Abstracts,* instincts are treated only under the topic "Animal Instinctive Behavior."

This editor rejects the notion of instincts altogether. So-called instinctive behavior is merely a response to specific-object properties, derived from the biological nature of the organism. Also, many apparently unlearned actions may not be unlearned at all. Behaviors such as a bird's flying south may represent the integration of activities already learned, such as abilities to fly and to establish direction, coupled with certain maturational changes in the organism itself.

In sum, the vast majority of authorities believe the term *instinct* to be of little use in explaining human behavior. Humans mature so slowly that they possess tremendous capacities for adaptability. Anyhow, the debate is muted, largely because it offers little worthwhile return. But a great many people persist in the belief that particular behaviors—for example, mothering behaviors—are natural, or instinctive.

## IMPRINTING AND CRITICAL PERIOD

Of more concern at present are two relatively new and closely related concepts, those of imprinting and critical period. Imprinting implies learning that can occur only during a comparatively brief period in the early life of the organism. Once learned, the behavior becomes almost as firm and as irreversible as though it were innate. Imprinting may well serve important adaptive functions. For example, since the young lamb becomes imprinted very early with its mother, it remains close by her side. Else it might well take off with "a casually encountered wolf as its mother with obvious and strikingly maladaptive consequences" (Krech, Crutchfield, & Livson, 1974, p. xvii).

Considerable research confirms the existence of imprinting phenomena. In a typical experiment, an animal imprinted, or exposed, to a human and deprived of contact with its own species during a brief critical stage becomes attached to the human instead of its own kind. For example, if the critical period for teaching mallards to follow humans is missed by even a few hours, and if during that period they have been exposed to a mother duck, they cannot be taught to follow humans.

At least one theory provides a plausible explanation for imprinting among animals and perhaps also for infants. According to three English biologists (Horn, Rose, & Bateson, 1973), specific biochemical changes in the nervous system for various species are very different in earlier and later development. The dramatically fast learning involved in imprinting derives from the unusual plasticity of the nervous system in the newborns of those species. It is uncertain whether anything like imprinting occurs among humans. Certainly, the baby does acquire, at around 6 months of age, a close attachment to its caretaker. At about the same time, babies begin to display a fear of strangeness. Hence, some psychologists entertain the idea that this brief span of time may represent the human counterpart to the subhuman's imprinting period (Krech, Crutchfield, & Livson, 1974).

Implicit within the concept of imprinting is the critical-period hypothesis: that certain experiences may have a far more profound effect at certain periods than at others. The concepts of critical period and of imprinting may be differentiated in several ways. Imprinting typically involves behaviors more basically rooted in the organism, whereas a critical period may involve any sort of learning, from very simple to extremely complex. Imprinted learning occurs early in life, a critical period at any time during life. Moreover, imprinting takes place in a very short period of time, whereas a critical period may span months, or even years. Typically, imprinting is confined to one brief period; but there may be two or even more critical periods for establishing a particular behavior. For example, there may be two critical periods for establishing sex role: early childhood and puberty.

Critical periods may relate both to animals and to humans. Among animals, critical periods are usually early. A dog owner can establish a firm bond with a puppy when it is between 3 and 8 weeks old. The puppy's sense organs are fully enough developed to permit awareness, but its cerebral cortex is still developing. These factors suggest that the affection somehow becomes built in. Among humans, critical periods generally occur early, but may occur at any stage. The period of early childhood has been called critical for establishing a sense of trust, and early adolescence for establishing a feeling of identity.

Let us consider a few examples. With regard to IQ there seems to be some time near the second birthday that is critical for complete recovery from the effects of deprivation (Bronfenbrenner, 1970). Children adopted before the age of 2 recover completely, or almost completely, from earlier retardation, whereas those adopted later continue to be retarded. Such findings suggest the need for very early educational intervention programs. In another study (Livson & Peskin, 1967), leisure-time activities in childhood were related to psychological adjustment at age 30. The most predictive period proved to be the years 8 to 11, which suggests that effective mastery of reality and social interaction are critical at this period. Still another study (Ali, 1973) suggests that the critical period for developing the individual dispositions that facilitate exploration have already been established by age 4 and may not be affected by increasing age or maturity. In this study, 4- and 5-year-old children who demonstrated exploratory behaviors became totally engrossed and remained relatively free from distracting anxieties. One small girl showed "emotional freedom and comfort; she explored the entire stimulus field very thoroughly, never was afraid or anxious to touch or play with anything. She had a tremendous capacity and ability to attract and sustain adult attention"(p. 325). By contrast, a low-competent child "did poorly on all exploratory tasks; she was withdrawn, inhibited, and sad all the time, unusu-

ally slow in movements and had difficulty in opening the plastic box"(p. 325).

The age of school entrance, writes Nash (1970), may also relate to a critical period. Note that all educational systems begin formal teaching of children between 5 and 7 years of age. Piaget himself designated the age of 7 as a major transitional point when the child is capable of intuitive understanding of relations between objects, and so-called concrete operations become possible. By this time presumably the Oedipal situation has been worked through, and the latency period has begun. During this latency period psychosexual development is slow, but social and cognitive development progress rapidly.

Certainly the critical-period concept, if valid, has significant implications for designing learning environments. It seems pretty certain that young children must have ample sensory experience, autonomy training, creative toys, and positive reinforcement, if they are to become competent people and superior learners later on. However, foundations that are critical for later developments may sometimes have no easily apparent relationship to them. For example, it seems critical for subsequent creative development that children establish foundations at an early age of self-confidence and autonomy. It also appears critical for the later acquisition of language and spelling skills that a child develop a respect for rules. However, this same characteristic, if overdeveloped, may prove critical in impeding later scientific and mathematical achievements.

Bruner (1971) relates the critical-period hypothesis to stage theory. He believes that the mastery of practically all human skills involves a series of hierarchical steps. Hence, efficiency requires that the learner take these steps in a particular order, consistent with the child's own stages of growth. Moreover, there seem to be optimal or critical times for educating children in particular abilities. The opposite is also true—that is, there are times when results are especially unfortunate if certain conditions do not prevail. For example, dietary deficiencies experienced by a child during the first month of life may interfere with the production of cortical (brain) cells. On the other hand, if the child experiences deprivation of protein later in life, after the central nervous system has stabilized, little or no damage is apparent (Cratty, 1970). Note, too, that having experiences during particular critical periods is more vital in some developmental areas than in others. That is, developments in affective, motor, and cognitive areas are not equivalent. For example, retardation in locomotion deriving from lack of opportunity for motor experience may not be permanent. However, the effect of inadequate or abnormal affective relationships may be enduring (Shapiro & Biber, 1972).

## ISSUES RAISED

Certain issues arise relative to each of these three concepts. As for instinct, several questions suggest themselves: If, as certain writers suggest, some human behaviors are instinctive, which behaviors are they? Also, if we have abandoned the concept of instinct for that of maturation, just how does maturation relate to learning in the development of behaviors? In working with animals, are we simply masking our ignorance by labeling as instinct those behaviors that we do not understand?

Other questions arise about imprinting. Does something akin to imprinting occur among humans? Have many of our unexplained likes or aversions sprung from imprinting-like experiences when we were infants? Would it be well to rig the infant's environment scientifically to ensure imprinting of a healthy and constructive nature? If fathers spent more time with their infant children, would father love become as important as mother love? Could machines be devised to facilitate desirable imprinting processes?

By contrast with instinct and imprinting, the concept of critical period is deemed of considerable significance for humans; but many questions about it remain. For instance, how should patterns of home and school training be organized to insure optimum learning? Are critical periods for all children essentially the same? Are such periods built in, the result of maturation, or are they the result of experiential sequences, or both? Among animals we look

for specific stages in maturation of sensory or motor functions in the central nervous system, but we are unclear on these matters with humans. For instance, we are still uncertain just how children acquire language and their own styles of speech. Anyhow, the attention shown this concept by researchers should yield fruitful hypotheses and, hopefully, certain practical applications during the next several years.

In the first selection Ladd Wheeler, Robert Goodale, and James Deese review earlier concepts of instinct, and explain the modern concept of the term. In the second excerpt John Nash discusses several studies of imprinting among animals and considers its possible relevance for humans. In the last selection Burton White and Jean Carew Watts tell why they believe that the 10- to 18-month period is especially critical in human development. They base this conclusion on the results of a longitudinal study that was designed to determine what types of child rearing are most effective. All three concepts—instinct, imprinting, and critical period—are still controversial, especially where humans are concerned.

## REFERENCES

Ali, F. Dimensions of competence in young children. *Genetic Psychology Monographs,* 1973, *88* (Second Half), 305–328.

Bronfenbrenner, U. Two worlds of childhood:U.S. and U.S.S.R. *Psychology Today,* February 1970, pp. 6; 8; 80.

Bruner, J. S. The process of education revisited. *Phi Delta Kappan,* 1971, *53*(1), 18–21.

Cratty, B. J. *Perceptual and motor development in infants and children.* New York: Macmillan, 1970.

Harlow, H. F., & Zimmerman, R. R. Affectional responses in the infant monkey. *Science,* 1959, *130,* 421–423.

Horn, G., Rose, S. P. R., & Bateson, P. P. G. Experience and plasticity in the central nervous system. *Science,* 1973, *181,* 506–514.

Krech, D., Crutchfield, R. S., & Livson, N. *Elements of Psychology* (3rd ed.). New York: Alfred A. Knopf, 1974.

Livson, N., & Peskin, H. Prediction of adult psychological health in a longitudinal study. *Journal of Abnormal and Social Psychology,* 1967, *72,* 509–518.

Nash, J. Critical periods: Time and rate in cognitive development. In *Developmental psychology: A psychobiological approach*. Englewood Cliffs, N.J.: Prentice-Hall, 1970.

Shapiro, E., & Biber, B. The education of young children: A developmental-interaction approach. *Teachers College Record,* 1972, 74(1), 55–79.

Sutton-Smith, B. *Child psychology*. New York: Appleton-Century-Crofts , 1973.

# Instincts

## Ladd Wheeler
## Robert A. Goodale
## James A. Deese

These relatively simple changes in the sensitivity of the nervous system to external stimulation lead us to consider the relation between the modifiability of our reactions and those components of behavior that are controlled by inborn patterns in the nervous system. The latter are what we usually refer to as *instincts*. Instincts are unlearned patterns of behavior, under the control of external stimuli (*releasers*) and internal conditions within the organism. The tendency to perform some instinctive act arises through the growth of the nervous system (Tinbergen 1951). The behavior emerges in its entirety when a particular external stimulus elicits it and the nervous system is ready to respond through its own development and the presence of hormones in the internal environment.

The concept of instinct, or innate patterns of behavior, was rejected by Watson and the

From *General Psychology*, by L. Wheeler, R. A. Goodale, and J. A. Deese. Copyright © 1975 by Allyn and Bacon, Inc. Reprinted by permission.

behaviorists. That rejection was due not only to Watson's extreme position on the influence of the environment, but also to the behaviorists' skepticism toward all preconceptions about the determinants of behavior. Remember that psychology, when it began, brought with it many ancient notions of what man is. In the desire to find basic truth, the behaviorists suggested that all things undefinable and unobservable be rejected until whatever man is becomes apparent from the objective data, rather than from assumed motives or influences.

At the time, much of the criticism and rejection of instinct by the behaviorists was deserved. After Darwin published his theory on evolution, textbook writers were fond of listing the many animal and human instincts that guided behavior. These lists differed widely from writer to writer and were largely based only on anecdote or logical argument (Bernard 1924). Early experiments aimed at discovering whether particular behaviors were instinctive or learned tended to come out in favor of the latter explanation. For example, baby chicks peck immediately after hatching, and many observers would regard that behavior as innate. Similarly, the fact that cats stalk and kill mice and rats is widely held to be instinctive. However, after a series of studies, Kuo (1932a, b, c, d) suggested that the chick actually learns to peck while in the egg. At an early stage, the chick's head is moved up and down by the beating of the embryonic heart. Later, the chick (still in the egg) responds to external stimulation by bending its head and opening and closing its beak. Much later, fluid entering the beak through these head movements is swallowed. Gradually, the movements of bending the head, opening and closing the beak, and swallowing become integrated into a single pattern, and that sequence provides the unborn chick with the opportunity to learn to peck immediately after hatching.

Kuo's (1930) investigation of rat-killing by cats showed that when kittens and rat pups were raised together in a single cage, the popularly predicted consequences never arrived. The rat did not cower before the cat with fear and trembling, and the full grown cat did not gaze at the rat hungrily. Far from an adversary relationship, the cat and rat "loved" each other, and one became restless and anxious whenever the other was temporarily removed from the cage.

Thus, when the concept of instinct was rejected in the early 1920s and 1930s as a valid explanation of behavior, there was little resistance in the United States. All the evidence and logic suggested that behaviors labeled as instinctive reflected only our ignorance of the true determinants of behavior, and that further study would reveal the many learning opportunities which were presently obscure (Beach 1955).

Some European biologists were not as convinced, however, that the notion of innate patterns could be so easily swept aside. Their continued investigation into innate behaviors and the mechanisms regulating the emergence of these behaviors has recently made the concept of innate patterns and predispositions very plausible indeed as an explanation of many animal behaviors and of many human behaviors. . . .

Lorenz, one of the leading contemporary spokesmen for the innate theory, points out that Kuo's observations of the embryonic chick in the egg "learning" to peck hardly explains the behavior of all birds. Some young birds, such as robins and thrushes, lift their heads and gape instead of pecking, and ducklings "shovel" with their bills rather than peck. Even if Kuo's explanation were accepted as evidence for learning how to peck, says Lorenz (1965), he would have to account for why what the chick learns in the egg is so perfect for what the chick must do to survive after hatching. In essence, Kuo is left to look for an "innate schoolmarm."

According to Lorenz, early learning theorists tremendously overrated the amount of learning that could possibly take place during early development. Consider, says Lorenz, the young swift—reared in a dark, narrow crevice with no opportunity to spread its wings, let alone beat them up and down. Nor can it attain a sharp visual image. Everything visual must be a blur for the swift, because the farthest point in its nest is nearer than the nearest point that the bird's eyes can focus on at that point in its development. Nevertheless, the moment a young swift leaves the nest, it not only flies, but it copes successfully with air resistance, updrafts, and turbulence; it can recognize and catch prey; and it can make a precise landing at a suitable place. A description of all information necessary to perform these behaviors successfully would fill many volumes; yet the swift puts it all together instantly. Any explanation of such complex integration, in such a brief time, by such an inferior learner (when compared to man), certainly strains the learning explanation, says Lorenz.

The modern concept of instinct, as defined by adherents such as Lorenz (1965) and Tinbergen (1951), is quite different from the concept rejected by the behaviorists, when it was defined as any complex pattern of behavior, universal to the species, which arises fullblown upon first presentation of the appropriate stimulus without any prior opportunity to learn the response. That definition essentially set up a two-category classification: learning and instinct. But instinct was defined as anything common to the species which could not be shown to have been learned. Thus, instinct became, in effect, a wastebasket into which behaviors fell automatically if evidence for learning them could not be found. That definition is what psychologists call a "negative definition:" Instinct is the *absence* of learning.

The modern definition of instinct is a positive definition; that is, a behavior is defined as instinctive only when the specific pattern of behavior being called instinctive is described and *the stimulus that releases that pattern is identified*. Thus, whereas such general behaviors as self-preservation, fighting, or reproduction were previously labeled instincts, nowadays behavior patterns described as instinctive are the smiling response of the human infant, the gaping response of the young herring gull, or the downward spiraling escape movements of the nocturnal moth. These instinctive patterns are specific fixed-action patterns and not the broad categories designated earlier that included many behaviors within them.

In addition, when a specific behavior is labeled instinctive, the stimulus that "releases" that behavior is identified. Instincts are presumed to contain their own energy supply, and that energy is released by the releasing stimulus. Instincts, then, are no longer defined by the absence of something (learning), but by the presence of something (the releaser). Thus, the releaser for picking up a human infant and cuddling it is the "babyish" shape of the infant's head. The releaser of the gaping response in young herring gulls in the nest is the red spot on the parent's beak.

As research and theoretical interpretation has continued, ethologists (students of behavior that occurs in natural settings) have broadened the range and complexity of behaviors presumed to be innately governed and released by innate releasing mechanisms (IRMs). For example, animals normally escape when a predator approaches (Lorenz 1966). However, if the predator reaches a position closer than a "critical distance" before the animal can escape, an attack is triggered instead of escape, and the trapped animal fights like the legendary cornered rat. Lorenz suggests that hunting "accidents" on wild game safaris are due to an unsuspecting hunter entering the thick underbrush and penetrating the animal's critical distance. Presumably, circus lion tamers play that game for thrills.

A more far-reaching application of the doctrine of innate behaviors and their releasers has been suggested by Lorenz in his book, *On Aggression* (1966). Lorenz believes the invention of weapons seriously upset the rules by which living organisms, humans in this case, get along together. Social animals are presumed to have inhibitory mechanisms that control aggression and prevent an animal from killing members of his own species. Among humans, killing of one another was less probable before weapons, because the intended victim could escape or could elicit the pity of the aggressor through screaming, crying, submissive gestures, and appeasing attitudes. Now, however, high-altitude bombers and nuclear missiles enable men to kill one another without directly witnessing the carnage. Thus, whatever inhibitory mechanisms are ordinarily available during a face-to-face encounter are no longer available.

Another example of an innate response, says Lorenz, is the response we call "patriotism," "militant enthusiasm," or "*esprit de corps.*" He sees it as a specialized form of communal aggression. A shiver runs down the back and along the outside of both arms. An emotional soaring causes elation, and the individual is ready to forsake all in the call of duty. Muscle tone increases, carriage stiffens, the head is raised, the jaw juts out, and the facial muscles take on the look of the film hero. Inhibitions against hurting or killing a fellow-species member lose their power. Originally, says Lorenz, that reaction was in response to a vital challenge to the small community of known members, held together by bonds of kinship, love, and friendship. As the social unit grew from the family to the country, certain customs, rites, and insignia began to symbolize that communal bond. As the symbolization process grew, however, it became detached from its human origins. Symbols could now be used to generate defense of one's country, or they could be used to make men want to go to war for "honorable and just" causes. Like any other instinct, communal patriotism has its releasers. The key releasing stimuli, says Lorenz, are (1) a threat to the social unit by some outside force, (2) the presence of an "enemy" from whom the threat emanates, (3) an inspiring leader figure, and (4) the presence of many individuals feeling the same emotion. Manipulation of these releasers by self-aggrandizing leaders or misguided government officials can cause men to kill their brothers in the name of the highest moral and ethical values (Lorenz 1966). According to Lorenz, the belief that human aggression is learned causes us to institute the wrong remedies. In so doing, we prevent the channeling of aggressive energy through harmless outlets and thus lead ourselves into worse predicaments.

For Lorenz and others, instinct is the foundation upon which learning rests. If changes in behavior can be wrought through learning, then learning must have some adaptive value. Learning must do something that assures the survival of a species, and that is why there is an evolutionary trend toward organisms with greater and greater capacities to learn. Learning occurs, however, only in behavior sequences where adaptation to local conditions must be made while playing out the inborn predispositions.

The interplay between learning and innate factors suggested by Lorenz (1957) can be seen in two examples. A raven, when nest-building begins to emerge, will carry all types of objects in its bill. Later, another component of nest-building emerges, namely a sideways quivering of the head, and the raven begins to carry only twigs and straw. The sideways motion catches the material in the nest, producing a satisfying reaction in the bird which causes him to let go of the twig. Since this satisfaction does not result when pieces of shingle or paper are brought to the nesting site (these materials do not catch when pushed sideways), the bird soon "learns" to choose the right materials.

A young dove, sexually mature, will begin to make nest-calling sounds. When the bird is given a nest for the first time, it doesn't appear to recognize it as a nesting site. In the process of nest-calling from here, there, and everywhere, the bird inevitably ends up in the nest at some point. What happens then is best described by Craig (1918), who performed the experiment: "he abandons himself to an orgy of nest-calling. . . , turning now this way and now that in the hollow, palpating the straw with his feet, wings, breast, neck and beak, and rioting in a wealth of new, luxurious stimuli."

For Lorenz (1965), adaptation for survival is the key principle. Since evolutionary progression shows that learning ability increases upon ascending the phylogenetic scale, then learning must have survival value. The more flexibility allowed to meet and change with local conditions, the greater are an organism's chances of survival. But learning is always in service to the survival mechanisms born into the species through evolutionary time. Therefore, although man may have fewer obvious innate patterns of response than lower organisms do, he still does have them and they determine his behavior in many ways. Visual processes, reflexes, growth of the nervous system and the like are relatively fixed, and their range of modifiability in the normal, healthy, intact organism is essentially uninfluenced by learning. Social bonds and feelings of safety,

for instance, are instincts man experiences only on the emotional level, and he is free to roam far and wide to achieve their satisfaction. A bird may be bound by the sight and feel of a crotch in a tree and a small range of suitable nesting materials in order to feel "at home." Man may use a wider variety of habitat and dwellings, but he must have an emotional feeling of being "at home" and secure.

Even that joy in beautifully executed movement that can cause us endlessly to practice dancing or skating or to pay to see professional athletes in superb condition is, says Lorenz, the subjective joy from a "perfection-reinforcing mechanism" that evolved to ensure economy of movement in survival activities. Some innate behavior patterns may even hinder us, as when the most rational and careful thinkers "lose their heads" and fall in love. And ganging up on the individual who diverges too much from the group norm ("fatty," "stinky," "fairy") may be an expression of instinctive group defenses, says Lorenz.

For Lorenz and his followers, there is no simple division into learned versus innate responses. There are many innate responses—the releasing mechanism, orientation mechanisms, eye-brain-muscle integrations, fixed action patterns (like the smile response of an infant)—and these innate responses are as different from one another as hands and feet are. Some patterns are entirely innate, and in some behavior chains learned elements fill the gaps between innate links, or even other innate patterns may fill the gap. But there are no chains or patterns of responses that are "only" learned (Lorenz 1965). With that, there seems little left for us but instinctively to move on.

## REFERENCES

Beach, F. A. The descent of instinct. *Psychological Review*, 1955, *62*, 401–410.

Bernard, L. L. *Instinct: A study in social psychology*. New York: Henry Holt, 1924.

Kuo, Z. Y. The genesis of the cat's response to the rat. *Journal of Comparative Psychology*, 1930, *11*, 3–35.

Kuo, Z. Y. Ontogeny of embryonic behavior in aves. I: The chronology and general nature of the behavior of the chick embryo. *Journal of Experimental Zoology,* 1932, *61,* 395–430. a

Kuo, Z. Y. Ontogeny of embryonic behavior in aves. II: The mechanical factors in the various stages leading to hatching. *Journal of Experimental Zoology,* 1932, *62,* 453–487. b

Kuo, Z. Y. Ontogeny of embryonic behavior in aves. III: The structural and environmental factors in embryonic behavior. *Journal of Comparative Psychology,* 1932, *13,* 245–271. c

Kuo, Z. Y. Ontogeny of embryonic behavior in aves. IV: The influence of embryonic movements upon behavior after hatching. *Journal of Comparative Psychology,* 1932, *14,* 109–122. d

Lorenz, K. Z. *The nature of instinct in instinctive behavior: The development of a modern concept.* New York: International Universities Press, 1957.

Lorenz, K. Z. *Evolution and modification of behavior.* Chicago: University of Chicago Press, 1965.

Lorenz, K. Z. *On aggression.* New York: Harcourt, Brace & World, 1966.

Tinbergen, N. *The study of instinct.* London: Oxford University Press, 1951.

# Human Imprinting

## John Nash

There has been some interest in the question of human infantile smiling since Darwin (1877) noted the first smile to appear at about forty-five days—not, of course, that Darwin was the first to observe that babies smile; he

From pp. 153–158 of *Developmental Psychology: A Psychobiological Approach,* by J. Nash. Copyright © 1970. Reprinted by permission of Prentice-Hall, Inc., Englewood Cliffs, New Jersey.

was merely early in wondering about its scientific significance. Gray (1958) has proposed that the smiling response is the human analogue of the following response in birds. J. P. Scott (1963) has suggested that in canine puppies tail wagging is the corresponding action and that each species makes a behavioral response that is within its repertoire at the time imprinting occurs. This may be the answer to the earlier argument about the necessity for active following.

Spitz and Wolf (1946) followed Kaila in studying the smiling response and showed that at first it could be brought about by anything rudimentarily resembling a human face but that later only a familiar face would be effective in producing it. In an orphanage population they found little smiling before two months of age and nearly 100 percent response between about three and five months. By the sixth month the smile would show only to a familiar adult face and was not given to strangers. Evidently by this age discrimination is possible; the findings also suggest attachment to specific persons. Ambrose (1963) has reported a study that is consistent with the results of Spitz and Wolf, but he found both the beginning and the end of the indiscriminate smiling period to be earlier in home-reared infants than in those in orphanages. His results, however, are based upon small numbers (four in each group). Both Gray (1958) and J. P. Scott (1963) regard this period of indiscriminate smiling as one in which the child is establishing social contacts. Before about five or six weeks these contacts are impossible, or at least difficult, and from the data on deprivation produced by Bowlby and others, it is concluded that the end of indiscriminate smiling also represents the end of the period of imprinting or of establishing social relations. If no social relationships are formed by this age, then all subsequent ones, especially those more intense and permanent ones we call "attachments," are rendered more difficult.

Apparently the smile is not in the early days a response specific to the face or its representation. Salzen (1963) has reported that it can be elicited by a change in brightness.

From studies of a large number of Russian

children, Kistyakovskaya (1965) has concluded that smiling in infants is a response not only to people but to a range of prolonged visual or auditory stimuli as well. Other "positive emotional responses" also accompany these stimuli, and both these responses and smiling are independent of the satisfaction of organic needs. She does not, however, regard smiling as an innate response.

Babies may be observed smiling to themselves, without any obvious stimulus being apparent and when the observer is hidden. Some naturalistic observations of this phenomenon might modify theorizing in this area. The fact that infants might smile spontaneously or in response to a broad range of stimuli would not necessarily invalidate the idea that smiling is primarily a social response; it could be, for example, that the human face is the commonest or most potent arouser, but this suggestion needs to be checked.

This emphasis on visual stimuli in the imprinting of the human infant arouses questions about blind children. There is no evidence to suggest that their socialization as adults is adversely affected, at least beyond what one could attribute directly to their handicap. It seems that some alternative method of imprinting is available. A number of studies show that the efficacy of imprinting in animals can be improved by adding auditory stimuli to the visual ones (Gottlieb, 1963). Also, auditory stimuli alone can elicit following in birds (Collias, 1952; Collias and Collias, 1956). It may be that in some species born blind, such as the cat, imprinting is essentially a nonvisual procedure. The role of auditory or other sensations in human imprinting has not been explored, but it is suggested that the literature that treats it as a specifically visual phenomenon may be oversimplifying the matter.

An important point about imprinting, for developmental theory, is that it appears to provide an explanation for the beginnings of socialization. J. P. Scott (1963) has spoken of primary socialization during the "smiling" period, when the infant becomes attached to the parents. This attachment is the first social relationship to be formed. From it the infant generalizes (by what Scott calls secondary socialization) attachments to the species to which the parents (and the infant itself) belong. That is, by way of this initial imprinting the young animal becomes a socialized member of its species.

Animals misimprinted to other species show a variety of abnormal social behaviors as adults. In many cases they will ignore their own kind and direct their attentions to those they had known in infancy. Sluckin (1965) has reviewed in a variety of species a number of cases of courtship behaviors that are directed toward an inappropriate object; for example, he talks of birds making their courtship display to men or even to inanimate objects, when imprinted to these things. Despite tall stories and ancient myths about infants reared by wolves, we have no reliable accounts of humans misimprinted in this way, though Harlow gives good accounts of rhesus monkeys imprinted to cloth mother surrogates. What we might have in humans is nonimprinted infants. Bowlby and others have spoken of the origins of psychopathy (better perhaps called sociopathy) in adults who as children were separated from their parents over the critical imprinting period (the smiling one) and who thus lack the initial primary socialization from which all later social relationships are assumed to derive.

Under natural conditions an animal misimprinted or not imprinted at all would have little chance of survival. This might be also true in many primitive human communities and the sociopath might be an artificial product of civilized societies. Not only is imprinting fairly permanent, but the results of nonimprinting are also long-lasting; the difficulties of producing normal social responses from sociopaths are notorious to clinicians.

From the summed data of a number of studies of children deprived of normal parental care at various times in the first three years it appears that the first three months are not critical to imprinting, that the period from three to six months is the critical one, and that susceptibility to imprinting may wane after six months. Schaffer and Emerson (1964), in a study of sixty infants, found an initial period of indiscriminate attachments to people, followed in the sixth to ninth months by specific attachments to those most consistently around them.

One question about imprinting is whether or not it is an all-or-none phenomenon. Many of the experimenters refer to the strength of the following response; it is evident that there are variations in this behavior that are correlated with environmental differences (and perhaps, too, though this seems unexplored, with genetic differences between individuals and strains). If, however, we regard imprinting not merely in the context of this specific behavior but also as the precursor of more varied social behaviors, then the question arises as to the relationship between early strength of following and later social responses. Are the weaker followers less responsive in their social interactions, or is there an all-or-none relationship so that there are no effective differences in imprinting? In this case any strength of imprinting above threshold would be effective, and in later life these early differences would be lost. There does seem to be an experimental answer to this question. Clinical observations do suggest degrees of imprinting.

Most of the literature treats imprinting as a one-way phenomenon, with offspring imprinting to their parents. A few writers speak of the reverse, parents imprinting to their young, and there is enough evidence to suggest that this is a real phenomenon, at least in some species.

In cats, according to Schneirla and Rosenblatt (1961), the odor of birth fluids plays an important role in forming the tie between the mother and her kittens. Blauvelt (1955) found that in goats the period immediately following birth is a critical one in the development of mother-young relationships. As soon as the kid leaves the mother's body, she licks it, and she keeps her head close to the kid lying on the ground until it can stand up and walk to her. If the mother is restrained from this licking after birth and is removed for a short time, she does not lick on return, and it may take a long time for the mother-kid relationship to be established. Even after only a few minutes of separation, the mother may be quite disturbed when the kid is reintroduced. If the mother is allowed to feed the kid before this separation, the reunion is much quicker afterward. It would seem that the effects of severance are permanent; Hersher et al. (1958) separated newborn kids from their mothers at times ranging from five to ten minutes after birth and kept them separated between thirty minutes and one hour. After the separation, the kids were helped to suckle from their own mother (apparently they could not do so successfully without help), after which there was no further interference for two to three months. At the end of this time the animals were tested by placing the mother in an experimental chamber with three kids, one of which was her own. Control mothers were highly selective in suckling their own kids, but the experimental ones spent significantly more time suckling others.

Collias (1956) has given experimental confirmation of what shepherds have long known, that the ewe is attracted to the newborn by odor. Normally a ewe will accept a young lamb in place of her own, but an orphan lamb can be transferred to a bereaved ewe only if the lamb is covered with the skin of her dead lamb for a time. If newborn lambs are separated from the mother for two to four hours following birth, the mother will reject them.

There is no information on this point over a wide range of species, but such data as there are suggest that lower down the scale these immediate postpartum experiences may be less vital. Labriola (1953) compared primiparous female rats whose young were born by Cesarean section with those having normal births. The Cesarean mothers did not have the opportunity of postpartum licking of the young, but on retrieving tests carried out at twenty-four hours after birth there was no difference between the two groups. The rat mother, who will quite readily adopt other young, is, however, able to recognize her own (Beach and Jaynes, (1956a, b).

Mother chimpanzees have been observed to show signs of recognition of their own offspring, even one year after separation from them, provided they had reared the young for the first year. Several of the domesticated species, such as fowls, will adopt birds of other species if they incubate the eggs of these birds themselves. In such cases they may be observed to peck at and chase away young that are different from the adopted ones, even though these "strangers" are of their own species (Ramsey, 1951). Tinbergen (1939) noted that parent herring gulls do not apparently discriminate between young gulls until their own brood is about five days old, after which time they recognize their own and chase off others.

The idea that human parents may imprint to their offspring has been suggested by Lorenz (1943). He points to the fact that infants of many species have features distinctive from those of the adult and that a protuberous forehead is common to many infants; he claims that this has sign-stimulus properties to adults and elicits parental behavior. The particular features of the human infant are the prominent forehead and the billowing cheeks (visible result of the sucking pads), which he calls the "kewpie-doll" configuration.

It is a common observation that an unwed mother often has great difficulty in giving up her baby for adoption after she has been exposed to it. If Lorenz's suggestion about the "kewpie-doll" sign stimulus is valid, it may be one perceptual cue that mediates the imprinting of human parents to their offspring. Reference has been made to individual differences in cuddling in babies: This may well be another crucial variable in the formation of an attachment, the "noncuddling" being less stimulating to the parent and hence less imprinted to.

Another feature of early parent-child interaction is related to eye-to-eye contact. A review of the literature on this topic has been given in Robson (1967). In his own observations he noted considerable individual variation in the nature of eye contact in the first six months. Some infants seemed actively to seek and engage this contact, whereas others merely made it, apparently uninterestedly. Some were noted to avoid contact. Robson discusses the implications of eye contact, noting among other things that parents are commonly delighted when it occurs and respond to it, whereas they are frustrated if the infant avoids it. This contact (or lack of it) may have important developmental sequelae, which one may

regard as an element in the imprinting of parents. A marked change in parental behavior, from "caretaker" role to affectionate attachment, is said to accompany imprinting.

Whether one should define such social attachments in the parent-offspring direction as imprinting is perhaps a matter of choice. If a strict definition is to imply a following response by offspring to movements in their parents (or a surrogate) that have some kind of innate basis, then parent-offspring attachments are excluded. If, on the other hand, imprinting is taken to imply the formation of a social attachment between two individuals, one of whom is an infant, and in which there is some kind of inbuilt readiness to respond to certain perceptual cues, then the term can apply to both directions.

If the existence of a critical period is to be considered an essential part of the definition of imprinting, clear evidence on whether or not such periods exist in parent-offspring imprinting in primates is needed. Such evidence is not at present forthcoming. Certainly the females of many nonprimate species will only suckle young, or accept them as offspring, while in specific hormonal states; in this sense critical periods do exist for these species. Assuming that the "kewpie-doll" sign gestalt already mentioned does operate, there is a significant time during which the human infant bears these features, which he loses in due course. This time would not, however, qualify as a critical period because it involves a change external to the parent, not within him. However, there could still be within the parent, conditions specifically postpartum and limited in time, that coincide with the existence of a specific sign gestalt in the offspring in such a way that the parent is particularly sensitive to some perceptual cues at this time. The argument will apply especially to the mother, but in those species in which both parents are involved in care of the offspring, the supposed sensitivity might be part of the species-specific equipment and present in both sexes. Although this analysis is highly speculative when applied to humans, it is worth bearing in mind in observations of human parental behaviors.

A point of psychoanalytic theory has been

the importance of the feeding process in attaching the infant to the mother; in such a way feeding plays a crucial role in socialization. Harlow (1958) has thrown doubt on this theory by his well-known experiments with rhesus monkeys, in which he showed that infants "fed" by a wire surrogate mother spent only enough time with "her" to feed and passed the greater part of their time with a cloth surrogate that was never associated with feeding. In a series of experiments he has convincingly demonstrated the strong and permanent affective tie that the infant monkey will form with the cloth surrogate mother, even though it is never fed by it, and the weakness of the link formed with the feeding wire surrogate. When frightened, the young monkey would seek comfort from the cloth surrogate and thus comforted would face a frightening object or explore an open field, whereas it could get no such assurance or support from the feeding wire surrogate. The feeding relationship is apparently irrelevant to the forming of these ties between infant and mother. Harlow suggests that tactile creature comfort derived from the soft and cuddly cloth surrogate is, in this tie, the crucial element and evidently one having considerable implications for development.

A couple of other studies with dogs also show the feeding relationship to be irrelevant to socialization. Brodbeck (1954) raised puppies during the critical period of socialization under two conditions: Half were fed by hand and the other half by machine, but all had the same amount of human contact. There was no difference between the groups in their attachment to people. Fisher (1955) reared fox terriers in isolation boxes throughout the period of socialization and fed them mechanically. They were released for regular intervals of contact with the experimenter and again their socialization to him was unaffected by their being divorced from feeding experience.

In discussing early social development, Bowlby (1951) and others have emphasized the importance of a consistent relationship with a single mother figure. These authors believe, in fact, that the child needs to be imprinted to a single mother. It certainly seems to be the case with some species that the infant does imprint to a specific individual; this is particularly true of the sheep, in which each lamb follows its mother and continues to do so into adulthood. This following is, in fact, the basis of the flocking behavior of the sheep, in which each follows the mother, who follows her mother, and so on up to the matriarch. However, in the early stages this seems to be not because the lamb is discriminating but because the mother is. As mentioned earlier, the mother will accept only her own offspring, which she recognizes on the basis of smell, and will chase off a stranger. The literature does not say for how long the lamb remains indiscriminate in this matter. It seems that in many other species, too, it is the parents who reject young to which they are not themselves imprinted (even if these are of her own species, as when a hen rears ducklings and rejects chicks). As already mentioned, the human infant is in the beginning quite indiscriminate so far as the smiling response is concerned, but even when he begins to distinguish strangers from familiar faces, he still continues to smile to each of the familiar faces, and there is no suggestion in the literature of any favoritism among the equally familiar ones. Now it may be that in the matricentric style of child rearing of our society there is one face in particular that is more constantly around than others, but in some other communities where infant care is shared, there must be a greater range of equally familiar faces, and it would be interesting to study the smiling response in relation to each of these. Imprinting, in social species at least, is essentially the attachment of an infant to his species, and it may be that we should not overemphasize the imprinting relationship between the infant and the mother specifically.

## EPILOGUE

Imprinting is a well-established phenomenon found in many species, and there is some evidence of its existence in the primates. On the basis that a feature of behavioral development apparently widespread across species would not be likely suddenly to disappear in humans, it is assumed that imprinting is a factor in human development also. This is admittedly not a strong argument, but it does have some supporting evidence to give it plausibility.

The discussion of the nature of imprinting, whether it is simply a form of association learning or some special kind of learning, is inconclusive on present evidence, which encourages one to make his own decision. It would seem reasonable to assume, with Hess, that imprinting is a special form of learning in which there is a genetically given present readiness to attach certain behavioral responses to certain stimulus patterns. There is genuine learning involved in that, to establish the bond, the environment must bring the responses and stimuli together during the critical period of maturation readiness; but because the organism is ready-primed, the learning proceeds swiftly. Once established, this learned response becomes a firm part of the organism's repertoire and is difficult (if not impossible) to alter.

To put it another way, the assumption is being made that imprinting is a biological predisposition to certain forms of learning. That is, the learning involved is of a special nature in that it has a lower threshold than some other forms. Most learning theories seem to imply an empty organism, a *tabula rasa,* at least for early learning, whereas with imprinting it would seem as if the organism comes with the learning already half-done. Whether this makes the learning process itself any different is an open question, and perhaps we do not have to assume that it does, in which case we can possibly reconcile Hess and Hinde. Maybe Hess is right in assuming some special readiness to learn in imprinting and Hinde correct in assuming that when the learning occurs it is associative.

The idea of special predispositions to certain learnings is an important one that will be referred to in other contexts. Imprinting may not be a unique phenomenon but one instance of a more general class of developmental events in which there is an innate predilection to particular learning. Because of this prepriming, some behaviors are easier to learn than others. Those who claim that all behavior is learned may be right, or largely so, but perhaps some behaviors are more learned than others. The others are those that are primed and that require less learning than those for which there is no constitutional precedent.

Whatever the nature of imprinting, it has marked consequences for the infants' subsequent relations with his parents and, by generalization, for all his later social interactions with his fellows. It is assumed that in humans the adult face provides the essential sign gestalt for triggering the imprinting response, which is smiling, though probably other stimuli are also effective. This mechanism occurs during a critical period between about three to six months of age. The possibility exists of imprinting (or some process similar to it) of parents to their offspring, and this possibility also has developmental implications.

The consequences of failure of imprinting are probably fatal to survival under natural conditions for most species, but the human infant can survive, physically. The psychological consequences to him may be extensive. If there is merely failure of imprinting without other perceptual deprivation, an individual of normal cognitive development, but with the deficiencies in social interactions that make up the sociopathic personality, may result. If, as is probably more often the case, conditions leading to failure of imprinting also reduce total stimulation, a sociopath of stunted cognitive development may be produced.

It is perhaps necessary to conclude with a cautious note to temper the somewhat enthusiastic account of imprinting given in this chapter. As Clarke (1968) has warned us, there are some qualifiers that need consideration. It could be that the influence and permanence of imprinting is, in fact, different from what is at present assumed by those who read much into it. Nevertheless, some important research is suggested by the work on imprinting, and even if the results of this research prove in the long run not quite what some of us could expect, the results may still advance our knowledge of human development.

# REFERENCES

Ambrose, J. A. The concept of a critical period for the development of social responsiveness. In B. M. Foss (Ed.), *Determinants of infant behavior* (Vol. 2). New York: Wiley, 1963.

Beach, F. A., & Jaynes, J. Studies of maternal retrieving in rats: I. Recognition of young. *Journal of Mammalogy*, 1956, *37*, 177–180. (a)

Beach, F. A., & Jaynes, J. Studies of maternal retrieving in rats: III. Sensory cues involved in the lactating female's response to her young. *Behaviour*, 1956, *10*, 104–125. (b)

Blauvelt, H. Dynamics of the mother-newborn relationship in goats. In B. Schaffner (Ed.), *Group processes: Transactions of the first conference*. New York: Josiah Macy, Jr., Foundation, 1955.

Bowlby, J. Maternal care and mental health. *W. H. O. Monographs*, 1951 (Serial No. 2).

Brodbeck, A. J. An exploratory study on the acquisition of dependency behavior in puppies. *Bulletin of the Ecological Society of America*, 1954, *35*, 73.

Clarke, A. D. B. Learning and human development. *British Journal of Psychiatry*, 1968, *114*, 1061–1077.

Collias, N. E. The development of social behavior in birds. *Auk*, 1952, *69*, 127–159.

Collias, N. E. The analysis of socialization in sheep and goats. *Ecology*, 1956, *37*, 228–239.

Collias, N. E., & Collias, E. C. Some mechanisms of family integration in ducks. *Auk*, 1956, *73*, 378–400.

Darwin, C. A biographical sketch of an infant. *Mind*, 1877, *2*, 285–294.

Fisher, A. E. *The effects of differential early treatment on the social and exploratory behavior of puppies*. Unpublished doctoral dissertation, Pennsylvania State University, 1955. Quoted in J. P. Scott, The process of primary socialization in canine and human infants. *Monographs of the Society for Research in Child Development*, 1963, *28*(1, Serial No. 85).

Gottlieb, G. Imprinting in nature. *Science*, 1963, *139*, 497–498.

Gray, P. H. Theory and evidence of imprinting in human infants. *Journal of Psychology*, 1958, *46*, 155–166.

Harlow, H. F. The nature of love. *American Psychologist*, 1958, *13*, 673–685.

Hersher, L., Moore, A., & Richmond, J. B. Effect of post partum separation of mother and kid on maternal care in the domestic goat. *Science*, 1958, *128*, 1342–1343.

Kistyakovskaya, M. Yu. O stimulakh vyzyvayushchikh polozhitel'nye emotsii u rebenka pervykh mesyatsev zhisni. [Stimuli that elicit positive emotions in infants.] *Voprosy Psikhologii*, 2, 129–140. (*Psychological Abstracts*, 1965, *39*, No. 11912.)

Labriola, J. Effect of caesarean delivery upon maternal behavior in rats. *Proceedings of the Society for Experimental Biology N. Y.*, 1953, *83*, 556–557.

Lorenz, K. Z. Die angeborenen Formen möglicher Erfahrun. [The innate conditions of the possibility of experience.] *Zeitschrift Fuer Tierpsychologie*, 1943, *5*, 235–409.

Ramsey, A. O. Familial recognition in domestic birds. *Auk*, 1951, *68*, 1–16.

Robson, K. S. The role of eye-to-eye contact in maternal-infant attachment. *Journal of Child Psychology and Psychiatry*, 1967, *8*, 13–25.

Salzen, E. A. Visual stimuli eliciting the smiling response in the human infant. *Journal of Genetic Psychology*, 1963, *102*, 51–54.

Schaffer, H. R., & Emerson, Peggy E. Patterns of response to physical contact in early human development. *Journal of Child Psychology and Psychiatry*, 1964, *5*, 1–13.

Schneirla, T. C., & Rosenblatt, J. S. Animal research panel 1960. *American Journal of Orthopsychiatry*, 1961, *31*, 223–291.

Scott, J. P. The process of primary socialization in canine and human infants. *Monographs of the Society for Research in Child Development*, 1963, *28*(1, Serial No. 85).

Sluckin, W. *Imprinting and early learning*. Chicago: Aldine, 1965.

Spitz, R. A., & Wolf, K. M. The smiling response: A contribution to the ontogenesis of social relations. *Genetic Psychology Monographs*, 1946, *34*, 57–125.

Tinbergen, N. On the analysis of social organization among vertebrates, with special reference to birds. *American Midland Naturalist*, 1939, *21*, 210–234.

# The Critical Period of Development

## Burton L. White and Jean Carew Watts

Many people who study the development of children have made statements about the special importance of particular age ranges. In this regard, we are no different. Our study, even though incomplete at this writing, has convinced us of the special importance of the 10- to 18-month age range for the development of general competence. At this time of life, for most children, several extremely important developments seem to coalesce and force a test of each family's capacity to rear children. The primary burden in most cases falls upon the mother.

Let us first characterize children during the second and third years of life, to help set the stage for explaining why we believe so strongly in the unique importance of the 10- to 18-month period. We will then summarize what we think we are learning about desirable child-rearing practices.

## THE CHILD AT ONE YEAR OF AGE

Most one-year-olds appear to resemble each other in a few interesting and fundamental ways. First of all, perhaps the hallmark of this age is curiosity. The one-year-old seems genuinely interested in exploring his world throughout the major portion of his day. Aside from mealtimes and the need to relieve various

From pp. 234–240 of "Discussions and Conclusions," by B. L. White. In *Experience and Environment: Major Influences on the Development of the Young Child* (Vol. 1), by B. L. White and J. C. Watts. Copyright © 1973. Reprinted by permission of Prentice-Hall, Inc., Englewood Cliffs, New Jersey.

occasional physical discomforts, his consuming interest is in exploration. This fact is confirmed by our task data, especially in the predominance of the *explore, mastery,* and *gain information—visual* experiences. Unfortunately, not all situations are optimal for nurturing that curiosity, nor are the rules governing exploratory behavior equivalent across homes. Nonetheless, the one-year-old is primed for expending enormous amounts of energy exploring and learning about his world.

The curiosity of the one-year-old is aided by his newly acquired ability to cover space. Whereas, at 6 months of age, he was limited to the places his mother kept him (i. e., crib, high chair, playpen, changing-table, bath, carriage, etc.), he can now either crawl, cruise, or walk wherever he wishes, subject to his mother's approval and the physical layout of the home. Unfortunately, he is not yet very skillful with his body, nor very knowledgeable about danger or destruction. On the one hand, he is capable of enormous amounts of intellectual and social learning and development of motor skills such as walking, climbing, and especially the use of his hands. On the other hand, razor blades, broken glass, and electrical equipment are to him only additional opportunities for exploration. In addition, fragile objects that are precious to other people engender no special treatment from him. This combination of factors alone places considerable stress on most mothers. But there is more.

The one-year-old is poised for fundamental development in social and language development as well. During the first year of life, there is little to suggest that infants are self-conscious or particularly thoughtful creatures. During the second year, however, one can observe the emergence of a sense of self. Increasingly, the child seems to assimilate ideas of who he is. His name comes to produce an appropriate and a special response from him. Gradually, he begins to use the terms "me" and "mine." Also during that second year, he begins for the first time to seriously engage in interpersonal contests. As many have noted before, a sense of autonomy begins to manifest itself during this period.

Along with a growing sense of self and independence, the child during the second year of life seems to be learning a great deal about his mother and her reactions. He studies her and approaches her often during this period and seems to develop a very strong attachment to her. Other human beings count, but not much compared to his mother, in most cases. Peers ordinarily spend very small amounts of time with him. Fathers may spend a bit more when we do not observe, but they still probably do not compare with the mother as centers of continuing interest (except in rare cases). During the second year, unlike any other time in his life, the child seems to develop in these directions in a manner that may produce a vigorous, secure, loving, and healthy social animal, or else may take other paths. By two, he may become a modest form of social tyrant whose major orientation during his waking hours is clinging to and dominating his mother,* or he may learn that his mother is rather unpredictable—sometimes, someone to fear, while at other times, someone who will protect him.

Before 8 or 9 months of age there is little reason to believe that infants understand words. By 36 months of age, they seem (in most cases) to be able to process most simple language. It is clear that a remarkable amount of language development is taking place beginning at about one year of age. Certainly, no analysis of the effects of child-rearing practices during this age period should ignore this fact.

A further point on one-year-olds concerns the issue of physical maturity. At one, some children look and behave very much like the average 9- or 10-month-old, while others appear several months advanced. The fact that walking ability emerges at about this time helps accentuate differences in maturity at this age. We suspect that part of the reason one cannot predict future development from a one-year-old's behavior is this factor. The commonly seen striking differences in physical maturity become much less marked by the time the child reaches two years of age, but at one they hinder prediction and also complicate the problem of effective child-rearing techniques.

## THE CHILD AT TWO YEARS OF AGE

Data about the two-year-old (24 to 27 months) are slightly less interesting to us than data about the one-year-old. The reason is that it appears the two-year-old has already taken shape, to a degree that suggests that many basic formative experiences are already behind him. Our test data, like that of many other studies, indicate that children who are going to develop well or poorly (during the preschool period, at least) begin to reveal which course they are on at about the middle of the second year of life.

The two-year-old is usually just emerging from a rather dramatic phase, the aforementioned emergence of his sense of agency. This has been manifest in many ways, but perhaps the most dramatic is reflected in our compliance/noncompliance data. As we discussed earlier, the one-year-old is generally an agreeable child, as are most three-year-olds, but sometime during the second year of life, our subjects begin asserting themselves, rejecting suggestions, ignoring commands, testing limits, and generally flexing their muscles. Some mothers cope well with this normal phenomenon, others not so well. Not all children have left this stage behind at two, and in many cases, children seem to carry the related conflicts along for many years.

Two-year-olds usually maintain a high level of intrinsic curiosity, but not as uniformly high as among one-year-olds. They are much more sophisticated about social relations, although their prime area of knowledge concerns their own family. They seem to have developed a standard inventory of social-interaction patterns to use with the family, and are usually more shy with strangers than one-year-olds. Their language capacities have increased dramatically, such that most everyday simple language is usually understood, if not ex-

*A major casualty of such a development is that normal intrinsic interest in exploring physical reality and mastering skills becomes subjugated to the social orientation. This division of interest may have profound importance.

pressed. They may now exhibit the capacity for "pretend" or fantasy behavior, and you may see signs of a budding sense of humor. They are now slightly more interested in television but still spend (on the average) no more than about one-half hour a day really attending to the screen. Their body control is now much advanced over the one-year-old, and they have moved on to practicing advanced motor skills like tricycle and wagon riding and climbing. Their play with objects involves more practicing of skills than exploration of object qualities, but they have not yet ordinarily begun to *construct products,* such as drawings, puzzles, or playhouses. Their capacity for sustained conversation is very limited, although they will listen to language for fairly long periods. Finally, their direction of interest still shifts rapidly, with typical units of experience lasting only twenty to thirty seconds or so, with the exception of occasional long periods of viewing television.

## THE SPECIAL IMPORTANCE OF THE 10- TO 18-MONTH PERIOD OF LIFE

At the beginning of this section we remarked that the 10- to 18-month period of life was of peculiar importance for the development of overall ability in children. In addition, we believe that families first reveal their level of capacity for child-rearing during this period. What follows is an explanation of why we think this way.

First of all, the development of the capacity for receptive language begins to become substantial at about 8 or 9 months of age. Our subjects developing *very well* (and those of other studies) first show fairly clear precocity, as compared with children developing poorly, at about 18 months. Variations in the language milieu prior to 8 months of age are far less likely to affect language and related development than are those occurring subsequently. Second, the emergence of locomotor ability in the form of crawling at about 9 or 10 months of age combines with several factors to place a great deal of stress on the primary caretaker. Locomobility plus intense curiosity, plus poor control of the body, plus ignorance of common dangers, plus ignorance of the value of things, plus ignorance concerning the rights of others, spells trouble. Third, sometime toward the end of the first year of life, two social developments of significance begin to undergo rapid development. Babies begin to reveal a growing awareness of themselves as agents, as beings with separate identities. The form of this identity appears to be shaped largely through social interactions with the primary caretaker. These interchanges also appear to shape the infant's basic orientation toward people in general. He typically reveals a very strong orienting tendency toward his mother and initiates very sizable numbers of overtures in her direction. He seems to be acquiring his basic style as a social animal.

To the degree that we are correct, then, most of the basic foundations of educational and general development will receive their shape and quality during this short interval. Now, we do not mean to say that the first 10 months of life are of no importance at all, nor that every child enters and leaves the critical stage at the same time. Certainly, a child has to be well nourished and well loved from birth. Furthermore, previous research by the senior author (White, 1971) seems to indicate that infants can probably derive much more pleasure and perhaps developmental gain from the first months of life than they now do. (Also see Hunt, 1961.) However, under current practices of child-rearing, whatever infants experience during their first months of life (except for extreme deprivation) does not apparently lead to important differential achievement by age one. Although differences in achievement are, of course, present in every group of one-year-old infants, developmental differences that are indicative of future educational performance do not appear to emerge until at least 18 months of age, if then.

We have said that important or predictive developmental divergence first becomes clear during the second year of life. Amplification of this key statement is necessary. We do not mean to say that all children test out as average throughout the first 18 months of life. Nor do we mean to say that scores for all children between 18 and 24 months of life immediately reflect their levels of ability for the rest of their lives. Between birth and 18 months of age, for example, a small percentage of children with serious developmental handicaps will score well below average on tests of general developmental status such as the Gesell, Griffiths, Bayley, and so on. An infant who repeatedly scores below 85 (one standard deviation below the mean in most cases) may indeed be manifesting what we are calling important developmental divergence. Such children constitute somewhat less than 17 percent of the population. Of these, some will ultimately develop normal or even superior ability; others will indeed never function at normal levels (see Knoblock and Pasamanick). Others will end up with moderate handicaps. The vast majority of children (over 82 percent) will regularly score above 85 on infant development tests with a central tendency of 100. However, whether they score 90 or 115 in this first year of life doesn't seem to tell us much about levels of function at age three and up.

Turning to the period from 18 months of age on, we suggest that children who will ultimately be exceptional in either direction (talented or of lower-than-average competence) will begin to reveal their direction of development first. Gradually, additional children will reveal predictive divergent advancement levels as a function of the degree to which they are exceptional. The modal child, by definition, will test at an average of 100 not only at 18 months but repeatedly throughout his developmental years, barring special educational experiences, test errors, and other factors that occasionally influence test performance. For some large but not surely identified number of children, then, developmental divergence will never be shown, simply because the average child, by definition, is nondivergent. He does, on the other hand, reveal divergence to some extent at 18 months and increasingly thereafter, in relation to the most exceptional children. By scoring around 100 regularly from 18 months on he reveals that he is neither particularly precocious nor particularly handicapped.

It seems to us that mothers are obliged to make at least three major sets of choices in regard to child-rearing practices during this period. The first choices become necessary when locomobility emerges (ordinarily in the form of crawling). The resultant potential for self-injury and for destructiveness, creation of clutter, and intrusion on the private domain of older siblings must be coped with by every family. The choices made vary widely and seem to link with subsequent developments in the child.

Some time late in the first year or into the second, mothers make a second important modification of their child-rearing practices. Sooner or later they become aware of their child's emerging capacity for language acquisition. Some choose to feed the growth of language by going out of their way to talk a great deal to their children. Some provide language input effectively by careful selection of suitable words and phrases and by exploiting the child's interest of the moment. Others provide a great deal of input but with considerably less skill and effectiveness. Other mothers show minimal attention to the language interests of their children or for other reasons provide negligible amounts of language input.

The third major shaping of fundamental child-rearing practices during this period appears to be triggered by the onset of negativism sometime after 14 or 15 months of age. The disappearance of the benign, easy-to-get-along-with 12-month-old is very disconcerting to many mothers. Negativistic behavior is usually experienced as stressful to some degree by all mothers. Styles of reaction to such behavior in children vary from the overpunitive all the way to the overacquiescent.

These three emerging phenomena—locomobility and its stressful consequences, language-learning ability, and negativism—force maternal reactions that become fairly fixed in most cases by the time the child is 18 months of age. It is this three-step creation of the early child-rearing styles that underlies our emphasis on the 10- to 18-month period of life.

## REFERENCES

Hunt, J. McV. *Intelligence and experience.* New York: Ronald Press, 1961.
Knoblock, Peter. Open education for emotionally disturbed children. *Exceptional Children,* 1973, *39*(5), 358–365.

Pasamanick, Benjamin. A tract for the times: Some sociologic aspects of science, race and racism. *American Journal of Orthopsychiatry,* 1969, *39*(1), 7–15.

White, B. L. *Human infants: Experience and psychological development.* Englewood Cliffs, N.J.: Prentice-Hall, 1971.

## SUGGESTIONS FOR FURTHER READING

Bateson, P. P. Length of training, opportunities for comparison, and imprinting in chicks. *Journal of Comparative and Physiological Psychology,* 1974, *86*, 586–589. In this study of domestic chicks, which involved giving the chicks a choice between a familiar stimulus and a novel one, length of training was found to have a marked effect. The longer they were exposed to the familiar stimulus, the more they attempted to approach it.

Dennis, W. *Children of the crèche.* New York: Appleton-Century-Crofts, 1973. This study in a Lebanese orphanage found that children reared in an impoverished orphanage for only the first two years of life were able to catch up in mental functioning after adoption. If adopted after that age, however, they remained retarded in proportion to the time spent in the orphanage beyond age 2.

Gordon, I. J. The beginnings of the self: The problem of the nurturing environment. *Phi Delta Kappan,* 1969, *50*(7), 375–378. Gordon cites significant research studies to establish the importance of the early years.

Hunt, J. McV., & Kirk, G. E. Social aspects of intelligence, evidence and issues. In R. Cancro (Ed.), *Intelligence: Genetic and environmental influences.* New York: Grune & Stratton, 1971. Children reared in impoverished, as compared to normal, environments proved significantly retarded in their mental and social development.

Klopfer, P. Is imprinting a Cheshire cat? *Behavioral Science,* 1967, *12*(2), 122–129. Dr. Klopfer, of the Department of Zoology, Duke University, reports that imprinting is not a unitary process, and that its motor and perceptual aspects can be independently manipulated.

Lazarus, R. S. *The riddle of man.* Englewood Cliffs, N.J.: Prentice-Hall, 1974, Chapter 6. The concept of instinct is examined within the general context of explaining the origins of aggression both in humans and in lower animals.

Scott, J. P. A time to learn. *Psychology Today,* October 1969, pp. 46–48; 66–67. The author describes his work with dogs in terms of critical-period phenomena and suggests implications of similar phenomena among humans.

Scrimshaw, N. S. Early malnutrition and central nervous system function. *Merrill-Palmer Quarterly,* 1969, *15*(4), 375–388. The author reviews relevant literature for both humans and animals and briefly summarizes conclusions.

Seitz, V., Seitz, T., & Kaufman, L. Loss of depth avoidance in chicks as a function of early environmental influences. *Journal of Comparative and Physiological Psychology,* 1973, *85,* 139–143. A relationship was established between imprinting and visual cliff performance among average chicks reared sequentially in two different environments. The findings are related to the question of environmental imprinting.

Suomi, S. J., & Harlow, H. F. Social rehabilitation of isolate-reared monkeys. *Developmental Psychology,* 1972, *6*, 487–496. After complete social deprivation from 4 to 12 months of age, monkeys ordinarily become permanently abnormal in their behaviors. However, the effect can be overcome to a certain extent.

Zajonc, R. B., Markus, H., & Wilson, W. R. Exposure, object preference, and distress in the domestic chick. *Journal of Comparative and Physiological Psychology,* 1974, *86*, 581–585. The results of this experiment suggested that imprinting is not an instantaneous or sudden attachment to the first object encountered. Rather, it represents a more gradual process that depends on repeated exposure to the object.

# 5
## Stage Theory

In recent years a considerable body of theory and research has been devoted to the concept of stage theory. According to this theory, various aspects of human development proceed by stages, each with its own special characteristics. While these stages follow no rigid chronological schedule, they are said to occur at roughly the same periods in development. Moreover, they are hierarchical, in that they follow a logical unvarying sequence, with each succeeding one dependent on those that have gone before.

It is easier to distinguish stages in certain areas of development than in others. Certainly almost everyone is familiar with stages of motor development because they are so visible. The infant learns to lift its head, roll, scramble forward by using its elbows; children learn to crawl before they proceed to the next stage, walking. Other aspects of development—for example, intellectual development—are more difficult to chart; hence, psychologists may differ somewhat concerning the number, duration, or significance of the stages involved.

Stage theory is no new creation but simply a revival of views deeply rooted in the past. Early advocates of this view were Aristotle and Rousseau, who suggested that educational experiences should be properly articulated with developmental stages (Muus, 1970). Centuries later, in the 1930s, the concept of life stages was popular at the University of Vienna.

The Vienna writers, especially Charlotte Bühler (1959), postulated five principal stages. During the first stage, childhood, an individual lives at home and is dependent on the family.

From age 12 to about 28, the individual engages in exploratory and preparatory activities, while deciding what to do with his or her life and establishing his or her independence. A person performs his or her major work in life from about age 28 to 50, after which activities decline. At 65 the person may retire, gradually restricting activities and loosening ties.

Sometimes, as in the preceding summary, life-as-a-whole is interpreted as proceeding by stages. In addition, different aspects of the developmental process are analyzed in terms of their own special developmental patterns—all of which, of course, become somehow articulated within any single individual. For example, Lawrence Kohlberg, one of the best known stage theorists, has applied stage theory to moral development. In the premoral stage, a child may simply do the "right thing" to receive rewards or avoid punishment. In the higher stage of conventional morality, a person is guided by convention and the need to feel approved by others. In a still more advanced stage, an individual's behaviors are chosen on the basis of what is best for the community. In the very highest stage, says Kohlberg, the individual is guided by his or her own personal system of values. The individual has tested and refined a set of values and has become committed to them. On the other hand, such an individual can be dangerous. A person's own perceptions, no matter how sincere, may prove untrustworthy unless that person has good judgment and a genuine concern for others. Would not Hitler fall in this category?

Two other well-known stage theories—

Freud's theory of sexual development and Piaget's outline of cognitive development—are described in our first reading by Ladd Wheeler, Robert Goodale, and James Deese. Piaget's theory was based on careful observation of European children in the 1920s, 1930s, and 1940s. His theory of intellectual development, as briefly summarized in our first reading, along with the work of his collaborators, students, and disciples, has had a tremendous impact on developmental theory and education.

Many researchers have attempted to replicate and test Piaget's theories; and most of them have confirmed his general sequence of cognitive development. Not all report the same timetable of stages, which are modifiable to some extent by the manipulation of the child's experience. Theorists also differ with Piaget in matters of interpretation and emphasis. Jerome Bruner agreed with Piaget that learning tasks fall in a logical hierarchy; however, Bruner placed greater stress on children's ability to grasp somewhat complex concepts if sufficiently simplified. The Russian psychologist Lev Vygotsky believed that thought had its roots in speech, whereas Piaget concluded that speech and reasoning developed along parallel paths.

Freud, whose theory is also summarized in the first reading, interpreted psychological development in terms of distinct psychosexual stages. According to Freud, an individual goes through oral, anal, phallic, latent, and genital stages in the process of attaining maturity.

The second reading, by the editor of this volume, helps to place stage theory in perspective. To date, certain general conclusions about stage theory have emerged; nevertheless, various issues—defined in the second reading—remain unresolved.

## REFERENCES

Bruner, J. S. *The process of education.* New York: Wiley, 1960.

Bruner, J. S. *Studies of cognitive growth.* New York: Wiley, 1966.

Bühler, C. *Der menschliche Lebenslauf als psychologisches Problem.* Göttingen: Verlag fur Psychologie, 1959.

Kohlberg, Lawrence. The cognitive developmental approach to moral development. *Phi Delta Kappan,* 1975, *51*(10), 670–673.

Muus, R. E. Theories of adolescent development—Philosophical and historical roots. In E. D. Evans (Ed.), *Adolescence: Readings in Behavior and Development.* New York: Dryden Press, 1970.

Rogers, D. *Child psychology.* Belmont, Calif.: Brooks/Cole, 1969.

Vygotsky, L. S. *Thought and language.* Cambridge, Mass.: Institute of Technology Press, 1962.

# Two Significant Stage Theories

## Ladd Wheeler
## Robert A. Goodale
## James Deese

### PIAGET'S THEORY OF COGNITIVE DEVELOPMENT

We have already noticed two important aspects of Piaget's theory of development. One is his emphasis upon the occurrence of developmental stages. Second is his notion of the development of conceptual intelligence from the sensorimotor intelligence of early childhood.

For Piaget, the use of language in young children is largely egocentric. It is not so much used for communication as it is for the overt expression of inner thought. Even when children are (from an adult point of view) communicating with one another, they do not do so in

From *General Psychology,* by L. Wheeler, R. A. Goodale, and J. A. Deese. Copyright © 1975 by Allyn and Bacon, Inc. Reprinted by permission.

the cognitive sense usually intended by that term. The transcription of conversations of young children shows that the verbal processes, activities, and underlying thought processes are more often parallel than interacting. A three-year-old might greet his friend by saying, "See my new ball," to which his friend replies, "I hurt my knee." The interchange bears no hint of the reciprocal interrelation that ordinarily characterizes adult conversation. Thus, for young children, speech is a tool of personal expression rather than of interpersonal communication. As the child grows older, his verbal processes are used to communicate with other people. Speech becomes less egocentric and more sociocentric.

After cognitive development passes through the sensorimotor stage to the stage of conceptual intelligence, there are, according to Piaget, the following well-defined phases: The pre-operational period, concrete operations, and formal operations (Piaget 1952; 1953; Inhelder and Piaget 1958). These phases are characterized by the emergence of qualitatively new kinds of functions at each step.

## Pre-Operational Period (Age 2 – 7)

*Intuitive Thinking*. The earliest kind of conceptual thought is purely intuitive. Children's concepts are concretely tied to the immediate appearance of things. Children younger than five or six years old group similar things together on the basis of some obvious characteristic. To the toddler, all animals are "doggies" or "kitties." The immediate perceptual resemblance among all small, furry animals overrides the adult's insistence that animals are classified on the basis of abstract, biological characteristics. To the occasional embarrassment of the young mother, toddlers regard all male adults as "daddy."

In addition to being tied to perceptual resemblance, there is a deficiency of *object permanence* in young children. A marble ball rolled into one end of a long tube may not be seen by the young child as the same marble when it emerges from the other end. It simply doesn't occur to the child that the two percep-

tions are related. The great insight that an object which disappears and reappears is still the same object doesn't come until later.

Abstractions that go beyond perceptual similarity simply exhaust the understanding of the young child, though he may accept the vocabulary of some things adults force upon him ("*Share* your toys"; "Janie is your *sister*"). One of the great insights developed from Piaget's work is the fact that concepts such as causality, volume, and time are radically different in young children from what they are in older children or adults.

*Causality*. A characteristic difference between the adult's conception of abstract notions and the child's concrete understanding of those same notions is to be found in the concept of causality. Children do have causal concepts, but these are hard for the adult to appreciate. The adult may try to mystify the young child with some trick of magic. He expects the child to react with something like, "Hey, how did you do that?" More than likely, however, the child will simply react with nonperplexed indifference. Something quite commonplace to the adult, however, such as a water fountain, may strike the child as strange and mystifying.

The preschool child's concept of causality is *animistic*—he attributes human characteristics to inanimate objects. He may know that buildings and automobiles are built by humans, but if he thinks about it at all, he is likely to attribute the origin of rocks or the motion of clouds to human agents as well. A resistant material, such as a stiff spring, may be regarded as willfully resistant. Fantasy to children may not seem to be fantasy. To them it seems perfectly reasonable that a wooden puppet can talk. Even the primary school child may be only dimly and unconvincingly aware of the inanimate nature of the ventriloquist's dummy. When the child begins to appreciate the division between the animate and the inanimate, the distinction may be capriciously and arbitrarily applied. The child does not immediately grasp the adult distinction. The animistic aspects of things simply become less important. If the toy hurts when you break it, it clearly suffers less than Tabby does when you step on her tail. The child begins by distinguishing between those things that react out of proportion to the applied force and those that passively receive what is done to them.

## Concrete Operations (Age 7–11)

Sometime between the ages of five and seven is a dramatic change in the way children think. They begin to change the basis of their thinking from immediate perceptual obviousness to concepts based on processes and relations. To adults, a quart of water is a quart of water, whether it is in a tall pitcher or a flat bowl. But the very young child cannot see that there is an abstract concept called amount or quantity which remains the same when the shape or form of something changes. In a word, the child cannot appreciate the concept of *conservation*—that quantity or volume can remain the same when shape changes. From an adult point of view, children make absurd mistakes. Most four-year-olds will tell you unhesitatingly that a tall, thin quart jar holds more than a short, fat quart jar. He may persist in this even when you pour the water from one container into the other right before his eyes. From the child's point of view, it is the adult's questions that are absurd. Of course there's more water in the thin pitcher, because the water height is "bigger!"

The child who has not grasped conservation sees objects as different according to the sensory impression they make upon him (the water level in this case). The child cannot appreciate that if one property of an object changes, the object may still remain the same. Thus, the child has difficulty in abstracting the constant quantity concept of two things that differ in size and shape, or perhaps even in color. Try the water jar experiment out on some three-, four-, or five-year-olds. The universality of it and the seeming absurdity of the child's answer is quite impressive.

*Mathematical Concepts.* Concepts like time, quantity, and shape are concepts of relation. The fundamental property of quantity is order—ordered relation among numbers. The number 3 is between the numbers 2 and 4, and the number 4, in turn, is between 3 and 5. These relationships are of great difficulty for the preschool child, and in his thinking about these things he is profoundly different from the adult. The child knows absolute and immediate things but he has difficulty putting them together. A preschool boy may know he has a brother (because you told him so), but he is confused, puzzled, and uncomfortable if you tell him his brother necessarily has a brother. Try asking him if his brother has a brother. The abstract rule of brotherly relations is beyond him.

Mathematical concepts provided Piaget (1953) with some of his best illustrations of the differences in modes of thought among children of different ages. While a child of four or five may be able to count, he does not understand the rules for assigning numbers to objects. Nor does he understand there must be a one-to-one correspondence between the same numbers of things in order for the concept of number to mean anything. Suppose we put down eight red chips spaced in a row. We ask a very young child to take out of a box exactly the same number of blue chips. What does he do? He makes a row of blue chips equally as long but packed closer together than the red chips. Thus, there are more of them in the row. A six-year-old will carefully place each blue chip opposite a red chip so as to make the same number. From this we can infer that the six-year-old has grasped the essential property of number, even though he is far from articulating the abstract principle.

Thus, at some point in his intellectual development the child is capable of seeing that amount and number are not defined by perceptual similarity, but by an operation that establishes relationships. He has reached the stage at which he can understand concrete operations. In the early part of this phase he can explain to you in his own way why one jar holds the same as the other ("because it isn't as tall but it's bigger around") or why it is necessary to count off one blue chip for each red chip ("because you have to have both the same"). The elementary school child can grasp the concrete relations in arithmetic, and he can do, by rote, extensions of these operations as in multiplication and division. He can solve arithmetic problems in fractions if the concept of fractions has been explained by reference to a pie or something similarly concrete.

## Formal Operations (Age 11–15)

Around the age of eleven or so, according to Piaget, the child is able to deal with formal or abstract relations. These are operations that can be performed in hypothesis, when the sequence of the operations need not be carried out concretely. It becomes possible for the typical child to understand arithmetic and mathematics as purely formal systems subject to the rules of logic. Armed with the abstract relations of logical reasoning, the child can now move on to deal with the problems of physics through the use of algebra and geometry. He can also deal with purely hypothetical questions without getting bogged down in irrelevant details.

The changes Piaget describes in human intellectual development are changes both in capacity and mode of thinking. Mode of thinking changes so radically that a child may not be able to understand how he thought a few years ago. In fact, Piaget suggests that the profound changes in way of thinking that occur between five and seven years may be one of the reasons for the failure to recall early childhood memories.

## THE PSYCHOSEXUAL STAGES

Coincident with the child's motor and cognitive development is the development of the child's "personality" (his usual mode of interacting with the world and handling his conflicts). We will describe one way of conceptualizing this development—Freud's. While there are other ways of describing personality development, Freud's was one of the first and has been the most influential for some time. Here we describe Freud's theory of psychosexual stages. *Psychosexual* relates to the fact that a child experiences desire and pleasure in focusing activities around a particular core of behaviors.

Freud believed there is a fixed succession of stages through which all individuals must pass on the way to maturity: the oral, anal, phallic, latency, and genital stages. Students find these names humorous when applied to personalities, but Freud was a physician, and the terms were natural to him. Had he said, instead, that there are important periods in everyone's life—the stage in which everything goes into the mouth, the stage of toilet training, the stage of identity as a boy or girl, the adventurous age, and the dating age—and that how others treat us during these stages is important for later social interactions, few would quarrel with his observations except to add a few more. In order to fully appreciate Freud, you have to learn to see some of his vocabulary as a kind of shorthand for summarizing a wealth of activities and processes under the single, most salient term.

## The Oral Stage

According to Freud, during the first year of life the mouth is the important *erogenous zone* (an area that gives intense pleasure), and the child desires stimulation through sucking, tasting, mouthing, swallowing, biting, and the like. A conflict arises between a child's incessant need to get and the limited amount of time and attention the parents will devote to that need. So the child inevitably experiences some frustration. If this frustration is severe, fixation at the oral stage may result. If the parents are too indulgent, the child will perceive their harried resentment and inconsistencies, and again fixation may result. *Fixation* at a psychosexual stage means that the conflicts and needs of that period continue to be major determinants of gratification and coping in the adult personality, despite their childish expressions.

In general, the "oral personality" is one who maintains the passive, clinging dependency of the nurtured infant all through life. For example, passive acceptance of sensory enjoyment, as in TV addiction or in being massaged, is one aspect of the oral personality.

## The Anal Stage

During the second year of life the child begins to acquire control of his anal sphincters, and the parents contemplate toilet training. The erogenous zone is now the anal orifice, and the child enjoys stimulation through withholding and eliminating feces. The conflict in the anal stage is between the child's desire to give or withhold feces according to his pleasure and the parents' desire that the child expel it at certain times and places. If the parents are too punitive or too indulgent, fixation may again result, this time around anal needs and conflicts.

The "anal retentive character" is one described in psychoanalytic theory as compulsively and excessively neat, emotionally constricted, highly opinionated and proud of his superior intelligence, condescending towards anyone who does not rely solely on the "facts," and stingy. The "anal expulsive character" is one whose house or desk is messy, his business affairs are in disorder, and he is "scatterbrained," excessively generous, is impulsive, and has scrawly handwriting and fights back by doing what is required at inappropriate times or in a way that others find unsatisfactory.

Freud saw the anal stage as critical to the development of creativity, since the child is aware of creating something personal which is an object of social interest. The fact that all children sooner or later play with their own feces is one manifestation of that burgeoning desire to mess around with the unknown. How the parents react to that event and other acts of curiosity and exploration at this age determines how eager and confident the child will be to "get into" and "play around with" something new.

## The Phallic Stage and Oedipal Conflict

From about the third through the fifth or sixth year of life, the primary erogenous zone is the genitals. The child enjoys stimulation of his own genitals (as in washing, scratching, holding, looking) and is interested in the genitalia of others. It is during this stage that the Oedipal conflict occurs, though the conflict is somewhat different for males than for females. Freud named this stage after the classic Greek hero who slays his father and marries his mother.

At the beginning of the phallic stage the young boy is closer to his mother than to his father because she has been more involved in his care and training. With his expanding thought processes the boy develops a desire to get all his mother's attention and affection, and he wishes daddy was out of the picture. In a vague way he connects his genital sensations to love for his mother and jealousy toward his father. He fantasizes about how babies are made and is curious about conversations between mom and dad that contain "double meanings" that pass right over his head. He wants "to hug mommy, too" when his parents embrace, and he becomes a frequent visitor to the bedroom "to sleep with mommy and daddy" (between them, of course), or to get mommy out of bed and give him some attention (give him breakfast, turn on the TV, find his shoes, or retrieve the hamster he let out). All this is not to say that the child fully understands the dynamics motivating him, of course.

The boy's longings produce conflict for two reasons. First, he fears retaliation (scolding, spanking) from a seemingly omnipotent father. Second, although he is jealous of his father, he doesn't want to lose his love and protection. The child translates all of this unconsciously into a fear of castration, since the conflict arose when the locus of bodily pleasure shifted from the anal region to the genitals.

The young boy's situation is further complicated by the fact that his mother rejects his wish for exclusive possession. This produces anger against her and a desire to eliminate her and take her place with his father. However, that, too, implies castration. So the boy experiences both castration anxiety and separation anxiety (loss of one or both parents).

As a consequence, the child abandons his irrational wishes, forgets he ever had them, and begins to identify with dad. This forgetting process Freud termed *repression,* which refers to the process whereby thoughts and memories that would bring on pain, fear, shame, guilt, or other undesirable emotions are prevented from entering consciousness, as when you "forget" a dentist's appointment. It is important to realize here that repression is a subtle process that occurs without conscious intent on the child's part. It is not an active "driving out of the mind" but simply a failure to remember.

The little girl, too, desires to possess her mother exclusively. But she cannot take her father's place because she doesn't have a penis. *Penis envy* creates shame and rage against the little girl's mother for having allowed her to be born without a penis. The child then turns to her father, desiring to take her mother's place with him. Her desire is not only rebuffed by the father, but she fears the genital injury that would follow if he penetrated and impregnated her, so she abandons and represses her wishes. The fact that none of us can remember such "ridiculous" thoughts only shows how well repression works.

It is interesting at this point to compare the physiognomy of the Oedipal stage child with that of the pre-Oedipal child. As discussed earlier, Lorenz hypothesizes that an infant has a quality of "babyishness" which serves to release mothering and protective behaviors in adults. But the babyish quality might lead to overprotection and "smotherlove" if continued and would therefore interfere with adult personality characteristics conducive to species survival. Has Lorenz discovered an innate releaser that changes enough by school age to bring about the Oedipal behaviors that Freud saw? Perhaps these physiological changes allow the child to begin to "grow up."

For both males and females, then, the Oedipal conflict consists of feelings of love and rage toward both parents, feelings of helplessness, and the need to give up Oedipal wishes. The child identifies with his parents and incorporates what he believes to be their values as his own. Up until that point, the child's morality depended upon whether his parents were watching him. But the Oedipal wishes were so strong, the child needs a permanent "watcher"

to guard him against recurrent urges, and so the development of "conscience" begins.

People fixated at the phallic stage need a great deal of recognition and appreciation. If they get it, they can be marvelous people to be with; if not, they may become depressed. In general, they seek the company of the opposite sex but shy away from deep commitments. The fixated male may be either effeminate or masculine, but in either case he is so in an obvious or inflexible way. The fixated female is likely to exaggerate her femininity by appearing, like a Southern belle, to be naive, pure, and somewhat childish; in fact, she may be either chaste or promiscuous.

The emotional pains the child experiences during the Oedipal stage—frustration of his wishes, fear of castration, the shame if his wishes are discovered, guilt from desiring one parent out of the way—are intense and require a drastic amount of repression to avoid unpleasant recurrences. Freud saw such strong repression as responsible for our inability to recall very much about our early childhood. Thus, what Piaget saw as a new mode of thinking emerging from neurological maturation and experience, Freud saw as a change in interest and attitude to avoid unpleasant memories. The result was, for Freud, the emergence of the latency stage.

## The Latency Stage

During this stage the child experiences a decrease in the intensity of oral, anal, and phallic drives. He goes to school and begins to take an interest in his physical and social environment. His temper tantrums and selfishness become inappropriate and largely disappear. He becomes a "good boy," "mother's helper," Cub Scout, rock collector, Little Leaguer, and any of the hundred other things that appear, on the surface, to have little similarity to the interests that occupied him earlier. Children who experience difficulty in keeping the thoughts and interests of those earlier stages "forgotten" may show exaggerated shifts away from those behaviors during the latency stage. Such children become very clean, very obedient, very asexual, very grown up, very moralistic, and so on. These traits constitute a defense against the anxiety that would be brought on by their opposites.

## The Genital Stage

Puberty and menarche signal the end of the latency stage and the start of the genital stage. Boys and girls begin to give up their avoidance of the opposite sex and find each other ''OK'' and interesting to talk to on occasion. The transition is not a smooth one, for the physiological changes of the genital stage renew some of the sexual and aggressive drives of the earlier stages. The anxiety experienced at these times is usually little understood by the adolescent, because earlier memories are mercifully hidden from conscious awareness. The boy may listen to dad one day and decide he's unreasonable the next. But playing baseball is more interesting with adulous girls on the sidelines, and going to a dance can be fun even if both sexes do spend most of their time arrayed against opposite walls. Saperstein (1955) interprets the boy's growing interest in pretty girls as a neutralized reincarnation of his Oedipal desires when mom was the most beautiful girl in the world. At adolescence the child begins to show some obstinacy and unruliness as a result of the increase in aggressive drive, and raids on the icebox or demands to wear lipstick are clear indications that muted oral drives are still intact.

For Freud, this reawakening of pleasure and desire in the genitals was appropriate to mature, heterosexual, non-incestuous interests. Individuals fixated at the oral and anal levels are primarily concerned with themselves—their own stimulation and interests, their own pleasure—and not with the needs and interests of others. Individuals fixated at the phallic stage have great difficulty interacting with others, and Freud mentioned the sexual exhibitionist and the homosexual as obvious examples. The individual who has safely arrived at the genital stage has a personality structure firmly based on sex-role identification, desexualized care and consideration for all maternal-like figures (for the boy) or paternal-like figures (for the girl). Such individuals have acquired the ability to interact easily with members of the opposite sex and to fall in love with at least one of them.

These descriptions of the Freudian stages and their personality types are oversimplified, and fixation is not all-or-nothing. No one completely escapes being influenced by the conflicts of early childhood, and no one becomes completely fixated at one stage. Since everyone has some residual influences from earlier stages, the question of maturity actually revolves around how much drive and pleasure survive to the genital stage of development to dominate the goals and behaviors of the adult personality.

## REFERENCES

Inhelder, B., & Piaget, J. *The growth of logical thinking from childhood to adolescence.* New York: Basic Books, 1958.
Piaget, J. *The origins of intelligence in children.* New York: International Universities Press, 1952.
Piaget, J. How children form mathematical concepts. *Scientific American,* 1953, *189*(5), 74–79.

# The Age-Stage Controversy

## Dorothy Rogers

Many of the laws and customs of our society are based on birthdays. For example, children are admitted to nursery school or first grade after a specific age, which is assumed to be a valid criterion of development. Also, an individual below a certain age is deemed a minor, not fully responsible for his or her acts. Similarly, chronological ages are assigned for determining an individual's fitness to enter school, drive a car, get married, or enter various legal contracts. At the other end of the maturity scale, people are dismissed from jobs or awarded pensions solely on the basis of age.

The organization of life tasks by ages and stages has given rise to certain questions and hypotheses to explain them. The so-called *age-stage hypothesis* suggests that children's development proceeds through relatively invariant behavioral stages that are progressively more mature and better defined. These stages are usually associated with particular ages. Indeed, one of the long-standing issues in child psychology is whether children follow the same basic sequence in their development.

## INTERPRETATIONS OF THE AGE-STAGE HYPOTHESIS

Perhaps Piaget (1932) has done more than anyone else to popularize the age-stage concept. He perceived children as progressing through sequential stages of conceptual development. For example, in the first stage of moral development, until about age 7, the child is a realist and judges deviant acts in terms of damage done. Finally, after certain intermediate stages, the child learns to apply principles differentially and to realize that rules can be altered. At the later stage, intent matters more than damage done. At the early stage, the child who breaks 15 cups is judged more wicked than one who breaks one cup, even though the first child's mishap was completely accidental, while the second child's involved disobedience.

In this country, Havighurst (1953) has proposed a series of life stages, emphasizing the developmental tasks to be accomplished at each stage. That is, if an individual is to function effectively at any given stage, he must have accomplished the tasks appropriate to preceding stages. For example, a child must become toilet-trained before he enters school.

Kohlberg (1970) has distinguished three major stages of moral development. In the pre-conventional stage of early childhood, the child simply does whatever leads to personal gratification. Next, in the conventional stage of later childhood, the child accepts the standards of parents and the community. Finally, in the post-conventional stage, the individual develops personal principles, sometimes conflicting with society's conventional morality.

Similarly, Peck and Havighurst (1960) have described five character types, ranging from the lowest, or amoral, to the highest, or rational-altruistic, type. Each stage in character development is deemed typical of a particular age-stage; and satisfactory moral development implies a regular progression to successively more mature character types.

According to Erik Erikson's theory (1950), children of different age groups exhibit correspondingly different behaviors in terms of life tasks and personality characteristics. Thus, the 5-year-old should be chiefly concerned with issues of autonomy versus shame and doubt; the 8-year-old should be concerned with initiative versus guilt; and the 11-year-old should be concerned about industry versus inferiority.

Other authorities, such as Hunt, Tanner, and Inhelder, also perceive development as sequential, but ascribe this orderliness to organismic-environmental interaction. Aside from the child's own developmental stage, the very nature of learning might seem to dictate a certain order. For instance, experience with concrete situations would naturally precede the capacity to derive a generalization from them.

Certain earlier writers, such as McGraw and Gesell, were prone to describe all individuals as developing at about the same pace. Thus, they described the 5-year-old as though all children aged 5 behaved in the same manner. Such a position emphasizes the importance of maturation in development and minimizes the impact of environment. Developmental-psychology textbooks are still shot through with statements that such-and-such behavioral manifestations occur at this or that age. Despite a common failure to make the point clear, the ages given are intended simply as averages. That is, if a girl's puberty is said to occur at about age 13, it is intended simply to mean that the average girl experiences puberty about then. However, chronological age has generally been discarded as a reliable criterion of development.

## CRITICISMS OF STAGE THEORY

There are various criticisms of the age-stage hypothesis. For one thing, in certain particulars many children do not move to more mature stages as a function of age. In one study Kahana and Kahana (1970) tested the validity of the concept of fixed stages in cognitive development, with reference to the dream concept among Hasidic children. The progression proved somewhat regular until about age 9, after which a new pattern emerged. Older subjects sometimes failed on levels of cognitive development passed by younger children. Hence, this study "did not support the invariance of the process of emerging cognitive structures in the development of the dream concept" (p. 288). It did underscore the significance of cultural influences in modifying the sequence of cognitive development. It suggests, too, that particular environments may even cause reversals in cognitive development.

In another study, Dulit (1972) reported a pretty clear sequence of stages—from sensorimotor to egocentric to concrete, through adolescence. However, after early adolescence there was no single path, but a dropout rate or branching into parallel tracks. Indeed, only "a modest proportion" of the few subjects engaged in formal thinking as defined by Piaget. Even among older adolescents, only 20–35% functioned at the formal level. That is, the formal stage of thinking "did not appear to be characteristic of adolescence in the sense of being routine, expected, or highly likely" (p. 298). Hence, for teenagers the formal stage represents a potential that only sometimes becomes an actuality; and even in adulthood this potential remains only partly developed.

Another study, lasting two years, and involving adolescents ages 13 to 18, disclosed that age does not in itself constitute a significantly relevant variable. Instead, developmental change is determined more by the cultural moment than by age. The adolescents as a group decreased in superego strength, social-emotional anxiety, and achievement during the 1970–1972 period, independent of their own ages. During the same years they all increased in independence (Nesselroade & Baltes, 1974).

Sequences may also be changed by manipulating the child's experiences. For instance, if infants spend their first few years in an orphanage and are then placed in a home where they have little contact with other children, but maintain a close contact with their foster parents, the so-called homosexual period may possibly precede the oedipal stage. Also, there is the factor of overlap. At any specific age, differences between individuals may outweigh the group averages. For instance, according to Erikson, adolescence is the age for establishing an identity; however, many youngsters have firmly established their identity before then and others never fully succeed in establishing one.

## DISTORTIONS OF STAGE THEORY

Stage theory is sometimes applied in distorted ways. Long before Piaget, society was growing more and more age-segregated, as life's various tasks were sorted by age groups. However, asserts Bronfenbrenner (1970), adults should become more involved in the lives of their children. Conversely, children should assume greater responsibilities within their own families, communities, and society at large. In another distortion of stage theory, school tasks are often rigidly bound to age periods. For example, boys and girls enter school at about the same age regardless of differences in their developmental timetables. However, boys experience an apparent lag in cognitive development simply because they take longer to mature (Kahana & Sterneck, 1972). Prolonged maturation might well prove an advantage because as long as the organism is developing it is more amenable to modification. Even within the same sex, the rate of maturing varies and should be taken into account.

Some persons, often educators, also make the mistake of too rigidly interpreting data derived from developmental research. If it is found that certain tasks are normally mastered at a particular stage, school curricula may be arranged accordingly;

> however, such tasks should not be thought of as discrete and belonging solely to a specific stage. A task can hardly be mastered successfully if the groundwork for its accomplishment is not laid earlier. For example, an adolescent will hardly establish an identity at adolescence unless he has made considerable progress toward that goal earlier. The developmental task theory also encourages the perception of development as a lock-step process. One performs Task No. 1, then Task No. 2, and so on, in that order. Actually, progress in mastering developmental tasks is overlapping and relatively continuous, though setbacks are normal. Moreover, the identification of such tasks, in so precise a fashion, tends toward crystalizing the life-curriculum prescribed for children, thereby obstructing the sort of critical reexamination and continuous modification needed in a rapidly changing society. . . .
>
> Finally, the concept of developmental tasks may be wrongly interpreted as implying that each life stage is simply an apprenticeship for what follows. Thus, the child's role would simply be an audition for the role he will play as an adult. Instead, each stage is important for its own sake but should provide a healthy base for later stages [Rogers, 1972, p. 73].

Most misapplications of stage theory derive from distortions in interpretation of writings and research on the topic. For example, Bruner (1960) declared that "The foundations of any subject may be taught to anybody at any age in some form" (p. 512). Bruner proceeded to make good his statement, by reducing advanced concepts to simpler versions more digestible by the young consumer. However, it only seems that Bruner's point of view differs from that of Piaget. Bruner did not mean that the child could skip stages in development. Rather, he meant that the subject itself may be manipulated in such a way as to make it appropriate to the child at any stage.

## POSITIVE CONTRIBUTIONS OF STAGE THEORY

Despite such distortions, which can and should be corrected, stage theorists have made significant and worthwhile contributions to developmental psychology. Stage theory pinpoints the need to determine the relative contributions of maturation and environment to characteristics manifest at particular stages. Only through experimental manipulation and variation of the environment can this question be answered. Perhaps maturation itself may even be altered instead of accepted as inevitably decreed at the instant of conception, through alteration of genetic makeup before birth. Stage research can help to decide what changes might be desirable, if and when such modifications become generally approved and feasible.

Stage theory has also helped adults to appreciate that children undergo important modifications in the progress of growth. Children's experiences must be properly articulated with their stage development, which proves no easy task. For example, the most effective school curriculum would provide children with tasks that they are only just ready to tackle.

> Accordingly, developmental psychologist Jerome Kagan has proposed a 'crest of the wave' theory of education. The child is seen as riding a wave in precarious balance. At any given age, he or she is just exactly ready for a few educational experiences. But the child is also in constant danger of either sliding back down the wave if it encounters too easy a lesson, appropriate to an earlier developmental stage, or of falling forward on its face if the lesson it encounters is too far beyond its capacity. The best curriculum should provide the appropriate experience at the right time. This intriguing idea has, unfortunately, not yet been developed to the point that teachers can identify with certainty what stages a particular child has reached and what lessons are best for him or her [Fantino & Reynolds, 1975, p. 345].

Stage research also provides helpful norms for determining whether a particular child's progression toward maturity is satisfactory. Although each individual has his or her own unique developmental pattern, significant diversions from more typical patterns of development at least raise the question: Is the observed deviation optimum for this child? It may well be, and, if so, it should be respected. On the other hand, without some kind of norms, abnormal lags and unhealthy deviations in development might not be detected and, if possible, corrected.

In fact, research in this area has very broad applications because differences at successive age periods inevitably dictate the age-grading of society. Yet, only if these stages be properly researched and interpreted can society operate with maximal efficiency. For example, most adults have wrongly assumed that children and young adolescents are rarely capable of major crimes. Yet statistics prove that numerous crimes are committed by individuals of this age. Undoubtedly, the whole concept of juvenile delinquency and its treatment needs reevaluation. Developmental-stage research also has obvious application to such varied areas as designing sports equipment, cars, and clothes, constructing houses and playgrounds, preparing foods, planning television programs, organizing educational curricula, and providing medical care—in fact, all major areas of human activity.

## QUESTIONS REGARDING THE AGE-STAGE CONCEPT

Various questions regarding the stage concept remain unresolved. The main question is: Do children go through invariant sequences in the various areas of their development? If so, do developmental sequences simply reflect genetically determined patterns? Or are such sequences simply the outcome of relatively constant ways that society arranges children's experiences? Is the order of behavioral development invariable or subject to change? Can it be that certain kinds of development are closely tied to maturational factors and others much

less so? At present there is general agreement that those behaviors that hinge closely on maturation follow correspondingly less variant patterns. For instance, the child will sit before standing and crawl before walking, because these activities hinge closely on unvarying sequences in physical maturation. Beyond this point, considerable disagreement arises.

A second basic question relating to the age-stage hypothesis is this: To what extent, if any, can a child's progress be hastened from one level to another? To date, no infant has acquired a proficiency in reading. But could infant experience be so engineered as to permit most children to read earlier than customary? With so much to be learned in today's complex world, this question holds considerable significance.

Another question involves the critical-period hypothesis discussed earlier in this book. Are some stages more significant than others? If so, at what periods should specific experiences take place? Among certain animals, if the infant fails to have normal social relationships, it cannot develop normal sex relationships later on (Harlow & Harlow, 1966). Are there similar critical periods in human development?

A further question is this: Can some stages in the various areas of development be skipped, or is each essential? Consider, for instance, Freud's concept of the child's psychosexual development as involving four stages, with a different kind of love object providing satisfaction in each stage. In the first, or narcissistic stage, the child is said to gain erotic satisfaction from himself. In the second, or Oedipal stage, the child becomes attached to the parent of the opposite sex. In the third, or homosexual stage, the child views as love objects members of his or her own sex. Finally, if all goes well, the individual becomes heterosexual, capable of mature love relationships with members of the opposite sex. Must children go through these stages in this order? May one or more be skipped altogether?

In sum, the majority of studies support the age-stage hypothesis; that is, children seem to go through generally invariant stages in certain areas of development. However, the minority of studies that refute the hypothesis should not be overlooked. Besides, many related questions have yet to be resolved. The sequences that have been reported have been derived from comparing children of different ages in the performance of the same task. Needed, but still rare, are longitudinal studies that trace the development of the same children over a period of time. Finally, even casual examination indicates that many so-called replications of research are actually somewhat different.

## REFERENCES

Bronfenbrenner, U. *Two worlds of childhood: U.S. and U.S.S.R.* New York: Russell Sage Foundation, 1970.

Bruner, J. S. *The process of education.* New York: Vintage Books, 1960.

Dulit, E. Adolescent thinking à la Piaget: The formal stage. *Journal of Youth and Adolescence,* 1972, *1*(4), 281–301.

Erikson, E. H. *Childhood and society.* New York: Norton, 1950.

Fantino, E., & Reynolds, G. S. *Contemporary psychology.* San Francisco: W. H. Freeman, 1975.

Gesell, A., & Armatruda, C. S. *Developmental diagnosis* (2nd ed.). New York: Hoeber, 1943.

Harlow, H. F., & Harlow, M. K. Learning to love. *American Scientist,* 1966, *54,* 244–272.

Havighurst, R. J. *Human development and education.* New York: Longmans, 1953.

Hunt, J. McV. *Intelligence and experience.* New York: Ronald, 1961.

Kahana, B., & Kahana, E. Roles of gratification and motor control in the attainment of conceptual thought. *American Psychological Association Proceedings,* 1970, *5,* 287–288.

Kahana, B., & Sterneck, R. Word association responses of children as a function of age, sex and instructions. *Journal of Genetic Psychology,* 1972, *120,* 39–48.

Kohlberg, L. Moral development and the education of adolescents. In E. D. Evans (Ed.), *Adolescents: Readings in behavior and development.* Hinsdale, Ill.: Dryden Press, 1970.

McGraw, M. B. Later development of children specially trained during infancy: Johnny and Jimmy at school age. *Child Development,* 1939, *10,* 1–19.

Nesselroade, J. R., & Baltes, P. B. Adolescent personality development and historical change:

1970–1972. *Monographs of the Society for Research in Child Development,* 1974, *39*(1), 1–79.

Peck, R. F., & Havighurst, R. J. *The psychology of character development.* New York: Wiley, 1960.

Piaget, J. *The moral judgment of the child.* New York: Harcourt Brace, 1932.

Rogers, D. Stage theory: Critical period related to adolescence. In D. Rogers, *Issues in adolescent psychology* (2nd ed.). New York: Appleton-Century-Crofts, 1972.

Tanner, J. M., & Inhelder, B. (Eds.). *Discussions on child development.* New York: International Universities Press, 1960.

## SUGGESTIONS FOR FURTHER READING

Dulit, E. Adolescent thinking à la Piaget: The formal stage. *Journal of Youth and Adolescence,* 1972, *1*(4), 281–301. After replicating two of Piaget's and Inhelder's 1958 formal-stage experiments, Dulit concludes that the formal stage differs appreciably from the earlier Piagetian stages. Early adolescence is the time when a single-path model of cognitive development becomes grossly inadequate. After that a more complex model becomes essential. Only a minority of children ever attain the formal stage of thinking.

Elkind, D. *Children and adolescents: Interpretive essays on Jean Piaget* (2nd ed.). New York: Oxford University Press, 1974. These 12 essays deal with basic Piagetian concepts, misunderstandings about how children learn, egocentrism in children and adolescents, the course of mental development, Piaget and education, and Montessori and Piaget.

Elkind, D., Hetzel, D., & Coe, J. Piaget and British primary education. *Educational Psychologist,* 1974, *11*(1), 1–10. This article constitutes an explanation of the relationship between British primary education and the philosophy of education implicit in the writings of Jean Piaget. While British primary education and Piaget approach children's learning from quite different directions, their conclusions are interpreted as in close agreement.

Gaudia, G. The Piagetian dilemma: What does Piaget really have to say to teachers? *Elementary School Journal,* 1974, *74*(8), 481–492. Certain questions are raised relating Piagetian theory to classroom practice. The point is made that Piaget himself made little effort to interpret his theories in ways that would permit easy application of his findings to classroom teaching.

Ginsburg, H., & Opper, S. *Piaget's theory of intellectual development: An introduction.* Englewood Cliffs, N.J.: Prentice-Hall, 1969. After outlining Piaget's biography, the authors describe his work and theories in clearly understandable language. Implications for education are also suggested.

Gould, R. Adult life stages: Growth toward self-tolerance. *Psychology Today,* September 1975, pp. 74–81. This analysis of life stages in adulthood lends better perspective to stage theory as a developmental concept, and it suggests possible relationships between adult and early stages of life.

Isaacs, N. *A brief introduction to Piaget.* New York: Agathon Press, 1972. These essays by the late scholar and educator, Nathan Isaacs, describe how the child gradually, by stages, learns about the world and how to deal with it. The emphasis is on Piaget's basic ideas.

Lickona, T. Piaget misunderstood: A critique of the criticisms of his theory of moral development. *Merrill-Palmer Quarterly,* 1969, *15*(4), 337–350. The author clarifies Piaget's position on eight criticisms often made of his theory. The accompanying discussion provides a framework for understanding the broader aspects of Piagetian theory.

Rebelsky, F., Conover, C., & Chafetz, P. The development of political attitudes in young children. *Journal of Psychology,* 1969, *73,* 141–146. This investigation of political knowledge and attitudes of children, ages 2 to 13, indicates an increase in information by age and greater information about controversial issues of the day than about the incumbent president. Learning patterns for political information are consistently age-related.

Resnick, R. J. A developmental and socioeconomic evaluation of perceptual integration. *Developmental Psychology,* 1969, *1,* 691–696. Urban, white, first-grade boys from two socioeconomic classes were randomly assigned to three training groups to examine the effects of experience on the development of perceptual abilities. Results showed that the developmental sequence for perceptual integrative abilities can be accelerated. Training is more effective with boys from an average than from a poor environment, and experiential factors are a significant aspect of perceptual development.

Riegel, K. F. Dialectic operations: The final period of cognitive development. *Human Development,* 1973, *16*(5), 346–370. While Piaget's interpretations capture a broad variety of childhood accomplishments, they fail adequately to represent the emotions and thoughts of creative mature persons.

Riley, M. W. The perspective of age stratification. *School Review,* 1974, *83*(1), 85–91. Stratification by age is discussed, with special emphasis on similarities between youth and old age.

Smart, M. S., & Smart, R. C. *Children— Development and relationships.* New York: Macmillan, 1972. This child-development book is organized by stages of development, utilizing a combination of Erik Erikson's stages of personality development and Jean Piaget's stages of cognitive development. Special attention is given to the early phases of development because of its significance in overall developmental patterns.

Uzgiris, I. C. Patterns of cognitive development in infancy. *Merrill-Palmer Quarterly,* 1973, *19,* 181–204. The Piagetian Scales developed by Uzgiris and Hunt were administered in order to determine stages in object-concept development.

Wadsworth, B. *Piaget's theory of cognitive development.* New York: David McKay, 1971. This book introduces the reader to the basic concepts of Piaget's theories of cognitive development in a "simplified, conceptual manner," with emphasis on those writings having special relevance to educational practice.

Weitz, L. J., Bynum, T. W., Thomas, J. A., & Steger, J. A. Piaget's system of 16 binary operations: An empirical investigation. *Journal of Genetic Psychology,* 1973, *123*(2), 279–284. In their 1958 work Inhelder and Piaget offered a single protocol as their only evidence that the completely developed formal-operational thinker employs all 16 binary operations of functional logic. In this replication of that study, involving a random sampling of 9-, 12-, and 16-year-olds, not one person used more than 5 of the 16 operations, and there was no developmental trend with regard to the number of operations used.

**The Age-Stage Controversy**

# 6

## Sex Role

Earlier in this century, growing individuals were generally categorized as children or adolescents, with little differentiation by sex. However, social-sex roles are now recognized as highly significant in human development, especially in cultures where they are highly polarized. Social-sex role refers to patterns of behavior that society deems appropriate for each sex. It suggests behaviors typical of the ideal male or female as defined by the culture.

Social-sex role is important for a variety of reasons. It defines the nature of much of one's behavior, including one's manner of dress and one's play and work activities. It also determines areas of discrimination and privilege. Sally may have a football, but Tommy may not have a doll. Sammy is permitted to slug it out with Bobby, but Edna is forbidden to sock Susie. To appreciate the importance of sex role, let the reader review his or her activities for one day and consider how each is somehow modified by sex role.

Note, too, that others modify their behaviors toward a child according to the child's sex. Hence, regardless of how a child feels about himself, he must cope with the image his sex creates in the minds of others. Perhaps Susie prefers so-called boys' games, yet she is expected to like the dolls given her at Christmas. In fact, even by the age of 2½ children have been made aware of sex-role expectations (Heise & Roberts, 1970).

## PERSPECTIVE ON MALE AND FEMALE SOCIAL-SEX ROLES

The male's stereotypic role holds many advantages, and some disadvantages. Basic social institutions foster the tradition of masculine superiority. The boy is often granted more freedom than the girl and is accorded positions of higher status and greater responsibility. Hence boys have a higher self-concept, initiate action more quickly, and feel less inhibited (Kagan, 1972). They are provided greater opportunities for developing competence and self-confidence. For example, boys' toys, as compared with girls' toys, are more expensive, complex, active, varied, and social. By contrast, girls' toys are more simple, passive, and solitary. (A Report on Children's Toys, 1972). Although boys and girls receive an equal number of gifts, 73% of boys' gifts are toys compared with 57% for girls, who often get cosmetics, jewelry, and clothes, instead of toys. Field workers observing in toy departments during the Christmas season saw not a single scientific toy purchased for a girl. The doctor's kit designated as a boy's toy had a stethoscope, a miniature microscope, a blood-pressure tester, and other instruments. The nurse's kit designated for girls was equipped with a nurse's apron, plastic silverware, play sick tray, and play food (Levy & Stacey, 1973).

Nevertheless, the boy's role has its liabilities—for example, it is narrow and hard to fulfill successfully. A boy must be all boy, although as a man he is granted more latitude. He is pressured more and more to succeed, because the family's status and livelihood will depend on him. His role is also portrayed as contrary to his best interest in the classroom. At least in elementary school, teachers are mostly women whose feminine attitudes, interests, and values permeate the classroom. Thus the classroom climate conflicts sharply with that of the boy's own peer culture. As a result, more traditionally masculine boys often have conflicts with their teachers. In one study (Sexton, 1970), only 31% of the most masculine boys behaved politely to their teachers, whereas 68% of the least masculine boys were polite to them. On the other hand, boys' disadvantage in women teachers' classrooms may be overrated. Teachers' negative criticisms are directed at boys' misbehaviors rather than at their academic performance (Brophy & Good, 1970). Furthermore, according to informal studies by the editor, most elementary-school teachers prefer boys to girls.

The female's role is also said to have certain advantages, most of which may be interpreted as disadvantages, too. The girl is sheltered; however, being sheltered may reduce her self-confidence. She is encouraged to develop warmth and nurturance, but unless tempered by strength, such traits may degenerate into emotionalism and weakness. She is granted the privilege of motherhood; but if motherhood becomes the focus of her existence, she has little to live for after the children leave home.

Even in childhood, girls anticipate a more circumscribed vocational choice. When children were asked "What do you want to be when you grow up?" girls aged 6 and 7 seemed little influenced by the women's liberation movement (Looft, 1971). By contrast, boys saw a wide range of opportunities open to them and named numerous occupational categories. Moreover, occupational foreclosure occurred earlier in girls; that is, boys were more susceptible to changing their initial choices. When asked what they wanted to be when they grew up, the boys most frequently replied football player (9) and policeman (4). Other choices included doctor, dentist, scientist, pilot, and astronaut. Of the 33 girls, 25 named either nurse (14) or teacher (11) as their first choice. The remaining choices included mother, stewardess, and sales clerk. None of the girls expressed a desire to follow such occupations as politics, science, or law. A few girls said they would be mothers, but none of the boys said they would be fathers.

Apparently, a high degree of femininity, in the traditional sense, is unhealthy for children of either sex. In a longitudinal study that involved a follow-up of children originally studied a dozen years earlier, femininity consistently related to negative self-evaluation in both boys and girls (Sears, 1970). For both sexes femininity was associated with poor self-concept as well as with aggression, fearfulness, and insecurity. In short, the hypothesis that poorly sex-typed children would have poor self-concepts was supported only for boys.

Not surprisingly, most boys like their role, whereas girls are less satisfied with theirs. By adulthood most females come to accept their role, although they often dislike certain features of it. However, individuals of both sexes vary in feelings about their sex role. The pretty girl who is accorded special status finds femininity rewarding; but the competitive, adventurous girl finds it frustrating and confining. The shy, indecisive boy finds difficult the sex role that the muscular athlete assumes with ease.

Although both sex roles hold certain disadvantages, society has made little conscious effort to modify them. Females are taught to be conformist and to make the best of whatever fate has been allotted to them. Most males are content with their role and largely unaware of subtle factors that work to their disadvantage. Both sexes form their ideas about sex role so early and so unconsciously that they believe differential sex behaviors to be rooted in biology, and hence insusceptible to change.

There is considerable disagreement concerning the proportionate part that genetics and culture play in fashioning social-sex roles. Certain sex differences appear so early as to suggest a genetic origin (Hutt, 1972). Even at 5 months of age, girl infants show less interest than boys in varied and novel stimuli and less tendency to explore (Stevenson & Lynn, 1971). However, no primary innate or genetic mechanisms predetermine psychosexual differences. In fact, almost all personality traits and behaviors traditionally associated with males or females, with the possible exception of aggressiveness, appear to be more socioculturally than biologically determined. When mistakes in an infant's sexual identity are made, the wrongly assigned role becomes permanently stamped in and as irreversible as if innately preordained (Money, 1963).

Nevertheless, the sex roles themselves, as culturally defined, can be changed, and indeed are changing. There is a certain growing flexibility within each of the sex subcultures, especially the female; and there has been a trend toward blurring the distinctions between the sexes (Rosenberg & Sutton-Smith, 1972). Nevertheless, modifications may be more apparent than real; that is, most changes are in peripheral areas. In one school where sex role as such was deemphasized, most children nevertheless chose identities consistent with their sex, while accepting others' preference for aspects of the opposite sex role. Another problem was cultural lag in materials provided for the school. For example, consider this typical children's song in an ultra-modern nursery school: "And the daddy went spank-spank, and the mommy went 'shh-shh' (The song concerned a child who had made noise on a bus.)" (p. 471). Although serious efforts have been made to reduce racist materials provided to children, far less attention has been given to deleting materials of a sexist nature (Joffe, 1971).

## QUESTIONS RELATING TO SEX ROLE

In any case, sex roles are currently in a state of flux with no clear consensus as to their present status or what they should become. Many subsidiary issues remain to be answered. How do sex roles differ in their finer distinctions? Will depolarization of sex roles increase or diminish heterosexual conflict? What should the respective responsibilities of home, school, and society-at-large be in identifying and effecting desired changes?

A related question is this: To what extent are sex roles rooted in biological differences? Certain sex differences appear so early in life and are so universally reported as to raise the question whether they are innate, and hence resistant to change. For example, boys are physically stronger, heavier, and more active even at birth. As a result, perhaps males are naturally better equipped than females for a vigorous, strenuous role. However, the evidence suggests that most distinctions in psychosocial sex roles are largely environmentally determined. If this is so, should a critical analysis and revision of sex roles be consciously undertaken?

The literature on sex roles covers many aspects of the subject and reflects highly diverse points of view. Our first selection, by Patrick Lee and Nancy Gropper, is especially stimulating. These two authors propose that the sex-role construct can be conceptualized more adequately in cultural than in psychosocial terms. They argue that a bicultural sex-role model is best and that boys and girls should have full and equal access to traditionally sex-typed educational and cultural resources. In the second selection, David Lynn discusses the biological and environmental bases of sex roles.

## REFERENCES

Brophy, J. E., & Good, T. L. Teachers' communication of differential expectations for children's classroom performance: Some behavioral data. *Journal of Educational Psychology,* 1970, *61,* 365–374.

Heise, D. R., & Roberts, E. P. M. The development of role knowledge. *Genetic Psychology Monographs,* 1970, *82* (First Half), 83–115.

Hutt, C. *Males and females.* New York: Penguin Books, 1972.

Joffe, C. Sex-role socialization and the nursery school: As the twig is bent. *Journal of Marriage and the Family,* 1971, *33,* 467–475.

Kagan, J. The emergence of sex differences. *School Review,* 1972, *80,* 217–227.

Levy, B., & Stacey, J. Sexism in the elementary school: A backward and forward look. *Phi Delta Kappan,* 1973, *55* (2), 105–109.

Looft, W. R. Sex differences in the expression of vocational aspirations by elementary school children. *Developmental Psychology,* 1971, *5,* 725–732.

Money, J. Developmental differentiations of femininity and masculinity compared. In S. M. Farber and R. H. L. Wilson (Eds.), *Potential of women.* New York: McGraw-Hill, 1963.

A report on children's toys. *Ms.,* December 1972, p. 57.

Rosenberg, B. G., & Sutton-Smith, B. *Sex and identity.* New York: Holt, Rinehart & Winston, 1972.

Sears, R. R. Relation of early socialization experiences to self-concepts and gender role in middle childhood. *Child Development,* 1970, *41,* 267–289.

Sexton, P. How the American boy is feminized. *Psychology Today,* August 1970, pp. 23–29; 66–67.

Stevenson, A. H., & Lynn, D. B. Preference for high variability in young children. *Psychonomic Science,* 1971, *23,* 143–144.

# Sex Role Culture and Educational Practice

## Patrick C. Lee and Nancy B. Gropper

The Bicultural Model provides us with a third language for describing the interaction of sex-role cultures. Its particular focus is on acquired cross-cultural compatibilities, similar-

From "Sex Role Culture and Educational Practice," by P. C. Lee and N. B. Gropper, Harvard Educational Review, 1974, *44*(3), 369–410. Copyright © 1974 by President and Fellows of Harvard College. Reprinted by permission.

ities, and consistencies. Its basic postulate, unlike the Difference Models, is that sex-role cultures need not be viewed as mutually exclusive alternatives. In fact, as will be argued below, one usually has membership in both cultures, although one's primary affiliation is usually with one culture or the other. Primary affiliation, however, does not rule out secondary affiliation, especially given the low degree of internal consistency within the cultures and the human capacity for knowing and comprehending much more than is expressed in behavior.

Social scientists have long recognized that there are two realms of human activity, one habitually translated into behavior while the other goes relatively unexpressed as underlying knowledge. Two people whose sex-typed behavior may be quite different may share the same underlying sex-role knowledge and range of sex-typed interests as may people with similar behavior. In either case, people's observable behavior provides a shaky basis for making inferences about anything beyond the lower limits of their underlying knowledge. According to learning theorists, behavior is a function of reinforcement, while knowledge is a function of learning. Thus, while boys and girls are reinforced to adopt behaviors typed to their own sex, they often learn through observation much about the behavior associated with the opposite sex. So while their sex-typed behavior may differ markedly, their sex-role knowledge may show considerable overlap. With different patterns of reinforcement, much of the cross-sex knowledge they carry could be easily translated into behavior, making them expressively as well as receptively bicultural.

Sex-role knowledge is the key to sex-role biculturalism. Since much of it is not subject to the vagaries of reinforcement, knowledge is relatively stable and cross-situational in nature. Sex-typed behavior, on the other hand, is often specific to those situations in which it has been reinforced. Thus, what is considered appropriately masculine behavior in one situation may be defined quite differently in another situation. The same, of course, holds for female-typed behavior. Mischel (1966, 1970, 1971) has argued repeatedly and persuasively that such evidence is cause for defining sex role more in situational terms and less as a generalized trait. Sex-role behaviors appear to be specific in several respects:

1. *Test Specific*. Different tests purporting to measure central aspects of sex role often correlate poorly with each other and thus have little predictive validity. Moreover, the same child often performs quite differently on two administrations of the same test (for examples, see Mischel, 1966, p. 67; 1970, p. 24).

2. *Response Specific*. Boys and girls both know how to be aggressive; they simply have different ways of expressing it. Girls show greater prosocial aggression, for example, verbal threats for breaking rules, while boys' aggressive responses tend to be physical (Mischel, 1966, p. 73). Madsen (1968) found that girls can also be physically aggressive, although it takes different forms from boys' physical aggression.

3. *Reward Specific*. Bandura (1965) found that boys imitated a physically aggressive model more than girls did. Introducing incentives for imitating, however, eliminated differences between the sexes, clearly indicating that girls had knowledge of aggressiveness, but needed reinforcement to translate their knowledge into behavior.

4. *Object Specific*. Males are expected to be physically aggressive with some males under some conditions, but not with other males, such as elderly men or distinguished citizens, and hardly ever with women (Mischel, 1966, p. 67). In other words, the aggressive behavior of a given male in one situation does not predict well to his response in another situation.

5. *Age Specific*. Cross-sex typing is particularly susceptible to age variation. Dependency in young boys, for example, is not correlated with dependency in adulthood (Kagan & Moss, 1962). Achievement behavior in females fluctuates with age and stage of life (Bardwick, 1971). During those periods when dependency and achievement are not expressed in behavior, we must assume that they still exist in terms of knowledge.

It seems, then, that the current status of sex-role culture is unstable, that it is characterized by much cross-cultural continuity and intracultural discontinuity, and that the ultimate demonstration of this is the existence of large numbers of bicultural individuals, in potential if not in fact. We have already mentioned the abstract notion that reinforcement releases knowledge into behavior, but we would like to describe some of the concrete forces which are currently releasing increasing numbers of people into some degree of functional biculturalism.

There are several broad social and economic movements which are serving as release mechanisms. The so-called youth culture, for example, places a high value on expressiveness among males and defines inexpressiveness as an undesirable personality trait (Balswick & Peek, 1971). Women's Liberation seems to be fostering a strong orientation toward competence among many women, as are changes in employment patterns. Three out of five working women now are married, and one in three married women is working (Clavan, 1970). The changing economic status of women and the enhanced geographic mobility of families have lessened the differentiation of intra-familial roles so that the parental models now presented to children are more bicultural than in the past (Knox & Kupferer, 1971). The offspring of working mothers tend more toward sex-role biculturalism than the children of non-working mothers (Hartley, 1960; Vogel *et al.*, 1970), and children, especially girls, from modern families are less sex-typed than those from more traditional families (Minuchin, 1965).

With the increasing divorce rate and the steady movement toward suburban residency, the incidence of father absence and low father availability is increasing, and boys have a diminishing supply of available adult male models during the early years of life. Regarding this the cross-cultural research of Burton & Whiting (1961) indicated that close mother-son relations, essentially excluding the father during the early childhood years, resulted in marked cross-sex identity for boys.

## BICULTURALISM IN FEMALES AND MALES

Females tend to be more bicultural than males. While male sex-role culture gravitates around one pole, females seem to operate in a bi-polar system. Females are expected to relate to an affiliative system of role prescriptions which attributes primacy to fecundity, intuition, and nurturance as indices of expressive mastery. Males, on the other hand, are required to enter the achievement system of role prescriptions which places value on status, power, and wealth as the criteria of instrumental mastery. Females are permitted, and occasionally encouraged, to relate to the highly desired achievement system, while males are usually discouraged from cultivating the kind of expressive skills ordinarily associated with the female sex role. The broader range of options open to females increases the probability of functional biculturalism among girls and women, while the typical male version of biculturalism is constructed from a more limited range of options.

The precursors to adult female biculturalism are evident in early childhood. Kohlberg (1966, pp. 117–120), for example, found that children already have marked sex-typed preferences by the age of four. After this boys continue to show a steady increase from a baseline of about 60 percent male-typed choices to a preference rate of 80 to 100 percent. Girls, however, do not appear to get above a 70 to 80 percent preference rate for female-typed choices. Brown (1957) compiled similar results on the *It Scale* choices of children from kindergarten through fifth grade. He found that girls were significantly more variable than boys in their sex-role preferences, that boys showed a much stronger preference for the male role than girls showed for the female role, and from the first through the fourth grades, girls preferred the male to the female role. Sutton-Smith (1972, pp. 405–413) found that, as children grow up, boys prefer fewer games, while girls seem to adopt the games which the boys have abandoned. This process continues until about nine years of age, when girls have a broad repertoire of games and boys have become highly specialized. The trend seems to be for girls to invade male categories of play, while boys retreat to fewer categories. These findings are suggestive of two pressures toward biculturalism in young girls. First, there is evidently less external pressure on girls to adopt

female-typed preferences than there is on boys to assume male-typed preferences. Second, girls probably feel some internal pressure to adopt the male-typed choices on which society places such high value. One must assume that girls know the difference between first and second place, and have the same inherent desire for status boys have.

A second precursor of female biculturalism may be the girls' tendency to imitate opposite-sex models more than boys do. Bandura, Ross, and Ross (1963) found that girls imitated a powerful male model more than boys imitated a powerful female model. In a study testing the complementary effect, Grusec and Brinker (1969) found that girls showed less same-sex imitation than boys. These studies indicate that models with desired attributes may be almost as salient as same-sex models. This poses no problems for boys since adult males in our society are generally viewed to have more desired attributes than adult females. Girls, however, indicate their conflict through their tendency to imitate male as well as female models.

The five studies presented above suggest that a common sex-role profile among females in American society would include a standard sex-role orientation or basic identity, but a strongly ambivalent sex-role preference, and a moderately ambivalent sex-role adoption. According to Biller (1971), the latter two are, respectively, functions of the parental value assigned to sex-typed phenomena and the degree of imitation of same-sex models. In another intriguing formulation, Burton & Whiting (1961) distinguished among three kinds of identity: attributed, subjective, and optative. These refer, respectively, to the sex role assigned to a person by society, how the person subjectively defines himself or herself in sex-role terms, and which sex role a person would opt for, if given the choice. Thus the fully sex-typed person would both internalize and prefer the sex role assigned by society. However, in a society like ours, where the male role is so highly valued, one should expect that convergence of the three kinds of identity would be more common in boys than in girls. The identity of girls should typically include at least some masculine characteristics. Using the models of Biller and Burton and Whiting, we would expect moderate to strong cross-sex preferences but not cross-sex identity in American females. The research cited on young children, and the high incidence of female movement into traditionally male economic, familial, social, and recreational roles would seem to confirm our expectation.

The roots of male biculturalism probably lie in the fact that, during the first few years of life, boys spend most of their time with their mothers. This close, prolonged, and primary association with an adult female has prompted several theorists to postulate that the boy's initial identification is with his mother rather than his father (Lynn, 1969; Mowrer, 1950; Bronfenbrenner, 1960). There has been too little systematic observation of the mother-infant relationship, and almost no research on father-infant interactions, so comparative statements about mother versus father influence during this period of life are based more on folk wisdom than on evidence (Kotelchuck, 1973). However, one startling finding is that, over the course of 24 hours, fathers spend an average of 37.7 seconds talking with their three-month-old infants (Rebelsky & Hanks, 1971), while mothers average almost two hours of verbalization with their infants in an eight-hour period (Moss, 1967). If these figures are even remotely indicative of the degree of exclusiveness of the early mother-son relationship, then it is surprising that boys are not more bicultural.

One can only assume that, during the early years of relatively low father availability, the boy's various caregivers (e.g., mother, baby-sitter, older siblings) encourage him to adopt a masculine orientation. Biller & Bahm (1971), for example, found that father-absent boys who perceived their mothers as encouraging aggressiveness had high masculine self-concepts, while those who did not perceive similar maternal encouragement tended to have low masculine self-concepts. This retrospective finding suggests the role the mother can play in male sex-role enculturation, even in the absence of the father altogether. Nevertheless, it would appear that the developmental precursor to biculturalism in males is their close and sustained relationship with the mother during the early formative years. Subsequent to this early period the typical boy experiences increasing, but not entirely successful, pressure to acquire a homogeneously male profile (Brown, 1957; Kohlberg, 1966; Sutton-Smith, 1972; and Fagot & Patterson, 1969). The same research indicates that girls typically experience a longer period of bicultural grace than boys enabling them to become more conversant with the epistemology, aspirations, and folkways of male sex-role culture.

# EDUCATIONAL IMPLICATIONS OF BICULTURALISM

Our analysis of sex-role culture in terms of the Bicultural Model indicates that males and females share a common range of sex-role information, interest, and aspirations, and that the developmental origins of these lie in early childhood. The language of biculturalism, however, does not drown out the language of cultural differences. As pointed out earlier, there are differences between the sex-role cultures, although they are clearly not as stable, persistent, or mutually exclusive as popular sex-role stereotyping suggests. For the school effectively to serve children who are increasingly bicultural while maintaining their basic identities as boys or girls, it must learn to speak both languages. We would like to reexamine teacher sex-role expectations, classroom space and materials, and teacher modeling value in terms of biculturalism.

# TEACHER SEX-ROLE EXPECTATIONS

Our suggestions here are directed primarily to the sensibility of the teacher, and represent extensions of our earlier recommendations about the interaction of pupil-role with sex-role expectations. The teacher should recognize that boys and girls are more alike than different and that, both biologically and culturally, there is more variation within than between the sexes.

Where sex differences exist, they are mostly behavioral and/or situational in nature, stemming from societal expectations, previous reinforcement, and habit. They are not necessarily an expression of all that children know or can know about sex-role culture. Nor are they representative of their potential repertoire of sex-typed behaviors.

On the contrary, given the current status of sex-role biculturalism, the teacher should expect more children than in the past to express academic preferences and career objectives which represent either reversals or blendings of past sex-role patterns. These should in no way be derogated or sacrificed to outmoded and maladaptive sex-role expectations. Nor should currently fashionable sex-role ideologies be used to coerce children to cross-sex type or to select their primary cultural affiliation on the basis of a spurious personal choice. We do not see the school as the place for tampering with the basic dimensions of identification; rather it can be a place for experimenting with traditionally sex-typed preferences, interests, and behaviors.

Finally, just as individual morality and justice dictate that educators ignore society's racial and class barriers to equal educational opportunity, they also dictate that sex barriers be ignored (Baumrind, 1972). None of this is to say that all social claims on the individual be ignored. On the contrary, in addition to appreciating the merits of orderly social change, we have already pointed out that society's current claims are specifically for change in economic patterns and social customs. Teachers who recognize the irrelevance of most traditional sex-role ideology are hardly mavericks. Everywhere they look they can find support for their efforts to give boys and girls equal access to the resources of the educational system.

## CLASSROOM SPACE AND MATERIALS

Children are partially sex-role enculturated by three or four years of age so teachers should expect some resistance to their adoption of bicultural behaviors, especially from young boys. Because girls are more bicultural, a biculturated classroom would at first seem to be a more congenial setting for girls. Boys, therefore, may require special support in order to overcome their initial resistance to realizing their bicultural capacity. In the early grades, this could probably be done rather easily, especially if the children came from modern, professional class families. At the higher elementary grades and in schools serving lower socioeconomic status populations, one should anticipate greater resistance from both girls and boys. By high school, however, adolescents become more responsive to the temper of the larger society and teachers might again expect a period of relative openness to sex-role biculturalism.

In order to indicate how the teacher can use classroom space and materials to expedite biculturalism, we will report a recorded nursery school observation, then suggest ways of dealing with the problem it depicts. In this incident a girl and a boy had already been assigned roles by a socially powerful girl in the housekeeping area. The powerful girl was the mother, the other girl was the dog, and the boy was the father. All children were four years old:

> The boy takes some playdough in a pot to the stove. He announces that he is cooking. The 'mother' says 'Daddies don't cook.' The 'dog' says the same thing. The boy moves back from the stove—he says in a quiet voice, 'My poppy cooks . . .' He stands off at a distance looking at the stove. He looks uncertain about what to do next. The teacher was watching the interaction and she tells the two girls that daddies sometimes do cook. The boy immediately returns to the stove and starts to cook.

One way of dealing with this problem, of course, was to directly intervene as this teacher did. By supporting the boy, she helped to counteract the natural conservatism of sex-role ideology among young children (Kohlberg, 1966, pp. 100–101). Due to their relatively undifferentiated cognitive structure, young children are not inclined toward subtle distinctions, but tend to think in more categorical terms. However, they are also very receptive to new learning, if the teacher gives them sufficient time and age-appropriate reasons. In this way the teacher becomes a stimulus for the child's cognitive accommodation.

Another way of dealing with problems of this kind would be to arrange classroom space and materials to break some of the traditional associations between sex role and areas, such as those found in Shure's study of classroom ecology (1963). For example, the teacher could combine the housekeeping and block areas. This would eliminate the necessity for boys and girls to pass into alien territory to share each other's resources. We have never seen this merger in a classroom, but we suspect that, given adequate teacher supervision, it would release many children into episodes of bicultural expression. With the passage of months some sustained bicultural activities should emerge. Moreover, it could serve as a precursor to subsequent blends of sex-typed areas in the later grades. Many advocates of the integrated curriculum have pointed out the artificiality of demarcating subject areas from one another (Blackie, 1967, p. 51). When one adds to this artificiality the unfortunate tendency for students to sex-type some subjects as male, for example, arithmetic, and others as female, for example, reading, we have a double basis for seeking interesting and potentially creative combinations of classroom activities and school subjects (Stein & Smithells, 1969).

## TEACHER MODELING VALUE

We would like to underscore and expand some of our earlier suggestions on Teacher Modeling Value. Because teachers are simultaneously professional and almost always female, they should give full vent to their usually large capacity for biculturalism. They should become involved in male-typed activities as spontaneously as in female-typed activities. We are not suggesting that female teachers try to become imitation males. This would be a ridiculous embarrassment to them and to their students. We are only suggesting that they be as bicultural as personal comfort will allow and that this may involve some concrete adjustments in their range of *expressed* interests, their activity rate, and the clothing they wear to work. In addition to having more fun, they would present an exciting and expanded range of modeling possibilities to their female students and create a more congenial setting for their male students.

From the bicultural point of view, we see a double value in exposing young children to more male teachers. First, there should be advantages for young girls because of their relative willingness to imitate male models. The male teacher could make his sex-typed competencies available to young girls through both modeling and direct teaching, thereby enhancing their already manifest tendency toward biculturalism. Second, there remains the problem of most boys' reluctance to imitate female models. Since male teachers of young children are generally quite nurturant, they could provide effective models of biculturalism to young boys. By involving themselves in female as well as male-typed activities, they could show boys that interest in feminine activities does not constitute a threat to masculine identity (Baumrind, 1972, pp. 173–174). It is doubtful that even an extraordinary woman could do this as successfully as an ordinary man could. It should be mentioned, however, that male teachers are not to be viewed as the special property of boys any more than female teachers would play this role with girls. Teachers of both sexes would be expected to make their sex-role cultural resources available to all children, irrespective of sex. Lest there be any confusion on this point, willingness and ability to provide such service should be a criterion for hiring male teachers; and for retaining female teachers.

## REFERENCES

Balswick, J. O., & Peek, C. W. The inexpressive male: A tragedy of American society. *Family Coordinator*, 1971, *20*, 363–368.

Bandura, A. Influence of models' reinforcement contingencies on the acquisition of imitative responses. *Journal of Personality and Social Psychology*, 1965, *1*, 589–595.

Bandura, A., Ross, D., & Ross, S. A. A comparative test of the status envy, social power, and secondary reinforcement theories of identifactory learning. *Journal of Abnormal and Social Psychology*, 1963, *67*, 527–534.

Bardwick, J. M. *Psychology of women: A study of biocultural conflicts.* New York: Harper & Row, 1971.

Baumrind, D. From each according to her ability. *School Review,* 1972, *80,* 161–197.

Biller, H. B. *Father, child, and sex role.* Lexington, Mass.: D. C. Heath, 1971.

Biller, H. B., & Bahm, R. M. Father-absence, perceived maternal behavior, and masculinity of self-concept among junior high school boys. *Developmental Psychology,* 1971, *4,* 178–181.

Blackie, J. *Inside the primary school.* London: Her Majesty's Stationery Office, 1967.

Bronfenbrenner, U. Freudian theories of identification and their derivatives. *Child Development,* 1960, *31,* 15–40.

Brown, D. G. Masculinity-femininity development in children. *Journal of Consulting Psychology,* 1957, *21,* 197–202.

Burton, R. V., & Whiting, J. W. M. The absent father and cross-sex identity. *Merrill-Palmer Quarterly,* 1961, *7,* 85–95.

Clavan, S. Women's liberation and the family. *Family Coordinator,* 1970, *19,* 317–323.

Fagot, B. I., & Patterson, G. R. An in vivo analysis of reinforcing contingencies for sex role behaviors in the preschool child. *Developmental Psychology,* 1969, *1,* 563–568.

Grusec, J. E., & Brinker, D. B. Reinforcement for imitation as a social learning determinant with implications for sex role development. Unpublished manuscript, University of Toronto, 1969.

Hartley, R. E. Children's concepts of male and female roles. *Merrill-Palmer Quarterly,* 1960, *6,* 83–91.

Kagan, J. E., & Moss, H. A. *Birth to maturity: A study in psychological development.* New York: Wiley, 1962.

Knox, W. E., & Kupferer, H. J. A discontinuity in the socialization of males in the U. S. *Merrill-Palmer Quarterly,* 1971, *17,* 251–261.

Kohlberg, L. A cognitive-developmental analysis of children's sex-role concepts and attitudes. In E. E. Maccoby (Ed.), *The development of sex differences.* Stanford, Calif.: Stanford University Press, 1966.

Kotelchuck, M. The nature of the infant's tie to his father. Paper presented at the Biannual Meeting of the Society for Research in Child Development, Philadelphia, April 1973.

Lynn, D. B. *Parental and sex-role identification: A theoretical formulation.* Berkeley, Calif.: McCutchan, 1969.

Madsen, C., Jr. Nurturance and modeling in preschoolers. *Child Development,* 1968, *39,* 221–236.

Minuchin, P. Sex-role concepts and sex typing in childhood as a function of school and home environments. *Child Development,* 1965, *36,* 1033–1048.

Mischel, W. A social-learning view of sex differences in behavior. In E. E. Maccoby (Ed.), *The development of sex differences.* Stanford, Calif.: Stanford University Press, 1966.

Mischel, W. Sex-typing and socialization. In P. H. Mussen (Ed.), *Carmichael's manual of child psychology* (Vol. 2). New York: Wiley, 1970.

Mischel, W., & Mischel, H. The nature and development of psychological sex differences. In G. S. Lesser (Ed.), *Psychology and educational practice.* Glenview, Ill.: Scott, Foresman, 1971.

Moss, H. A. Sex, age, and state as determinants of mother-infant interaction. *Merrill-Palmer Quarterly,* 1967, *13,* 19–36.

Mowrer, O. H. Identification: A link between learning theory and psychotherapy. In O. H. Mowrer, *Learning theory and personality dynamics.* New York: Ronald, 1950.

Rebelsky, F., & Hanks, C. Fathers' verbal interaction with infants in the first three months of life. *Child Development,* 1971, *42,* 63–68.

Shure, M. B. Psychological ecology of a nursery school. *Child Development,* 1963, *34,* 979–992.

Stein, A. H., & Smithells, J. Age and sex differences in children's sex-role standards about achievement. *Developmental Psychology,* 1969, *1,* 252–259.

Sutton-Smith, B. *The folkgames of children.* Austin, Tex.: University of Texas Press, 1972.

Vogel, S. R., Broverman, I. K., Broverman, D. M., Clarkson, F. E., & Rosenkrantz, P. S. Maternal employment and perception of sex roles among college students. *Developmental Psychology,* 1970, *3,* 384–391.

# Determinants of Sex Roles

## David B. Lynn

Sex-role development seems to be an interaction of (1) biologically rooted potentials that predispose males and females toward some behaviors more than others; (2) parent-child relationships, seemingly inherent in the typical family pattern, that predispose each sex toward certain roles; and (3) both blatant and subtle cultural reinforcements of traditional masculine- and feminine-role prescriptions. To understand the meaning of these three forces, let's use as an illustrative example the clearly demonstrated greater aggressiveness of males.

## (1) BIOLOGY

Among the elements interacting to produce sex-role development are the biologically rooted potentials that predispose males and females toward some behavior more than another (in this case, toward more aggression in males). A trait that is more characteristic of one sex than the other is likely to have a biological component if it (1) occurs in that sex when the child is very young (has had less time to learn), (2) is more characteristic of that sex in nearly all cultures, (3) is also more characteristic of the sex in other primates, and (4) is consistent with findings on hormones.

A stronger biological predisposition toward aggressiveness in males than in females is suggested by the fact that the greater aggressiveness of males occurs at an early age, is found in most cultures throughout the world, and is found in other primates as well as in man (Mitchell et al., 1967). The idea of the biologi-

From *The Father: His Role in Child Development,* by D. B. Lynn, pp. 142–146. Copyright © 1974 by Wadsworth Publishing Company, Inc. Reprinted by permission of the publisher, Brooks/Cole Publishing Company, Monterey, California.

cal origins of male aggressiveness is also supported by recent evidence that male-hormone treatment of pregnant primates increased the incidence of rough-and-tumble play among their female offspring and decreased their tendency to withdraw from the threats and approaches of others. In humans, too, girls who (because of their mothers' medical treatment) were affected by male hormones while still in the mother's uterus later showed more vigorous activity and more tomboyish behavior than did other girls (Money & Ehrhardt, 1968).

## (2) FAMILY

Other components interacting to produce sex-role development are parent-child relationships that predispose each sex toward certain roles. In this case, let's examine aggression in males. An almost universal human experience is that Mother is the primary caretaker of the infant. Consequently, the first and principal person to whom the baby forms an attachment is usually the mother (Schaffer & Emerson, 1964). Since she is the first person after whom he patterns himself, he takes on some of her characteristics and often reacts in the way she would without being aware of doing so.

Inherent in the typical family pattern, in which Mother is the caretaker, is the demand that the boy shift from his initial identification with the mother to identification with the masculine role, while no shift is demanded of the girl. In our culture, certainly, the girl has the company of her same-sex parental model for identification (the mother) much more than the boy has the company of his same-sex model (the father).

The father, in his role as instrumental leader, is often alert to the boy's need to break his initial identification with the mother. He may sense that the boy requires a "push" in order to make the shift from mother-identification to masculinity. We say "Try to be a man" to males and "Be a woman" to females (Johnson, 1963). The father believes that development of assertiveness (if not aggression) is essential if the boy is to take his instrumental role in the world, and he may encourage aggression in the way he acts with him.

He may treat his boy in such a way that, to reciprocate in the relationship, the boy must act tough and show aggression. He may, for example, put gloves on his very young son and play at boxing with him.

The mother, too, treats her sons and daughters differently beginning in their infancy (Lewis, 1972). Lewis observed that mothers talked to, handled, and touched their 6-month-old daughters more than their sons. When observed seven months later, the daughters, in turn, talked to and touched their mothers more than the sons did. If a woman does not openly encourage her son's aggressiveness, she may wink at it. Rhesus monkey mothers also treat their male and female infants differently. They punish the male infant earlier and more often but restrain, protect, and have more physical contact with the female infant (Mitchell, 1968).

The girl does not need to assert herself in the same way the boy does, since she does not shift from her initial identification with the mother. Because her mother is playing the expressive role, she is a model of the peacemaker, not of the aggressor. The father may treat his girl very differently from the way he treats his boy, unlike the mother, who may treat them similarly, considering them both simply children (Goodenough, 1957). Girls receive more affection, attention, and praise; boys are subjected to greater pressure and discipline. This distinction is maintained chiefly by the father (Bronfenbrenner, 1961).

Ironically, the more masculine father may most enhance femininity in his girls as well as masculinity in his boys (Heilbrun, 1965). Upon reflection, however, one recalls that the popular notion of very masculine men is that they want men to be men and women to be women—''feminine'' in the traditional sense—and the irony disappears. A father who plays a strong instrumental role in the family as a whole may be very expressive with his little girl. He may flirt, tease, and pamper his daughter, even when she is only 3 or 4 years old, in such a way that to reciprocate in the relationship she must react with affection, gentleness, docility, and coquetry rather than with aggression. The same father may treat his little boy in

a way that elicits aggression. For the boy to receive his father's approval he must be aggressive, and for the girl to do so she must not be.

## (3) SOCIETY

Society provides numerous blatant role prescriptions of aggressiveness for males, the most obvious being the conscription of young men into the military, where in wartime they are explicitly expected to kill. Although there are women in the American military, they are not allowed combat roles. A more subtle role prescription for aggression is provided by military toys. Boys are given toy soldiers to play with and girls are given dolls—toy soldiers are preparing boys to fight wars and dolls preparing girls to be mothers. The male heroes in novels, on TV, and in films (such as ''007,'' James Bond) are usually extremely violent; in contrast to these, the most vicious heroine seems gentle. Like it or not, a society's popular heroes and heroines tend, to some extent, to become role models (Bandura & Walters, 1963).

Football and other contact sports encourage male aggression. Even teachers discourage boys from being ''sissies,'' if they do not actively encourage aggression. Most cultures reinforce females in nurturance, dependence, obedience, and home-centered activities and discourage aggression that would be tolerated in males (Barry, Bacon, & Child, 1957). Animal studies provide some evidence that the attachment of some female primates to the mother lasts longer than that of males—so long, in fact, that there are social groupings made up of a grandmother, her daughters, and the daughters' female offspring (Maccoby & Masters, 1970). Societies tend to capitalize on traits for which there is a biological predisposition, thus reinforcing some traits in males and others in females.

So all three components, biology, family, and society, seem to be involved in producing males that are typically more aggressive than females. Although the discrepancy between males and females in aggression is more clearcut than in many other traits, the same elements probably coalesce to produce many other sex differences as well. To ask which is the most important component in producing a sex-role characteristic is like asking which is the most important element in producing snow among moisture, low temperature, and so on. They are all essential to produce snow; but whether the snow is very wet with large flakes or very dry with small ones depends on the nature of each element. Likewise, biology, family, and society are all involved in producing sex-role characteristics, but how each characteristic is expressed will depend on the nature of each of the ingredients. For example, parents can interact with a boy in a way that will inhibit his aggression or with a girl in a way that will enhance hers. Some societies (such as the Tchambuli of New Guinea) produce relatively aggressive women and passive men (Mead, 1935), apparently overriding a biological predisposition toward the opposite pattern.

It may be that the mother plays a larger part as a model of femininity for girls than the father does as a sex-role model for boys. Other male playmates, heroes in books, in films, and on TV, and even mother and schoolteachers may play a relatively large part in defining masculinity for boys. Moreover, mothers are typically a salient and available model for girls, who are usually more oriented toward home and its family members than boys anyway. Although the girl models after both parents, her femininity may be more a by-product of her identification with her mother than is the masculinity of a boy from identification with his father. The boy has one problem of shifting from patterning himself after the mother and a second problem in identifying with his father because of the modern father's lack of salience. The boy is seldom, if ever, with his father as he engages in his vocation, although both boy and girl are often with the mother as she carries out her household activities. Consequently, the father as model for the boy is like a map showing the major outline but lacking most details, whereas the mother as model for the girl might be thought of as a detailed map. The boy will not acquire masculinity simply as a by-product of identification with his father.

All of this is not to say that the father is unimportant in the boy's acquisition of sex-role behavior. Studies of father absence show that he is very important. We have seen how the father can relate to the boy in such a way that, to reciprocate, he must behave in a masculine fashion. Thus he is critical in the boy's achievement of sex-role characteristics, not so much by acting as a salient model as by defining standards of masculine behavior and exacting adherence to these standards.

## REFERENCES

Bandura, A., & Walters, R. H. *Social learning and personality development.* New York: Holt, Rinehart & Winston, 1963.

Barry, H., III, Bacon, M. K., & Child, I. L. A cross-cultural survey of some sex differences in socialization. *Journal of Abnormal and Social Psychology,* 1957, *55,* 327–332.

Bronfenbrenner, U. Some familial antecedents of responsibility and leadership in adolescents. In L. Petrullo & B. M. Bass (Eds.), *Leadership and Interpersonal Behavior.* New York: Holt, Rinehart & Winston, 1961.

Goodenough, E. W. Interest in persons as an aspect of sex differences in the early years. *Genetic Psychology Monographs,* 1957, *55,* 287–323.

Heilbrun, A. B., Jr. An empirical test of the modeling theory of sex-role learning. *Child Development,* 1965, *36,* 789–799.

Johnson, M. M. Sex role learning in the nuclear family. *Child Development,* 1963, *34,* 319–333.

Lewis, M. Parents and children: Sex-role development. *School Review,* 1972, *80,* 229–240.

Maccoby, E. E., & Masters, J. C. Attachment and dependency. In P. H. Mussen (Ed.), *Carmichael's manual of child development* (Vol. 2). New York: Wiley, 1970.

Mead, M. *Sex and temperament in three primitive societies.* New York: Wm. Morrow, 1935.

Mitchell, G. D. Attachment difference in male and female infant monkeys. *Child Development,* 1968, *39,* 611–620.

Mitchell, G. D., Arling, G. L., & Moller, G. W. Long-term effects of maternal punishment on the behavior of monkeys. *Psychonomic Science,* 1967, *8,* 209–210.

Money, J., & Ehrhardt, A. A. Prenatal hormonal exposure: Possible effects on behavior in man. In R. P. Michael (Ed.), *Endocrinology and human behaviour.* London: Oxford University Press, 1968.

Schaffer, H. R., & Emerson, P. E. The development of social attachments in infancy. *Monographs of the Society for Research in Child Development,* 1964, *29,* (2, Serial No. 94).

# SUGGESTIONS FOR FURTHER READING

Biller, H. B. Father dominance and sex-role development in kindergarten-age boys. *Developmental Psychology,* 1969, *1*(2), 87–94. Three aspects of sex role were considered: orientation (self-perception of femaleness or maleness), preference (individual preference for either sex role), and adoption (an individual's masculinity or femininity as viewed by others). Of these three aspects of sex role, father dominance influenced orientation most and adoption least. The boy's perception of his father's relative dominance was more related to the boy's masculine development than was the actual degree of his father's dominance in father-mother interaction.

Block, J. H. Conceptions of sex role: Some cross-cultural and longitudinal perspectives. *American Psychologist,* 1973, *28,* 512–526. The effects of socialization are related to sexual identity, and a framework is presented for explaining sex-role definition. Research suggests that culturally determined sociological processes broaden the sex-role definition of males but limit that of females.

Chasen, B. Sex-role stereotyping and prekindergarten teachers. *Elementary School Journal,* 1974, *74*(4), 220–235. After reviewing research relevant to sex roles in young children, Chasen reports a study of 24 prekindergarten teachers' beliefs about the differential roles of boys and girls in their classes.

Entwisle, D. R., & Greenberger, E. Adolescents' views of women's work role. *American Journal of Orthopsychiatry,* 1972, *42,* 648–656. A study was made of ninth-grade children's views of women's work. Differences in such views were analyzed according to the respondents' age, sex, race, social class, and IQ.

Fagot, B. I. Sex-related stereotyping of toddlers' behaviors. *Developmental Psychology,* 1973, *9*(3), 429. Subjects 20 to 25 years of age who had had little or no contact with young children designated each of 38 behaviors of 2-year-olds as appropriate for boys, girls, or both sexes. Only six behaviors were sex-typed by more than five subjects. In general, roughhouse play, play with transportation toys, and aggressive behavior were considered masculine, whereas playing with dolls, dressing up, and looking in the mirror were considered feminine. More males sex-typed behaviors than did females, perhaps because females are permitted more latitude in their own behaviors.

Hartley, R. E. Children's perceptions of sex preference in four culture groups. *Journal of Marriage and the Family,* 1969, *31*(2), 380–387. Boys and girls, ages 5 to 8, from four culture groups supplied endings to stories involving a girl or boy for adoption. In three of the four groups, females were represented as more likely to be chosen. Interesting speculation is offered concerning the significance of the results.

Hirsch, G. T. Non-sexist childrearing: Demythifying normative data. *Family Coordinator,* 1974, *23*(2), 165–170. The author challenges mental-health authorities and behavioral scientists to examine their common acceptance of stereotyped sex roles. She illustrates how so-called scientific evidence is used to support such stereotypes and suggests details for programs of nonsexist childrearing.

Hutt, C. *Males and females.* New York: Penguin Books, 1972. This book provides a synopsis of much of the psychological and biological research relating to differences between the sexes. Although it offers no new information, it does afford fresh interpretations and insights.

Inselberg, R. M., & Burke, L. Social and psychological correlates of masculinity in young boys. *Merrill-Palmer Quarterly,* 1973, *19*(1), 41–47. This study compares the personality characteristics, self-concepts, and reputations of kindergarten boys with various masculinity ratings. Implications of the findings are then discussed.

Joffe, C. Sex-role socialization and the nursery school: As the twig is bent. *Journal of Marriage and the Family,* 1971, *33*(3), 467–475. This study was designed to determine the nursery school's role in teaching sex-role expectations. Both the school's policy concerning sex roles and children's perceptions of them are analyzed.

Levy, B., & Stacey, J. Sexism in the elementary school: A backward and forward look. *Phi Delta Kappan,* 1973, *55*(2), 105–109. Sex-typing is demonstrated to permeate the curriculum, the extracurriculum, teacher behaviors, and the whole school structure in ways especially damaging to children.

Lewis, M. Parents and children: Sex-role development. *School Review,* 1972, *80*(2), 229–240.

Children's sex-role development is discussed in terms of parental attitudes toward children's sex. The consequences of differential parental behaviors and sex differences in adult social patterns are related to early socialization processes.

Oliver, L. Women in aprons: The female stereotype in children's readers. *Elementary School Journal*, 1974, *74*(5), 253–259. An analysis of five children's stories discloses differences in sex role to which boys and girls are commonly exposed.

Saario, T. N., Jacklin, C. N., & Tittle, C. K. Sex role stereotyping in the public schools. *Harvard Educational Review*, 1973, *43*, 386–416. The school's stereotyping of sex roles is investigated in three major areas: elementary-school readers, educational-achievement tests, and curriculum.

Vroegh, K. Masculinity and femininity in the elementary and junior high school years. *Developmental Psychology*, 1971, *4*(2), 254–261. The correlates of masculinity and femininity, as defined by teachers and children in grades 1–3, 4–6, and 4–8, were determined. In addition, an effort was made to define developmental trends in masculinity and femininity.

Ward, W. D. Process of sex-role development. *Developmental Psychology*, 1969, *1*(2), 163–168. Ward decides that sex-role preferences are established for both sexes by the age of 5; sex-role identification occurs earlier for girls than for boys; sex-role preference precedes sex-role adoption for both sexes; and the three measures are independent.

# 7
## Maternal Deprivation

One of the most strongly held beliefs in current psychology is that children need their mothers and that maternal deprivation, of whatever nature, leaves unhealthy effects. However, the situation is not clear-cut. For one thing, there are all sorts of parental deprivations, including those that stem from death, divorce, the mother's employment, hospitalization of the child, or mere neglect. Deprivation may involve lack of psychological parenting, as well as lack of parenting in the more conventional sense. Separation may be brief or lengthy, intermittent or permanent. It may be the child rather than the mother who is away from home, as in an institution, foster home, day nursery, or hospital. The effects of deprivation may stem from mother absence as such or from factors associated with her absence. For example, the child may suffer not only from loss of the mother's love and nurturance, but also from lack of toys, special foods, or other things that she customarily provides. In fact, the child may suffer more from the absence of environmental stimulation than from deficient mothering. That is, institutional care may be harmful not because the mother is absent, but because caretakers are too busy to provide experience of a sufficiently varied or stimulating nature.

A smaller number of studies have been made of paternal deprivation—caused by war, desertion, divorce, or employment away from home—than of maternal deprivation. On the basis of studies done thus far, the specific effects of maternal as opposed to paternal deprivation correspond to the different roles of mother and father; otherwise, the same general principles apply.

Interest in maternal deprivation derives, historically, from the plight of infants in institutions. During the 1930s and 1940s research studies by Goldfarb (1945), Spitz (1945), and others suggested that children deprived of normal relationships with their mothers would suffer dire consequences. Spitz contrasted the adjustment of infants reared in a foundling home with those living in a prison nursery. In the foundling home, babies received good physical care but were kept in curtained cribs and deprived of contacts with caretakers. By contrast, infants in the prison nursery spent some time every day with their mothers, receiving individual love and care. The infants in the foundling home suffered loss of sleep and appetite, which made them susceptible to disease, and occasionally death. Spitz interpreted these results to mean that a child deprived of the all-important mother-child relationship might languish and even die. In 1952 Bowlby reviewed research on the topic to that date and concluded that typical behaviors resulting from maternal deprivation included lying, stealing, inability to relate to others, and a curious lack of emotional response. However, considerable doubt has been cast on these earlier conclusions. Institutions can be organized—by providing a low adult-child ratio, plenty of toys, and other facilities—so as to compensate for such deficiencies as Goldfarb and Spitz described.

Recently questions regarding maternal

deprivation have focused mainly on mothers who work. For example, how adequate are day-care centers, the common repository of working mothers' children? The same principle applies as with institutions for foundlings: the overall effect of such centers depends on the quality and type of program involved. In general, children in well-run day-care centers fare as well as or better than those reared at home. In one study a home-reared group declined in developmental quotient at 30 months, while day-care infants significantly improved in their developmental levels (Caldwell, Wright, Honig, & Tannenbaum, 1970).

In other research, Fowler (1972) describes a day-care program with favorable social and physical dimensions, including staff, buildings, and equipment. As a result of these conditions, the vast majority of the children prospered both interpersonally and cognitively. They were also friendly to strangers, the girls considerably more than the boys. Both sexes gained on mental test scores, the girls more than the boys; in fact, 64% of the girls, but only 31% of the boys, gained 20 IQ points or more. Perhaps when exposed to values and methods that emphasized autonomy, achievement, and intellectual curiosity for both sexes, the girls' parents began to compensate for the lower independence and expectations that they had earlier bestowed on them. Boys, on the other hand, were already developing along the course of their upper intellectual potential; thus there was less room for growth. Advantaged children gained more than disadvantaged children, perhaps because the disadvantaged parents lacked the psychological or socioeconomic resources to maintain the methods prescribed. In fact, half of the disadvantaged children failed to gain, declined markedly, or dropped out because the family could not sustain efforts to help. Nevertheless, the great majority of the total group gained. Hence, concludes Fowler, the issue hinges on the quality of care and education, in either home or institution.

It has traditionally been assumed that the home environment is the optimum place for rearing a baby; however, the evidence gained here suggests that day-care centers can provide equally healthy settings. They may also pro-

vide a bonus in social adaptation and intellectual development. Indeed, group day care can be perceived not as a competing, but as a complementary resource for bringing up children, especially for disadvantaged families and working mothers. Day-care children are still with parents for some hours every day and all the weekend. It may well be that the quality, not quantity, of parent-child interaction is important in evaluating the effects of the absence of either or both parents.

The question then arises: Will children deprived of attending such centers suffer? Again, the answer depends on the quality of care at home. Children of well-off, resourceful parents may have ample social contacts, considerable travel, and plenty of educational toys. On the other hand, children tied closely to their mothers, with little other contact, have little chance to develop broad social relationships. Nor do they have a chance to explore the world outside their home (Yudkin & Holme, 1963). In addition, a mother's feelings of powerlessness are conveyed to her children and affect their coping abilities (Bruner, 1970).

Another factor that relates to this issue is the mothers' own adjustment. Many mothers who would otherwise prefer to work remain at home with young children because they feel they should. In consequence, they often feel bored, isolated, and frustrated. On the other hand, mothers who continue their careers also do most of the domestic work at home. In consequence, women in such families often carry almost unbearable strains which filter through to the children (Yudkin & Holme, 1963/1969).

Overall, the influence of maternal employment depends on the particular family situation and on the social setting. In certain cases, the working-mother phenomenon may reduce another problem, that of excess mothering. The child who is unduly mothered may become overly dependent. Nevertheless, observe Yudkin and Holme (1963/1969), most of the literature stresses "the value of the exclusive mother-child relationship and ignores the possibility, or even the need, for its dilution" (p. 138). Of course, sheer quantity of mothering may not determine excessive mothering in the psychological sense. A mother may be physically present, but remain so aloof as to have little impact.

A related question is this: Can a child have too many mothers? Sometimes a child may be "mothered" by several adults or older siblings. Again, the answer is quality, not structure of care. There is no clear evidence, observes Yarrow (1961), that multiple mothering, without concurrent deprivation or stress, results in personality damage.

By now we should face this question: Just how essential is the biological mother to the mothering process? It is popularly assumed that she is inevitably tied to the infant's life because of her maternal instinct, a notion based on the historical fact that women usually nourish and raise children. In fact, few so-called authorities question the concept that the mother is the one who must do the mothering. However, observes Yarrow (1961), it is scientifically untenable to assume that women are naturally superior as child rearers and socializers, without corresponding studies of the effect of father-infant reaction on the subsequent development of the child. Indeed, fathers may sometimes provide as good or better mothering than mothers. Or even siblings may do the job—or so animal research suggests. In one experiment (Suomi, Collins, & Harlow, 1973) rhesus-monkey infants were reared from birth with their mothers in a common pen and then separated from them permanently at 60, 90, or 120 days of age. Half the young monkeys were housed individually following separation, while the other half were housed in pairs. The age of separation made no significant difference, but the monkeys housed alone suffered considerably more disturbance. Those that were housed together proved no different in social development from the monkeys reared with their mothers. Furthermore, even less conventional mother surrogates may be found. A grandmother, or sibling, or babysitter, or even a father might provide "mothering" equally as well as the biological mother. Or perhaps during the first weeks of life machines might supply the very young infant's basic needs.

Research concerning maternal deprivation is still inadequate partly because of faulty design and interpretation. Much of the confusion arises from ambiguous terminology, improper interpretation, and overgeneralization. There is little agreement as to just what behaviors mothering includes, or what mother love means. Besides, certain matters have been largely ignored—for example, the residual effects of maternal deprivation on specific children. If the interval between deprivation and the measurement of its effects is long, the effects of deprivation can hardly be untangled from innumerable intervening factors. In a study by Rheingold and Bayley (1959), a group of infants who received constant mothering for eight weeks were compared with another group who received routine institutional care. At the conclusion of the experiment, the experimental subjects showed some superiority; but a year later they were superior only in amount of vocalization in social tests. Another important question is this: Are there critical periods in which deprivation may have much greater impact than it would in others? In one study, kittens separated from their mothers at the age of 2 weeks were more fearful and aggressive, and more disturbed by intense stimulation, than a second group separated at weaning age or a third group separated at the age of 12 weeks (Seitz, 1959).

In our first selection, Rochelle Wortis reviews the most significant studies of the infant's attachment to, and separation from, the mother and questions the common assumption that the biological mother must be the one primarily responsible for the child. She believes that certain fundamental changes in child-rearing practices might prove beneficial for both mother and child. In the second selection, Lois Hoffman reviews research concerning maternal employment, especially in terms of deprivation theory.

# REFERENCES

Almquist, E. M., & Angrist, S. S. Role model influences on college women's career aspirations. *Merrill-Palmer Quarterly*, 1971, *17*(3), 263–279.

Bowlby, J. *Maternal care and mental health.* Geneva: World Health Organization, 1952 (Monograph Series No. 2).

Bruner, J. *Poverty and childhood.* Paper presented at Merrill-Palmer Institute, Detroit, 1970.

Caldwell, B. M., Wright, C. M., Honig, A. S., & Tannenbaum, J. Infant day care and attachment. *American Journal of Orthopsychiatry,* 1970, *40,* 397–412.

Fowler, W. A. A developmental learning approach to infant care in a group setting. *Merrill-Palmer Quarterly,* 1972, *18*(2), 145–175.

Goldfarb, W. Psychological privation in infancy and subsequent adjustment. *American Journal of Orthopsychiatry,* 1945, *15,* 247–255.

Kappel, B. E., & Lambert, R. D. Self worth among the children of working mothers. Unpublished manuscript, University of Waterloo, 1972.

Lambert, T. A. Generations and change. *Youth and Society,* 1972, *4*(1), 21–45.

Propper, A. M. The relationship of maternal employment to adolescent roles, activities, and parental relationships. *Journal of Marriage and the Family,* 1972, *34,* 417–421.

Rheingold, H., & Bayley, N. The later effects of an experimental modification of mothering. *Child Development,* 1959, *30,* 363–372.

Seitz, P. F. D. Infantile experience and adult behavior in animal subjects: II. Age of separation from the mother and adult behavior in the cat. *Psychosomatic Medicine,* 1959, *21,* 353–378.

Spitz, R. A. Hospitalism: An inquiry into the genesis of psychiatric conditions in early childhood. In R. S. Eissler, A. Freud, H. Hartmann, & M. Kris (Eds.), *The psychoanalytic study of the child* (Vol. 1), New York: International Universities Press, 1945.

Suomi, S., & Harlow, H. F. Social rehabilitation of isolate-reared monkeys. *Developmental Psychology,* 1972, *6,* 487–496.

Suomi, S., Collins, M. L. & Harlow, H. F. Effects of permanent separation from mother on infant monkeys. *Developmental Psychology,* 1973, *9*(3), 376–384.

Yarrow, L. Maternal deprivation: Toward an empirical and conceptual re-evaluation. *Psychological Bulletin,* 1961, *58,* 459–490.

Yudkin, S., & Holme, A. *Working mothers and their children.* London: Sphere Books, 1969. (Originally published, 1963.)

# The Acceptance of the Concept of the Maternal Role by Behavioral Scientists: Its Effects on Women

## Rochelle Paul Wortis

*"The maternal 'instinct' is a comfortable male myth; a woman can only give freely if she is in a position where she does not feel deprived herself."* [12]

The purpose of this review is to reexamine critically the importance of the concept of "mothering" and to suggest that much of the evidence employed in psychological studies of the importance of the mother for the development of infants and children is based on assumptions that are scientifically inadequate. Furthermore, modern psychology, with its emphasis on individual advancement, individual achievement, and individual development, has encouraged the isolation of the adult woman, particularly the mother, and the domestication and subordination of females in society.

I am here challenging a concept that has for generations been viewed as a biological and social necessity. It is important, however, to discuss some of the contradictions inherent in our system of child-rearing that have overwhelming negative, oppressive effects on half the population (women) and on all infants who develop in the environment of the nuclear family, with its prevailing emphasis on the mother-infant socialization process.

From "The Acceptance of the Concept of the Maternal Role by Behavioral Scientists: Its Effects on Women," by R. P. Wortis, *American Journal of Orthopsychiatry,* 1971, *41*(5), 733–746. Copyright © 1971 by the American Orthopsychiatric Association, Inc. Reprinted by permission.

There are four basic questions to bear in mind when reading the literature on mother-infant interaction:

1) Is it a biological fact that, in the human species, the mother is the most capable person to socialize the infant?

2) Is it a biological fact that the human newborn seeks out the mother (rather than the father) or a female (rather than a male) as the figure to which it naturally relates best, needs most, and attaches itself to socially?

3) Socially, what criteria should we employ to define whether it is beneficial for the infant to form a strong bond of attachment to one woman?

4) Is it beneficial for the mother to assume the principal responsibility for the care and socialization of the young child?

We must begin with the understanding that we all have a strong prejudice about the need for "mothering" because we were all mothered. In a society such as ours, in which mothering is the principal mode of rearing children, any variant pattern that occurs (such as "multiple mothering," infants being raised by their fathers, or group rearing of infants) is considered abnormal. Participants in such variant patterns are constantly reminded of the "fact" that what they are doing is an exceptional alternative, a poor substitute for the "normal" pattern. This implies that they could never equal or improve upon the norm.

Margaret Mead has long been questioning the provincialism of studies of mother-infant interaction by Western psychologists and psychiatrists. In particular, Mead criticized the emphasis on the exclusive mother-infant bond. She emphasized that the conscious care of the infant is a cultural, not a biological invention. Therefore, whether or not the mother is the principal figure in the developing child's environment is a socio-cultural question and not a biological one. According to Mead, diversified kinds of attachment relationships have been successful in other cultures.[24] In our society, on the other hand, the vast majority of women are conditioned to expect that the child-rearing function will be their major, individual responsibility.

# ATTACHMENT

The "Attachment Function," as defined and elaborated by John Bowlby,[7] is a dual process through which the infant develops a strong psychobiological need to maintain proximity with the mother while the mother has a strong psychobiological need to maintain proximity with the infant. Attachment behavior usually begins to appear at around four to six months and, during the first year of life, a strong affectional bond develops.[1, 7] An "autonomous propensity" by the mother and infant to develop attachment toward each other is assumed by Bowlby's theory. This aspect of the theory will be discussed later in this paper.

The primacy of the mother-infant attachment bond is contradicted by Schaffer and Emerson's[35] study of attachment. They described three different stages in the development of attachment behavior: an "asocial" stage, in which the infant actively seeks optimal stimulation from *all* aspects of the environment; a "presocial" stage, in which the infant indiscriminately seeks proximity to objects that give it satisfaction; and, finally, a "social" stage, in which attachments to specific individuals occurs. Schaffer and Emerson concluded that:

> To focus one's enquiry on the child's relationship with the mother alone would therefore give a misleading impression of the attachment function. . . . In certain societies multiple object relationships are the norm from the first year on: the relevant stimuli which evoke attachment behaviour are offered by a number of individuals and not exclusively one person, and a much more diversified system of attachments is thus fostered in the infant. (pp. 70–71)

That there is no evidence for the assumption that attachments must be confined to only one object, the mother, nor that all other attachments are subsidiary to the mother-infant bond, was one of the findings of their study. They concluded that:

> Whom an infant chooses as his attachment object and how many objects he selects depends,

we believe, primarily on the nature of the social setting in which he is reared and not on some intrinsic characteristic of the attachment function itself." (p. 71)

Finally, Schaffer and Emerson suggested that while the mother tends to be present in the child's environment for most of the time, this does not guarantee that she will provide the quantity and quality of stimulation necessary for optimal development of the infant. A recent experimental-observational study by Kotelchuck,[20] one of the few studies on father-infant interaction, demonstrated that one-to-two year old infants are equally attached to their fathers and mothers. Furthermore, the strength of attachment to fathers correlated with the degree to which the fathers cared for their children during their development.

## SEPARATION

The principal argument used to encourage women to devote their constant attention to newborns is based on the suggested deleterious effects of mother-child separation (the "Bowlby-"[5] or "Spitz-hypothesis"[38, 39]). Most of the studies of mother-child separation have been based, however, not on normal separation of infants from their parents, but on institutionalized children. Because of the physical and social sterility of many hospitals and orphanages, these children often suffered from inadequate environmental and human stimulation.[10, 44] The mother-child separation studies have not provided an adequate history of "the reasons which led to the children studied being uprooted from their homes or about the conditions in which they lived before this happened," according to Barbara Wootten.[43]

> One can hardly assume that the boys and girls found in a Children's Home constitute a fair sample of the child population generally: something unusual either in themselves or their environment must have happened to account for their being deprived of ordinary family life.[43] (p. 146)

Yarrow's[44] review of studies published between 1937 and 1955 concluded that most of the studies of institutionalized infants selected subjects who were already under treatment for emotional or personality disturbances. Furthermore, they were lacking in data on the early conditions of maternal care. In addition, Yarrow wrote,

> The dramatic character of these changes [i.e., reactions of infants to separation from the mother] has overshadowed the significant fact that a substantial portion of the children in each study did not show severe reactions to separation. (p. 474)

Casler[10] concluded that,

> none of the clinical or institutional studies ostensibly supporting the "Spitz-Ribble hypothesis" really does so, simply because none is able to demonstrate that probable causes of the adverse effects of institutionalization, other than maternal deprivation, are inoperative. (p. 12)

Casler further described several studies in which institutionalized babies showed no ill effects. Pinneau, who published several articles[30, 31, 32] dissecting methodological inadequacies of the Spitz and Ribble studies, concluded that

> It may well be that the burden of blame for the uncritical acceptance of his work does not rest with Spitz, who has published his results as he sees them, but rather with those who have acclaimed his work, and whose research training should enable them to make a critical evaluation of such research reports.[32] (p. 462)

Positive alternatives to traumatic separation of infant and mother have not been sufficiently discussed in the psychological literature. In fact, there seems to have occurred a dangerously unscientific extrapolation of assumptions from studies of institutionalized infants to the much more common situation in which infants leave their homes for part of the day, are cared for by other responsible individuals, and are returned again to their homes. As a result, women are taught to believe that infants require their undivided attention during the first two or three years of life, at least. The way our society is structured, this attitude functions to confine the woman physically (to her home) and socially (to her family unit). Neil O'Connor[28] observed:

> There is some danger that by analysing one source of emotional disturbance, such as mother-child separation, the interaction of the society and the family may be neglected, and the family considered as if it were an isolated unit, which alone determines the behaviour of individuals in all their social relations. (p. 188)

On this matter, Margaret Mead[23] wrote:

> At present, the specific biological situation of the continuing relationship of the child to its biological mother and its need for care by human beings are being hopelessly confused in the growing insistence that child and biological mother, or mother surrogate, must never be separated, that all separation, even for a few days is inevitably damaging, and that if long enough it does irreversible damage. This . . . is a new and subtle form of antifeminism in which men—under the guise of exalting the importance of maternity—are tying women more tightly to their children than has been thought necessary since the invention of bottle feeding and baby carriages. Actually, anthropological evidence gives no support at present to the value of such an accentuation of the tie between mother and child. . . . On the contrary, crosscultural studies suggest that adjustment is most facilitated if the child is cared for by many warm friendly people. (p. 477)*

Finally, returning to the experience of natural separation between parents and children, none of the studies of children of working mothers has demonstrated systematic differences between children who are home all the time and children whose mothers work.[45, 46] However, because the Bowlby-Spitz hypothesis has had such a profound impact on child-rearing practice, legislators, employers and educators have refused to provide sufficient adequate free childcare for working women.[46] Consequently, working women are usually forced to find their own, individual solutions to the child-care problem. Even in "dual-career" families (families in which the mother and father both have professional careers), the men and women tend to accept as inevitable that women should take on the major responsibility for the organization of child-care and the household in addition to their career responsibilities.[33] The consequence is that the women in such families carry the strain of both career and family problems. Apparently this is a major problem in Eastern European socialist countries as well as in Western society.[33, 46]

The excellent reviews mentioned above, on the subject of separation and institutionalization, share in criticizing overgeneralizations that have been drawn from separation studies. Several reviewers[10, 44] attempted to analyze the objective variables that the mothering function provides for the healthy growth and emotional security of the developing infant. However, none has sufficiently questioned the concept that the mother must be the one who does the mothering. Yudkin and Holme[46] wrote:

> Most of the literature, however, tends to stress the value of the exclusive mother-child relationship and to ignore the possibility or even the need, for its dilution. This is to attempt to justify a particular, local and almost certainly, temporary, economic and cultural pattern as an eternal biological law. This can only do a disservice to both the mothers and the children. (p. 138)*

## NATURALISM AND INSTINCT THEORY

The assumption that the biological mother must be the major responsible adult in the infant's life is intimately related to the theory that women have an instinct to mother. The assumption is based on observations, from the earliest recorded history, that confirm that

---

*From "Some Theoretical Considerations on the Problem of Mother-Child Separation," by M. Mead, *American Journal of Orthopsychiatry,* 1944, *24,* 471–483. Copyright © 1944 by the American Orthopsychiatric Association, Inc. Reprinted by permission.

*From *Working Mothers and their Children,* by S. Yudkin and A. Holme. Copyright © 1963 by Michael Joseph Ltd. This and all other quotes from these authors reprinted by permission.

women are usually the ones who nurture and raise children, specifically their own children.* It remains an assumption, or hypothesis, however, that what we observe and describe naturalistically is what is biologically correct or socially optimal. John Stuart Mill wrote:

the unnatural generally means only uncustomary, and . . . everything which is usual appears natural. The subjection of women to men being a universal custom, any departure from it quite naturally appears unnatural. (quoted in Millett,[25] p. 94)

In the words of one reviewer:

While most of us will continue to believe in the importance of mothering during infancy, we must recognize that this belief has more the characteristics of a faith and less the basis of demonstrated fact. (Ericksen, quoted in Casler,[10] p. 9)

Ethology, the study of animals in their natural environments, has had a strong influence on recent practice in human developmental psychology. Bowlby[6] has been one of the principal protagonists in the trend to return to naturalistic observations of human and animal behavior:

Until recent years, most of the knowledge available about mother-infant interaction in humans was either anecdotal or else a result of reconstructions based on data derived from older subjects. In the past decade, however, enquiries have been begun which have as their aim the systematic, descriptive and causal study of what actually occurs during a baby's interaction with the humans who care for him. (p. xiii)

However, ethologists, carrying out descriptive studies of behavior, have not approached their observational tasks bias-free. The discipline of ethology has long been linked with instinct theory, which attributes the organization of

complex patterns of species-typical behavior to hypothetical, pre-formed biological models.[22, 42] On the human level, instinct theory emphasizes the biological pre-destination of psychological characteristics:

The Freudian view of man's nature starts from the assumption that he is really a nonsocial or even an antisocial creature. His primary needs are not social but individual and biological. This means that society is not essential to man but is something outside his nature, an external force to whose distorting pressures he is victim.[4] (p. 96)

Critics of instinct theory have stressed its neglect of the social and developmental history of the organisms being observed and its failure to view the organism as one that both affects and is affected by the biosocial environment in which it develops.[21, 36] Bowlby's theory of attachment behavior[1, 7] is an interactionist one. However, it assumes that there are certain features of the environment that the infant is biologically structured to be particularly sensitive to. The theory assumes that the environment of the newborn is optimal, and that the infant is biologically predisposed to adapt to it. As summarized by Ainsworth,[1]

ethologists hold that those aspects of the genetic code which regulate the development of attachment of infant to mother are adapted to an environment in which it is a well-nigh universal experience that it is the mother (rather than some biologically inappropriate object) who will be present under conditions which facilitate the infant's becoming attached to her. (pp. 995–996)

Such a theory is conservative because it neglects the enormous range of sociocultural environments into which newborn infants are thrust and idealizes the mother-infant couple, which, as Orlansky[29] pointed out long ago, is "one conforming to an ideal-typical norm held by Western psychiatrists." (p. 15)

It is frequently argued that the human female, like other mammals, is biologically best equipped to respond to the needs of a newborn because of her long period of biological, hormonal and psychological priming during pregnancy. It has been suggested, for instance,

*An entertaining and informative article by Una Stannard[40] attempts to document that "Women have the babies, but men have the maternal instinct." In her historical paper, Stannard reminds us that the major books and manuals telling women how to be good mothers have been written by men.

that in the period immediately after birth, mothers may be particularly sensitive to the needs of their babies.[7] This may indeed be true. However, it is also true that a woman who has just had her first child, and who has not previously handled, fed, or cared for an infant, has great difficulty in the first days of the baby's life in establishing feeding, whether it be by breast or bottle. New mothers often have to be told how to hold the baby, burp it, bathe it, and dress it. Of course, most women learn how to care for their infants quite efficiently within a short period of time, through practice and determination.

Recent studies have demonstrated that infants play an active role, even in the first weeks of life, in getting their needs satisfied. There is now extensive literature on the way in which the infant actively initiates social interaction and is capable of modifying the behavior of the adult who cares for it.[3, 41] This means that the infant helps the adult to develop appropriate responses that will bring about the satisfaction of its needs. This, in turn, means that, given a socially acceptable alternative, the mother need not be the principal caretaker of her own infant, although many women may still want to enjoy this responsibility.

Most evidence today indicates that the factors that are important for healthy infant and child development are: consistent care; sensitivity of the caretaking adult(s) in responding to the infant's needs; a stable environment, the characteristics of which the growing infant can learn to identify; continuity of experience within the infant's environment; and physical and intellectual stimulation, love, and affection. "There is no clear evidence," Yarrow[44] wrote, "that multiple mothering, without associated deprivation or stress, results in personality damage." And Mead[24] wrote,

The problem remains of how to separate the necessary protection of a child who has been isolated in an exclusive pair relationship with the mother—of a type which cannot be said to be natural at a human level, because it actually does not permit participation by the father, care of the dependent older siblings, and ties with the three-generation family, all of which are human experiences—from advocacy of the artificial perpetuation or intensification or creation of such conditions of exclusive mother-child dependence. (p. 58)

Unlike other reviewers,[17, 27, 46] who advocate reforms for women that would alleviate the strains of dual or triple careers, while basically accepting the assumption that only women can perform the mothering function, I would like to emphasize that it is scientifically unacceptable to advocate the natural superiority of women as child-rearers and socializers of children when there have been so few studies of the effects of male-infant or father-infant interaction on the subsequent development of the child.

The acceptance of the concept of mothering by social scientists reflects their own satisfaction with the status quo. The inability of social scientists to explore or to advocate alternatives to current child-rearing practices is due to their biased conception of what should be studied and to their unwillingness to advocate social change. As Myrdal and Klein[27] recognized,

the sentimental cult of domestic virtues is the cheapest method at society's disposal of keeping women quiet without seriously considering their grievances or improving their position. It has been successfully used to this day, and has helped to perpetuate some dilemmas of home-making women by telling them, on the one hand that they are devoted to the most sacred duty, while on the other hand keeping them on a level of unpaid drudgery. (p. 145)

The time has come to evaluate more critically the ways in which the home and the single mothering figure *fail* to provide the kind of environment that is optimally stimulating or satisfying to the growing infant.

## MOTHERS' FEELINGS AND THE NEEDS OF WOMEN

A young housewife[12] writes:

I feel it should be more widely recognized that it is in the very nature of a mother's position, in our society, to avenge her own frustrations on a small, helpless child; whether this takes the form of tyranny, or of a smothering affection that asks the child to be a substitute for all she has missed. (p. 153)

It is important to recognize that many young mothers have ambivalent feelings about the responsibility of motherhood. Hannah Gavron's[13] survey of women in London showed that:

the majority of wives, both working-class and middle-class, appear from the discussion of their own views on home and work to be essentially on the horns of a dilemma. They want to work, feel curiously functionless when not working, but at the same time they sense their great responsibilities towards the children. In both groups those who were at home gave the children as their main reason for being there. (p. 122)

My own experience, studying the development of feeding behavior in infants, corroborates this. I studied mature, healthy, full-term babies, all the products of normal pregnancies and deliveries. The mothers were not tense or unhappy women with unusual medical or psychological histories. Yet, many of the women expressed the same conflicts: boredom, sense of isolation being home alone with the baby, desire to be able to get back to work, and doubts about finding adequate child-care facilities should they have the opportunity of getting employment. Most of the women, whether they wanted to work or not, had the feeling that it would be wrong to go out to work because it might somehow endanger the infant's well-being. The study of Yarrow and her colleagues[45] demonstrated that "Mothers who prefer to work but out of a sense of 'duty' do not work report the most problems in child rearing." (p. 122)

The negative effects of too intensive a relationship developing between mother and child, leading to a clinical pattern of "overprotection," are discussed by Myrdal and Klein.[27] Herzog[17] gives passing mention to the fact that "it is no secret that some mothers are not loving, and some who are do not want to devote themselves exclusively to infant or child care."

(p. 18). A recent book[11] on child-rearing restates the problem:

The role in which most contemporary theorists of child development cast the mother makes it hard for her and hard for her children. What's more, the evidence indicates that she has been *mis*cast. No matter how seriously she takes the demand on her for omnipotence, and no matter how omnipotent the performance she turns out, there is no guarantee that the act will come off. All too often the child fails to reflect the best parents' most studious try for perfection. (p. 14)*

We must now turn our attention to the home. We are taught that the best environment for the growth and development of a healthy child is provided within the individual home. The home environment, however, is socially sterile because mobility, outside stimulation, exchange of ideas and socially productive relationships are severely limited there:

The isolated woman at home may well be kept "in touch" with events, but she feels that the events are not in touch with her, that they happen without her participation. The wealth of information which is brought to her without any effort on her part does not lose its vicariousness. It increases rather than allays her sense of isolation and of being left out.[27] (p. 148)

Yudkin and Holme[46] discuss the effects of the physical and social isolation of small families in which:

a large number of children are tied almost exclusively to their mothers for the first five years of life, having little opportunity to meet any other people or to develop the beginnings of social relationships, let alone to explore the world outside their own home, until the sudden and dramatic beginning of their school life. Such isolation is obviously likely to increase the closeness and intensity of the relationship between the mother and her young children and

---

*From *Your Child Is a Person*, by S. Chess, A. Thomas, and H. Birch. Copyright © 1965 by The Viking Press, Inc. Reprinted by permission.

may well have an effect on the type of adult personality that results, but whether the effect is good or bad is another matter. (pp. 137–138)

An English housewife [12] wrote:

Housework is housework, whoever does it. It is a waste socially, psychologically, and even economically, to put me in a position where my only means of expressing loyalty to [the baby] is by shopping, dish-washing and sweeping floors. I have trained for teaching literature to university students; it would be far more satisfying to guide a nursery class with Carl in it than it is to feel too harassed by irrelevant jobs to pay his development much attention. (p. 148)

The home, therefore, is physically restrictive and, for many women, is felt to be socially restrictive as well. In the home, one's economic and personal tensions and problems are most pronounced. These factors have a profound effect on the mother and child confined to the home, and are a principal influence on the physical, intellectual, and social development of children coming from different social class backgrounds. Bruner's[8] recent review of studies dealing with the cognitive development of children from different social class backgrounds, is rich in examples of the complex way in which feelings of powerlessness by the mother are conveyed to the children and affect the children's ability to cope with their environment.

Current studies of mother-child interaction in the United States, comparing children of working-class mothers with children of middle-class mothers, have ostensibly demonstrated the "cognitive superiority" of the latter. The conclusions of such research are that working-class mothers have to be taught to behave like middle-class mothers. The form of implementation recently adopted to help these women and their children is to teach working-class women how to provide optimal maternal stimulation to the child within the home environment. However, no programs are implemented to provide working-class women with the advantages of class privilege that middle-class women enjoy, since it is beyond the power of the behavioral scientist to effect such changes in the social and economic status of the people concerned (*How Harvard Rules Women,*[18] pp. 66–74). Hunt's[19] recommendation that parent-child centers become the focus of intervention programs by professionals to teach "competence" to poverty mothers and their children was aptly criticized by Gordon,[14] who wrote:

Hunt is proposing a strategy that, like most formal education, essentially seeks to upgrade black and poor people by identifying all those things that are "wrong" with them, and changing those things. Such a strategy, with its implied criticism and its prescription for the adoption of goals and values of the oppressors, should hardly be imposed upon a group by outsiders, no matter how well intentioned. More effective programs of assistance are likely to come from among the people themselves. (p. 41)

One might add that the people, in this case working-class mothers, might feel that other individuals should be involved in the process of child-rearing and that the responsibility for the socialization of children should not rest on the mothers alone.

In the past and present, day-care programs for children have been officially encouraged during periods of economic strain, when women's labor was necessary for production. Neither economics nor women's needs to get out of the home, however, are sufficient justification for child-care centers. Good day-care programs are a necessity for infants and children because they encourage the development of cooperative social interaction during a period of life in which, in modern Western society, children receive insufficient experience with other trusting, loving, dependable children and adults. In the words of two day-care workers:[16]

It is well documented that attitudes toward work, race, sex (including male/female roles), initiative, and cooperation are formed during the first five years of life. It follows that we need to be seriously concerned with what happens inside the day care center.

What goes on between the child and the environment (whether it's a home or a day care center) affects the kind of capacities that the child will have as an adult. The ability to feel deeply and be sensitive toward other people, the ability to trust oneself and use one's initiative, the ability to solve problems in a creative and collective way—these all can be given their foundation or stifled in the first five years.

By the age of 4 children are taking in the idea that a woman's place is in the home. Three and four year old children are already learning that it's better to be white. They are learning to follow directions and rules without asking why. They are learning how to deny their own feelings and needs in order to win approval from adults.

These are examples of learning that most commonly result from early childhood experiences. These are elements of the invisible curriculum that usually forms the child's environment in our society. (pp. 27–28)*

Recognizing the social needs of mothers and infants, some investigators have begun to encourage entry into day nurseries at much earlier ages than is customary. While these efforts were, at first, strongly criticized by workers in the field, the findings were very encouraging: assessments made at thirty months showed that children from lower-class families who were enrolled in a day-care center from about one year of age did not differ from home-reared children in the strength of attachment to their mothers. Likewise, mothers of day-care infants did not show any differences from home-mothers in intensity of attachment to their infants. The study[9] showed that, while the home-reared group declined in developmental quotient at thirty months, the day-care infants increased in developmental level.

I am convinced that new studies will continue to demonstrate that stable, loving, stimulating group environments can produce healthy, affectionate, bright youngsters, and that, quite early in life, infants can spend a good part of their day away from their homes and parents without adverse consequences. The problem ahead of us is to analyze the rela-

tionship between the nuclear family and the functioning of society, and to study and create the conditions under which the home ceases to confine the woman and the child to social and productive isolation. The fact is that, in modern Western society, no other institutions offer the adult the comfort, the emotional security, the loyalty, and the emotional dependability that the modern family provides. Even saying this, it is necessary to recognize the converse, that for many children and women, the modern family is a prison, breeding repression, unequal relationships and authoritarian conformity.* I am cautious, however, not to suggest that we overthrow the family and substitute other institutions as alternative child-rearers. To do this would be impossible at this stage because of the already mentioned positive value of the family, and because we have not consciously experimented sufficiently with alternatives that could successfully replace it.

## DISCUSSION

The creation of alternative life styles, work patterns, or economic change, cannot be successfully imposed on people or prescribed for them without their cooperation. The creation of any alternative processes, when it involves major changes from historical precedent, is a political problem as well as an educational or psycho-social one. For people to attempt alternatives within this society, they must feel the necessity for change and feel that they are not alone in their efforts to create it. People do not attempt to create even small changes in their lives if they lack the confidence or the ability or the power to make them work. In short, programs that would produce the conscious articulation of goals and criteria for positive social change cannot be undertaken without the initiative of the people who are going to be involved.

Acting on the basis of the common sense of oppression experienced by women in society, the women's liberation movement has begun to analyze the relationship between some transitional and long-range goals which, if won,

*From "On Day Care," by L. Gross and P. Macewan, *Women: A Journal of Liberation*, 1970, *1*(2), 27–28. Copyright 1970 by Women: A Journal of Liberation, 3028 Greenmount Ave., Baltimore, Md., 21218. Reprinted by permission.

*The evolution of the family and its relationship to societal structure has been the basis for a good deal of study and renewed analysis.[15, 26, 34]

could significantly change women's status in society. The women's liberation movement will not be satisfied, for example, with equality with men if that equality is defined simply in terms of employment opportunity or work status; in present society, that would mean that they give up one oppressive situation (subjugation in the home) to step into another oppressive situation (exploitation at work). Nonetheless, in order for women to participate in efforts to create more meaningful and rewarding work experiences, they must achieve the transitional goal of shared work with men in the home around the housekeeping and child-rearing functions. This means that ways have to be found in which men can begin to take a more active part in home life and in emotional and social interaction with infants. The encouragement of male participation in early childhood socialization requires, for its success, the transformation of existing social and educational institutions because men today are not prepared to assume major shares of responsibility either in home-making or in child-rearing. As Sweden has already done, sex-role stereotyping in books (children's and adults') and in advertising has to be ended in order to discourage traditional practices of sex-differentiated behavior. Paid paternity leaves for men and greater opportunities for fathers to participate in the care of newborns is recognized as essential. Men have to be involved more in early education, from day-care to primary schools. Unless nurseries and schools are staffed by men as well as women, the responsibility for the socialization of children will continue to fall upon women and they will continue to feel that other social responsibilities are not within their domain. This was apparently the experience of women in the kibbutzim in Israel. At the beginning, women were encouraged to share in the heavy work with men, but men were not similarly encouraged to share in the care of children. As a result, women became overburdened with the strain of both kinds of responsibilities and gradually dropped out of the productive branches. A sexual division of labor persists to this day in the kibbutzim. Only women work as nurses and infants' teachers.[37]

For men and women to share in the care of infants while maintaining jobs, then in their capacity as workers both men and women have to be able to work shorter hours without losing pay. The extra time would be used for child care either at home or in cooperatively organized day care centers at work or in the community. Group day care is considered by the women's liberation movement to be a more progressive alternative to family day care because it removes children and adults from the isolating and non-productive environment of the home, substituting a social environment in which infants and adults may interact with each other in large, unrestrictive spaces with many objects and toys to share. The socialization process, therefore, becomes less individualistic for the children and more cooperative for the adults. It follows that parental control of the organization and staffing of day-care centers is essential. The new, radical generation of parents do not want dumping grounds for their children, but rather centers of exciting educational activity and play in which children and adults share collectively in the process of growing up. Dissatisfied with the racist, sexist, and middle-class-biased education that children receive in public schools, the radical day-care movement wants day care that is organized and controlled by the people in their communities who wish to create a more democratic, equalitarian society for their children.[16]

A final word needs to be said about alternatives to the nuclear family, in particular the new movement toward communalism. Seen in the most positive of perspectives, a small percentage of the American population is attempting to establish stable communal living arrangements as a way of socializing productive relationships in the living place. Cooking, shopping, cleaning, child care, and social relationships are being shared by all who live together.

The renaissance of communalism can be seen to develop out of the women's liberation philosophy. The women's liberation movement helped to convince women that their oppression did not develop from their internal inadequacies, but was the natural outgrowth of problems inherent in the structure of our society. By forming social and political bonds as a group, rather than as individual women, it has been possible for women to experience new and better forms of social relationships and to begin successfully to create some of the changes necessary before all women can, in fact, be liberated. Breaking down alienating forms of social relationships can be seen to be a first step in the process of transforming society. A recent paper on "The Liberation of Children"[2] concludes:

"If we want to change society we can begin by changing the kind of people we are and the kind of children we raise. People who are more loving, more concerned about each other, more secure and less competitive will have attitudes that are contrary to the ones on which our society is based, and while the creation of new attitudes is not in itself a revolution, perhaps it helps create the preconditions."

## REFERENCES

1. Ainsworth, M. 1969. Object relations, dependency, and attachment: a theoretical review of the infant-mother relationship. Child Developm. 40:969–1025.
2. Babcox, D. 1970. The liberation of children. Up From Under 1(1):43–46 (Up From Under, 339 Lafayette St., New York, N.Y. 10012).
3. Bell, R. 1971. Stimulus control of parent or caretaker behavior by offspring. Developmental Psychol. 4:63–72. (Invited address, 1968. Division of Developmental Psychology, 76th Annual Convention, American Psychological Association).
4. Birch, H. 1953. Psychology and culture. In Basic Problems in Psychiatry, J. Wortis, ed. Grune & Stratton, New York.
5. Bowlby, J. 1951. Maternal Care and Mental Health. World Health Organization Monogr., Geneva.
6. Bowlby, J. 1961. Foreword. In Determinants of Infant Behaviour. B. Foss, ed. Methuen & Co., London.
7. Bowlby, J. 1969. Attachment and Loss. Vol. I. Attachment. The Hogarth Press and the Institute of Psychoanalysis, London.
8. Bruner, J. 1970. Poverty and Childhood. Paper presented at Merrill-Palmer Institute, Detroit.
9. Caldwell, B., et al. 1970. Infant day care and attachment. Amer. J. Orthopsychiat. 30:397–412.
10. Casler, L. 1961. Maternal deprivation: a critical review of the literature. Monographs Soc. Res. Child Developm. 26(2) ser. #80:1–64.
11. Chess, S., Thomas, A., & Birch, H. 1965. Your Child Is A Person. Viking Press, New York.
12. Gail, S. 1968. The housewife. In Work. R. Fraser, ed. Penguin Books, London.
13. Gavron, H. 1968. The Captive Wife. Penguin Books, London. (first published by Routledge & Kegan Paul, London, 1966).
14. Gordon, E. 1971. Parent and child centers: their basis in the behavioral and educational sciences. An invited critique. Amer. J. Orthopsychiat. 41:39–42.
15. Gordon, L. 1970. Families. New England Free Press, 791 Tremont St., Boston.
16. Gross, L., & Macewan, P. 1970. On day care. Women: A Journal of Liberation 1(2):26–29. (Women: A Journal of Liberation, 3011 Guildford Ave., Baltimore, Md. 21218).
17. Herzog, E. 1960. Children of Working Mothers. U. S. Dept. of Health, Education and Welfare, Children's Bureau, Washington, D. C.
18. How Harvard Rules Women. 1970. The arrogance of social science research: manipulating the lives of black women and their infants. New England Free Press, Boston.
19. Hunt, J. McV. 1971. Parent and child centers: Their basis in the behavioral and educational sciences. Amer. J. Orthopsychiat. 41:13–38.
20. Kotelchuck, M. 1971. The nature of the child's tie to the father. Unpublished Ph.D. thesis, Harvard University.
21. Lehrman, D. 1953. A critique of Konrad Lorenz's theory of instinctive behavior. Q. Rev. Biol. 28:337–363.
22. Lorenz, K. 1935. Companionship in bird life. In Instinctive Behavior, C. Schiller, ed., 1957, International Universities Press, New York.
23. Mead, M. 1954. Some theoretical considerations on the problem of mother-child separation. Amer. J. Orthopsychiat. 24:471–483.
24. Mead, M. 1962. A cultural anthropologist's approach to maternal deprivation. In Deprivation of Maternal Care. A Reassessment of its Effects. Public Health Papers, #14, World Health Org., Geneva.
25. Millett, K. 1970. Sexual Politics. Doubleday & Co., New York.
26. Mitchell, J. 1966. Women: the longest revolu-

tion. New Left Review, 40(Nov-Dec). (Available as a pamphlet from New England Free Press, Boston).

27. Myrdal, A., & Klein, V. 1968. Women's Two Roles (2nd ed.). Routledge and Kegan Paul, London.

28. O'Connor, N. 1956. The evidence for the permanently disturbing effects of mother-child separation. Acta Psychol. 12:174–191.

29. Orlansky, H. 1949. Infant care and personality. Psychol. Bull. 46:1–48.

30. Pinneau, S. 1950. A critique on the articles by Margaret Ribble. Child Developm. 21:203–228.

31. Pinneau, S. 1955. The infantile disorders of hospitalism and anaclitic depression. Psychol. Bull. 52:429–452.

32. Pinneau, S. 1955. Reply to Dr. Spitz. Psychol. Bull. 52:459–462.

33. Rapoport, R., & Rapoport, R. N. 1969. The dual career family: A variant pattern and social change. Human Relations 22:3–30.

34. Reich, W. 1962. The Sexual Revolution (3rd ed). The Noonday Press (Farrar, Straus and Giroux), New York.

35. Schaffer, H., & Emerson, P. 1964. The development of social attachments in infancy. Monographs Soc. Res. Child Developm. 29(3):ser. #94.

36. Schneirla, T. 1956. Interrelationships of the 'innate' and the 'acquired' in instinctive behavior. *In* L'Instinct Dans le Comportement des Animaux et de l'Homme. P. Grasse, ed. Masson et Cie, Paris.

37. Spiro, M. 1965. Children of the Kibbutz. Schocken Books, New York. (First published by Harvard Universities Press, 1958).

38. Spitz, R. 1945. Hospitalism: An inquiry into the genesis of psychiatric conditions in early childhood. Part I. Psychoanal. Stud. Child 1:53–74.

39. Spitz, R., & Wolf, K. 1946. Anaclitic depression: an inquiry into the genesis of psychiatric conditions in early childhood (II). Psychoanal. Stud. Child 2:313–342.

40. Stannard, U. 1970. Adam's rib, or the woman within. Transaction 8:24–35.

41. Thomas, A., et al. 1963. Behavioral Individuality in Early Childhood. New York University Press, New York.

42. Tinbergen, N. 1951. The Study of Instinct. Clarendon Press, Oxford.

43. Wootten, B. 1959. Social Science and Social Pathology. Allen and Unwin, London.

44. Yarrow, L. 1961. Maternal deprivation: Toward an empirical and conceptual reevaluation. Psychol. Bull. 58:459–490.

45. Yarrow, M., et al. 1962. Child-rearing in families of working and non-working mothers. Sociometry 25:122–140.

46. Yudkin, S., & Holme, A. 1969. Working Mothers and Their Children. Sphere Books, London. (First published by Michael Joseph, London, 1963).

# Effects of Maternal Employment on the Child—A Review of the Research

## Lois Wladis Hoffman

In a previous review of the literature on the effects of maternal employment on the child, we pointed out that the earlier view that maternal employment had a great many effects on the child, all of them bad, had been replaced by a new outlook—that maternal employment had no effects at all (Hoffman, 1963a). We assumed that maternal employment did have an effect. What the effect was might depend on the nature of the employment, the attitude of the working mother, her family circumstances, the social class, whether employment is full or part time, the age and sex of the child, the kinds of child care arrangements that are set up, and a whole host of other conditions, but until the

Reprinted from *Developmental Psychology*, 1974, *10*(2), 204–228. Copyright 1974 by the American Psychological Association. Reprinted by permission.

research questions had been properly defined and explored, we were not prepared to concede that there was no effect. While studies of maternal employment as a general concept yielded little, it was suggested that examining the effects under specified conditions might prove more fruitful. To demonstrate, we tried to show that when the relationships between maternal employment and a child characteristic were examined separately for various subgroups, interesting patterns were revealed. Thus, juvenile delinquency did seem to relate to maternal employment in the middle class, although it did not in the lower class. Part-time maternal employment seemed to have a positive effect on adolescent children, although this was not equally true for full-time employment or for younger children. The lack of consistent findings with respect to the effects on the child's independence or academic achievement was tied to the failure to examine these relationships separately for each sex. And the mother's attitude toward employment was seen as an important aspect of the situation that would affect her child-rearing behavior and thus mediate the impact of her employment on the child.

It was our hope that such speculations would give rise to new empirical investigations, but the intervening years have produced few studies of maternal employment. About the same time our review was published three others appeared: Stolz, 1960; Siegel and Haas, 1963; and Yudkin and Holme, 1963. Perhaps the overall impression given was not that maternal employment required more careful study, but that it should not be studied at all. Most of the more recent studies reviewed here were only incidentally interested in the effects of maternal employment on the child, and the few that focused on this variable were modest in scope.

On the other hand, it was previously noted that segments of the American population that contributed more than an equal share of the working mothers—blacks and single-parent families in particular—were not studied at all. A few investigators have begun to fill this gap (Kreisberg, 1970; Rieber & Womack, 1968; Smith, 1969; Woods, 1972).

Moreover, there have been some methodological improvements. Few studies today would lump boys and girls together, and most consider relationships separately for each social class. Several studies have, in fact, focused only on one class—the professional mother being a particularly popular subject currently (Birnbaum, 1971; Garland, 1972; Hoffman, 1973; Holmstrom, 1972; Jones, Lundsteen, & Michael, 1967; Poloma, 1972; Rapoport & Rapoport, 1972). These studies have, in turn, revealed the need to consider both the education of the parents and the nature of the mother's job. The new studies indicate that the mother who works as a professional has a very different influence than one who works in a less intellectually demanding and less prestigious position. Since women's jobs often underuse their talents and training, education and the nature of the job are important singly and also in interaction.

Even methodologically, however, the studies leave much to be desired. Very few controlled on family size or ordinal position, although these variables relate to both maternal employment and most of the child characteristics studied. Failure to match on these may give an advantage to the working mother, since her family is smaller, and small family size contributes positively to cognitive abilities, particularly in the lower class (Clausen & Clausen, 1973). The need to control on more than one variable simultaneously is apparent in a number of reports, while the crudeness of the social class control is a problem in others.

But the most distressing aspect of the current research situation is the lack of theory. The typical study uses the sniper approach—maternal employment is run against whatever other variables are at hand, usually scores on intelligence tests or personality inventories. Even when a study indicates a complex pattern of findings or results counter to the accumulated research, no attempt is made to explain the pattern or reconcile the discrepancy.

Furthermore, the typical study deals only with two levels—the mother's employment status and a child characteristic. The many steps in between—family roles and interaction patterns, the child's perceptions, the mother's feelings about her employment, the child-rearing practices—are rarely measured. As previously noted (Hoffman & Lippitt, 1960), the distance between an antecedent condition like maternal employment and a child characteristic is too great to be covered in a single leap. Several levels should be examined in any single study to obtain adequate insight into the process involved.

To help counteract the generally atheoretical aspect of so much of the maternal employment research, the present review tries to organize the data around five basic approaches.

## HYPOTHESES ABOUT THE EFFECTS OF MATERNAL EMPLOYMENT ON THE CHILD

What is the process by which maternal employment might affect the child? The ideas, whether implicit or explicit, that seem to guide the research and discussion can be classified into five general forms:

1. Because the mother is employed, she, and possibly her husband, provide a different model of behavior for the children in the family. Children learn sex role behavior largely from their parents. To the extent that a different role is carried out by the working mother than the nonworking mother, the child has a different conception of what the female role is. The self-concept of girls is particularly affected.

2. The mother's emotional state is influenced by whether or not she is employed, and this affects her interaction with her children.

3. Employed and nonemployed mothers probably use different child-rearing practices, not only because the mother's emotional state is different but also because the situational demands are different.

4. Because of her regular absences from the home, the working mother provides less personal supervision of her child than does the nonworking mother; and it is usually assumed that the supervision is less adequate.

5. Again, because of the working mother's regular absences from the home, the child is deprived, either emotionally or cognitively, or perceives her absence as rejection. In the sections that follow we examine each of these hypotheses and report the relevant research.

The ultimate dependent variables that have been studied—that is, the child characteristics that are the focus of attention—can be classified as follows: (a) the child's social attitudes and values; (b) the child's general mental health and social adjustment and independence or dependence specifically; and (c) the child's cognitive abilities, achievement motivation, and intellectual performance. These are considered throughout the article. In addition, however, data on maternal employment and the child's academic achievement are reviewed in a separate section because much of these data are from simple two-level studies in which it is impossible to say what hypotheses are involved.

### The Working Mother as Role Model

Hartley (1961) has observed that one experience common to all children of working mothers is that they "are exposed to a female parent who implements a social role not implemented by the female parents of other children [p. 42]." Since the child learns sex roles from observations of his parents, maternal employment influences his concept of the female role. More importantly, since one of the earliest statuses assigned to the child is that of gender, maternal employment presumably affects the female child's concept of herself and the behavior expected of her.

There is an impressive array of data to support this theory. Hartley (1961) found that elementary-school-age daughters of working mothers, in comparison to daughters of nonworking mothers, are more likely to say that both men and women typically engage in a wide variety of specified adult activities, ranging from using a sewing machine to using a gun and from selecting home furnishings to climbing mountains. That is, the daughters of working mothers indicated more similarity in the participation of men and women. They saw women as less restricted to their homes and more active in the world outside.[1]

That the division of labor between husband and wife is affected by maternal employment is well established. Husbands of employed women help more in household tasks including child care. While considerable traditionalism remains and working women engage in more domestic tasks than do their husbands, the division of household tasks is nonetheless more egalitarian when the mother is employed (Blood & Hamblin, 1958; Hall & Schroeder, 1970; Holmstrom, 1972; Kligler, 1954; Szolai, 1966; Walker, 1970b; Weil, 1961). Furthermore, this difference is reflected in the children's perceptions, as seen in Hoffman's (1963b) study of children in the third through sixth grades and Finkelman's (1966) more recent study of fifth and sixth graders. Children five years of age and older whose mothers work are more likely to approve of maternal employment (Duvall, 1955; Mathews, 1933), and King, McIntyre, and Axelson (1968) reported that ninth graders whose mothers worked viewed maternal employment as less threatening to the marital relationship. These investigators also found that the greater the father's participation in household tasks, the more accepting of maternal employment were the adolescent boys and girls.

Furthermore, daughters of working mothers view work as something they will want to do when they are mothers. This was reported by Hartley (1960) in her study of elementary school children and in four studies of adolescent girls (Banducci, 1967; Below, 1969; Peterson, 1958; Smith, 1969). It was also found in college women (Almquist & Angrist, 1971; Zissis, 1964) and as a background factor among working professional women (Astin, 1969; Birnbaum, 1971).[2] Douvan (1963) and

Roy (1963) found that adolescent daughters of working mothers were, in fact, more likely to be already employed.

Another closely related group of findings dealt with the attitudes toward women's roles in general. Are working mothers' children less likely to endorse a traditional or stereotypic view of women? Douvan (1963) found that the daughters of working mothers scored low on an index of traditional femininity.[3] Vogel, Broverman, Broverman, Clarkson, and Rosenkrantz (1970) studied the relationship between the sex role perceptions held by male and by female college students and their mothers' employment. Sex role perceptions were measured by having subjects describe the typical adult male and the typical adult female by checking a point along a continuum between two bipolar descriptions. Previous work with this scale had indicated which descriptions were more typically assigned to each sex and also which traits were seen as positive or negative. In general, the positively valued stereotypes about males included items that reflected effectiveness and competence; the highly valued female-associated items described warmth and expressiveness. Both male students and female students with employed mothers perceived significantly smaller differences between men and women, with the women being more affected by maternal employment than were the men. Furthermore, the effect of maternal employment was to raise the estimation of one's own sex; that is, each sex added positive traits usually associated with the opposite sex—daughters of working mothers saw women as competent and effective, while sons of working mothers saw men as warm and expressive.

---

[1]When asked to indicate which activities women liked and disliked, the daughters of working mothers reported more liking and less disliking of all activities—household, work, and recreation.

[2]Studies of children usually deal with maternal employment at the time of the study. Adult subjects, on the other hand, typically report past employment, for example,

"when you were growing up," and one does not know how old the child was at the time of the employment. The age of the child is also ambiguous in studies in which samples have been selected in terms of a characteristic of the mothers, since the ages of the children may vary.

[3]The fact that daughters of working mothers are lower on traditional femininity should be kept in mind in evaluating studies like Nelson's (1971) that use pencil-and-paper personality inventories. Many of these inventories are biased toward the very questionable assumption that traditional femininity is the healthy pattern for girls (Constantinople, 1973; Henshel, 1971; Lunneborg, 1968).

This result is consistent with that of an interesting study by Baruch (1972a). College women were administered a measure developed by Goldberg (1967) in which subjects are presented with a number of journal articles and asked to judge the quality of the article and of the author. Half of the articles are given female names as authors, and half are given male names. Previous research by Goldberg had indicated that college women tend to attach a lower value to the articles attributed to women authors. Baruch found that the daughters of employed women were significantly different from the daughters of full-time housewives in that they did not downgrade the articles attributed to women. Thus, the daughters of working mothers were less likely to assume lower competence on the part of women authors: "it is women whose mothers have not worked who devalue feminine competence [Baruch, 1972a, p. 37]." Meier (1972) also found among college students that maternal employment was positively related to favoring social equality for women. The most equalitarian ideology was held by daughters of women in high-status occupations.

The relationship between maternal employment and sex role ideology is not perfectly clear, however, particularly when a multi-dimensional sex role ideology scale is used. For example, Baruch, in the above study, developed a 26-item Likert-type scale to measure attitudes toward careers for women. Scores on this scale, which dealt with the desirability of a career orientation in women, the compatibility of the career and family roles, the femininity of the career woman, and women's ability to achieve intellectual excellence, were not related to maternal employment per se. Rather, a positive attitude toward the dual role resulted when the respondent's mother worked and also had successfully integrated the two roles.

With a somewhat comparable sample—wives of graduate students in the Boston area—Lipman-Blumen (1972) found no relationship between employment of the wife's mother and responses on a measure of sex role ideology. This scale consisted of six items dealing with whether women belong in the home carrying out domestic duties and child care, with men responsible for the financial support

of the family. In an earlier study, Hoffman (1963c) used two separate scales: one dealing with husband-wife division of labor and the other with attitudes toward male dominance. These two scales were administered to mothers, not daughters, and to a less educated sample than Lipman-Blumen's, representing also a broader range of social class. The expected relationship was found on the first scale: That is, working mothers favored a less traditional division of labor than nonworking mothers, but no relation was obtained between employment and attitudes toward male dominance.

Not only is the role represented by the working mother different in content from the role represented by the nonworking mother, but the motivation to model the working mother appears to be stronger. Thus, Douvan (1963) found that adolescent daughters of working mothers were more likely to name their mothers as the person they most admired; and Baruch (1972b) found that college women with working mothers were more likely to name their mothers as the parent they most resembled, and the one they would most want to be like.

It is clear that the effects of maternal employment considered in this light must be different for males and females. For one thing, although maternal employment might affect all children's concepts of the woman's role, it should affect only the girls' self-concept, unless the mother's working also reflects something about the father. Douvan found that lower-class adolescent boys whose mothers work full time are less likely than those whose mothers do not work to name their father as the person they most admire. In the lower class, the mother's employment may communicate to the child that the father is an economic failure. McCord, McCord, and Thurber (1963) also found in their study of lower-class boys from intact families that the sons of women who were employed during the boys' preadolescent years were significantly more likely than were the sons of full-time housewives to indicate disapproval of their fathers. Since these two studies were done, maternal employment has become much more prevalent, and it might therefore be expected that the finding would no longer be obtained. However, two recent Canadian studies reported the same pattern. Kappel and Lambert (1972) found in their study of children 9 to 16 years old that the sons of full-time working mothers in the lower class evaluated their fathers lower than did the sons of other full-time working mothers and lower than did the sons of the part-time or nonworking mothers in any class.[4] Propper (1972) found that in a predominantly working class sample, the adolescent sons of full-time working mothers were less likely than were the sons of nonworking mothers to name their father as the man they most admired. The finding by Vogel and his colleagues (1970) discussed previously suggests, on the other hand, that at least among middle-class males the father whose wife works may be seen as a more nurturant figure, possibly because of his taking over some of the child care roles. In any case, maternal employment more clearly defines the mother's role change than the father's, and thus the effect on the daughter may be more pronounced.

Nevertheless, there have been few studies of the effect of maternal employment on the daughter's self-esteem, and they have not always found the expected results. Thus, Baruch (1972b) found no relationship between maternal employment and the self-esteem of college women as measured by the Coopersmith Self-Esteem Inventory. She reported that the daughters of working mothers with positive career attitudes tended to have higher self-esteem, but this relationship was not statistically significant. Kappel and Lambert (1972), using a semantic-differential-style self-esteem measure with 3,315 9- to 16-year-old Canadian children, found that the daughters of nonworking mothers were lower in self-esteem than were the daughters of part-time working mothers but higher than were the daughters of full-time working mothers. The daughters of full-time working mothers did have higher self-esteem than did those of the nonworking group, however, when any one of the following conditions existed: The mother worked for self-oriented reasons, was very satisfied with work, or was a professional.

Despite the inconclusive findings on self-esteem, for girls maternal employment seems to contribute to a greater admiration of the mother, a concept of the female role that includes less restriction and a wider range of activities, and a self-concept that incorporates these aspects of the female role. Douvan (1963) found the adolescent daughters of working mothers to be relatively independent, autonomous, and active, and there are suggestions from other studies that this may be true for younger girls as well (Hoffman, 1963a). For boys, maternal employment might influence their concept of the female role, but what the effects are on their attitudes toward their father and themselves depends very much on the circumstances surrounding the mother's employment.

It would seem, then, that the daughter of a working mother would have higher academic and career aspirations and show a higher level of actual achievement. Considerable evidence for this comes from studies of college women. Almquist and Angrist (1971) found that career-oriented college women were more likely to be the daughters of working women; and Tangri (1969) found that college women who aspired to careers in the less conventionally feminine areas were more likely to be the daughters of working women. In studies of highly educated professional women, both Ginzberg (1971) and Birnbaum (1971) found maternal employment a significant background factor.

Studies of the achievement motivation or academic success of younger children provide neither overwhelming support nor clear refutation of the role-model explanation. On the whole the data are consistent with such a theory, but the investigations have not been designed to pinpoint the process by which the independent and dependent variables are linked. Thus, many studies have not examined the relationships separately for male and female subjects—an essential step for applying the results to the role-model hypothesis. For example, Powell (1963) obtained projective-

[4] This finding was obtained from Tables 3 and 5 of the Kappel and Lambert study and was not discussed by the authors.

test measures of achievement motivation from subjects four times, at ages 9, 10, 11, and 12. The children of working mothers had higher achievement motives, but the relationship was significant only at age 9. However, even though Powell was working from a modeling theory, the data were not reported separately by sex. Jones et al. (1967), using a similar measure, compared sixth-grade children of professionally employed mothers with a matched sample whose mothers were full-time housewives. The children of professional women showed a higher achievement motive, but the difference was not statistically significant. The relationship might have been stronger in these two studies if the girls had been examined alone.

In some cases the predicted child behavior may not be found because there is a counterinfluence at work. For example, the study by Kappel and Lambert (1972) suggests that when the mother's employment involves conflict and difficulties, as is sometimes the situation with full-time employment, the daughter's self-esteem is not enhanced.

In other cases, the empirical data seem to support the role-model rationale, but other processes may be at work that could also explain the result. For example, the study by Jones et al. (1967) showed that children of professional mothers were better readers than were the children of full-time housewives. Although their subjects were matched by socioeconomic status, the professional mothers were better educated than were the housewives, more time was spent with the child in reading activities, and their homes included more books. One wonders whether modeling was the process involved or the more stimulating home environment that the professionally employed mothers provided. In short, while the parental roles in the employed-mother family may serve as an influence in a particular direction, other factors associated with maternal employment might exert influence in the same direction. As noted earlier, the conceptual gap between maternal employment and a child trait is too great to be covered in simple two-level studies. A better test of the hypothesis would require examining the many intervening steps in the modeling

process: (a) the content of the roles, (b) the attitudes toward the roles, (c) the child's motivations to model various aspects of the roles, and (d) the development in the child of the skills needed to implement the appropriate behaviors.

Nevertheless, it does seem clear that when a mother works she provides a different model of behavior for the children in the family, particularly for the girls. Further, the hypothesis that this difference is important for the daughter's concept of sex roles, and thus presumably her self-concept, makes sense. Traditional sex role stereotypes in America assign a lower status to women than to men and include the view that women are less competent. Maslow, Rand, and Newman (1960) described as one effect, "the woman in order to be a good female may feel it necessary to give up her strength, intelligence or talent, fearing them as somehow masculine and defeminizing [p. 208]." Another effect has been empirically documented by Horner (1972)—that women who dare to achieve do so with anxiety and ambivalence about their success. The role of working mother is less likely to lead to traditional sex role stereotypes and more likely to communicate competence and the value of the woman's contribution to the family. She may have higher status in the family and represent to her daughter a person who is capable in areas that are, in some respects, more salient to a growing girl than are household skills.

To summarize: Considering the four major dependent variables from the standpoint of the role-model theory, the data indicate that maternal employment is associated with less traditional sex role concepts, more approval of maternal employment, and a higher evaluation of female competence. This in turn should imply a more positive self-concept for the daughters of working mothers and better social adjustment, but there are only indirect data on this. There is some support for the idea that daughters of working mothers are more independent because of modeling their more independent mothers. Evidence also suggests that the daughters of working mothers have higher achievement aspirations, but it has not yet been demonstrated that the actual abilities of the child are affected by the different role model provided by the working mother.

## The Mother's Emotional State

*Morale.* The assumption that the mother's emotional state is influenced by whether or not she is employed and that this affects her adequacy as a mother underlies several different approaches. One type of hypothesis, for example, relies on the commonly accepted belief that good morale improves job performance. Since this theory has validity in the industrial setting (Roethlisberger & Dickson, 1939), why not in the home? In fact, there is some support for it. Yarrow, Scott, deLeeuw, and Heinig (1962) examined, by means of interviews with mothers of elementary school children, the child-rearing patterns of four groups of mothers: (*a*) mothers who worked and preferred to work, (*b*) mothers who worked and preferred not to work, (*c*) nonworking mothers who preferred to work, and (*d*) nonworking mothers who preferred not to work. Among the nonworking mothers, satisfaction with their lot made a significant difference: The satisfied nonworking mothers obtained higher scores on a measure of adequacy of mothering. However, satisfaction did not differentiate the working mothers. One should keep in mind that when this study was conducted it was more socially acceptable to say, "Yes, I am working, but I wish I could be home all the time with my children" than it was to say, "Yes, I am home all day with my children, but I wish I were out working." Thus, some of the dissatisfied workers may not have been as dissatisfied as they indicated. By the same token, the dissatisfaction of the homemaker may have been more extreme, and her dissatisfaction more closely linked to the mothering role itself; that is, the very role with which she was indicating dissatisfaction included mothering. Indeed, of all four groups, the lowest scores on adequacy of mothering were obtained by the dissatisfied homemaker. (The highest, by the satisfied homemaker.) Furthermore, the investigators considered the motives for choosing full-time homemaking: Those women who stressed duty as the basis for the choice had the lowest scores of all.

The question of the dissatisfied nonworking mothers is interesting. Would the working mother who enjoys her work be dissatisfied as a full-time homemaker? In the practical sense, this may be the real issue; and the Yarrow et al. (1962) data suggest that the satisfied working mother may not be as adequate a parent as the satisfied nonworking mother but she is more adequate than the dissatisfied nonworking mother. Birnbaum (1971) in an interesting study compared professionally employed mothers with mothers who had graduated from college "with distinction" but had become full-time homemakers, that is, women who had the ability to pursue professional careers had they so chosen. Both groups were about 15 to 25 years past their bachelor's degree at the time they were interviewed. With respect to morale, the professional women were clearly higher. The nonworking mothers had lower self-esteem, a lower sense of personal competence—even with respect to child care skills, felt less attractive, expressed more concern over identity issues, and indicated greater feelings of loneliness. The nonworking mothers were even more insecure and unhappy in these respects than was a third sample of professional women who had never married. Asked what they felt was missing from their lives, the predominant answer from the two groups of professional women was time, but for the housewives it was challenge and creative involvement.

The mothers were also compared with respect to orientation toward their children. In response to the question, "How does having children change a woman's life," the full-time homemakers stressed the sacrifice that motherhood entailed significantly more often than did the professional women. The professional women answered more often in terms of enrichment and self-fulfillment. Although both groups mentioned the work involved and the demanding aspects of motherhood, the homemakers stressed duty and responsibility to a greater extent. The homemakers indicated more anxiety about their children, especially with regard to the child's achievements, and they stressed their own inadequacies as mothers. In response to a projective picture showing a boy and his parents with a crutch in the background, the homemakers told more dramatic, depressed, and anxious stories. With respect to the growing independence of their children, the professional women responded positively, while the homemakers indicated ambivalence and regret. They seemed to be concerned about the loss of familiar patterns or their own importance.

There are no direct data in the Birnbaum (1971) study on the children themselves, but the pattern of the able, educated, full-time homemakers suggests that they would have shortcomings as mothers, particularly as their children approached adolescence. At that time, when the child needs a parent who can encourage independence and instill self-confidence, the anxieties and concerns of these women and their own frustrations would seem to operate as a handicap.

There are additional studies suggesting that when work is a source of personal satisfaction for the mother, her role as mother is positively affected. Kligler (1954) found that women who worked because of interest in the job were more likely than were those who worked for financial reasons to feel that there was improvement in the child's behavior as a result of employment. Kappel and Lambert (1972) found that the 9- to 16-year-old daughters of full-time working mothers who indicated they were working for self-oriented reasons had higher self-esteem and evaluated both parents more highly than did either the daughters of full-time working mothers who were working for family-oriented reasons or the daughters of nonworking mothers. In this study the measures of the mother's motives for working and the child data were obtained independently. In the studies by Yarrow et al. (1962), Birnbaum (1971), and Kligler, the mother was the source of all the data. Woods (1972) found that in a study of fifth graders in a lower-class, predominantly black urban area where almost all of the mothers were employed, mothers who reported a positive attitude toward employment had children who obtained scores on the California Test of Personality indicating good social and personal adjustment.

*Role Strain.* Another dimension of morale that has been studied focuses on the strain of handling the dual roles of worker and mother. The general idea is that whatever the effect of maternal employment under conflict-free circumstances, the sheer pressure of trying to fill these two very demanding roles can result in a state of stress that in turn has a negative effect on the child. Thus, the main thrust of Kappel and Lambert's (1972) argument is that part-time employment, and full-time employment when it involves minimal conflict, have a positive effect; full-time employment under most conditions, however, involves strain and therefore has adverse effects. In Douvan's (1963) study of adolescent children in intact families, the only group of working-mother children who indicated adjustment problems were the children of full-time working mothers in the lower class. This group of working mothers was the one for whom the strain of the dual role seemed to be the greatest.

In contrast, Woods (1972) found the children of full-time workers to be the best adjusted. Her sample, however, was all lower class from a population in which most mothers were employed and included many single-parent families. Under these circumstances, the full-time employed mothers may have been financially better off than were the others and may have had more stable household arrangements to facilitate their employment. The mother's positive attitude toward employment related to the child's adjustment, as noted above, but also her satisfaction with child care arrangements contributed to a positive attitude toward employment. In a sense then, although full-time employment of lower-class mothers did not seem to have adverse effects on the child as suggested in the other two studies, strain as manifested in dissatisfaction with child care arrangements may have exerted such an influence.[5] To some extent the attitude to-

[5]The study does not indicate whether the woman's satisfaction reflected the objective conditions or not; the mother's perceptions and the child's report of the situation were significantly but not highly related.

ward employment generally may reflect the mother's feeling of role strain.

*Guilt.* Still another possible emotional response to employment is that the working mother feels guilty about her work because of the prevailing admonishments against maternal employment. While this may result in some appropriate compensation for her absence from home, it may also be overdone.

There is evidence that working mothers are very concerned about whether or not their employment is "bad" for their children, and they often feel guilty. Even Birnbaum's (1971) happy professional mothers indicated frequent guilt feelings. Kligler (1954) also noted that the working mothers experienced anxiety and guilt and tried to compensate in their behavior toward their children. Some evidence for guilt on the part of the working mother and the effects of this on the child is provided in a study by Hoffman (1963b). Third- through sixth-grade children of working mothers were studied, with each working-mother family matched to a nonworking-mother family on father's occupation, sex of child, and ordinal position of the child. The data included questionnaires filled out by the children, personal interviews with the mothers, teacher ratings, and classroom sociometrics. The working mothers were divided into those who indicated that they liked working and those who disliked it. Working mothers who liked work, compared to the nonworking matched sample, had more positive interaction with the child, felt more sympathy and less anger toward the child in discipline situations, and used less severe discipline techniques. However, the children of these working mothers appeared to be less assertive and less effective in their peer interactions. Their intellectual performance was rated lower by teachers, and their scores on the school intelligence tests were lower. Also, these children helped somewhat less in household tasks than did the children of nonworking mothers. Thus, the overall pattern seemed to indicate that the working mother who liked work not only tried to compensate for her employment but may have actually overcompensated. These data were collected in 1957 when popular sen-timent was opposed to maternal employment. As a result the women may have felt guilty about working. In trying to be good mothers, they may have gone too far, since the children's behavior suggested a pattern of overprotection or "smother love."

The mothers who did not like work, on the other hand, showed a very different pattern. They seemed less involved with the child; for example, they indicated less frequent disciplining and somewhat fewer positive interactions, as compared to nonworking mothers. The children helped with household tasks to a greater extent than did the children of nonworking mothers. They were also more assertive and hostile toward their peers. Their school performance as rated by their teachers was lower, although they did not perform more poorly on the school intelligence tests. The total pattern suggested that these children were somewhat neglected in comparison to the nonworking matched sample. The working mothers who disliked work had less reason to feel guilty, since they were working for other than self-oriented reasons.

*Effects on the Child.* A complicated picture is presented if the data on the working mother's emotional state are considered in relation to the child characteristics cited earlier as most often linked to maternal employment: (*a*) the child's attitudes, (*b*) mental health and social adjustment and independence-dependence specifically, and (*c*) cognitive abilities and orientations. First, with respect to the attitude toward maternal employment itself, there are some indications that the tendency of working mothers' children to have a positive attitude is enhanced when the employment is accompanied by a minimum of conflict and strain for the mother (Baruch, 1972a; King et al., 1968).

Moving on to the more complex dependent variables, it appears that when maternal employment is satisfying to the mother, either because it is more easily incorporated into her activities or because it is intrinsically gratifying, the effects on the child may be positive. The effects are more clearly positive—as indicated by various measures such as an "adequacy of mothering" score, the child's self-esteem, the child's adjustment score on the California Test of Personality, and attitudes toward parents—when this situation is compared either to that of the full-time housewife who would really prefer to work (Yarrow et al., 1962) or to maternal employment when it is accompanied by strain and harassment (Douvan, 1963; Kappel & Lambert, 1972; Woods, 1972). There are even indications that in some situations, as when the children are approaching adolescence and older or when the mother is particularly educated and able, the working-mother role may be more satisfying than is the role of full-time housewife and that this may make the working mother less anxious and more encouraging of independence in her children (Birnbaum, 1971). On the other hand, there is also evidence that the working mother with younger children who likes to work might feel guilty and thus overcompensate, with adverse effects for the child in the form of passivity, ineffectiveness with peers, and low academic performance (Hoffman, 1963b). Thus the data about the mother's emotional state suggest that the working mother who obtains satisfaction from her work, who has adequate arrangements so that her dual role does not involve undue strain, and who does not feel so guilty that she overcompensates is likely to do quite well and, under certain conditions, better than does the nonworking mother.

## Child-Rearing Practices

Concern here is with whether the child of a working mother is subject to different child-rearing practices and how these in turn affect his development. To some extent this topic is covered in other sections. In discussing the different role models presented in the working-mother families, for example, we indicated that the child-rearing functions are more likely to be shared by both parents. The fact that the child then has a more balanced relationship with both parents has generally been viewed with favor. The active involvement of the father has been seen as conducive to high achievement in women, particularly when he is supportive of independence and performance (Ginzberg,

1971; Hoffman, 1973), and to the social adjustment of boys (Hoffman, 1961) as well as to the general adjustment of both boys and girls (Dizard, 1968).

Data also indicate that the working mother's family is more likely to include someone outside the conjugal family who participates in the child care (Hoffman, 1958; U.S. Department of Labor, 1972). This situation undoubtedly operates as a selective factor, since the presence of, for example, the grandmother makes it easier for the mother to go to work; but the effects of this pattern have not been widely examined. The specific issue of multiple mothering and frequent turnover in babysitters is discussed later in the article, primarily in terms of effects on the infant and the young child when these issues are most meaningful.

In discussing the guilt sometimes felt by the working mothers, it was suggested that they sometimes try to compensate for their employment, in some cases overdoing it. There is considerable evidence that working mothers particularly in the middle class do try to compensate. In some studies, this is made explicit by the respondents (Jones et al., 1967; Kligler, 1954; Rapoport & Rapoport, 1972), while in others it is revealed in the pattern of working-nonworking differences obtained. As examples of the latter, Yarrow and her colleagues (1962) found that the college-educated working mothers compensated by having more planned activities with children, and the professional mothers in Fisher's (1939) early study spent as many hours with their children as did the full-time homemakers. Finally, Jones et al. found that the mothers employed as professionals spent more time reading with their sixth-grade children than did nonworking mothers, though this was part of a generally greater stress on educational goals, not just compensation for employment.

When the working mother tries to make up for her employment, she often makes certain implicit judgments about what the nonworking situation is like. These may be quite inaccurate. The working mothers in Hoffman's (1963b) study who required less household help from their children than did the nonworking mothers are a case in point. And, in general, the non-working mother is not necessarily interacting with her child as much as is imagined or as pleasantly. There is a great deal of pluralistic ignorance about the mothering role, and many mothers may be measuring themselves against, and trying to match, an overidealized image. It is possible that the nonworking mother spends relatively little time in direct positive interaction with her child, and thus the working mother's deliberate efforts might end up as more total positive interaction time. With respect to the amount of time spent in total child care, comparisons indicate that the nonworking women spend more time (Robinson, 1971; Walker & Woods, 1972). These reports, however, are geared toward other purposes and are not helpful in providing information about parent-child interaction. In most cases, working and nonworking women are compared without regard to whether or not they are mothers. Obviously the nonworking women include more mothers, and thus they do, as a group, spend more time in child care. Even when only mothers are compared, the number of children in the family and the children's ages are not considered, and the kind of child care is often not specified. Just how much of the day does the nonworking mother spend interacting with the child? This is an unfortunate gap in our knowledge.

*Independence Training.* Several studies have focused on whether the working mother encourages independence and maturity in her children more than does the nonworking mother. The answer seems to depend on the age of the child and the social class or education of the mother. In the work of Yarrow and her colleagues (1962), the working mothers who had not gone to college were more likely to indicate a stress on independence training and to assign the children a greater share of the household responsibilities. The college-educated working mothers did not show this pattern and in fact showed a nonsignificant tendency in the opposite direction. The subjects in this study were similar to Hoffman's (1963b) respondents in that the children were of elementary school age; thus it is interesting that the college-

educated working mothers in the former study exhibit a pattern similar to the working women who liked work in the latter study. Burchinal and Lovell (1959) reported for somewhat older children that working mothers were more likely to stress independence, and a stress on independence and responsibility can be inferred as more characteristic of the working mothers in the national sample study of adolescent girls reported by Douvan (1963), although the data rely more on what the girl is like than on parental child-rearing practices. Birnbaum's (1971) study of professionally employed mothers also suggests an encouragement of independence. The age of these children varied. The study by Von Mering (1955) is often cited as evidence that professional mothers stress independence training in elementary-school-age children, but since there were only eight mothers in the sample, such conclusions do not seem justified.[6]

A longitudinal study of lower-class boys from intact families, begun in the 1930s, suggests that the relationship between maternal employment and independence training is contingent upon the family milieu (McCord et al., 1963). Data obtained when the boys were between 10 and 15 years old showed that among the families judged to be stable by a composite index, working mothers were less overprotective and more supportive of independence than were nonworking mothers. These differences were not obtained for the unstable families, and the sons of the working mothers in this group proved to be the most dependent subjects in the entire sample. Because their mothers did not seem to be the most encouraging of dependency, their dependent behavior was interpreted by the authors as a response to feelings of rejection rather than to parental patterns of independence training.

[6] Propper (1972) found that the adolescent children of working mothers were more likely to report disagreements with parents but were not different from the children of nonworking mothers with respect to feelings of closeness to parents, parental interest, or support. The overall pattern may indicate more tolerance of disagreement by the working mothers rather than a more strained relationship. This interpretation fits well with the general picture of working mothers encouraging independence and autonomy in adolescent children.

The data are quite sketchy, but the general picture is that except for the working mothers of younger children (elementary school age) who are educated or enjoy work and possibly the working mothers in unstable families, working mothers stress independence training more than do nonworking mothers. This is consistent with what one would expect. It has already been indicated that the more educated working mothers try to compensate for their employment. Thus they would be expected to avoid pushing the younger children into maturity, stressing the nurturant aspects of their role to make up for their absence at work. As the child grows older, independence is called for. To the nonworking mother the move from protector and nurturer to independence trainer is often very difficult. For the working mother, on the other hand, the child's growing independence eases her role strain. Furthermore, the psychological threat of becoming less essential to the child is lessened by the presence of alternative roles and sources of self-worth.

The evidence for the effect of this pattern on the child is not definitely established. Two of the studies, Hoffman's (1963b) and McCord et al.'s (1963), examined data at each of the three levels: employment status, child-rearing behavior, and child characteristics; but the findings are ambiguous. Hoffman did not directly examine the relationship between maternal behavior and the child characteristics; McCord and her colleagues did and failed to find a significant association between independence training and independence. None of the other relevant maternal employment studies obtained separate data on the child-rearing patterns and the child characteristics. On the other hand, several child development studies that have no data on maternal employment have found that parental encouragement of independence relates to high achievement motivation, competence, and achievement behavior in both males and females (Baumrind & Black, 1967; Hoffman, 1972; Winterbottom, 1958).

*Household Responsibilities.* Most of the data indicate that the child of the working mother has more household responsibilities (Douvan, 1963; Johnson, 1969; Propper, 1972;

Roy, 1963; Walker, 1970a). The exception to this generalization is again the mothers of younger children who are more educated or who enjoy work. Although working mothers may sometimes deliberately avoid giving the child household responsibilities, such participation by children has generally been found to have a positive, not a negative, effect (Clausen, 1966; Johnson, 1969; Woods, 1972). Obviously, this does not mean overburdening the child, but expecting the child to be one of the effectively contributing members of the family seems conducive to the development of social adjustment and responsibility.

*Parental Control.* What other effects of maternal employment on child-rearing practices might be expected? One hypothesis might be that the working mother leaves her child more often without care or supervision. This is the focus of the next section, but by and large, there is little evidence that this is the case. On the other hand, because of the demands imposed by the dual role of worker and mother, the working mother might be stricter and impose more conformity to a specified standard. That is, just as reality adaptation might lead her to encourage the child in independence and to take on household responsibilities, she might also be expected to demand more conformity to rules so that the household can function smoothly in her absence. There is some evidence for this pattern among the less educated groups. Yarrow et al. (1962) found that the children of working mothers in their noncollege group were generally under firmer parental control than were the children of nonworking mothers. Woods (1972) found more consistency between principles and practice in the discipline used by the full-time working mothers in her lower-class, predominantly black sample. However, Yarrow et al. found greater inconsistency in their college-educated working mothers.

Still another possibility is that the working mother is milder in discipline because of conscious efforts to compensate the child or because of higher morale. Hoffman's (1963b) working mothers, especially those who liked work, used less severe discipline and indicated

**Effects of Maternal Employment on the Child**

**131**

less hostility in the discipline situation than did the nonworking mothers. It should be noted that the focus in this study was not on the content of the discipline but on its severity. Thus the data do not indicate whether the children were under more or less firm control but only that the discipline used was milder.

There are a few studies, such as those that compared the child-rearing views of working and nonworking mothers and found no meaningful differences (Kligler, 1954; Powell, 1963), that are not reviewed here, but we have included most of the available data on maternal employment and child-rearing practices. It is surprising how few investigations of maternal employment have obtained data about actual child-rearing behavior. Most of the studies have simply related employment to a child characteristic and then later speculated about any relationship that might be found. If the daughters of working mothers are found to be more independent or higher achievers, one cannot tell if this is a product of the working mother as model, the fact that the father is more likely to have had an active part in the girl's upbringing, the result of the fathers in working-mother families being more likely to approve of and encourage competence in females, or whether it is because these girls were more likely to have been encouraged by their mothers to achieve independence and assume responsibilities. All of these intervening variables have been linked to female independence and achievement (Hoffman, 1972, 1973).

## Maternal Absence and Supervision

The most persistent concern about maternal employment has to do with the sheer absence of the mother from the home while she is working and the fear that this represents a loss to the child in terms of supervision, love, or cognitive enrichment. Much of the earlier research on maternal employment and juvenile delinquency was based on this hypothesis: The mother was working, the child was unsupervised, and thus he was a delinquent. There is some support for this theory, despite the fact that maternal employment and delinquency do not relate as expected. In the study of lower-class boys carried out by Glueck and Glueck (1957), regularly employed mothers were no more likely to have delinquent sons than were nonemployed mothers. However, inadequate supervision seemed to lead to delinquency whatever the mother's employment status, and employed mothers, whether employed regularly or occasionally, were more likely to provide inadequate supervision. McCord and McCord (1959) also found a tie between supervision and delinquency in their longitudinal study of lower-class boys (which, unlike the Gluecks', included only intact families), but there was little difference between the working and nonworking mothers with respect to adequacy of supervision (McCord et al., 1963). Furthermore, the tie between the adequacy of supervision and social adjustment conceptualized more generally is not conclusively established. In the study by Woods (1972) of lower-class fifth-grade children, inadequate supervision did not have a statistically demonstrable adverse effect on boys, although unsupervised girls clearly showed lower school adjustment scores on tests of social relations and cognitive abilities.[7] Delinquency per se was too rare in this sample for any comparison, and the relationship between maternal employment and the adequacy of supervision was not examined.

Even less is known about the linkage of these three variables—maternal employment, supervision, and delinquency—in the middle class. Although middle-class working mothers express concern about finding adequate supervision for their children and although a number

---

[7] The sex differences in the Woods study are both intriguing and difficult to interpret. In most child development studies, the girls show ill effects from too much supervision or control, while the boys typically suffer from too little (Becker, 1964; Bronfenbrenner, 1961; Hoffman, 1972). This may reflect the higher level of control generally exercised over girls, so that the low end of the scale for girls is not as low as for boys, either objectively or subjectively. However, there have been very few child development studies of the lower class, and it is possible that the lack of supervision is more extreme than in the typical child development sample. Thus the middle-class girl who is unsupervised relative to other middle-class girls may not represent the level of neglect encountered by Woods.

of publications stress the inadequacy of supervision in families in which the mother works (Low & Spindler, 1968), it is not clearly established that the children end up with less supervision in either social class. Furthermore, although the adequacy of supervision seems related to delinquency in the lower class, this relationship is not established for the middle class. Nye (1958), for example, found a curvilinear relationship—both high and low supervision moderately associated with delinquency. It may seem obvious that these three variables should be linked in both the middle and the lower class, but there is little empirical documentation.

Ignoring now the issue of supervision, what is the relationship between maternal employment and delinquency? In our previous review, we suggested that there did seem to be a relationship between maternal employment and delinquency in the middle class. This relationship was found by Nye (1963) using a self-report measure of delinquent behavior and Gold (1961) who used police contact as the measure; in both studies the relationship was obtained for the middle class and not for the lower class.[8] Glueck and Glueck (1957), studying only lower-class subjects, found no tendency for the sons of regularly employed women to be delinquent despite the fact that their sample included broken homes, a variable that relates to both delinquency and maternal employment. They did find the sons of the "occasionally" employed women to be delinquent, but the occasionally employed group was clearly more unstable than were those in which the mother worked regularly or not at all. They were more likely to have husbands with poor work habits and emotional disturbances, poor marriages, or to be widowed or divorced. The Gluecks saw the occasionally employed mother as working "to escape household drudgery and parental responsibility," but, in another view, the question is not why

they went to work, since their employment was obviously needed by the circumstances of their lives, but why they resisted regular employment. The delinquency of their sons seemed more a function of family instability, the inadequacies of the father, or something about the mothers not being employed more regularly, rather than a function of maternal employment per se.

Two studies already mentioned supplement these ideas. McCord et al. (1963) found no tendency for maternal employment to be associated with delinquency when the family was stable, but in the unstable families the sons of working mothers did have a higher delinquency rate. The higher frequency of delinquency was clearly not simply due to the instability; family instability did relate to delinquency, but maternal employment in the unstable family further increased the risk.

Woods' (1972) study, which included results of psychological tests and information gathered from teachers and school and community records, found that the full-time, steadily working mother seemed to be a positive factor in the child's social adjustment. The subjects were 142 fifth graders, all the fifth graders in the school, and 108 had working mothers. Clearly, in this context, in which maternal employment is the common, accepted pattern, its meaning to parents and children is quite different. The author suggests that full-time maternal employment is a requirement of family well-being in the economic circumstances of these families and as such is respected and appreciated.

Woods' (1972) interpretation is consistent with our own earlier hypotheses about the meaning of maternal employment particularly among blacks (Hoffman, 1963a) and with other data (Kriesberg, 1970). A basic theme throughout both the earlier review and the present one is that the context within which maternal employment takes place—the meaning it has for the family and the social setting—determines its effects. In addition, the positive influence of full-time maternal employment in the lower class raises the question again of why some lower-class women resist full-time employment when their situation obviously

[8]There are two other recent studies (Brown, 1970; Riege, 1972) in which no relationship was found between maternal employment and juvenile delinquency. Since there was no separate examination by social class or attention to relevant mediating variables, these studies are not illuminating in this discussion.

calls for it. What characterizes these nonworking or irregularly employed mothers? They have less ego strength, less competence in terms of physical or emotional health, training or intellectual ability, or more children. The Gluecks' (1957) data indicate that the occasionally employed mothers were the most likely to have a history of delinquency themselves. In short, in addition to the value of the mother's employment to the family, the differences may reflect selective factors, and the employed mothers in these circumstances may be healthier, more competent, or in better circumstances with respect to family size.[9]

Consistent with Woods' (1972) interpretation is the fact that the children in the study with extensive responsibility for the household tasks and the care of siblings showed higher school achievement.[10] Like their mothers they were cooperating with realistic family demands. The author is aware, however, that the causality might be reversed, that is, that mothers give competent children more responsibilities. There are also other interpretations: For example, firstborn children particularly in lower income families usually show higher academic performance, and they are also the ones more likely to be given household tasks.

To summarize, the hypothesis that maternal employment means inadequate supervision has been primarily invoked to predict higher delinquency rates for the children of working mothers. There are data, although not very solid, that in the lower class, working mothers provide less adequate supervision for their children and that adequacy of supervision is

linked to delinquency and social adjustment, but there is not evidence that the children of working mothers are more likely to be delinquent. The data suggest instead that full-time maternal employment in the very low social class groups represents a realistic response to economic stress and thus, because of selective factors or effects, may be correlated with more socially desirable characteristics in the child. Adequacy of supervision has rarely been studied in the middle class, although here there is some evidence for a higher delinquency rate among working mothers' children.

## Maternal Deprivation

*The School-Age Child.* For school-age children, there is very little empirically to link maternal employment to maternal deprivation. Although Woods (1972) suggests that full-time employment may represent rejection to the middle-class child, there is no evidence of this. While it has been commonly assumed that maternal employment is interpreted by the child as rejection, the evidence, as indicated above, suggests that the children of working mothers tend to support the idea of mothers working. Furthermore, as maternal employment becomes the norm in the middle, as well as in the lower, class it seems even less likely that the sheer fact that a mother is working would lead to a sense of being rejected.

The evidence as to whether the working mother actually does reject the school-age child has already been covered in earlier sections of this review. The general pattern is that the working mother, particularly in the middle class, makes a deliberate effort to compensate the child for her employment (Hoffman, 1963b; Jones et al., 1967; Kligler, 1954; Poloma, 1972; Rapoport & Rapoport, 1972; Yarrow et al., 1962) and that the dissatisfied mother, whether employed or not and whether lower class or middle class, is less likely to be an adequate mother (Birnbaum, 1971; Woods, 1972; Yarrow et al., 1962). The idea that maternal employment brings emotional deprivation to the school-age child has not been supported (Hoffman, 1963a; Peterson, 1958;

---

[9]There are data that indicate that children from large families, particularly in the lower class, show lower school performance than do children from smaller families (Clausen & Clausen, 1973). Perhaps, then, it is not that full-time employment has a positive effect but that the full-time employed mothers have fewer children and the positive effect is a function of smaller family size.

[10]These findings seem somewhat inconsistent with Douvan's (1963) suggestion that the lower-class daughters of full-time working mothers were overburdened with household responsibilities. Douvan's subjects were older, and thus it is possible that they were more heavily burdened than were the fifth graders and more resentful of their duties. Douvan's sample was also white, while Woods' was predominantly black.

Propper, 1972; Siegel & Haas, 1963; Yudkin & Holme, 1963). In part this may be because the working mother is often away from home only when the child is in school; and if her work is gratifying in some measure, if she does not feel unduly hassled, or if she deliberately sets about to do so, she may even spend more time in positive interaction with the child than does the nonworking mother. While this can sometimes be overdone and compensation can turn into overcompensation (Hoffman, 1963b), it may also be one of the important reasons why maternal employment has not been experienced by the school-age child as deprivation. In drawing action conclusions from the research, it is important to keep this in mind. The absence of negative effects does not mean that the mother's employment is an irrelevant variable; it may mean that mothers have been sufficiently concerned to counterbalance such effects effectively.

*Infancy.* More recently attention has focused on the possible adverse effects of maternal employment on the infant and the very young child. The importance of attachment and a one-to-one relationship in the early years has been stressed by Spitz (1945), Bowlby (1958, 1969), and others (Yarrow, 1964). Although most of this research has been carried out on children in institutions with the most dramatic effects demonstrated among children whose infancy was spent in grossly deprived circumstances, it nevertheless seems clear that something important is happening during these early years and that there are critical periods when cognitive and affective inputs may have important ramifications throughout the individual's life. Concern has been generated about this issue because of the recent increase in maternal employment among mothers of infants and young children and also because of the new interest in day care centers as a means of caring for the preschool children of working mothers. As these two patterns emerge, the effects of maternal employment must be reevaluated. In this section we review the evidence that has been cited on one side or the other of these issues. As we shall see, however, we really know very little.

The research on maternal deprivation suggests that the infant needs a one-to-one relationship with an adult or else he may suffer cognitive and affective loss that may, in extreme conditions, never be regained. The importance of interactions in which the adult responds to the child and the child to the adult in a reciprocal relationship has been particularly stressed (Bronfenbrenner, 1973). There is some evidence of a need for cuddling (Harlow & Harlow, 1966) and a need for environmental stimulation (Dennis & Najarian, 1957; Hunt, 1961). These studies are often cited as evidence for the importance of the mother's full-time presence in the home when the infant is young.

Extending these findings to the maternal employment situation may be inappropriate, however. Not only were the early Bowlby (1953, 1958) and Spitz (1945) data obtained from studies of extremely barren, understaffed institutions, but later research suggested that the drastic effects they had observed might be avoided by increasing the staff-child ratio, by providing nurses who attended and responded to the infants' cries, smiles and vocalizations, and by providing a more stimulating visual environment. Further, the age of the child, the duration of the institutionalization, and the previous and subsequent experiences of the child all affect the outcome (Rheingold, 1956; Rheingold & Bayley, 1959; Rheingold, Gewirtz, & Ross, 1959; Tizard, Cooperman, Joseph, & Tizard, 1972; Yarrow, 1964). Most important, however, institutionalization is not the same as day care, and day care is not the same as maternal employment. The inappropriateness of the studies of institutionalized infants to maternal employment has also been noted by Yudkin and Holme (1963), by Yarrow (1964), and by Wortis (1971).

In addition, there is no evidence that the caretaker has to be the mother or that this role is better filled by a male or a female. There is some evidence that the baby benefits from predictability in handling, but whether this is true throughout infancy or only during certain periods is not clear, nor is it clear whether the different handling has any long-lasting effects. Studies of multiple mothering have produced conflicting results (Caldwell, 1964). Child psychologists generally believe that there must be at least one stable figure to whom the infant forms an attachment, but this is not definitely established, and we do not know whether the periodic absence from the infant that is likely to go along with the mother's employment is sufficient to undermine her potential as the object of the infant's attachment.

Nevertheless, a number of child development studies suggest that within the normal range of parent-child interaction, the amount of expressive and vocal stimulation and response the mother gives to the infant affects his development (Emerson & Schaffer, 1964; Kagan, 1969; Lewis & Goldberg, 1969; Moss, 1967). Furthermore, although the attempts to increase cognitive performance through day care programs have not been very successful, attempts to increase the mother-infant interaction in the home appear to have more enduring effects (Bronfenbrenner, 1973; Levenstein, 1970, 1971). While there is no evidence that employment actually affects the quantity or quality of the mother-infant interaction, the voluntary employment of mothers of infants and young children has not heretofore been common, and it has rarely been studied. It is therefore important to find out whether the mother's employment results in less (or more) personal stimulation and interaction for the infant.

In addition to the importance of stimulation and interaction and the issue of emotional attachment for the infant, there are less fully explored questions about the effects on the mother. Bowlby (1958) and others (Hess, 1970) believe that the mother-child interaction is important for the development of the mother's "attachment," that an important source of maternal feeling is the experience of caring for the infant. Yudkin and Holme (1963), who generally approve of maternal employment in their review, stress this as one of the real dangers of full-time maternal employment when the child is young:

We would consider this need for a mother to develop a close and mutually satisfying relationship with her young infant one of the fundamental reasons why we oppose full-time work for mothers of children under 3 years. We do not say that it would not be possible to combine the two if children were cared for near their mothers so that they could see and be with each other during the day for parts of the day, and by such changes in households as will reduce the amount of time and energy needed for household chores. We are only stating that this occurs very rarely in our present society and is unlikely to be general in the foreseeable future and that the separation of children from their mothers for eight or nine hours a day, while the effects on the children may be counteracted by good substitute care, must have profound effects on the mother's own relationship with her young children and therefore on their relationship in the family as they grow older [pp. 131–132].

The issue of day care centers is not discussed in this review in any detail; however, our ignorance is almost as great here. While the cognitive advances expected from the Head Start day care programs were not adequately demonstrated (Bronfenbrenner, 1973), neither were there negative effects of these programs (Caldwell, Wright, Honig, & Tannenbaum, 1970). Obviously, the effects of day care centers for working mothers' children depend on the quality of the program, the time the child spends there, what happens to the child when he is not at the day care center, and what the alternatives are.

Arguments on either side of the issue of working mothers and day care often use data from studies of the kibbutzim in Israel, since all kibbutzim mothers work and from infancy on the child lives most of the time in the child centers. Some investigators have been favorably impressed with the development of these children (Kohn-Raz, 1968; Rabkin & Rabkin, 1969), while others have noted at least some deleterious consequences (Bettelheim, 1969; Spiro, 1965). In fact, however, these data are probably quite irrelevant. According to Bronfenbrenner (1973), these children spend more time each day interacting with their parents than do children in the more conventional nuclear family arrangement, and the time they spend together is less subject to distractions. The whole living arrangement is different, including the nature of the parents' work and the social context within which interaction takes place. The mother participates a great deal in the infant care, breast feeding is the norm, and both parents play daily with the child for long periods and without other diversions even as he matures. Thus, the Israeli kibbutz does not provide an example of maternal deprivation, American day care, or maternal employment as it is experienced in the United States.

There have been few direct attempts to study the effects of the mother's employment during the child's infancy. These few have had two special problems with which to cope: (*a*) Observed differences in infancy are difficult to interpret in terms of long-range adjustment; and (*b*) because the pattern of going to work when one had an infant was previously unusual, there were often special surrounding circumstances that made it difficult to ferret out the effects of employment per se. One way to handle the first problem is to compare older children with respect to their mothers' earlier employment. For example, Burchinal (1963) examined intelligence scores and school adjustment for a large sample of children in the seventh and eleventh grades. Children whose mothers had been employed when the child was three years old or younger were compared to children whose mothers were employed only when the child was older or whose mothers were never employed. Very few statistically significant results were obtained.

The second problem plagued the study by Moore (1963). In an intensive, longitudinal study, Moore compared children of elementary school age in Great Britain with respect to their mothers' employment history, with particular consideration given to the nature of the child care arrangements that the working mother established. However, the groups contrasted were different in ways other than whether or not the mother was employed at certain points in the child's life. Thus, one observed difference was that the children who had been left by their mothers from early infancy showed more dependent attachment to their parents than did any other children in the study and they also exhibited other symptoms of insecurity such as nail-biting and bad dreams; however, Moore also indicated that the mothers who started

work early in the child's life did not themselves seem as attached to the child. While this latter observation could have been a result of the mother's not having had as much close contact with the child, it is also possible that these mothers were different from the start and the child's disturbance reflected this more than it reflected the mother's employment. Since these mothers had sought employment when few mothers of infants worked, they may have been a more psychologically distinct group than one would now find. Indeed, Moore's case studies reveal patterns of emotional rejection, and in some cases the mother explicitly went to work to escape from the child. Furthermore, the mothers who went to work full time before their children were two years old often had difficulty finding good mother substitute arrangements, and the data indicate that the stability of the child care arrangements was an important factor affecting the child's adjustment.

Obviously the effects of maternal employment on the infant depend on the extent of the mother's absence and the nature of the substitute care—whether it is warm, stimulating, and stable. However, while studies of maternal employment and the school-age child by and large offer reassurance to the working mother, we have very little solid evidence concerning the effect on the younger child.

## MATERNAL EMPLOYMENT AND THE CHILD'S ACADEMIC ACHIEVEMENT

Probably the child characteristics that have most often been examined in relation to maternal employment are those pertaining to academic achievement. These are reviewed separately, since in most cases the data are too skimpy to be interpreted in terms of the five approaches discussed above. Included are studies of academic aspirations (usually whether or not the child plans to go to college), achievement motivation, intelligence test scores, and school performance. Most of the studies lack a guiding theory or even post hoc interpretations; the investigator rarely tries to explain why his data are consistent or inconsistent with other studies. The result is a hodgepodge of findings. The more recent studies have analyzed the data separately for sex and social class, and this has resulted in complex patterns, but there is no apparent order in these patterns. Until this issue is tackled with more theoretical sophistication, there will be little illumination.

## College Plans

Why would one expect college plans to be affected by the mother's employment? Possibly because it means extra money in the house, one might predict that the children of the employed women, if the husbands' incomes were equated, would be more likely to plan on college. In fact, mothers often indicate they are working to help finance their children's college education. Possibly daughters, modeling an active, occupation-oriented mother, would be more likely to seek college when their mothers worked. This second hypothesis might be affected by what kind of work the mother engaged in, particularly what kind of work in relation to her education, and also by how the mother felt about her employment. None of these necessary additional pieces of data are available in the pertinent studies, so an interpretation of the results is impossible.

Roy (1963) found that among rural high school students the children of working mothers were more likely to plan to go to college than were the children of nonworking mothers. This was true for both sexes, although a general impression from the tables is that the relationship was stronger for girls. (The report does not indicate if this sex difference was statistically significant.) On the other hand, the children of working mothers in the town sample were less likely to go to college. (Here the difference for girls appeared very slight.) The research supported the investigator's point that even within the same generally rural area residence in the town or on farms was a meaningful distinction, but the data are insufficient for interpreting the results.

Banducci (1967) also examined the relationship between desires and plans for college and maternal employment, reporting the data separately by sex and father's occupation. His sample consisted of 3,014 Iowa high school seniors living with both parents. Three occupational levels were considered—laborer, skilled worker, and professional—presumably representing socioeconomic levels generally; "professional" in this study did not necessarily connote high educational achievement. For most subjects, males and females, maternal employment was positively associated with desires and plans for college. But for the group classified as professional, the opposite relationship prevailed: The daughters of working mothers were significantly less likely to expect to go to college, and the sons of working mothers were less likely to expect to go or to aspire for college, the latter relationship being significant. How can we interpret this curious pattern of findings? Did the presence of a working mother indicate the lower socioeconomic end of the professional group? Were the working mothers in this group employed in a family business, and thus the family was less education oriented? As indicated below, the sons of these women also had lower grade point averages, so there was something different about them, but whether an effect of maternal employment or some other peculiarity of this particular subsample was uncovered, it is impossible to say with the available information.

The several studies of college and professional women that indicate maternal employment is associated with more ambitious career goals have already been cited (Almquist & Angrist, 1971; Birnbaum, 1971; Ginzberg, 1971; Tangri, 1969).

## Achievement Motives

There are two studies of children's achievement motives in relation to maternal employment. Both measured achievement motives by scoring projective responses according to the scheme developed by McClelland and Atkinson (Atkinson, 1958). Powell (1963) obtained achievement motivation scores and maternal employment data longitudinally for subjects at each of the following ages: 9, 10, 11, and 12. The children of employed mothers showed higher achievement motivations at each age level, significantly for age 9. Several years after the Powell study was published, Jones et al. (1967) carried out a similar study with sixth graders. They found a parallel but nonsignificant relationship. No mention was made of the earlier study. How valuable it would have been if they had replicated Powell's work by presenting data for 9-, 10-, 11-, and 12-year-olds! Neither study analyzed the data separately for boys and girls, although, as indicated earlier, Powell's "modeling" hypotheses would suggest that the relationship might have been stronger for girls than for boys.

## IQ Scores

Two studies of the lower socioeconomic class indicate that maternal employment and IQ scores are positively related. Woods (1972) in her study of fifth graders found that full-time maternal employment was associated with higher intelligence test scores as measured by the California Test of Mental Maturity, and Rieber and Womack (1968), studying preschoolers, found that more of the children of working mothers fell in the highest quartile on the Peabody Picture Vocabulary Test. Both of these studies included blacks and single-parent families, and the latter also included families of Latin American background.

The researchers who examined the relationship between maternal employment and intelligence test scores in more middle-class samples found more complex results. Hoffman (1963b) found that in a sample of white, intact families, the children of working mothers who liked work had lower IQ scores than did the matched children of nonworking mothers. The children of the working mothers who disliked work, however, were not different from the nonworking matched group.

Rees and Palmer (1970) presented a particularly interesting and complicated analysis of longitudinal data from a number of different studies. Their samples varied, but by and large they represented a higher socioeconomic group than the above three studies. Data were analyzed separately for boys and girls, with impor-

tant differences appearing. In general, maternal employment related to high IQ in girls and low IQ in boys. Using as the independent variable the mother's employment status when the child was 15, they found that the daughters of working mothers had higher IQs at age 6 and around age 15, although there was no relationship for age 12. Was the working mother of the 15-year-old also working when the child was 6? We do not know. The relationships for the boys were the opposite. The data were interpreted by the investigators as reflecting a general association between nontraditional femininity and higher IQ in girls: That is, the working mother represented to her daughter a less traditional view of femininity.[11] This theory suggesting a negative relationship between traditional femininity and achievement in girls has been discussed more fully by Maccoby (1966) and by Hoffman (1972); and data tying maternal employment to nontraditional femininity were discussed earlier in this review.

## Academic Performance

Hoffman (1963b) found that the elementary-school-age children of working mothers showed lower school performance than did the matched sample with nonworking mothers, using teacher ratings of performance to measure the dependent variable. Nolan (1963) found no difference for rural elementary school children and a difference favoring the children of working mothers in high school, but this study did not even control on social class. Neither of these studies reported the data separately by sex.

Two more recent studies of elementary school children were carried out in which attention was directed to whether or not the mother was employed in a professional capacity. In one, the reading achievement of the sixth-grade children of professionally employed mothers was compared to the reading achievement of full-time housewives' children who were matched by social class, sex, age, and IQ

[11]Another finding of their analysis consistent with this interpretation is that girls who had a brother either just older or just younger also had higher IQs.

(Jones et al., 1967). The study indicates that the children of the professional mothers were more proficient. It also suggests why, for these parents spent more time in reading activities with the children and had more plans for the children's education, there were more books in the home, and the mothers were better educated. The data were not analyzed separately for boys and girls. It is important to point out as one implication of this study that matching on social class is not the same as matching on education, and matching on the father's occupation is not the same as matching on income or life style.

The difference between employed mothers and professionally employed mothers is also indicated in the study by Frankel (1964) of intellectually gifted high school boys. High and low achievers matched on IQ scores were compared. The low achievers were more likely to have working mothers, but the high achievers were more likely to have professional mothers. Although the socioeconomic status as conventionally measured did not differentiate the groups, the education of the mothers (and possibly both parents) did. While the higher achievement of the children of professional mothers is easily interpreted, it is not clear why the low achievers tended to have nonprofessional working mothers. Frankel described these women impressionistically as dissatisfied and hostile. This judgment may or may not be valid, but it would be worthwhile to compare women working at various levels of jobs in terms of both selective factors and the effects of employment on the mother's psychological state. It might be noted that in Levine's (1968) study of women's career choice, the mother's education was found to be more important than whether or not the mother worked; Tangri (1969) found the mother's employment the more important.

Moving into the high school age, most studies found no differences in school achievement. Thus neither Nye (1963) nor Nelson (1969) reported significant differences, nor did Keidel (1970) in a comparison that matched on academic ability. In Burchinal's data (1963) one of the few relationships that remained significant despite controls introduced on socioeconomic status was the lower school grades of the eleventh-grade boys whose mothers were currently working. Roy (1963) also found adolescent sons of working mothers to have lower school grades, although only in his town sample. Banducci also reported differences in grades: Sons of working mothers in the socioeconomic class called professional had significantly lower grades than did the sons of nonworking mothers, but in the class labeled "skilled worker" the opposite relationship prevailed, the sons of working mothers having significantly higher grades than did the sons of the nonworkers. No other differences in school grades were significant. Of the several comparisons by Banducci (1967) of scores on the Iowa Tests of Educational Development, a standardized achievement measure, the sons of working mothers in the lowest socioeconomic group, laborers, had higher scores than did the nonworking-mother sons in that class. Brown (1970) found lower scores on the California Achievement Test for the middle-class eighth- and ninth-grade sons of working mothers.

Farley (1968) compared the self-reported grade point averages of students in an introductory sociology course at Cornell University. The males who indicated their mothers were employed also reported significantly higher grades. There was no relationship for females. No variables were controlled. If the data were more solidly established, it would be interesting, since several studies indicate that maternal employment is prevalent in the backgrounds of women who pursue professional careers, but whether their college grades were better has not been established.

## Summary of the Findings on Academic Achievement

Although there are some indications that maternal employment is positively associated with high school children's college plans, the opposite relationship has occasionally been shown. Per capita family income has not been controlled in these studies, however, and maternal employment may sometimes reflect low income as well as indicate augmented income.

There is evidence, however, that college-educated daughters of working mothers have higher career aspirations and achievements. Furthermore, in one study using longitudinal data, daughters of working mothers obtained higher intelligence test scores at 6 and 15 years of age. Two of the hypotheses discussed in this article, the modeling theory and the idea that independence training is stressed by working mothers, are particularly pertinent to the achievement of girls, and both predict higher achievement for the daughters of working mothers.

On the other hand, we suggested in an earlier review (Hoffman, 1963a) that sons of working mothers may not fare so well. This view receives a modest amount of support, and the data suggest that the sons of working mothers in the middle class show lower academic performance. In the lower class, however, better academic performance is associated with maternal employment for both sexes.

## GENERAL SUMMARY

The research reviewed in this article has been organized around five general hypotheses that seem to be implicitly involved in the expectation that maternal employment affects the child, with an additional section dealing with effects on academic achievement. These hypotheses are not mutually exclusive, and the various processes in fact interact—sometimes reinforcing one another, sometimes counteracting. An aim of the social scientist interested in this topic should be to ascertain the conditions under which one process or another would operate and how these would interact. It is important to understand the effects of maternal employment at this level so that predictions and action implications are meaningful in the face of a changing society.

## REFERENCES

Almquist, E. M., & Angrist, S. S. Role model influences on college women's career aspirations. *Merrill-Palmer Quarterly*, 1971, **17**, 263–279.

Astin, H. S. *The woman doctorate in America.* New York: Russell Sage Foundation, 1969.

Atkinson, J. W. (Ed.) *Motives in fantasy, action, and society.* Princeton, N. J.: Van Nostrand, 1958.

Banducci, R. The effect of mother's employment on the achievement, aspirations, and expectations of the child. *Personnel and Guidance Journal,* 1967, **46**, 263–267.

Baruch, G. K. Maternal influences upon college women's attitudes toward women and work. *Developmental Psychology,* 1972, **6**, 32–37. (a)

Baruch, G. K. Maternal role pattern as related to self-esteem and parental identification in college women. Paper presented at the meeting of the Eastern Psychological Association, Boston, April 1972. (b)

Baumrind, D., & Black, A. E. Socialization practices associated with dimensions of competence in preschool boys and girls. *Child Development,* 1967, **38**, 291–327.

Becker, W. C. Consequences of different kinds of parental discipline. In M. L. Hoffman & L. W. Hoffman (Eds.), *Review of child development research.* New York: Russell Sage Foundation, 1964.

Below, H. I. Life styles and roles of women as perceived by high-school girls. Unpublished doctoral dissertation, Indiana University, 1969.

Bettelheim, B. *The children of the dream.* London: Macmillan, 1969.

Birnbaum, J. A. Life patterns, personality style and self esteem in gifted family oriented and career committed women. Unpublished doctoral dissertation, University of Michigan, 1971.

Blood, R. O., & Hamblin, R. L. The effect of the wife's employment on the family power structure. *Social Forces,* 1958, **36**, 347–352.

Bowlby, J. A. Some pathological processes engendered by early mother-child separation. In M. J. E. Senn (Ed.), *Infancy and childhood.* New York: Josiah Macy, Jr. Foundation, 1953.

Bowlby, J. A. The nature of the child's tie to his mother. *International Journal of Psychoanalysis,* 1958, **39**, 350–373.

Bowlby, J. A. *Attachment.* New York: Basic Books, 1969.

Bronfenbrenner, U. Some familial antecedents of responsibility and leadership on adolescents. In L. Petrullo & B. M. Bass (Eds.), *Leadership and interpersonal behavior.* New York: Holt, Rinehart & Winston, 1961.

Bronfenbrenner, U. Is early intervention effective?

Paper presented at the biennial meeting of the Society for Research in Child Development, Philadelphia, March 1973.

Brown, S. W. *A comparative study of maternal employment and nonemployment.* (Doctoral dissertation, Mississippi State University) Ann Arbor, Mich.: University Microfilms, 1970, No. 70–8610.

Burchinal, L. G. Personality characteristics of children. In F. I. Nye & L. W. Hoffman (Eds.), *The employed mother in America.* Chicago: Rand McNally, 1963.

Burchinal, L. G., & Lovell, L. Relation of employment status of mothers to children's anxiety, parental personality and PARI scores. Unpublished manuscript (1425), Iowa State University, 1959.

Caldwell, B. M. The effects of infant care. In M. L. Hoffman & L. W. Hoffman (Eds.), *Review of child development research.* New York: Russell Sage Foundation, 1964.

Caldwell, B. M., Wright, C. M., Honig, A. S., & Tannenbaum, J. Infant day care and attachment. *American Journal of Orthopsychiatry,* 1970, **40,** 397–412.

Clausen, J. A. Family structure, socialization, and personality. In L. W. Hoffman & M. L. Hoffman (Eds.), *Review of child development research.* Vol. 2. New York: Russell Sage Foundation, 1966.

Clausen, J. A., & Clausen, S. R. The effects of family size on parents and children. In J. Fawcett (Ed.), *Psychological perspectives on fertility.* New York: Basic Books, 1973.

Constantinople, A. Masculinity-femininity: An exception to a famous dictum? *Psychological Bulletin,* 1973, **80,** 389–407.

Dennis, W., & Najarian, P. Infant development under environmental handicap. *Psychological Monographs,* 1957, **71** (7, Whole No. 436).

Dizard, J. *Social change in the family.* Chicago: University of Chicago, Community and Family Study Center, 1968.

Douvan, E. Employment and the adolescent. In F. I. Nye & L. W. Hoffman (Eds.), *The employed mother in America.* Chicago: Rand McNally, 1963.

Duvall, E. B. Conceptions of mother roles by five and six year old children of working and nonworking mothers. Unpublished doctoral dissertation, Florida State University, 1955.

Emerson, P. E., & Schaffer, H. R. The development of social attachments in infancy. *Monographs of the Society for Research in Child Development,* 1964, **29**(3, Serial No. 94).

Farley, J. Maternal employment and child behavior. *Cornell Journal of Social Relations,* 1968, **3,** 58–70.

Finkelman, J. J. Maternal employment, family relationships, and parental role perception. Unpublished doctoral dissertation, Yeshiva University, 1966.

Fisher, M. S. Marriage and work for college women. *Vassar Alumnae Magazine,* 1939, **24,** 7–10.

Frankel, E. Characteristics of working and nonworking mothers among intellectually gifted high and low achievers. *Personnel and Guidance Journal,* 1964, **42,** 776–780.

Garland, T. N. The better half? The male in the dual profession family. In C. Safilios-Rothschild (Ed.), *Toward a sociology of women.* Lexington, Mass.: Xerox College Publishing, 1972.

Ginzberg, E. *Educated American women: Life styles and self-portraits.* New York: Columbia University Press, 1971.

Glueck, S., & Glueck, E. Working mothers and delinquency. *Mental Hygiene,* 1957, **41,** 327–352.

Gold, M. *A social-psychology of delinquent boys.* Ann Arbor, Mich.: Institute for Social Research, 1961.

Goldberg, P. Misogyny and the college girl. Paper presented at the meeting of the Eastern Psychological Association, Boston, April 1967.

Hall, F. T., & Schroeder, M. P. Time spent on household tasks. *Journal of Home Economics,* 1970, **62,** 23–29.

Harlow, H., & Harlow, M. H. Learning to love. *American Scientist,* 1966, **54,** 244–272.

Hartley, R. E. Children's concepts of male and female roles. *Merrill-Palmer Quarterly,* 1960, **6,** 83–91.

Hartley, R. E. What aspects of child behavior should be studied in relation to maternal employment? In A. E. Siegel (Ed.), *Research issues related to the effects of maternal employment on children.* University Park, Penn.: Social Science Research Center, 1961.

Henshel, A. Anti-feminist bias in traditional measurements of masculinity-femininity. Paper presented at the meeting of the National Council on Family Relations, Estes Park, Colorado, August 1971.

Hess, H. Ethology and developmental psychology. In P. Mussen (Ed.), *Carmichael's manual of child psychology.* New York: Wiley, 1970.

Hoffman, L. W. *Effects of the employment of mothers on parental power relations and the division of household tasks.* Unpublished doctoral dissertation, University of Michigan, 1958.

Hoffman, L. W. The father's role in the family and

the child's peer group adjustment. *Merrill-Palmer Quarterly,* 1961, **7,** 97–105.

Hoffman, L. W. Effects on children: Summary and discussion. In F. I. Nye & L. W. Hoffman (Eds.), *The employed mother in America.* Chicago: Rand McNally, 1963. (a)

Hoffman, L. W. Mother's enjoyment of work and effects on the child. In F. I. Nye & L. W. Hoffman (Eds.), *The employed mother in America.* Chicago: Rand McNally, 1963. (b)

Hoffman, L. W. Parental power relations and the division of household tasks. In F. I. Nye & L. W. Hoffman (Eds.), *The employed mother in America.* Chicago: Rand McNally, 1963. (c)

Hoffman, L. W. Early childhood experiences and women's achievement motives. *Journal of Social Issues,* 1972, **28**(2), 129–155.

Hoffman, L. W. The professional woman as mother. In R. B. Kundsin (Ed.), *A conference on successful women in the sciences.* New York: New York Academy of Sciences, 1973.

Hoffman, L. W., & Lippitt, R. The measurement of family life variables. In P. Mussen (Ed.), *Handbook of research methods in child development.* New York: Wiley, 1960.

Holmstrom, L. L. The two-career family. Paper presented at the conference of Women: Resource for a Changing World, Radcliffe Institute, Radcliffe College, Cambridge, April 1972.

Horner, M. S. Femininity and successful achievement: A basic inconsistency. In J. M. Bardwick, E. Douvan, M. S. Horner, & D. Gutman, *Feminine personality and conflict.* Belmont, Calif.: Brooks/Cole, 1972.

Hunt, J. McV. *Intelligence and experience.* New York: Ronald Press, 1961.

Johnson, C. L. *Leadership patterns in working and nonworking mother middle class families.* (Doctoral dissertation, University of Kansas) Ann Arbor, Mich.: University Microfilms, 1969, No. 69–11, 224.

Jones, J. B., Lundsteen, S. W., & Michael, W. B. The relationship of the professional employment status of mothers to reading achievement of sixth-grade children. *California Journal of Educational Research,* 1967, **43,** 102–108.

Kagan, J. Continuity of cognitive development during the first year. *Merrill-Palmer Quarterly,* 1969, **15,** 101–119.

Kappel, B. E., & Lambert, R. D. Self worth among the children of working mothers. Unpublished manuscript, University of Waterloo, 1972.

Keidel, K. C. Maternal employment and ninth grade achievement in Bismarck, North Dakota. *Family Coordinator,* 1970, **19,** 95–97.

King, K., McIntyre, J., & Axelson, L. J. Adolescents' views of maternal employment as a threat to the marital relationship. *Journal of Marriage and the Family,* 1968, **30,** 633–637.

Kligler, D. The effects of employment of married women on husband and wife roles: A study in culture change. Unpublished doctoral dissertation, Yale University, 1954.

Kohn-Raz, R. Mental and motor development of kibbutz, institutionalized, and home-reared infants in Israel. *Child Development,* 1968, **39,** 489–504.

Kreisberg, L. *Mothers in poverty: A study of fatherless families.* Chicago: Aldine, 1970.

Levenstein, P. Cognitive growth in preschoolers through verbal interaction with mothers. *American Journal of Orthopsychiatry,* 1970, **40,** 426–432.

Levenstein, P. Verbal interaction project: Aiding cognitive growth in disadvantaged preschoolers through the Mother-Child Home Program July 1, 1967–August 31, 1970. Final report to Children's Bureau, Office of Child Development, U. S. Department of Health, Education, and Welfare, 1971. (Mimeo)

Levine, A. G. Marital and occupational plans of women in professional schools: Law, medicine, nursing, teaching. Unpublished doctoral dissertation, Yale University, 1968.

Lewis, M., & Goldberg, S. Perceptual-cognitive development in infancy: A generalized expectancy model as a function of the mother-infant interaction. *Merrill-Palmer Quarterly,* 1969, **15,** 81–100.

Lipman-Blumen, J. How ideology shapes women's lives. *Scientific American,* 1972, **226**(1), 34–42.

Low, S., & Spindler, P. *Child care arrangements of working mothers in the United States.* (Children's Bureau Publication 461) Washington, D. C.: U. S. Government Printing Office, 1968.

Lunneborg, P. W. Stereotypic aspect in masculinity-femininity measurement. Paper presented at the meeting of the American Psychological Association, San Francisco, September 1968.

Maccoby, E. E. Sex differences in intellectual functioning. In E. E. Maccoby (Ed.), *The development of sex differences.* Stanford, Calif.: Stanford University Press, 1966.

Maslow, A. H., Rand, H., & Newman, S. Some parallels between sexual and dominance behavior of infra-human primates and the fantasies of patients in psychotherapy. *Journal of Nervous and Mental Disease,* 1960, **131,** 202–212.

Mathews, S. M. The development of children's attitude concerning mothers' out-of-home employment. *Journal of Educational Sociology,* 1933, **6**, 259–271.

McCord, J., McCord, W., & Thurber, E. Effects of maternal employment on lower-class boys. *Journal of Abnormal and Social Psychology,* 1963, **67**, 177–182.

McCord, W., & McCord, J. *Origins of crime.* New York: Columbia University Press, 1959.

Meier, H. C. Mother-centeredness and college youths' attitudes toward social equality for women: Some empirical findings. *Journal of Marriage and the Family,* 1972, **34**, 115–121.

Moore, T. Children of working mothers. In S. Yudkin & H. Holme (Eds.), *Working mothers and their children.* London: Michael Joseph, 1963.

Moss, H. A. Sex, age, and state as determinants of mother-infant interaction. *Merrill-Palmer Quarterly,* 1967, **13**, 19–36.

Nelson, D. D. A study of school achievement among adolescent children with working and nonworking mothers. *Journal of Educational Research,* 1969, **62**, 456–457.

Nelson, D. D. A study of personality adjustment among adolescent children with working and nonworking mothers. *Journal of Educational Research,* 1971, **64**, 1328–1330.

Nolan, F. L. Effects on rural children. In F. I. Nye & L. W. Hoffman (Eds.), *The employed mother in America.* Chicago: Rand McNally, 1963.

Nye, F. I. *Family relationships and delinquent behavior.* New York: Wiley, 1958.

Nye, F. I. The adjustment of adolescent children. In F. I. Nye & L. W. Hoffman (Eds.), *The employed mother in America.* Chicago: Rand McNally, 1963.

Peterson, E. T. The impact of maternal employment on the mother-daughter relationship and on the daughter's role-orientation. Unpublished doctoral dissertation, University of Michigan, 1958.

Poloma, M. M. Role conflict and the married professional woman. In C. Safilios-Rothschild (Ed.), *Toward a sociology of women.* Lexington, Mass.: Xerox College Publishing, 1972.

Powell, K. Personalities of children and child-rearing attitudes of mothers. In F. I. Nye & L. W. Hoffman (Eds.), *The employed mother in America.* Chicago: Rand McNally, 1963.

Propper, A. M. The relationship of maternal employment to adolescent roles, activities, and parental relationships. *Journal of Marriage and the Family,* 1972, **34**, 417–421.

Rabkin, L. Y., & Rabkin, K. Children of the kibbutz. *Psychology Today,* 1969, **3**(4), 40.

Rapoport, R., & Rapoport, R. The dual-career family: A variant pattern and social change. In C. Safilios-Rothschild (Ed.), *Toward a sociology of women.* Lexington, Mass.: Xerox College Publishing, 1972.

Rees, A. N., & Palmer, F. H. Factors related to change in mental test performance. *Developmental Psychology Monograph,* 1970, **3**(2, Pt. 2).

Rheingold, H. The modification of social responsiveness in institutional babies. *Monographs of the Society for Research in Child Development,* 1956, **21**(2, Serial No. 63).

Rheingold, H., & Bayley, N. The later effects of an experimental modification of mothering. *Child Development,* 1959, **30**, 363–372.

Rheingold, H., Gewirtz, J. L., & Ross, H. W. Social conditioning of vocalizations in the infant. *Journal of Comparative and Physiological Psychology,* 1959, **52**, 68–73.

Rieber, M., & Womack, M. The intelligence of preschool children as related to ethnic and demographic variables. *Exceptional Children,* 1968, **34**, 609–614.

Riege, M. G. Parental affection and juvenile delinquency in girls. *The British Journal of Criminology,* 1972, **12**, 55–73.

Robinson, J. B. Historical changes in how people spend their time. In A. Michel (Ed.), *Family issues of employed women in Europe and America.* Leiden, Netherlands: E. J. Brill, 1971.

Roethlisberger, F. J., & Dickson, W. J. *Business Research Studies.* Cambridge, Mass.: Harvard Business School, Division of Research, 1939.

Roy, P. Adolescent roles: Rural-urban differentials. In F. I. Nye & L. W. Hoffman (Eds.), *The employed mother in America.* Chicago: Rand McNally, 1963.

Siegel, A. E., & Haas, M. B. The working mother: A review of research. *Child Development,* 1963, **34**, 513–542.

Smith, H. C. *An investigation of the attitudes of adolescent girls toward combining marriage, motherhood and a career.* (Doctoral dissertation, Columbia University) Ann Arbor, Mich.: University Microfilms, 1969, No. 69–8089.

Spiro, M. E. *Children of the kibbutz.* New York: Schocken Books, 1965.

Spitz, R. A. Hospitalism: An inquiry into the genesis of psychiatric conditions in early childhood. *Psychoanalytic Studies of the Child,* 1945, **1**, 53–74.

Stolz, L. M. Effects of maternal employment on children: Evidence from research. *Child Development,* 1960, **31**, 749–782.

Szolai, A. The multinational comparative time

budget: A venture in international research cooperation. *American Behavioral Scientist,* 1966, **10,** 1–31.

Tangri, S. S. Role innovation in occupational choice. Unpublished doctoral dissertation, University of Michigan, 1969.

Tizard, B., Cooperman, O., Joseph, A., & Tizard, J. Environmental effects on language development: A study of young children in long-stay residential nurseries. *Child Development,* 1972, **43,** 337–358.

U. S. Department of Labor, Women's Bureau. *Who are the working mothers?* (Leaflet 37) Washington, D. C.: U. S. Government Printing Office, 1972.

Vogel, S. R., Broverman, I. K., Broverman, D. M., Clarkson, F. E., & Rosenkrantz, P. S. Maternal employment and perception of sex roles among college students. *Developmental Psychology,* 1970, **3,** 384–391.

Von Mering, F. H. Professional and nonprofessional women as mothers. *Journal of Social Psychology,* 1955, **42,** 21–34.

Walker, K. E. How much help for working mothers?: The children's role. *Human Ecology Forum,* 1970, **1**(2), 13–15. (a)

Walker, K. E. Time-use patterns for household work related to homemakers' employment. Paper presented at the meeting of the Agricultural Outlook Conference. Washington, D. C., February 1970. (b)

Walker, K. E., & Woods, M. E. Time use for care of family members. (Use-of-Time Research Project, working paper 1) Unpublished manuscript, Cornell University, 1972.

Weil, M. W. An analysis of the factors influencing married women's actual or planned work participation. *American Sociological Review,* 1961, **26,** 91–96.

Winterbottom, M. R. The relation of need for achievement to learning experiences in independence and mastery. In J. W. Atkinson (Ed.), *Motives in fantasy, action, and society.* Princeton: Van Nostrand, 1958.

Woods, M. B. The unsupervised child of the working mother. *Developmental Psychology,* 1972, **6,** 14–25.

Wortis, R. P. The acceptance of the concept of the maternal role by behavioral scientists: Its effects on women. *American Journal of Orthopsychiatry,* 1971, **41,** 733–746.

Yarrow, L. J. Separation from parents during early childhood. In M. L. Hoffman & L. W. Hoffman (Eds.), *Review of child development research.* New York: Russell Sage Foundation, 1964.

Yarrow, M. R., Scott, P., deLeeuw, L., & Heinig, C. Child-rearing in families of working and nonworking mothers. *Sociometry,* 1962, **25,** 122–140.

Yudkin, S., & Holme, A. *Working mothers and their children.* London: Michael Joseph, 1963.

Zissis, C. A study of the life planning of 550 freshman women at Purdue University. *Journal of the National Association of Women Deans and Counselors,* 1964, **28,** 153–159.

## SUGGESTIONS FOR FURTHER READING

Breitveld, J. P. Mother and child in Africa—A brief conversation with Thomas Lambo. *Psychology Today,* September 1972, pp. 62–64. This short article about the African style of mothering helps provide perspective on the significance of mothering, or the lack of it, in our own society.

Hofer, M. A. Physiological responses of infant rats to separation from their mothers. *Science,* 1970, *168,* 871–873. The data derived from separating rat pups from their mothers are discussed in terms of the maternal-deprivation literature and the specific mechanisms disrupted by mother-infant separation.

Hoffman, L. W. Effects of maternal employment on the child—A review of the research. *Developmental Psychology,* 1974, *10*(2), 204–228. In this excellent review of research, findings concerning maternal employment are related to maternal role, child-rearing practices, concepts of maternal deprivation, children's achievement motivation, and academic performance.

Hogan, R. The terror of solitude. *Merrill-Palmer Quarterly,* 1975, *21*(1), 67–74. In this review of Bowlby's *Attachment and Loss,* Hogan considers his thesis that adult psychopathology often stems from deprivation of attachment figures, especially mothers, in infancy.

Rutter, M. *Maternal deprivation.* Baltimore: Penguin Books, 1972. This short volume affords a comprehensive evaluation of important theories and research relating to maternal deprivation.

Rutter, M. Maternal deprivation reconsidered. *Journal of Psychosomatic Research,* 1972, *16*(4), 241–250. Children were observed at successive stages in their growth in terms of maternal-deprivation factors. The syndrome of acute distress is probably due in part to disruption of the bonding process, but not necessarily to the mother. Certain emotional disabilities are perceived as the result of failure to establish attachments in the first three years of life.

**Effects of Maternal Employment on the Child**

Stayton, D. J., Ainsworth, M. D. S., & Main, M. B. Development of separation behavior in the first year of life: Protest, following, and greeting. *Developmental Psychology*, 1973, *9*(2), 213–225. In this longitudinal study of 26 infants, aged 15 to 24 weeks, separation and greeting responses were examined, such behaviors being plotted at 3-week intervals. Findings are discussed within the broad context of overall social development.

Stern, G. G., Caldwell, B. M., Hersher, L., Lipton, E. L., & Richmond, J. B. A factor analytic study of the mother-infant dyad. *Child Development*, 1969, *40*(1), 163–181. Ratings of 30 mothers and their 1-year-old infants yielded nine factors based on composites of maternal and child behaviors and personalities. The reciprocal nature of the interactions supports the contention that maternal behavior has definite consequences.

Tizard, B., & Rees, J. A comparison of the effects of adoption, restoration to the natural mother, and continued institutionalization on the cognitive development of four-year-old children. *Child Development*, 1974, *49*, 92–99. A study of 65 children, aged 4½ years, who had spent two to four years in an institution was undertaken in order to determine the effects of living in institutions and of maternal deprivation accruing to such experience.

# 8

## The Role of the Father

Early psychological literature focused on the mother, and studies of child-rearing practice were confined almost exclusively to the mother's relationship to the child. By contrast, the father was the anonymous member of the family. Where he was mentioned at all, he was conceded but small importance in child rearing. In recent years the father has won increasing regard, although he is still accorded far less attention by researchers than the mother.

## REASONS FOR RESEARCHERS' NEGLECT OF THE FATHER

There are various reasons for researchers' long neglect of the father. In Western society, at least, motherhood has been treasured, almost sanctified, whereas fatherhood has inspired relatively little emotion. In colonial times, the son learned a trade at his father's side; but after the industrial revolution, the father moved out of the home and left the boy's rearing to the mother. In consequence, for a long interim the father's role was largely vestigial; and the mother was deemed the key figure in the child's rearing.

For another thing, the stress on infancy as the critical period in human development accentuated the belief in maternal influence. Psychoanalytic emphasis on basic habit training in shaping personality placed the mother in a crucial position. Furthermore, the role of

mother is institutionalized, whereas the role of father is still somewhat ill-defined and diffuse.

In addition, girls, but not boys, are trained from early childhood for their parental role. The girl is inducted into the mother role through playing with dolls, assisting the mother at home, and taking domestic-science courses in school. No parallel training for fatherhood exists for boys. Not surprisingly, few boys seem able or willing to picture themselves as future fathers. Note also that child-care publications are directed almost wholly to mothers.

Finally, the mother is simply more accessible than the father to researchers. The factor of accessibility alone often accounts for emphasis on, or neglect of, any specific segment of the population. Similarly, note the relatively meager research relating to the upper class and to children of the pre-nursery-school age.

## PERSPECTIVE ON THE FATHER'S CURRENT ROLE

However, various influences are converging to change the trend and to give substance to the concept of fatherhood. Shorter workdays and longer vacations have restored the father to the bosom of his family, at least for greater segments of time. Coincidentally, he has done much to reorient the family's way of life. Nowadays he joins the family on vacations and outings; and he spends more time with his son at such pursuits as gardening and tinkering in the home workshop. Nevertheless, he spends less time showing his children his occupation.

The father's function in the family has been further modified by the increasing depolarization in sex roles, especially in the middle class. Since the male is now less insistently masculine than in former times, the father can acknowledge and develop his more nurturant traits. A by-product of this trend has been a more permissive attitude toward affectional relationships between father and child. Neighbors smile benignly on the father who plays with his children. In fact, modern society not only permits, but actually encourages, warm father-child relationships.

As a result, the psychological distance between father and child has narrowed. No longer does the father feel compelled to remain aloof, the awesome symbol of family power and knowledge. Younger, better-educated men, especially, are coming to take real pride in fatherhood. They refuse to perceive their role as unimportant and insist on fathering their children in more than the biological sense. They play with their children and help bathe and feed them, without threat to their masculine self-image.

Of course, there are exceptions to the trend. First- and second-generation Americans often follow the patriarchal patterns of the old country. Working-class men have been slower than their wives to adopt middle-class patterns of child rearing. Even in the same subculture, men's concepts of fatherhood may differ. A particular father may be uncertain of his own manhood and afraid to be loving toward his children.

The changing concept of fatherhood holds great significance for child rearing. The father's increasing contact with the small child is especially noteworthy since it holds considerable import for the child's future development. Establishing a sound basis for cognitive development, including creativity, for example, relates especially to paternal influence (Carlsmith, 1964). While the mother still spends far more time with the infant than does the father, there is no evidence that the impact

of influence is directly proportionate to the amount of association involved.

The father is conceded an especially important part in his children's acquisition of sex role. He serves as a sex-identification figure for his son, and as a mature male model to whom his daughter may relate. Perhaps this function is especially important now, when sex roles are becoming more confusing. In fact, the father may be even more important in determining the quality of the child's sex role than is the mother. The mother tends to treat both sexes as children, whereas the father more clearly differentiates his treatment of daughters and sons.

In addition, the father is often conceded the dominant role even in the woman's own bailiwick, the home. His income partially dictates where the family lives. His occupation largely determines the family's social status and, indirectly, who the children's friends will be. Furthermore, it is he who interprets the outer world to the family. As he discusses his job, or business, or politics, children pick up odd bits of information and gradually build concepts of the larger society. Besides, the father is typically more dominant and aggressive than the mother; hence, his relationships with the children, though fewer than the mother's, may have greater impact, at least for equivalent lengths of contact. When he speaks to the child, he expects to be heard.

Some of the father's influence is indirect. For example, the mother consults the father about decisions affecting the children, although she is the one who carries them out. Also, she involuntarily transmits to the children her own feelings of content or discontent as a wife. If the father fails to respect her sexual or affectional needs, or her requirements as a person, the mother unconsciously transmits feelings of anxiety and unhappiness to her children.

In one respect, the father's role has diminished, and it is well that it has. In pioneer days, the father was the harsh disciplinarian, the final authority who inspired fear in the small child. Certainly, the presence of such an awesome figure did little to increase the small child's self-confidence. The boy's view of his father as all-powerful might block the development of his own ego. The girl might easily come to fear males and reject them or, just as bad, to develop a feeling of inferiority to males and a dependent, submissive attitude toward them.

## STATUS OF RESEARCH ON THE FATHER

Such studies of the father's role as exist are still too few to represent a fair appraisal of his influence. A number of studies are concerned with the child's relationship to the father alone, or to the father as compared to the mother. In order to assess the father's role adequately, there must be more research and continuing research. Since his role is rapidly changing, findings may become quickly outdated. Furthermore, since it varies with the culture or subculture involved, overgeneralizations should be avoided. Few studies have performed the significant task of interviewing the father himself concerning his role.

Probably the most adequately treated area of father research concerns the father's impact on his son's problem behaviors, especially as related to delinquency. Much of this work has come from sociologists, who have contributed some of the most significant research concerning the father's role. Other important data have come from anthropologists, especially from their studies of primitive societies. The father has also received some attention in psychotherapy, in terms of his role both in causing and in treating children's disorders. Some of the best research has concerned the child's identification with the father.

A handful of studies relate to paternal deprivation, as opposed to the large number concerned with maternal deprivation. Research results on this topic are conflicting. On the one hand, various studies indicate that children of both sexes experience difficulties in personality development (Bigner, 1970). However, recent investigations report no significant differences

in sex-role preference or masculine behaviors between boys with or without fathers in the home (Sutton-Smith, Rosenberg, & Landy, 1968; Thomes, 1968). Other male siblings and peers may assume part of the fathering role where younger father-absent children are concerned. Indeed, research indicates that older siblings may play a significant role in assisting with the young boy's sex-role development by serving as male role-models (Bigner, 1970; Santrock, 1970).

Other questions have received even less attention. What should the father's role ideally be? How will women's increasing liberation affect the father's role? How do fathers perceive their own role? How can boys be prepared more effectively for their role as fathers?

In the first selection that follows, David Lynn outlines critical issues relating to the father's role in modern Western society. It is from his book *The Father: His Role in Child Development,* which treats the father both in cultural perspective and in the father-child relationship. In the second selection, Jerry Bigner summarizes the most significant research on the topic and derives certain significant implications.

## REFERENCES

Bigner, J. J. *The effects of sibling influence on sex-role development in young children.* Unpublished doctoral dissertation, Florida State University, 1970.

Carlsmith, L. Effect of early father absence on scholastic aptitude. *Harvard Educational Review,* 1964, *34,* 3–21.

Santrock, J. W. Paternal absence, sex typing, and identification. *Developmental Psychology,* 1970, *2,* 264–272.

Sutton-Smith, B., Rosenberg, B. G., & Landy, F. Father absence effects in families of different sibling composition. *Child Development,* 1968, *39,* 1213–1222.

Thomes, M. M. Children with absent fathers. *Journal of Marriage and the Family,* 1968, *30,* 89–96.

# Fathers and America in Transition

## David B. Lynn

### FATHER ABSENCE AND DETACHMENT BECAUSE OF WORK DEMANDS

One of the factors eroding the father's position in the family is the nature of work today in urban-industrial societies. Fathers now work away from the home, so that a degree of father absence is taken for granted. This has not been true throughout history, nor is it true in all cultures today (exceptions are the craftsman and the farmer on a small plot); but in our society the absence of the father through death or divorce can be considered simply an extreme on the prevailing continuum of father absence.

First, consider fathers who are executives, scientists, high-level technicians, professors—the "executive-professional men." Second, consider unskilled to skilled laborers—the "working man." Do these two groups differ in the degree of father absence?

Ours is popularly considered to be the age of leisure, and for the worker there is validity to that belief. Ironically, work hours have been increasing for the executive-professional man as the workingman's hours have been decreasing. The executive-professional does not punch a time clock—but neither is he expected to limit his workday to eight hours. Since the supply of executive-professional men is insufficient to meet the expanding needs of an increasingly complex society, the demands on his time have been growing, and so has his workweek.

Harold Wilensky's (1961) study of working hours showed that a growing minority of urban males in the United States usually work 55 hours a week or more. At least a third of the lawyers, professors, small proprietors, and middle managers in Wilensky's sample worked that long. He found that some of the men in the upper strata worked many extra hours, week after week, reaching a truly startling lifetime total (Wilensky, 1967). The time of many executive-professional men is absorbed not only in work but also in transit, since they often live in the suburbs and work in the city. A typical day for one of these men might start before the children rise, with a hurried breakfast followed by a tedious trip to the office, either by commuter train or by a tense and frustrating drive on a crowded freeway. He may arrive home, worn from work and a tiresome commute, briefcase in hand, so late that the younger children are already in bed and the older ones fully occupied in their own affairs. He is denied the leisurely family dinner, with shared experiences. After dining with his wife or alone, he may work on material brought from the office.

This typical day may actually underrepresent the extent to which work absorbs the executive-professional. He may also work weekends or, if not, may flee the tensions of the job (and, incidentally, the family) to relax with tennis or golf partners, recuperating for the demands of the coming week. In addition, he is frequently away from home on business trips. It is not, however, his vocation alone that absorbs his energies and draws the professional-executive man from his family. He is frequently active in civic affairs, from a genuine sense of responsibility.

Other working fathers must also frequently be absent from the family. The salesman must often travel, the serviceman may have duty overseas, and the small businessman spends long hours struggling to become established.

A positive personal commitment to work generally declines in importance as one descends the status hierarchy, because the nature of one's job loses intrinsic appeal. Hence work at the lower socioeconomic levels entails limitations in income and life style but allows more time that can be devoted to one's family. Even so, some workers let their job separate them from their family. Legitimate economic need or the seduction of the credit economy entraps families into debts that can be paid only through overtime or "moonlighting." Moreover, although the working man is less likely to devote his spare time to civic activities, it is traditional for him to spend a night out with "the boys." Also, with some men the stultifying routine of the factory and the deadening journey to and from work cause such reactions as aggression or apathy at home, alienating them from their family.

Working men are much less likely than professional-executive fathers to see child rearing as part of their parental duties. They are more likely to regard children as the wife's domain, almost as though the children belonged to her, not to them. Although the working father's rhetoric of authoritarianism may be strong, and he is likely to be punitive, the professional-executive father usually possesses more genuine authority in the home. The working father is less likely to exert family leadership or even to support the mother's authority.

The activities that working men engage in may be more appealing to little boys of all classes than professional-executive activities. All little boys enjoy watching carpenters, demolition crews, automobile mechanics, and firemen, and they admire the things such men do. The professional-executive father's career, in contrast, may not be understood or appreciated by a small child but becomes increasingly valued as he grows older. As he matures, the working man's son's identification with his father may weaken, and he may become disenchanted with the family (Benson, 1968).

Although the possibilities for father detachment are real, many professional-executive and working fathers can and do balance work and family involvement. Moreover, many craftsmen and farmers on small plots (occupations characteristic of a previous era), although physically present with the family, may lack the time, energy, or motivation to become involved. Work serving as an escape from family hassles is not new.

Of course, our pluralistic country is composed of families of varied cultural and ethnic heritage, and the roles that fathers play vary accordingly. These diverse patterns are treated in a later chapter.

## FRAGMENTATION OF THE FAMILY BECAUSE OF SEPARATE INTERESTS

It is not simply the absence or preoccupation of the father, however, that weakens his impact on his children. The family is fragmented as never before by the disparate interests of its members. A youth culture, more compelling in America than in other countries, attracts even young children away from the family toward peers who share their separate interests and values. Mother, too, especially in the middle class, may be absorbed in her own social and community responsibilities. These diverse interests may leave a family little in common to talk about when they are together. The result may be a home environment that dulls the father's effectiveness. But diverse interests need not inevitably fragment the family. In loving families with genuine involvement in one another, diverse interests give them more to talk about and enrich their lives.

## THE KNOWLEDGE EXPLOSION AND THE RAPIDITY OF CHANGE

Another development sabotaging the father's influence in the family is the knowledge explosion. The growth of knowledge is now so rapid that even the most intelligent and intellectually oriented man cannot stay abreast of all that is taught his children in the public school or absorbed through television. His ignorance of that which is new undermines his traditional role as the fountain of knowledge in the home. It is hard for a man to be a convincing source of knowledge when he cannot help his third-grade child with the "new math," does not know the names of the emerging African nations, and is less knowledgeable of space technology than his elementary-school child.

The knowledge explosion is the source of ever-accelerating change in virtually every facet of the culture. With the rapidity of technological change and innovation comes a concomitant revolution of values. Consequently, every adult is living in a transformed, unfamiliar world, something like a stranger in a foreign land. The world is not the world he knew as a child. Like a foreign country, it may be exciting and invigorating—even awe-inspiring—but it isn't comfortable; it isn't home. To youth, however, the contemporary world *is* home, and they are oriented in it. It is therefore not very surprising that the natives (youth) should feel a superiority to the foreigners (adults), who don't know their way around. A roughly analogous situation was that of the children of immigrants in the nineteenth and early twentieth centuries, who generally felt shame for parents tied to old-world values. They turned to their peers, who shared with them the values of the new world. For the youth of today, as well as for the immigrants' children, the values transmitted from the past seem of little utility. Youth are ''where it's at''; their parents aren't. Something is happening, but Mr. Jones does not know what it is (Dylan, ''Ballad of a Thin Man,'' 1965).

Some consequences of the knowledge explosion may not directly devalue the father for the child but may undermine a man's confidence in himself and thus indirectly have the same result. The knowledge explosion may produce so much that is new in a man's vocation that he feels the constant threat of falling hopelessly behind. His diminished boldness and loss of certainty may be subtly perceived by his child and leave him vulnerable, contributing to his insecurity in the father role.

Because of the knowledge explosion, the almost universal tribal threat of displacement by younger men occurs earlier in a man's life than before. The almost inevitable hostility toward younger men in response to this threat may generalize to a man's own son. This condition is exacerbated when a youth scorns the achievements of his father's generation and rejects his way of life—for example, by demeaning the value of traditional education, hard work, and material well-being and by living without plans for the future in unconventional and disordered quarters with unconventional relationships among the residents. This contempt for older achievements and values is the ultimate repudiation of his father's way of life and can only damage a father's effectiveness.

## THE CHANGING NATURE OF SEX ROLES

Another development that undermines a man's confidence, and thus indirectly his relationship with his children, is the changing nature of sex roles. Assertion of women's rights to egalitarian relationships with men threatens traditional male dominance, often eroding men's confidence. Regardless of the justice of the demands and the more wholesome relationships between the sexes that should obtain once equality is achieved, the transition period is stressful for many men.

There is not only a vocational threat and a threatened loss of authority in the home but a sexual threat as well. With sexual emancipation, women, as well as men, feel entitled to sexual fulfillment. In our recent past a woman was not expected to enjoy sex; rather, she was expected to submit passively for her husband's pleasure, not her own. Although sexual relations with such a passive partner may not have produced sexual ecstasy, they certainly did not challenge a man's prowess. Now, with women demanding equal sexual satisfaction, a man is challenged. There is now the underlying threat that, if he does not satisfy her, she may reject him; even if this is not a threat, he may lose self-esteem because of his own sense of failure.

## DIVORCE

Another social development combines with those already mentioned to tax the stability of marriage further: the belief in the right to personal fulfillment, in the justice of terminating relationships that fail to provide fulfillment, and in the immorality of maintaining those that do not. This belief runs counter to the value that traditionally supported the institution of marriage—''for better or for worse, till death do us part.'' Without arguing the merits of either value, it is obvious that the latter contributes to the continuance of marriage and the former to its breakup. Within the present value system, a person whose mate is unstimulating emotionally, sexually, or intellectually might feel completely justified in terminating the marriage and guilty for prolonging it.

Another condition that may contribute to the instability of marriage is the lack of permanence and stability in the culture as a whole (if we assume that lack of permanence in one sphere discourages permanence in another). Few people live as adults in the neighborhoods where they grew up; those who do may find that childhood friends have left and the neighborhood has been transformed.

Friendships formed in adulthood are abandoned as we move from place to place seeking vocational advancement. Perhaps it bolsters a marriage to remain in touch with the people and the environment that surrounded the couple at the time of their marriage—a condition that is rare today. In addition, perhaps we grow accustomed to change in a changing world, and marriage becomes simply another sphere of life in which change is possible or even probable.

The extremely high divorce rate should not lull us into the comfortable assumption that since it is frequent it could not possibly be tragic. One of the obvious consequences of divorce is that, in all but the rare instances in which the father is awarded custody, divorce separates the child from his father, a condition that may be compensated for to some extent by visits of varied length and frequency. Even so, a child may feel somehow responsible for the breakup, angry toward one or both parents, rejected by one or both, or torn by conflicting loyalties to both. In addition, the child often has the problem of adjusting to a stepfather, with the likelihood of a conflict of loyalties between stepfather and real father and between mother and stepfather. The child may also find it difficult to adjust to his father's new wife.

A father's resentment against paying child support may complicate his relationship with his child. He may hope that his former wife will remarry quickly so that he can stop "shelling out" money for alimony. Child support may be such a financial burden that he cannot remarry; he resents the children for it and feels guilty about his resentment. If he does remarry, there may be a strained and artificial quality in acting as father to his new wife's children.

If a father lives near his former family, he may become a "weekend father" (Klemesrud, 1969) with visiting privileges, who takes his children on the weekend to playgrounds, parks, and museums. This period, which should be reserved for reacquaintance, tenderness, affection, and reassurance of mutual love, may be turned into a frenetic search for new and exciting diversions (helicopter rides, bay cruises) to compensate for underlying emotions of resentment, guilt, competition with the mother for the child's love, and fear that the child will report boredom back to the mother.

In contrasting our current family problems with those of the past, it should be noted that, as the divorce rate has gone up, the death rate has gone down. More men are now separated from their children by divorce but fewer by death.

## HOPE FOR THE FATHER-CHILD RELATIONSHIP

The contemporary social revolution has some bright features that may have positive implications for the father-child relationship. There is a resurgence of humanism accompanied by greater self-awareness, increased sophistication concerning interpersonal relationships, a desire for affectionate interaction, and much good will. Many fathers are more genuinely motivated to meet the individualistic needs of their children, are less likely to impose their own ambitions and hopes on their children, are less authoritarian and arbitrary, and are much less austere and unapproachable than fathers of the recent past. For these reasons their anguish is particularly acute when social forces conspire to sabotage their best intentions. Perhaps these underlying positive values, coupled with anguish over failure to actualize them, can be developed as motivating forces for discovering more compatible social structures from which satisfactory father-child relationships could emerge.

## SUMMARY

Developments that lessen the impact of the father on the family include father absence and detachment stemming from work demands, fragmentation of the family stemming from separate interests, the knowledge explosion and the rapidity of change, the changing nature of sex roles, and divorce.

It is easy to lose perspective on the father by focusing too narrowly on contemporary problems. It may help to turn from the human condition altogether and examine paternal behavior in other animals. Following that, a look at the evolution of the family from man's early origins and at fathers in other cultures will prepare the way for further exploration of the current scene.

## REFERENCES

Benson, L. *Fatherhood: A sociological perspective.* New York: Random House, 1968.

Dylan, B. Ballad of a thin man. M. Whitmark & Sons (ASCAP). In B. Dylan's record album, *Highway 61 Revisited*. Columbia Album CL 2389, 1965.

Klemesrud, J. Pride, guilt drive most "weekend fathers" to work too hard at entertaining their children. *The Sacramento Bee,* June 3, 1969. (New York Times News Service.)

Wilensky, H. L. The uneven distribution of leisure: The impact of economic growth on "free time." *Social Problems,* 1961, *9,* 32–56.

Wilensky, H. L. Work as a social problem. In H. S. Becker (Ed.), *Social problems: A modern approach.* New York: Wiley, 1967.

# Fathering: Research and Practice Implications

## Jerry J. Bigner

There are several approaches concerning the role of the father in the family. These include: (a) the family unit, having developed in accordance with man's own evolution, became a predominantly monogamous unit in which the father played a significant role (Westermarck, 1921); (b) the role of fatherhood became a social invention in which the father provided for the nurturance of both wife and children (Mead, 1949); and (c) the family organization imposed on the male the duties of family life as retribution for sexual rights with the wife and defined his role as the father to be peripheral, temporary, and relatively immaterial. (Klineberg, 1954) Goode (1964) has cited these complex socio-sexual variables as the principle factors which bind the male to the family grouping.

Regardless of these theoretical postulations concerning the reasons *why* the father remains in the family group, there is a dearth of data available in the literature concerning fathering *per se* and the isolation of those behavioral variables which make the role take on its significance. In contrast, there is a relative wealth of data concerning the importance of mothering and its implications for subsequent psychosocial functioning in life. The works of Spitz (1949), Bowlby (1951), Harlow (1958), and others have pointed out significant variables which emphasize the necessity of the development of a close mother-child relationship in the early years of the child's life.

Reprinted from *Family Coordinator,* 1970, *19*(4), 357–362. Copyright 1970 by National Council on Family Relations. Reprinted by permission.

## CONCEPTIONS OF FATHERING

Traditionally, the concept of the father has been that of provider and head of the family group. Waller and Hill (1951) aptly describe his role as a parent within this framework:

"Because the father knew what the child should become, he did not seek to understand the child as an individual; he prescribed the activities which were for the child's good, and he placed emphasis on giving things to and doing things for the child. He was interested in the child's accepting and attaining goals established exclusively by himself, and he found satisfaction in the child's owing him a debt which could be best repaid by obedience and by bringing honor to the family." (Waller and Hill, 1951, 411)

With the shift from a relatively simple agrarian to a complex industrial society, distinct changes have occurred in the conceptions of masculinity, femininity, parenthood, and fatherhood in particular. The change in the conceptualization of fatherhood has been investigated and labeled as developmental in nature. (Duvall, 1946; Elder, 1949) Its elements are in sharp contrast to the traditional concept of fatherhood. This view has been defined best by one of Elder's research subjects:

"A good father is interested in what his child does, helps his child to be interested in what the father does, and wants to help the child attain his own goals." (Waller and Hill, 1951, 415)

The difficulties inherent in these two conceptualizations of fatherhood are particularly evident in the case of men who are foreign-born, sons of immigrants, or members of lower socio-economic classes. Because they have acquired an internalized, traditional concept of fatherhood, they feel that the man who loves his sons and demonstrates his affections openly to them is soft and non-masculine. In order to counteract these feelings and to conform to cultural ideals, these men become excessively strict and harsh in interacting with their sons with the result being the development of "bullyish" traits in the sons. (Bartemeier, 1953; Tasch, 1957)

Schvaneveldt, Fryer, and Ostler (1970) have taken a somewhat divergent approach in seeking to assess the relative "goodness" or "badness" of parents. Focusing on interviews with middle-class nursery-school children, girls more frequently perceived a "good" father as one who displayed affection to others, while a "bad" father was one who disciplined, failed in domestic matters, and was emotionally cold. Boys more frequently mentioned a "good" father as one who played with them and a "bad" father as one who disciplined them.

It may be said that whatever teaching the father does for his children is accomplished more by example than by precept. This contention is supported by the work of Stolz, et al., (1954) who have shown that many fathers feel inadequate in carrying out their prescribed roles, especially in such areas as discipline, companionship, and instruction of character traits to their children. This feeling is accentuated in fathers who have been separated from their children for a relatively long period of time, particularly during the child's preschool years.

Aberle and Naegele (1952) have argued that the middle-class father has developed a set of values and attitudes, based on his occupational role, which serves not only to shape the expectations held for his children but also by which he evaluates their behavior. When fathers said they had "no plans" for their sons in regard to their future occupation, it was implied that any occupation was suitable provided it was a middle-class occupation. On the other hand, a majority of fathers expected their daughters to marry while considering a career only as a possibility. In evaluating their school-age sons' present behavior, it was found that fathers tended to focus primarily on those general character traits conducive to success in a middle-class occupational role, e.g., the development of initiative, responsibility, etc. Furthermore, fathers expressed more concern over male than female first-borns, and even less over later-born females. Thus, it was concluded that fathers' attitudes and expectations differed toward sons and daughters.

# RESEARCH ON FATHERING

There are only two areas which have received research attention concerning the role of fathering: (a) the effects of the father-son relationship on masculine development; and (b) the effects of father-absence on sex-role identification in boys and on family functioning. Even more significantly, there have been no studies dealing with specific behaviors which might commonly be thought to constitute the concept of fathering *per se*. McCandless (1967) has suggested that fathers are unwilling perhaps to cooperate in research studies due to occupation commitments. Seeley, *et al.,* (1956) also have suggested that fathers view male child development and research experts "as inadequate men who have not been able to make the grade in the *really* masculine world." (Seeley, *et al.,* 1956, 194)

Essentially, it has been found that sex-role development in boys is facilitated by a warm, rewarding, nurturant father who openly expresses interest in his son's development of aggressiveness and other culturally prescribed masculine traits. (Mussen and Distler, 1959; Biller and Borstelmann, 1967) For the most part, studies investigating this topic have not utilized actual father-son interaction measures nor corresponding correlations between the masculinity of the father and of the son.

Kagan (1958) has delineated three conditions necessary for the establishment of an optimally strong masculine identification in boys: (a) the model (father) must be perceived as nurturant to the child; (b) the model must be perceived as being in command of desired goals, e.g., power, love from others, and as being competent in tasks which the child regards as important; and (c) the child must perceive some basis of similarity of external attributes between himself and the model. Kagan (1964) has stated that the child, whose male identification model exhibits traditional masculine behavior, does not perceive a great degree of discrepancy between his own behavior and that of his peers' upon school entrance as does the child who identifies with a father who does not exhibit such sex-role behavior. Thus, the value of having a traditionally-oriented father who manifests "appropriate" sex-role behavior is considered by Kagan to be more of a necessity than a disadvantage to the child.

The lack of data on fathering is accentuated particularly in the area of father-daughter interaction as illustrated by a comprehensive review of the literature by Biller. (1970)

It has been found that father-absence occurs more frequently among lower-class families and among Negro families in all social classes. (Mischel, 1961; Deutsch and Brown, 1964) Studies have shown that father-absence produces a number of behavior problems as well as deleterious effects on intellectual and personality development. However, there appears to be some confusion at the present time concerning the effects of father absence on the male child and on family functioning. Psychological studies have tended to find that father absence produces deleterious effects while sociological studies have tended to find no such effects on children's development.

It is commonly held by exponents of Freudian theory that the absence of the father during the preschool and middle-childhood years predisposes the boy to sexual inversion. (Neubauer, 1960) Data from more recent research appears to support the possibility of the presence of critical periods in masculine development particularly during the early childhood years. Money (1965) and Hampson (1965) have concluded that sex-role concepts appear to be difficult to change after the third year of life. The actual timing of the father's absence from the family appears to be a crucial variable in that subjects have been reported to be less masculine if the father's absence occurred during the first four years of life. (Hetherington, 1966; Biller, 1969) The future difficulties experienced in sex-role identification by boys whose fathers were absent in infancy has been supported by crosscultural data presented by Whiting, Kluckhohn, and Anthony (1958) and Burton and Whiting. (1961) These studies have found that many societies exclude the father from interaction with sons during infancy, emphasizing instead a close mother-son relationship. Masculine behavior became strongly reinforced during preadolescence and adolescence, primarily through initiation rite experiences. The resulting difficulty was a "sexual identification conflict" due to the repression of the feminine identification.

The relative feminization of males as a result of the absence of the father from the family setting has been one of the more prominent findings of studies conducted in previous years. This general finding has been cited by numerous authors who have presented data showing that both male and female children experience deleterious personality development due not only to the father's absence but also to changes in the mother's shift to more authoritarian childrearing patterns. (Sears, Pintler, and Sears, 1946; Sears, 1951; Stolz, *et al.,* 1954; Lynn and Sawry, 1959) More recent investigations have reported the finding of no significant differences in sex-role preference or in masculine behaviors between children with and without the presence of the father in the home. (Miller, 1961; Greenstein, 1966; Barclay and Cusumano, 1967; Biller, 1968; Herzog and Sudia, 1968; Sutton-Smith, Rosenberg, and Landy, 1968; Thomes, 1968) It should be noted, however, that discrepancies in these findings may be attributed to the methodological and theoretical differences between the various investigations.

## IMPLICATIONS

Nash (1965) has taken the view that Western society may be characterized as "mother-centered" in its childrearing approaches and that the rearing of children is considered to be largely a female responsibility. Since the mother does play an important role during the early stages of a child's development and some men are somewhat hesitant to enter into this relationship, mothers perhaps can aid their children's development by creating situations in which the father is encouraged to exercise his role. This might be accomplished through specific tasks which would be the sole responsibility of the father. An example would be bathing the children. In addition, bedtime

schedules can be easily arranged so that the father can be allowed at least some time during the day to be with his children.

A man usually considers his occupation to be the focal point of his fathering behavior. An active attempt on the part of both parents and teachers to increase children's understanding of just what the father does during his working hours would be helpful in developing a concept of this aspect of the father's role. Preschool and elementary programs should include teaching units on fathers' occupations which include field trips to see fathers actively involved in their work. This type of unit may be tied in easily with units on introducing children to the "community helpers," e.g., policemen, doctors, mailmen, etc.

The father's role in the sex education of his children should be emphasized as well since this is an important area in which the father can truly exercise his role. Parent and family life educators can aid parents by offering more specific avenues of instruction on the "hows" and "whys" of this area of fathering. Klein (1968) has provided an excellent source for helping fathers in this manner.

Community programs as Big Brothers of America, Boys' Clubs, YMCA Indian Guide, Scouts, and athletic programs provide numerous opportunities for the active involvement of boys and their fathers or father substitutes. As research has suggested, these programs could aid in shaping the young boy's personality development as early as the second or third year.

Since preschool aged boys who lack consistent father-figures have been found to seek attention from almost any available male, it would appear that preschool and elementary programs would achieve a greater impact on boys if more male teachers were involved in all areas of curriculum. (Ostrovsky, 1959; McCandless, 1967) Preschool programs such as Project Head Start could aid father-absent children in their intellectual and personality development by employing male personnel. It is possible that their presence would complement and complete the "enriched environment" which is provided by such programs.

The encouragement of older male siblings and peers to take an active role in fathering behavior appears to be a plausible solution for younger father-absent children. Recent research has shown that an older sibling has an important role in aiding a child's sex-role development by acting as an additional role model. (Bigner, 1970; Santrock, 1970)

There are many descriptions available of therapeutic programs and techniques for working with children of father-absent homes. (Meerloo, 1956; Wylie and Delgado, 1959; Neubauer, 1960; Forrest, 1967; Stoller, 1968) In addition, therapeutic groups such as Parents Without Partners have served to help many mothers and children from father-absent homes. (Freudenthal, 1959; Schlesinger, 1966; Burgess, 1970)

The assumption made frequently, implicitly or explicitly, that the mother has the major effect on the child's development and that the father's role has dubious importance is being tested gradually by researchers. Research has shown that the father's greatest impact on his children occurs primarily in those areas involving psychosexual, personality, social, and intellectual development. In essence, current research has suggested that there is more to the parent-child relationship than that involving the mother and the child.

# REFERENCES

Aberle, David F. and Kasper D. Naegele. Middle-class Father's Occupational Role and Attitudes toward Children. *American Journal of Orthopsychiatry, 1952,* **22,** 366–378.

Barclay, A. G. and D. Cusumano. Father-Absence, Cross-Sex Identity, and Field-Dependent Behavior in Male Adolescents. *Child Development, 1967,* **38,** 243–250.

Bartemeier, Leo. The Contribution of the Father to the Mental Health of the Family. *American Journal of Psychiatry,* 1953, **110,** 277–280.

Bigner, Jerry J. The Effects of Sibling Influence on Sex-Role Development in Young Children. Unpublished Doctoral Dissertation, Florida State University, 1970.

Biller, Henry B. A Note on Father-Absence and Masculine Development in Lower Class Negro and White Boys. *Child Development,* 1968, **39,** 1003–1006.

Biller, Henry B. Father-Absence, Maternal Encouragement and Sex-Role Development in Kindergarten Age Boys. *Child Development,* 1969, **40,** 539–546.

Biller, Henry B. and Lloyd J. Borstelmann. Masculine Development: An Integrative Review. *Merrill-Palmer Quarterly,* 1967, **13,** 253–294.

Biller, Henry B. and Stephan D. Weiss. The Father-Daughter Relationship and the Personality Development of the Female. *Journal of Genetic Psychology,* 1970, **116,** 79–94.

Bowlby, John. *Maternal Care and Mental Health.* Monograph Series No. 2. Geneva: World Health Organization, 1951.

Burgess, Jane K. The Single-Parent Family: A Social and Sociological Problem. *The Family Coordinator,* 1970, **19,** 137–144.

Burton, Roger V. and John W. M. Whiting. The Absent Father and Cross-Sex Identity. *Merrill-Palmer Quarterly,* 1961, **7,** 85–95.

Deutsch, Martin and B. Brown. Social Influences in Negro-White Intelligence Differences. *Journal of Social Issues,* 1964, **18,** 24–35.

Duvall, Evelyn M. Conceptions of Parenthood. *American Journal of Sociology,* 1946, **52,** 193–203.

Elder, Rachel A. Traditional and Developmental Characteristics of Fatherhood. *Marriage and Family Living,* 1949, **11,** 98–100, 106.

Forrest, Tess. The Paternal Roots of Male Character Development. *Psychoanalytic Review,* 1967, **54,** 51–68.

Freudenthal, Kurt. Problems of the One-Parent Family. *Social Work,* 1959, **4,** 44–48.

Goode, William J. *The Family.* Englewood Cliffs, N.J.: Prentice-Hall, 1964.

Greenstein, Jules M. Father Characteristics and Sex-Typing. *Journal of Personality and Social Psychology,* 1966, **3,** 271–277.

Hampson, John L. Determinants of Psycho-sexual Orientation. In F. A. Beach (Ed.), *Sex and Behavior.* New York: Wiley, 1965.

Harlow, Harry F. The Nature of Love. *American Psychologist,* 1958, **13,** 213–220.

Herzog, Elizabeth and Cecelia E. Sudia. Fatherless Homes: A Review of Research. *Children,* 1968, **15,** 177–182.

Hetherington, E. Mavis. Effects of Paternal Absence on Sex-Typed Behaviors in Negro and White Preadolescent Males. *Journal of Personality and Social Psychology,* 1966, **4,** 87–91.

Kagan, Jerome. The Concept of Identification. *Psychological Review,* 1958, **65,** 296–305.

Kagan, Jerome. Acquisition and Significance of Sex Typing and Sex Role Identity. In M. Hoffman and L. Hoffman (Eds.), *Review of Child Development Research,* Vol. 1. New York: Russell Sage Foundation, 1964, 137–168.

Klein, Ted. *The Father's Book.* New York: Ace Publishing Corporation, 1968.

Klineberg, Otto. *Social Psychology.* (Rev. ed.) New York: Holt, 1954.

Lynn, David B. and William L. Sawry. The Effects of Father Absence on Norwegian Boys and Girls. *Journal of Abnormal and Social Psychology,* 1959, **59,** 258–262.

McCandless, Boyd R. *Children: Behavior and Development.* (2nd ed.) New York: Holt, Rinehart, Winston, 1967.

Mead, Margaret. *Male and Female.* New York: Morrow, 1949.

Meerloo, Joost A. M. The Father Cuts the Cord: The Role of the Father as Initial Transference Figure. *American Journal of Psychotherapy,* 1956, **10,** 471–480.

Miller, Barbara B. Effects of Father Absence and Mother's Evaluation of Father on the Socialization of Adolescent Boys. Unpublished Doctoral Dissertation, Columbia University, 1961.

Mischel, William. Father-Absence and Delay of Gratification. *Journal of Abnormal and Social Psychology,* 1961, **63,** 116–124.

Money, John. Psychosexual Identification. In J. Money (Ed.), *Sex Research: New Developments.* New York: Holt, Rinehart, Winston, 1965.

Mussen, Paul and Luther Distler. Masculinity, Identification, and Father-Son Relationships. *Journal of Abnormal and Social Psychology,* 1959, **59,** 350–352.

Nash, John. The Father in Contemporary Culture and Current Psychological Literature. *Child Development,* 1965, **36,** 261–297.

Neubauer, Peter B. The One-Parent Child and His Oedipal Development. In *Psychoanalytic Studies of the Child,* Vol. 15. New York: International Universities Press, 1960, 286–309.

Ostrovsky, Everett S. *Father to the Child: Case Studies of the Experiences of a Male Teacher.* New York: Putnam, 1959.

Santrock, John W. Paternal Absence, Sex Typing, and Identification. *Developmental Psychology,* 1970, **2,** 264–272.

Schlesinger, Benjamin. The One-Parent Family: An Overview. *Family Life Coordinator,* 1966, **15,** 133–137.

Schvaneveldt, Jay D., Marguerite Fryer, and Renee Ostler. Concepts of "Badness" and "Goodness" of Parents as Perceived by Nursery School Children. *The Family Coordinator,* 1970, **19,** 98–103.

Sears, Pauline S. Doll-Play Aggression in Normal Young Children: Influences of Age, Sex, Sibling Status, and Father's Absence. *Psychological Monographs,* 1951, **65,** Entire No. 323.

Sears, Robert R., Margaret H. Pintler, and Pauline S. Sears. Effects of Father Separation on Preschool Children's Doll Play Aggression. *Child Development,* 1946, **17,** 219–243.

Seeley, John R., R. Alexander Sim, and Elizabeth W. Loosley. *Crestwood Heights: A Study of the Culture of Suburban Life.* New York: Basic Books, 1956.

Spitz, Rene. The Role of Ecological Factors in the Emotional Development in Infancy. *Child Development,* 1949, **20,** 145–155.

Stolz, Lois M., *et. al. Father Relations of War Born Children.* Stanford: Stanford University Press, 1954.

Sutton-Smith, Brian, B. G. Rosenberg, and Frank Landy. Father Absence Effects in Families of Different Sibling Composition. *Child Development,* 1968, **39,** 1213–1222.

Tasch, Ruth J. Interpersonal Perception of Fathers and Mothers. *Journal of Genetic Psychology,* 1957, **87,** 50–65.

Thomes, Mary M. Children with Absent Fathers. *Journal of Marriage and the Family,* 1968, **30,** 88–96.

Waller, Willard and Reuben Hill. *The Family: A Dynamic Interpretation* (Rev. ed.) New York: Holt, Rinehart, Winston, 1951.

Westermarck, Edvard A. *History of Human Marriage.* New York: MacMillan, 1921.

Whiting, John W. M., Richard Kluckhohn, and Albert Anthony. The Function of Male Initiation Ceremonies at Puberty. In E. E. Maccoby, T. M. Newcomb, and E. L. Hartley (Eds.), *Readings in Social Psychology.* New York: Holt, 1959, 359–370.

Wylie, Howard I. and Rafael A. Delgado. A Pattern of Mother-Son Relationship Involving the Absence of the Father. *American Journal of Orthopsychiatry,* 1959, **29,** 644–649.

## SUGGESTIONS FOR FURTHER READING

Aldous, J. Children's perceptions of adult role assignment: Father absence, class, race and sex influences. *Journal of Marriage and the Family,* 1972, *34*(1), 55–65. In order to determine their perceptions of adult role assignments, low-income preschool white and black children from father-absent and father-present homes were interviewed. A similar comparison was made of middle- and lower-class preschool father-present children's adult role perceptions.

Biller, H. B. Father absence and the personality development of the male child. *Developmental Psychology,* 1970, *2*, 181–201. The effect of father absence on the son was found to depend on various factors, including sociocultural milieu, time and length of father's absence, availability of surrogate models, and maternal behaviors.

Biller, H. B. *Father, child, and sex role.* Lexington, Mass.: Heath Lexington Books, 1971. Research relevant to the father's influence on his children's personality development is examined and interpreted. Although some of the author's conclusions are frankly speculative, this book provides an excellent summation of research on the topic.

Biller, H. B., & Weiss, S. D. The father-daughter relationship and the personality development of the female. *Journal of Genetic Psychology,* 1970, *116,* 79–93. Research is reviewed concerning the father's influence on his daughter.

Davids, L. Foster fatherhood: The untapped resource. *Child Welfare,* 1973, *52,* 100–107. The competencies and incompetencies of foster fathers are analyzed and suggestions made for improving the quality of foster fatherhood.

Greenberg, M., & Morris, N. Engrossment: The new-born's impact upon the father. *American Journal of Orthopsychiatry,* 1974, *44,* 520–531. This study was designed to determine the impact of the first newborn upon the father. In clinical interviews specific aspects of the developing bond between father and newborn were observed and underlying reasons for such development hypothesized.

Hetherington, E. M. Effects of father absence on personality development in adolescent daughters. *Developmental Psychology,* 1972, *7,* 313–326. The effects on adolescent daughters of father absence, because of death or divorce, are reported and analyzed.

Kopf, K. E. Family variables and school adjustment of eighth-grade father-absent boys. *Family Coordinator,* 1970, *19*(2), 145–150. In this study of father-absent boys, their school adjustment related positively to their participation in household tasks and to the mother's positive or neutral attitude to the father. Adjustment was unrelated to degree of father absence, age of child at separation, son's ordinal position, sex of siblings, or prior father-son relationships.

Leonard, J. The fathering instinct. *Ms.,* November 1974, pp. 52–53; 56; 112. A writer/editor offers a delightful account of his own experiences in fathering and taking care of two small children.

Pedersen, F. A., & Robson, K. S. Father participation in infancy. *American Journal of Orthopsychiatry,* 1969, *39,* 466–472. This study, undertaken to define normal father-infant relationships, revealed a wide variation among a homogeneous middle-class group. No factor proved consistent for infants of both sexes. Father relations were revealed as more significant than previous research would suggest.

Radin, N. Father-child interaction and the intellectual functioning of four-year-old boys. *Developmental Psychology,* 1972, *6,* 353–361. Twenty-one lower-class and 21 middle-class fathers were observed interacting with their 4-year-old sons in order to determine the relationship among paternal child-rearing practices, sex-role preference, and intellectual functioning in young boys. Nurturance and restrictiveness accounted for over a third of the variance in the boys' IQ. Distinctive class differences were found, including a negative association among lower-class boys between IQ and male sex preference.

Santrock, J. W. Paternal absence, sex typing, and identification. *Developmental Psychology,* 1970, *2,* 264–272. Structured doll play and maternal interviews were used to determine the effects of paternal absence, and its relationship to older siblings and a father substitute.

Schvaneveldt, J. D., Fryer, M., & Ostler, R. Concepts of "badness" and "goodness" of parents as perceived by nursery-school children. *Family Coordinator,* 1970, *19*(1), 98–103. Nursery school children, ages 3 to 5, were twice interviewed about what constitutes "goodness" or "badness" in mothers and fathers. The results are related to other research.

Wohlford, P., Santrock, J. W., Berger, S. E., & Liberman, D. Older brothers' influence on sex-typed, aggressive, and dependent behavior in father-absent children. *Developmental Psychology,* 1971, *4,* 124–134. This study, which involved very poor black preschool girls and boys, concerns the role of the older male sibling as a surrogate male role-model for father-absent children.

**Fathering:
Research and
Practice
Implications**

**161**

# 9

## Optimal Patterns of Child Rearing

Despite the vast literature having to do with home and child rearing, little of it concerns broader aspects of the process. Instead, most studies concern very limited aspects of child rearing, such as the father-son relationship, or discipline, or language training. The matter of fitting the pieces together to determine what constitutes an effective comprehensive design of child rearing has been largely ignored.

The reasons for this neglect of broader patterns are easy to understand. For one thing, the effects of child rearing are a long-term matter; hence, expensive longitudinal studies are required to assess them. Second, there are many kinds of children and an equally varied assortment of parents; hence, no single child-rearing pattern may be optimal for all. Consider, too, the sophisticated task of determining how subprocesses in a broad design of child rearing fit together—a jigsaw requiring all the expertise psychologists can muster to fit together. Finally, child rearing relates to the cultural context in terms of time, place, and circumstance; hence, conclusions must be continually modified in terms of the context within which child rearing occurs.

Regardless of the quality of more ambitious research projects, many issues will remain. How can the significance of any specific aspect of child rearing be properly related to the total design? How can findings derived from studying one population of subjects be extrapolated to other groups? Who is to decide what outcomes for children are desirable? How can children best be prepared for a fast-changing world?

In our first selection, Burton L. White and Jean Carew Watts describe the most important characteristics of the child's primary caretakers, as derived from their longitudinal research already cited in Issue No. 4. From the same study they also arrive at "best guesses" regarding effective child-rearing practices. In the second selection, Urie Bronfenbrenner tells what is wrong about child care in America and suggests ways that it might be improved. (You will note the first selection includes references to "A" and "C" mothers. As you might guess, "A" means best and "C" means less than best.)

# Important Characteristics of Primary Caretakers

## Burton L. White and Jean Carew Watts

The responsibility for child-rearing currently rests in the hands of the mother in American society. That situation may change if and

From pp. 240–244 of "Discussions and Conclusions," by B. L. White. In *Experience and Environment: Major Influences on the Development of the Young Child* (Vol. 1), by B. L. White and J. C. Watts. Copyright © 1973. Reprinted by permission of Prentice-Hall, Inc., Englewood Cliffs, New Jersey.

when day care for infants becomes more prevalent. We believe the ideas we are espousing will be relevant to good infant day-care practices as well as to home rearing of children. What then can we say in a succinct fashion about optimal characteristics of mothers? We can divide the problem into a few major components.

## Attitudes and Values

The performance of a mother derives in part from her attitudes and values. It is also significantly affected by her resources, both material and psychological. We can single out at least the following areas of importance with respect to attitudes and values: life in general, young children, the formative role of infancy, possessions, housekeeping, and safety.

*Life in General.* A woman who is seriously depressed or very angry or unhappy about life probably cannot do a good job of getting her young child off to a good start. None of our successful mothers have such attitudes toward life, while a few of our unsuccessful mothers do.

*Young Children.* Some mothers don't seem to really enjoy their children during the one-to-three age range. They spend as little time as possible with them, and when they interact with them, they don't seem to get much pleasure from the experience. Some of our mothers who do poorly fall into this category, others of them do not; virtually all our successful mothers seem to derive a great deal of pleasure from their children during this age range.

*The Formative Role of the One- to Three-Year Age Range.* Mothers seem to vary considerably on this dimension. We doubt that many of our C mothers believe strongly that this period of life has profound significance for development. On the other hand, not all A mothers do either. It is our impression that many of our A mothers perform excellently without any measurable degree of commitment to this thesis. They seem to spontaneously

grant their infants generous measures of attention and consideration, simply as a part of a natural way of life.

*Possessions.* There is a fair degree of incompatibility between a strong desire to preserve the contents of one's home and the normal tendency toward nonmalicious destructiveness in infants. The mother who is very concerned about her possessions is in for trouble. She has basically three routes to take. She can physically prevent her child from contacting many items in the home by the habitual use of playpens, cribs, and gates. We suspect this route produces frustration and stunting of curiosity in infants. She may allow the child the run of the house and attempt to prevent damage by stopping the child with words or actions when he appears about to break something. This route is often unsuccessful because of the child's limited understanding of words and normal development of negativism. At the very best, it results in a mother who is very frequently saying "No, don't touch that" to her child. Another practice is to allow the child to roam, and to accompany him in an attempt at constant supervision combined with gentle redirection. This route is very time- and energy-consuming, and few mothers can afford it.

*Housekeeping.* Very few of our A mothers are meticulous housekeepers. Most of them seem to have accepted the idea that an infant and a spotless home are incompatible. The problem is often aggravated by a husband who insists on a spotless home, in part because he doesn't realize how much work is entailed. The paths a mother of an infant may take to maintain a spotless home are similar to those for the preservation of possessions, and the pitfalls are similar.

*Safety.* We have already described the potential for self-injury that every infant has. The danger is very real. Again, mothers vary widely in how they deal with danger. And again, most of the ways that reduce the danger carry with them the real possibility of reducing the child's normal curiosity and development.

About all our study tells us so far is that our A mothers are usually more inclined than our C mothers to take risks on this score with their one-year-olds. There is some research that suggests that children have more built-in controls than we give them credit for. The work on depth perception by Gibson and Walk (1960), for example, suggests that by the time children begin to crawl, they can skillfully discriminate depth and furthermore are inclined to avoid moving off safe positions and injuring themselves. There are certain African tribes that allow their infants access to sharp weapons and utensils, with no apparent serious injuries resulting. It is our impression that infants are generally far more careful about protecting themselves than we think. We do not mean to suggest that no caution need be exercised. Earlier, we alluded to the problems of razor blades, broken glass, and so on, but there is a middle ground in the treatment of the problem of safety, and some mothers are markedly overprotective to the point where they seem to interfere too much with good development.

## MOTHERING, A VASTLY UNDERRATED OCCUPATION

We will begin with the bold statement that the mother's direct and indirect actions with regard to her one- to three-year-old child, especially during the second year of life, are, in our opinion, the most powerful formative factors in the development of a preschool-age child.

Further, we would guess that if a mother does a fine job in the preschool years, subsequent educators such as teachers will find their chances for effectiveness maximized. Finally, we would expect that much of the basic quality of the entire life of an individual is determined by the mother's actions during these two years. Obviously, we could be very wrong about these declarative statements. We make them as very strong hunches that we have become committed to, as a kind of net result of all our inquiries into early development.

Let us quickly add that we believe most women are capable of doing a fine job with their one- to three-year-old children. Our study has convinced us that a mother need not necessarily have even a high school diploma, let alone a college education. Nor does she need to have very substantial economic assets. In addition, it is clear that a good job can be accomplished without a father in the home. In all these statements we see considerable hope for future generations.

## BEST GUESSES ABOUT MOST EFFECTIVE CHILD-REARING PRACTICES

Our A mothers talk a great deal to their children, and usually at a level the child can handle. They make them feel as though whatever they are doing is usually interesting. They provide access to many objects and diverse situations. They lead the child to believe that he can expect help and encouragement most, but *not all* the time. They demonstrate and explain things to the child, but mostly on the child's instigation rather than their own. They prohibit certain activities, and they do so consistently and firmly. They are secure enough to say "no" to the child from time to time without seeming to fear that the child will not love them. They are imaginative, so that they make interesting associations and suggestions to the child when opportunities present themselves. They very skillfully and naturally strengthen the child's intrinsic motivation to learn. They also give him a sense of task orientation, a notion that it is desirable to do things well and completely. They make the child feel secure.

Our most effective mothers do not devote the bulk of their day to rearing their young children. Most of them are far too busy to do so; several of them, in fact, have part-time jobs. What they seem to do, often without knowing exactly why, is to perform excellently the functions of designer and consultant. By that I mean they design a physical world, mainly in the home, that is beautifully suited to nurturing the burgeoning curiosity of the one- to three-year-old. It is full of small, manipulable, visually detailed objects, some of which were originally designed for young children (toys), others normally used for other purposes (plastic refrigerator containers, bottle caps, baby-food jars and covers, shoes, magazines, television and radio knobs, etc.). It contains things to climb, such as chairs, benches, sofas, and stairs. It has available materials to nurture more mature motor interests, such as tricycles, scooters, and structures with which to practice elementary gymnastics. It includes a rich variety of interesting things to look at, such as television, people, and the aforementioned types of physical objects.

In addition to being largely responsible for the type of environment the child has, this mother sets up guides for her child's behavior that seem to play a very important role in these processes. She is generally permissive and indulgent. The child is encouraged in the vast majority of his explorations. When the child confronts an interesting or difficult situation, he often turns to his mother for help. Although usually working at some chore, she is generally nearby. He then goes to her and usually, but *not always,* is *responded to* by his mother with help or shared enthusiasm, plus, occasionally, an interesting, naturally related idea. These ten- to thirty-second interchanges are usually oriented around the child's interest of the moment rather than toward some need or interest of the mother. At times, under these circumstances, the child will not receive immediate attention. These effective mothers do not always drop what they are doing to attend to his request, but rather if the time is obviously inconvenient, they say so, thereby probably giving the child a realistic, small taste of things to come.

These mothers very rarely spend five, ten, or twenty minutes teaching their one- or two-year-olds, but they get an enormous amount (in terms of frequency) of teaching in "on the fly," and usually at the child's instigation. Although they do volunteer comments opportunistically, they react mostly to overtures by the child.

These effective mothers seem to be people with high levels of energy. The work of a young mother without household help is, in spite of modern appliances, very time- and energy-consuming. Yet we have families subsisting at a welfare level of income, with as many as eight closely spaced children, that are doing every bit as good a job in child-rearing during the early years as the most advantaged homes. (A Russian-type "Hero of the People" award ought to go to such remarkable women.)

## REFERENCE

Gibson, E. J., & Walk, R. D. The visual cliff, *Scientific American*, 1960, *202*, 64–71.

# Who Cares for America's Children?

## Urie Bronfenbrenner

I shall be short, but not very sweet. America's families and their children are in trouble. Trouble so deep and pervasive as to threaten the future of our nation. The source of the trouble is nothing less than a national neglect of children, and of those primarily engaged in their care; and neglect of America's parents.

We like to think of America as a child-centered society, but our actions belie our words. A hard look at our institutions and ways of life reveals that our national priorities lie elsewhere. The pursuit of affluence, the worship of material things, the hard sell and the

Reprinted from *Young Children*, 1971, 26(3), 157–163. Copyright 1971 by National Association for the Education of Young Children. Reprinted by permission.

soft; the willingness to accept technology as a substitute for human relationships; the imposition of responsibility upon families without support, and the readiness to blame the victims of evil for the evil itself, have brought us to the point where a broken television set or a broken computer provokes more indignation and more action than a broken family or a broken child.

Our national rhetoric not withstanding, the actual patterns of life in America are such that children and families come last. Our society expects its citizens first of all to meet the demands of their jobs, and then to fulfill civic and social obligations. Responsibilities to children are to be met, of course, but this is something one is expected to do in his spare time.

But when, where and how? In today's world, parents find themselves at the mercy of a society which imposes pressures and priorities that allow neither time nor place for meaningful activities and relations between children and adults, which downgrade the role of parent and the functions of parenthood, and which prevent the parent from doing the things he wants to do as a guide, friend and companion to his children.

The frustrations are greatest for the family of poverty, where the capacity for human response is crippled by hunger, cold, filth, sickness and despair. No parent who spends his days in search of menial work and his nights in keeping rats away from the crib can be expected to find the time, let alone the heart, to engage in constructive activities with his children or serve as a stable source of love and discipline. The fact that some families in poverty do manage to do this is a tribute to them, but not to the society or community in which they live.

For families who can get along, the rats are gone but the rat race remains. The demands of a job, or often two jobs, which claim mealtimes, evenings and weekends as well as days; the trips and moves one must make to get ahead or simply hold one's own; the ever increasing time spent in commuting; the parties, the evenings out, the social and community obligations; all of the things one has to do if he is to meet his primary responsibilities produce a situation in which a child often spends more time with a passive babysitter than with a participating parent or adult.

Even when the parent is at home, a compelling force cuts off communication and response among family members. Although television could, if used creatively, enrich the activities of children and families, it now only undermines them. Like the sorcerer of old, the television set casts its magic spell, freezing speech and action, turning the living into silent statues so long as the enchantment lasts. The primary danger of the television screen lies not so much in the behavior it produces—although there is danger there—as in the behavior it prevents; the talks, the games, the family festivities and arguments through which much of the child's learning takes place and through which his character is formed. Turning on the television set can turn off the process that transforms children into people.

In our modern way of life it is not only parents of whom children are deprived, it is people in general. A host of factors conspire to isolate children from the rest of society: the fragmentation of the extended family, the separation of residential and business areas, the disappearance of neighborhoods, the elimination of small stores in favor of supermarkets, zoning ordinances, occupational mobility, child labor laws, the abolishment of the apprentice system, consolidated schools, television, telephones, the substitution of the automobile for public transportation or just plain walking, separate patterns of social life for different age groups, the working mother, the delegation of child care to specialists; all these manifestations of progress operate to decrease opportunity and incentive for meaningful contact between children and persons older or younger than themselves.

And here we confront a fundamental and disturbing fact: *Children need people in order to become human*. The fact is fundamental because it is firmly grounded both in scientific research and in human experience. It is disturbing because the isolation of children from adults simultaneously threatens the growth of the individual and the survival of the society. The young cannot pull themselves up by their own bootstraps. It is primarily through observing, playing and working with others older and younger than himself that a child discovers both what he can do and who he can become, that he develops both his ability and his identity. It is primarily through exposure and interaction with adults and children of different ages that a child acquires new interests and skills, and learns the meaning of tolerance, cooperation and compassion.

Hence, to relegate children to a world of their own is to deprive them of their humanity and to deprive ourselves of humanity as well. Yet, this is what is happening in America today. We are experiencing a breakdown in the process of making human beings human. By isolating our children from the rest of society, we abandon them to a world devoid of adults and ruled by the destructive impulses and compelling pressures, both of the age-segregated peer group and the aggressive and exploitive television screen. By setting our priorities elsewhere and by putting children and families last, by claiming one set of values while pursuing another, we leave our children bereft of standards and support, and our own lives impoverished and corrupted.

This reversal of priorities, which amounts to a betrayal of our children, underlies the growing disillusionment and alienation among young people in all segments of American society. Those who grew up in settings where children, families, neighborhoods and communities still counted are able to act out their frustration in positive ways through constructive protest, through participation and through public service. Those who come from circumstances in which the family, the neighborhood and the community could not function—be it in slum or suburb—can only strike out against an environment they have experienced as indifferent, callous, cruel and unresponsive. One cannot condone the destruction and violence manifested by young people in widely disparate and desperate parts of our society. But one can point to the roots of a process which if not reversed will continue to spread.

The failure to reorder our priorities, the insistence on business as usual, and the continued reliance on rhetoric as a substitute for radical reforms can have only one result: the far more rapid and pervasive growth of alienation, apathy, drugs, delinquency and violence among the young and among the not so young in all segments of our national life. We face the prospect of a society which resents its own children and fears its youth.

What is needed is a change in our patterns of living which will once again bring people back into the lives of children, and children back into the lives of people. But how? The verse in Isaiah says, "a little child shall lead them." I propose we act upon that text. But perhaps to do so one must speak not in the language of Isaiah, but in the language of our contemporary times.

What I am proposing is the seduction of America by its children. What do I mean? Let me give you some examples, concrete actions we could take at all levels in our society: business, industry, mass media, communities, local, state and Federal governments, right down to the local neighborhood; concrete actions that would have the effect of bringing people back into the lives of children, and back into the lives of people.

One of these suggested actions comes from the U. S. S. R., which is not the only country that does this; it's also done in Scandinavia. This is the custom for which there's no English word, so I've used the word "adoption," in which a business or an industry adopts a group of children or a children's program with the aim of becoming friends, of acquainting children with the people who work in the world of work.

My colleague in the Forum Planning Committee, Dr. David Goslin of the Russell Sage Foundation, decided to Americanize this idea, because he felt, as I do, that the values are human rather than parochial. He persuaded the *Detroit Free Press* to try an experiment. Recently that newspaper saw in its composing room, press room, dispatch room, city room and other offices, young children 12 years of age from two schools in the city of Detroit. It was a fascinating thing to watch.

When we first talked to the people at the *Free Press* they said, "Gee! kids? You know we're a newspaper here. What will we do with them, sit there all day and watch them? Besides, you know this is a busy place." As one lady in the advertising section said to me, "Professor, you mean you're going to have kids around here—you really mean that?"

On the last day, that same lady said to me, "Professor, it's going to be so lonely here next week—those kids are easier to talk to than people." They were from two schools, one in a slum area, the other in a middle-class area, both black and white. The children were just themselves. They said things like, "This is a place to meet, a way to understand people." "If every kid in Detroit and all around the United States got to do this, I don't think there would be so many problems in the world." It was a two-way street that came alive there. People rediscovered children, and children rediscovered people.

## OTHER ACTIONS CAN BE TAKEN

Another idea is the notion of encouraging business and industry to place day care centers in or near the place of business—not as the only location for day care and preschool centers, but as one of the options available to parents, so that during the coffee breaks and during the lunch hours, people could visit the kids. Perhaps then children would once again become a subject of conversation in places where children don't get talked about as much as they used to.

We are about to propose that every moderately sized place of business or branch of a business in the country establish a Commission on Children to ask how the policies and practices of that business affect the lives of their employees and their children as family members. On such a commission, obviously the employees as well as the management and the union should participate.

We recommend that business explore and maximize half-time and part-time jobs for comparable rates of pay and status so that those parents who choose to work part-time may do so, instead of having to make the choice between full-time work or full-time no work, or part-time work at a reduced rate of pay, reduced status and reduced job security. We're talking about flexible work schedules so that parents can be at home when the kids arrive at home.

We emphasize especially family-oriented industrial planning and development: so that when plants are established, locations are determined and housing is planned, consideration is given to the fact that employees have families and have to be concerned with how and where they can spend time as families. It should be kept in mind in planning the buildings, the apartments and residences that there will be children and parents living in these places. In short, we are asking for a family-oriented business and industrial policy in America. We speak also of actions to be taken in the realm of the mass media and the advertising industry.

We ask that urgent attention be paid to the creation of an entirely new kind of television programming, one which no longer casts the viewer in the role of a passive and isolated bystander, but which instead involves family members and neighbors in activities with each other. That is, involving children, adults, older kids, younger kids and grandparents in games, conversations and joint creative activity. And we assert that there is nothing inherent in television technology which precludes this kind of possibility.

The community, of course, is the family of families. And it is there, perhaps, more than anywhere else that the family needs support. Because the thesis I am presenting to you is that just as children cannot function unless they have healthy and human parents and caretakers, parents and all those who carry the responsibility for children in our society need the support of the community and of the society in order for them to be able to function effectively in their roles. It is not the family that's breaking down, it is not the staff of people engaged in work with children that is breaking down, it is the support in the society for the family and for those who are faced with the responsibility and the delight of raising a new generation of human beings that is being withdrawn.

There are many other measures we are considering. I will mention one or two, in relation to the schools. We point out the sterility of courses in parent education for junior and senior high school, where there are no children in evidence. We suggest that preschool programs and Head Start centers be located in or near school programs, that school curricula utilize these as learning opportunities and opportunities for responsibility. Then the older children get some notion of what a child is like, what a child's needs are and how much fun a child is, so we do not have a generation of young people who don't discover what a child is until they have one.

These are new kinds of suggestions. They bring difficulties, but they also bring promise. They bring a very important element into the lives of older school-aged children. If one looks at the problems of human development cross-culturally, as I've been privileged to do during this past decade, one is struck by the fact that American society is characterized by the inutility of children. We in our own country do not give children anything really important to do. We give them duties, not responsibilities. And yet, there are things they could do if we but looked around.

One of the most important responsibilities that the older child can have, both as an individual and as a group, is responsibility for the young. Evidence indicates that older children are very effective as models, as re-enforcers, as praise-givers to the young, but in our age-segregated society such opportunities are seldom given.

## OLDSTERS OFFER VITAL ASSISTANCE

Similarly, there is another group for whom children can be a delight and a genuine help, and who in turn can serve a very important purpose in providing a humanizing experience for children. I refer to older people. The pleasure which a child gets from recognizing how much he's appreciated by an older person is a special kind of pleasure on both sides.

It's perhaps paradoxical that in our discussions and preparation for the White House Conference on a forum which is to deal with children and families, we make very few recommendations to families. Our position is essentially this: that given sun, soil, air and water, a plant does not need to be told how to grow. If America's parents, and those bearing the responsibility for the upbringing of the young, are given the place and the power and the prestige, to enable them to function as guides, companions and sources of love and discipline for children; and to have a decisive role in determining the environments and programs in which our children live and grow, the great majority of these parents and these professional workers will be able to take full advantage of that opportunity to enhance the quality of life both for children and for the nation.

There is but one caution to be borne in mind. The crucial factor, of course, is not how much time is spent with a child, but how the time is spent. A child learns, he becomes human, primarily through participation in challenging activity with those whom he loves and admires. It is the example, challenge and re-enforcement provided by people who care that enable a child to develop both his ability and his identity. An everyday example of the operation of this principle is the mother who daily talks with her young child and, usually without thinking much about it, responds more warmly when he uses new words or expressions or new motions. And as he does so, she gradually introduces new and more complex activities in her activity with the child.

So it is this way, in work and in play with children: in games, in projects, in shared responsibilities with parents, adults and older children, that the child develops the skills, motives and qualities of character that enable him to live a life that is gratifying both to himself and to those around him. But this can happen only in a society that lets it happen, and makes it happen, a society in which the needs of families and children become a primary concern, not merely of special organizations and interest groups, but of all the major institutions—government, industry, business, mass media, communities, neighborhoods and individual citizens.

It is the priorities that they set that will determine our children's present and America's future.

# SUGGESTIONS FOR FURTHER READING

Busse, T. V. Child-rearing antecedents of flexible thinking. *Developmental Psychology,* 1969, *1,* 585–591. The quality of fifth-grade boys' flexible thinking was related to the behavior, attitudes, and social class of their mothers and fathers. In some cases, parental factors bore a linear relationship to flexible thinking; in others a moderate "control" position seemed most effective.

Eron, L. D., Huesmann, L. R., Lefkowitz, M. M., & Walder, L. O. How learning conditions in early childhood—including mass media—relate to aggression in late adolescence. *American Journal of Orthopsychiatry,* 1974, *44,* 412–423. This ten-year longitudinal study disclosed strong evidence that aggression is learned and that children's aggressive behaviors relate strongly to models of behavior to which they have been exposed. The sexes respond differently to these models because of differences in their own past experiences.

Granzberg, G. The psychological integration of culture: A cross-cultural study of Hopi type initiation rites. *Journal of Social Psychology,* 1973, *90,* 3–7. A previous study of child-rearing patterns among Hopi Indians is compared with present ratings of child indulgence, compliance, and initiation among 32 primitive societies. The results indicate a crossculturally significant relationship between the child-rearing pattern of indulgence followed by compliance training and group initiation rites featuring the use of masks and/or disciplinary whipping.

Hunt, J. McV., & Eichorn, D. H. Maternal and child behaviors: A review of data from the Berkeley Growth Study. *Seminars in Psychiatry,* 1972, *4,* 367–381. This article describes the Berkeley Growth Study, a longitudinal study begun in 1928, of mental, physical, motor, and behavioral development from infancy to adulthood. Analyses are made of the consistency of maternal and child behaviors, their interaction, and their relationship to mental development. Maternal behavior patterns, especially those that were consistent over a period of time, were judged to shape the developing behaviors of the child, which, in turn, influenced the child's intellectual development.

Korner, A. F. Early stimulation and maternal care as related to infant capabilities and individual differences. *Early Child Development and Care,* 1973, *2,* 307–327. Recent research is reviewed concerning the capabilities of newborns and their individual differences. Infants are probably more capable of organized responses than has been assumed, but they are especially dependent upon maternal care. In the earliest weeks of life the mother provides affective and cognitive stimulation for the infant.

Madsen, M. C., & Kagan, S. Mother-directed achievement of children in two cultures. *Journal of Cross-Cultural Psychology,* 1973, *4,* 221–228. Mother-child pairs both in a small Mexican town and in Los Angeles were observed in experimental situations in which the mother controlled rewards given the child for success or failure. Mothers of both groups rewarded their children for success; however, the Mexican mothers gave more rewards for failure and chose easier achievement goals.

McIntyre, R. W. Parenthood training or mandatory birth control: Take your choice. *Psychology Today,* April 1973, pp. 34–39; 132–133; 143. Compulsory parent training and licensing are recommended instead of the hitherto haphazard modes of child rearing.

Mussen, P., & Beytagh, L. A. M. Industrialization, child-rearing practices, and children's personality. *Journal of Genetic Psychology,* 1969, *115* (Second Half), 195–216. This study was designed to determine the consequences for child-rearing practices and on children's personality structure of the family's shift from an agricultural to an industrial mode of life. The study involved 63 Puerto Rican boys, ages 9 to 12, and many of their parents. The data refuted the common hypothesis that industrialization produces psychological maladjustment and disorganization. Instead, the industrialized children and their parents proved to have sounder psychological health, stability, and optimism.

Robinson, H. B., Robinson, N. M., Wollins, M., Bronfenbrenner, U., & Richmond, J. Early child care in the United States of America. *Early Child Development and Care,* 1973, *2,* 359–582(Monograph). This discussion of major societal contexts associated with child care in the United States covers such topics as child-rearing techniques, day care, adoption, health care, and socioeconomic-class differences. Recommendations and predictions are made for the future.

Weissman, H. N. Disposition toward intellectuality: Its composition and its assessment. *Journal of General Psychology,* 1970, *82,* 99–107. This study involves a determination of life-history factors—including modes of child rearing—of persons showing creative, superior, and adaptive performance, and ways of identifying such individuals.

Whiting, B. B. Folk wisdom and child rearing. *Merrill-Palmer Quarterly,* 1974, *20*(1), 9–19. New approaches are discussed relating to child-rearing practices, including the use of folk wisdom, published documents, and social-science research. Also discussed are conditions that may explain Americans' dependency on specialists and the American youth's current antiprofessionalism.

Yarrow, M. R. Research on childrearing as a basis for practice. *Child Welfare,* 1973, *52,* 209–219. Research on child rearing has followed several paths and yielded important findings; however, an approach to "totality of rearing" is needed for today's society.

# 10

## Patterns of Discipline

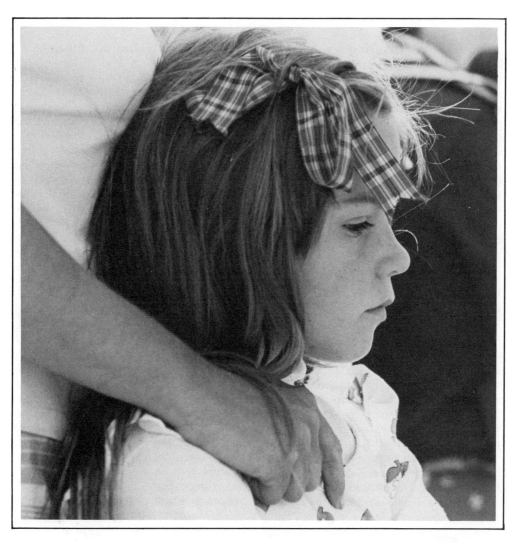

In developmental psychology, patterns of discipline are often classified in two ways: as negative or positive, in terms of reinforcement, and as power-oriented or love-oriented. Positive reinforcement refers to rewarding approved behaviors, and negative reinforcement to punishing disapproved ones. In power-oriented discipline, the parent lays down the law and swiftly punishes the child who disobeys. By contrast, love-oriented techniques utilize praise, warmth, and reasoning, coupled with withdrawal of love when the child disobeys. Love-oriented discipline is not to be confused with ultrapermissive discipline, which connotes an absence of controls.

## HISTORICAL PERSPECTIVE ON DISCIPLINE

In the days of our forefathers, the "spare-the-rod" philosophy ruled supreme, and many a child felt its impact—literally. A central theme in literary works was a need to impose strict discipline on a child, virtually from infancy. The child was perceived as being born with a corrupt and selfish nature, a "fact" that posed problems for parents (Demos, 1974). The schoolroom counterpart of this philosophy embraced such devices and ideals as detention halls, conduct grades on report cards, and pin-drop quietness. In the first third of this century, this no-nonsense attitude was reinforced by the behaviorists, who believed that children should not be coddled.

However, in the period that followed, a trend toward permissiveness set in, sparked by progressive educators and psychoanalysts. Parents and educators alike were warned against thwarting the child, lest he develop neuroses. The dictum "Spare the rod, spoil the child" was displaced by "Wield the rod and warp the child." More recently, severe punishment and strict discipline have been associated with such personality traits as conformity, rigidity, and poor progress in creative thinking. Nevertheless, warnings began being sounded that the pendulum was swinging too far, and that we were developing a soft generation, without tough fiber. One result was a revival of the get-tough approach in education.

Meanwhile, psychologists and therapists took refuge in a cautious middle-of-the-road position, advocating a recipe of flexible firmness flavored with warmth. Parents were counseled to make it easy for children to obey, but when punishment was necessary, to punish sparingly, and in such manner as to "teach" the child. Parents themselves, deprived of their traditional prerogative of cracking down on the incorrigible child, and without a specific formula to take its place, wavered somewhat uncertainly between more and less permissiveness. Concurrently, researchers, armed with computers, grants of increasing size, and assorted hypotheses, sought to determine the modes of discipline used and their effects on the child. They reported much significant data, without arriving at firm conclusions.

## FACTORS RELATING TO TYPE OF DISCIPLINE

Many and often obscure factors relate to the type of discipline employed. However, according to Bronfenbrenner (1961), lower-class patterns of punishment favor the boy, middle-class patterns the girl. Boys, he asserts, are undermined by the love-oriented techniques of the middle classes, whereas girls have more freedom in middle-class than in lower-class homes. Boys thrive under the patriarchal regime of the lower class, whereas girls benefit from the matriarchal authority of the middle class. However, concludes Bronfenbrenner, both sexes thrive best in equalitarian households.

Culture is also a factor in type of discipline employed. A comparison of Jewish, Chinese, and Protestant mothers, all in the United States, disclosed that Chinese mothers are especially restrictive in child-rearing attitudes while Jewish and Protestant mothers are far more permissive (Kriger & Kross, 1972). Children reared permissively are more likely than more authoritatively reared children to become independent and to develop a high need for achievement. Restrictive behaviors have also been linked with underachievement in school (Davids & Hainsworth, 1967).

Even within the same culture, individual patterns of control vary according to the personalities of the parents involved. A parent lacking real convictions may waver uncertainly in manner of control. A henpecked husband with unfulfilled power needs may be unable to tolerate forwardness either in son or in daughter.

## POWER- VERSUS LOVE-ORIENTED DISCIPLINE

The most generally recommended pattern of discipline today is the relatively permissive, love-oriented pattern. Guilt feelings, it is assumed, help to control the child's behavior in the absence of authority. It is also argued that parental firmness provides the child with clear guidelines and a feeling of security. However, love-oriented techniques typically produce guilt and nonaggression. Boys, especially, who are trained to turn the other cheek may be ill prepared for a competitive society. Moreover, the threat of withdrawal of love may jeopardize independence.

The effect of power-oriented discipline, says Lang (1969), depends on how it is handled. Children whose parents deal autocratically toward them assume little responsibility themselves. By contrast, children who hold unusual power grow selfish and insensitive to others. When parents and children share power, the children are relatively responsible and responsive to the needs of others. Where the situation is simply one of anarchy, and no control is manifest by either parents or children, children become indifferent and unable to respond to others. The power approach, as imposed by any authority, raises an interesting issue. As Milgram (1974) points out, "obedience is as basic an element in the structure of social life as one can point to" (p. 603). He notes that some sort of authority system is required for any form of communal living.

Certain psychologists, including the editor of this volume, question both power- and love-oriented techniques. Guilt feelings, inculcated through withdrawal of love, may cause the child to reject himself. Besides, the good behaviors produced by love-oriented discipline may derive from the need to please the parent, rather than from a more logical base. For the rest of his or her life, an individual may have difficulty adopting a course contrary to that learned in childhood, despite every evidence that another course of behavior is wiser.

Power-oriented punishment, too, is dangerous, and to be reserved for emergencies, for reasons already stated. Perhaps the best formula is this: to manipulate the environment so as to encourage good behavior, and to reward it frequently. Bad behavior should be ignored, to the extent practicable, or "maneuvered" into becoming good behavior. For instance, instead of whipping Junior for surreptitiously taking a look at his gun, Dad explains guns and the dangers involved. However, he keeps the gun well away from temptation until the boy is mature enough to understand. Finally, the parents should exercise the sort of self-discipline and respect for others that encourages imitation. Also, in infinite subtle ways they should inculcate in the child such self-respect that the child will choose modes of behavior that are consistent with a healthy self-image.

## POSITIVE VERSUS NEGATIVE REINFORCEMENT

A related aspect of the discipline issue is whether positive or negative enforcement procedures produce more desirable results. Positive reinforcement suggests rewarding approved behaviors which, in turn, makes them more probable. It may involve such rewards as gifts, praise, or any other evidence of approval. Negative reinforcement is just the reverse, providing punishment for disapproved responses so that they will, henceforth, not recur. Negative reinforcement may involve rebukes, corporal punishment, a raised eyebrow, a sharp tongue, or any other evidence of disapproval. A certain amount of research, especially with animals, supports the use of negative reinforcement or aversive control of behavior under certain circumstances (Neale, 1969).

Other studies indicate that negative reinforcement techniques are more effective than rewards with children (Meyer & Offenbach, 1962; Meyer & Seidman, 1961; Penney & Lipton, 1961). It is simply impossible, declares Ausubel (1957), for children to learn what is not tolerated or disapproved merely by approving desired behaviors. That is, punishing specific responses may have an educative effect. Nevertheless, punishment often has unfavorable effects. Ordinarily it does not eliminate the troublesome behaviors, at least over the long haul; nor does it indicate what behaviors are desirable. Finally, punishment may have various unfortunate side effects, such as creating in the child fear, tension, and withdrawal, or unfavorable associations with learning.

On the other hand, most psychologists stress the need for positive reinforcement; that

is, the child is somehow rewarded for making the approved response (Clarizio & Yelon, 1967). At the start such rewards may have to be tangible in nature and coupled with verbal social reinforcers—for example, "I like the way you performed in that situation today." Reinforcers can gradually be shifted from the concrete into language and symbolic forms of reward.

After surveying the research, Howe (1972) concludes that in the long run punishment is generally ineffective in controlling behaviors, and that there are unpredictable side effects. According to Eron, Walder, and Lefkowitz (1970), studies of parent-child relationships, without exception, indicate that punitive parents have poorly adjusted children. Moreover, the harsher the punishment the more acute its effects. Hence, strong demands are being made for legislation protective of children. Such "primitive punitiveness," observes Maurer (1974), should be abandoned. "When as an adult the erstwhile battered child shoots 18 people from a Texas tower, kills 14 nurses in a Chicago residence, or slays a movie colony party in Hollywood, the blood is on the hands of those who would give aid and comfort to the punishing parents who shaped these lives without learning that corporal punishment is an ethical evil" (pp.623–624).

Of course, one should keep in mind that what is reward or punishment for one child may not be for another. The spanking that may have a traumatic effect on a highly sensitive child may be almost welcome to another who has trouble getting his parents' attention at all. The child who has come to expect praise only after he has truly earned it may derive more pleasure from such signs of approval than does another who is indiscriminately approved no matter what he does.

## SELECTED VIEWS ON DISCIPLINE

Many writers have offered their own prescriptions for good discipline. For example, Snider and Murphy (1975) recommend positive modes of control based on acceptance and respect for the child. Cole and Cole (1970) recommend plenty of praise for good behavior and sparing yet firm reprimands and punishments. Parents themselves favor firm discipline for children. In a 1969 Gallup Poll 49% believed that teachers were not strict enough, whereas only 2% believed they were too strict.

According to findings of the Harvard Human Development Preschool Study (White & Watts, 1974) cited earlier, researchers concluded that certain principles of discipline are in order; first, that the adult in the home should not try to win all arguments with the child, especially around the middle of the second year when the child begins being negative. Nor should efforts be made to keep the child from cluttering the house. Tampering with the environment is a symptom of a curious, healthy baby. The child should not be surrounded with edicts and rules, but should be permitted to do what he or she desires to do so long as it is safe. Nor should the parent attempt to force basic habits, such as toilet training, on the child. By the time the child is 2 or over such training will be easy. Nor should parents worry if they must say no to the child from time to time (White & Watts, 1974).

Note that much of the research regarding modes of child rearing compares the effects of directly contrasting conditions, one extreme presumably conducive to optimal development and the other to various emotional or social disturbances. Among the polarities thus studied have been breast- versus bottle-feeding, early versus late toilet-training, and in the present case, power-oriented versus love-oriented discipline. Implicit in such research is the assumption that smaller amounts of the variable under consideration will similarly affect the child to a proportionately less degree. For instance, in the matter of maternal deprivation, if complete absence of the mother is concluded to have adverse effects, then lesser deprivation, as in maternal employment, is presumed to have negative, though lesser, effects.

In the area of discipline, if power-oriented methods prove bad, even moderately stern discipline is also presumed to have similar, though milder, negative effects. However, the issue hardly resolves itself into an either-or proposition. Probably some combination of permissiveness and punishment is best. Or possibly no one method or blend of methods is best; instead, perhaps the method chosen had best be adapted to the situation and personalities immediately involved. However, even where practices are individually tailored to situations, they undoubtedly reflect some general philosophy of punishment and discipline.

Bronfenbrenner (1961), for one, believes the either-or position is unjustified. Instead, he encourages thinking in terms of optimal patterns of control, rather than choosing between polar extremes of power-oriented or love-oriented control. Sometimes strict control may be required—for example, to produce immediate obedience in an emergency. In more usual circumstances, simply reinforcing approved behavior with a warm smile or pat on the back might be all that is needed.

The implications of the whole discipline issue and its components are vast. What are the effects of such negative reinforcements as nagging, scolding, and corporal punishment? Is love-oriented discipline conducive to developing guilt feelings and dependency? In constructing teaching machines, should incorrect replies simply be not rewarded, or be punished? Do low grades on report cards spur the child to do better, or discourage better performance?

In our first reading, Donald Baer defends punishment as a legitimate means of changing undesirable behaviors. He believes that causing the child a small amount of pain is justifiable if it spares him much greater pain in the future. In the second reading, Diana Baumrind summarizes certain of her own conclusions about child rearing as derived from her own extensive research.

## REFERENCES

Ausubel, D. *Theory and problems of child development.* New York: Grune & Stratton, 1957.

Bronfenbrenner, U. The changing American child: A speculative analysis. *Journal of Social Issues,* 1961, *17,* 6–18.

Clarizio, H. F., & Yelon, S. L. Learning theory approaches to classroom management: Rationale and intervention techniques. *Journal of Special Education,* 1967, *1*, 267–274.

Cole, M., & Cole, S. Russian nursery schools. In *Readings in educational psychology.* Del Mar, Calif.: CRM Associates, 1970.

Davids, A., & Hainsworth, P. Maternal attitudes about family life and child rearing as avowed by mothers and perceived by their under-achieving and high-achieving sons. *Journal of Consulting Psychology,* 1967, *31*, 29–37.

Demos, J. The American family in past time. *American Scholar,* 1974, *43*, 422–446.

Eron, L., Walder, L. O., & Lefkowitz, M. M. *Learning of aggression in children.* Boston: Little, Brown, 1970.

Howe, M. J. A. *Understanding school learning: A new look at educational psychology.* New York: Harper & Row, 1972.

Kriger, S. F., & Kross, W. H. Child-rearing attitudes of Chinese, Jewish, and Protestant mothers. *Journal of Social Psychology,* 1972, *86*(Second Half), 205–210.

Lang, L. H. Responsibility as a function of authority in family relations. *Dissertation Abstracts,* 1969, *29*, 3668–3669.

Maurer, A. Corporal punishment. *American Psychologist,* 1974, *29*, 614–626.

Meyer, W. J., & Offenbach, S. I. Effectiveness of reward and punishment as a function of task complexity. *Journal of Comparative and Physiological Psychology,* 1962, *55*, 532–534.

Meyer, W. J., & Seidman, S. B. Relative effectiveness of different reinforcement combinations on concept learning of children at two developmental levels. *Child Development,* 1961, *32*, 117–127.

Milgram, S. The dilemma of obedience. *Phi Delta Kappan,* 1974, *55*, 603–606.

Neale, D. C. Aversive control of behavior. *Phi Delta Kappan,* 1969, *50*, 335–338.

Penney, R. K., & Lipton, A. A. Children's discrimination learning as a function of reward and punishment. *Journal of Comparative and Physiological Psychology,* 1961, *54*, 449–451.

Snider, S. J., & Murphy, W. C. Discipline—What can it teach? *The Elementary School Journal,* 1975, *75*, 299–303.

White, B. L., & Watts, J. C. *Experience and environment: Major influences on the development of the young child* (Vol. 1). Englewood Cliffs, N.J.: Prentice-Hall, 1974.

# Let's Take Another Look at Punishment

## Donald M. Baer

*When Bill was 12 he became sexually aroused watching girls go down a playground slide with their panties exposed. His fantasies during masturbation soon centered about this incident, and probably because of the powerful reinforcing effects of orgasm, the association between panties and sexual arousal soon became habitual. His fetish for women's panties persisted for more than 20 years. Even when Bill was in his early 30s, his sexual thoughts centered around panties—he would buy panties or steal them from department stores or clotheslines, and he would wear them and fondle them while he masturbated.*

*Bill's relations with women were strained; he was impotent, and very unhappy. He went for help to Malcolm Kushner, then psychologist at the Veterans Administration Hospital in Coral Gables, Florida. Bill agreed to participate in an unusual therapy program that used electric shock.*

*During therapy sessions when Bill held panties or looked at pictures of women in panties he received a painful electric shock in his forearm. He would tolerate the shock for as long as he could. When he wanted the shock to end, he would say "stop" and simultaneously put the panties or pictures aside.*

*Bill and the therapist repeated this procedure 12 times in every 20-to-30-minute session, with three such sessions per week. Gradually Bill's obsession with panties decreased, and after 14 weeks he reported that panties no longer aroused him.*

*At this point, the therapist concentrated on Bill's impotence. With the help of a considerate and patient girl friend, Bill gradually over-*

Reprinted from *Psychology Today Magazine,* 1971, 5(5), 32–37ff. Copyright © 1971 by Ziff-Davis Publishing Company.

*came his anxieties about being with women.*

*Once, after the conclusion of therapy, Bill had to appear in court for a traffic violation. He became anxious and apprehensive, and reported that thoughts of women's panties began to recur—although he could dismiss them from his mind if he tried. Such mild recurrences occurred twice in three months after the punishment sessions ended. Both times the therapist gave him booster sessions, and the impulses promptly disappeared.*

*Eighteen months later Bill remained free of his fetish and no substitute symptoms had appeared. He was married, a new father, and reported that his sexual life was normal.*

In recent years, many behavior therapists have studied punishment as a therapeutic tool. Behaviorists define punishment in terms of behavior; a punisher is any stimulus that reduces the frequency of the behavior that precedes it. Electric shock very often acts as a punisher, but in cases in which it does not, it is a contradiction to say "I applied punishment but the behavior did not decrease." In general, behaviorists have found punishment to be one of the fastest, most effective techniques available for helping people rid themselves of troublesome behaviors.

By the usual standards of science these findings ought to evoke admiration: scientists successfully applied research findings to problems that had not responded to therapy and they relieved patients of misery. Had the findings been a vaccine against some disease, there would have been headlines and congratulations. But the treatment is not called "vaccination," it is called "punishment." The word brings with it images of anger, whips, screams. So instead of celebrating a new scientific advance, we feel apprehensive; we look for a hint of sadism.

Punishment is a natural part of everyone's learning history. A child learns to walk in part to avoid the pain of falling down. Everyone learns to avoid doing those things that result in pain. This process operates even while we sleep. A small boy who rolls off the bed is punished immediately by colliding with the floor; he soon learns to limit his nocturnal tossings.

But we have a peculiar ambivalence toward pain. We can see that pain is a good teacher as long as it is inflicted by inanimate objects—hard floors, hot radiators, sharp knives. But somehow, pain inflicted by a human being seems different—barbaric and repellent.

I think that much of our revulsion regarding the use of punishment is based on a reaction against the truly inhumane conditions of many years ago that recur in literature—headmasters with canes, slave masters, prison turnkeys with whips, bullies, orphanage overseers, snake-pit mental hospitals. We like to think of such practices as long past, so when a therapist speaks objectively about the uses of punishment, we react as if he were asking us to forget all the years of progress and humane reform.

Another source of resistance is the Freudian notion that where there is neurosis there was some early trauma. We assume that the long-range side effects of punishment must be disastrous. Also, we assume that even if the symptoms are removed, the underlying conflict will remain and will manifest itself in other symptoms. But among hundreds of studies, only a few have found evidence for anything like symptom substitution. The concept appears to be a myth.

*For six months June could not stop sneezing. The 17-year-old girl's case was one of the most baffling her many doctors had ever seen. June had consulted neurologists, endocrinologists, allergists, urologists, psychiatrists and hypnotists; she had tried a pharmacopoeia of medicines, but she kept sneezing.*

*When Kushner first saw her, June was sneezing at a rate of once every 40 seconds. It did not affect her eating or sleeping, which suggested that the sneezes may have been psychological. Kushner decided on an unusual therapy program. He placed a microphone around June's neck and connected it to a voice key and a shock source. When the girl sneezed, the sound relay triggered a brief but painful electric shock through electrodes connected to her fingers.*

*At the end of only one day's therapy, after she had worn the apparatus only four and a half hours, June stopped sneezing.*

*From then on, therapy sessions helped her develop more appropriate ways of dealing with her environment.*

*Five years have passed since June's six-month sneezing jag. She is now 22 and since that day in Kushner's office, she has not been bothered again by her singular compulsion.*

Our resistance to the use of punishment is based on moral grounds, not scientific ones. But the moral position that pain is bad and should always be avoided becomes itself immoral when it prevents us from helping persons who have learned behavior that puts them in even greater pain. Unfortunately, many of our public institutions promote just that kind of learning.

*Jimmy, a retarded seven-year-old, functioned at the level of a two-year-old. He bit his hands repeatedly, until they were swollen, bleeding and infected. Nurses finally made him wear boxing gloves or arm splints that prevented him from bending his elbows. The child's hand-biting problem intensified when he was on the hospital ward. He would cry in pain, yet continue to tear the flesh from his hands until nurses held his hands away from his mouth.*

I suggest that Jimmy was taught his behavior. He was rewarded for hand-biting, rather than for more desirable behavior, because the nurses and caretakers were busy. They could ignore Jimmy when he was engaged in acceptable behavior, but they had to respond whenever he bit himself. Eventually they became accustomed to Jimmy's continuous hand-biting; they would intervene only when he was more destructive than usual. In this way, they reinforced self-destruction that got progressively worse. They could not have done a better job if they had purposely designed a training program to instruct Jimmy in his own self-mutilation.

Of course, the nurses had no such intention—they were just doing their jobs, reacting with professional care and attention toward their patient, and with human sympathy toward a child in pain.

My indictment is only a hypothesis, of course, and it will probably never be proven directly. No behavior therapist would train a child to bite the flesh off his hands just to prove how easily it can be done by social influence in an institutional setting.

Jimmy's behavior probably would have died out if the nurses had attended to him systematically when he was not biting his hands and had ignored him when he was. But this would have worked only if everyone had participated 100 per cent of the time. When Malcolm Kushner suggested this to the personnel on the hospital ward, he found most of them reluctant to go along with such a program. They felt it would be inhumane and cruel to ignore a child who was in pain.

Kushner decided that the fastest way to relieve Jimmy of his pain would be to subject him briefly to even more pain. He applied electrodes to Jimmy's leg, and shocked him every time he put his hand in his mouth. After only two sessions of less than an hour each, the boy quit biting his hands. His infections began to heal, and the nurses were so impressed with the sudden change that they readily assisted in later booster sessions to maintain this behavior and they cooperated in a broader therapeutic program to help the boy develop more desirable social behavior.

Jimmy's case is extreme. Behavior therapists usually work with patients who are not so disturbed and whose pains are more mental than physical. But whether the therapist deals with self-mutilation, drug addiction, alcoholism, or such quirks as excessive blinking, the moral formula remains the same: a small number of brief, painful experiences is a reasonable exchange for the interminable pain of a lifelong maladjustment. If people think someone looks silly blinking his eyes every couple of seconds, they may decide to stay away from him, especially when they find themselves beginning to blink with him. Enduring a few brief shocks may be a small price to pay to rid oneself of a socially disruptive habit.

Of course, there are alternative therapies—one therapist might prefer to use positive, painless methods; another might want to get at the underlying dynamics of the problem, not just the symptoms.

But how long will it take? That, in my opinion, is the critical question for the moralist.

For as one therapist tries his ostensibly more benevolent or more basic methods, the patient continues to undergo daily punishment while he awaits a cure. Not to rescue a person from his unfortunate habits is to punish him, to leave him in a state of recurrent punishment.

The therapist who humanely avoids inflicting pain on his patients has no moral superiority over another therapist who gives a patient electrical punishment so that he may escape social punishment. The basic questions are which punishment is tougher, and which lasts longer? We have a bookkeeping problem here, not a moral one.

Critics of punishment say that it doesn't actually weaken behavior—it only suppresses behavior for as long as the punishing stimulus is present. This criticism at first seems valid, because a response that has disappeared after punishment often returns when the punishing stimulus is removed. But frequently this event is an artifact of the experiment and not an inherent characteristic of punishment itself.

For example, if a rat usually receives food when it presses a bar, but gets no food while a red light is on, it will soon learn to stop pressing the bar while the red light glows. Similarly, if when punishment is present a behavior does not receive its usual reward, the response may decrease because the punishing stimulus has come to act as a red light—as a signal that no reward is forthcoming. When the punishing stimulus is removed, the behavior may resume quickly, giving the impression that the punishment effect was only temporary.

There are recurrent, dramatic findings that the effects of punishment are often permanent and irreversible. A behavior that has been punished only a few times may never recur. Such dramatic success is a blessing to therapists, but a headache to theorists. If the experimenter decides to stop punishing a certain response, a subject who has ceased responding anyway will have no way to find out about this new contingency. So it is often hard for the theorist to tell whether a behavior has really been unlearned or merely suppressed. Of course, this distinction is of little importance to the patient concerned—as long as a troubling behavior is gone, it makes little practical sense to argue over why it is gone. The effects of punishment are often quick and long-lasting.

*Ivar Lovaas, Benson Schaeffer and James Q. Simmons report on their work with five-year-old identical twin boys who had been diagnosed as schizophrenic. The boys would not speak or respond to other persons. They each spent 70 to 80 percent of their time rocking back and forth, fondling themselves, or moving their hands and arms in repetitive, stereotyped movements. At other times they would go into tantrums–screaming, throwing objects, and hitting themselves.*

*Lovaas and his colleagues punished the boys with brief electric shock for their self-stimulation and tantrums. Although they scheduled three punishment sessions, the self-stimulation and tantrums virtually ceased after the first session and did not recur for 11 months. By then the experimenters were concentrating on therapy designed to train the boys to be more socially responsive.*

Punishment works. The technique is simple, and so is the technology. Anyone with a hand to swing is equipped with a punishing device. Mail-order catalogs list a number of inexpensive and reliable cattle prods that deliver punishing but undamaging electric shocks.

Because punishment is so efficient and simple, there is danger that it could become the first or even the exclusive behavioral technique of carelessly trained therapists. That would indeed be tragic. For one thing, punishment is painful, and the essence of my argument is that we should have as little pain as possible. Punishment should only be used when it will eliminate a behavior that produces even greater punishments. It is essential, I believe, that therapists who use punishment learn a wide range of other behavioral techniques so that they will use punishment only in limited cases, when it is clearly the treatment of choice.

Another danger in the indiscriminate use of punishment is a phenomenon called secondary punishment. Any stimulus that is associated consistently with punishment and with nothing else tends to acquire a punishing function itself. If a dog jumps up on the couch and someone yells "No!" while slapping him on the snout, the word "no" itself will soon act as a punisher. This principle also applies to the persons administering the punishment. If the therapist, teacher or parent who applies punishment becomes himself a punishing stimulus, he should expect all the typical responses— escape, avoidance, aggression, and attempts to have him removed. Kushner, Lovaas, Todd Risley and other behavior therapists take extensive—monumental—care to limit punishment, and they always combine it with repeated positive reinforcement of other behaviors.

In recent years, researchers have reported successful results using punishment to cure such diverse problems as smoking, tics, suicidal ruminations, jealousy, thumb-sucking, nail-biting, homosexuality, exhibitionism, alcoholism, dangerous wall-climbing and habitual coughing.

But punishment works better with some problems than with others. For example, some cases of stuttering, phobia and avoidance behavior have actually intensified when therapists attempted to use punishment.

Thus, there are many unanswered questions. We need to know when punishment is likely to work well and when it is not. We need to know what conditions are likely to help a person retain at home the lessons learned with punishment in the therapist's office. To answer these questions, we will have to do research on punishment. And to do the research, we will have to allow responsible researchers to use punishment. And to do that we will have to overcome our unreasoned revulsion to the whole idea. Punishment is not a barbaric atavism that civilized men must always avoid. It is a legitimate therapeutic technique that is justified and commendable when it relieves persons of the even greater punishments that result from their own habitual behaviors.

# A Position on Childrearing

## Diana Baumrind

I would like now to move from a report of research findings into a presentation of some of my conclusions about childrearing. I want to make clear that experts in the field disagree just as parents do. The meaning I derive from my research findings is affected by my personal values and life experience, and is not necessarily the meaning another investigator would derive.

I have been quoted as opposing permissiveness, and to a certain extent that is true. I would like to describe my position on permissiveness in more detail. I think of the permissive parent as one who attempts to behave in a nonevaluative, acceptant and affirmative manner toward the child's impulses, desires and actions. She consults with him about policy decisions and gives explanations for family rules. She makes few demands for household responsibility and orderly behavior. She presents herself to the child as a resource for him to use as he wishes, not as an ideal for him to emulate, nor as an active agent responsible for shaping or altering his ongoing or future behavior. She allows the child to regulate his own activities as much as possible, avoids the exercise of control, and does not insist that he obey externally defined standards. She attempts to use reason and manipulation, but not overt power, to accomplish her ends.

The alternative to adult control, according to Neill, the best known advocate of permissiveness, is to permit the child to be self-regulated, free of restraint, and unconcerned about expression of impulse, or the effects of his carelessness. I am quoting from *Summerhill* now:

From *Some Thoughts About Childrearing: A Talk Presented to the Children's Community Center in Berkeley, California, May 14, 1969,* by Diana Baumrind.

*Self-regulation means the right of a baby to live freely, without outside authority in things psychic and somatic.* It means that the baby feeds when it is hungry; that it becomes clean in habits only when it wants to; that it is never stormed at nor spanked; that it is always loved and protected (1960, p.105, italics Neill's).

*I believe that to impose anything by authority is wrong. The child should not do anything until he comes to the opinion—his own opinion— that it should be done* (1960, p. 114, italics Neill's).

Every child has the right to wear clothes of such a kind that it does not matter a brass farthing if they get messy or not (1960, p. 115).

Furniture to a child is practically nonexistent. So at Summerhill we buy old car seats and old bus seats. And in a month or two they look like wrecks. Every now and again at mealtime, some youngster waiting for his second helping will while away the time by twisting his fork almost into knots (1960, p. 138).

Really, any man or woman who tries to give children freedom should be a millionnaire, for it is not fair that the natural carelessness of children should always be in conflict with the economic factor (1960, p. 139).*

Permissiveness as a doctrine arose as a reaction against the authoritarian methods of a previous era in which the parent felt that her purpose in training her child was to forward not her own desire, but the Divine Will. The parent felt that since the obstacle to worldly and eternal happiness was self-will, that the subduing of the will of the child led to his salvation. The authoritarian parent of a previous era was preparing his child for a hard life in which success depended upon achievement, and in which strength of purpose and ability to conform were necessary for success. With the advent of Freudian psychology and the loosening of the hold of organized religion, educated middle-class parents were taught by psychologists and educators to question the assumptions of their own authoritarian parents. Spock's 1946 edition of *Baby and Child Care* advocated the

*From *Summerhill: A Radical Approach to Child-rearing,* by A. S. Neill. Copyright © 1960 by Hart Publishing Company. Reprinted by permission.

psychoanalytic view that full gratification of infantile sucking and excretory and sexual impulses were essential for secure and healthful adult personalities. The ideal educated, well-to-do family in the late 40's and 50's was organized around unlimited acceptance of the child's impulses, and around maximum freedom of choice and self-expression for the child.

However by 1957 Spock himself changed his emphasis. He said, in the 1957 edition of his famous book, "A great change in attitude has occurred and nowadays there seems to be more chance of conscientious parents getting into trouble with permissiveness than with strictness."

I would like now to examine certain of the assumptions which have been made in support of permissiveness, most of which, when examined in a research setting, have not been supported.

1. One assumption previously made was that scheduled feeding and firm toilet training procedures have as their inevitable consequences adult neuroses. This apparently is not so. Unless the demands put upon the infant are unrealistic—as might be the demand for bowel training at five months—or the parent punishes the infant cruelly for failure to live up to her demands—scheduled feeding and firm toilet training do not appear to be harmful to the child.

2. A second assumption, that punishment, especially spanking, is harmful to the child, or not effective in controlling behavior, is also not supported by recent research findings. On the contrary, properly administered punishment has been shown by the behavior therapists to be an effective means of controlling the behavior of children. This hardly comes as a surprise to most parents. Brutal punishment *is* harmful to the child. Threats of punishment not carried out are harmful to the child. A parent who threatens to punish must be prepared to deal with escalation from the child by prompt administration of punishment. She cannot appease. Otherwise the threat of punishment will actually *increase* the incidence of undesirable behavior, since it is just that undesirable behavior which will cause the parent to cancel the punishment, in an attempt to appease the child.

While *prompt* punishment is usually most effective, it is important for the parent to be certain that the child knows exactly why he is being punished, and what kind of behavior the parent would prefer and why. While extremely rapid punishment following a transgression works best in training a rat or a dog, a human child is a conscious being and should be approached as one. It should not be enough for a parent, except perhaps in critical matters of safety, to *condition* a child to avoid certain kinds of behavior by prompt punishment. The parent's aim is to help the child control his own behavior, and that end requires the use of reason and the bringing to bear of moral principles to define what is right and what is wrong conduct.

Properly administered punishment, then, provides the child with important information. The child learns what it is his parent wants, and he learns about the consequences of not conforming to an authority's wishes.

3. A third assumption that advocates of permissiveness have made is that unconditional love is beneficial to the child, and that love which is conditional upon the behavior of the child is harmful to the child. I think that the notion of unconditional love has deterred many parents from fulfilling certain important parental functions. They fail to train their children for future life and make them afraid to move towards independence. Indulgent love is passive in respect to the child—not requiring of the child that he become good, or competent, or disciplined. It is content with providing nourishment and understanding. It caters to the child and overlooks petulance and obnoxious behavior—at least it tries to. The effect on the child of such love is often not good. Once the child enters the larger community, the parents are forced to restrict or deprive. Accustomed as the child is to immediate gratification, he suffers greater deprivation at such times than he would if he were not accustomed to associating discipline with love. He does not accept nor can he tolerate unpleasant consequences when he acts against authority figures. Such a child, even when he is older, expects to receive, and is not prepared to give or to compromise. The rule of reciprocity, of payment for value re-

ceived, is a law of life that applies to us all. The child must be prepared in the home by his parents to give according to his ability so that he can get according to his needs.

The parent who expresses love unconditionally is encouraging the child to be selfish and demanding while she herself is not. Thus she reinforces exactly the behavior which she does not approve of—greedy, demanding, inconsiderate behavior. For his part, the child is likely to feel morally inferior for what he is, and to experience conflict about what he should become. I believe that a parent expresses her love most fully when she demands of the child that he become his best, and in the early years helps him to act in accordance with *her* image of the noble, the beautiful and the best, as an initial model upon which he can create (in the adolescent years) his own ideal.

On the other hand, I do believe that to the extent that it is possible, a parent's *commitment* to the child should be unconditional. That is, the parent should stay contained *in* the experience with the child, no matter what the child does. Parental love properly expressed comes closest in my mind to the Christian notion of *Agape*. The parent continues to care for the child because it is her child and not because of the child's merits. Since she is human, the quality of her feeling for him depends upon the child's actions, but her interest in his welfare does not depend upon his actions and is abiding. This abiding interest is expressed not in gratifying the child's whims, nor in making few demands upon him, nor in approval of his actions, nor even in approving of what he is as a person. Unconditional *commitment* means that the child's interests are perceived as among the parent's most important interests, and that (no matter what the child does) the parent does not desert the child. But the love of a parent for a child must be demanding—not demanding of the unconditional commitment it offers—but rather demanding of the reciprocal of what it offers. The parent has the right—indeed, the duty—to expect obedience and growth towards mature behavior, in order that she can discharge her responsibilites to the child, and continue to feel unconditional commitment to his welfare. (Only parents are required, as an expression of love, to give up the object of that love, to prepare the object of love to become toatally free of the lover).

## AUTHORITATIVE VERSUS AUTHORITARIAN PARENTAL CONTROL

Now that I have discussed the concept of permissiveness in childrearing, I would like to explain the distinction which I make between *authoritarian* and *authoritative* parental control.

I think of an *authority* as a person whose expertness befits him to tell another what to do, when the behavioral alternatives are known to both. An authority does not have to *exercise* his control, but it is recognized by both that by virtue of his expertness and his responsibility for the actions of the other, he is fit to exercise authority in a given area.

By *authoritative parental control* I mean that, in relation to her child, the parent should be an authority in the sense just defined.

1. *In order to be an authority, the parent must be expert.* It seems to me that many parents and teachers have come to the conclusion that they are not expert on matters which pertain to the young people placed in their charge. Therefore, since they are not expert, they abandon their role as authorities. I think instead that they should become more expert. Parents often do need more information about children of all ages than they have, in order to be expert. But much of what a parent needs to know she can learn from observing her child and listening to him. A parent must permit her child to be a socialization agent for her, as well as the other way, if the parent is to acquire the information about the child and his peer group that she needs in order to make authoritative decisions about matters which affect the child's life. Unlike the authoritarian parent, the authoritative parent modifies her role in response to the child's coaching. She responds to suggestions and complaints from the child and then transmits her own more flexible norms to her child. In this way, by becoming more expert, the parent legitimates her authority and increases her effectiveness as a socializing agent.

2. *In order to be authoritative, the parent must be willing and able to behave rationally, and to explain the rationale for her values and norms to the child.* The parent does not have to explain her actions all the time to the child, especially if she knows that the child knows the reason but is engaging in harrassment. But a parent does need to be sure that she herself knows the basis for her demands, and that the child also knows, within the limits of his understanding, the reasons behind her demands.

In authoritarian families the parent interacts with the child on the basis of formal role and status. Since the parent has superior power, she tells the child what to do and does not permit herself to be affected by what he says or does. Where parents do not consult with children on decisions affecting the children, authority can only rest on power. As the child gets older and the relative powers of parent and child shift, the basis for parental authority is undermined. Even the young child has the perfect answer to a parent who says, "you must do what I say because I am your mother," and that answer is, "I never asked to be born." The adolescent can add, "Make me," and many say just that when parents are unwise enough to clash directly with an adolescent on an issue on which the adolescent has staked his integrity or autonomy.

3. *In order to be authoritative, the parent must value self-assertion and willfulness in the child.* Her aim should be to prepare the child to become independent of her control and to leave her domain. Her methods of discipline, while firm, must therefore be respectful of the child's actual abilities and capacities. As these increase, she must share her responsibilities and perogatives with the child, and increase her expectations for competence, achievement, and independent action.

I believe that the imposition of authority even against the child's will is useful to the child during the first six years. Indeed, power serves to legitimate authority in the mind of the child, to assure the child that his parent has the power to protect him and provide for him.

The major way in which parents exercise power in the early years is by manipulating the reinforcing and punishing stimuli which affect the child. What makes a parent a successful reinforcing agent or an attractive model for a child to imitate is his effective power to give the child what he needs—i.e., the parent's control over resources which the child desires, and his willingness and ability to provide the child with these resources in such a manner and at such a time that the child will be gratified and the family group benefitted. Thus, practically as well as morally, gratification of the child's needs within the realistic economy of the family, is a precondition for the effective imposition of parental authority. An exploited child cannot be controlled effectively over a long period of time. The parent's ability to gratify the child and to withhold gratification legitimates his authority. The child, unlike the adolescent, has not yet reached the level of cognitive development where he can legitimate authority, or object to its imposition, on a principled basis.

By early adolescence, however, power based on physical strength and control of resources cannot and should not be used to legitimate authority. The young person is now capable of formal operational thought. He can formulate principles of choice by which to judge his own actions and the actions of others. He has the conceptual ability to be critical even though he may lack the wisdom to moderate his criticism. He can see clearly many alternatives to parental directives; and the parent must be prepared to defend rationally, as she would to an adult, a directive with which the adolescent disagrees. Moreover, the asymmetry of power which characterizes childhood no longer exists at adolescence. The adolescent cannot be forced physically to obey over any period of time.

When an adolescent refuses to do as his parent wishes, it is more congruent with his construction of reality for the parent simply to ask him, "why not?". Through the dialogue which ensues, the parent may learn that his directive was unjust; or the adolescent may learn that his parent's directive could be legitimated. In any case, a head-on confrontation is avoided. While head-on confrontation won by the parent serves to strengthen parental authority in the first six years, it produces conflict about adult authority during adolescence.

Although a young person need feel no commitment to the social ethic of his parents' generation, he does have, while he is dependent upon his parents, a moral responsibility to obey rational authority, i.e., authority based on explicitly, mutually-agreed-upon principles. The just restrictions on his freedom provide the adolescent with the major impetus to become self-supporting and responsible to himself rather than to his parents.

## THE RELATIONSHIP OF INDIVIDUAL FREEDOM TO CONTROL

To an articulate exponent of permissiveness in childrearing, such as Neill, freedom for the child means that he has the liberty to do as he pleases without interference from adult guardians and, indeed, with their protection. Hegel, by contrast, defines freedom as the appreciation of necessity. By this he means that man frees himself of the objective world by understanding its nature and controlling his reactions to its attributes. His definition equates the concept of freedom with power to act, rather than with absence of external control. To Hegel, the infant is enslaved by virtue of his ignorance, his dependence upon others for sustenance, and his lack of self-control. The experience of infantile omnipotence, if such he has, is based on ignorance and illusion. His is the freedom to be irresponsible, a very limited freedom, and one appropriate only for the incompetent.

For a person to behave autonomously, he must accept responsiblity for his own behavior, which in turn requires that he believe the world is orderly and susceptible to rational mastery and that he has or can develop the requisite skills to manage his own affairs.

When compliance with parental standards is achieved by use of reason, power, and external reinforcement, it may be possible to obtain obedience and self-correction without stimulating guilt reactions. To some extent the parent's aggressiveness with the child stimulates counteraggressiveness and anger from the child, thus reducing the experience of guilt and of early internalizations of standards whose moral bases cannot yet be grasped. When the child accepts physical punishment or deprivation of privileges as the price paid for acts of disobedience, he may derive from the interaction greater power to withstand suffering and deprivation in the service of another need or an ideal and, thus, increased freedom to choose among expanded alternatives in the future.

Authoritarian control and permissive noncontrol both shield the child from the opportunity to engage in vigorous interaction with people. Demands which cannot be met or no demands, suppression of conflict or sidestepping of conflict, refusal to help or too much help, unrealistically high or low standards, all may curb or understimulate the child so that he fails to achieve the knowledge and experience which could realistically reduce his dependence upon the outside world. The authoritarian and the permissive parent may both create, in different ways, a climate in which the child is not desensitized to the anxiety associated with nonconformity, nor willing to accept punishment for transgressions. Both models minimize dissent, the former by suppression and the latter by diversion or indulgence. To learn how to dissent, the child may need a strongly held position from which to diverge and then be allowed under some circumstances to pay the price for nonconformity by being punished. Spirited give and take within the home, if accompanied by respect and warmth, may teach the child how to express aggression in self-serving and prosocial causes and to accept the partially unpleasant consequences of such actions.

The body of findings on effects of disciplinary practices give provisional support to the position that authoritative control can achieve responsible conformity with group standards without loss of individual autonomy or self-assertiveness.

# REFERENCE

Neill, A. S. *Summerhill: A radical approach to childrearing.* New York: Hart, 1960.

# SUGGESTIONS FOR FURTHER READING

Chance, P. After you hit a child, you can't just get up and leave him; you are hooked to that kid. *Psychology Today,* November 1973, pp. 76–84. This conversation with Ivar Lovaas chiefly concerns the control of autistic children; however, the ideas expressed raise interesting questions concerning behavior control in general.

Elder, G. Adult control in family and school. *Youth and Society,* 1971, *3,* 5–35. Public opinion concerning school discipline is considered in historical and comparative perspective.

Ladd, E. T. Regulating student behavior without ending up in court. *Phi Delta Kappan,* 1973, *54,* 304–309. Suggestions are made for coping with children's misbehaviors at school that take fully into account today's focus on student's rights and anti-authoritarianism.

LaVoie, J. C. The effects of an aversive stimulus, a rationale, and sex of child on punishment effectiveness and generalization. *Child Development,* 1973, *44,* 505–510. The relative effectiveness of various modes of reinforcement were examined and related to the sex of the children involved. The results were then contrasted with those obtained in other research.

LaVoie, J. C. Type of punishment as a determinant of resistance to deviation. *Developmental Psychology,* 1974, *10,* 181–189. Laboratory punishment paradigm, with first- and second-grade children as subjects, was used to assess the comparative effectiveness of an aversive stimulus, withholding of resources, withdrawal of love, reasoning alone, and reasoning combined with praise. The results are discussed in terms of sex of child, mode of reinforcement, and anxiety arousal.

LaVoie, J. C., & Looft, W. R. Parental antecedents of resistance-to-temptation behavior in adolescent males. *Merrill-Palmer Quarterly,* 1973, *19,* 107–116. Parental behaviors, including type of discipline and ease of communication between parent and son, were related to their teenage sons' potential discipline problems.

McNeil, E. B. *Human socialization.* Belmont, Calif.: Brooks/Cole, 1969. Pp. 145–150. McNeil discusses three concepts of discipline: the mental hygienist's view, the life-space approach, and the "cook-book" style. This is a brief, but readable and perceptive discussion.

Milgram, S. The dilemma of obedience. *Phi Delta Kappan,* 1974, *55,* 603–606. The author examines the moral question of whether or not one should obey when commands conflict with one's conscience. He examines experiments relevant to this question and considers how unthinking obedience may lead to losing sight of the broader consequences of one's behaviors. The problem of obedience, therefore, becomes a matter of considerable social concern. Students may note comments on this article by Robert L. Ebel and Lawrence Kohlberg in the pages just following Milgram's article.

Neale, D. C. Aversive control of behavior. *Phi Delta Kappan,* 1960, *50,* 335–338. The author appraises the relative advantages of positive and negative reinforcement; and he notes, in particular, laboratory evidence for the superiority of aversive or negative control.

# 11

## Alternative Family Life-Styles

A major feature in contemporary America has been the emergence of certain alternative family life-styles that differ significantly from that of the traditional household—husband, wife, and children, living apart from their relatives, with the woman as homemaker and the father as breadwinner. The alternative, or "counter-culture family is a social unit composed of more than two adult members, living in a legally unconventional situation, with or without children, obviously not in total alignment with the dominant mores of our conjugal family model" (Whitehurst, 1972, p. 395). Such families include groups living together in single-parent households, and two-parent families united by social rather than legal contracts.

## CHARACTERISTICS OF ALTERNATIVE FAMILIES

Although these family styles have distinctive variations, they generally share certain characteristics. All grew out of the counterculture movement of the 1960s and early 1970s, when young adults began questioning the ideological and personal values of traditional America. They have many functions, including provision for food, shelter, clothing, happiness, and financial support of family members; procreation, care, and socialization of the children; and interpersonal support in personal and family crises (Cogswell & Sussman, 1972). They emphasize such values as affection,

openness, and expression of sensuous pleasures, both with the child and with each other. They also value good health, natural foods, and natural childbirth (Eiduson, Cohen, & Alexander, 1973).

Their child-rearing practices are especially distinctive and, in many respects, successful. Babies are often carried on the mother's back and accompany her most of the time, at least during the first year of life. Initially close parent-child relationships are common; however, children move rapidly toward self-reliance at 2½ to 3 years. The change begins after the child is weaned and the mother returns to before-pregnancy activities. Meantime the child has developed a generalized sense of trust because of being switched among mothers for breast-feeding or because of multiple caretakers, often older siblings. According to traditional family stereotypes even older children are portrayed as somewhat inept, requiring constant caretaking by both parents and contributing little to the family. Nevertheless, older children can be quite effective socialization agents for young children, in many respects more so than the parents themselves.

Such families may have other positive values, too. Since there is minimal discrimination between sex roles, children can realize their broadest potential without fear of transcending sex barriers. Moreover, since their parents refuse to be hemmed in by tradition and unduly manipulated by others' carping criticism, they develop a greater feeling of personal freedom and a trust in the integrity of their own views.

The children of alternative-type families also experience considerable social interaction. The middle-class nuclear family may isolate children from broad social contacts. By contrast, certain alternative families serve, in effect, as extended families, providing their children contacts with different kinds of people. Thus they have a variety of role models and a better chance to find ones compatible with their own dispositions (Cogswell & Sussman, 1972).

Note, too, that the very concept of alternative life-styles suggests that the family should be molded to the needs of its members. One form of oppression, declares Tucker (1974), has been universal—that children have had no alternatives but to live with their parents or be housed in some jail-like alternative. We have glorified the nuclear family as the sole valid family mode, although many children might flourish better under some other system. Besides, everyone should try to understand and appreciate different modes of life. Adults not living in nuclear families include single persons with or without children, married people without children or with stepchildren, couples with grown children, homosexual couples, elderly people in nursing homes, and so forth.

## DISADVANTAGES OF ALTERNATIVE FAMILY STYLES

On the other hand, living in alternative style families has its hazards. For one thing, such families are often deprived of medical and social welfare services, either by law or by local agencies' interpretation of the law (Cogswell & Sussman, 1972). For another, persons who disregard long-standing tradition must often cope with adverse criticism. For example, a father who performed most of the domestic duties in his home tells how neighbors reacted:

When Amy [my daughter] was born, I quit my job in Boston to stay home and take care of her. This was not really very liberated. I disliked my job; I wanted to write a book.

Our neighbors, strangers, disapproved. The idea of a grown man staying home during the day to care for a baby was subversive. . . . To see me in the middle of the afternoon pushing my daughter up a hill in a stroller, or carrying her strapped to my back like kitchen utensils for an Alpine ascent, was offensive. . . .

Finally, I had to explain to the mailman that I was a writer. . . . He relayed this information to the neighborhood. It was exculpatory. Writers, properly, are presumed strange, but not dangerous [Leonard, 1974, pp. 52–53].

It may be argued that weaknesses within the nuclear family derive not from the concept itself, but from burdens unfairly imposed on it. Skolnick and Skolnick (1971) contend that "not only is the nuclear family a faultily constructed piece of social engineering, but it also, in the long run, contains the seeds of its own destruction" (p. 29). However, Gaylin (1971) argues that we have placed an undue burden on the nuclear family by expecting it to fulfill all our affiliative needs—an impossible and unreasonable task. In consequence, "the critics step in and condemn the family for its failures, using the example of modern youth. Their search for new life styles—the burgeoning of communal living, 'free communits,' and so on, have all been used as arguments that the modern American family has failed to meet the needs of postindustrial man" (p. 76).

The trouble is, pursues Gaylin, we may be "throwing out the baby with the bath" (p. 76). Even if the family has not been able to meet all the unusual demands placed upon it, it has somehow managed to instill in its members a feeling of community that they transfer to situations outside the family structure. Note, too, that experimental family styles often revert to the traditional model. In societies that have tried to mandate communal rather than nuclear family life, notably in Russia and Israel, there has been a gradual return to more traditional forms of family life.

Certainly, many questions regarding the relative worth of different family styles remain to be answered. What is the long-term effect on children's adjustment and personalities? In what ways, and to what degree, will such modes of child rearing affect socialization in traditional households? When parents retreat from experimental marriage forms to more traditional settings, what is the effect on their children? Do they have difficulty adapting to the new mode of life and to neighbors who have been reared in more traditional ways? What is the relative effect on boys and girls, or on younger and older children? What are the differences in children's adjustment according to specific family alternatives? Are certain of these alternatives better for some children than others? Do the children of such marriages seek similar family forms when they establish their own families of procreation, or do they follow more traditional patterns? What adjustments should society make for dealing with such families and for providing family services to them, taking into account their special characteristics and the needs of the children involved?

The answers to such questions are vital, because the potential significance of alternative families far exceeds what their small numbers might suggest. They serve as testing grounds for life-styles that may be adapted in part to more traditional modes of life. The persons involved are often bright and ingenious, and many of the ideas that they evolve about family life may prove quite useful. Certainly, in rapidly changing times these "laboratories" of family-life research may suggest ways that the institution of the family should be modified. Otherwise, it may not possess the integrity or viability to meet the demands of generations to come.

The articles that follow provide two quite interesting and provocative views of counterculture families. In the first, Brian T. Shanley compares nuclear- and communal-family models in terms of the values they represent and encourage in their children. In the second, Robert Rath and Douglas McDowell report a study of counterculture families in noncommunal settings in Pennsylvania. The parents were interviewed regarding their child-rearing goals, values, and practices, and problems involved in their children's schooling. Needed, but still lacking, are data derived from longitudinal studies of children growing up in alternative types of families.

## REFERENCES

Cogswell, B. E., & Sussman, M. B. Changing family and marriage forms: Complications for human service systems. *Family Coordinator*, 1972, *21*, 505–516.

Eiduson, B. T., Cohen, J., & Alexander, J. Alternatives in child rearing in the 1970s. *American Journal of Orthopsychiatry*, 1973, *43*, 720–731.

Gaylin, N. L. The family is dead—long live the family. *Youth and Society*, 1971, *3*, 60–79.

Leonard, J. The fathering instinct. *Ms.*, November 1974, pp. 52–53; 56; 112.

Skolnick, A., & Skolnick, J. *Family in transition: Rethinking marriage, sexuality, child-rearing, and family organizations*. Boston: Little, Brown, 1971.

Tucker, Y. Y. The child within. *Ms.*, September 1974, pp. 70–71; 94–95.

Whitehurst, R. N. Some comparisons of conventional and counterculture families. *Family Coordinator*, 1972, *21*, 395–401.

# Communalism Versus the Nuclear Family: An Analysis of Alternative Models

## Brian T. Shanley

When one examines Erikson's classic model of psychosocial development and judges the nuclear American family as a primary agent of such development, serious questions arise concerning the value of the prevailing family

Reprinted from *Child Welfare*, 1972, *51*, 618–626. Copyright 1972 by Child Welfare League of America, Inc. Reprinted by permission.

structure. Does the conventional family promote personal growth and the self-actualization of its members, or does it simply preserve the status quo? Does it facilitate the formation of healthy personalities, or does it stifle such development, as Jourard suggests?(5:43)

These questions are not new: Plato proposed the elimination of the family, as we know it, in *The Republic*. But an unprecedented number of young Americans are actively pursuing alternatives to the traditional family structure, and this is a new phenomenon. There have been isolated attempts at such experiments throughout our history, the most notable being the Oneida Community, which involved about 300 persons for a period of 30 years during the 19th century. But in the last decade, attempts at intentional communities have proliferated across the country, and appear still to be on the increase. Although precise figures are unobtainable, it has been estimated that more than 10,000 persons are now involved in such efforts.(4:28) Roszak identifies this trend as a clear manifestation of the counterculture that he sees emerging in our technocratic society.(8:201) Hedgepeth concurs:

> Historically and biologically, it's no freak thing that's happening now. When a person senses, even subconsciously, a deprivation of some particular dimension to his life he silently craves it, like the dietary needs of pregnant women that so often seem irrational. These young migrants quietly sense the cruelly shattered status of a society erected on a cult of rigid, nonemotional "Individualism." And in response, they hunger now for community. They crave the sensation of becoming whole with other human beings, of being a part of a larger thing. Rather than wanting to continue splitting up, specializing, pigeonholing the entire planet, they have upon them the urgent urge to put things back together.(4:30)*

*From *The Alternative: Communal Life in New America,* by W. Hedgepeth and D. Stock. Copyright © 1970 by William Hedgepeth. This and all other quotations from this source are reprinted by permission of Macmillan Publishing Co., Inc.

These are the youth who were reared on Dr. Benjamin Spock by parents who withdrew from extended families to go it alone at producing new members for society. Several unforeseen problems arose in these isolated nuclear families, chief among them being the position of centrality that children held. As a result of this centrality, parental needs became fulfilled chiefly through the children, and not through interaction with other adults. Parsons suggests that these parents were reliving their own childhood through participation in their children's lives.(7) Beyond this, the introjection of parental values was constantly sought by the parents as evidence of their influence. If it was not forthcoming, the parents felt that they had failed in their job of child rearing. If it was forthcoming, it was most likely at the expense of whatever insights the child might have gained had he been free to experience a broader variety of human contacts.

This unilateral relationship was inconsistent with the "passion to explore" that Spock felt should be cultivated in a child.

But it was consistent with the manner in which the parents themselves had been reared in their extended families and so seemed natural. For understandable reasons, they felt their traditions were worth preserving: They had been through the depression and war, and had worked hard to provide a comfortable existence for their children; and now they were able to pamper their offspring with material goods and thus enrich their lives.

But these children were soon to begin questioning that comfortable existence, and resisting what to them was a shallow existence. Since their economic security was assured, they saw no need for the tradition-directedness nor the goal-orientation that dominated their parents' personalities. An affluent society provided them with several years' time in which to develop these feelings in relative comfort, and in the company of their peers. And so the "passion to explore" did develop. But it developed not with adult guidance, but in reaction to it.

What had evolved since is basically an alternative life style. It is difficult to categorize

**Communalism vs. the Nuclear Family**

**193**

or define this style: indeed, it arose in part to protest the compartmentalization that marks American life in general. But it involves a search for intimacy, and seeks a basic change in the quality of human relations. The communal experiments, I think, best exemplify the spirit of this search. In a recent year the FBI reported the arrest of more than 90,000 juvenile runaways.(8:33) Many of this number were in search of such alternative living arrangements. This paper examines the communal living arrangement, vis-a-vis the isolated nuclear family, in reference to the Erikson model of psychosocial development. The communal experiments taking place in America are quite diverse. As Downing writes:

> The tribal family members act out a Camelot-like legend, seeking a brotherhood and sisterhood of sharing, loving and growing. Sadly, they often frustrate their own yearnings through naivete, inexperience or lack of discipline. Their expressed social ideal is that of equality of all members in a freely giving, freely receiving cooperative; their reality is different, ranging from traditional tribal systems headed by the Old Man or the Mother; to fairly stable, hard-working cooperatives; to loose peer groups of limited duration cohabiting in one dwelling; to isolated, anarchic, fear-laden situations similar to Golding's novel, *The Lord of the Flies*.(2:120)

This discussion refers chiefly to the first two types of arrangements that Downing lists, in that they are the more viable. The failure rate of American communes is high, especially among the latter types listed by Downing. This is due chiefly, I think, to lack of planning or resources. Rarely do members abandon a commune due to a rejection of the original concept.

It should be kept in mind that any attempt to establish a commune in this country is made in the context of a subculture at odds with the dominant culture. For this reason I use as a model of the communal unit the kibbutz of Israel, which is fully sanctioned by its society.

The kibbutz has been able to develop over a 3-generation span, and is thus more suitable for objective evaluation than are the American experiments. Where essential cultural differences exist—and they do to a certain extent—I point them out.

## TRUST VS. MISTRUST

In the nuclear family, an infant is given loving and protective care by his mother from the time of infancy on a regular basis. At the age of 6 months, he is able to differentiate between his mother and outsiders, and recognizes the security that she offers him.

In the kibbutz, within days of birth, the child is taken away from the mother, and placed with other infants under the charge of a *metapelet,* or nurse, who provides professional care. From the very start a pattern is established: the *metapelet* cares for the child's physical needs, and the mother, on a limited basis, cares for his emotional needs. The mother is permitted to breast-feed the infant up until the age of 6 months, by which time he must be weaned. His imprinting is derived from a variety of sources. He is taught from the earliest age that the kibbutz is his home, and that all its members are his family. He is cared for 24 hours a day, but by different persons.

The average American commune is not yet nearly so structured as the kibbutz, and yet all retain the concept that its members form a family. It may sound somewhat crude to state it in this way, but it is nonetheless true: private property is frowned upon, whether it be material goods or children. Communitarians maintain that real trust develops when an infant always feels secure, and not only when he's in the presence of one person. Conversely, mistrust is far more likely to develop when one person—who may die or be ill or just be occupied with other matters—is relied upon exclusively for security.

The basic conflict between the two models could be expressed in terms of quantity versus quality. The commune offers constant care, but cannot offer the deeply personal care that a good mother can provide. Basic trust in a generalized other should develop naturally in a commune, while a deep trust in a significant other can develop in the nuclear family.

## AUTONOMY VS. SHAME, DOUBT

In the average nuclear family, a child is instructed in the various do's and don't's—in accordance with the parent's value system—

from the earliest age. Such matters as correct table manners and proper hygiene are drilled into him. The child is made aware of his family's socioeconomic identity and is taught how to act in accordance with that status, thus encouraging the development of a personal superego that will conflict with the ego.

Bettelheim questions whether a personalized ego can exist in a kibbutz, suggesting a positive relationship between the absence of private property and the absence of private emotions.(1:235, 281) Values are formed chiefly by the peer group with which the child lives. Whatever superego demands arise have been created by a collective, communal ego. In a consensus community, to obey the superego is to obey the only external environment that exists. Thus, a child experiences far less conflict than in a nuclear family.

I think that the same generally holds true in American communes, to whatever extent they are organized on a no-value basis. But there is considerably more contact between adult and child, and a certain degree of value orientation is inevitably imparted. Many adults seek to keep such influence to a minimum.

> Sometimes, the adults' desire to communalize their children is so intense that girls will have intercourse with several males during their most fertile days so no one will know who the father is. Because of the strong belief in natural childbirth, as held by the majority of communitarians, babies are most often born completely out of the reach of official sources. This means that just as there are no marriage licenses, so also there are no birth certificates—and hence, no social security numbers or any other tags or digits or ways of being classified and kept track of by the Establishment. The child, then, becomes a total nonperson, so far as the straight world is concerned, completely insulated from the impersonal mechanisms of society, including, most importantly, the draft. To further ensure nonidentification, the children often bear only mystical names or descriptive Indian-style titles, like "Sweetwater" or "Cloud" or sometimes the names of the communes themselves.(4:127)

The primacy of the peer group in a commune serves to minimize sources of shame and doubt and to maximize autonomy. This contrasts with the extreme pressure exerted by the superego on a nuclear family child to conform to his parents' expectations, and the subsequent guilt feelings that are provoked.

## INITIATIVE VS. GUILT

The collective superego of the communal setting provides a basic contrast to the personalized superego of the nuclear family. There is not nearly so much distance between child and model, in that the model is diffuse and the child always has peer group support. When role playing takes place, it is more diversified than in the nuclear family, where role playing can often consist merely of parent playing.

And yet it is chiefly a group role that is played. This is especially true in the kibbutz, where a child has virtually no time that he can call his own. In contrast, American communes allow much greater opportunity for individual initiative, with far less emphasis on comradeship.

What both communal settings share is reference to a generalized other rather than to the all-powerful parents. These children are free to engage in what Jean Piaget calls their collective monologues, and thus develop the ability to interact freely, unhampered by parental attitudes. What they are hampered by, to varying degrees, is the sense of collectiveness, or usness, which can give rise to group guilt feelings, and restrict the child's ability to make personal decisions.

## INDUSTRY VS. INFERIORITY

"Work," writes McLuhan, "does not exist in a nonliterate world." Communitarians do not perform tasks, but acts of self-expression. Children contribute to the communal economy from the earliest age by participation in such activities as gardening. Bettelheim writes that the children of the kibbutz just naturally develop self-sufficiency and that they value this as superior to whatever work patterns might exist in the outside world. This is in striking contrast to the middle-class American child, who is constantly frustrated by his apparent uselessness in society, and the extent of schooling that is required for him to fill a vital role.

In urban American communes, traditional work roles are negatively valued, but are nonetheless accepted for brief periods of time, when necessary in order to meet communal needs. Children—in theory—are fully equal members of the commune, and thus have no reason to feel inferior. In some cases mothers are collecting AFDC benefits, and thus the children might be contributing to the sustenance of the community. But they make their important contribution as individuals in the interdevelopmental process, which completely transcends work roles.

## IDENTITY VS. IDENTITY CONFUSION

It is at this stage that the average adolescent enters into a psychosocial moratorium, in which he integrates the preceding elements of personality formation.

In many communal settings, and particularly in the kibbutz, this task is already completed: The individual's identity is the group's identity and has been firmly established as such. There is no need to consider the demands that might be placed on one's development by ideological commitment: A commitment has already been made to the communal way of life, which often—in the case of the kibbutz—has its own ideology. The outside world is considered foreign and alien. Its occupations, from which other youth are struggling to make a choice, appear irrelevant.

It is at this stage that many American youth become attracted to the concept of communal living—in a refusal to assume a standardized societal role. For they find that those roles that society offers them are lacking as outlets for personal creativity and growth—qualities that they have come to expect in their lives within an affluent society. Many other youth compromise a pursuit of personal development in favor of the material security assured them by embracing a societal role. And a few struggle against great odds to achieve self-actualization within an established role.

At first glance, then, it would appear that the communal arrangement virtually eliminates the great task of identity formation for the young. But as Bettelheim writes of kibbutz adolescents:

> While their place in society is assured, the place is designated by their elders, from whose yoke—however gentle—they wish to fight free. Most of all, though finding one's place in society is much easier, *it is not much of a finding of oneself,* because no personal doing won them the place.(1:243)

No personal decision had to be made, and the question arises whether a personal decision could be made.

## INTIMACY VS. ISOLATION

According to Erikson, a clear sense of personal identification is an essential prerequisite to intimacy. In accord with this theory has been the observation that kibbutz children, while intense in their relations with one another, are incapable of intimacy: they do not possess strong personal emotions and thus cannot exchange them.(1:160)

The resultant sense of isolation is clearly manifest in the members' xenophobic attitudes toward other living conditions.(1:250)

Erikson has pointed out that American youth who don't successfully cope with the crisis of intimacy can go through life maintaining highly stereotyped interpersonal relations and not advance further on the developmental scale. But at least they have a chance to achieve intimacy, as difficult as the task might be in a technocratic society. How ironic it is that while communes are currently being sought by many youth for this purpose, those reared in communes appear incapable of reaching the same level of development.

The question may rightly be asked whether the kibbutz experience need necessarily apply to American efforts at communal living. Although there is no certain answer, I would be inclined to answer in the affirmative. Among second-generation kibbutzim, there was a marked decline in the Zionist influence that distinguished the experiments initially; among the third generation, such influence is virtually nonexistent.(1:289) If one assumes that current American experiments are going to evolve into more structured form, it is difficult to escape the conclusion that effects similar to those of the kibbutz would follow. It might be noted that the Oneida experiment ended in its third generation, at which time these effects would become clearly visible.

## GENERATIVITY VS. STAGNATION

But to return to those effects: Generativity is defined as "the concern for establishing and guiding the next generation."(3:138) One cause for the retardation of this impulse, according to Erikson, is an excessive self-love based on a too strenuously self-made personality. It is precisely such a self-love that communal peer-group members constantly reinforce upon one another.

I think it can be safely said that most young parents now emerging from nuclear families have at least the desire to guide their children's generation. The kibbutzim clearly disavows such a role, and one of the most basic characteristics of the emerging American experiments is self-preoccupation.(2:123)

According to Erikson, such personalities can never ripen, but can only stagnate, and ultimately lead to despair. Again, the groundwork for such a development is laid in adolescence, with the rejection of a personal identity.

## INTEGRITY VS. DESPAIR

The limited data compiled on the aging kibbutzim seem to bear out Erikson's theory. Although they retain the same physical security that they gained upon entering the kibbutzim, they seem to have lost their enthusiasm. Writes Yonina Talmon:

Even those who in the process of aging seem well ordered and well balanced very often feel defeated. In many cases we found a consider-

able discrepancy between our evaluation of the degree of adjustment achieved by an elderly member, on the one hand, and his own self-evaluation, on the other. We found that many of the aged tended to underrate the advantages and overrate disadvantages . . . rely on organizational changes rather than on ideological reorientation and personal resocialization. They do not realize the need for a deliberate cultivation of flexibility in role.(9:112)

She goes on to point out the marked tendency of these aged to cling to their family members. This irony is further compounded by Erikson's description of a key element in the achievement of integrity: "a sense of comradeship with men and women of different times and of different pursuits . . ."(3:139)

One might argue that few aged individuals from any background reach the final stage in Erikson's model, and that the kibbutz at least assures their basic security. Bettelheim discussed the merits of the kibbutz educational system in the same context—that although it rarely produced exceptional students with leadership potential, it did guarantee a respectable middle-level performance by all. This writer doesn't believe that in either context universal mediocrity should be held as an ideal.

## CONCLUSIONS

As Otto has written, "The actualizing of our human potential is closely bound to the regeneration of our human institutions."(6:112) The proponents of alternative family structures can learn much from one another; to continue to head in separate directions is to assure the continued credibility of the charge that we function at 6% of our capacity.(6:111)

Although neither the nuclear family nor the communal arrangement is perfect, each has clearly demonstrated benefits for psychosocial development. They have both reflected the crucial importance and dynamic character of the adolescent stage of development.

We should keep these thoughts in mind when dealing clinically with identity crises, and resist the urge to uphold any given model as

Communalism vs. the Nuclear Family

**197**

definitive. What we should aim for is a synthesis of those insights that have been provided by alternative models, and a recognition that only through further experimentation can we hope to gain fresh insights into the developmental processes.

## REFERENCES

1. Bettelheim, Bruno. The Children of the Dream. New York: Macmillan, 1969.
2. Downing, Joseph J. "The Tribal Family and the Society of Awakening," in The Family in Search of a Future, Herbert Otto, editor. New York: Appleton-Century-Crofts, 1970.
3. Erikson, Erik. Identity: Youth and Crisis. New York: W. W. Norton, 1968.
4. Hedgepeth, William, and Stock, Dennis. The Alternative: Communal Life in New America. New York, Macmillan, 1970.
5. Jourard, Sidney M. "Reinventing Marriage: The Perspective of a Psychologist," in The Family in Search of a Future.
6. Otto, Herbert. "The New Marriage: Marriage as a Framework for Developing Personal Potential," in The Family in Search of a Future.
7. Parsons, Talcott, et al. Family Socialization and Interaction Process. New York: Free Press, 1955.
8. Roszak, Theodore. The Making of a Counter Culture. New York: Doubleday, 1969. Conservative estimates are that about 600,000 ran away from home in 1970 (U S. News and World Report, April 24, 1972, p. 38).
9. Talmon, Yonina. "Aging in Israel, a Planned Society," in Middle Age and Aging, Bernice Neugarten, editor. Chicago: University of Chicago Press, 1968.

# Coming Up Hip: Child Rearing Perspectives and Life Style Values Among Counter Culture Families

## Robert A. Rath & Douglas J. McDowell

Over the past decade in the United States, there has been developing among young people a culture with values and norms that appear as marked departures from those of the larger society. These changes surfaced and received considerable publicity in the 1950's with the Beats and were carried forth in the 1960's by both hippies and activists. Hippies have more or less withdrawn from American society and appear currently to be engaged in a variety of trial and error attempts to develop alternatives to existing values and institutions, while activists are working in various capacities toward changing traditional society (Roszak 1969, esp. Ch 2). Both categories are working to establish options to the values and life styles of contemporary American society and with some exceptions, the objectives for each are quite similar.

As a population cohort, these people have recently begun to establish families of their own and many are in various stages of attempting to transmit these alternative values to their offspring. This study is primarily concerned with a descriptive analysis of this socialization process from the perspectives of counter culture parents.[1] Focus is on certain life style

Reprinted from Sociological Symposium, Fall 1971, 7, 49–60. Copyright 1971 by Sociological Symposium. Reprinted by permission.

[1]The terms "hippie" and "counter culture adherent" are used interchangeably throughout this paper.

value orientations as a context for child rearing and on child rearing practices and goals.

The counter culture, like the culture of the dominant society, is not homogeneous; rather, it includes numerous diverse elements and styles. With respect to family organization, distinctions can be drawn between individuals living in communal fashion and those maintaining no essential commitments beyond the immediate nuclear family. While life style and value differences between the two are no doubt observable, the existence of an ethic and perspective common to the counter culture (Roszak 1969:1-83) suggests that perhaps there are more similarities than differences, at least on basic issues such as child rearing.

This study dealt exclusively with counter culture families living in noncommunal settings although views on communal living arrangements were discussed with respondents. Decisions to concentrate on families in noncommunal situations were based on estimates that this category presently includes the vast majority of counter culture adherents and that at this point in time, the possibility seems remote that communal systems will become a dominant mode of counter culture family organization. If the counter culture endures, it will likely do so in the context of varying degrees of contact with the larger society and apart from the cultural isolation that a relatively autonomous commune might provide. This would seem to pose a variety of problems for parents attempting to rear children according to alternative or possibly deviant values. Thus, a second research concern was to investigate some problems and consequences of contacts with the dominant society. At several points in the analysis respondents' views are compared with recollections and perceptions of their own experiences in their families of orientation.

## PROCEDURES

Data were obtained from a nonrandom selection of counter culture families through "focused interviews" (Merton 1956) constructed to obtain respondents' views on values in relation to life style, socialization goals and child rearing practices. There were twenty-six respondents comprising thirteen families which were defined to include one adult male, one adult female and at least one child.

Families were identified and contacted with the help of peer informants familiar with counter culture "communities" in specific areas of Pennsylvania. Other persons known to be involved in the life of these communities were also asked to comment on the extent to which potential study families were considered "members" of the counter culture, hippies or "freaks."[2] Consensus among their peers that the individuals in particular families did in fact belong to the counter culture was a main criterion for including those families in the study. Study families also served as informants and suggested contacting other families for possible inclusion in the study.

Other criteria used to identify and select families for study were: (1) self-identification as counter culture adherents (pre-interview criterion); and (2) identification with counter culture values (post-interview criterion). Potential respondents were contacted and questioned concerning their awareness of a commitment to counter culture life styles. Decisions to interview them were based upon their professed identity with these alternative norms. Post-interview decisions to include particular families in the study were predicated on responses to a general checklist of counter culture values and attributes incorporated in the interview guide. These included: (1) life style values such as "doing your own thing," tolerance for individual differences (the right of others to do their own thing), learning and knowing through direct personal experience, developing intimate primary relationships with others, encouraging free and open expression of emotions, negating competition and material acquisition and irreverent or rebellious attitudes toward conventional society; and (2) stereotyped normative patterns such as drug use, strong

[2] "Freak" is another term for hippie. Unlike the designation hippie, which is seen as an invention of the mass media (or at least promulgated by them for "negative" reasons) the word freak is viewed as an in-group invention connoting affection. It is also used to denote obsessions or addictions to a variety of things: food, drugs (e.g., "speed freak"), activities, etc.

interest in rock music, use of "health foods," interest in astrology and the occult, distinctive clothing styles and for males long hair, beards and mustaches. All thirteen families interviewed expressed support for all or most of these ideas and values and were retained for further study.[3]

Although an interview guide was used to insure that all topics were covered, the questioning was kept relatively informal and unstructured, a style that is in keeping with counter culture values that question nearly all forms of structured activities. Respondents preferred to "rap" (i.e., engage in a face-to-face, give and take kind of communication where individuals "really" express the way they feel and because of the relatively unstructured format, interviews took the form of "rap sessions" concerning their values, family and children. Pursuing the topics that interested them most, all respondents appeared to talk openly and willingly and frequently volunteered the required information without being asked. All interviews were recorded on tapes in the respondents' homes. Major areas discussed in the interviews centered on general life style values and how they related to family and children, marital and family role structure, the family in relation to the larger society, socialization goals and child rearing philosophies, approaches and methods. Interview data were

supplemented by observations made in the home and subsequent conversations with about half of the respondents.

## CHARACTERISTICS OF RESPONDENTS

For the most part, respondents fit the recent descriptions of counter culture adherents reported in both popular and social science literature. Typically, they were from relatively affluent, socially privileged homes. Most were reared in what they characterized as a fairly permissive and liberal atmosphere where parents were described as showing too little concern and interest in the lives of their children (Keniston 1968:32).

In general, respondents were from suburban or small urban areas in Pennsylvania, their fathers were likely to be in white collar occupations and their religious background typically was Protestant. Most were between the ages of twenty and twenty-four, had received some college training in nontechnical and nonbusiness fields, and had educational aspirations beyond the undergraduate college degree level.

## SOCIALIZATION GOALS

Socialization goals may be viewed as attempts on the part of parents to inculcate in their children qualities and characteristics that they value and view as desirable. They are idealized conceptions of the kind of person they would like their child to be and the values they would like him to internalize. Goals also imply that those professing them have some sense of how they might be attained which, respondents claimed, centered on teaching by example, on practicing what is preached, on not doing what you don't want your child to do. Also stressed was the idea that child rearing was not a process that could be separated from other events and behaviors within the home, rather, it was part of the business of living in a family situation.

Major socialization goals for counter culture parents included at least the following:

[3] While a more precise method of determining who belongs to the counter culture might be desirable, the very nature of the counter culture value system would seem to render this impossible. There are no formalized entrance requirements and no recognized set of attributes or behaviors that would positively identify one as a member or nonmember. Within the counter culture there are references to the "straight" society or "square" world but there seems to be little set agreement on what this comprises or who is "straight" and who is "hip." At present, it seems, one can be "hip" in more or less degree, a notion explicit in hippie typologies developed by Howard (1969), Yablonsky (1968) and Simmon & Trout (1967:27–32). Variability was also found among present study families; some were obviously more hip than others. That is, they were described by peer informants as "a really freaky couple," they identified strongly as freaks and the authors' impressions, based upon analysis of views expressed during the interview, confirmed these judgments. There were high degrees of correspondence among these three criteria for all thirteen families.

(1) Development of the child's creative potential to its fullest (self-actualization).
(2) Development of self confidence, a positive self-image and independence at an early age.
(3) A sense of responsibility to self and others (not hurting others).
(4) Openness to change and experimentation.
(5) An ability to relate interpersonally with others in an open and honest way (no "game-playing"), especially with parents.
(6) Tolerance and appreciation of individual differences and the rights of others.
(7) Attitudes of cooperation and sharing.
(8) An appreciation that life should be lived to its fullest.
(9) Openness toward sex and sexuality and an appreciation of it as a normal human activity.
(10) Respect for the family and parental values (not obedience).
(11) A questioning stance toward all norms, rules and authority.
(12) A capacity to express emotions openly and freely.
(13) Strong commitments to peace and nonviolence.

Notable qualities not mentioned were obedience, respect for authority, a work ethic, religious commitments, competitiveness and success in the traditional sense of achieving wealth and prestige. In fact, most of these were devalued, especially obedience to rules that "don't make sense" and work where the prevailing attitude was "if it doesn't feel good, don't do it." Also devalued was following the advice of "experts" in relation to child rearing. The manner in which parents went about child rearing was seen to stem from their own personal experiences and self-understanding, "common sense" and "just being in tune with the child's needs."

The family was seen as providing a "nurturing environment" for the individual child and adult, while the nuclear family was described by most as an environment in which the individual could develop his emotional, creative and intellectual potential. Self development within the counter culture involves "doing your own thing," while being a member of

a family group necessarily involves duties and responsibilities. This would seem to involve a conflict between individual autonomy and family responsibilities. To the extent that conflict was present, it was dealt with by emphasizing the developmental potential for the individual as a family member rather than its limiting aspects. While recognizing that marital and parental roles impose certain duties, most respondents seemed to feel that these roles also opened avenues for new experiences and facilitated development of the individual and thus they perceived no real conflict for themselves.

All parents recognized that there was likely a divergence between these ideals and the realities of their situation, due in part from their rejection of many dominant cultural values and practices while remaining involved with the general social structure through which they are expressed and realized. Achievement of these ideals was also inhibited by the fact that respondents were socialized by different standards and values and only in relatively recent years had they adopted counter culture values and norms. This inhibiting effect of parental and societal values, norms and beliefs passed on to respondents from their families of orientation, peers and society were referred to as "hang-ups" which they were attempting to overcome and prevent passing on to their children.

## CHILD REARING PRACTICES

Running throughout discussions of child rearing practices were several key themes centering on the human need to receive and give love and affection in an open and uninhibited way, active involvement of both parents in the life of the family (especially in child care and rearing) and relating to the child as a unique individual with rights of his own, especially the right to order his own environment (permissiveness). All respondents claimed to be strongly committed to these three ideas. They are examined below in relation to respondents' own views and the perceived practices of their parents.

## PARENTAL AFFECTION AND INVOLVEMENT

While professing commitment to affection and involvement, many respondents also claimed that this was not the case for their own parents and their own childhood experiences. On the contrary, no respondents described their own relationships with their parents, either as a child or an adult, as being characterized by open displays of love and affection and it was on this dimension that they saw themselves diverging widely from the values and practices of their parents. Whether or not their parents were affectionate toward them is not at issue. The important point seems to be that respondents perceived affection to be lacking and in the context of their own families claimed to be encouraging openness in displaying emotions, especially love and caring.

This strong emphasis on openly displaying affection was closely linked to parental involvement in the child rearing process. While all respondents stressed involvement of both parents, most also made special mention of the father's role in socialization and the desirability of the male parent taking an active part in the family, home and child rearing. While parental involvement in the socialization process was seen to have positive consequences for the children providing them with role models and a sense of belonging as well as values and guidelines for behavior, it was also related to fulfillment of individual companionship needs. All respondents considered companionship an important family function and in contrasting their views with those of their parents claimed that this was another area where they were doing things differently.

Their parents were frequently described as "too busy" to become involved in family activities. It was generally recognized that this was usually a result of involvement with activity related to their fathers' occupation, a perception that reinforced a desire on their part to work only at jobs that permitted the individual freedom to devote time and energy to the family. Similar views were expressed regarding females both in relation to work outside the home and household chores. While there was a desire expressed to include family members in most all of one's activities, employment, school and/or other interests necessitated that time be spent apart from the family. Thus, the companionship function, as it is in most family situations, was closely linked to the amount of free time available, especially for fathers in relation to their job demands. However, all individuals professed a commitment to working out a life style that would permit maximum amounts of time to be devoted to family activities.

For the most part, companionship revolved about recreational activities that were developed and carried out primarily by the family as a unit rather than in those provided by other units in society or ones in which members engaged as individuals. Activities mentioned by respondents were those which minimized monetary cost and maximized involvement and being together. These activities included: "doing things around the home" (e.g., playing musical instruments, watching television, having friends visit, "making things," playing games), traveling, camping, picnicking, visiting friends, walking and hiking, bicycling and attending auctions. Companionship was claimed by all to be an important family function through which members could provide one another with mutual affection and a sense of belonging.

## PERMISSIVENESS

Sixteen respondents described their parents as permissive and ten as strict in relation to the establishment of rules and their enforcement. On the other hand, all respondents voiced commitments to permissiveness in relation to their own children. The ten that described their parents as strict registered strong dissatisfaction with this approach and were determined not to subject their children to inflexible rules of conduct. As many put it, "You make rules when you're up tight about things and there are just not that many things that put us up tight." Most rules seemed to pertain to avoiding situations that would place the child in obvious physical danger (e.g., playing in areas where there was heavy automobile traffic).

This was also generally true for the other sixteen persons. Their dissatisfactions with parental approaches to child rearing did not include permissiveness. They would retain this approach and if anything permit their children even greater latitudes. But they emphasized permissiveness only as it was also accompanied by parental involvement (companionship) in the socialization process and by open displays of love and affection on the part of the parent toward the child. Without involvement and affection, it was recognized that permissiveness is likely to be construed by the child as *not caring* on the part of the parent or as was the case with a number of respondents, the freedom permitted them as children came to be defined as benefitting the parents rather than themselves. As one person put it, "They [his parents] gave us a lot of freedom. They were permissive as hell. But it was all a lot of crap. It just gave them the time to do their money making, social climbing thing." All respondents seemed committed to avoiding similar definitions of the situation on the part of their children. This was to be accomplished through child rearing approaches that stress affection and involvement as well as permissiveness. These points in turn suggest the following hypothesis: permissive approaches to child rearing, unless perceived by children to be accompanied by appropriate parental involvement and sufficient affection, will come to be defined as: (1) not caring on the part of the parents and/or (2) to the advantage of (i.e., freedom for) the parents rather than the child.

In a similar vein, parental involvement in the life of a child was viewed as positive only as it was also accompanied by affection and permissiveness. This point was emphasized especially by eight females who described their parents as having been "involved" in their upbringing (no males described their parents in this manner). Four of these women said that parental involvement was accompanied by permissiveness and four claimed that strict rules were enforced and parental authority emphasized. Each reflected negatively on their experiences. Where parental involvement was ac-

companied by permissiveness and affection was lacking, the involvement was seen as superficial. Where involvement was not accompanied by permissiveness, it was judged as parental domination. Similar thoughts and agreements were voiced by most other respondents as these issues were discussed. These views suggest that specific child rearing practices are not perceived in an isolated way; nor is it likely that they can be divorced from the values implicit in them. Whatever approaches to socialization parents utilize, it seems likely that the child experiences them in a context and does not react to them apart from that context. It would also appear that children perceive, interpret and evaluate parental practices according to their own needs and desires (e.g., affection, freedom) rather than in terms of parental intentions and wishes.

In relation to permissiveness, all parents claimed to be willing to grant their children the freedom to develop and define their own values and way of life. Since they felt that they had redefined the culture of their parents and peers, they saw no alternative but to permit their children the same autonomy. Most expressed hopes that some degree of continuity would be established between the generations but recognized the possibility that their children might develop an entirely unique or different culture or might return to the way of life of the "straight" society. Parental views on this matter were summed up generally by the idea that their childrens' lives were their own, that "they have to do their thing just as we did ours."

## FAMILY & SOCIETY

The values of counter culture American youth have been the subject of numerous recent studies, essays and books (Berger 1967, 1971; Brown 1969; Carey 1968; Davis 1967; Dworkin 1969; Flacks 1967, 1971; Gouldner 1970; Hopkins 1968; Howard 1969; Keniston 1965, 1968; Nisbet 1970; Roszak 1969; Simmon & Trout 1967; Simmons & Winogard 1968; Suchman 1968; Toynbee 1968; Yablonsky 1968). Their views on American society and its institutions are well documented and in the main are characterized by varying degrees of estrangement from the dominant culture accompanied by a disengagement or refusal to participate in mainstream institutions. In more or less degree, but without exception, the twenty-six individuals included in the present study manifested all or most of the commitments and dissatisfactions typically associated with people of the counter culture. Some of them are reiterated here as they related to family life and child rearing.

Conflict resulting from contact with mainstream institutions was apparent in varying degrees but seemed to pose problems only as it affected the family situation and in resolving differences there was general agreement that some compromises were more tolerable than others. Where concessions were tolerable or did not seem to be required, conflicts were defined as "minor hassles" or simple harrassment. Where they involved important values and principles, conflict was defined as serious and led frequently to speculation about the possibility of "dropping out" which usually meant subsistence farming on a rural commune.

Minor hassles typically included harrassment over hair and clothing styles, displaying such things as peace symbols and drug use (especially marijuana). Frequently, these problems required little or no adjustment in respondents' life styles. Marijuana use, because it is illegal, was an exception. All respondents defined it as legitimate and used it regularly which necessitated taking certain precautions including concealing their activity from the children. Their main concern was not over precautions as such, but over the limited breech in interpersonal openness between parent and child in order to protect the parent from possible detection and prosecution.

Serious conflict resulted from the structure and nature of the larger society and posed problems about which respondents as individuals could do little other than protest or withdraw. These included most of the values and practices usually associated with counter culture opposition: war, violence, military conscription and spending, prejudice, discrimination and the structure of opportunity, public education and the nature of work and the economy.

A majority of respondents in one form or another had been involved in organized political protests aimed at change while four persons had been active in Students for a Democratic Society. All had withdrawn from these activities agreeing that it was a waste of time in that "nothing was accomplished." Underlying discussions of political involvement as a way of instituting change was a pervasive sense of frustration and powerlessness. The general attitude was "who needs it" coupled with a belief that "the most effective kind of politics is your own life style," by which was meant that change would occur as individuals altered their values and behavior (Roszak 1969:168). All respondents were committed to this idea and in varying degrees claimed to be practicing it in their individual lives and particularly in relation to their families.

Although they admitted to being "political drop-outs," they did not see themselves as less active or radical with respect to commitments to change. Rather, according to their discussions, it seems that their radicalism had shifted to a personal and family level where there was an attempt to structure relationships in terms of counter culture values and in opposition to many values perceived to be operative in the dominant culture. Thus, the changes that could not be implemented in the larger society could be accomplished within the home and family. Satisfactions in the short run stemmed from a personally rewarding life style and in the long run from expectations that the children would be both cause and effect of similar life style shifts throughout society. There was not always a perceived connection between the parents' past frustration in bringing about change and the hopes expressed for the children.

## DILEMMAS OVER EDUCATION AND WORK

All parents saw the possibility of serious conflicts developing over the education of their children and in relation to earning a livelihood. In each of these areas, contact with the larger society could not be avoided and compromises were inevitable. The compromises, in turn, involved some basic principles and central values on which respondents were reluctant to give ground.

In relation to education, the conflict was similar to that faced by the Amish when confronted with compulsory school attendance for their children in non-Amish schools (Hostetler 1970: 193–208). As with the Amish, counter culture parents viewed the culture of the public schools along with its teaching methods and subject matter as inimical to their own values and positively dysfunctional to the kind of society in which they wished to live and help create for their children. Specific criticism centered on artificially compartmentalized learning, required conformity, mass nature of education, crowded classrooms, preaching "blanket patriotism," failure to stimulate creativity, overly structured learning situations, failure to emphasize the arts and overemphasis on authority and competition. In short, virtually all of the central values of American public education outlined by Williams (1970:334$f$) were attacked except the creed of democratic values. A number of respondents voiced approval of the emphasis placed in public education on teaching democratic ideals but claimed that either the values could not be learned because they were taught by authoritarian methods or if they were learned the school undermined its credibility in that it did not practice what it preached.

Estrangement from American public education was virtually total but as only one of the families had a school-aged child, the problem was not yet a reality for most parents and few had come up with any concrete ways of dealing with it other than simply complying with the law. For most, the obvious alternatives were unrealistic, e.g., developing private or alternative schools, moving to areas where the public schools were in keeping with their values. Although the Amish have been successful in establishing "alternative" schools for themselves in some places, one can only speculate on whether similar developments will occur on a large scale among people of the counter culture.

Because some suitable options were available, conflict over earning a living posed less of a dilemma. While a few persons were considering subsistence farming as an alternative to working in jobs that were linked fast to the American economy, most were resigned to working for wages, salaries or profits. However, an acceptable job had to meet certain criteria, the most important being that it offered the individual sufficient freedom and personal autonomy. Corporate, bureaucratic positions were rejected out of hand while most gravitated or aspired to teaching positions or self-employment which included careers in music, art, the professions and retail businesses such as restaurants, "head shops" and art galleries.

The potential for conflict did not stem from work itself but from the nature of work in the American economy. First, it was perceived that the wage and salary structure virtually forces males to become full time breadwinners in the family, a role that most of them did not want because it limited their freedom and took them out of the home. It also inhibited any attempt to develop equalitarian roles within the family thus driving them into a traditional division of labor where females assume homemaker tasks and males become wage earners. This produces the conditions for the second dilemma in that males are consequently limited with regard to taking an active part in child care and rearing. There was a general recognition that work in the context of the American economy was basically incompatible with their ideas on family structure, roles and relationships, a factor that led to searches for occupations that would permit them the time and freedom to become more involved with home and family.

Issues such as education and earning a living led all respondents at one time or another to consider communal living and a more or less complete withdrawal from contact with the larger society. Three females had rejected the idea on the grounds that there would be "too many constraints." All others were still considering the possibility, six of them to the point of making plans and inquiries into acquiring land. Communes were envisioned as "real communities" where inhabitants could structure their own lives and institutions and negatively valued social pressures would be minimal.

## DISCUSSION

The counter culture family paralleled closely in form and function the companionship family discussed by Burgess and Locke (1945). The companionship family, hypothesized as an emergent form, signaled "a transition from an institution with family behavior controlled by the mores, public opinion and law to . . . family behavior arising from the mutual affection and consensus of its members" (Burgess & Locke 1945:26). Although precise measurement of the extent of this shift was not possible within the present study, the counter culture family appears to be striving to reach the companionship ideal. This conclusion seems valid in all respects except in the area of family functions. While the companionship family as an ideal type permits society to assume responsibility for economic, educational, recreational, religious and productive functions, the noncommunal counter culture family has recognized a need and in some instances is moving to assume greater control in these areas. Thus, it appears to be diverging from the companionship-institutional continuum as described by Burgess and Locke to an entirely different dimension. This divergence appears to be a result of a recognition that American social institutions are mutually supportive, closely interrelated and increasingly organized around utilitarian norms. These factors interact to create a social situation incompatible with the companionship family ideal. The ideal has not yet become part of the institutionalized structure of the larger society and those seeking to realize it in their daily lives are faced with the task of altering their relationship to mainstream institutions by assuming some of the tasks ordinarily performed by them.

Counter culture parents recognized the family's potential for creating changes in society and discussed socialization as an important change inducing process. The family was viewed largely as an independent rather than dependent variable instituting basic value changes to which the larger society would eventually be compelled to respond. However, specific child rearing practices did not appear to differ greatly from trends described by several writers as emerging among middle class parents in general "toward modes of responses involving greater toleration of the child's impulses and desires, freer expression of affection, and increased reliance on 'psychological' methods of discipline" as well as shifts in the role of fathers as providers of affection (Bronfenbrenner 1961:6). From respondents' perspectives, they were closer to achieving this than most other American families. However, because of the similarities noted, questions must be raised concerning the extent and nature of these changes and differences vis-a-vis shifts in family form and function that are already in process.

But from another perspective, counter culture respondents recognized the pervasiveness of norms such as utility, rationality and impersonality while they approached child rearing with personal and expressive values. Values provide an important context for the development of specific child rearing processes and "the child's acquaintance with the values implicit in various socialization practices may be more important than the manifest content he learns from these activities" (Inkeles 1961: 624). If this is true, then the values held by children of the counter culture should in some degree reflect their parents' opposition to dominant values and institutions in American society.

## REFERENCES

Becker, H. *Outsiders: studies in the sociology of deviance.* New York: Free Press, 1963.

Berger, B. Hippie morality—more old than new. *Transaction.* 5 (1967) 19–27.

Berger, B. *Looking for America.* Englewood Cliffs: Prentice-Hall, 1971.

Bronfenbrenner, U. The changing American child —a speculative analysis. *Journal of Social Issues.* 17 (1961) 6–18.

Brown, M. The condemnation & persecution of Hippies. *Transaction.* 7 (1969) 33–46.

Burgess, E., & Locke, H. *The family: from institu-*

tion to companionship. New York: American Book, 1945.

Burgess, E. The family in a changing society. *American Journal of Sociology*. 53(1948) 417–421.

Burgess, E. Values and sociological research. *Social Problems*. 2 (1954) 16–20.

Carey, J. *The college drug scene*. Englewood Cliffs: Prentice-Hall, 1968.

Davis, F. Why all of us may be hippies someday. *Transaction*. 5 (1967) 10–18.

Dworkin, G. The Hippies: permanent revolution? *Dissent*. 16 (1969) 180–183.

Flacks, R. The liberated generation. *Journal of Social Issues*. 23 (1967) 52–75.

Flacks, R. *Youth & social change*. Chicago: Markham, 1971.

Gouldner, A. *The coming crisis of Western sociology*. New York: Basic Books, 1970.

Hopkins, J. *The Hippie papers*. New York: New American Library, 1968.

Hostetler, J. *Amish society*. Baltimore: John Hopkins Press, 1970.

Howard, J. The flowering of the hippie movement. *The Annals*. 382 (1969) 44–55.

Inkeles, A. Social structure & socialization. *Handbook of socialization theory & research,* edited by D. Godlin. Chicago: Rand McNally, 1961.

Keniston, K. *The uncommitted: alienated youth in American society*. New York: Harcourt, Brace & World, 1965.

Keniston, K. *Young radicals: notes on committed youth*. New York: Harcourt, Brace & World, 1968.

Merton, R., M. Fiske, & P. Kendall. *The focused interview*. Glencoe Free Press, 1956.

Nisbet, R. *The social bond*. New York: Knopf, 1970.

Roszak, T. *The making of a counter culture*. Garden City: Doubleday, 1969.

Simmon, G., & G. Trout. Hippies in college: from teeny-boppers to drug freaks. *Transaction*. 5 (1967) 27–32.

Simmons, J., & B. Winogard. *It's happening: a portrait of the youth scene today*. Santa Barbara, Calif.: Marc-Laird Publications, 1968.

Suchman, E. The 'hang-loose' ethic & the spirit of drug use. *Journal of Health and Social Behavior*. 9(1968) 145–155.

Toynbee, A. As it was in Rome . . . . *Horizon*. 10 (1968) 26.

Williams, R. Jr. *American society*. New York: Knopf, 1970.

Yablonsky, L. *The Hippie trip*. New York: Western, 1968.

## SUGGESTIONS FOR FURTHER READING

Bedell, J. W. Reorganization in the one-parent family: Mother absent due to death. *Sociological Focus,* 1971–72, *5*(2), 84–100. This study concerns the changes in tasks and role relationships of the father and children in families after the mother has died.

Berger, B., Hackett, B., & Millar, R. M. The communal family. *Family Coordinator,* 1972, *21*, 419–427. This anthropological investigation of communes on the West Coast of the United States verifies the image of the commune. It also analyzes its functions in terms of economic bases, ideologies, marital and child relationships, and problems associated with child rearing.

Constantine, L. L., & Constantine, J. M. Group and multilateral marriage: Definitional roles, glossary and annotated bibliography. *Family Process,* 1971, *10*, 157–176. The research reported here relates to 16 multilateral marriage groups in the United States. Parties to such a marriage include at least three persons, each of whom is married to at least two other members of the conjugal unit.

Eiduson, B. T. Looking at children in emergent family styles. *Children Today,* 1974, *3*(4), 2–6. Emergent family styles are briefly described in terms of types of persons involved, varieties of living style, and their effect on parents and children, as well as other aspects of their living arrangements.

Hohnstrom, L. L. *The two-career family*. Cambridge, Mass.: Schencken Books, 1972. Seven two-career families were compared with seven traditional families where the wife's energies were devoted primarily to housekeeping and homemaking. The roles of each spouse and problems of child rearing are analyzed and compared in these two major family forms.

Keller, S. Does the family have a future? *Journal of Comparative Family Studies,* 1971, *2*, 1–14. The universality of any single type of family is portrayed as unfortunate. Also discussed are challenges to the contemporary nuclear family, cultural influences on family styles, and potentials for future change.

Levine, S. V., Carr, R. P., & Horenblas, W. The urban commune. *American Journal of Orthopsychiatry,* 1973, *43*, 149–163. This analysis of 30 urban communes involves consideration of members' backgrounds, motivations for joining, ideology, child care, and implications for society.

Olson, D. H. Marriage of the future: Revolutionary or evolutionary change? *Family Coordinator,* 1972, *21,* 383–393. This article concerns changes taking place in the institution of marriage and the family, processes involved in the mating-dating game, changing sexual patterns in society, and alternative family life-styles.

Ramey, J. W. Communes, group marriages, and the upper-middle class. *Journal of Marriage and the Family,* 1972, *34,* 647–655. Interviews held with 80 couples exploring the feasibility of communal living deal with their reasons for involvement, including the potential effects on their children.

Ramey, J. W. Emerging patterns of innovative behavior in marriage. *Family Coordinator,* 1972, *21,* 435–456. Patterns of innovative behavior in marriage are discussed including free love, dyadic marriage, swinging, open marriage, communes, and group marriage. Comments are made about the effect on children of living in such situations.

Van Meter, M. J. S. Teaching about changing life styles. *Family Coordinator,* 1973, *22,* 171–182. A graduate seminar entitled Contemporary Issues on the American Family dealt with options for life-styles within marriage and other questions especially relevant to the times.

Whitehurst, R. N. Some comparisons of conventional and counterculture families. *Family Coordinator,* 1972, *21,* 395–401. Traditional and countercultural families are compared in terms of eight activity areas, ranging from religion and leisure-time use to economics and child rearing. Both family forms are analyzed with regard to their implications for social control and personal growth.

Zimmerman, C. C. The future of the family in America. *Journal of Marriage and the Family,* 1972, *34,* 323–333. The study reported here concerns trends in the American family system and predictions of changes by the end of the century.

# 12

## Social Class as a Factor in Child Rearing

In the 1940s a series of research reports made Americans aware that they lived in a class society. Social scientists analyzed American communities in the same manner that anthropologists study primitive societies. People were classified as belonging to the same class if they normally ate or drank together, conversed intimately, as in social cliques, or married into one another's families. All investigators were impressed with the high degree of agreement that all informants showed as to where any specific individual belonged in the social hierarchy.

We still use such expressions as "wrong side of the tracks" and "the 400." The very term "upward mobility" suggests that different social levels persist. Even children are aware of social-class distinctions, at least by the fourth grade; and brighter children may be aware of such distinctions in the first grade. From an early age they unconsciously absorb, through hearing their elders, notions about the privileged and the poor.

Social-class levels differ from one section of the country to another. In Eastern cities, upper-upper and lower-upper classes can be differentiated; however, in communities of the Midwest and Far West, there is little distinction between the two upper classes. In both East and West, the upper-middle class is made up of business and professional people, but lacks the wealth and social prestige of the upper classes. The lower-middle class is composed of such persons as clerical or retail workers who live in the "wrong" part of town. The difference between the upper-lower and lower-lower classes is largely one of moral considerations. The upper-lowers are said to be poor, honest, and ambitious, and the lower-lowers shiftless, dirty, and disorderly.

## FACTORS THAT RETARD OR PROMOTE SOCIAL-CLASS DISTINCTIONS

Cultural leveling, or the reduction in distinctions between social classes, is said to proceed through such factors as mass media, desegregation of schools, and minimum-wage laws. Heavy taxes on the upper classes and labor-union membership and welfare programs for the lower classes have reduced the economic distance between them and, accordingly, the differences in their life-styles. As members of the lower classes become property owners, they naturally acquire certain middle-class values, such as a regard for law and order, a belief in the right to profits, and a concern for civic conditions. Also, the mass media continually expose lower-class children and their parents to middle-class values. And educational programs such as Head Start and college scholarships help to equalize educational opportunities.

Also helping to close gaps between the social classes is a two-way process of acculturation. Middle-class life-styles are copied by the lower classes, but lower-class values may also filter into the middle class, as lower-status persons mingle with, or rise into, the middle class. Many persons with lower-class backgrounds now graduate from college and teach school, where they unconsciously disseminate residual traces of their lower-class origins.

Other factors serve to retard the leveling of social classes. For one thing, it is almost axiomatic among behavioral scientists that providing the broadest possible opportunities for developing intellectual potential would increase, not decrease, differences in achievement—hence also in social status. Another factor is the common desire of many people, especially less secure ones, to look down on someone else. They can only feel satisfied with their own status by feeling superior to many others. This tendency is reflected in, and fostered by, the competitiveness of our society. The urge to get ahead implies getting ahead of someone else.

As upper and lower classes are artificially absorbed into the middle class, that class tends to fractionate into subclasses, which, to all practical purposes, become new social classes. Moreover, specialization in today's technological society tends to segregate the population into groupings according to skills, educational levels, and sociocultural milieu—for instance, urban, suburban, or rural. Any such segregation tends to result in distinctive sets of attitudes, beliefs, and behaviors. Although some of this differentiation is of a cross-sectional nature—that is, different but equal—the differences may also be perceived hierarchically. Inevitably, the various groupings will be perceived as having differential status within the society; and they will, in effect, preserve the social-class system, if not explicitly, certainly implicitly.

## SOCIAL-CLASS DISTINCTION REGARDING CHILDREN

Research turns up other important distinctions, especially in modes of child rearing. Upper-class mothers compared with working mothers are more tolerant of their children's aggressions. They also recognize more completely the emotional complexities in child rearing, more adequately meet their baby's physical needs, and encourage more interaction. Working-class mothers hold their infants for longer periods of time primarily as a means of prohibiting them from crawling around and getting into things (Tulkin, 1973). Working-class mothers also have less confidence that they can influence their children's development. They feel more powerless, overwhelmed, and helpless.

Social class also influences the status assigned to different members of the family (Jacob, 1974). In middle-class families with an 11-year-old son, the parents are relatively equal, and both are more influential than the son. In middle-class families with a 16-year-old son, the boy becomes more influential at the expense of his mother, while the father's influence remains the same. The father is generally secure as the most powerful family member, with mother and adolescent son vying for second place. The chief difference between lower- and middle-class families in this regard is the lower-class father's loss of influence in relation to his adolescent son. In lower-class families, the 16-year-old son often exceeds his father as the most influential family member (Jacob, 1974).

Social class relates somewhat differently to boys and girls (Kagan, 1972). The relationship between social class and cognitive achievement is closer for girls. Perhaps one reason is that the girl is more likely to adopt her family's values, while the boy is more exposed to values outside the home. Economically disadvantaged mothers project their own sense of powerlessness and inadequacy onto their daughters more than onto their sons, and they are more likely to praise their sons' simple accomplishments. Upper-middle-class mothers are more likely to criticize incompetent behavior in their daughters than in their sons. Parents of all social levels have concern for their sons' advancement, but mothers from different social and educational backgrounds differ in their concern for the intellectual development of their daughters.

## LIMITATIONS OF CULTURALLY AND ECONOMICALLY DEPRIVED CHILDREN

Recent interest in social class has focused chiefly on lower-class deprivation. This concept—deprivation—applies to environments devoid of stimulating characteristics. Thus, environments may be deprived without appearing to be: although not specifically stunting development, neither do they encourage it. A truly enriching environment must be both supportive and challenging. In this regard children in economically deprived families fare poorly. Also in such families many children are born prematurely, many suffer from iron-deficiency anemia, and 35% have not been completely immunized (Richmond, 1974).

Such children also suffer other disadvantages. According to Kellaghan and McNamara (1972), social class is related to intelligence— that is, the lower the social class the lower the measured intelligence. However, other research suggests that mental tests are biased in favor of the white middle class (Knowles & Shah, 1969). There seems to be no proof that differences exist in original mental potential according to sex, race, or social class. Nevertheless, disadvantages within lower-class families limit whatever potential their children may have. Even during their first year, middle-class infants respond more to mothers' and strangers' voices than do lower-class children, perhaps because they experience more verbal stimulation from their mothers. Middle-class infants also look more at the mother and at the stranger after hearing their voices (Tulkin, 1973).

Ordinarily lower-class children possess a lower self-concept; however, lower-class nonwhite children often have a higher self-concept than do lower-class white children (Trowbridge, 1970). Black children in particular have profited from such slogans as "Black is beautiful" and from the struggle for social respectability, which has given them something to fight for.

Certain social-class effects operate in quite subtle ways—for example, regarding time perspective. In a study of two groups of eighth-graders (Zelen & Zelen, 1970), one predominantly black and lower-class, the other white and middle-class, no significant differences were found in total life-span expectations. Both groups estimated that they had already lived a third of their lives. The underprivileged group estimated their achievements to date as approximately 43% of their total life achievements, the more favored group as 31% of the achievements they anticipated in life. Apparently, the higher-class children felt they had more to expect from the future.

Many lower-class children also belong to culturally disadvantaged racial and ethnic minorities, who do not share equally in opportunities available to children of the dominant culture. For example, they may speak their own dialects and languages quite fluently but have trouble with speaking standard English. Children who find that members of the dominant culture, especially their teachers, criticize their customs and speech, may reject them and even themselves. Until recently our country, with its melting-pot tradition, viewed groups that insisted on retaining their identity as strange, lower-class, or even unpatriotic. However, nowadays the new and growing acceptance, even approval, of pluralism in lifestyle and culture is changing this situation. Growing numbers of philosophers, educators, and even so-called average citizens, are coming to appreciate contributions of the racial and ethnic minority groups among us.

## PROGRAMS FOR DISADVANTAGED CHILDREN

In recent years, widespread interest has focused on helping disadvantaged children, especially in early grades. Such children require books, pictures, and toys that most children simply take for granted; and they need language training if they are to achieve in classrooms where standard English is the rule. Programs designed for these groups, including the so-called Head Start classes, vary greatly in type and results. In one study (Hertzig & Birch, 1971), after three years of special training from ages 3 to 6, children showed no gains in IQ. However, in cases where mothers had been trained to help, such programs have had positive results (Starr, 1971). Nor can the effect of such programs be measured simply by gains in IQ, for such an approach negates the importance of progress on other dimensions. These include improvements in such areas as health, social adjustment, attitude, and familiarity with the dominant culture. While children should respect their own culture, they should nevertheless be sufficiently well versed in ways of the dominant culture to accommodate adequately to it.

Studies designed for improving the lot of culturally deprived children typically report progress, varying with the adequacy of the program involved. In one such study (Specter & Cowen, 1971), six inner-city infants, aged 10 to 24 months, with severe social and verbal deficiencies, were seen three times a week for several hours by college-student volunteers. The program was restricted to children with greater than 25% overall retardation. As a result of this saturated enrichment program, the childrens' social and verbal development dramatically improved. However, most follow-up studies of such efforts report erosion, or even erasure, of gains unless efforts are maintained. In effect, such programs serve largely as "a momentary palliative," and nothing short of improving ghetto living conditions can provide the quality of help desired (Specter & Cowen, 1971).

For a better perspective on this discussion, keep in mind several points. For one thing, we have treated education for the disadvantaged in relation to early-childhood programs simply because that is where it has most often occurred. More effective progress depends on adapting programs to the needs of all subcultural groups, on all grade levels, and even in college. Yet special help in upper grades has been either inappropriate or disgracefully neglected (Schultz & Auerbach, 1971). With regard to compensatory education at any level, many gains—for example, in attitude, self-concepts, and social competence—may not be easily measured. Moreover, gain itself is defined in terms of middle-class standards. Does the child gain by becoming more middle-class in attitudes and behaviors? Most authorities nowadays advise that these children develop pride in their own culture and share it with others. They learn to value diverse ways of life, each for its own special contributions, instead of perceiving them on levels, from better to worse. In fact, the so-called deprived family does not, in its own eyes, feel deprived until it is labeled as such. As Tulkin and Konner (1973) point out, "deprivation is largely in the eyes of the beholder, which suggests that intervention should proceed on the basis of a much wider knowledge of consequences of different sets of experiences than we now have" (p. 49).

Implicit in the foregoing discussion, as well as in the vast literature on social class, are many questions. What are the special strengths of the lower classes? What special disadvantages do middle- and upper-class children sustain? Human nature being what it is, is social stratification inevitable? How can social programs for disadvantaged children, of any social class, be made more effective? How can lower-class children maintain the strengths peculiar to their class while accommodating to, or perhaps moving into, the dominant middle-class culture?

In the first article that follows, Steven Tulkin reviews and interprets data concerning the effect of social class on children's development. Although the chief emphasis is on matters of cultural deprivation, some of the discussion relates specifically to middle-class children. In the second article, David Bachelor and Rosalie Donofrio also discuss poor children, but from a more specific perspective. They examine current images of poor children, take issue with certain popular concepts of deprivation, and suggest ways to improve the situation.

## REFERENCES

Hertzig, M. E., & Birch, H. G. Longitudinal course of measured intelligence in preschool children of different social and ethnic backgrounds. *American Journal of Orthopsychiatry*, 1971, *41*, 416–426.

Jacob, T. Patterns of family conflict and dominance as a function of child age and social class. *Developmental Psychology*, 1974, *10*, 1–12.

Kagan, J. The emergence of sex differences. *School Review*, 1972, *80*, 217–227.

Kellaghan, T., & McNamara, J. Family correlates of verbal reasoning ability. *Developmental Psychology*, 1972, *7*, 49–53.

Knowles, R. T., & Shah, G. B. Cultural bias in testing: An exploration. *The Journal of Social Psychology*, 1969, *77*, 285–286.

Schultz, C. B., & Auerbach, H. A. The usefulness of cumulative deprivation as an explanation of educational deficiencies. *Merrill-Palmer Quarterly*, 1971, *17*, 27–39.

Specter, G. A., & Cowen, E. L. A pilot study in stimulation of culturally deprived infants. *Child Psychiatry and Human Development*, 1971, *1*(3), 168–171.

Starr, R. H., Jr. Cognitive development in infancy: Assessment, acceleration, and actualization. *Merrill-Palmer Quarterly*, 1971, *17*, 153–186.

Trowbridge, N. T. Self concept of disadvantaged and advantaged children. Paper presented before the American Educational Research Association, Minneapolis, March 1970.

Tulkin, S. R. Social class differences in infants' reacting to mothers' and strangers' voices. *Developmental Psychology*, 1973, *8*, 137.

Tulkin, S. R., & Konner, M. J. Alternative conceptions of intellectual functioning. *Human Development*, 1973, *16*, 33–52.

Zelen, S. L., & Zelen, G. J. Life-span expectations and achievement expectancies of under-privileged and middle-class adolescents. *Journal of Social Psychology*, 1970, *80*, 111–112.

# An Analysis of the Concept of Cultural Deprivation

## Steven R. Tulkin

The term "cultural deprivation" is commonly used to summarize the presumed reasons why lower-class and minority group children show deficits in the development of "intellectual skills." However, there are serious limitations to the validity of the concept of cultural deprivation, and psychologists and educators should reevaluate their roles in programs which attempt to "enrich" the lives of "deprived" populations. The cultural deprivation concept is limited in that (*a*) it does not advance psychology as a science because it does not focus attention on how specific experiences affect developmental processes; (*b*) it ignores cultural relativism; and (*c*) it neglects political realities, which are likely to be primarily responsible for many of the traits observed in deprived populations. The limitations described under *a* are discussed only briefly, since they are likely to be most familiar to social scientists.

## THE IMPORTANCE OF PSYCHOLOGICAL PROCESSES

The concept of cultural deprivation has often made it easy for social scientists to overlook the importance of the *processes* by which environmental experiences influence development. Jessor and Richardson (1968) stated:

To speak, for example, of maternal deprivation as an explanation is to attempt to account for certain characteristics of infant development by

Reprinted from *Developmental Psychology*, 1972, 6(2), 326–331 and 338–339. Copyright 1972 by the American Psychological Association. Reprinted by permission.

the absence of the mother rather than by the presence of some specifiable set of environmental conditions. While mother absence may be a useful and convenient way to summarize or symbolize the conditions which will likely be present, the important point is that development is likely to be invariant with or related to the conditions which are present, not with those which are absent [p. 3].

Research concluding that social class or racial differences are found on particular developmental or intellectual tasks does not further understanding of development, unless we examine the actual processes that contributed to the differences. Wolf (1964) urged researchers to distinguish between status variables (class, race, etc.) and process variables (the actual *experiences* of children which contribute to their cognitive growth). He rated parents on 13 process variables descriptive of interactions between parent and child. The items fell under the headings of parental press for academic achievement and language development, as well as provision for general learning. He found a correlation of .76 between these process variables and IQ measures of fifth-grade students. Similarly, Davé (1963) obtained a multiple correlation of .80 between process variables and school achievement. These are substantially higher than the correlations of .40 to .50 which are typically reported between socioeconomic status and measures of intelligence or school achievement.

## NEED FOR CULTURAL RELATIVISM

Many authors who discuss deprived populations appear to disregard cultural relativism, despite the attempts—predominantly from anthropologists—to emphasize the importance of cultural relativism in understanding minority subcultures in the United States. Writers have enumerated certain characteristics of black American culture, for example, which can be traced to the cultural patterns of its African origin (Herskovits, 1958). Other authors have argued that particular minority groups possess cultures of their own, which have "developed out of coping with a difficult environment"

here in the United States (Riessman, 1962). Despite the recognition of the need for relativism, middle-class Americans, including professionals, have difficulty remaining relativistic with regard to minority cultures. Gans (1962) discussed the difficulties encountered by middle-class "missionaries" in understanding the Italian-American subculture he studied in Boston's West End. He observed that West End parents made frequent use of verbal and physical punishment, and commented that "to a middle-class observer, the parents' treatment often seems extremely strict, and sometimes brutal." Gans, however, felt that

> the torrents of threat and cajolery neither impinge on the feelings of parental affection, nor are meant as signs of rejection. As one mother explained to her child, "We hit you because we love you." People believe that discipline is needed constantly to keep the child in line with and respectful of adult rules, and without it he would run amok [pp. 59–60].

Another example of a subcultural pattern which is foreign to middle-class observers was reported by Lehmer (1969). She noted that Navajo children would not compete for good grades in school, and explained that Navajo customs emphasized cooperation, not competition: "In Navajo tradition, a person who stands out at the expense of his brother may be considered a 'witch' [p. D-4]." Does this low need for achievement reflect cultural deprivation or cultural difference?

Why is it so difficult for outsiders to acknowledge subcultural behavior patterns? Gans (1962) believed that the difficulty stemmed from the observers' missionary outlook:

> [They] had to believe that the West Enders' refusal to follow object-oriented middle-class ways was pathological, resulting from deprivations imposed on them by living in the West End. They could not admit that the West Enders acted as they did because they lived within a social structure and culture of their own [pp. 151–152].

In fact, Gans had earlier stated that one of the tenets of West End life was a rejection of "middle-class forms of status and culture." In other words, it was culturally valued to be culturally deprived.

The difficulty of achieving a relativistic approach to the study of subcultures has made research difficult, because minority group children are constantly evaluated by middle-class standards. One issue of current interest to psychologists is whether black ghetto residents are less able to communicate verbally, or are simply less proficient in "standard English." It is claimed by many researchers that lower-class subjects are verbally deficient, and the deficits are "not entirely attributable to implicit 'middle-class' orientations [Krauss & Rotter, 1968]." Other experts have argued that black English is a fully formed linguistic system in its own right, with its own grammatical rules and unique history (Baratz & Shuy, 1969; Labov, 1967; Stewart, 1967, 1969a). These critics have stated that black language is "different from standard American English, but no less complex, communicative, rich, or sophisticated [Sroufe, 1970]"; and argued that research reporting language "deficits" among black children reflects only the middle-class orientation of the research instruments and procedures. Supporting this argument, Birren and Hess (1968) concluded that

> studies of peer groups in spontaneous interaction in Northern ghetto areas show that there is a rich verbal culture in constant use. Negro children in the vernacular culture cannot be considered "verbally deprived" if one observes them in a favorable environment—on the contrary, their daily life is a pattern of continual verbal stimulation, contest, and imitation [p. 137].

Similarly, Chandler and Erickson (1968) observed *naturally occurring* group interaction and reported data which disputed the findings of Bernstein (1960, 1961) and others that middle-class children more commonly used "elaborated" linguistic codes while lower classes typically spoke with "restricted" codes. Chandler and Erickson found that the use of restricted or elaborated linguistic codes was not as closely related to the social class of speakers as had been suggested by other researchers.

Both inner-city and suburban groups . . . were found to shift back and forth between use of

relatively "restricted" linguistic codes and relatively "elaborated" codes. These shifts were closely related to apparent changes in the degree of shared context between group members. Examples of extremely abstract and sophisticated inquiry among inner-city Negro young people were found in which a highly "restricted" linguistic code was employed [p. 2 ].

If black English and standard English are simply different languages, one cannot be seen as more deficient than the other (Sroufe, 1970). Most schools, however, demand that students use standard English, and frequently black children who have been classified by their schools as "slow learners" are able to read passages of black English with amazing speed and accuracy (Stewart, 1969b). Similarly, Foster (1969) found that the introduction of nonstandard English dialect increased the ability of tenth-grade disadvantaged students "to comprehend, to recall, and to be fluent and flexible in providing titles for verbal materials." Black students ($N = 90$) also scored higher than white students ($N = 400$) on Foster's (1970) Jive Analogy Test (H. L. Foster, personal communication, 1971).

This argument does not imply that the teaching of standard English is an infringement of the rights of minority cultures. It is necessary that students learn standard English, but there is a difference between emphasizing the development of positive skills which may facilitate a successful adaptation to a particular majority culture versus devaluating a group of people who may not emphasize the development of these particular skills. As Baratz and Baratz (1970) suggested, research should be undertaken to discover the *different* but not pathological forms of minority group behavior. "Then and only then can programs be created that utilize the child's differences as a means of helping him acculturate to the mainstream while maintaining his individual identity and cultural heritage [p. 47]."

## An Objective Look at the Middle Class

The cultural bias of middle-class America has not only hindered an appreciation of the attributes of minority cultures, but it has also prevented an objective evaluation of middle-class culture. Psychologists do not write about the "deficiencies" of the middle class, but the cultural relativist might find a great deal to write about. Coles (1968) suggested that it may be appropriate to label middle-class children deprived, because

> they're so nervous and worried about every-thing they say—what it will mean, or what it will cost them, or how it will be interpreted. That's what they've learned at home, and that's why a lot of them are tense kids, and, even worse, stale kids with frowns on their faces at ages 6 or 7 [p. 277].

Similarly, Kagan (1968) hypothesized that middle-class children were more anxious about failing than lower-class children. He noted that lower-class children may be less anxious about making a mistake and, therefore, more likely to answer questions and make decisions "im-pulsively." Most people would agree that an impulsive style could be a hindrance to the development of abstract analytical thinking, but researchers have paid little attention to the possible virtues of an impulsive (or "spontan-eous," "nonanalytical") style, and have not considered the consequences of attempting to discourage this style. Maccoby and Modiano (1966) spoke to this point in their discussion of differences among children in Mexico City, Boston, and a rural Mexican village. They noted that people socialized into the modern industrial world often lose the ability to experi-ence. "They are," the authors suggested, "like people who see a painting immediately in terms of its style, period, and influences, but with no sense of its uniqueness [p. 268]." Maccoby and Modiano concluded by caution-ing that

> as the city child grows older, he may end by exchanging a spontaneous, less alienated rela-tionship to the world for a more sophisticated outlook which concentrates on using, exchang-ing, or cataloguing. What industrialized man gains in an increased ability to formulate, to reason, and to code the ever more numerous bits of complex information he acquires, he may lose in decreased sensitivity to people and events [p. 269].

But it is quite doubtful if psychologists would call him culturally deprived.

## Relativism toward Other Cultures

Psychologists frequently label American minority groups as culturally deprived, but they are less likely to make value judgments about other cultures. In fact, social scientists are reasonably tolerant of child-rearing prac-tices observed in other cultures which would be devaluated if they were found in a minority group in the United States. Rebelsky and Abeles (1969), for example, observed Ameri-can and Dutch mothers with their 0–3-month-old infants. They found that a Dutch baby typi-cally slept in a low closed bed with a canopy overhead. Dutch mothers kept the infant's room cool—"for health reasons"—necessi-tating infants being "tightly covered under blankets, often tied into the crib with strings from their sheets." Further, the authors re-ported comparisons showing that "American mothers looked at, held, fed, talked to, smiled at, patted, and showed more affection to their babies more often than did Dutch mothers." These findings, however, were not used to condemn Dutch mothers. The authors related the differences in parental behavior to cultural variations in the parents' conceptions of in-fancy. For example, they noted that

> Even if a [Dutch] parent sees a child awake and wanting to play or look around, . . . he is not likely to respond to this wish or to the behavior which implies this wish because of fear of "spoiling" the baby (stated by 9 of the 11 mothers in Holland), or because of the belief that a baby in this age range should sleep and not play or stay awake [pp. 16–17].*

Observations also revealed that Dutch in-fants had fewer toys with which to play. By 3 months of age, almost half of the Dutch babies still had no toys within sight or touch. The au-thors explained that Dutch mothers were con-cerned that "toys might keep the babies awake, or overstimulate them." There were also cul-tural differences in the mothers' reactions to their infants crying.

*From "Infancy in Holland and in the United States," by F. Rebelsky and G. Abeles. Unpublished paper. Reprinted by permission.

Crying meant a call for help to U. S. mothers; they often reported lactating when they heard the cry. In Holland, crying was considered a part of a baby's behavior, good for the lungs and not always something to stop. In addition, though a mother might hear the cry in Holland and interpret it as a hunger cry, she still would not respond if it was not time for the scheduled feeding [pp. 7–8].

Rebelsky and Abeles did not suggest that Dutch mothers were rejecting or depriving their infants. They did not argue that intervention was necessary to change the patterns of mother-infant interaction. They concluded, instead, that both United States and Dutch cultures "may be training very different kinds of people, yet with each culture wanting the ones they produce." Such data reported for a group of lower-income American mothers might be followed by a call for a massive intervention program, or possibly the removal of the infants from their homes.

A similar cultural comparison was reported by Caudill and Weinstein (1966, 1969) who investigated maternal behavior in Japan and in the United States. The authors reported that American mothers talked more to their infants, while Japanese mothers more frequently lulled and rocked their infants. These differences were seen as reflecting different styles of mothering:

> The style of the American mother seems to be in the direction of stimulating her baby to respond . . . whereas the style of the Japanese mother seems to be more in the direction of soothing and quieting her baby [1966, p. 18].

In both cultures, the "style" of mothering was influenced by the prevailing conception of infancy. Caudill and Weinstein (1969) reported that in Japan

> The infant is seen more as a separate biological organism who from the beginning, in order to develop, needs to be drawn into increasingly interdependent relations with others. In America, the infant is seen more as a dependent biological organism who, in order to develop, needs to be made increasingly independent of others [p. 15].

American mothers, following their conception of infancy, pushed their infants to respond and to be active; Japanese mothers, also following their conception of infancy, attempted to foster reduced independent activity and greater reliance on others. As a part of this pattern, the Japanese tended to place less emphasis on clear verbal communication. Caudill and Weinstein reasoned that "such communication implies self-assertion and the separate identity and independence of the person" which would be contrary to the personality which Japanese mothers were attempting to build into their children. Thus, in Japan, as in Holland, mothers related to their infants in a manner consistent with their beliefs and values.

Caudill and Weinstein (1966) also reported data showing that according to American "standards," the Japanese infants might be considered "deficient." They engaged in less positive vocalization and spent less time with toys and other objects: "The Japanese infant," they said, "seems passive—he spends much more time simply lying awake in his crib or on a *zabuton* (a flat cushion) on the floor [p. 16]." The authors further reported that a study by Arai, Ishikawa, and Toshima (1958) found that—compared to American norms—Japanese infants showed a steady decline on tests of language and motor development from 4 to 36 months of age. Caudill and Weinstein, however, remained relativistic. They commented that although Arai, Ishikawa, and Toshima seemed somewhat distressed that the "Japanese mothers were so bound up in the lives of their infants that they interfered with the development of their infants in ways which made it difficult to meet the American norms," Caudill and Weinstein (1969) did not share the Japanese authors' concern over the lack of matching the American norms: "We do not believe that the differences we find are necessarily indications of a better or a worse approach to human life, but rather that such differences are a part of an individual's adjustment to his culture [p. 41]." Again, it is doubtful if the same conclusion would have been reached had the data been collected from a minority subculture in the United States.

A final example of the need for cultural

relativism involves a study of Ashkenazic and Sephardic Jews in Brooklyn (Gross, 1967). Both groups were solidly middle class, and lived only two blocks apart. Both had been long established in this country and spoke English in their homes. On entering school, however, the Ashkenazic children averaged 17 points higher on a standard IQ test, a disparity similar in magnitude to that often reported between children of white suburbs and black slums.

Gross pointed out that it is generally assumed that inferior performance in school necessarily reflects deprivation and lack of opportunity. He argued, on the contrary, that each culture has its own ideas of what is important—some emphasize one skill, some another. Despite their children's lower IQ scores the Sephardic mothers were not deprived, however one defines the term: "In many cases they had minks, maids, and country homes." The Sephardic mothers were all native born, high school graduates, and none worked. The children "were blessed with privilege, money and comfort, but their level of academic readiness was similar to that of their underprivileged Israeli counterparts."

Gross explained that the difference was related to cultural tradition: The two communities represented different routes into the middle class—the Ashkenazim through success in school and the Sephardim through success in the marketplace. The author concluded that educational unpreparedness could be found among the "financially well-to-do" as well as among the lower classes, and suggested that this finding should be a "caution signal to social engineers." Gross questioned those who advocate changing lower-class blacks to conform to the life styles and values of middle-class whites, and suggested that there was an element of "white colonialism" in the attempt to "reshape the economically underprivileged in the image of the education-minded intellectually oriented academicians."

Gross's final point merits expansion, because intervention is becoming a big business in the United States today. The federal government is spending large amounts of money on intervention programs, and some social scientists fear that the interventionists will totally disregard subcultural systems in their attempts to "save" the "deprived" children.

> When we force people of another culture to make an adjustment to ours, by that much we are destroying the integrity of their personalities. When too many adjustments of this sort are required too fast, the personality disintegrates and the result is an alienated, dissociated individual who cannot feel really at home in either culture [Lehmer, 1969, p. D-4].

Why is it so common for researchers to remain relativistic in their discussions of socialization practices in other nations, while being intolerant of subcultural differences among lower-income and minority groups in this country? One could propose that each nation socializes its children according to prevailing cultural values so that regardless of the fact that practices in other nations are different, children in each country develop the personalities and intellectual skills needed for success in their own particular social systems. This theory would argue that it is inappropriate to apply cultural relativism to subcultures because a person's success remains defined by the majority culture. Keller (1963), for example, argued that "cultural relativism ignores the fact that schools and industry are middle class in organization and outlook."

Cultural relativism and success in "schools and industry," however, are *not* mutually exclusive. It is possible to teach children the skills needed for articulation with the majority culture, while encouraging them to develop a pride in their own family or cultural heritage, and to utilize the particular skills which their own socialization has strengthened. A majority culture can, however, promote a narrow definition of success in order to ensure that the power of the society remain in the hands of a relatively select group within the society. Thus, by maintaining that any deviation from the white middle-class norm represents cultural deprivation, the white middle class is guarding its position as *the* source of culture—and power—in this nation.

# REFERENCES

Arai, S., Ishikawa, J., & Toshima, K. Developpement psychomoteur des enfants Japonais. *La Revue de Neuropsychiatrie Infantile et d'Hygiène Mentale de l'Enfance,* 1958, **6,** 262–269. Cited by W. Caudill & H. Weinstein, Maternal care and infant behavior in Japan and America. *Psychiatry,* 1969, **32,** 41.

Baratz, J. C., & Shuy, R. W. (Eds.) *Teaching black children to read.* Washington, D. C.: Center for Applied Linguistics, 1969.

Baratz, S. S., & Baratz, J. C. Early childhood intervention: The social science base of institutional racism. *Harvard Educational Review,* 1970, **40,** 29–50.

Bernstein, B. Language and social class. *British Journal of Sociology,* 1960, **11,** 271–276.

Bernstein, B. Social class and linguistic development: A theory of social learning. In A. H. Halsey, H. Floud, & C. A. Anderson (Eds.), *Education, economy and society.* Glencoe, Ill.: Free Press, 1961.

Birren, J. E., & Hess, R. Influences of biological, psychological, and social deprivations on learning and performance. In *Perspectives on human deprivation.* Washington, D. C.: Department of Health, Education, and Welfare, United States Government Printing Office, 1968.

Caudill, W., & Weinstein, H. Maternal care and infant behavior in Japanese and American urban middle class families. Bethesda, Md.: National Institute of Mental Health, 1966. (Mimeo)

Caudill, W., & Weinstein, H. Maternal care and infant behavior in Japan and America. *Psychiatry,* 1969, **32,** 12–43.

Chandler, B. J., & Erickson, F. D. *Sounds of society: A demonstration program in group inquiry.* (Final Rep. No. 6-2044) Washington, D. C.: United States Government Printing Office, 1968.

Coles, R. Violence in ghetto children. In S. Chess & A. Thomas (Eds.), *Annual progress in child psychiatry and child development.* New York: Brunner/Mazel, 1968.

Davé, R. H. The identification and measurement of environmental variables that are related to educational achievement. Unpublished doctoral dissertation, University of Chicago, 1963.

Foster, H. L. Dialect-lexicon and listening comprehension. Unpublished doctoral dissertation, Teachers College, Columbia University, 1969.

Foster, H. L. Foster's Jive Lexicon Analogies Test. Series II. Buffalo: Office of Teacher Education, State University of New York, 1970. (Mimeo)

Gans, H. J. *The urban villagers: Group and class in the life of Italian-Americans.* New York: Free Press of Glencoe, 1962.

Gross, M. *Learning readiness in two Jewish groups.* New York: Center for Urban Education, 1967.

Herskovits, M. *The myth of the Negro past.* Boston: Beacon Press, 1958.

Jessor, R., & Richardson, S. Psychosocial deprivation and personality development. In *Perspectives on human deprivation.* Washington, D. C.: United States Government Printing Office, 1968.

Kagan, J. On cultural deprivation. In D. C. Glass (Ed.), *Environmental influences.* New York: Rockefeller University Press, 1968.

Keller, S. The social world of the urban slum child: Some early findings. *American Journal of Orthopsychiatry,* 1963, **33,** 823–834.

Krauss, R. M., & Rotter, G. S. Communication abilities of children as a function of status and age. *Merrill-Palmer Quarterly,* 1968, **14,** 161–174.

Labov, W. Some sources of reading problems for Negro speakers of nonstandard English. In A. Frazier (Ed.), *New directions in elementary English.* Champaign, Ill.: National Council of Teachers of English, 1967.

Lehmer, M. Navajos want their own schools. *San Francisco Examiner and Chronicle,* December 14, 1969.

Maccoby, M., & Modiano, N. On culture and equivalence. I. In J. S. Bruner, R. R. Olver, & P. M. Greenfield (Eds.), *Studies in cognitive growth.* New York: Wiley, 1966.

Rebelsky, F., & Abeles, G. Infancy in Holland and in the United States. Paper presented at the meeting of the Society for Research in Child Development, Santa Monica, March 1969.

Riessman, F. *The culturally deprived child.* New York: Harper & Row, 1962.

Sroufe, L. A. A methodological and philosophical critique of intervention-oriented research. *Developmental Psychology,* 1970, **2,** 140–145.

Stewart, W. A. Sociolinguistic factors in the history of American Negro dialects. *The Florida FL Reporter,* 1967, **5**(2).

Stewart, W. A. Linguistic and conceptual deprivation—fact or fancy? Paper presented at the meeting of the Society for Research in Child Development, Santa Monica, March 1969. (a)

Stewart, W. A. On the use of Negro dialect in the teaching of reading. In J. C. Baratz & R. W. Shuy (Eds.), *Teaching black children to read.* Washington, D. C.: Center for Applied Linguistics, 1969. (b)

Wolf, R. M. The identification and measurement of environmental process variables related to intelligence. Unpublished doctoral dissertation, University of Chicago, 1964.

# Poor Children: Images and Interpretations

## David L. Bachelor & Rosalie S. Donofrio

## INTRODUCTION

After years of neglect, benign and otherwise, the poor child has come to the forefront of research in education. The national conscience is twinging and the rush for remediation is on. Studies focusing on the poor child are abundant and a thorough review of the literature would be exhausting, as well as futile. It would be futile because the literature on the poor child tends to lack imagination and illustrates an unwillingness to test out a variety of interpretations. The literature tends to present a hit-and-run approach to the learning problems of the poor. It seems that researchers and educators are trying to find a one-shot method for dealing with poor children's problems based on preconceived notions of the origins of the problems. Interpretations of poor children's performance are made, new methods implemented, outcomes reported, but no consistent progress seems to be made. Research and replication based on alternative theoretical foundations is necessary. The aim of this paper

Reprinted from *Sociological Symposium*, Fall 1971, 7, 1–13. Copyright 1971 by Sociological Symposium. Reprinted by permission.

is to integrate three of the images of the poor child and his performance that have emerged from the recent literature. Out of such a synthesis it is hoped that a new, more realistic, image of the poor child will emerge and provide the basis for a new theoretical foundation.

The topics of poverty, child development and intervention programs have generated an enormous literature in the last decade or so. Though this literature illustrates a variety of approaches and is based on a variety of data, the great majority of the writings utilize essentially the same interpretations and produce the same image of the poor child: he has failed to make the same general developmental advances accomplished successfully by his middle-class counterpart. The dominance of the deprivation theory in the interpretation of poor children's school performance is almost unquestioned and is certainly the most commonly used one. The theory influences most of the interpretive writing on poor children and almost all of the empirical reports.

A relatively rare counter-theme recently developing is the argument that growing up poor does develop useful skills and encourages certain kinds of talent. Since this point of view is held by comparatively few writers, it therefore may be unnoticed by people who should be aware that there may be alternative interpretations of poor children's school performance.

The purpose of this paper is to review a representative sampling of writings illustrating the two general themes already outlined. Though these themes appear to be opposed and even irreconcilable, a few recent papers and research reports may provide interpretations that synthesize the contending images of poor children. Criticism of past work and a review of the more recent synthesizing point of view will make up the final section.

## IMAGES OF THE POOR CHILD AS DEPRIVED

Obviously not all writers who adhere to the general theory of deprivation agree on all the particulars: some stress economic forces as a cause of deprivation; others would emphasize a rural background; the rest would blame the quantity and quality of interaction in the home. Despite the disagreement on the specifics, the image of the child generated by these writers is one of deficiencies. They imply and sometimes specifically outline a common view of the poor child and of the mechanisms affecting his performance in school and in the job market.

There is perhaps no more succinct statement concerning the lack of "socially useful" skills among the "disadvantaged child" than the one made by Havighurst in 1964:

> There is substantial doubt that the socially disadvantaged children in our big cities have any positive qualities of potential value in urban society in which they are systematically better than the children of families who participate fully in the mass cultures. . . As a group they are inferior in tests of spacial perception, for example, as well as in tests of vocabulary and arithmetic. (Havighurst 1964, pp. 28–29)

The author does concede that "the difference between the socially disadvantaged and the mass culture is less on tests of certain non-verbal skills than on tests of more verbal and abstract abilities" (Havighurst 1964:29).

The image of the poor child is developed more specifically and at greater length by Bereiter, Engleman, & colleagues:

> From our earlier work in teaching concrete logical operations it became evident that culturally deprived children do not think at an immature level: many of them do not think at all. That is, they do not show any of the mediating processes which we ordinarily identify with thinking. They cannot hold onto questions while searching for an answer. They cannot compare perceptions in any reliable fashion. They are oblivious of even the most extreme discrepancies between their actions and statements as they follow one another in a series. . . . They cannot give explanations at all, nor do they seem to have any idea of what it is to explain an event. The question and answer process which is the core of orderly thinking is completely foreign to most of them. (Bereiter et al 1966:107)

The authors maintain further that the language of the "culturally deprived" child is not merely an underdeveloped version of standard English, "but is basically a non-logical mode of expressive behavior" (Bereiter 1966:112). These descriptions of the poor child, of his lack of abilities, and his deficiencies in elementary skills provide the basis for the major authors' much publicized academically oriented preschool.

The previous statement describing the weakness of poor children's speech agrees with the descriptions developed by the British sociolinguist Bernstein.

(1) Short, grammatically simple, often unfinished sentences with a poor syntactical form stressing the active voice.
(2) Simple and repetitive use of conjunctions (so, then, because).
(3) Little use of subordinate clauses to break down the initial categories of the dominant subject.
(4) Inability to hold a formal subject through a speech sequence; thus a dislocated informational content is facilitated.
(5) Rigid and limited use of adjectives and adverbs.
(6) Constraint on the self-reference pronoun; frequent use of the personal pronoun.
(7) Frequent use of statements where reason and conclusion are confounded to produce a categoric statement.
(8) A large number of statements/phrases which signal a requirement for the previous speech sequence to be reinforced: i.e., "Wouldn't it? You see? You know?" etc. This process is termed "sympathetic circularity."
(9) Individual selection from a group of idiomatic phrases or sequences will frequently occur.
(10) The individual qualification is implicit in the sentence organization; it is the language of implicit meaning. (Bernstein 1961, 1960)

Bernstein does not use the same words that Bereiter uses to describe this language pattern. That he agrees with much of what Bereiter says is strongly implied by the term he uses to describe this language pattern: The restricted code.

The experiments carried out by Martin Deutsch and his associates have led them to develop the concept of sensory deprivation. He finds poor children to have inferior auditory and visual discrimination, time judgement, sense of number, and other basic concepts. In other papers he described what he calls a severe and general language impoverishment (Deutsch 1965, 1963).

The broad picture of the child as drawn by these authors is one of deficiencies and failures. The poor child lacks a variety of skills because he has failed to develop as quickly or as well as the better-off child. It should be emphasized that the image of the poor child under the theory of deprivation is a relative one: he fails to grasp or to utilize skills or knowledge that is assumed to be firmly within the capabilities of the average middle class youth of the same age.

The basis for these deficiencies is strongly implied and often discussed by the authors mentioned in this paper and the many others who share a similar view of the poor child. To paraphrase the authors as concisely as possible the origins of deprivation stem from the home. The quality and quantity of interaction in the typical economically poor urban milieu retards the development of critical skills and abilities. The quality of verbal and non-verbal interaction is such that logical operations, questioning, listening, seeing, judging, scheduling and so on are not practiced or encouraged. The material and objects available in the home for the child to manipulate and perceive are felt to be few and to lack in sensory variety. Crowded conditions, noise, and the lack of organization in the home are felt to be the causes of disabilities labeled sensory deprivation.

Such an image of poor children is built on school grades, drop-out rates, and most often, performance on standard tests of intelligence or achievement. It seems that this image is most popular because it has the weight of empirical evidence on its side. As Havighurst (1964) points out, there is an impressive array of data that appears to indicate that the poor child cannot perform up to the standard of his better off counterpart. The finding that poor, and often minority, children score one standard deviation below the mean on standard IQ tests is nearly universal (Carlson & Henderson 1950; Jensen 1961, 1969; Pasamanick 1951; Shuey 1966).

## IMAGES OF THE POOR CHILD AS ABLE

A few writers on the topic relevant to this paper appear to work from assumptions which are rather different than the ones used by the deprivation theorists. Though they do not say so in so many words they seem to feel that the simple fact of growing up in a poor and difficult environment is evidence that the child has acquired some competencies. We should recognize these skills and attempt to build upon them in the school situation.

One of the earliest and most influential proponents of this view of the poor child is Frank Riessman. In *The Culturally Deprived Child* he argues that poor children have a distinctive learning style and termed it a "concrete learning style." Such a mode of learning is quite different from the learning habits of the middle-class child and the practices typically found in public schools; hence, the failure of poor children to perform "adequately." Riessman concedes that the children he calls disadvantaged or lower class may be retarded in reading, knowing how to ask and answer questions, and what he terms general school know-how. The author argues, however, that emphasizing the weaknesses of the poor child obscures the real skills and potentials that he has. The school, according to Riessman, actively fails the physically oriented slow learner by not utilizing his concrete learning style and physical interest as one avenue to abstract thinking. He suggests using activity involvement, for example role playing, as a general constructive response to poor or disadvantaged children (Riessman 1962, 1961).

Two other images of the poor child agree in general with Riessman, but where he supplies some plan of action (no matter how vague) the other two authors merely attempt to catalogue the skills and strengths of the child. It is made clear that if we are to succeed in changing these children, we have to build on what strengths they have. Furthermore, it seems that "the key issue in looking at the strengths of the inner city child is the importance of not confusing difference with defect" (Eisenberg 1967:85).

These strengths can be described as deriving from the impoverished environment in which poor children grow up. Such skills may be labeled Practical Knowledge or simply more experience with the seamy side of life.

> Their understandings are more often economic than aesthetic. Their interests are less concerned with romantic love than with the duties, difficulties, and conflicts of life in a family which is trying to survive in adversity. (McCreary 1966:49)

Other kinds of strengths are described in the following way:

(1) Strong In-Group Feelings: One cultural strand of working-class existence which is powerfully reinforced by the life experience of socially disadvantaged youths is an impulse toward mutual aid, fellow feeling, or reciprocity. Those on the bottom or those who have been driven into a corner by economic deprivation or ethnic discrimination and injustice, sharing adversity and misfortune with others, are likely to learn to share also their resources of a material and spiritual nature. (Ibid, 50)
(2) Self-Reliance and Autonomy: Independence and self-sufficiency, associated with the realistic if sometimes harsh life experiences of such youth make for a maturity and responsibility frequently found with these individuals. Such independence can often lead to clashes when school personnel attempt to control poor children and get them to act like other children. (Ibid, 51)
(3) Physically and Visually Oriented: The style of the inner city children is physical and visual. To engage these children in watching a movie, or a class play where they act it out, or a role-playing exercise where they pretend to be the storekeeper and customers will teach them how to behave. There is much greater likelihood of getting the children to be able to give verbal descriptions of what happened than if you simply challenged the children with a verbal stimulus. (Eisenberg 1967:83)
(4) Externally Oriented: These children are externally oriented rather than introspective. Questions about how people feel and think are less meaningful to them than questions about what people do. (Ibid, 84)*

*From "Some Positive Characteristics of Disadvantaged Learners and their Implications for Education," by

In addition these writers tend to agree that the poor child learns concretely and has a physical oriented learning style similar to Riessman's outline.

The image derived from these writings [see also Glatt 1965] on the child living in economically deprived conditions differs in important respects from the image presented in the first section of this paper. The first group of authors emphasized deficiencies; the second skills and abilities. The difference could be thought of as only differences in emphasis or priorities; the first group tend to emphasize things that have to be done, the deficiencies that have to be made up; the second group focuses on the skills children have and that can be built upon in the school or intervention program context. However, this description of the differences between the two sets of writers obscures some fundamental differences in starting points and end results. Those authors whose work fits under the deprivation heading tend to see poor children as collections of deficiencies, who react to their environment at a low, intuitive level. These children are seen as little more than animals, illogical, uncommunicative, and with little or none of the intellectual apparatus which characterizes the rest of us humans. Intervention programs, special classes in the public schools have as their job doing what the home and parents have failed to do. School, according to the deprivation theorists, must often originate the cognitive structures that are assumed not to exist.

The second set of authors presents an image that is more humane, human, right-feeling, and based on much weaker evidence. It strikes us as a more realistic view of the child to hold that he has both strengths and weaknesses, although it may be that few of the strengths and most of the weaknesses are precisely in those activity areas rewarded or punished by school and middle-class society. Economic deprivation, growing up poor, may result in the weakening of the development of certain types of intellectual abilities. Such disabilities may be irreversible or they may not. However, to as-

E. McCreary. In S. Webster (Ed.), *Knowing the Disadvantaged Learner*, Part I. Copyright © 1966 by Staten W. Webster. Reprinted by permission.

sume that growing up poor robs one of basic logical skills such as speech is to provide evidence of selective blindness on the part of some authors.

Nevertheless, those writers who argue that surviving in the harsh environment of poverty develops some abilities base their contentions mostly on intuition and guess. Some of the abilities appear to constitute very good guesses, some appear to be derived from the author's own misperceptions of what it means to be poor. (Glatt 1965)*

Indeed, reading some of this material easily gives the impression that the writers believe there is something precious in being poor; an impression that does damage to the validity of their major point that poor children do learn some skills. We are faced with the dilemma of wanting to believe the second image on emotional grounds but have to believe the first because all of the "hard" evidence seems to support the deprivation theory. Fortunately some recent research appears to provide a third image of the poor child and it is to this alternative that we turn.

## SITUATIONAL BIASES AND COPING SKILLS

Recent research indicates that some measure of synthesizing can now be introduced which will give a fairer and more useful image of the poor child. In the fundamentally important area of language, Labov has reinterpreted some of the findings and analysis. He states that the

> . . .linguistic behavior reported by Bereiter is merely the product of a defensive posture which children adopt in an alien and threatening situation. Such behavior can be produced at will in

any group of children and can be altered by changing the relevant sociolinguistic variables. (Labov 1969:1)*

In other words, Labov does not necessarily take issue with the results of interviews with poor children or other methods of getting language samples from them; he does argue that the data derived from such situations is typically misinterpreted. He maintains that asymmetrical situations in which a large, controlling adult runs an interview with a small, controlled child, a situation "where anything he says can literally be held against him" (Labov 1969:6), results in the child avoiding saying anything. Furthermore, "if one takes this interview as a measure of the verbal capacity of the child, it must be his capacity to defend himself in a hostile and threatening situation" (Labov 1969:6).

The bulk of Labov's report details the initial, non-verbal performances of Black children in the interview situation. Slowly, by altering the symmetry of the interview setting (interviewer sitting on the floor with the child, "rapping" with him in dialect, and allowing the child to bring his best friend to the session) a much fuller and richer sampling of the child's language repertory was gained. Labov goes on to analyze the interview data and to make a strong argument that such speech is a flexible and logical mode of communication. He generalized from the interview material:

> One can now transfer this demonstration of the sociolinguistic control of speech to the other test situations—including I.Q. and reading tests in school. The power relationships in a one-to-one confrontation between adult and child are too asymmetrical. This does not mean that some Negro children will not talk a great deal when alone with an adult, or that an adult cannot get close to any child. It means that the social situation is the most powerful determinant of verbal behavior and that an adult must enter in the right social relation with a child if he wants to find out what a child can do: that is just what many teachers cannot do. (Labov 1969:11)

*As an example some of the authors cited in the second section of this paper maintain that deprivation somehow intensifies cooperation among the poor. That may occur, but so might it encourage selfishness in using up the little you have before someone else takes it away. The latter mode of behavior seems to prevail among Black male floaters in Washington, D. C. See Elliot Liebow, *Tally's Corner,* Boston: Little, Brown and Co., 1967; Zahava D. Blum & Peter H. Rossi, in *On Understanding Poverty,* ed. by Daniel P. Moynihan. New York: Basic Books, 1969, pp. 343–397.

Houston in the examination of some of the assumptions [the author refers to them as "myths"] concerning the language of poor children agrees with the preceding points. She concurs with Labov on the crucial role of sociolinguistic variables in the speech performance of children:

> To be sure, lack of reinforcement for linguistic behavior must have an effect on the young child. Most probably, it is effective in limiting the use of language in non-reinforcing contexts. (Houston 1971:950)

More specifically the author cites some research she did among Black children in northern Florida. Two registers or ranges of language styles which have in common their appropriateness to a given situation or environment were found among these children.

> These registers were termed by us the School and Non-school registers, because the first appeared primarily in school settings and with teachers and the second in other settings. However, the school register also was used with all persons perceived by the children as in authority over them or studying them in any way . . . and in formal and constrained situations . . . One may note that the characteristics of the School register include most of the observations given . . . as indications of disadvantaged nonfluency. It should be added that the content expressed in this register tends to be rather limited and non-revelatory of the children's attitudes, feelings and ideas. (Houston 1971:952–53)

The situational variation in use of language, switching of registers and of styles within registers, may be a specific instance of what has been referred to in another report as "coping" or "survival" skills (Bachelor et al 1970). Language itself is not a skill but is more in the nature of an innate property of the organism (Lenneberg 1964, 1966; Chomsky 1965); but, the collecting, interpreting of cues, and reacting to them linguistically can be seen as a skill—one so securely internalized as to be used unconsciously. And, coping skills means those sensitivities to cues and modes of reacting to them which has allowed the child growing up in poverty to survive physically and psychically.

The research done at the child development centers of the Albuquerque Comprehensive Child Care and Development Project infer something of the existence of survival skills. It was found that among approximately 75 children aged two years six months to five years eleven months the mean scores on the Peabody Picture Vocabulary Test (PPVT) were just about one standard deviation below the national mean. (The mean IQ score for the sample was 84.9.) The mean IQ scores obtained from a sub-sample of 25 children on the Wechsler Pre-school and Primary Scale of Intelligence (WPPSI) was 85.16. By contrast, the mean Social Quotient (SQ) for these children was more than one standard deviation above the national mean on the Vineland Scale of Social Maturity (VSMS). The VSMS is an observer scored test which attempts to measure a child's independence from adult help by means of items asking whether or not a child can perform a given task, i.e., feed himself, dress himself, take trips alone and so on (Bachelor et al 1970).

The depressed scores of these children on the PPVT and WPPSI may illustrate the impact of the sociolinguistic variables discussed by Labov and Houston. Scores on the VSMS, however, may be interpreted as signifying the children's early acquisition of skills necessary to cope with a poverty environment, in this instance the early development of independence. If such coping skills are encouraged in a poverty milieu, the VSMS is, at best, a very limited sampling of such behavior since it concentrates on at-home activities. The poor child usually enters the street or peer group environment at a very early age (as compared to middle-class children); perhaps there is a large component of street skills or abilities to deal with the environment outside the home within any set of coping or survival skills. The work at the Child Development Project is now concentrated on specifying situational factors influencing performance and coping or survival skills.

A final consideration in developing a realistic image of the poor child comes from basic research in psychology and deals specifically with children's imagery and learning of paired-associate (PA) words. It has been found that in a sample of 432 children, grades 1, 3, and 6 in schools stratified by socio-economic characteristics, low strata children performed on the PA experiment just as well as the high strata children. This finding contradicted the author's hypothesis that low strata children should also show less learning facilitation when compared to high strata children in the PA experiment. The authors discussed the findings in this manner:

> The relatively high degree of learning proficiency observed among children from low strata schools is at once the most puzzling and most promising aspect of the present results. . . . The teachers of the children from the low strata schools corroborated the simplistic inference indicated by standardized test performance in describing their students as being slow to learn and difficult to teach . . . A more likely interpretation of the discrepancy is that it occurs because of pronounced differences between the conditions of learning that are characteristic of the laboratory . . . three ends of such differences may be distinguished. First, greater control of the focus of the child's attention is achieved in the laboratory than in the classroom . . . Second, the requirements of the child's task are explicitly detailed to a much greater extent in the laboratory than in the classroom. Third, in the laboratory case, the information necessary for the child to make a judgement about the adequacy of his performance is inherent in the learning materials themselves, whereas in the classroom such information is typically made available only in the teacher's reaction to the child's behavior and not within the boundaries of the task itself. (Rohwer et al 1968:29–30)*

In another place the major writer calls attention to findings that there are apparently differing developmental trends in children's use of imagery in learning between middle-class and lower-class Black children. (Rohwer 1970:401) These developmental variations in

imagery could be attributed to sociolinguistic variables due to the manner in which the experiments were carried out. However, it is just as plausible to maintain that the necessity of responding to quite different environments influences the development of different mnemonic and learning structures at different times among poor and not-so-poor children.

The image of the poor child which appears to be emerging from the literature just discussed is more human, but it is still obscure in several crucial areas. It is clear that the poor child is not the retarded little beast some imply he is. He appears to have decided linguistic and behavioral skills, though in many respects it is very hard to describe them yet with any precision. From this review of more balanced, although inferential and heuristic, studies it appears that the core of the problem of the inferior school performance of the poor child can be relieved by getting the child to perform better in school situations, on the one hand, and on the other by getting the schools and teachers to see that their image of poor children is all too often punitive and obtuse.

## CONCLUSIONS AND IMPLICATIONS

Where do we go from here? Common sense dictates that something must be done to or for or with the poor child in order to place him on a competitive level with his middle class counterpart. The writers feel that two channels for change are available: changing the schools and development of new pre-school or intervention programs.

Pre-school or intervention programs are probably the easiest route, because they remove remediation and prevention from the schools. Ideally, intervention programs prepare the child to be assimilated into an ongoing system. Intervention programs are too new to have documented their successes; only their failings are documented.

Head Start critics are abundant (Cawley 1968; Circirelli 1969; Coleman 1966; Jensen 1969; Kean 1970; Osborn 1969; Shore 1971; Van 1971). But, even a cursory look at the literature reveals that the criticisms leveled are as inconclusive as the praise given these programs. As with most innovations, only time will accurately pinpoint their specific strengths and weaknesses, and as for the battles presently being waged for and against such programs, they are probably very healthy for academics, in general. As is evidenced in the first section of this paper, the view of the poor child has been far too complacent, far too pejorative. Authorities on deprivation assumed that deficiencies are cumulative; a child from a poor background entered school at a slight disadvantage and underwent a steady decline. By the sixth grade he was as much as three years behind his grade level. But what of the benefits of intervention programs? Could they not also be cumulative? It is not inconceivable that lower class children helped by their coping skills and a kick-off from a properly articulated intervention program, could enter school at a slight disadvantage and begin a steady incline; by sixth grade they could be two or three years ahead of grade level (Strickland 1971:7). Granted, the assumption is tenuous, but maybe not altogether unwarranted. As with any assumption, time will tell; it is the hope of these writers that intervention programs will not be cast aside until such time as enough hard data can be generated to either prove or disprove their merits.

For now, intervention programs may be justified on the grounds that since generally they aren't subject to any of the public school red tape, they are an excellent proving ground for innovations in both child and teacher training. They have opened communications between home and school. They provide jobs, dignity, and money for residents of poor neighborhoods and therefore prop up the economy while freeing parents for work and leisure. Their medical services and meals enable the child to learn better or at least live a more comfortable life. Perhaps these are reasons enough to silence critics until data is available. Arthur Jensen (1969) says that intervention programs are not useful, because they do not raise IQ substantially; their only benefit to the child is in raising his grade point average. It is an opinion of these writers that better grades are justification enough for continuance of these programs, since grades bear some positive relationship to success in employment.

Changing the schools is a knotty problem. The concept of school is deceptive; school exists as a separate entity capable of working changes upon those who enter, but generally incapable of change within itself. As people have accepted IQ scores as the only valid assessment of intelligence, so they accept the school as the only place one can learn; it is looked upon as the supreme holder of knowledge. Anyone who fails to learn is deficient, or defective. But schools are now the subject of serious scrutiny. Educators are aware that IQ's are not the only measure of intelligence. Can schools, as they presently exist, be the only place where one can learn? Intelligence, aptitude, learning, call it what you may, is nothing more than behaving efficiently in a particular situation (Maslow 1944). For the poor child the intelligence test may not be a justifiable situation for measuring the efficiency of behaving; the school may also be the incorrect situation for judging the learning abilities of poor children.

Issue can be taken with the deprivation theorists and the school on two levels. First, it must be shown that IQ and achievement tests, and the masses of data generated through their use, somehow do not measure skills and competencies of poor children validly or that tests do not take in all the socially useful skills developed in children. Arthur Jensen (1961) clearly demonstrated that although intelligence tests aptly identified middle class children of high and low ability, they were inefficient in categorizing the intellectual capacities of poor children. Other studies of this kind have been mentioned in sections II and III; more are needed. We speak of beginning the educational process "where the child is at." More investigation into the strengths of poor children may reveal where the "AT" is really at (Sears 1966:7).

Secondly, failure in the public school is seen by the deprivation theorists as originating largely outside the school and in the home. The child entering school from a poor home is seen as disadvantaged because he has not been taught certain things in the home. The public schools may not succeed in helping this child, but such failure is after the fact. Such reasoning is dangerous . . . "because it diverts attention from the real defects of our educational system to the imaginary defects of the child" (Labov 1969:2). We feel that if the school fails it is because it does not recognize the child's needs and respond to them. Schools for poor children should begin at different developmentally earlier points than they do for the typical middle-class child. Whether or not the poor child can or will ever catch up is not an issue dealt with very often, but when it is, the conclusions are usually pessimistic. But, deprivation theorists and the schools cannot be blamed entirely. Pessimism is usually the easiest way out. An optimistic view of the poor child's future may cost time, money, and will involve a serious rocking of the boat.

Regardless of the formidable odds, these writers would like to present some suggestions for changing schools. To begin, we must rid ourselves of the missionary zeal with which we attack poor children. No, not everyone should nor wants to be WASP. Secondly, we must not delude ourselves by thinking that poverty is precious or charming. On the contrary, the poor "trip" is a "bummer." Thirdly, we must examine what happens in the schools that causes poor children to fail. Surely, the high drop out rate must indicate that schools are also failing. Along these lines Labov states:

> Before we impose middle class verbal style on children from other cultural groups, we should find out how much of this is useful for the main work of analyzing and generalizing, and how much is mere stylistic—or even dysfunctional. In high school and college middle class children spontaneously complicate their syntax to the point that instructors despair of getting them to make their language simpler and clearer. In every learned journal one can find examples of jargon and empty elaboration—and complaints about it. Is the 'elaborated code' of Bernstein really so flexible, detailed and subtle as some psychologists believe? Is it not also turgid, redundant, and empty? Is it not simply an elaborated style, rather than a superior code or system?
> Our work in the speech community makes it painfully obvious that in many ways working-

class speakers are more effective narrators, reasoners, and debaters than middle-class speakers who temporized, qualify, and lose their argument in a mass of irrelevant detail. Many academic writers try to rid themselves of that part of middle-class style that is empty pretension, and keep that part that is needed for precision. But the average middle-class speaker that we encounter makes no such effort; he is enmeshed in verbiage the victim of sociolinguistic factors beyond his control. (Labov 1969:12)*

Susan Houston (1971) refers to school and home registers of language. Both are now incorporated at the university level; perhaps they should be allowed to function interchangeably in the elementary classroom. Critics would say that poor children only use a restrictive code and are therefore non-verbal. But, the reader is asked to think: what code, restrictive or elaborated, do teachers use when addressing poor children (Hess 1970)?

Developmental psychology as proposed by Erickson points out that children between the ages of roughly 6–11 are characterized by feelings of industry versus inferiority.† At these ages there is marked competition for excellence and status permeated by the dread of failure. Although success is not always necessary to reduce the feelings of inferiority, the child must be made to know that his efforts are appreciated and respected. This can probably be best accomplished by reducing comparisons among peers such as eliminating grades and tracking. As schools are now, they only seem to increase the poor child's feeling of inferiority.

As the final, and perhaps most simplistic suggestion, we should like to suggest that poor children are a dilemma to the schools because they are ambiguous. They do not conform to the means of prediction and control used on middle-class children. Poor children do not look, smell, talk, act, or think like middle-class children. They are indeed confusing because the trained incapacity so prevalent in the

---

*Perhaps the authors should give thought to this allegation?

†Personal communications: S. Roll, Dept. of Psyc. UNM.

schools is inappropriate in the light of the changed situation, i.e., poor children (Merton 1961). Perhaps the easiest method of guaranteeing success for poor children is to throw out the old rules, accept their ambiguity, and let the children lead the teachers in the learning process.

# REFERENCES

Bachelor, L., et al. *Learning Among Poor Children: Test Constructs & Coping Skills.* Albuquerque Research Report, no. 1. Albuquerque: Albuquerque Comprehensive Child Care and Development Project, 1970.

Bereiter, C., et al. An academically oriented preschool for culturally deprived children. *Preschool Education Today,* edited by F. Hechinger, 105–35. New York: Doubleday, 1966.

Bernstein, B. Social class & linguistic development: a theory of social learning. *Economy, Education & Society,* edited by A. Halsey, J. Floud & C. Anderson, 288-308. New York: Free Press, 1961.

Bernstein, B. Language & social class. *British Journal of Sociology* 11 (1960) 271–76.

Carlson, H., & N. Henderson. The intelligence of american children of mexican parentage. *Journal of Abnormal & Social Psychology* 45 (1950) 544–51. This latter study found that from age six to eleven the performance of Mexican children on IQ tests declined relative to the Anglo control group (page 548).

Cawley, J. Learning aptitudes among pre-school children of different intellectual levels. *Journal of Negro Education* 37 (1968) 179–83.

Chomsky, N. *Aspects of the Theory of System.* Cambridge: MIT Press, 1965.

Circirelli, V., et al. *The Impact of Head Start: An Evaluation of the Effects of Head Start on Children's Cognitive & Effective Development.* Washington, D C: Office of Economic Opportunity, 1969.

Coleman, J., et al. *Equality of Educational Opportunity.* Washington, D C: U. S. Printing Office, 1966.

Deutsch, M. The role of social class in language development & cognition. *American Journal of Orthopsychiatry* 34 (1965) 78–88.

Deutsch, M. The disadvantaged child & the learning process. *Education In Depressed Areas,* edited by A. Passow, 170–81. New York: Columbia University Teachers College, 1963.

Eisenberg, L. Strengths of the inner city child. *Education of the Disadvantaged Child,* edited by A. Passow, 78–88. New York: Holt, Rinehart & Winston, 1967.

Glatt, C. Who are the ddp deprived children? *Elementary School Journal* 65 (1965) 407–13.

Havighurst, R. Who are the socially disadvantaged? *Journal of Negro Education* (Summer 1964) 20–29.

Hess, R., & V. Shipman. Early experiences & socialization of cognitive modes in children. *Learning In Social Settings,* edited by M. Miles & W. Charters, Jr. Boston: Allyn & Bacon, 1970.

Houston, S. A re-examination of some assumptions about the language of the disadvantaged child. *Child Development* 41 (1971) 947–63.

Jensen, A. Environment, heredity & intelligence. Compiled from *Harvard Educational Review* 39 (1969).

Jensen, A. Learning abilities in mexican-american children. *California Journal of Educational Research* 12 (1961) 147–59.

Jensen, A. Learning abilities in mexican-american & anglo-american children. *California Journal of Educational Research* 12 (September 1961) 147–57.

Jensen, A. How much can we boost IQ & scholastic achievement. *Harvard Educational Review* 39 (Winter 1969) 81.

Kean, J. Impact of head start: an evaluation of the effects of children's cognitive & effective development. *Childhood Education* 46 (1970) 449–51.

Labov, W. The logic of non-standard english. *Monograph Series On Language & Linguistics,* edited by J. Alatis, 1–42. Washington, D C: Georgetown University Press, 1969.

Lenneberg, E. The natural history of language. *The Genesis of Language: A Psycholinguistic Approach,* edited by F. Smith & G. Miller, 219–52. Cambridge: MIT Press, 1966.

Lenneberg, E. A biological perspective of language. *New Directions in the Study of Language,* edited by E. Lenneberg, 65–88. Cambridge: MIT Press, 1964.

Maslow, A. What intelligence tests mean. *Journal of General Psychology* 31 (1944) 85–93.

McCreary, E. Some positive characteristics of disadvantaged learners & their implications for education. *Knowing the Disadvantaged Learner,* edited by S. Webster, part 1. San Francisco: Chandler, 1966.

Merton, R. Bureaucratic structures & personality. *Complex Organizations,* edited by A. Etzioni, 48–60. New York: Free Press of Glencoe, 1961.

Osborn, D. Some gains from the head start experience. *Childhood Education* 44 (1969) 8–11.

Pasamanick, B. The intelligence of american children of mexican parentage: a discussion of uncontrolled variables. *Journal of Abnormal & Social Psychology* 46 (1951) 598–602.

Riessman, F. *The Culturally Deprived Child.* New York: Harper & Row, 1962.

Riessman, F. & S. Miller. The culture of the underprivileged: a new look. *Social Problems* (Summer 1961) 86–97.

Rohwer, W., Jr., et al. Grade level, school strata & learning efficiency. *Journal of Educational Psychology* 59 (1968) 26–31.

Rohwer, W., Jr. Images & pictures in children's learning: research results & educational implications. *Psychology Bulletin* 73 (1970) 393–403.

Rossi, P., & Z. Blum. Class, status & poverty. *On Understanding Poverty,* edited by D. Moynihan, 36–63. New York: Basic Books, 1969.

Sears, R. Introduction. *Learning About Learning,* edited by J. Bruner. Washington, D C: Department of Health, Education & Welfare, 1966.

Shore, M., & N. Milgram. The effectiveness of an enrichment program for disadvantaged young children. *American Journal of Orthopsychiatry* 43 (1971) 442–49.

Shuey, A. *The Testing of Negro Intelligence.* New York: Social Science Press, 1966.

Strickland, S. Can slum children learn? *American Education* (July 1971).

## SUGGESTIONS FOR FURTHER READING

Caldwell, B. M. A decade of early intervention programs: What we have learned. *American Journal of Orthopsychiatry,* 1974, *44,* 491–496. A pioneer in compensatory education for economically disadvantaged children summarizes what has been learned from a decade of experimentation.

Coyle, F. A., & Eisenman, R. Santa Claus drawings by Negro and white children. *Journal of Social Psychology,* 1970, *80,* 201–205. White and black children, aged 4 to 8, each colored a Santa Claus face with crayons. Both races tended to portray Santa as Caucasian; however, the particular colors used were different.

Fort, J. G., Watts, J. C., & Lesser, G. S. Cultural background on learning in young children. *Phi Delta Kappan,* 1969, *50*(7), 386–388. Studies of children from Jewish, black, Chinese, and Puerto Rican cultures suggest how particular early family experiences affect the child's subsequent learning ability. Each ethnic group apparently transmits its own combination of intellectual strengths and weaknesses.

Herzog, E. An essay review . . . Psychosocial deprivation: What we do, don't, and should know about it. *Children,* 1969, *16*(6), 238–240. This review describes the results of a study by the National Institute of Health, designed to make a broad-based assessment of psychosocial deprivation, in order to identify gaps in knowledge and understanding, and to suggest implications for research policy and social-action programs. A vast amount of useful knowledge is pulled together, including a consideration of what still needs to be learned.

Herzog, E., & Lewis, H. Children in poor families: Myths and realities. *American Journal of Orthopsychiatry,* 1970, *40,* 375–387. The writers examine certain popular fallacies about disadvantaged children and their families that can obstruct effective services and interventions.

Jacob, T. Patterns of family conflict and dominance as a function of child age and social class. *Developmental Psychology,* 1974, *10,* 1–12. Patterns of family dominance and conflict are analyzed according to children's age, sex, and social class. Of special interest are results that suggest that the adolescent gains influence at the expense of the mother in middle-class families, whereas they gain at the expense of the father in lower-class families.

Lichtenwalner, J. S., & Maxwell, J. W. The relationship of birth order and socioeconomic status to the creativity of preschool children. *Child Development,* 1969, *40,* 1242–1247. Young middle-class and firstborn children outscored lower-class and later-born children when administered an object-identification originality test.

Lucco, A. A. Cognitive development after age five: A future factor in the failure of early intervention in the urban child. *American Journal of Orthopsychiatry,* 1972, *42,* 847–856. The cognitive development of the disadvantaged child is treated in terms of Piagetian theory, current educational practices, and suggested improvements.

Messer, S. B., & Lewis, M. Social class and sex difference in the attachment behavior of the year-old infant. *Merrill-Palmer Quarterly,* 1972, *18,* 295–306. This study was designed to determine differences among 13-month-old infants in free play situations, according to social class and sex. The behaviors observed included style of play, toy preference, vocalizing, movement about the room, and infant-mother touching.

Meyers, E. O. Doing your own think: Transmission of cognitive skills to inner city children. *American Journal of Orthopsychiatry*, 1974, *44*, 596–603. "Think" workshops, designed to help Harlem parents experience fun in thinking with their children, produced significant gains in the cognitive skills of both generations.

Schroeder, R. S., & Flapan, D. Aggressive and friendly behaviors of young children from two social classes. *Child Psychiatry and Human Development*, 1971, *2*, 32–41. Descriptions of children's nursery-school behaviors are used to determine social-class differences in overly aggressive and friendly acts. Social-class differences are suggested to explain these findings.

Seltzer, R. J. The disadvantaged child and cognitive development in the early years. *Merrill-Palmer Quarterly*, 1973, *19*, 241–252. The origin of the cultural-deprivation syndrome, as it relates to cognitive development, is treated in terms of what both the mothers and the infant bring to the situation.

Soares, A. T., & Soares, L. M. Self-perception of culturally disadvantaged children. *American Educational Research Journal*, 1969, *6*, 31–46. Disadvantaged as compared with advantaged children in segregated urban schools, grades 4 through 8, had more positive self-perceptions. The challenge is to preserve this positive self-image while instilling a more realistic and higher level of aspiration.

Trowbridge, N. Self-concept and socioeconomic status in elementary school children. *American Educational Research Journal*, 1972, *9*, 525–537. In this study of children, ages 8 to 14, those of low socioeconomic status made higher self-concept scores than children of middle socioeconomic status, in both sexes, among blacks as well as whites, in both rural and urban areas. Sex and age differences were also found.

Tulkin, S. R., & Cohler, B. J. Childrearing attitudes and mother-child interaction in the first year of life. *Merrill-Palmer Quarterly*, 1973, *19*, 95–106. Interaction was observed between mothers and their firstborn baby girls who were approximately 10 months of age, and differences in their behaviors were studied according to social class. Comment is also made concerning improvements that should be made in this type of research.

Zigler, E. Social class and the socialization process. *Review of Educational Research*, 1970, *40*, 87–110. The author reviews available research in order to define social-class differences in various aspects of society's processes of socialization.

# 13
## Education of the Very Young Child

Interest in early education has derived from various factors, including animal research. Animal studies have confirmed the belief that early experience is crucial. For example, rats raised in cages filled with "toys" and provided experiences in running mazes developed thicker, heavier cortexes than did deprived rats (Bennett, Diamond, Krech, & Rosenzweig, 1964). Apparently, reduction in early sensory stimulation impairs intellectual development.

## FACTORS THAT SUPPORT EARLY EDUCATION

Other writing and research apply directly to humans. Interest was focused on early training by a classic study in which a psychologist read selections of Greek drama to his son at regular intervals from the age of 15 months until age 3 (Burtt, 1941). At the age of 8 the boy learned the original material read to him more quickly than similar material encountered for the first time. At this age the saving in time was 27%. The experiment was repeated at age 18 with no savings at all. Although the results were thus inconclusive, significant questions were raised.

Nor should the young child be regarded as the unwilling pawn of the sadistic adult who willy-nilly imposes on him some learning experience. Even the very young child shows an amazing desire to know; he handles, explores, and manipulates whatever he can reach. Is it not wise, therefore, to capitalize on this neophyte learner's potential? If so, is it not best that young children be provided the expert help that only trained professions can provide?

The rapidly growing phenomenon of the working mother has also increased interest in early education. Traditionally, mothering for the young child has been deemed essential; hence, much interest focuses on the day school's capacity to serve as substitute. While older children fare as well as children of parents who stay at home, there is little solid evidence concerning the very young child (Hoffman, 1974). Apparently, much depends on the quality of day care provided.

Any day-care program, to be successful, should meet the following criteria (Heinecke, Friedman, Prescott, Puncel, & Sale, 1973). (1) It should take into account all aspects of the child's development. (2) The experiences provided should meet each child's individual needs, within practical limitations of course. (3) Children should be encouraged to explore and make choices in order to develop coping skills. (4) The program should encourage "a variety and balanced expression of feelings—joy, anger, pride, sorrow, affection, sympathy, etc."(p. 11). (5) The child should be helped to adapt to persons and environments outside the home. (6) Services provided should complement, not displace, family functions. (7) Various types of care should be provided in order to permit options. (8) Professional services should be available to families. (9) Programs should take into account ethnic and racial differences. (10) There should be continuous communication between day-care center and family. (11) Day-care personnel should have knowledge of the child's family experience, in order to articulate the day-care program with it.

Another impetus to early childhood education has been the growing concern for disadvantaged children. It is widely accepted that a child's school performance depends on his or her having had an adequate foundation in terms of preschool experience. That is, the child entering school should bring the sort of informal experiences that constitute an adequate foundation for more formal learning. Yet lower-class parents often fail to provide their children adequate training in more elaborate forms of communication (Schoggen & Schoggen, 1971). Moreover, the often overworked parents and crowded homes fail to provide the supportive yet challenging environments that children need. Although progress in early skill development derives from "internal biological sources," it must be stimulated and shaped by the environment. In other words, even in early years, the child's environment must be consciously designed to facilitate the development of social and cognitive skills.

Other factors, too, argue for early training. The growing complexity of life and the proliferation of knowledge make it imperative that children begin their acquisition of knowledge early. They need to establish the sort of basic skills and attitudes that will make them lifelong learners, capable of continually readapting to a fast-changing world. Moreover, in times when more and more young people aspire to higher degrees, early education seems imperative, lest an individual's race be lost at the outset. Among disadvantaged children, especially, preschool learning appears essential if they are to have any place in the educational sun.

Again, the stress on interpersonal adjustment in a society where most leisure and work activities proceed in groups makes social abilities crucial, and research suggests that the bases for such competence should be laid early. At home a mother may develop dependency in her children, thus reducing the possibility that the children may find equivalent satisfaction with their peers. Besides, the mother may lack the time, skill, and facilities for providing her child with the necessary social training. By contrast, at school every child may be guaranteed experiences appropriate to his or her personality and age level by persons especially trained for the task.

Considerable research underscores the effectiveness of early education. For example, after attendance at a certain preschool program in Ogden City, Utah, disadvantaged children scored higher after they reached first grade on nine different measures of achievement than did a matched group of children who had not attended a preschool program.

Many authorities also reject the warning that early schooling somehow poisons the essence of childhood. The notion of childhood, notes Goodman (1971), "can be stiflingly sentimental and can be employed to keep children away from challenging activities so that they remain retarded and ignorant. Thus children are emotionally exploited simply to serve the fantasies of regressed adults"(p. 4).

## PROBLEMS RELATING TO EARLY CHILDHOOD EDUCATION

On the other hand, there are those who caution against uncritically embracing programs of early childhood education. They deplore the trend toward the school's reaching deeper and deeper into childhood, threatening even to pluck the infant from its cradle. Young children, argue this group, need plenty of maternal love within the sanctuary of the home, if they are to develop feelings of security in their formative years. The young child consigned to an impersonal school has little chance to establish an identity. He or she is forced into a mold and caught up in a treadmill of routine—forced to become a child without the opportunity of being a baby.

As for the social advantages presumably offered at school, perhaps children would profit still more from completely informal play with their peer groups. Perhaps the child who spends part of the day at school and the rest at home, at all times under the care of adults, will become too dependent on them. Moreover, the child must first have experienced a warm dependent relationship with the parents before he or she can feel secure enough to be accepted by peers.

Other theorists have argued that if learning experiences are introduced prematurely, learning may proceed so slowly that the child perceives no progress. Consequently, the child becomes bored and negatively oriented toward intellectual tasks. Persons with this point of view have at their tongue-tip numerous citations of research that indicate that children with nursery-school training generally show no advantage over those without it. But their opponents counter by saying that it is the quality of early education that counts.

## QUESTIONS TO BE ANSWERED

Certainly the question is a great deal more complex than the simple issue: is early formal training desirable or not? There are many related questions. If it is granted that early education is desirable, what type is most effective? One issue is whether preschools should be run along traditional free-play lines or whether they should be structured to elicit the greatest possible cognitive development at the earliest possible age. Perhaps the answer lies somewhere between. Kodman (1970) reported considerable success with a balanced program in preschool, divided between a prescriptive and a child-centered permissive curriculum. The program was pupil-centered, innovative, and permissive, but also involved particular objectives in perceptual, motor, language, and cognitive development. Children participated in activities designed to improve their self-concept, trust, self-confidence, and creativity.

Other questions abound. What type of stimulation has the greatest impact? At what ages are the results of different kinds of stimulation especially effective? And what sort of children should be involved? Perhaps early education is indicated solely for the only child who lacks social contacts, or for children whose homes are unhappy or without stimulation. It must also be decided whether a child will miss anything essential through being away from home for a good part of each day. Finally, a practical question is involved: how can a country overwhelmed by debt afford the luxury of schools for the very young? On the other hand, if such education is proved vital, the question might be rephrased: can the country afford *not* to provide it?

The state of California has decided that such education is indeed worth the cost, despite warnings from some quarters. In our first selection, Raymond Moore, Robert Moon, and Dennis Moore raise questions about the wisdom of California's plan; in the second article, Burton White defends it. Certainly, educators across the country will be watching to determine what the outcomes will be.

## REFERENCES

Bennett, E. L., Diamond, M. C., Krech, D., & Rosenzweig, M. R. Chemical and anatomical plasticity of the brain. *Science,* 1964, *146,* 610–619.

Burtt, H. E. Experimental study of early childhood memory: Final report. *Journal of Genetic Psychology,* 1941, *58,* 435–439.

Goodman, P. Introduction. In P. Adams, L. Berg, N. Berger, M. Duane, A. S. Neill, & R. Ollendorf, *Children's Rights.* New York: Praeger, 1971.

Heinicke, C. M., Friedman, D., Prescott, E., Puncel, C., & Sale, J. S. The organization of day care: Considerations relating to the mental health of child and family. *American Journal of Orthopsychiatry,* 1973, *43,* 8–22.

Hoffman, L. W. Effects of maternal employment on the child—A review of the research. *Developmental Psychology,* 1974, *10,* 204–228.

Kodman, F., Jr. Effects of preschool enrichment on intellectual performance of Appalachian children. *Exceptional Children,* 1970, *36,* 503–507.

Schoggen, M., & Schoggen, P. *Environmental forces in the home lives of three-year-old children in three population subgroups.* DARCEE Papers and Reports, Vol. 5, No. 2, John F. Kennedy Center for Research on Education and Human Development, George Peabody College, Nashville, Tennessee, 1971.

# The California Report: Early Schooling for All?

## Raymond S. Moore,
## Robert D. Moon,
## Dennis R. Moore

The United States is currently witnessing one of its most remarkable educational developments—a drive for earlier and earlier schooling for all children which appears to be either overlooking or ignoring many of the most important findings of developmental research. While such oversight is not new to American education, in this instance the evidence and implications are not only clear, but also warn of formidable costs—first, in tax moneys, and second and far more important, in possible damage to young children.

A look at the early schooling (ES) movement reveals many developments, e.g., mounting problems of child behavior, parents chafing at the "shackles" of parenthood, inadequate and unregulated care of children, and federal and state interest in early schooling. Educators are intrigued by research which points up the rapid early development of intelligence. (See Bloom's review, *Stability and Change in Human Characteristics*.[1]) But many of these well-intentioned people overlook scientific findings which point in other directions than that in which early childhood education is now generally going, e. g., studies on early *vs.* later school admission, neurophysiology, cognition, and maternal deprivation. If such findings are not carefully considered, early childhood educators may threaten the very childhood development they design to improve.

In order to develop a fair and somewhat comprehensive viewpoint, the Hewitt Re-

Reprinted from *Phi Delta Kappan*, June 1972, 615–621ff. Copyright 1972 by Phi Delta Kappan, Inc. Reprinted by permission. A more complete presentation of this report is made in *Better Late than Early* by R. S. Moore and D. R. Moore, Reader's Digest Press, New York.

search Center has involved leading educators, legislators, scholars, and researchers at local, state, and national levels from coast to coast in a review of early childhood research. A limited cross-section of the resulting analysis is presented here.

We acknowledge, of course, the need of special education for the seriously disadvantaged or handicapped. There is also a need to care for children who have handicapped parents or whose parents are compelled to work. No position is taken here against early intervention where indicated by research. The principal questions we shall treat here are: What is the best kind of intervention or care for young children? What is generally the best—and most financially feasible—environment for early childhood development (ECD)?

We will attempt 1) to analyze typical goals of early schooling proponents, 2) to examine their use of research in support of their conclusions, 3) to see what systematic research actually says about typical ES programs and proposals, and 4) to report some practical solutions growing out of research and experimentation. In order to maintain a sharp focus this will be done primarily with reference to one state—California.

The report of the California Task Force on Early Childhood Education[2] is relatively middle-of-the-road as ES proposals go. For example, it proposes to take schooling at first only down to four-year-olds, rather than to children aged three or three and one-half as planned in New York State and Houston. The task force plan may soon be presented to the California legislature. Because California has long been among the pioneers in U. S. education, it will exercise a telling influence among other states. Yet the California proposal, with some variations, appears typical of current ES rationale.

## TYPICAL EARLY SCHOOLING GOALS

The California Task Force offers a philosophy and goals that would build on a substantial body of research:

The past decade has produced a new body of educational, psychological, and medical research documenting the crucial importance of the first eight years of life. And we are convinced that these early years are critical in determining the future effectiveness of our citizens and in the long-range prevention of crime, poverty, addiction, malnutrition, neurosis, and violence.[3]

The report assumes that "even though research is still in progress and conclusions continue to evolve, enough evidence is in" to justify certain goals, namely, "to bring about the maximum development of every child" down to age 4.[4] And it is proposed that this goal will be accomplished by providing for *academic* as well as personal development and requiring "school districts to restructure and expand existing programs."[5]

## TYPICAL USE OF RESEARCH

The California goal of maximum development surely is consistent with the ideals of most Americans. The report cites many examples of ECD research and experimentation which it assumes will provide substance for its implementation plan. Yet in no case does it clearly show how this research supports its plan. In fact certain research quoted in the report actually contradicts the task force's conclusions that *schooling* under carefully selected teachers is desirable for *all* four-year-olds. For example:

1. Harold Skeels's study[6] of orphanage children is quoted as demonstrating how the young child, given a favorable environment, can make marked intellectual growth. But the report does not continue its analysis to show that Skeels's "environment" was an institution in which *retarded teenagers* provided the orphans a *warm, free, one-to-one, continuing* mother or mother-surrogate relationship. Skeels's study had little to do with academic instruction or credentialed teaching.

2. The report quotes findings of the White House Conference of 1970: "We must free ourselves from our antiquated and erroneous beliefs that school is the only environment in which creativity is enhanced and learning takes place, or that the teacher is the sole agent of such achievements."[7]

3. Another task force item cites the June, 1971, report of the Education Commission of the States, which says in part:

It is not recommended that states establish formal classroom pre-school programs for all three- and four-year-olds because there is no evidence that all children need a structured group experience if they are receiving some kind of systematic training and because there are viable, less expensive alternatives.[8]

4. The report calls for "at least one adult to every ten children"[9] in educating four-year-olds. Yet every experiment quoted in the report in which adult-child ratios were given (six out of eleven examples) the adult-to-child ratio was 1:5 *or less,* or a need for at least four to six times the number of adults required for a standard kindergarten-primary grade ratio of 1:20 to 1:30. Although the California cost proposals are still in the formative stages, Superintendent Wilson Riles is counting on a per-child annual cost of about $500 to $600. Yet one of the documents quoted in the report (*Preschool Breakthrough*[10]) notes that the prekindergarten experience of New York State sees an annual $1,800-per-child cost as necessary for "adequate day care" and "much more if the program reaches a desirable standard."

In view of such examples as this, it is difficult to understand how the task force concludes that all four-year-olds should be provided academic schooling. And the discrepancy between research and projected implementation goes much farther. Unfortunately, California's proposal is not an isolated illustration of such disparity, as Earl Schaefer, one of the nation's leading early childhood education specialists, notes:

. . . Although much of this [ECD] research data has been generated during the last decade, earlier studies of intellectual development have motivated the current volume of research. Unfortunately, interpretations of the significance of this data, although they have guided the course of research, have as yet had minimal impact on educational planning. . . .[11]

This may be one of the reasons for the findings of William Rohwer (University of California, Berkeley) and others that "the research and development phases of early childhood programs have succeeded but the implementation phases, thus far, have largely failed."[12]

While there is evidence of some desirable effects of ES programs for disadvantaged children, the assessment of failure of large-scale programs is related primarily to academic or cognitive achievement, a goal strongly stressed in the California report.[13] Referring to a number of large-scale ES programs it studied, the U. S. Commission on Civil Rights concluded that "A principal objective of each was to raise academic achievement of disadvantaged children. Judged by this standard the programs did not show evidence of much success."[14] The Westinghouse/Ohio University study found Head Start to have been "ineffective in producing any [lasting] gains in cognitive and affective development" and stressed the present "limited state of knowledge" about what would constitute effective intervention.[15]

## WHAT SYSTEMATIC RESEARCH SAYS

For the purposes of this report, key factors in three types of studies will be considered among many on which there is substantial research evidence: 1) studies comparing early and later school entrants; 2) neurophysiological research, including brain changes which affect vision, hearing, cognition, etc.; and 3) maternal deprivation studies.

These will be followed by a brief review of research on family attitudes toward children and comparisons between the home and the school as alternatives for early childhood development.

### Early and Late School Entry

Most academic schooling, it will be assumed, eventually rests upon an ability to read. In turn, Nila Smith points out, "Dozens of investigations indicate that reading maturation accompanies physical growth, mental growth, emotional and social maturity, experiential background, and language development."[16] Willard Olson found that "children of the same age and the same grade location are regularly found to differ by as much as four or five years in their maturation and their readiness to perform tasks."[17]

The question then is not only, Is the child *ready* for school? but even more important, Does he demonstrate his readiness by sufficient maturity to *sustain* learning? and, Will the early starter be *as well or better motivated and less frustrated and anxiety-ridden* than the one who starts later? A wide variety of studies provides the answers. H. M. Davis reports, for example, the matching of two groups of children as to sex, age, intelligence, and home conditions:

> The American Educational Research Association matched two groups of children as to sex, age, intelligence, and home conditions. One group began reading at the age of six, the other at the age of seven. In two years the late-beginning group had caught up with the early-beginning group. After the first two years, these two groups were joined in classes. At the end of their seventh school year the children who began a year later were one year ahead of the early beginners.[18]

Inez King[19] reports an Oak Ridge, Tennessee, study of two groups totaling 54 children who were five years and eight months to five years and 11 months old when they started school. They were compared with 50 children who started at six years and three months to six years and eight months of age. Stanford Achievement Tests at the end of grade six showed a distinct difference, strongly in favor of the older group. In this study, of the 11 children who were retained, only one had started after six years of age; 19 boys and 16 girls of the younger group appeared to be maladjusted in some way, while only three boys and three girls from the older group were considered maladjusted.

ECD studies involving retention of learning have been done at virtually all grade and socioeconomic status (SES) levels, with remarkably uniform results. B. U. Keister[20] reported that five-year-olds could often develop enough skills to get through first-grade reading, but the learning was generally not retained through the summer vacation. Other comparisons of reading achievement of early and late starters were made by Marion Carroll[21] in the third grade, Joseph Halliwell and Belle Stein[22] in the fourth and fifth grades, and Richard Hampleman[23] in the sixth. All found generally that later entrants significantly excelled those who started earlier. Similar studies with similar results have also been reported by Elizabeth Bigelow,[24] Inez King,[25] Lowell Carter,[26] Clyde Baer,[27] Donald Green and Sadie Simmons,[28] and Margaret Gott.[29] There are many more.

John Forrester[30] did a vertical study of 500 grade 1-12 children in the Montclair, New Jersey, public schools. The very bright but very young pupils at the time of school entrance did not realize their school success potential. From junior high on, 50% of them earned only C grades. However, the very bright but older group excelled generally throughout their school careers.

While many of these studies were undertaken with a combination of low and middle SES children, higher SES groups perform similarly. Paul Mawhinny[31] reports how children from Detroit's elite Grosse Pointe, Michigan, families were selected by psychologists because they were considered mature enough or of sufficient potential to be admitted to kindergarten before age five. But after 14 years an evaluation was made of all who remained in the Grosse Pointe schools. More than one-fourth of the selected group were below average or had repeated a grade.

Arnold Gesell and Frances Ilg, after extensive research and clinical analyses, found that school tasks such as reading, writing, and arithmetic "depend upon motor skills which are subject to the same laws of growth which govern creeping, walking, grasping." The resulting awkwardness and immaturity "are often sadly overlooked by teachers and parents":

When the school child was a baby the adult attitudes tended to be more reasonable. One did not say he should walk at this or that age. Feeling confident that he would walk at the most seasonable time, one was more interested to observe the stage and degree of his preliminary development. If reading readiness and walking readiness are appraised on similar grounds, more justice is done the child.[32]

## Neurophysiology and Cognition

The findings of neurophysiologists, psychologists, and medical personnel are remarkably similar in their timing of stages at which children are normally ready to think abstractly, or organize facts, and to sustain and retain learning without undue damage or strain. Many neurophysiological studies demonstrate significant changes in brain patterns which occur between ages seven and eleven. These include impressive experiments which lead one to question if children should be required to participate in regular academic instruction until they are at least eight years old. Some researchers and scholars suggest even until adolescence, e. g., Rohwer[33] and Fisher.[34]

A number of studies of the young child's brain, including Penuel Corbin's, Jean Nicholson's, G. C. Lairy's, W. E. Nelson's, and very recent studies by David Metcalf and Kent Jordan,[35] show that appreciable brain changes take place from birth into adolescence, including the shifting of control from the emotional centers to the reasoning centers. They point to ages seven to eleven or twelve as this important period during which a child eventually develops the ability to sustain high cortical thought.

A. Davis[36] records Paul Yakovlev's findings that the child's brain is not fully insulated or completely developed until after seven years, and sometimes not until age ten or later. H. G. Birch and M. Bortner[37] and M. Bortner and H. G. Birch[38] found that until these ages young children and brain-damaged adults were inaccurate in the perception of shapes and grossly inaccurate in attempts to reproduce them.

The findings of cognitive psychologist Jean Piaget coincide remarkably with those of the neurophysiologists. Willis Overton summarizes Piaget's four major steps in the development of the child:

> . . . (a) the sensory motor period—birth to two years; (b) the preoperational period—two years to seven years; (c) the period of concrete operations—seven to eleven years; and (d) the period of formal operations between eleven and fifteen years.[39]

Overton notes that the change from preoperational to concrete operational periods of childhood finds the very young child involved in direct perception relationships with a minimum of reasoning. So this child relates quantity to shape and form of objects, but if the shape or form is changed he is confused. He must also change the quantity. For instance, he cannot understand how a low, wide glass can hold as much water as a tall, narrow one. It is not until he is seven or eight or later that he becomes a fully "reasonable" creature. As he goes through this transition he begins to reason abstractly instead of limiting himself to direct relationships.[40]

Millie Almy's replication of Piaget's work demonstrated "that only 48% of the second-grade children in the middle class school, with a mean chronological age of seven years and four months, were able to conserve in all three of the [Piagetian] tasks"[41] which were designed to measure cognitive maturity in terms of abstract thinking normally required for primary grades. Almy concludes that "failure to begin to conserve [Piaget's term for ability to understand certain problems] at an early age may be associated with a failure to grasp much that goes on in the classroom and elsewhere."[42]

William Rohwer sees schooling as an intrusion on the child's freedom to learn associatively during his preoperational years. He found "little evidence to support the rationale for progressively lowering the age of required school entrance if by evidence one requires data demonstrating a positive effect of early school entrance on later school achievement." He suggested that schooling, as commonly understood, be delayed "several years."[43]

Psychiatrist J. T. Fisher supports this thesis from clinical observation and affirms a need for a primary effort in behalf of the home. Speaking for greater initial freedom for developing a strong affective base for later stability in cognition, and incidentally for nongradedness, he says:

> Psychologists have demonstrated that a normal child commencing his education in adolescence can soon reach the same point of progress he would have achieved by starting to school at five or six years of age. I have often thought that if a child could be assured a wholesome home life and proper physical development, this might be the answer to a growing problem of inadequate classroom space and a shortage of qualified teachers—and the instinctive reluctance of all of us to hand over tax dollars for anything that doesn't fire bullets.[44]

Torsten Husén,[45] in a widely circulated international study, found a strong negative correlation between early entry age and attitudes toward school. D. Elkind[46] found no support for "the claims of lastingness of pre-school instruction, [but] . . . evidence in the opposite direction . . . . The longer we delay formal instruction, up to certain limits, the greater the period of plasticity and the higher the ultimate level of achievement." He sees frustrated, anxiety-ridden, "intellectually burned" children who lose motivation for intellectual success which they deserve.

## Visual Maturity

Findings on the child's visual system are highly similar to those of his brain: The processing of visual stimuli in the brain traces the same electrical path as do the impulses involved with cognitive activity that occur between the thalamus and the cortex. Therefore, if these connections are not completed in their development, the visual signals will not be interpreted clearly, according to James Chalfant and Margaret Scheffelin. These authors add that

> The processing of visual stimuli at the higher cortical levels involves: (a) visual analysis, the separation of the whole into its component parts; (b) visual integration, the coordination

of mental processes; and (c) visual synthesis, the incorporation or combination of elements into a recognizable whole. A review of literature reveals a variety of cognitive tasks requiring the analysis, integration, and synthesis of visual information.[47]

Luella Cole[48] observed that some children are unable to fixate on objects at close range until age seven or eight or later. Stanley Krippner[49] notes how hard it is to explain to parents that it is not the child's eye that reads but his brain. Chalfant and Scheffelin[50] confirm that "the retina is an outward extension of the cerebral cortex." Thus the visual system is not ready for reading until the brain is relatively mature.

An interesting longitudinal illustration of this relative maturity is provided by Moselle Boland's report of a paper presented by a Texas ophthalmologist at the 1963 meeting of the Texas Medical Association:

> Dr. Henry L. Hilgartner said there has been a tremendous increase in nearsightedness in [Texas] school children in the past 30 years. . . . He blames use of their eyes for close school work at an early age. . . . The constant pull of the eye muscles to do close work, he said, causes the eyeball to become larger. This is the basic defect in nearsightedness. . . . Prior to 1930, he said, 7.7 children were farsighted to every one nearsighted. . . . In 1930, Texas compulsory school age was lowered from seven to six years. Today, he added, five children are nearsighted for every one farsighted. . . . "I believe the chief cause is children being required to start school at the early age of six instead of being allowed to grow for another year or two," Dr. Hilgartner commented.[51]

Ruth Strang[52] and Homer Carter and Dorothy McGinnis[53] note that when children cannot adjust to the difficulties and discomforts of tasks requiring close vision, they simply give up trying to read.

Carter and McGinnis explain how the six small muscles of each eye must coordinate precisely to focus on near objects and produce only a single mental image. At six years the "visual mechanism" is still "unstable."[54]

Luella Cole[55] and others report also that not more than 10% of five-year-olds can see any difference between "d" and "b" or "p" and "q." Not until children are eight years old can one "be perfectly certain the eyes are mature enough to avoid such confusions."

## Auditory Maturity and Other Factors

As a child matures there is a progressive increase in sound discrimination. According to Carter and McGinnis,[56] this ability to differentiate similar speech sounds is considered by many investigators to be of prime importance in successful reading. If a child is unable to hear the difference in sounds, he will be unable to reproduce the sound correctly in speaking. This would also handicap him in recognizing written words, since improper pronunciation would lead him to expect a different spelling of the word. Luella Cole[57] notes specifically: "If he has normal six-year-old ears he will still be unable to distinguish consistently between the sounds of 'g' and 'k' and 'm' and 'n,' 'p' and 'b' or any other pair of related sounds."

H. G. Birch and A. Lefford[58] did not find intersensory maturity emerging until the children are at least seven or eight years of age. Joseph Wepman[59] found that in some children the combination of auditory discrimination and memory—"ability to retain and recall speech sounds"—is not well developed until the age of nine.

## Maternal Deprivation

When a child is taken from home for early schooling or remains at home without loving care from someone he trusts, research says to expect mental and emotional problems which affect his learning, motivation, and behavior. John Bowlby presented evidence, formulated a statement of principle, and defined maternal deprivation in his 1951 report to the World Health Organization:

> . . .the infant and young child should experience a warm, intimate, and continuous rela-

tionship with his mother (or permanent mother-substitute) in which both find satisfaction and enjoyment. . . .

A state of affairs in which the child does not have this relationship is termed "maternal deprivation." This is a general term covering a number of different situations. Thus a child is deprived even though living at home if his mother (or permanent mother-substitute) is unable to give him the loving care small children need. Again, a child is deprived if for any reason he is removed from his mother's care.[60]

He reiterated this view nearly 20 years later, reporting that in the Western world much the commonest disturbances of attachment "are the results of too little mothering, or of mothering coming from a succession of different people." And these disturbances "can continue for weeks, months, or years"—or may be permanent.[61]

Many ES proponents believe that the young child needs social contact outside the home. There are a number of reasons to doubt that he does. Research is specific. Marcel Geber's work in Uganda demonstrates, much like Harold Skeels's, that such attention or deprivation reaches beyond the emotional responses of young children.[62] Using tests standardized by Arnold Gesell, Geber tested over 300 Uganda babies during their first year. The babies for the most part were from low-SES, tribal-oriented families in which mothers were child-centered, continually caressing, cuddling, and talking to their little ones. He found these infants to be superior to Western children in physiological maturation and coordination, adaptability and sociability, and language skills. It may be observed that African children often do mature earlier than Westerners. Yet Geber reports that in his sampling those babies from relatively high-SES Uganda families with less maternal contact but more involvement in formal training were much less mature in the above qualities than the babies of the low-SES mothers.

L. J. Yarrow also reports that "besides the retardation of development caused through emotional factors, maturation in adjustment is markedly slowed by deprivation of sensory,

social, and affective stimulation when a child cannot be with his mother."[63] Bowlby adds that even partial deprivation "brings in its train acute anxiety, excessive need for love, powerful feelings of revenge, and . . .guilt and depression."[64]

## The Mother's Attitude

The mother's acceptance of her role is of greatest importance in the child's development. Mary Ainsworth found

. . . significant differences . . . when the mothers were grouped in terms of satisfaction with their role, whether the homemaker or the worker role. Dissatisfied mothers, both working and nonworking, reported undesirable child-rearing practices and attitudes more frequently than mothers who were satisfied with their role.[65]

Education and reassurance of parents thus become a vital concomitant of any ECD program, whether in the home or in school, whether the mother works or not, but particularly with the mother who does not have a wholesome appreciation of her role. Thus, says Bowlby, numerous direct studies

make it plain that, when deprived of maternal care, the child's development is almost always retarded—physically, intellectually, and socially—and that symptoms of physical and mental illness may appear. . . and that some children are gravely damaged for life.[66]

Some educators believe that parents are either too ignorant or obsessed with a desire for freedom to be willing to give their children the care they need for optimum development. A number of studies demonstrate that this is not necessarily so. Louise Daugherty,[67] Robert Hess and Virginia Shipman,[68] Mildred Smith,[69] Hylan Lewis,[70] and Phyllis Levenstein[71] found that parents are concerned, regardless of socioeconomic status. When Mildred Smith took study-help materials to homes and induced parental help, 90% of the homes responded, and of these 99% of the parents asked that the program be continued.

Levenstein[72] not only found generally that if approached rightly, disadvantaged mothers "take seriously the family's responsibility to lay groundwork for school learning," but also noted that their "aspirations for their children are very similar to those of middle-income mothers." The fact that the mother saw the practical teacher as less effective than she, yet sensed her own inadequacies, suggests as the more urgent role of the state the development of home education programs for adequate parenthood.

## School vs. Home

Then should the young child be taken from home to be trained in a school? There may be cases of acute or extreme deprivation where this is necessary. Yet Bowlby insists, on the basis of many investigations, that "children thrive better in bad homes than in good institutions," and children "apparently unreasonably" are even attached to bad parents. "It must never be forgotten," Bowlby observes,

> . . . that even the bad parent who neglects her child is nonetheless providing much for him. . . . Except in the worst cases, she is giving him food and shelter, comforting him in distress, teaching him simple skills, and above all is providing him with that continuity of human care on which his sense of security rests.[73]

Burton Blatt and Frank Garfunkel found it necessary to reject the research hypothesis of their own study involving low-SES children who "were at least two years away from entering the first grade." They concluded that (a) the home is more influential than the school, (b) the school can do little without strong home support, (c) disadvantaged parents "are often anxious to cooperate," and (d) school organization and requirements are often "foreign" to these parents who in turn are blamed by the school for not readily accepting them.[74]

Special education would certainly appear to be indicated for many specific cases of disability such as speech, vision, hearing, cerebral palsy, severe mental retardation, and certain neuroses, psychoses and advanced emotional problems. Yet it is difficult to find research support for *generalized* early schooling as described in the California Task Force report. In fact it is difficult to understand, in the face of substantial evidence to the contrary, how educators can justify existing generalized schooling down to ages five and six, or compulsory education below age eight.

On the other hand, certain child-care needs must be met. These are not generalized needs, but are specific problems growing out of parents' inability to care for their young children, e.g., physical or psychological handicaps, ineptness, immaturity, or severe economic stress requiring the mother to work. Any lesser reason which simply accomodates a growing demand for parental "freedom" must, in terms of research findings, be considered parental dereliction. And while research may not yet always be definitive in placing the blame, there is considerable evidence that points toward maternal deprivation and early schooling as primary reasons for childhood maladjustment, motivational loss, poor retention, deterioration of attitudes, visual handicaps, and a wide variety of other physical and behavioral problems, including minimal brain dysfunction.

In summary, research and comparisons of school entry ages clearly point to the need 1) to delay any type of educational program that proposes or permits sustained high cortical effort, or strain on the visual or auditory systems, before the child is seven or eight, and for 2) a warm, continuous mother or mother-surrogate relationship (without a succession of different people) until the child is at least seven or eight.

Investigators (Daugherty, Hess and Shipman, Levenstein, Lewis, Smith, *et al.*) have shown that parents, when clearly shown their children's needs, overwhelmingly respond to them. Likewise, other researchers (Rohwer, Elkind, Husén, *et al.*) make clear that the earlier children go to school the more likely they are to develop negative attitudes toward school.

## SOME PRACTICAL SOLUTIONS FROM RESEARCH

So the closer the child's early environment can be kept to his home (or other home with a low adult-to-child ratio) which may provide a continuous warm and free growing place, the more likely his maximum development will be. And this home should neither propose nor permit such learning as violates the child's normal developmental crescendo.

### Parent Education

With some of these principles in mind, Susan Gray,[75] Phyllis Levenstein,[76] David Weikart,[77] Ira Gordon,[78] and others have been experimenting with home schooling. While research does *not* indicate the need for schooling as such, there is much to be learned from these researchers toward effective parent education which can lead to appropriate pre-school environments regardless of cultural background or socioeconomic status. And indeed, if as psychiatrist J. T. Fisher infers, the state desires to save money, one of the most effective ways may be to help in the development of "wholesome home life."[79]

### Home Schools

Both Susan Gray and Phyllis Levenstein experimented with home schools. Levenstein describes her successful experience with such a program which she calls the "Mother-Child Home Program."[80] Because of the resistance of some mothers, particularly of low-SES families, to *teacher* visitation, she calls the professional visiting personnel "toy demonstrators." Gray notes that "the potential [of the home] is sometimes difficult to tap but it is there."[81]

Such programs may well provide a *modus operandi* for such child care as is really necessary and avoid heavy capital and operating costs which California's present proposal is certain to bring.

There is now a sufficient research base to suggest several procedures in lieu of early schooling as commonly conceived. The state should:

1. Carefully restudy the needs of its children in the light of research. It should realize that research provides no more reason for early schooling for all four-year-olds simply because they have intelligence than it does for early sex for twelve-year-olds simply because they have generated reproductive equipment. They must await the development of balancing factors. Great damage may be avoided.

2. Embark upon a massive parent education program, assisting first those who are in greatest need, but educating all parents, by all media available, concerning the developmental needs of their children. Parents who are neither handicapped nor forced to work should be helped to better understand their privileges and responsibilities as parents, to see that "freedom" sacrificed now will bring larger benefits later.

3. Make such provisions as are necessary for all exceptional children: the severely handicapped or disabled or others requiring special education. Even here research indicates that programs should be kept as close to the home as practicable.

4. Take an interest in providing care for the relatively normal children of handicapped parents or those forced to work, by selecting homes nearby, if possible, as home-schools. Those homes and mothers (or other adults) who are qualified would be selected for their warmth, continuity, aptness for children, and dedication to their welfare. These may well be operated as enlightened care centers on a small adult-to-child ratio (normally not more than 1:4 or 1:5), and might be subsidized by the state where parents cannot meet the costs. Traveling teachers on state or local payroll could monitor these home-schools to see that they were provided adequate materials and equipment and to coordinate them with existing ADC and other social service programs.

## CONCLUSION

It would be hard to find an area of educational research more definitive than that on child development and school entry age. It is difficult to see how planners can review this evidence and conclude that four- or five-year-olds generally should be in school, much less three-year-olds.

Goals of maximum development of the child are generally sound, but research says that California's proposed way to reach them can only lead to greater trouble. In short, it appears that California's planners, and others with similar plans, have either overlooked or ignored or seriously misinterpreted responsible research. If such evidence is questioned, then further research should be undertaken before legislating in areas so delicate as the young child's mind. Meanwhile, scientific evidence comparing the validity of the home and the school as early childhood environments clearly favors the home.

It is hoped that the California legislature and the State Board of Education will ponder these facts and that other legislators and educators—federal, state, and local—will also consider carefully the dangers of veering from the guidelines which research has supplied.

## REFERENCES

1. Benjamin S. Bloom, *Stability and Change in Human Characteristics.* New York: John Wiley & Sons, 1964, p. 88.
2. "Report of the Task Force on Early Childhood Education." Sacramento, Calif.: Wilson Riles, State Superintendent of Public Instruction, and the State Board of Education, November 26, 1971, p. 29.
3. *Ibid.,* p. 1.
4. *Ibid.,* p. 1.
5. *Ibid.,* p. 10.
6. Harold M. Skeels, *Adult Status of Children with Contrasting Early Life Experiences: A Follow-Up Study.* Monograph of the Society for Research in Child Development, No. 105. Chicago: University of Chicago Press, 1966, pp. 1–68.
7. White House Conference on Children and Youth, 1970, *Report to the President.* Washington, D. C.: U. S. Government Printing Office, 1970, pp. 97–98.
8. Education Commission of the States, *Early Childhood Development, Alternatives for Program Development in the States.* Denver, Colo.: The Commission, 1971.
9. *Ibid.,* p. 3.
10. *Ibid.,* p. 40.
11. Earl S. Schaefer, "Toward a Revolution in Education: A Perspective from Child Development Research," *The National Elementary Principal,* September, 1971, p. 18.
12. William D. Rohwer, Jr., "On Attaining the Goals of Early Childhood Education." (Paper presented at OEO Conference on Research in Early Childhood Education, Washington, D. C., 1970.)
13. *Ibid.,* pp. 1–5, 17–19.
14. U. S. Commission on Civil Rights, *Racial Isolation in the Public Schools,* Vol. 1. Washington, D. C.: Government Printing Office, 1967, p. 138.
15. Westinghouse and Ohio University, "The Impact of Head Start: An Evaluation of the Effects of Head Start on Children's Cognitive and Affective Development," in *The Disadvantaged Child,* Joe L. Frost and Glenn R. Hawkes, editors. Boston: Houghton Mifflin, 1970, pp. 197–201.
16. Nila B. Smith, "Early Reading: Viewpoints," in *Early Childhood Crucial Years for Learning,* Margaret Rasmussen, editor. Washington, D. C.: Association for Childhood Education International, 1966, pp. 61–62.
17. Willard C. Olson, *NEA Journal,* October, 1947, pp. 502–03.
18. H. M. Davis, "Don't Push Your School Beginners," *Parent's Magazine,* October, 1952, pp. 140–41.
19. Inez B. King, "Effect of Age of Entrance into Grade 1 upon Achievement in Elementary School," *Elementary School Journal,* February, 1955, pp. 331–36.
20. B. U. Keister, "Reading Skills Acquired by Five-Year-Old Children," *Elementary School Journal,* April, 1941, pp. 587–96.
21. Marion Carroll, "Academic Achievement and Adjustment of Underage and Overage Third-Graders," *The Journal of Educational Research,* February, 1964, p. 290.
22. Joseph W. Halliwell and Belle W. Stein, "A Comparison of the Achievement of Early and Late Starters in Reading Related and Non-Reading Related Areas in Fourth and Fifth Grades," *Elementary English,* October, 1964, pp. 631–39, 658.
23. Richard S. Hampleman, "A Study of the Comparative Reading Achievements of Early and Late School Starters," *Elementary English,* May, 1959, pp. 331–34.
24. Elizabeth Bigelow, "School Progress of Underage Children," *Elementary School Journal,* November, 1934, pp. 186–92.
25. King, *op. cit.*

26. Lowell Burney Carter, "The Effect of Early School Entrance on the Scholastic Achievement of Elementary School Children in the Austin Public Schools," *Journal of Educational Research*, October, 1956, pp. 91–103.

27. Clyde J. Baer, "The School Progress and Adjustment of Underage and Overage Students," *Journal of Educational Psychology*, February, 1958, pp. 17–19.

28. Donald Ross Green and Sadie Vee Simmons, "Chronological Age and School Entrance," *Elementary School Journal*, October, 1962, pp. 41–47.

29. Margaret Ellen Gott, *The Effect of Age Differences at Kindergarten Entrance on Achievement and Adjustment in Elementary School.* (Doctoral dissertation, University of Colorado, 1963.)

30. John J. Forrester, "At What Age Should Children Start School?," *The School Executive*, March, 1955, pp. 80–81.

31. Paul E. Mawhinny, "We Gave Up on Early Entrance," *Michigan Education Journal*, May, 1964, p. 25.

32. Arnold Gesell and Frances L. Ilg, *The Child from Five to Ten.* New York: Harper and Brothers, 1946, pp. 388–89.

33. Rohwer, *op. cit.*, p. 37.

34. James T. Fisher and Lowell S. Hawley, *A Few Buttons Missing.* Philadelphia: J.B. Lippincott Company, 1951, pp. 13–14.

35. Penuel H. Corbin (master's thesis in pediatrics, University of Minnesota, 1951. NA Med Library, W4A, 9C791E, 1951, C1); Jean M. Nicholson *et al.*, *EEG and Clinical Neurophysiology*, Vol. 8, 1956, p. 342; G. C. Lairy *et al.*, *EEG and Clinical Neurophysiology*, Vol. 14, 1962, pp. 778–79; W. E. Nelson, *Textbook of Pediatrics.* Chicago: Saunders Co., 1967, p. 1088; David Metcalf and Kent Jordan, "EEG Ontogenesis in Normal Children," in *Drugs, Development, and Cerebral Function*, W. Lynn Smith, editor. Springfield, Ill.: Charles C. Thomas, 1972, pp. 127–28.

36. A. Davis, *Regional Development of the Brain in Early Life.* Cambridge, Mass.: Harvard University Press, 1964.

37. H. G. Birch and M. Bortner, "Perceptual and Perceptual Motor Dissociation in Brain Damaged Patients," *Journal of Nervous and Mental Diseases*, 1960, p. 49.

38. M. Bortner and H. G. Birch, "Perceptual and Perceptual Motor Dissociation in Cerebral Palsied Children," *Journal of Nervous and Mental Diseases*, 1960, pp. 103–8.

39. Willis F. Overton, "Piaget's Theory of Intellectual Development and Progressive Education," in *Yearbook of the Association for Supervision and Curriculum Development, 1972.* Washington, D. C.: The Association, pp. 95–103.

40. *Ibid.*, p. 103.

41. Millie Almy, Edward Chittenden, and Paula Miller, *Young Children's Thinking.* New York: Teachers College Press, Columbia University, 1966.

42. *Ibid.*, p. 99.

43. Rohwer, *op. cit.*, pp. 7–8.

44. Fisher, *loc. cit.*

45. Torsten Husén, *International Study of Achievement in Mathematics*, Vol. II. Uppsala: Almquist and Wiksells, 1967.

46. D. Elkind, "Piagetian and Psychometric Conceptions of Intelligence," *Harvard Educational Review*, 1969, pp. 319–37.

47. James C. Chalfant and Margaret A. Scheffelin, *Central Processing Dysfunctions in Children: A Review of Research* (Ninds Monograph 9). Washington, D. C.: U. S. Department of Health, Education, and Welfare, 1969.

48. Luella Cole, *The Improvement of Reading, with Special Reference to Remedial Instruction.* New York: Farrar and Rinehart, Inc., 1938.

49. Stanley Krippner, "On Research in Visual Training and Reading Disability," *Journal of Learning Disabilities*, February, 1971, p. 16.

50. Chalfant and Scheffelin, *op. cit.*, p. 23.

51. Moselle Boland, "Going to School Too Soon Blamed for Eye Troubles," *Houston Chronicle* (Texas), April 30, 1963.

52. Ruth Strang, *Diagnostic Teaching of Reading.* New York: McGraw Hill, 1964, pp. 164–65.

53. Homer L. J. Carter and Dorothy J. McGinnis, *Diagnosis and Treatment of the Disabled Reader.* London: MacMillan, Collier-MacMillan Ltd., 1970.

54. *Ibid.*, p. 48.

55. Cole, *op. cit.*, p. 284.

56. Carter and McGinnis, *op. cit.*, pp. 51–52.

57. Cole, *op. cit.*, p. 282.

58. H. G. Birch and A. Lefford, "Intersensory Development in Children," *Monographs of the Society for Research in Child Development*, No. 89, 1963.

59. Joseph M. Wepman, "The Modality Concept—Including a Statement of the Perceptual and Conceptual Levels of Learning," in *Perception and Reading*, Proceedings of the Twelfth Annual Convention, International Reading Association, Vol. 12, Part 4, pp. 1–6. Newark, Dela.: The Association, 1968.

60. John Bowlby, *Maternal Care and Mental Health.* Geneva: World Health Organization, 1952.

61. John Bowlby, *Attachment and Loss,* Vol. I. Attachment. New York: Basic Books, 1969.

62. Marcel Geber, "The Psycho-Motor Development of African Children in the First Year, and the Influence of Maternal Behavior," *Journal of Social Psychology,* 1958, pp. 185–95.

63. L. J. Yarrow, "Separation from Parents During Early Childhood," in *Child Development Research* I, Martin and Lois Hoffman, editors. New York: Russell Sage Foundation, 1964, p. 127.

64. Bowlby, *op. cit.,* p. 12.

65. Mary D. Ainsworth *et al.,* "The Effects of Maternal Deprivation: A Review of Findings and Controversy in the Context of Research Strategy," in *Deprivation of Maternal Care, a Reassessment of Its Effects.* New York: Schocken Books, 1966, p. 117.

66. Bowlby, *op. cit.,* p. 15.

67. Louise G. Daugherty, *NEA Journal,* December, 1963, pp. 18–20.

68. Robert D. Hess and Virginia C. Shipman, "Maternal Attitudes Toward the School and the Role of Pupil: Some Social Class Comparisons," in *Developing Programs for the Educationally Disadvantaged,* A. Harry Passow, editor. New York: Teachers College Press, Columbia University, 1968, pp. 127–28.

69. Mildred Beatty Smith, "School and Home: Focus on Achievement," in *Developing Programs for the Educationally Disadvantaged,* A. Harry Passow, editor. New York: Teachers College Press, Columbia University, 1968, pp. 106–7.

70. Hylan Lewis, "Culture, Class, Poverty, and Urban Schooling," in *Reaching the Disadvantaged Learner,* A. Harry Passow, editor. New York: Teachers College Press, Columbia University, 1970, p. 24.

71. Phyllis Levenstein, "Learning Through (and From) Mothers," *Childhood Education,* December, 1971, pp. 130–34.

72. *Ibid.,* p. 132.

73. Bowlby, *op. cit.* (fn. 60), pp. 67–68.

74. Burton Blatt and Frank Garfunkel, *The Education of Intelligence,* Washington, D. C.: The Council for Exceptional Children, 1969.

75. Susan W. Gray, "The Child's First Teacher," *Childhood Education,* December, 1971, pp. 127–29.

76. Levenstein, *op. cit.*

77. David P. Weikart, "Learning Through Parents: Lessons for Teachers," *Childhood Education,* December, 1971, pp. 135–37.

78. Ira J. Gordon, "The Beginnings of the Self: The Problem of the Nurturing Environment," *Phi Delta Kappan,* March, 1969, pp. 375–78.

79. Fisher, *op. cit.,* pp. 13–14.

80. Levenstein, *op. cit.,* p. 134.

81. *Ibid.,* p. 127.

# Preschool: Has It Worked?

## Burton L. White

What have we learned about preschool education in the past decade? In the early 1960s, the federal government became seriously concerned with the education of children less than six years of age.

Children whose earliest school performances were below average often fell further behind the longer they went to school, it was found. Indeed, this pattern was very common, especially in lower-income population areas. Project Head Start was conceived to deal with this national problem.

Since then, Head Start has attempted preventive or remedial education in thousands of settings for many children, at a cost of many hundreds of millions of dollars. A variety of educational programs have been tried with many different kinds of children, 3 to 6 years of age.

Reprinted from *Compact,* July/August 1973, 6–7. Copyright 1973 by Education Commission of the States. Reprinted by permission.

After nearly a decade of such activity, at least one central fact is clear: Given our current resources, a poorly developing 3-, 4-, or 5-year-old is not often converted to an average or above-average elementary school student. As far as academic effects are concerned, Head Start has clearly not worked for most of the target population.

I do not mean to say that Head Start has had no important benefits. Certainly, there have been substantial health benefits. Certainly, more families have a heightened awareness of educational issues in early childhood. There may even be benefits for the social development of Head Start children that we have not yet measured. But, as for the central goal of heading off educational underachievement, the results have been disappointing.

Early signs of the inadequate benefits of Head Start prompted the federal government to begin two new programs. The first, Project Follow Through, rested on the assumption that continuation of special educational assistance was needed to maintain preschool gains. Enrichment programs in the elementary years were tried. As far as I can tell, such programs have shown even fewer positive results than Head Start.

The second program rested on the assumption that Head Start began too late—that children had to be reached before they became three years old. Called the Parent-Child Center Project, it was designed to provide preventive education during the first three years of life. Unfortunately, shortly after its inception, the country experienced an economic recession and funds for government programs in education were cut back severely. As a result, we have accumulated little or no evidence to date on the effectiveness of parent-child centers.

The events of the past decade have led me to three rather momentous conclusions:

If a 3-year-old is six months or more behind in academically relevant areas, such as language and problem-solving skills, he is not likely to ever be successful in his future educational career. There are exceptions to this generalization, but the results of Head Start, Follow Through and other remedial programs clearly support this statement for large numbers of American children.

We have apparently overemphasized the role of the schools in the total education of children.

We have apparently underemphasized the role of the family as the child's first educational delivery system. We do not prepare prospective parents to help children acquire the foundation for formal education.

At least four fundamental areas can be identified as part of the foundation normally achieved in some fashion in the years before a child enters the first grade.

*1. Language development.* From about the age of 6 to 8 months on to about 36 months, most children acquire the ability to understand most of the language they will use in ordinary conversation throughout their lives. No educator denies the central role of language in a child's educational career.

*2. Social attachment, social style and basic self-perceptions.* Much recent research has described how babies form their first vital social relationship (usually to their mother), how they adopt their first social style and how they form their early impressions of themselves during the first three years of life. Much of that research also has indicated strongly the underlying importance of those social developments for a child's future educational success.

*3. The development of curiosity and intrinsic interest in learning.* Nothing alive is more curious or more interested in exploration and learning than the typical 8-month-old baby. It is difficult to destroy or even badly suppress that urge during the first months of an infant's life. Sadly, the compelling urge to learn found in nearly every baby, rich or poor, is not invulnerable beyond the first year of life. By age two or three, many babies are much less curious, much less interested in learning for its own sake. Often the causes of such educational set-backs are clearly discernible in the child-rearing practices in the home.

*4. Learning to learn skills.* Jean Piaget, the Swiss student of the origins of children's intelligence, has stimulated much recent intensive research on that topic. Suffice to say that most children look fine in this area up to the middle of the second year of life, but that many begin to fall behind at that point.

Not everyone in early education would endorse this description of developmental processes in the early years; many professionals would. I believe the evidence for the special importance of development in the first three years is very convincing. What, then, are the ramifications for public policy?

I have noted that by three years of age identifiable educational deficits have already developed in many children. This conclusion is now beyond dispute. Moreover, such deficits often do not appear until the middle of the second year of life. Each month that passes subsequently finds more future underachievers. If we are to sponsor preventive education, it has to be from the first year of life on. Since most infants receive their early education in their homes—and quite informally as a consequence of child-rearing practices of the family—we will have to provide support for the family or somehow arrange for infants to go to school.

Our research of the last eight years at the Harvard pre-school project has focused on how a minority of families from many backgrounds regularly do an outstanding job of rearing their children during the first years of life. We have become convinced that the job is best done in the home by the family.

We have also concluded that most families have the potential to do the job. We have observed first-rate development in low-income homes in situations where there are many closely spaced children, where the mother holds a part-time job and where the marriage is shaky or nonexistent. Such successes notwithstanding, most families need help and our educational system isn't providing it.

How can we let a child with a hearing problem, for example, pass through the period of primary language acquisition without remedial attention? I have not discussed the related problem of the stress of rearing infants and toddlers that debilitates mothers and handicaps marriages, but such concerns really ought to be dealt with, as well.

Recently, with funds from private foundations, we initiated a pilot program in Brookline, Mass., that illustrates possible new directions in public education. Initiated by Robert Sperber, Brookline's superintendent of schools, and directed by Donald Pierson, a partnership of physicians, psychologists and educators is now working with over 200 families with newborn babies. The program's central goal is to provide every reasonable support to each family to help it do the best job of early education it is capable of.

One major focus of the program is the comprehensive assessment of the educational status of each child, from birth until entrance to kindergarten or the first grade. The second major focus is family support. We have created a neighborhood resource center where parents can obtain a wealth of information about children and child rearing. They can privately view films and video tapes, borrow toys or books and talk to professionals in social work, pediatrics or early education. They can even leave their child in our care to get away for a few hours from the continuous responsibility and stress of child rearing.

We hope that providing professional guidance to families from birth will help prevent what we perceive to be a widespread and often needless waste of human potential during the preschool years.

Isn't it time we took a good look at why we wait to start educating children at age five or six when children start to learn at birth?

## SUGGESTIONS FOR FURTHER READING

Bronfenbrenner, U. Is early intervention effective? *Teachers College Record,* 1974, *76,* 269–303. An examination of certain of the best-known intervention programs of the past decade provides significant evidence regarding the potential effectiveness of such education.

Early childhood education for all. *Phi Delta Kappan*, 1972, *53*, 610–621. This special section on early schooling contains four articles that examine many, sometimes contrasting, views on this topic.

Fowler, W. The effect of early stimulation: The problem of focus in developmental stimulation. *Merrill-Palmer Quarterly*, 1969, *15*, 157–170. Fowler suggests optimizing early environmental control by deriving salient principles from the developmental histories of precocious children. He suggests models of long-term stimulation programs as well as details of curriculum and instruction.

Gray, S. W., & Kraus, R. A. The early training project: A seventh-year report. *Child Development*, 1970, *41*, 909–924. This article concerns an investigation designed to determine whether school experiences could be so organized as to offset progressive educational retardation of children from low-income homes. The present report describes a follow-up at the end of the fourth grade of a preschool intervention program for children from low-income families.

Kagan, J., & Whitten, P. Day care can be dangerous. *Psychology Today*, July 1970, pp. 37–39. Attendance at day-care centers is discussed in terms of children's basic needs, possible dangers that such attendance might pose for satisfying those needs, and recommendations for group care of children.

Karnes, M. B., Teska, J. A., & Hodgins, A. S. The differential effects of four programs of classroom intervention on the intellectual and language development of 4-year-old disadvantaged children. *American Journal of Orthopsychiatry*, 1970, *40*, 58–76. The differential effects of four types of preschool programs, representing a continuum from the traditional to the highly structured, are evaluated. The four forms are the traditional, the community-integrated, the Montessori, and the experimental.

Karnes, M. B., Teska, J. A., Hodgins, A. S., & Badger, E. D. Educational intervention at home by mothers of disadvantaged infants. *Child Development*, 1970, *41*, 925–935. This report concerns a 15-month program designed to enable mothers of young disadvantaged children to compensate for the developmental deficiencies often found in culturally and economically deprived families.

LaCrosse, E. R., Jr., Lee, P. C., Litman, F., Ogilvie, D. M., Stodolsky, S. S., & White, B. L. The first six years of life: A report on current research and educational practice. *Genetic Psychology Monographs*, 1970, *82* Second Half), 161–266. This monograph provides an excellent summary of current research concerning the first six years of life and its implications for education.

Meier, F. The new nursery-school program at Greeley, Colorado. *Developmental Psychology*, 1969, *1*, 178. Meier describes a nursery-school program especially designed to implement the most promising current practices in early education. This program and a parallel Responsive Environment Nursery School program are compared in terms of their effectiveness with underprivileged children.

Meierhenry, W. C., & Stepp, R. E. Media and early childhood education. *Phi Delta Kappan*, 1969, *50*, 409–411. A review of recent research indicates the growing significance of skillfully designed equipment in nursery school.

Moore, R. S. Further comments on the California report. *Phi Delta Kappan*, 1973, *54*, 560–561. Potential dangers are identified in California's program for educating young children.

Painter, G. The effect of a structured tutorial program on the cognitive and language development of culturally disadvantaged infants. *Merrill-Palmer Quarterly*, 1969, *15*, 279–294. The investigation reported here was designed to evaluate the effectiveness of various preschool programs for culturally disadvantaged children.

Senn, M. J. E. Early childhood education to what goals? *Children*, 1969, *16*, 8–13. Senn discusses various philosophical and experimental approaches to early childhood education in terms of basic values involved.

Shane, H. G. The renaissance of early childhood education. *Phi Delta Kappan*, 1969, *40*, 369; 412–413. Shane reviews factors in the renaissance of early childhood education, including current developments in this area.

Shapiro, E., & Biber, B. The education of young children: A developmental-interaction approach. *Teachers College Record*, 1972, *74*, 55–79. This paper details the premises, goals, and characteristics that distinguish a particular approach to educating young children.

Preschool: Has
It Worked?

# 14

## School-Related Issues

Society has a large stake in providing its children the most effective education possible; however, even the best informed persons disagree on what type is best. In fact, conflict over the goals and processes of education is one of the most characteristic features of any dynamic society. And perhaps it will always be, because changing times call for new solutions.

The issues involved are global and analytic, large and small, extending to every aspect of educational practice. Hence, it would be folly to attempt here even to list, without discussion, all the issues in education. Instead our aim is twofold: to identify a few of the more prominent issues in children's education and to present a sampling of views on the topic. In two other chapters, relating to early education and to career education, certain questions concerning children's schooling will be treated separately. Certainly, the school's significant role in almost every child's life compels attention to this area of his or her experience.

## ALTERNATIVE MODES OF SCHOOLING

One basic issue is this: what sort of alternatives to the traditional school are most effective? Of course, the concept of alternative schools simply suggests options in education. Among these are educational parks and learning centers that focus learning resources in one area and make them available to the whole community. Ethnic, multicultural, and bilingual schools stress ethnic and racial understanding and cultural pluralism. Dropout centers and school academies provide for needs of special groups. The term *free school* connotes unusual freedom. Ordinarily such a school is private and stresses motivation and personal development of the individual. In one sense free schools are the nonpublic-school type of open education. In one such school, the Santa Barbara (California) Community School, there is a "core curriculum of literature, science, and social studies [but] the classes follow the interests and preferences of the students" (Stretch, 1970, p. 77).

In the best-known alternatives, open schools and open classrooms, learning activities are organized around individual motivation and interest centers. Schools without walls involve learning activities throughout the community, with much community interaction. Ideally, the teacher in the open classroom is perceived as a facilitator rather than director of learning. When the child is ready to be challenged, the teacher, who is presumably ever alert to teachable moments, helps make them meaningful (Moss, 1972). The open-classroom model of the British Infant School permits children to be themselves and to develop in such manner as may be compatible with them. It stresses individual discovery, creative activities, and first-hand experiences. Its philosophy is that knowledge cannot be neatly compartmentalized and that play and work are complementary (Moss, 1972).

**School-Related Issues**

**253**

The open-education classroom, effectively operated, can produce other desirable outcomes as well. Children may assume responsibility for their own actions. They learn self-discipline and how to become involved on a long-term basis in tasks of their own choosing. They develop autonomy, self-confidence, and respect for others. They accept, and are in touch with, their own inner selves; and they are not afraid of feeling and fantasy.

While various alternative schools have their distinctive markings, in general they share certain characteristics in varying degrees. They afford real alternatives to the traditional school program. They are innovative and act as clearing houses for new ideas, anticipating the future. They maintain flexible programs that can be modified as need and experience suggest. They are responsive to, and vary according to, the special needs of their clientele, including the children, their parents, and the entire community, all of whom work closely with the teacher. Their openness relates not necessarily to the physical environment, but to a certain approach to learning. This approach means embracing all resources in a particular area and remaining open to new ideas. They have broad objectives including mastery of basic skills, enhancement of personality characteristics, and preparation of children for their role in society. They also make available a wide range of subject matter, learning environments, and means of work (Robinson, 1973). Their flexibility permits accommodation to many personality types, modes of work, cognitive styles, and talents. No single type of alternative school is deemed best for all kinds of students. Therefore, the stress in particular schools may be on selected emphases or combinations thereof. Students themselves, meantime, can choose that type of school most compatible with their own tastes and needs (Barr, 1973).

Such schools, when efficiently run, have certain desirable by-products. They provide ideas for more traditional schools, which may then decide to make needed modifications. Children in alternative schools typically enjoy learning because it relates to their personal goals and because their learning environments are appealing, stimulating, and varied. They develop certain desirable characteristics, including autonomy, responsibility, and self-respect. They are given opportunities for proving their responsibility; and in the process they learn to respect themselves. Students who have trouble adapting to traditional schools may find that certain special schools meet their particular needs.

Nevertheless, alternative-school programs may involve certain hazards. Certain children may need more structure or focus on basic skills than most such schools provide. Other children's dispositions and cognitive styles may be better adapted to traditional schools. For example, some children may find the constant stimulation and social interaction in alternative schools distasteful or overwhelming. Or activities may be so loosely organized that concepts and generalizations are neglected. Moreover, the organization of such activities may disregard the hierarchical development of certain concepts—for example, in mathematics and science. That is, the sequence of concepts required for learning particular subject-matter disciplines may be neglected to the point that important gaps develop. Often, too, the planning required for making such programs truly effective, plus the in-service training that teachers need to conduct them properly, may be grossly inadequate.

## MISCELLANEOUS ISSUES

Other questions concern the child's curriculum—for example, how relevant it should be to "real life." Should the focus be on abstract principles, culture, and aesthetics or on more "practical" matters? If the real-life curriculum be chosen, should content be geared to children as children or to children as future adults? Some authorities say that the best preparation for adulthood is experiencing childhood fully, with all the play, fantasy, and exploration that it entails. Others believe that children can appreciate quite mature, true-to-life problems if they are adapted to their level of experience.

Controversy also surrounds the question of process versus content. Should the greater emphasis be on learning facts, laws, theories, and generalizations, or on the processes or operations by which knowledge is acquired? The process curriculum is chiefly concerned with identifying basic processes of learning and selecting subject matter that involves those processes. The process advocates argue that knowledge is becoming so vast, and is changing so rapidly, as to make it impractical to make the acquisition of knowledge the school's primary goal. Instead, children should focus on how to retrieve knowledge and how to deal with it, in whatever form it may be encountered.

Nevertheless, a minority of educators defend the worth of content for its own sake. From this point of view, outcomes are identified first and processes are chosen to help students attain them. The means are judged simply in terms of what they achieve. Process itself is meaningless without ideas and content to support it. Of course, the real issue relates to degree of emphasis. Any educator knows that process and content cannot be treated in a strictly either-or fashion.

Other questions concern the selection of content for textbooks. Should children's readers reflect a serene world peopled by do-gooders and plain Janes? Or should they reflect the world as it is, with all its deviant as well as good-citizen types? Should the language used be cleaned up, or should it represent all the varied, sometimes colorful—even obscene—terms encountered in all walks of society?

Another question, which has subsided somewhat of late, concerns programmed instruction, through the use of computers or programmed textbooks. Such instruction involves a series of problems to be answered. The pupil proceeds through problems organized in sequence, each built on the preceding ones; after each answer, the pupil learns whether it was right or wrong. Advocates of programmed instruction claim that it individualizes and facilitates learning, without sacrifice of human values. Its opponents, however, claim that programmed learning fosters boredom and passivity.

Other issues in children's education are as broad and complex as the educational process itself. What forms of evaluation should be used? What are the most effective modes of discipline? Should teachers' effectiveness be measured in terms of proven achievement of previously selected outcomes? How can children be helped to prepare for an unpredictable future?

In the first reading, Philip DeTurk and Robert Mackin describe, with enthusiasm, certain features of alternative schools. In the second article, Mortimer Smith examines a wide variety of alternatives being tried or suggested for education today. Although he discovers some good in certain innovations, he believes that, for the most part, their virtues have been vastly overrated.

## REFERENCES

Barr, R. D. Whatever happened to the free school movement? *Phi Delta Kappan,* 1973, *54,* 454–457.

Moss, J. F. Growth in reading in an integrated day classroom. *The Elementary School Journal,* 1972, *72,* 308.

Robinson, T. E. Full turn of the wheel. *Phi Delta Kappan,* 1973, *54,* back cover.

Stretch, B. B. The rise of the "free school." *Saturday Review,* June 20, 1970, pp. 76–79.

# Lions in the Park: An Alternative Meaning and Setting for Learning

## Philip DeTurk
## Robert Mackin

Much of the energy of the alternative schools movement is devoted to finding financial backing, convincing school boards, soliciting community support, gaining sufficient "autonomy" for experimentation, and offering enjoyable and varied experiences for students. But the question, How much learning is going on? is often lost in the shuffle. Survival and maintenance concerns sometimes overshadow its purpose for being. In fact, that purpose—learning—can become damnably bothersome. To be sure, the purpose is addressed rhetorically:

> We want young people to learn more than grammar and geometry. We want them to learn in affective as well as cognitive areas. We want them to learn responsibility, self-direction, and self-esteem. We want them to learn how to relate to others and how to enjoy learning. We want them to learn how to learn. . . .

Beautiful words are written, but what do they mean and how are they realized? How do you reassure a skeptical board, a troubled parent, a frustrated teacher, a bored student, or even yourself that learning is actually taking place in the alternative school?

One question to ask is whether learning is taking place in the regular school. What makes schooling generally acceptable is the pretense that this is the case. To many parents (and kids and teachers and school board members), homework, teacher certification, and subject matter, bolstered by an evaluation system of testing and grading, give a powerful legitimacy and provide a security that "learning" prevails. The institutionalization of schooling, with its polished and understandable norms, "guarantees" that a service is being provided. Most importantly, from our standpoint, these same standards are also the grounds upon which alternative schools are usually and unfortunately judged.

In light of these accepted learning standards, how do we interpret the following situation? David is a 14-year-old student at the Alternative School in Marion, Massachusetts. Since the age of 8, when he stole a boat from the Marion harbor and sailed out to Buzzard's Bay overnight, he has been in continual hot water with the police and school officials alike. Clearly, his only reason for attending school—even an alternative school—was that he was required to do so. Within the school he stood apart from everyone and everything. The staff took a simple tack; Don't make "school-like" academic expectations of David. Be patient. Concentrate upon making the environment a comfortable and welcome place by treating him honestly and with respect. A breakthrough finally came. After Christmas vacation, David stood up during the morning group meeting and asked, to the amazement of everyone, if there were other people interested in "organizing an English literature group" with him.

In retrospect, we would interject several questions for our fellow educators to consider: Did learning take place for David during those preceding three months? Did David undergo any changes in attitude or behavior? Did his trust in people increase? Did his self-concept and ability to relate to others improve? Obviously, from the data provided, the reader cannot produce meaningful answers. But the answers are not so much the issue here as are the questions. Clearly, we must recognize that there are different priorities for different students at different times. How do we begin to address these varied concerns within alternative schools?

Reprinted from *Phi Delta Kappan*, 1973, *54*(7), 458–460. Copyright 1973 by Phi Delta Kappan, Inc. Reprinted by permission.

Differences in backgrounds, self-concepts, socializing abilities, and the like require different "success contexts." It becomes essential for alternative schools to ask and re-ask themselves the fundamental question, What is learning? in order to create such contexts in as personalized ways as possible. We suggest further that the school must view the way the student values himself and his needs, the way the student relates to other people, and the way the student operates within the institution of schooling. Within each of these dimensions lie variables that will affect what a student learns at a given place or time.

## SETTING INDIVIDUAL LEARNING PRIORITIES

In the Pasadena Alternative School, David and Greg learned their math not because of expert math instructors, but because of special private trips to the park where they alone fought imaginary lions; because of their own post office where they operated a student information center; and because of hours spent at a parent farm and a parent cooking class where they planted, prepared, and ate not-so-imaginary food; and because school for the very first time was the very best place they could think of being. David and Greg, two 9-year-olds, one Jewish and one black, learned their times tables because a Mexican-American mother devoted practically every day as a volunteer to bring them together, to make them happy, and to give them a sense of importance.

Students come into the alternative school, just as they do in any school, with different social, academic, and psychological backgrounds. The alternative school genuinely attempts to accommodate to those differences. Each student must learn what the learning options are, which ones he is interested in, and how deeply he wants to learn within each option he chooses. Comments which some Pasadena students made in the spring of 1972 about their Alternative School experience reveals this range of needs and interests:

I've been independent, have been able to do what I wanted to do—like reading books, ob-

serving nature—that I never paid attention to before.

When I read, I read what I want to read about, like my pigeons, instead of reading out of an old regular school book with boring stories.

I didn't want to take French or typing, and now I feel I really like them.

Never had any intentions to take photography and things like that before. They really turned me on.

As was the case with David and Greg, academic content is sometimes secondary to an environment which stresses and builds interpersonal relationships and self-confidence. The learner must learn how to be comfortable in order that he may be receptive to learning of any kind. He must learn how to learn.

To establish a school environment which allows students and staff to set differing learning priorities we need to develop programs with several dimensions.
—accepting each individual as an individual and as a contributing group member,
—making school acceptable and comfortable,
—defining new responsibilities for teachers,
—developing new responsibilities for students, and
—recognizing additional sources of learning.

## ACCEPTING EACH PERSON AS A HUMAN BEING

In Marion, Massachusetts, in 1972, camping trips enhanced the "community" approach to learning. These trips took place during school, after school, on weekends or vacations. On one trip to Vermont, 15 high school students and two staff members confronted each other well into the night, dealing with a wide range of personal problems. "Fantastic" was the word they used to describe the experience, an experience which allowed many of them to learn things about themselves—through the feedback of others—that they had never known.

At this same school (Bent Twig was the name they chose), daily soccer games with 20 or more on a side included kids with the widest range of ability. Since the ages ranged from four to 16, however, everyone had a place. The superintendent of schools, when he realized the kinds of kids who were excited about athletics for the first time, called the "physical education program" at Bent Twig the "best in the state."

## MAKING SCHOOL AN ACCEPTABLE RESOURCE FOR LEARNING

One of the more subtle goals of the alternative school is to rebuild for the students a trust in the school as a place to learn and a belief that learning is a respectable and meaningful activity.

In a June survey at Pasadena, parents agreed that fostering a "joy of learning" was the greatest achievement of the Alternative School. Students called it a "freedom to learn." One student cited her greatest achievement as "loosening up to do work, overcoming my own resistance to work, getting interested in things and wanting to learn them."

This freedom to learn results from a redefinition of teaching. In the alternative school, the teacher transcends the traditional intellectual relationship with students. One youngster remarked, "I learned to make friends with teachers, to know them as persons in their own life." Another added, "Since the school is not forcing knowledge on students, they really want to learn."

## THE TEACHER HAS NEW RESPONSIBILITIES

An undergraduate intern in Pasadena wrote, "The students received a fresh idea of what a teacher should be and most importantly could be." The teachers in the alternative school do consider a student's academic progress, but they also consider his interests and relationships with specific staff members and other students, home situation, and, of course, needs. The staff tries to provide an appropriate environment conducive to learning for the particular child. Teachers try to localize the problems so that they are not prescribing aspirin for a broken arm or math drill for a broken heart. In the case of Greg and David, the prescription called for lions in the park.

## THE LEARNER ALSO HAS RESPONSIBILITIES

A student might spend 50% of his time on his own writing a book, or artistically-inclined students might spend a day and a half each week in the art museum completely unsupervised. There were student-initiated learning experiences in the Pasadena Alternative School last year. One Pasadena student said: "I have learned to get along with all ages, and I have learned from little kids as much as I have learned from teachers." Another remarked: "I learned about cutting diameters in wood by teaching Blake, who cut it wrong." A third student commented: "I learned to do for myself, because if I don't do for myself, nothing will get done."

Students, with the help of adults and other students, begin to learn that learning is something which they must control, not something which is done to them. Freedom to learn requires individual responsibility. At a residential alternative school for 14- to 20-year-olds in Jefferson, New Hampshire, one option allowed students to tutor younger children in the town. Tutors were paid for this work, but half of their pay was kept in a school savings account. If students broke their own community rules—in this case taking a car, having sexual relations, or using drugs or alcohol—they lost their savings.

## THE TEACHER DOES NOT DO ALL THE TEACHING

In our alternative schools, students and adults become part of a learning community. Teaching and learning become a single act by a single person, or by a group! At the Alternative

School in Jefferson, no one on the staff could teach foreign languages. Two students, one Puerto Rican and one French-Canadian, took over the task. The format was simple—students wishing to take French or Spanish sat at the French table or at the Spanish table for all meals and during that time were not allowed to speak English.

At the same school, each student taking English through using media learned different skills of film making—camera operation, lighting, developing—and was then required to teach "his" skill to the others in the class.

The entire institution of schooling has been built around the role of the teacher as attorney, judge, and jury of learning. The presumption follows, therefore, that learning has a causal relationship to teaching. In the alternative school, however, learning can go on without teaching and teaching can go on without teachers!

In the alternative schools we have worked with, everyone becomes "teacher"—the teacher's wife who comes in twice a week for jewelry class, the white mother who devotes her mornings to one black high school boy, the black high school boy who devotes his mornings to one white mother, the grandmother who comes in to teach geology, the sheriff who holds a mock trial, the mother who teaches sewing at home, the mother who teaches yoga in school, the intern who helps individual students with their math, the three university students who give science demonstrations, the secretary who teaches typing, the alternative school student who teaches what she has learned in the art museum about ceramics to other alternative school students, and the learning community who teach each other the meaning of respect and privacy and sharing and need.

## LEARNING BECOMES A STUDENT RATHER THAN A TEACHER AGENDA

Bringing the student as well as the teacher into the evaluating role, and stretching the context of learning beyond the school walls, introduces some dramatic pedagogical questions:

—Why do we identify certain things as "subjects"?

—Why do we have requirements?

—Why are some subjects more important or "major"?

—What is curricular and what is extracurricular?

—How do we define "teacher"?

—What is a school?

—What is learning?

A junior high girl in Pasadena wrote that in public schools almost everything is done for the student:

> There the teacher tells him what to do and he does it regardless of its value to learning. In this school, the kid will be the judge about what books and materials will be useful to his learning, with some exceptions. . . . Self-motivation comes from within and the atmosphere and classes will try to be ones that will bring it out and develop it.

Not all student analyses of their learning are comforting or complimentary to the alternative school. One high school student in the Pasadena Alternative School made the following comment half-way into the first semester: "My achievements? I've met 45 new people and learned a few things about others: Is that going to help me for college?"

But at the same time a friend wrote:

> I've learned more in these two months than in two years of my other school, and that is the sincere truth. I've learned algebra, poetry, politics, and in an interesting way. I've learned about leather, clay, jewelry, photography, witchcraft, Black Panthers, typing, and little kids.
>
> Most of all I've learned about people and myself and a little bit about how our minds work. I've learned that I learn when I'm given freedom—more than when I'm imprisoned in school. I like the Alternative School, and I'm for the way we are trying to revolutionize the old system of learning, which I hate.

"College" or "revolution," learning to these students is obviously in the eye of the beholder. And the breadth and depth of learning (or lack thereof) are important dimensions which are often unaccounted for in traditional evaluations of student progress.

In summary, the alternative school itself is learning some things about learning. There are many questions which are unanswered, and there are also a host of new questions to ask. The authors suggest that educators who look at the evaluation of learning in schools keep the questions as well as the answers (grades or whatever) in mind. Are we asking these questions?

—Are students learning to learn?

—Are they preparing for future learning competence by building self-confidence, gaining an appreciation of group structures, using the school and other resources in a productive way?

—Is a student learning to overcome his special set of obstacles to effective learning?

—Is a student learning what there is to learn and which of those options he wants to take advantage of?

Learning in these terms requires a very broad alternative context, a context that allows each student to develop his potential. Does learning take place in the alternative school? The answer depends on the individual under consideration, what is meant by learning, and who is making judgment. If the alternative school has done nothing else, it has at least made us sensitive to the depth and scope of this essential educational concern.

# Educational Innovations: Treasure and Dross

## Mortimer Smith

Those who complain of the slow pace of change in social institutions ought to be encouraged by what is happening these days in American elementary and secondary schools. The natural tendency of schools has always been toward ossification, but in recent years the school system has been unable to resist the general push within the society to topple entrenched traditions, and has inaugurated ambitious instructional and organizational changes. These are taking place under the general heading of "innovation," a word that manages to suggest something more novel, glamorous and dramatic than simple "change."

The willingness to experiment and to abandon old methods and programs is in evidence in all parts of the country. In a high school in Montgomery County, Maryland, there are no bells, failure is never entered on a student's transcript, and there is a flourishing "hall culture," which means that on any given day you can find students sprawled on the floor in the halls, playing guitars or reading or gossiping. A middle school in Florida consists of a large open floor space with no partitions dividing teaching areas, library and chemistry lab, the whole looking a little like Grand Central Station with wall-to-wall carpeting. In Fairfax County, Virginia, a high school student serves as a voting member of the school board and receives a salary of $3,000 a year. In Berkeley, California, there is an "alternative" high school where everyone is encouraged to do his

Reprinted from "Educational Innovations: Treasure and Dross," by Mortimer Smith, *The American Scholar*, Volume 43, Number 1, Winter, 1973–74. Copyright © 1973 by the United Chapters of Phi Beta Kappa. Reprinted by permission of the publishers.

own thing and where the principal is quoted as saying: "We just don't consider anything that we can't enforce as an infraction." (A student put it another way: "Everything we want, we get.") In scores of school districts in North Dakota, as well as in many individual schools throughout the country, the curriculum is based on the "open classroom" concept, an innovation not easily defined but one that calls for informality and "creativity," freedom of movement for the child, a soft-pedaling of the pressure for academic success, and a somewhat excessive amount of tie-dyeing, lying on the floor, field trips, and the collecting of gerbils and turtles. In some schools reading is taught with the aid of the initial teaching alphabet, a phonetic alphabet that adds twenty new symbols to the conventional alphabet, and results in compositions ("Wee can reed and wee can riet on a pees of paeper") that remind one vaguely of the prose style of Josh Billings and Artemus Ward. In other schools children are trying to learn to read by a system that presents words and sounds in color—forty-seven different colors; the *t* sound becomes "the magenta sound," the *s* sound, "the pearly green sound." Some school systems use computers in teaching the basic skills; some remain open all year; others have abandoned report cards or have done away with grades or have established "storefront" schools. Voucher plans are in effect in a few places, giving parents the right to choose among a number of public schools. Some schools have entered into "performance contracting" with private firms to teach the basic skills, usually with financial penalties exacted against the company if the students show poor achievement.

These are but a few of the educational innovations that have been tried in the last few years. Another that is advocated probably should be described as a terminal operation rather than an innovation—the idea of "deschooling" advanced by Ivan Illich and by the late Paul Goodman and others. The advocates of deschooling believe that compulsory education laws, degrees, diplomas and formal courses are evils and that young people can learn all they need to learn by roaming the community, free from the restraints and com-

promises inevitable in the social institution of the school. The theory behind deschooling is that the only cure for a headache is decapitation.

Why such a clamor for innovation? Why such a demand for any new method or program so long as it is radically different from the old? Perhaps the demand for change can be put in perspective by considering some recent educational history. After World War II, dissatisfaction with public education accelerated rapidly and by the late 1950s, spurred in part by Sputnik, the critics had drawn up a fairly precise bill of complaints. They charged poor teacher preparation; low achievement among pupils in the basic skills, especially in reading; inadequate standards for the academic subjects; a proliferation of nonessential or trivial courses; and the domination of public education by a rigid and often anti-intellectual establishment consisting of the schools of education, state department of education, the United States Office of Education, and national teacher associations. There were, of course, honorable exceptions to the prevailing view in all these institutions, but after World War II "one of the striking features of American thought," in the words of the late Richard Hofstadter (in his *Anti-Intellectualism in American Life*), "was the appearance within professional education of an influential anti-intellectualist movement." Hofstadter's contention was that the dominant group in professional education believed that practical training in being family members, consumers and citizens was the primary aim of education, not intellectual development and cumulative knowledge.

By the early 1960s, when the problems of educating the "disadvantaged" in so-called ghetto schools came to the fore, the critics added some new items to their original bill of complaint, asserting that many city schools were dreary places staffed by administrators and teachers who were indifferent to, or contemptuous of, their students, and that city school systems were more often than not inflexible and stultifying bureaucracies.

These criticisms were made from a particular philosophical point of view about the purposes of schools; that is, the critics believed that while schools might have subsidiary purposes, the primary purposes are to teach the essential skills and transmit the heritage of civilized man and in the process to train the intelligence and to stimulate the pleasures of thought. The critics naturally wanted change, change that would strengthen the curriculum, improve the quality of teaching and eliminate some of the academic trivia.

As one of the veterans of the educational controversies that arose in the years after World War II, I cannot remember that any of us ever used the word "innovation" when we discussed plans for reforming the schools. Even so late as ten years ago that word had not yet appeared in the *Education Index*. In the most recent volume of this index the entries under "innovation" are measured in columns. With the change in terminology came a shift in philosophical bias. While some of the more mechanical current innovations are philosophically neutral, others stem from points of view about education that are at odds with the older tradition that the school ought to be a place where intellect, if not counted supreme, is at least respected. The movement for innovation has introduced a new form of anti-intellectualism to American schools, based not on adjustment to the social environment, which is the form the older anti-intellectualism took, but on asserting the supremacy of feeling over intellect.

Those who want rational changes in the schools and who are working for realizable reforms find some of the current innovations useful and demonstrably effective. Others are bizarre, if not nonsensical, and seem to take little note of the realities of the school situation. In sorting out the vast number of innovations I discern four categories of persons who now advocate change for American schools. The first group are the utopian society-changers who believe schools are the rotten instrument of a rotten society and should be destroyed and rebuilt. (Some of them—Illich, for example—are stronger on the demolition than the reconstruction.) The second group are the neo-progressives who want schools to be places of freedom, joy and ecstasy. They are probably influenced more by the late A. S. Neill and his

Summerhill School than by the Lincoln School-Progressive Education Association tradition of American progressivism. The third group are the technicians who think that our shortcomings can be corrected by the large-scale introduction of machinery and other packaged aids in the instructional program, aids they hope to make teacher-proof. And finally, there are those, among whom I number myself, who might be called the renovators. I am not particularly attached to the term—it sounds like patching up and disguising rather than changing things fundamentally—but in lieu of a better word I use it to refer to those who believe that the basic structure and many of the aspects of school organization are sound but who think that we must repair the damage that has resulted from faulty aims and methods and inadequate teachers.

The utopian society-changers are represented by such men as Ivan Illich, Edgar Z. Friedenberg, the late Paul Goodman, and to a certain degree, John Holt. The latter, in his early and immensely popular books, proved to be an old-fashioned progressive searching for better ways to motivate and teach young children, but more recently he seems to have lost faith in the usefulness of direct teaching. Increasingly his position seems to be that tests, teachers and subject matter are so corrupting that schools are not salvageable. His position is similar to that of another popular teacher-writer, James Herndon, who states in *How to Survive in Your Native Land* that the school "is *absolutely irrelevant* to the lives of children, who don't need school at all." Goodman and Friedenberg's opposition to schools seems to be grounded in philosophical anarchism, in a distaste for all institutional and group activity. Friedenberg is particularly incensed that young Americans in school and college are serfs, prisoners in a cruel adult world, who are "powerless and without resources." This remark was made at the end of the sixties, a decade when several college presidents were harried from office and many educational institutions were intimidated and even shut down by these "powerless" student-serfs. Paul Goodman was convinced that schools are a waste of time and often contended that the child up to the age of twelve needs no formal subjects and that the present eight-year curriculum of the elementary school could be telescoped into four months. (That's right, *months.*)

I do not know that all of the critics mentioned agree completely with Illich's demands for dismantling the school system. They are all certainly in agreement with him that, as presently constituted, schools are the natural enemies of youthful spontaneity and youthful eagerness to learn and that the educational process ought to be revitalized and revolutionized as part of the larger scheme to rebuild the present unsatisfactory society. I vacillate in my judgment of the practical influence of these men. Sometimes they appear to be simply a little coterie of eccentrics who write laudatory reviews of one another's books in the *New York Review of Books.* They do seem, however, to have an influence among new and idealistic young teachers who are nervous about exerting authority in the classroom; and a rather masochistic educational establishment continues to give them a forum at innumerable conferences. But surely it is unrealistic to believe that any considerable number of educators and parents could be brought to accept the radical proposals of the society-changers.

I suppose there is a certain amount of overlapping between the second group of innovators, the neo-progressives, and the society-changers. The former, like the latter, are profoundly unhappy with American schools, but they are not so pessimistic about the possibilities for reform, believing that schools can be rejuvenated if only we will stop using academic attainment as the chief measure of effectiveness. The neo-progressive movement, especially as reflected in the open classroom concept, has been strongly influenced by Charles E. Silberman's *Crisis in the Classroom,* one of the most popular educational books of recent years. Although Silberman has more respect for intellectual matters and academic accomplishment than most of the other neo-progressives, his book is primarily a sober and lengthy sermon exposing American schools as grim, joyless and coercive places, and recommending various informal pedagogical practices that suggest he might have been communing with the ghosts of William Heard Kilpatrick and Teachers College Columbia circa 1920.

The neo-progressives are inclined to think that a teacher who asserts authority, organizes his subject and gives tests is an enemy of the children. In a large number of innovations, including many (certainly not all) of the programs that come under the general heading of the open classroom, the "cognitive" has given way to the "affective," which often means that feeling takes place over thought, emotion over intellect, spontaneous action over reflection. The purpose of schools—so runs the argument—is not to exercise Johnny's mind; it is to make him feel good, to enhance his self-image. It does not seem to occur to some of these advocates of "affective" education that Johnny's image of himself is powerfully enhanced when he discovers that he can read and write and do his sums.

The older progressive movement in education had its extremists, but the best advocates of the child-centered school never thought that the child at the center meant any diminution of the role of intellectual training. Nor were the older progressives inclined to accept the sentimental legend of the Beautiful Children and the Ugly Adults. Today's neo-progressives bring to mind a *New Yorker* cartoon of several years ago that showed a school principal talking to a juvenile menace and his mother. The schoolman was saying: "Mrs. Minton, there's no such thing as a bad boy. Hostile, perhaps, aggressive, recalcitrant, destructive, even sadistic. But not bad."

The sentimentalism of the neo-progressives is particularly unfortunate when applied to inner-city schools. When they dismiss academic accomplishment for students in these schools as "irrelevant" or at best peripherally important, express impatience with Negro parents who want the schools to teach their children to read, extoll such claimed lower-class values as energy, spontaneity, and direct sense gratification, and encourage the use of a supposedly valid language known as black English—when the neo-progressives impose this sort of sentimentalism on the inner-city schools, they drive one more separatist wedge between races and between classes.

My third group of innovators, the technicians, differ radically from the first two groups. Not for them the freewheeling flexibility and the preoccupation with the psyche of the learner that mark the other groups. As producers of packaged curricula, some of which are of the machine variety and some not, their programs are highly structured and designed to teach precise segments of a curriculum. Around the technicians a new industry has sprung up in recent years that produces classroom computers, data-processing systems, programmed instruction materials, and other curriculum materials, mostly designed to be teacher-proof.

The "hardware boys" who sell this equipment are not the only ones who are sanguine about the future of technology in the schools. John W. Gardner, not one given to intemperate statement, expressed the view, when he was secretary of Health, Education and Welfare, that "the judicious use of videotape, programmed instruction, computer-assisted instruction and other new approaches holds promise of a truly immense gain in the availability of the highest quality of instruction. I'll say something even stronger. It is, in my opinion, the *only* hope for a radical upgrading of educational quality on a massive scale."

In my view, computer-assisted instruction (C.A.I.) is most useful as elementary drill at the rote level of what-does-five-plus-three-equal or with any subject matter that calls for exact responses. Reading instruction by the look-and-say, Dick-and-Jane method is no better when transferred from the basal reader to the machine. The qualities of imagination and interpretation and speculation cannot be built into the machine. And often equipment that is advertised as being designed with the individual student in mind is run with the protection of the machines in mind. Anthony G. Oettinger in his excellent book on the myths of educational innovation (*Run, Computer, Run*) says that in one language laboratory the printed rules state, "Please do not ask unnecessary questions about [this equipment]" and "No one is an individual in the laboratory."

Whatever the virtues of technological innovations—and I for one do not dismiss all such innovations as useless— they have failed to make much of an impact on the schools. Ten years ago reading instruction was to be revolutionized by the talking typewriter. Today this miracle device, along with many other machine programs, seems to have gone the way of the Edsel. Perhaps the most ambitious project in computer-assisted instruction, Stanford University's Institute for Mathematical Studies in the Social Sciences, sends its programs by leased wire to not much more than one hundred schools, hardly an impressive figure. Seven years ago an assistant United States commissioner of education, and an enthusiast for C.A.I., predicted that by 1976 computers would be operational in twenty-five percent of our schools, surely a fantastically optimistic estimate. Accurate figures are hard to find, but in 1970 a survey by the research division of the National Education Association showed that less than one percent of teachers responding to the survey had used C.A.I. in their classes. After years of generous foundation and government support, the technological revolution in schools simply has not arrived.

In talking with educators and parents about current innovations, one senses a growing caution, sometimes even disillusionment. There are many indications of dissatisfaction. Last year the Ford Foundation issued a reflective report on its ten-year support of the Comprehensive School Improvement Plan, which plan was aimed at "legitimizing the concept of innovation in public school programs and at testing various kinds of innovation." For the most part, the innovations the plan helped to finance were changes in arrangements and materials: programmed instruction, filmstrips, modular scheduling, changed seating plans, removal of walls, et cetera. The Ford report is a frank appraisal that comes to the conclusion that many of the innovations were a disappointment and that the results did not come close to justifying the $30 million that the project cost. Harold Howe II, vice-president of Ford's division of education and research, has been quoted as saying that "we're getting a little more humble. The old idea that we could build a better model and that it would serve as a lighthouse for other school systems was naïve.''

The more extreme innovations have also come in for reexamination, often by the practitioners themselves. One of the most unstructured of the innovative schools, John Adams High in Portland, Oregon, where the teacher "tells the student neither what he is to do, what he is to learn, nor how," is taking a second look at its program. In an article in *Phi Delta Kappan,* the head of the instructional program at the school, Allen L. Dobbins, indicated that the students themselves were expressing unhappiness with their unlimited freedom. Some of them thought "they weren't learning anything, that teachers didn't make them do any work." In the new city of Reston, Virginia, an elementary school that has been operating for some time as an open-space school, has now erected six-foot-high partitions in the hope of cutting down on noise and visual distraction and to provide space for chalkboards and the students' papers—in short, the open-space school is closing up again.

Even some of the utopian, society-changers are uneasy. Neil Postman, professor of education at New York University, a self-described radical, dissident, and hater of the school establishment, has decided that he cannot accept Ivan Illich and, quoting the Declaration of Independence on the unwisdom of changing long established governments for light and transient causes, says the same passage is relevant to schools. Jonathan Kozol, who is angry with the whole American economic and social system, including the schools, nevertheless has decided to operate his own "free-school" for poor children along traditional lines. He thinks affluent young teachers who are slumming in the free schools ought to teach the basic skills to poor children instead of encouraging them to "make clay vases, weave Indian headbands, play with Polaroid cameras, climb over geodesic domes."

What, then, are the prospects for needed reforms in the schools? Certainly they are poor if we are looking for some kind of miracle pill—a new social order, a way to change the hearts of men, a foolproof machine, some ideal rearrangement of space, the cultivation of joy unconfined in the lives of teachers and schoolchildren. My own conviction is that we must fall back on the recommendations of my last category of advocates of change, the renovators. These may not have the "dramatic," "exciting" and "dynamic" characteristics that the utopians look for in schemes for change, but for the long pull they may be the most effective.

I cannot in a short article offer a precise blueprint for reform but can simply indicate some "areas," as we say in education, where reform may be realizable. But first of all, I think the renovators want to settle the matter of aims and purposes. Any proposals they make for change are grounded in the conviction that schools exist to *teach,* to provide young people—all young people, not only the mentally superior—with knowledge that will be useful both in the utilitarian, vocational sense, and in the sense of providing some inner resources by which to live. In the process of education it must be assumed that the teacher knows more than the student and must have authority over him, exercised, one hopes, not capriciously but with humanity, understanding and benevolence.

Operating from these premises about education, the renovators maintain that some needed reforms can be achieved if we are content, or at least willing, to proceed patiently and without expectation of instant miracles. Among these reforms are better teacher education, improved reading instruction, higher aspirations for disadvantaged children, and the breaking down of educational bureaucracies.

Some progress is being made with several of these reforms. Although low reading achievement, especially in the large cities, is still something of a national scandal, there is evident around the country a refreshing willingness to buck the "reading establishment" with its outmoded whole-word method of teaching reading and to experiment with some of the effective phonics-based programs now available. An increasing number of teachers and principals are ignoring the sociological folklore about the traumatizing effect of "middle-class" education on children in the ghetto and are making the teaching of the basic skills their prime responsibility. And some progress is being made, in some places, in breaking down educational bureaucracies into manageable units. Unfortunately the "community control" movement has often been used by ideologues for noneducational purposes, but decentralization and honest lay participation in the conduct of schools are now possible realities.

At the heart of all reform of the schools, of course, is the problem of how to obtain and train good teachers. We could make some dent in this problem if we would increase our efforts to encourage bright rather than mediocre high school students to enter teaching, if undergraduate work for the prospective teacher were confined to broad liberal education with the how-to-courses limited to summer sessions and internships, and if we could obtain some relief from the systems of tenure and automatic pay scales now in effect. Under the present system it is difficult to get rid of the incompetent or to pay preferential salaries to the competent.

This is not an easy time for those who see the necessity for change in the schools and are trying to work out rational principles for reforms that can operate successfully in the existing system. (Not being a utopian, I assume that the system is going to be around for a while.) It is not an easy time because on the one hand the innovators urge us either to tear down or completely remake the school system and on the other hand the reports of James Coleman and Christopher Jencks seem to tell us that what the schools do doesn't make any difference in the future lives of the students. Perhaps the first step on the road to effective change in the schools is resistance on the part of educators and parents to all absolutist positions.

## SUGGESTIONS FOR FURTHER READING

Alternative educational programs: Promise or problems? *Educational Leadership*, 1974, *32*, 83–127. This special section, embracing 11 brief articles concerning alternative schools, deals with the philosophies and practices of such schools, problems and issues relating to them, illustrative programs, and how to organize them.

Bremer, J. & Von Moschzisker, M. *The school without walls: Philadephia's parkway program.* New York: Holt, Rinehart & Winston, 1971. An experimental innovative high school without walls is described and testimonials from teachers and students are provided.

Britton, J. O., & Britton, J. H. Schools serving the total family and community. *Family Coordinator*, 1970, *19*, 308–316. The community school is discussed with regard to organization, contributions to adults and children, activities, mode of organization and operation, and overall significance.

Cass, J. Are there really any alternatives? *Phi Delta Kappan*, 1973, *54*, 452–453. Cass concludes that the forms of innovation have displaced the substance and suggests ways of avoiding these pitfalls.

Dillon, S. V., & Franks, D. D. Education for competence. *Elementary School Journal*, 1973, *74*(2), 69–77. This description of certain open education schools in Kansas City provides a view of activities in such schools, a glimpse of teachers' and children's reactions to experiences there, and commentary on philosophies involved in such education.

Elliott, A. Student tutoring benefits everyone. *Phi Delta Kappan*, 1973, *54*, 535–538. This innovation, which involves more capable or older children helping less capable or younger ones, has proved consistently successful, but has failed to be widely exploited.

*Harvard Educational Review*, 1972, *42*(3). This special issue contains five articles by well-known authorities concerning various aspects of alternative schooling. Collectively the articles describe the varieties of such schools, their aims, practices, advantages and drawbacks, ideological bases, and political problems relating to them.

Havighurst, R. J. Curriculum for the disadvantaged. *Phi Delta Kappan*, 1970, *51*, 371–373. Havighurst predicts social changes in the 1970s that can reduce the need of special curricula for disadvantaged children. He recommends changes that should be made.

Karnes, M. B., Teska, J. A., & Hodgins, A. S. The effects of four programs of classroom intervention on the intellectual and language development of 4-year-old disadvantaged children. *American Journal of Orthopsychiatry*, 1970, *40*, 58–76. The study reported here was designed to determine the differential effects of four preschool intervention programs.

Kozol, J. Free schools: A time for candor. *Saturday Review of Education,* March 4, 1972, pp. 51–54. Kozol describes errors that free schools commonly make and suggests what they must do if they are to survive.

Minuchin, P., Biber, B., Shapiro, E., & Zimiles, H. *The psychological impact of school experience.* New York: Basic Books, 1969. Fourth-grade classes of four elementary schools, classified as modern or traditional, were studied in order to determine which type of environment was more favorable for children's social and intellectual development.

Pressman, H. Schools to beat the system: Can we open the gates of the ghetto and let the children out? *Psychology Today,* October, 1969, pp. 58–63. The author discusses special problems of education in urban ghetto areas and suggests better approaches.

Rathbone, C. H. Examining the open education classroom. *School Review,* 1972, *80,* 521–549. Rathbone describes the open-education classroom in detail and evaluates both its presumed advantages and possible disadvantages. He considers four of its aspects in particular: the organization of time, the organization of instruction, the organization of groups of children, and the organization of space.

Robinson, D. W. Alternative schools: Challenge to traditional education? *Phi Delta Kappan,* 1970, *51,* 374–375. Robinson discusses alternative schools, or those that apply variant views on method and curriculum to educating children. This movement is sprinkled with "super-Summerhills" and opportunities for experimenting with innovations.

Smith, M. CBE views the alternatives. *Phi Delta Kappan,* 1973, *54,* 441–443. The Council on Basic Education concludes that the alternatives movement has fallen far short of providing for basic needs and goals of education.

Sullivan, J. Open—traditional—What is the difference? *Elementary School Journal,* 1974, *74,* 493–500. This study was designed to determine whether pupils in an open classroom differ from traditionally taught pupils in creative thinking, creative writing, and self-confidence, especially when facing new problem-solving situations.

Weber, L. *The English infant school and informal education.* Englewood Cliffs, N. J.: Prentice-Hall, 1971. This well-done account is based on observation of schools for young children in England.

# 15
## Television

For decades, research has been concerned with the effects of mass media, such as comic books and radio; however, the effect of television may be greater, simply because it involves stimulation by both sight and sound. Besides, television involves more children, and more hours, than these other media ever did. In fact, 96% of American homes have at least one television set, and the average home set is turned on for at least six hours a day (Holden, 1972). Most children—9 out of 10—become well acquainted with television before they begin to make out any printed words whatsoever. In fact, preschool children are the single heaviest televiewing audience in the United States. After they enter school they watch television a bit less, but even between ages 6 and 13 remain dedicated televiewers. In short, television provides the single greatest common experience of American children.

Several reasons explain children's addiction to television. At least someone in the family has the set turned on much of the day; and small children, confined to the house most of the time, cannot escape its influence. Later, listening habits are reinforced as they and their peers discuss programs and incorporate TV plots in their games. Furthermore, television provides absorbing entertainment with no exertion to the viewer.

Despite its importance, children's televiewing receives little guidance, either at school or home. In one study (McLeod, Atkin, & Chaffee, 1972), only a third of parents controlled the kinds of programs their children saw. Only one parent in 12 actually prevented his or her children from viewing undesirable programs (Rarick, 1973). However, some evidence suggests that restricting the child's viewing of television may do more harm than good.

## POSITIVE EFFECTS OF TELEVISION

Certainly television has its strong points, even for child viewers. It permits identification with exciting and attractive people and provides kinds of experience that the child may yearn for but lack. It has important indirect effects as well. It often modifies the child's speech, manners, and morals in desirable ways. It constitutes an adjunct to learning, especially for children from poorer homes with little chance for wide experience.

Television also overcomes the barriers of time and space. It brings the world into the child's own home. For the first time, children are able to see the world's history being made before them. They see famous figures, and hear them, first-hand, discussing significant issues. Despite many programs of dubious worth, there are also magnificent presentations of opera, drama, ballet, and musicals. Never before have children been exposed so young or so often to the very finest of the world's cultural offerings. Thus, painlessly and pleasantly, children absorb a wealth of information, so that they are more sophisticated than ever before. Such learning could be increased many times over, some persons declare, if the potential of television were more fully realized.

Television plays a particularly important part in preparing children to enter school. Special programs pave the way for school experience, and when the fledgling scholar first goes to school, the situation possibly seems less strange. Televiewing also promotes reading readiness by introducing children to a richer vocabulary and wider experiences than they otherwise might have.

Perhaps television also makes some positive contributions to family life. It may draw family members together, both literally and figuratively. The mother uses the TV set as a baby-sitter to soothe and preoccupy the child while she has other things to do. On the other hand, television may interfere with the family's pursuing other activities together. Father and son may prefer watching a ball game to working together in the basement shop. The television program may replace the parent's bedtime story or place an indefinite moratorium on family picnics.

## THE CATHARSIS ISSUE

Television is sometimes said to provide healthy catharsis for unhealthy emotions. In other words, experiencing an unhealthy emotion vicariously—perhaps through televiewing—is claimed to drain it off, thus reducing the likelihood that stress will build and cause emotions to erupt (Chaffee & McLeod, 1971). However, most studies suggest the opposite—for example, that viewing violent programs increases hostile feelings in the viewer and a proneness to hostile action (Liebert, Neale, & Davidson, 1973).

On the other hand, note that research about television violence often involves only boys. Such programs might have a more positive effect on girls, at least where females are portrayed as successful aggressors. A measure of aggression—more than most females possess and less than many males possess—appears optimal for personality and cognitive development. Theoretically, therefore, girls might benefit from a moderate diet of aggressive behavior, whether direct or vicarious.

To date, we can only speculate about such matters. Much of this type of research is carried out in controlled experiments, and we lack evidence concerning the catharsis controversy on the basis of children's free-ranging behaviors in natural environments (Liebert, Neale, & Davidson, 1973). Does it matter if a child who views an aggressive cartoon is more likely than another who did not view it to break a balloon? Would he be more likely in real life to smash somebody's head open simply because he had looked at a crime program? Or may television simply trigger aggression in already aggressive persons, an act that might as easily be triggered by something else?

## NEGATIVE EFFECTS OF TELEVISION

The possible ill effects of television may be both direct and indirect. Fatigue, nightmares, and hypertension are labeled as by-products of this invader of the family living room. It is also feared that children may imitate characters who are villainous, weak, or fraudulent. In addition, television may deprive children of time needed to develop their various talents. Finally, television can be a time-waster if the programs involved are of little or no value.

Television is also said to provide a simplistic view of the world. The complexities of human interaction are reduced to 22- or 44-minute miniatures. It seems that "life becomes like a sandwich. On one piece of bread are the 'good guys' and on the other are the 'bad guys,' and violence, because it is faster and more appealing, becomes the repetitive spread" (Rue, 1974, p. 78). Television also stereotypes people according to occupation, sex, and other categories. Such stereotypes may be realistic in duplicating those of the real world, but children might better be exposed to programs that break down such stereotypes.

Perhaps the chief criticism of television is that it portrays excessive violence. On this subject, the Surgeon General's Scientific Advisory

Committee on Television and Social Behavior (1972) reported at least two major conclusions. First, although experiments with television indicate that children do indeed engage in imitative behavior, not all children are incited to aggressive behavior by seeing violent films. Second, the way children respond to violent material is a function of the context in which it is presented, whether it is perceived as reality or fantasy, whether the outcome is favorable or unfavorable as a result of the violence, and so forth.

Other negative effects of television are less direct. For instance, televiewing may keep a child up unduly late at night. Unless parents take a firm hand, it also becomes an obstacle to doing homework. Another problem is the sheer amount of time absorbed by television. What might a child be doing with this time that could have greater payoff? Is the child spending sufficient time playing, reading, or working on the thousand-and-one traditional projects of childhood?

## RESEARCH PROBLEMS

Research concerning the impact of television involves several problems. The effects are cumulative and long-term. Any one show involves many different parts, characteristics, and characters. A single television show may have many simultaneous effects, to which children may differentially respond, including subject matter, style, theme, character portrayal, and others. Such research also involves much subjective judgment—for example, concerning what constitutes a good or bad influence or what certain terminology means. Even the nature of violence is not clear (Holden, 1972). In three studies of programming, football was ignored by one research team, classified as highly violent by another, and classified as nonviolent by the third. In addition, conflicting conclusions abound. For example, one group of researchers reported that the relationship between aggression and televiewing was as strong or stronger for girls than for boys; but another found no relationship at all between girls' aggression and their televiewing.

## OTHER QUESTIONS

Other issues involved in children's televiewing are these: How great is the long-term impact of television? Just how early may a child be affected? We might assume that the child is influenced in some manner by television, even from birth. For much of a baby's waking time, the sights and sounds of television impinge upon its senses. To what extent does the effect of televiewing vary from child to child? One child may become so well satisfied with television's fantasy world as to feel no challenge in the world of reality. Another child may be stimulated by the very same program to more productive and creative performance than might otherwise be achieved.

Implicit in these general questions are many subsidiary ones. To what extent should children's programs be censored? If children are to cope adequately with a complex society, should they see all manner of human beings portrayed, including those commonly deemed less desirable? Are advertisers being permitted to brainwash Americans with whatever brand of propaganda their clients desire? What is the school's role in shaping children's televiewing habits?

In the first article that follows, Aimee Leifer, Neal Gordon, and Sherryl Graves review the literature regarding the effects of television on aggressive and prosocial behavior and social attitudes. This selection is excerpted from a longer article that also deals with the structure of the television industry and factors that influence programming. In the second article, Vincent Rue considers the impact of television on children and the parents' role in their children's televiewing experience. Certain principles are suggested for improving children's televiewing situation.

## REFERENCES

Chaffee, S., & McLeod, J. *Adolescents, parents, and television violence.* Paper presented at the annual meeting of the American Psychological Association, Washington, D. C., September 1971.

Holden, C. TV violence: Government study yields more evidence, no verdict. *Science,* 1972, *175,* 608–611.

Liebert, R. M., Neale, J. M., & Davidson, E. S. *The early window.* New York: Pergamon, 1973.

McLeod, J., Atkin, C., & Chaffee, J. Adolescents, parents, and television use. In *Television and Social Behavior: Vol. 3. Television and Adolescent Aggressiveness.* Washington: U. S. Government Printing Office, 1972.

Rarick, D. Parental evaluations of television violence. *Educational Broadcasting Review,* 1973, *7,* 34–43.

Rue, V. M. Television and the family: The question of control. *The Family Coordinator,* 1974, *23,* 73–81.

Surgeon General's Scientific Advisory Committee on Television and Social Behavior. *Television and growing up: The impact of televised violence.* Washington: U. S. Government Printing Office, 1972.

# Children's Television: More Than Mere Entertainment

## Aimee Dorr Leifer
## Neal J. Gordon
## Sherryl Browne Graves

Knowledge of the relationship between children and television has increased with the popularity of the medium. Research supports the conclusion that television can influence

From "Children's Television: More than Mere Entertainment," by A. D. Leifer, N. J. Gordon, and S. B. Graves, *Harvard Educational Review,* 1974, *44*(2), 213–245. Copyright 1974 by President and Fellows of Harvard College.

children's social behavior and attitudes. Children who watch programs depicting interpersonal violence display increased aggressiveness, but television can also encourage socially valued behavior. Moreover, children change their attitudes about people and activities to reflect those encountered in television programs. Thus, we conclude television is not only entertainment for children, it is also an important socializer of them.

The directions this socialization takes are determined primarily by the television industry which bears responsibility for broadcast content. It is a commercial industry which relies upon action, conflict, and proven formulas to attract the large viewing audiences needed to obtain advertising revenues. The number of participants in production, commercial sponsorship, and broadcasting is small, which further accounts for the lack of diversity in programming.

Changes in available content can occur most easily through industry action, although federal agencies and the public can also bring about such changes. We believe the desirable function television can serve in socializing children would be enhanced by greater diversity in television content combined with more broadcasting of programs produced especially for children and greater parental direction of children's viewing. Parents have the opportunity to use television to further their childrearing goals and the paper ends by considering a number of strategies they can use to achieve this.

## THE GUIDING LIGHT: TELEVISION AS A SOCIAL INFLUENCE

### Television and Aggression

There is now enough research to suggest viewing televised aggression contributes to aggressive behavior in children and adolescents. The demonstrated effects have implications beyond specific aggressive content and suggest that television can influence social behavior in general.

While there is no clear consensus on the

definition of aggression (Weiss, 1969), operational definitions usually focus on specific physical actions causing injury or discomfort to a person or damage to property (Surgeon General's Scientific Advisory Committee on Television and Social Behavior, 1972).

George Gerbner (1972a) has analyzed the agents, means, consequences, time, place, setting, frequency, and program format for violence every season since 1967. Gerbner reports that children's cartoons were the most violent programming among both prime-time (Monday through Friday evenings) and Saturday morning network television offerings during the years 1967–69, a finding recently supported by Barcus (1971, 1972). Gerbner analyzed ninety-five cartoons and found only four did *not* contain violence, defined as the overt expression of physical force intended to hurt or kill. He analyzed 762 leading characters and reports that 67 percent were involved in some violence, most often as a victim (the recipient of violence). Most men were involved in violence, as well as about half the women. If women were involved, they faced a greater risk of being victims.

Laboratory research has demonstrated that children will become more aggressive after exposure to aggressive programming. This was first shown in experiments conducted in the early sixties (e.g., Bandura, Ross & Ross, 1963; Lovaas, 1961; Mussen & Rutherford, 1961). Similar work has been conducted continuously in the succeeding decade. In one such study (Leifer & Roberts, 1972), four groups of preschoolers were compared: one saw an aggressive program and then played alone with toys; another saw a non-aggressive program and played with the same toys; a third saw the aggressive program and predicted how they themselves would resolve interpersonal conflict; and the fourth saw the non-aggressive program and predicted how they would resolve conflict. The programs were videotapes of twelve-year-old boys who either displayed aggression against toys and each other or played constructively with the toys and each other. Children who saw aggression were much more likely than the other children to commit aggression themselves, such as hitting an inflated clown, throwing a ball at a woman in the room with them, and shooting a dart gun. They were also more likely to say they would use aggression to resolve interpersonal conflicts.

In other work Leifer and Roberts (1972) examined how children of various ages would resolve interpersonal conflict after watching full half-hour television programs which contained varying amounts of violence. Children who saw the more violent programs were more likely to resort to aggression. This effect was most marked in children twelve years of age or younger and diminished as children matured. The programs varied in terms of how socially acceptable the motives for aggression were and how good the consequences were to the aggressors, but these variations had little influence. This probably occurred because the programs presented good and bad consequences, as well as good and bad reasons, for aggressing. Some programs had the theme that all aggression was bad, while others conveyed the message that aggression by the "good group" was useful. Young children apparently had difficulty, however, extracting these themes from the aggression and counter-aggression in each program. Thus, the amount of aggression in the program became the significant factor influencing their subsequent behavior.

Another significant factor in television programming is the degree of similarity between the setting portrayed on the screen and the child's actual surroundings. The greater the similarity between the two, the more likely the child will be to imitate aggression (Meyerson, 1966). Another factor is the presence of co-viewers with the child. Hicks (1968) reports that children who view an aggressive program with an adult who offers a variety of positive comments about the program ("Boy look at him go" . . . "He sure is a tough guy") will subsequently show more aggression in a post-test situation with this adult than will other children who had seen the same programs with the same adult but had heard the adult offer negative evaluations ("He shouldn't do that"). These effects do not appear when preschoolers are tested by an adult different from the one who viewed the program with them.

While the generality of the early experimental studies is limited because they take place in the laboratory, they all demonstrate that children can learn aggression simply by observing it. Approximately 40 percent of this learning is retained by four-and-five-year-olds after an interval of eight months (Hicks, 1965). If the televised model is rewarded for aggression, the child is more likely subsequently to aggress (Bandura, 1965), and parental evaluation or instruction regarding the permissibility of aggression can alter the amount of aggression (Hicks, 1968). These earlier efforts have been summarized by Baker and Ball (1969) and Goranson (1970).

More recent research on the effects of aggression has moved from experimental situations to those that more nearly reflect the daily lives of children (e.g., Friedrich & Stein, 1973; Parke, *et al.,* 1972; Steuer, Applefield & Smith, 1971). In nearly all cases these studies find increased aggression in the child's normal social interactions after watching television programs containing aggression. For example, Steuer, Applefield and Smith (1971) watched five matched pairs of preschoolers play together for ten ten-minute sessions over a period of two weeks. Then for eleven sessions they watched the children play after one child in each pair had seen a regular, violent Saturday morning cartoon while the other had seen the same cartoon with the violence removed. The child who saw the ordinary cartoon soon increased his or her hitting, kicking, choking, and pushing the other child. The victims did not increase their aggressiveness.

In another naturalistic study Friedrich and Stein (1973) showed aggressive cartoons (*Batman* and *Superman)* to preschool children three days a week for the middle four weeks of the nine-week school session and observed children during the entire nine-week session. Children who saw the programs showed a decline in tolerance of delay and rule obedience. For the children initially high in aggression, the programming increased their interpersonal aggression, while there was no effect on children initially low in aggression.

In addition to studies of preschoolers, there have been three recent naturalistic studies of the effects of exposing adolescents to ag-

gressive programming. The first by Feshbach and Singer (1971) asked boys residing in various schools to watch one of two television schedules for six weeks. The first schedule included aggressive programs such as *Superman* and *The FBI* and the second consisted of nonaggressive programs such as *Bewitched* and the *Flintstones*. The nonaggressive schedule was modified during the experiment, however, to allow boys to watch *Superman,* a favorite whose absence was bitterly protested. Boys' physical and verbal aggression were rated by teachers and observers before, during, and after the eight-week experiment. In contradiction to other studies, the authors concluded that boys who watched aggressive programs continued in their usual patterns of behavior, while boys who watched nonaggressive programs became more aggressive.

This study and the interpretation of the data have been subjected to numerous legitimate criticisms (e.g., Liebert, Davidson & Sobol, 1972; Liebert, Sobol & Davidson, 1972). In response to Feshbach and Singer two independent groups of researchers conducted similar studies, exercising care to avoid some of the pitfalls of the original study. One of these is nearly a duplicate of the original work (Wells, 1972), while the other employed similar subjects and methods but exposed boys to films rather than television programs (Parke *et al.,* 1972). Both studies found that boys exposed to aggressive television and film became more aggressive than boys exposed to nonaggressive material. The preponderance of evidence with adolescents, as well as preschoolers, therefore, suggests that exposure to everyday television containing aggression results in more aggressive behavior in viewers' everyday lives.

Such results and increasing concern for violence in American society led in 1971 to substantial federal support for an investigation of the relationship between children's aggression and their viewing of television violence. The results of the twenty-three research projects funded for this investigation are contained in the report of the Surgeon General's Scientific Advisory Committee on Television and Social Behavior (1972). The Committee cautiously concluded that there is "a preliminary and tentative indication of a causal relation between viewing violence on television and aggressive behavior; an indication that any such causal relation operates only on some children . . . and an indication that it operates only in some environmental contexts." Recently, Jesse Steinfeld, the former Surgeon General, stated more strongly that, "These studies . . . make it clear to me that the relationship between televised violence and antisocial behavior is sufficiently proved to warrant immediate remedial action" (1973, p. 38).

## Television and Socially Valued Behaviors

If television can effectively increase aggressive behavior, it conceivably can encourage other forms of interpersonal interaction. Researchers are finding some indications that socially valued behaviors can be communicated through television.

When we discuss "socially valued" or "prosocial" behaviors, we mean actions generally supportive of others within the existing social system. We include cooperation, nurturance, altruism, and self-control. But several difficulties arise in defining these behaviors. It is necessary to specify whose values, since value systems differ as do people. In addition, a particular behavior may be valued in some people and not in others. In most cases, for instance, aggressive behavior by policemen apprehending criminals is acceptable, but it is not appropriate for a child to hit her or his friend to resolve a conflict. Even prosocial behaviors, such as sharing, helping, cooperation, and self-control, can be used in anti-social ways. For example, successful bank robbers cooperate in crime, and minority members exercise self-control to maintain a social system relatively unresponsive to their needs. It is important to consider what the behaviors are, who values them, and in what contexts they are appropriate.

We know of no detailed content analyses of positive interactions occurring between people on television. Presumably the absence of detailed analyses in this area reflects a prior concern with harmful rather than beneficial effects of television viewing. Early researchers asked what is wrong with television more often than they asked what is, or could be, right. Recently, the Children's Television Workshop conducted a series of studies to determine the effectiveness of television as a teacher of cooperative behavior (Paulson, McDonald & Whittemore, 1972). They videotaped a series of short segments showing children and adults cooperating, sharing, combining resources, and helping each other. Children who viewed these segments during a regular *Sesame Street* program were more likely to cooperate and share than children who did not see them. The more minutes of positive social behavior they viewed the more likely they were to engage in similar behavior. Unfortunately, researchers did not find that children generalized the positive social behavior to new situations. Generalization of aggression does occur. The reasons for this difference are unclear. Perhaps transfer is more difficult with positive social behavior, or the children may not have seen enough instances of positive social behavior.

Leifer's current research builds upon this earlier work by the Children's Television Workshop (Leifer, 1973). Using a range of *Sesame Street* social material, she is trying to identify the factors that encourage positive social behavior and understand how they interact with the initial social skills of the viewer. She also is assessing the relationship between children's cognitive abilities and the messages they can acquire. Preschool children are observed in a number of different situations. In one they are given a sheet of paper and three felt-tip pens and asked to draw a house. Over a two-week period they watch six half-hour programs which contain only social material from *Sesame Street*. The programs include a segment portraying two men who are asked to draw a house on one piece of paper. The men initially fight over the available space and then decide to cooperate by drawing one large house. At the end of the two weeks the children are again asked to draw a house. Most improve their ability to work together and draw a reasonable facsimile. This example could be dismissed because the test so closely approximated what was performed on television. Perhaps the children obliged by doing what was expected. But the results still illustrate that children will copy behaviors portrayed on television when they believe they are appropriate.

Friedrich and Stein (1973) also examined the possibility that television could teach socially valued behavior. Children who watched four weeks of *Misterogers* showed greater self-control by persisting in tasks, obeying rules, and tolerating delays than children who watched four weeks of informational films (Friedrich & Stein, 1973). When interacting with other children, those from lower socioeconomic families showed more cooperation, nurturance, and verbalization of feelings after watching *Misterogers*. Films (O'Connor, 1972) have also been used to teach shy children strategies for joining a group of other children, such as standing near them and offering them a toy.

The studies on socially valued behaviors are encouraging. They use naturalistic approaches, which increase confidence in their generalizability, and indicate that television can teach children social behavior most parents value.

## Television and Social Attitudes

It would be surprising if television could affect children's behaviors and not affect their attitudes, yet we have less evidence that television influences attitudes than behavior. By social attitudes we mean children's beliefs, thoughts, values, and opinions regarding a variety of social issues (e.g., patriotism and the roles and abilities of minority groups, men, and women).

Television content has been analyzed in certain areas relevant to social attitudes. Analyses have been done which focus on the roles men and women, as well as whites and minorities, may play. The majority of characters seen on adult programs (Gerbner, 1972a) and children's programs (Mendelson & Young, 1972; Ormiston & Williams, 1973; Sternglanz & Serbin, 1974) are white males,

frequently portrayed with positive personality characteristics, such as competency, leadership, and bravery. Women and minorities suffer by comparison. In addition, content analyses of aggression on television suggest that "violence is a legitimate and successful means of attaining a desired end" and "it is to be expected that law enforcement officers will be as violent as the most violent citizens" (Baker & Ball, 1969, p. 335).

Influence of the visual media on children's attitudes was demonstrated as early as the 1930's. As part of a series of studies of the effects of feature films on children (see Charters, 1933, for a summary), seven- to twelve-year-olds watched one, two, or three films. The investigators looked for an effect on attitudes, the persistence of that effect over time, and the cumulative effects of more than one film (Peterson & Thurstone, 1933). Popular Hollywood-made films, such as *Birth of a Nation, All Quiet on the Western Front,* and *Journey's End,* were used. Peterson and Thurstone found that children changed their attitudes, making them more consistent with the values presented in eleven of the twelve films. For example, children developed positive attitudes towards Germans and Chinese and negative attitudes towards war. These changes persisted for as long as eighteen months, and children who saw two or three films changed attitudes more than children who saw one.

*Sesame Street* and the *CBS National Citizenship Test* recently have demonstrated again that the media can influence children's attitudes. In national studies children who watched *Sesame Street* for two years had more positive attitudes toward school and members of various races than did children who watched less (Bogatz & Ball, 1971). Adolescents who watched the *CBS National Citizenship Test* changed their attitudes more in the directions advocated by the program than non-viewers and the differences persisted at least six months later (Alper & Leidy, 1970). These differences are apparently due to program content rather than to personal characteristics of those who viewed. Viewers and non-viewers did not differ in knowledge or attitudes about topics not presented in the program.

Although few other empirical studies exist on the relationship between children's attitudes and television presentations, the available evidence supports the contention that children's attitudes are influenced by television.

## AS THE WORLD TURNS: FUNCTIONS OF TELEVISION

Television entertains and informs. This is a role the industry wishes to fulfill and the viewing public appreciates. Entertainment is necessary if the industry is to interest viewers in large enough numbers to attract commercial sponsors. But while entertaining, television influences intellectual and social development. Consequently, it may be important to place less emphasis on entertainment or information and to use television for promoting healthy development in children. The industry's use of violent action may create attractive programming, but it also can encourage aggressive behavior in some viewers. Fortunately, we may not have to choose between entertainment and positive socialization, since some popular and entertaining programs can influence children beneficially (e.g., *Zoom, Misterogers, Sesame Street, Fat Albert).*

Many justify current television content by their belief that it reflects reality. Yet there are some glaring discrepancies between the world as it is and the world presented on television. Only about 20 percent of all the characters on television are women (Gerbner, 1972a; Sternglanz & Serbin, 1974), while women comprise slightly more than half the population. Minority characters on children's programs are uniformly well-mannered and homogeneous (Mendelson & Young, 1972; Ormiston & Williams, 1973), whereas minority members vary in personalities as much as any group. On television, murder and mayhem are most likely to occur between strangers or near-strangers (Gerbner, 1972a); in real life most murderers' victims are their spouses, lovers, or family members (Federal Bureau of Investigation, 1970).

Television content may present general, subtle, and unconscious evaluations of various groups and actions. For example, it is no secret that women have been devalued by society. The few women who appear on television are rarely in positions of respect or prestige. Thus, while not deliberately attempting to reflect a devaluation of women, their relative exclusion and unflattering portrayal may be considered an accurate reflection of this devaluation.

Whether judged psychologically or statistically, reality is difficult to define in our multicultural nation. To argue that television does now or ever could present the real—or the ideal—is to simplify both what is real and what is ideal. Reality to one American is often unreality to another, and what is ideal to some of us is not at all ideal to others. It is important for us to realize that American television can never present a single real or ideal system with which most Americans would be comfortable.

Television, whether or not it accurately reflects our social system, does contribute to forming this social system. At the very least it helps to socialize a new generation of children into an already existing pattern. To the extent that television does not reflect reality, it socializes children into a fictitious social system, where criminals are always caught, minorities and the elderly are rarely seen, guilty people always break down under a good lawyer's barrage of questions, problems are solved in an hour, and things usually work out for the best.

Thoughtful leaders in television, as well as the disaffected and disenfranchised, claim that television is an instrument of political oppression (Clark, 1972; Gerbner, 1972b). They believe it has systematically excluded, ridiculed, regulated, or stereotyped members of various groups within our nation (Clark, 1972). In the past, non-whites often have been excluded from television programming, and when they were included, it was often with ridicule. Today, members of these groups usually appear in roles which actively support the current system, as policemen, soldiers, secretaries, and nurses (Clark, 1969). These portrayals may affect the attitudes and behavior of us all and serve to perpetuate the existing social order.

Those responsible for program production are sometimes accused of deliberately using television to oppress certain groups. This is difficult to support or refute. Appealing to viewers with purchasing power may mean neglecting viewers with limited funds (often minorities) and in this sense television is systematically working to the advantage of those already dominant in the society. Content appearing to oppress certain groups may also arise from the unconscious ideologies of television writers, producers, and directors. As the Bems (1971) have so effectively demonstrated for women, people occasionally revert to unconscious cultural stereotypes. For example, a woman may know that her ideology and professional role demand she assert herself in meetings with men. On most occasions she will do this, but sometimes unconsciously she will slip back into a more demure, passive, stereotypically feminine role. Stereotyped programming probably often occurs in a similar unconscious way. If our assertion that television influences children's social attitudes and behavior is correct, then it is important to examine the best ways to use this socializing power. To begin, we need to understand how television content is currently selected by the industry.

## REFERENCES

Alper, S. W., & Leidy, T. R. The impact of information transmission through television. *Public Opinion Quarterly,* 1970, **33,** 556–562.

Baker, R. K., & Ball, S. J. (Eds.). *Mass media and violence.* Vol. XI, *Report to the National Commission on the Causes and Prevention of Violence.* Washington, D. C.: U. S. Government Printing Office, 1969.

Bandura, A. Influence of models reinforcement contingencies on the acquisition of imitative responses. *Journal of Personality and Social Psychology,* 1965, **1,** 589–595.

Bandura, A., Ross, D., & Ross, S. A. Imitation of film-mediated aggressive models. *Journal of Abnormal and Social Psychology,* 1963, **66,** 3–11.

Barcus, F. E. *Saturday children's television. A report of television programming and advertising on Boston commercial television.* Boston: Action for Children's Television, July, 1971.

Barcus, F. E. *Network programming and advertising in the Saturday children's hours: A June and November comparison.* Boston: Action for Children's Television, 1972.

Bem, S. L., & Bem, D. J. Case study of a nonconscious ideology: Training the woman to know her place. In D. J. Bem (Ed.), *Beliefs, attitudes, and human affairs.* Belmont, Cal.: Brooks/Cole, 1971.

Bogatz, G. A., & Ball, S. *The second year of Sesame Street: A continuing evaluation.* Princeton, N. J.: Educational Testing Service, 1971.

Charters, W. W. *Motion pictures and youth: A summary.* New York: Macmillan, 1933.

Clark, C. C. Television and social control: Some observations on the portrayal of ethnic minorities. *Television Quarterly,* 1969, **8,** 18–22.

Clark, C. C. Race, identification, and television violence. In G. A. Comstock, E. A. Rubinstein, & J. P. Murray (Eds.), *Television and social behavior,* Vol. 5. Washington, D. C.: U. S. Government Printing Office, 1972.

Federal Bureau of Investigation. *Crime in the United States, Uniform Crime Reports—1970.* Washington, D. C.: U. S. Government Printing Office, 1970.

Feshbach, S., & Singer, R. D. *Television and aggression.* San Francisco: Jossey-Bass, 1971.

Friedrich, L. K., & Stein, A. H. Aggressive and prosocial television programs and the natural behavior of preschool children. *Society for Research in Child Development Monograph,* 1973, **38,** No. 4.

Gerbner, G. Violence in television drama: Trends and symbolic functions. In G. A. Comstock & E. A. Rubinstein (Eds.), *Television and social behavior,* Vol. 1. Washington, D. C.: U. S. Government Printing Office, 1972. (a)

Gerbner, G. Communication and social environment. *Scientific American,* 1972, **227,** 152–162. (b)

Goranson, R. Media violence and aggressive behavior: A review of experimental research. In L. Berkowitz (Ed.), *Advances in experimental social psychology,* Vol. 5. New York: Academic Press, 1970.

Hicks, D. J. Imitation and retention of film-mediated aggressive peer and adult models. *Journal of Personality and Social Psychology,* 1965, **2,** 97–100.

Hicks, D. J. Effects of co-observers' sanctions and adult presence on imitative aggression. *Child Development,* 1968, **39,** 303–309.

Leifer, A. D. Television and the development of social behavior. Paper presented at the biennial meetings of the International Society for the Study of Behavioral Development, Ann Arbor, 1973.

Leifer, A. D., & Roberts, D. F. Children's responses to television violence. In J. P. Murray,

E. A. Rubinstein, & G. A. Comstock (Eds.), *Television and social behavior,* Vol. 2. Washington, D. C.: U. S. Government Printing Office, 1972.

Liebert, R. M., Davidson, E. S., & Sobol, M. P. Catharsis of aggression among institutionalized boys: Further discussion. In G. A. Comstock, E. A. Rubinstein, & J. P. Murray (Eds.), *Television and social behavior,* Vol. 5. Washington, D. C.: U. S. Government Printing Office, 1972.

Liebert, R. M., Sobol, M. D., & Davidson, E. S. Catharsis of aggression among institutionalized boys: Fact or artifact? In G. A. Comstock, E. A. Rubinstein, & J. P. Murray (Eds.), *Television and social behavior,* Vol. 5. Washington, D. C.: U. S. Government Printing Office, 1972.

Lovaas, O. I. Effect of exposure to symbolic aggression on aggressive behavior. *Child Development,* 1961, **32,** 37–44.

Mendelson, G., & Young, M. *A content analysis of black and minority treatment on children's television.* Boston: Action for Children's Television, 1972.

Meyerson, L. The effects of filmed aggression on the aggressive responses of high and low aggressive subjects. Dis., University of Iowa, 1966.

Mussen, P. H., & Rutherford, E. Effects of aggressive outcomes on children's aggressive play. *Journal of Abnormal and Social Psychology,* 1961, **63,** 461–464.

O'Connor, R. D. Modification of social withdrawal through symbolic modeling. In K. D. O'Leary & S. G. O'Leary (Eds.), *Classroom management.* New York: Pergamon Press, 1972.

Ormiston, L. H., & Williams, S. *Saturday children's programming in San Francisco, California: An analysis of the presentation of racial and cultural groups on three network affiliated San Francisco television stations.* San Francisco: Committee on Children's TV, 1973.

Parke, R. D., Berkowitz, L., Leyens, J. P., West, S., & Sebastian, R. Movie violence and aggression: A field experimental approach. Unpublished manuscript, Fels Research Institute and University of Wisconsin, 1972.

Paulson, F. L., McDonald, D. L., & Whittemore, S. L. An evaluation of Sesame Street programming designed to teach cooperative behavior. Monmouth, Ore.: Teaching Research, 1972.

Peterson, R. C., & Thurstone, L. L. *Motion pictures and the social attitudes of children.* New York: Macmillan, 1933.

Schramm, W., Lyle, J., & Parker, E. B. *Television in the lives of our children.* Stanford: Stanford University Press, 1961.

Steinfeld, J. L. TV violence *is* harmful. *Reader's Digest,* April, 1973, 37–45.

Sternglanz, S. H., & Serbin, L. An analysis of the sex roles presented on children's television programs. *Developmental Psychology,* 1974, in press.

Steuer, F. B., Applefield, J. M., & Smith, R. Televised aggression and the interpersonal aggression of preschool children. *Journal of Experimental Child Psychology,* 1971, **11,** 442–447.

Surgeon General's Scientific Advisory Committee on Television and Social Behavior. *Television and growing up: The impact of televised violence.* Washington, D. C.: U. S. Government Printing Office, 1972.

Weiss, W. Effects of mass media of communication. In G. Lindzey & E. Aronson (Eds.), *Handbook of social psychology.* Boston: Addison-Wesley Press, 1969.

Wells, W. D. Television and aggression: A replication of an experimental field study. Unpublished manuscript, University of Chicago, 1972.

# Television and the Family: The Question of Control

## Vincent M. Rue

With the click of an "on" switch some 25 years ago, a new era of communication had unknowingly been illumined. Whether or not the "medium is the massage" as McLuhan (1967) would have us believe, or merely the message, is peripheral to the extent of its social penetration and pervasiveness. Phenomenolog-

Reprinted from *Family Coordinator,* 1974, *23*(1), 73–81. Copyright 1974 by National Council on Family Relations. Reprinted by permission.

Dr. Vincent Rue is Executive Director of the National Alliance for Family Life Foundation, 10734 Paramount Boulevard, Downey, California, 90241.

ically, television is more common to us than any race, creed, or political affiliation, electromagnetically living in 98.5 percent of American homes (*Television Factbook,* 1969–70). The medium is both modern yet moldy, master yet mistress, magnificent yet merciless, and mindful yet often mindless. As a unique intervening variable in mankind's development, television is a present composite of these paradoxes and more, more than we now know and more than we might have ever suspected. This paper will discuss the significance of television in family life. It will highlight pertinent viewing influences on family members, patterns of control, and present suggestions for improvement.

As far back as 1948, television was perceived as "practically a member of the family" (Coffin, 1948, 550). Today, the average American family views television some 6.12 hours per day, representing one fourth of a lifetime, or well over one third of all one's waking hours.[1] When these figures are broken down to account for individual use, the impact of television use is startling.[2] In short, television has become a constant resident in the American home.

Ironically, however, this electronic invader, so intimately ingrained in family life, is not oriented toward the family. Instead, it caters to the individual who may or may not be a member of a family. In the presence of the TV, the family tends to observe behavior that is more parallel, or individual-oriented, than interactive (Walters and Stone, 1971). In this sense, television is a familial activity only in the limited sense of one's being "in the same room with other people" (Maccoby, 1951, 427). Consequently, the tendency to decrease family conversation is increased in TV

families, transforming them from a "social group characterized by conversation, to an audience . . . silently gazing" (McDonagh, 1950, 122). Research by Bogart (1956), Coffin (1948), and Pearlin (1959) confirms television's major reorganizational effect on family life in recreational-leisure time activities with a general overall decrease in the amount of family communication. A simple behavioral circle might be constructed on the basis of these studies and others: the more we watch, the less we talk; the less we talk, the more we need to watch. All of this has led one author to proclaim: "either burn all television sets in the home or learn how to use them more judiciously" (Koprowski, 1973, 234).

## THE NATURE OF TELEVISION

Any mention of control of television use by parents, adults, adolescents, or children must necessarily include the contribution of those who make the programs possible, namely, the television industry itself.

First and foremost television is a money-making enterprise whose profit-making motives for existence must supercede all other considerations. At the same time television exists for citizens, since, in a real way, the airwaves are owned by the public (Communications Act, 1934). In order to balance these two competing interests the Federal Communications Commission regulates the broadcasting industry through licensure which demands that television stations be responsive to the public interest, convenience, and necessity of their local audience.[3]

---

[1]Nielsen survey, cited in *Change,* February, 1972, 11.

[2]According to Looney (1971, 55): "By the time a child is fourteen and in the eighth grade, he has watched the violent assault or destruction of nearly 18,000 human beings on television. During an average year, an older child attends school 980 hours and watches TV 1,340 hours, so that by the time he graduates from high school, he will have spent between 11,000 and 12,000 hours in the classroom and more than 22,000 hours in front of the television set, with perhaps 5,000 of those hours consumed by 350,000 commercial messages."

[3]The networks are not licensed. They are essentially a specialized service industry which provide programs to the affiliated stations over lines rented for the most part from the telephone company. Each commercial network owns and operates five licensed stations, the maximum permissable for one corporation. The networks sell advertising time on their programs, and give 30 percent of that revenue to the local stations which accept a program. The sale price of a commercial minute and the station's share are a direct function of audience size. Typical prices of popular shows are $60,000 to $75,000 per commercial minute, running $100,000 or more for specials. The above considerations mean that networks and stations choose their programs so that they have the largest possible audience at the lowest production cost consistent with audience drawing power (adapted from "The Advocates," October 3, 1971).

Any change in the existing structure or function of the television industry must then be understood in terms of its circular sustenance. Both responsible and irresponsible TV broadcasting is usually born of the networks, sponsored by independent commercial interest, unseen by federal agencies, bypassed by educators, nurtured by uninvolved (perhaps even uninterested or unsuspecting) parents, and consumed by indigested young and old. In turn, these viewers are influenced by what they see (violent or not violent), paired with multitudinous sponsoring advertisements: what they see, they are told, they must become. Viewers are then transformed into consumers of TV goods and philosophy which, in turn, promotes conglomerate commercial interests reinforcing the networks to continue producing a particular type of program. The bulk of this happens with almost nonexistent federal government involvement, nor investigative concern by child development and family relations specialists.

It should be remembered, however, that the medium of television is inherently neutral, in that it is an entertaining informational platform extending over time and the populace. In effect:

> It teaches law-breaking and law-enforcement equally well. It teaches the evil and the brutal as easily and completely as the good or the kind. What it teaches depends on the hands that control it, however wisely or ignorantly or innocently. It will teach what it *shows,* no matter whether it *intends* to teach this or not (Skornia, 1970, 2).

## PATTERNS OF TELEVISION CONTROL

Amidst inclement responses of industry abuse, the positive functions of family television viewing bear goal-oriented explication. In its own unique way television (1) provides information, fun, enjoyment, and pleasure; (2) it brings parents and children a broader view of life than exists in or around the family context; (3) it makes the unspeakable discussable by providing opportunities for expressing emotions which have never had occasion to surface,

such as love, hate, ambition, and accomplishment; and (4) it makes possible vicarious learning experiences for experimentation and self-growth (cf. Ziferstein, 1966).

The impact of television on children has received widespread attention in the literature, but little concern on the air. While there have been hundreds of studies in this area, 35 out of 44 major market television stations do not have as many as fourteen hours per week of children's programs (Jennings and Jennings, 1971).[4]

Perhaps the two most comprehensive studies ever undertaken regarding children and television were done in England by Hilde Himmelweit, A. N. Oppenheim, and Pamela Vince (1958), and in North America by Wilbur Schramm, Jack Lyle, and Edwin Parker (1961). Both studies found that the greater part of children's TV is adult programs, e.g., Westerns, crime, drama; that TV is most often used as a form of entertainment and escape; that TV reorganizes leisure time activities, reducing play time and dominating the child's leisure; that the greater the degree of parent-child conflict, the more television watched; that children are more frightened by realistic rather than stylized violence; that too early exposure to violent and stressful programs is also frightening; that TV to some extent makes children passive; and that TV makes its biggest impact when the child cannot turn to parents or friends for additional information. Schramm found little to no discrimination of adult program viewing by adults or children. Very often in cases where the TV is left on children view indiscriminately like their parents. Schramm recommends that parents use their examples as potently as possible (cf. Dominick and Greenberg, 1972), and

---

[4]This is not to say there are no high quality TV shows for children. Recent specially produced children's TV fare should be cited and lauded. For example, the Corporation for Public Broadcasting (CPB) enables Sesame Street, Mr. Roger's Neighborhood, and The Electric Company. This Fall, ABC hosts The ABC Afternoon Special, Kid Power, Curiosity Shop, Make a Wish, The Jackson Five, The Osmonds, and the Saturday Superstar Movie. NBC hosts Take a Giant Step, Talking with a Giant, and Mr. Wizard. CBS hosts Captain Kangaroo, In the News, You are There, and Children's Film Festival.

ing process, pointing out some of the "reality opportunities" as they are broadcast.

The case for discriminating use of television and parental control for children can be made in that it is taken as axiomatic here that children are human beings, not adults, and are a special interest group, with special and unique capabilities, needs, and interests in amusement, stimulation, discipline, education, recreation, moral development, imagination, and others. The following hour analysis of television air time might also lend credence to the need for selectivity in the programs children watch. A typical week for the 63 network prime-time hours broadcast looks like this: 35 hours—violent and melodrama series, and movies; nine hours—drama; nine hours—comedy; seven hours—variety; two hours—sports; and one hour—public affairs (*Better Radio and Television,* 1973, 2). According to Gerbner's TV violence index, the 1972 fall shows have a higher violence rating than ever: NBC—71 percent, ABC—67 percent, and CBS—57 percent (*Behavior Today,* October 2, 1972, 3).

Yet, abundant evidence indicates that there is generally little control of television viewing by parents for their children. In 1962, Hess and Goldman found that (1) while mothers view themselves as the most competent in regulating the television their children watch, they apparently are making little effort to supervise and regulate either type or quantity of TV viewing, (2) the father's role is mostly marginal, and (3) the young child is left to regulate his own viewing.

In 1970, preschool children were watching an average of 54 hours of TV a week, nearly 64 percent of their waking hours (Looney, 1971, 55). Lyle and Hoffman (1972) found that television was extremely popular with the 158 preschoolers they studied, and that they frequently made their own programming decisions.[5] Musgrave (1969) found that 53 percent of the 600 parents of eleven-year-olds studied did not

prohibit their children from watching any programs and 40 percent did not encourage the watching of specific programs. Steiner (1963) reported a laissez-faire attitude on the part of most parents who oppose television and practically no restrictions by those parents who only show signs of concern. While Rarick (1973) found a significant degree of concurrence between mother and father as to the desirability of a TV program for their child, he found that in only half of the 24 families studied did parents discuss programs with their children. Conjointly, one third said that they attempted to control the kinds of programs their children viewed, but only one out of twelve parents actually prevented their children from viewing undesirable programs.

Generally, the parents who do control their children's television do so for two broad reasons: (1) fear that their child may be adversely affected by premature exposure to the adult world and (2) a general belief that TV viewing is less important for a child than other activities (Barcus, 1969). But the dilemma of control is compounded by a number of factors. There is some support to indicate that restricting the child's viewing of TV may actually do more harm than good (cf. McLeod, Atkin, and Chaffee, 1972). Moreover, one study found that children do not prefer the kinds of programs their parents feel are most desirable for them to see (Rarick, 1973).

Barcus (1969) made a major contribution in this area by presenting a typology of parental controls over children's TV viewing (see Figure 1). The question of control of television use then becomes a matter of definition of type, degree, and temporality. In his studies, Barcus found evidence to suggest that there is both positive and negative parental controls exerted on both formal and informal levels. Conceivably, the type and degree of control can appropriately vary by age of the child and the viewing occasion, but more research is needed to determine the appropriate levels of intervention and the effects of this control in relation to group viewing where different age children are simultaneously viewing the same TV set.

The apparent fact that most parents do not control the TV their children watch might be

---

[5]For a detailed examination of television in the lives of preschool-age children, see J. Cazeneuve and P. Bendano, La Television y Los Ninos Menores de Cinco Anos (Television and Children under Five Years Old). *Revista Espanola de la Opinion Publica,* 1971, **23,** 49–54.

explained by any of the following reasons: parents hold a generally positive attitude about TV and its use; the negative effects of programs are overridden by the overall positive effects achieved; lack of time for continuous supervision or discussion; inexperience or unwillingness; the futility of uni-directional value development; the lack of experience, confidence, knowledge, or skills to discuss TV with their children; the non-differentiation between an entertaining and learning context.[6] In short, parental control of TV use mirrors myriad paradoxes:

> . . . television helps to educate the child, but watching it interferes with his education. It helps keep him busy and out of mischief, but it also keeps him too busy to do his chores. It keeps the kids in when you want them in, which is good, except for some of the bad things they see. And it keeps them in when you want them out, which is bad even if they see good things (Steiner, 1963, 95).

While there is some indication that parents might be more concerned about the development of moral values than violence (Rarick, 1973), beyond a doubt, the most insistent public focus on TV has been regarding violence in society and its antecedent stimuli, pervasive in the mass media (cf. Emery, 1959; Mussen and Rutherford, 1961; Zion, 1963; Wilson, 1971; Halloran, Brown, and Chaney, 1970; Steiner, 1963; Feshback and Singer, 1971; and Bandura, 1971). That the issue remains heated is testimony to the inconclusiveness of past research efforts and the cumulative contradictions amassed in the Kefauver hearings of 1951, the Dodd hearings of 1961–62, the Report of the National Commission on the Causes and Prevention of Violence in 1969, and now the recent Report of the Surgeon General's Scientific Advisory Committee on Television and Social Behavior in 1972.

A basic unanswered question has perplexed the empirical study of televised violence and viewer response: What is the relationship of what children bring to television to what television brings to them? The polarization of scientific opinion that televised violence adversely affects viewers is represented in the affirmative by the studies of Bandura and associates (1971), and in the negative by the research of Feshback and Singer (1971).

The most costly and comprehensive examination of television and violence has recently been completed by the twelve-member Surgeon General's Scientific Advisory Committee (*Television and Growing Up: The Impact of Televised Violence,* 1972). Undoubtedly marred by conservative membership selection, vested interests, and overly vague conclusions (Sterling, 1973), it nonetheless concluded its two million dollar study with the following two implications:

1. While imitative behavior is shown by most children in experiments on that mechanism of behavior, the mechanism of being incited to aggressive behavior by seeing violent films shows up in the behavior of only some children who were found in several experimental studies to be previously high in aggression. (The same held true for the field studies.)
2. There are suggestions in both sets of studies that the way children respond to violent film material is affected by the context in which it is presented. Such elements as parental explanations, the favorable or unfavorable outcome of the violence, and whether it is seen as fantasy or reality may make a difference (18).[7]

Regardless of these findings, the power of television would seem to be significant in that the billion dollar TV advertising market yearly

---

[6]Industry inattentiveness and the lack of parental concern and action in controlling children's television has prompted the establishment of a number of educational and advocacy-oriented organizations which provide helpful publications for parents, teachers, etc.: Action for Children's Television, 46 Austin St., Newtonville, Mass.; National Association for Better Broadcasting, 373 N. Western Ave., Los Angeles, Calif.; Citizens Communication Center, 1812 N St., N. W., Washington, D. C.; and Action on Safety and Health, 2000 H St., N. W., Washington, D. C.

[7]For a capsule view of this work, see C. Atkin, J. Murray, and O. Nayman. The Surgeon General's Research Program on Television and Social Behavior: A Review of Empirical Findings. *Journal of Broadcasting,* 1972, **16,** 21–35.

*Figure 1.* Theoretical Model of Types of Parental Controls Over Children's TV Viewing*

|  |  | *Control Prior to Viewing* | *Control During Viewing* | *Control After Viewing* |
|---|---|---|---|---|
| Positive Forms of Control | Formal | Screening<br>Selecting<br>Suggesting program for child | Discussion<br>Interpretations<br>Changing Channel to another program | Answering questions<br>Discussion of things viewed |
| | Informal | *De facto:*<br><br>adult selection & viewing | Viewing with children explaining | Praising things learned |
| Negative or Restrictive Forms of Control | Formal | Restrictions on:<br><br>1. content, programs<br>2. time<br>  a) # hours permitted<br>  b) certain hours<br>3. until completion of other activities | Shutting off set<br>Switching Channels | Forbidding future viewing |
| | Informal | *De facto:*<br>adult selection and viewing | Scolding child while viewing | Scolding child for things learned |

*From "Theoretical Model of Types of Parental Controls Over Children's TV Viewing," by F. E. Barcus, *Television Quarterly*, 1969, 66. Reprinted by permission of The National Academy of Television Arts and Sciences.

bears witness to the effectiveness of TV's influencing not only what you buy, but more importantly, who you are. Why not also in regard to violence?

From a slightly different perspective, for many children television has become a soothing pacifier and an effective one, because "like a sorcerer, it can tell stories, spin dreams, play enchanting music, make children laugh, even teach them jingles to sing—in short, it is an unfailingly entertaining companion" (Hayakawa, 1971, 106). But when TV's companionship role is escalated is it not conditioning children to over-expect ever stimulating interaction and uni-directional-giving friendships? For adults so encompassed, entertained, and consoled by television's unreality, is it not probable that their reality will inevitably become irritating? Perhaps television is saying something of the caliber of family interaction that in its constant luminescence we fail to see.

Someone once chided: we are what we eat. What does a steady diet of soap operas say about a housewife's marriage, particularly her information-stimulation inputs, i.e., her husband and friends? For that matter, what games are played by an uninterested husband who eagerly turns on television sports, but turns off marital or familial interaction? Television not only provides a diagnostic glimmer of relationship adequacy, but it also presents unlimited materials for classroom and family discussion of value development, love, marriage, family life, etc.

An additional point needs to be made about companionship and television use. Both from the perspective of the child and adult, human beings are very selective in choosing friends. The process of "friend selection" is usually ritualistic and elaborate. Yet television, in most cases uninvited, has been and is becoming more of an "ever attentive friend" for an increasing number of viewers as weekly hours of TV watching indicates. Because it poses no physical threat as would an undesirable stranger, TV has all the time it wants to say and do whatever it wants. Maybe as we become citizens of a post-industrial society, its relationship role will become ever more critical for many.

From the viewpoint of socialization, who and how often should we be asking: "Are the values TV portrays good enough for emulation?" For the most part, television exhibits a simplistic world view, flirting with unreality. The complexities of human interaction are reduced to 22 or 44 minute miniatures.[8] One can't help but think then that life becomes like a sandwich. On one piece of bread are the "good guys" and on the other are the "bad guys," and violence, because it is faster and more appealing, becomes the repetitive spread. But is this really what families want? Or is it simply what they get? Or is it so because too many have abrogated their public responsibility in voicing concern? Or perhaps more cogently, is it so because families are unable to voice their concerns amidst the roar of the television industry and network domination?

## IMPLICATIONS

By and large, parents expect the television industry to regulate and be responsible for itself. But network accountability is secondary to economic accountability, and this in turn very often supercedes program suitability to family preferences. Federal concern has been, for the most part, punting the responsibility back to the family living room. Consequently, all roads lead back to the family, which terminally pleads "stress-overload" and "over-expectation" but to ears that do not hear.

In conjunction with the recommendations made by the National Association for Better

[8]This is not to say that there are no programs which starkly confront reality. "The Family Game: Identities for Young and Old" is a TV show produced by WQED which deals with problems and issues facing families today and attempts to bridge the generation gap. Public television's serial broadcast of the Loud family might serve as an excellent focal point for discussing communication and marriage and family relations within and outside of the context of the family living room.

Broadcasting, this author posits ten recycled principles for remedial reconsideration and action in improving responsible television:

1. That controlled television use in the family is a requisite for individual and familial growth.
2. That parents watch at least some of the programs their children and adolescents watch, and in collaboration with them, establish rules and guidelines for the optimum use of television.
3. That open and frank discussion of television use, type of programs watched, and program content be encouraged by all family members, including marital units.
4. That children and adolescents are special audiences of TV consumers, and as such, merit special protection and programming responsibility suitable to their appropriate level of growth and maturity; and that child development and family relations specialists play a major role in age-related maturity and capability specification, and identification of program suitability.
5. That parents have a major responsibility to communicate to their children their own judgments about taste, and attitudes toward television viewing, including crime, cruelty, violence, sex, profanity, and all forms of exploitation.
6. That TV programs which incorporate sadism, "crime for fun" brutality as the basis for entertainment, "the portrayal of violence as a solution, and the picturing of details of crime and sadism which blunt feelings of compassion and humanity" (N.A.B.B., Policy Statement) do not reflect adequate responsibility to the "public interest, convenience, or necessity" (F.C.C. Licensing Requirements), and hence, should not be allowed the privilege of being publicly broadcast.
7. That both the television industry and independent commercial interests bear and share in all of the above mentioned responsibilities with special concern for exploiting the young, and adequate consumer participation in the type and amount of programs decided to be produced and broadcast.
8. That the federal government, through its regulatory arms (F.C.C. and F.T.C.) also share in this responsibility with the power of coercing the television industry to conform to these principles; that it establish as

rules Action for Children's Television's three recommendations proposed in 1971; that it more actively and stringently enforce "truth in advertising;" that it prohibit existing commercial advertising practices from children's television; that it generally diminish the amount and type of advertising on adult programs; and that it keep television competition fair by insuring that those broadcasters who seek to be conscientious and initiate programming change are not penalized in doing so.

9. That responsibility for improving the quality of television rests first with the broadcasting profession, second with commercial sponsors, third with family TV viewers, fourth with educators, and fifth, with representative federal agencies.

10. That both the public and the television industry be educationally reminded that the air and airwaves are public property; that the privilege of using these airwaves is indeed a right given with corresponding responsibility expected, and that the implications of public ownership of television need greater identification, publication, and actualization for substantial broadcasting responsibility to be achieved.

## CONCLUSION

These principles lay no claim to comprehensiveness or finality. Rather, they are presented as an initial attempt to counteract and correct the misnomer that primary television responsibility rests with the consumer. In conjunction with these principles, a number of unasked and unanswered questions have been raised and explored, especially regarding potential advantages and disadvantages of television use in the family. It is suggested that acknowledgement and concern for the resolution of these questions become a vital part of academic investigation in child development and family relations, rather than being sporadically subject to federal study or left to the vested interests of network sponsored research. Hence, even though television caters to individual interests, its mode, degree, and consequence of expression are all of familial and social concern. The aim of this presentation then is to prompt interest and impetus for

changing a perspective which has given inadequate consideration to the importance of television as a family member and its social-psychological utility.

## REFERENCES

Bandura, A. The Impact of Visual Media on Personality. In J. Segal (Ed.) *The Mental Health of the Child.* Rockville, Maryland: National Institute of Mental Health, 1971.

Barcus, F. E. Parental Influence on Children's Television Viewing. *Television Quarterly,* 1969, **7**(3), 63–74.

Bogart, L. *The Age of Television: A Study of Viewing Habits and the Impact of TV on American Life.* New York: Frederick Unger, 1956.

Coffin, T. Television's Effects on Leisure-Time Activities. *Journal of Applied Psychology,* 1948, **32,** 550–558.

Dominick, J. and B. Greenberg. Attitudes Toward Violence: The Interaction of TV Exposure, Family Attitudes, and Social Class. In *Television and Social Behavior.* Volume III: *Television and Social Learning.* Washington: U. S. Government Printing Office, 1972.

Emery, F. Psychological Effects of the Western Film: A Study in Television Viewing: II, The Experimental Study. *Human Relations,* 1959, **12,** 215–232.

Feshback, S. and R. Singer. *Television and Aggression.* San Francisco: Jossey-Bass, 1971.

Halloran, J., R. Brown, and D. Chaney. *Television and Delinquency.* Leicester: Leicester University Press, 1970.

Hayakawa, S. Who's Bringing Up Your Children? *Catholic Digest,* May, 1971, 105–108.

Hess, R. and H. Goldman. Parents' Views of the Effects of TV on Their Children. *Child Development,* 1962, **33,** 411–426.

Himmelweit, H., A. Oppenheim, and P. Vince. *Television and the Child.* London: Oxford University, 1958.

Jennings, R. and C. Jennings. *Programming and Advertising Practices in Television Directed to Children: Another Look.* Newtonville, Mass.: Action for Children's Television, 1971. (xerox)

Koprowski, E. Business Technology and the American Family: An Impressionistic Analysis. *The Family Coordinator,* 1973, **22,** 229–234.

Looney, G. The Ecology of Childhood. In *Action for Children's Television.* New York: Avon Press, 1971.

Lyle, J. and H. Hoffman. Explorations in Patterns of Television Viewing by Preschool-Age Children. In *Television and Social Behavior.* Volume IV: *Television in Day-to-Day Life — Patterns of Use.* Washington: U. S. Government Printing Office, 1972.

Maccoby, E. Television: Its Impact on School Children. *Public Opinion Quarterly,* 1951, **15,** 421–444.

McDonagh, E. TV and the Family. *Sociology and Social Research,* 1950, **35,** 113–122.

McLeod, J., C. Atkin, and J. Chaffee. Adolescents, Parents, and Television Use. In *Television and Social Behavior.* Volume III: *Television and Adolescent Aggressiveness.* Washington: U. S. Government Printing Office, 1972.

McLuhan, H. M. *The Medium Is the Massage.* New York: Random House, 1967.

Musgrave, P. How Children Use Television. *New Society,* 1969, **13,** 277–278.

Mussen, P. and E. Rutherford. Effects of Aggressive Cartoons in Children's Aggressive Play. *Journal of Abnormal and Social Psychology,* 1961, **62,** 461–464.

Pearlin, L. Social and Personal Stress and Escape in Television Viewing. *Public Opinion Quarterly,* 1959, **23,** 255–259.

Rarick, D. Parental Evaluations of Television Violence, *Educational Broadcasting Review,* 1973, **7**(1), 34–43.

Schramm, W., J. Lyle, and E. Parker. *Television in the Lives of Our Children.* Stanford, Calif.: Stanford University, 1961.

Skornia, H. Television Teaches What It Shows. Reprint from *Better Radio and Television,* 1970. Los Angeles: National Association for Better Broadcasting.

Steiner, G. *The People Look at Television.* New York: Alfred Knopf, 1963.

Sterling, C. Broadcasting Textbooks 1971–72. *Educational Broadcasting Review,* 1973, **7**(1), 44–53.

Surgeon General's Scientific Advisory Committee on Television and Social Behavior. *Summary Report to the Surgeon General: Television and Growing Up–The Impact of Televised Violence.* Washington: U. S. Government Printing Office, 1972.

*Television Factbook 1969–70.* Washington: Television Digest, 1969, 25.

Walters, J. and V. Stone. Television and Family Communication. *Journal of Broadcasting,* 1971, **15,** 409–414.

Ziferstein, I. The Use and Abuse of Children's Time. Reprint from *Better Radio and Television,* 1966. Los Angeles: National Association for Better Broadcasting.

# SUGGESTIONS FOR FURTHER READING

Ambrosino, L. Do children believe TV? *Children Today,* 1972, *1*(6), 18–19. This brief article considers the question: do children believe what they see on television? Note especially the references on the topic at the end of the article.

Barcus, F. E. Parental influence on children's television viewing. *Television Quarterly,* 1969, *8*(3), 64–65; 70–71. This study suggests that parents exercise greater influence on children's televiewing than has been shown by previous research.

Drabman, R. S., & Thomas, M. H. Does media violence increase children's toleration of real life aggression? *Developmental Psychology,* 1974, *10,* 418–421. This study concerned children's responses to real-life aggression after observation of fictional violence.

Eron, L. D., Huesman, L., Rowell, L., Monroe, M., & Waldes, L. O. How learning conditions in early childhood, including mass media, relate to aggression in late adolescence. *American Journal of Orthopsychiatry,* 1974, *44,* 412–423. A ten-year longitudinal study yields strong evidence that aggressive behaviors are learned, that models of such behaviors are especially important, and that girls and boys develop differently because of differential learning patterns.

Friedrich, L. K., & Stein, A. H. Aggressive and prosocial television programs and the natural behavior of preschool children. *Monographs of the Society for Research in Child Development,* 1973, *38* (4, Serial No. 151). The showing of three types of television programs (aggressive, prosocial, and neutral) to 93 nursery school children was related to changes in their behaviors over a period of several weeks.

Harrison, A., Jr., & Scriven, E. G. TV and youth: Literature and research reviewed. *Clearing House,* 1969, *44,* 82–90. Available research is reviewed to determine to what extent, and in what ways, youth have been influenced by television.

Holden, C. TV violence: Government study yields more evidence, no verdict. *Science,* 1972, *175,* 608–611. Conclusions are given relative to the Surgeon General's report on the effect on youth of watching violence on television. Also discussed are problems encountered in making the study and negative criticisms incurred.

Liebert, R. M., & Baron, R. Some immediate effects of televised violence on children's behavior. *Developmental Psychology*, 1972, *6*, 469–475. This investigation tested the hypothesis that exposure to televised violence would increase the willingness of children to hurt another child.

Palmer, E. L. Can television really teach? *American Education*, 1969, *5*(7), 2–6. The author tells why it is hard to teach 3- to 5-year-old children by television and describes a program designed to achieve this purpose.

# 16
## Children's Values

In recent years increasing attention has been devoted to children's values. The term *value* represents the worth ascribed to something. It defines what goals are desirable. Values can refer to concrete objects, abstractions, persons, or anything. Values may be attached to beauty, books, toys, or breakfast food. An individual's values may be inferred from observing his behavior; however, they cannot always be identified from casual observation. For example, we may assume that a certain child values learning because he always turns in his assignments; however, it may simply be that he is a conformist and does what the teacher says.

Values may be acquired in several ways, one being through imitation (Silberman, 1970). In addition, children learn through reinforcement. Whatever rewards or satisfies them acquires value. The process is gradual, as an individual comes to acquire increasingly more sophisticated standards of worth. Society has always taken a hand in shaping children's values—for example, in colonial times by "bringing a six-year-old to court for petty theft and hanging him, and having nine-year-olds pick straw in the factory, not because their labor was useful, but to teach them good work habits" (Goodman, 1971, p. 2).

Several factors account for the current interest in children's values. For one thing, parents have no reliable set of values to teach the young. Times and circumstances are changing so fast that society's values are fuzzy, like a picture out of focus. Children are thus confronted with conflicting values, perhaps causing them to pursue zigzag patterns of behavior. Their values, instead of becoming a steady compass, chart no definite course. Also of concern is the growth of technology, and the dehumanization it is often said to entail. "The idea of brotherhood is not new," writes Eisenberg (1973), "but what is special to our times is that brotherhood has become the precondition for survival" (p. 222).

The schools in particular have reaped considerable criticism concerning the values they teach. For example, Silberman (1970) criticizes the school's emphasis on docility and passivity. Moreover, to the extent that students are simply rewarded for doing busy work and memorizing, they gain little credit for being creative. Others call the schools' approach simplistic, because they do little to encourage students to achieve more complex, highly cognitive, and sophisticated values. Instead educators simply encourage compliance with rules and values that reinforce the dominant social system (Farnen & German, 1973). Moreover, elementary-school textbooks concerning legal and ethical behaviors often present a distorted view. The prevailing myth insists that everyone is equal before the law, has an equal chance to become President, and is equally capable of achieving success within our free enterprise system.

If values of dubious worth are sometimes taught, it becomes vital to determine which have most worth. Many values have been named as essential, and we suggest only a sampling here. According to Counts (1969), children should learn the ideals of human dignity and the inalienable rights of justice, freedom, and equal opportunity. Kagan (1973) suggests that a child needs to learn values that serve the needs of society, especially "faith, honesty, humanity." He wants children rated on the basis of humanism and not just on academic achievement, as in reading and mathematics. Such values are basic to our tradition; but we should also view other cultures' values to gain perspective on our own. As Tulkin and Konner (1973) point out: "Western psychology has much to learn from studying nonliterate thinking and non-Western systems such as Zen. We must not continue to support the notion that the skills of white middle-class Americans are the only desirable skills or the best skills, or that white middle-class American child-rearing practices represent the model toward which all parents should strive" (p. 49).

Also at issue is determining how values might best be taught. Certainly, such teaching should be realistically geared to what the child can absorb. It should be integrated with problem-solving methods so that children can see the implications of what they do and develop principles (Silberman, 1970). The problems involved should be realistic: adults should not play ostrich with society's dilemmas, if children are to become equally concerned and establish intelligent positions concerning them. Moreover, confrontation with realistic problems lets children test their values in real-life situations. In the process, they develop feelings of involvement and responsibility for decision-making.

Adults may also encourage children to criticize the status quo and to devise valid substitutes for what now exists. Many individuals become quite adept at opposing what exists but feel little responsibility for suggesting something to take its place. Although children's own solutions may be simplistic, they nevertheless provide the underpinnings for more sophisticated solutions to follow.

Certain issues relating to children's values have been suggested in the foregoing, but there are others. How can children learn to adapt values to changing times? How can they be helped to sort out values in an increasingly pluralistic society? How can emerging values be anticipated? Does censorship of textbooks prevent children from realistically appraising diverse, even commonly disapproved, values?

In the first selection that follows, Gisela Konopka tells how children acquire values and identifies the factors that shaped her own values. In the second article, Diane Ravitch discusses issues and views regarding moral education. In particular she considers whether the school has the right to indoctrinate students or the obligation to teach values. What is also needed, in addition to such discussions, is large-scale and continuing research to keep tabs on children's values in a fast-changing environment. While considerable research of this nature is available concerning adolescents, we have only limited empirical evidence concerning what children value.

## REFERENCES

Counts, J. S. Do teachers have the right to indoctrinate? *Phi Delta Kappan,* 1969, *51,* 186–189.

Eisenberg, L. On the humanizing of human nature. *Impact,* 1973, *23,* 213–224.

Farnen, R. F., & German, D. B. The jurisprudence of youth and adults: Some research findings. *Youth and Society,* 1973, *4,* 443–482.

Goodman, P. (Ed.). *Children's rights.* New York: Praeger, 1971.

Kagan, J. Exploring childhood. *Children Today,* 1973, *2*(2), 13–14.

Silberman, C. E. *Crises in the classroom: The remaking of American education.* New York: Random House, 1970.

Tulkin, S. R., & Konner, M. J. Alternative conceptions of intellectual functioning. *Human Development,* 1973, *16,* 33–52.

# Formation of Values in the Developing Person

## Gisela Konopka

*Some day all of us will sit as equals around a table while the great feast of brotherhood will be held. . . . It will take some time until this visit will be celebrated, but the time will come when we will truly be united and fight against the great evils of the world, perhaps even against death—whose earnest system of equality is at least not as offensive to us as the mocking system of inequality due to privilege that exists while we are alive.*

*Don't mock us, future reader. Each time believes that its struggle is the most significant one. To me, mine is truly like a religion. . . . I don't want glorification, but you may put a sword on my coffin because I tried to be a brave soldier in the struggle to free men to become truly human.*

This value-laden statement, with its call for the brotherhood of men and the significance of fighting for the equality of human beings, was not written in the 1970s in the United States. It was written in 1829 by the poet, Heinrich Heine. It bears testimony that the struggle in regard to value systems and the translation of them into practice is not new. This does not reassure us comfortably or alleviate our present concerns, but it does provide perspective. As a person constantly involved with value problems in application, I see the great anxiety expressed at this time almost all over the world in regard to value changes. One feels so frightened because in retrospect the past seems solid

From "Formation of Values in the Developing Person," by G. Konopka, *American Journal of Orthopsychiatry*, 1973, *43*(1), 86–92 and 95–96. Copyright © 1973 by American Orthopsychiatric Association, Inc. Reprinted by permission.

and clear—which in reality it never was. Anxiety is heightened by the fear that all values are lost and that we enter an age of pure cynicism. This fear is not totally unfounded: We live in a period of mysticism (*e.g.*, the interest in astrology) accompanied by cynicism—companions through the ages. Yet there are also totally different indications of value changes: a struggle to find genuine new ones, or new experiences of formerly held values.

When I was in Thailand, the Minister of Youth told me that, for centuries:

> There were three columns in our society which were considered unshakable. The first one was an acceptance of our religion, Buddhism. The second one was the acceptance of the complete authority of the king and of the patriarchal family. The third was our belief in fate and an acceptance of fate, whatever it brought us. All three columns shake today, and the third one has almost crumbled.

In my opinion, he expressed the outstanding change in value-determined behavior occurring in this century: Assertion of the individual's or the group's right to change his, her, or its own fate has not only become desirable but has taken the form of an injunction, a duty. This is contrary to centuries-old acceptance of class, caste, or racist systems. It even diminishes the significance of members of privileged groups fighting for the rights of others. *Self-assertion* is seen as a higher value.

Surely, the existence of people fighting for their own rights is not new. Peasant revolts and revolutionary movements are examples of this. Yet new is the worldwide acceptance of a responsibility for self-assertion and a practical and theoretical rejection of acquiescence, of meekness, of submission to fate. And with this new mood or value-determination goes renewed inquiry into the means of achieving one's goals. The urgency of debate on which media are "right," "wrong," "ethical," or "humane" cuts across age, racial, and national lines; and the answers are not always looked for in traditional precepts, but, with increasing frequency, in individual conscience. This I see as the one general trend in value changes, and its universality may have occurred because of the fast communication possible almost everywhere in the world. The exceptions are only strict dictatorships, which can close the borders of idea communication as well as the ones of physical entrance of strangers.

I want to focus on value formation within individuals. They certainly are part of the world around them. I must clarify first what I mean by values, of what kind of value formation I will speak. In an old dictionary of sociology,[1] the definition of value reads:

> Value is strictly a psychological reality, and is not measurable by any means yet devised. It is to be sharply distinguished from utility because its reality is in the human mind, not in the external object itself. . . . Ultimate values are axiomatic. . . . Their existence may be discovered by social or psychological research, but neither their validity nor their justifiability can be demonstrated. They are, at the same time, the final sources of the motivation of all conscious rational telic behavior.

This definition makes it clear that we are talking about abstracts, and about something that *ought* to be. Reality may or may not coincide with it. This may be in the realm of esthetics (taste) or ethics (relationships among human beings). It is to the latter value formation that I will address myself. It is my theoretical premise that *value formation within the individual is a developing phenomenon*. It is born out of an interacting process between the individual and the systems in which he finds himself, changing in different age periods; the individual himself changes and is being changed.

I could probably label my orientation as one of the developmental social psychologist. Yet I must add the biases derived from various philosophies, and the cautious approach of the historian. The value framework from which I speak is also hard to label according to established "schools of thought." I am partially a "humanist," and partially influenced by several religious denominations. I am definitely not a behaviorist, nor a strict Freudian, yet influenced by Freud and Adler and some of his other followers.

I have no intention of presenting my life history, but in trying to think through various influences that I consider important in having shaped my own value orientation, I found a kind of case example of the theory of developmental value formation. Let me share this with you in a short version in order to move from there to more general conclusions.

I grew up in a partially conservative, partially modern Jewish tradition, with a focus on the importance of the "here and now" and a missionary zeal for justice. Growing up in Berlin, I was permeated by German-Jewish idealism, but my parents and many of my relatives made me love Eastern mysticism, and very early—almost unconsciously—I learned to enjoy the value of variety among people. War—my mother's tears and my father's leaving; the standing in long lines for food— intensified a sense of the importance of fighting injustice.

As a young child, long before the advent of the Nazis, I experienced the terror of being considered inferior: After an incident in school when I, then eight years old, protested such injustice, I was told by my own father that I should never strike back, that "Jews are on this earth to suffer." Yet this same father had given to me the literature on socialism that advocated striking back, and in school we discussed Heinrich von Kleist's *Michael Kohlhaas,* the symbol of the stubborn fighter for human rights, and made him our hero. There were more contrasting influences: At the age of eleven I was severely castigated by my Jewish contemporaries for having too much knowledge of Christianity and loving the great painters, such as Durer and Michelangelo, who depicted Christian themes. I fought the Rabbi who called Jesus a bastard child and read the New Testament avidly, as well as stories by Scholem Aleichem.

In adolescence I joined a Jewish Youth Movement and then one related to the socialist labor movement. We studied the mysterious meaning of Gothic architecture and fought for women's rights. I terrified my poor father by pointing out how the Jewish religion considers women inferior and he tried to convince me otherwise. Among ourselves, we young people fought passionately over Freud and Adler and took sides; we read Bellamy, Upton Sinclair, and Herman Hesse (utopianism, socialism, and romanticism). We discussed Marxism until deep into the night, and compared it with Fabianism and other philosophies. During that time, I made a lasting decision, intellectually and emotionally, that the theory of Marxist materialism was not for me, in fact that it was absurd. It meant painful separation from former friends who had made the opposite ideological decision; value determination began to influence our lives strongly. Kant's ethic, with his stress on "the moral law within you," was intensified by reading and working with followers of Leonard Nelson (a German philosopher after World War I). He placed stress on making this moral law real in society, both through education and political action:

> Pedagogics is the systematic guidance of the individual toward virtue; its aim is to make him capable of fulfilling his ethical tasks. Politics is the systematic guidance of society toward a just condition, a condition in conformity with the postulates formulated in the theory of Right.[3]

Around the age of 18 or 19 years, my friends and I avidly read the newer social philosophers, Compte, Spencer, and Weber. They seemed to confirm what we thought, but did not move us deeply. More influential was the thinking of Plato, who seemed to describe such an ideal democratic society, but who turned out to be an elitist for intellectuals. It seems that all my life I am still fighting Plato when I disagree with elitist schools or educational systems that separate people on the basis of intellectual capacity. There were also nights of reading Augustine. His social order, based on love with justice towards everyone, seemed to be an ideal combination of the Judeo-Christian environment in which I found myself. But then, I did not agree with his separation of sinners from the saved. With some slight amusement, I find many young radicals today to be good old Augustinians, dividing the world exactly in the same—and to me, simplistic—way.

The strongest influence continued to be Kant and his followers. Kant understood

human relations, and stressed that human society can only be valuable if it is founded on social and political justice. Kant's essay on eternal peace, written in 1795, was so significant for young people who had lived through war and revolution. Even in his complex language, one could find the opposition to and the rationale for opposition to slavery and to all forms of human exploitation. And Kant so early established the demand that the human individual never be considered an "object."

> A state is not (like the soil on which it is placed) a possession. It is a society of men. Nobody, but the individual himself, can decide about himself.[2]

But, next to reading, the strongest influences on value formation came from life experiences—waiting for days in unemployment offices for a job, working in dirty factories and seeing the plight of mothers with young children, the struggle to gain an education while working for human rights. The advent of the Nazis, including the preceding desperate attempt to prevent their gaining power, was certainly a decisive value-intensifying event. It did not "shape" values; those had been developed in the growing-up years. A philosophy of "realistic idealism" demanded active involvement in the struggle against a power that considered one race superior to another. It also gave strength to withstand adversity. Placed into a standing coffin after having been spat at by a Nazi guard, and listening to some victims crying out in despair, I found myself almost calm; strength came through the inner knowledge that it was right to have actively fought this inhumanity, and not become a passive victim.

Events following this experience, books read, theories discussed never again shaped value orientation so considerably. The experience of human relations in a wide variety of nations and cultures widened the horizon, but did not substantively form new values. In the United States, some intensification of the existing philosophical orientation came from thinkers in the applied fields, *e.g.*, John Dewey, Eduard C. Lindeman, and the development of social group work as a way of putting human rights into practice. The extraordinary opportunity of meeting a wide variety of people, especially of diverse racial origin, broadened the sense of common humanity in a more experiential way than had ever been possible before coming to this country.

Out of this web or symphony of varying value influences, I can crystallize my evolving value system as accepting two basic absolute values:

1. The importance of the dignity of each individual.

2. The responsibility of men for each other.

Those coincide with values expressed by many great religions and humans, even though they may differ on the origins of those values:

The Judeo-Christian injunction says, "Love thy neighbor like thyself."

The Humanist postulates, "All men are brothers."

"The whole of humanity shall be a united people" (Ramakrishna, India's religious reformer).

"Wound no others, do no one injury by thought or deed, utter no word to pain thy fellow creatures" (the Code of Manu, Hindu).

"Harm no living thing" (Buddhist).

"Never do to others what you would not like them to do to you" (Confucius).

"The moral law within you" (Kant).

Those are only a few examples.

My view of man is psychosocial, seeing the individual as a whole, interacting constantly with others and with the systems and subsystems in which he or she finds himself or herself. My thesis is that:

1. The formation of values is a developmental process in the life of the individual within his culture and subculture.

2. It is a constant, never-ending one through the total life span, but with a peak in adolescence.

3. It is an intellectual as well as an emotional process.

4. Finally—outside of the early childhood years—it is an active process, the person himself or herself interacting with the influences impinging on him or her.

The concept that value systems can be handed down to another human being like an old garment or even a mantle, and the concept of "society" shaping totally the person's value system are both far too simplistic. The human being, his mind and emotions, are constantly acted upon as well as acting. The stages of value formation in the individual human development are varied and have their own characteristics. I will enlarge on this developmental theory of value formation, since I think it has significant meaning for relationship between the generations and for education in its widest sense.

During the first three years or so of his development the child will take his values directly from his closest human environment, parents and siblings, who in turn are part of the wider culture. The child does not question. He deeply incorporates those values at that time, in fact so much so that it is later hard for him to recognize them as values. Values related to body functions, for example, are intensely incorporated at that time. A perfect example of this are toilet habits in different cultures. In most western societies, defecation is done in a sitting position and this is considered "right." In many oriental cultures, the squatting position is considered the only right one. Relationships to other people are strongly incorporated at this time. This is not exclusively a Freudian concept. Cultural anthropologists have recorded observations of the trusting and gentle behavior of young children who have been raised in cultures where they are held closely to the body of either mother or father, and where no harsh methods, like slapping, are used to curb their instincts. A young oriental girl once said to me, "I'm glad I was not raised like so many kids here. I don't like to shout or hit. I never was hit in my life by my parents." This was not an expression of superficial politeness, but of an early instilled value of gentleness and concern for other human beings.

Though a three-year-old does not question the values under which he grows up, he resists them frequently. He or she asserts his or her own interests. Inside, the child begins a sifting through of what is accepted, what is rejected. This is mostly related to emotional reaction to other people. In psychoanalytical theory, this is described as the phenomenon of identification. The child incorporates attitudes of the beloved person. He resists openly—or by pretended adjustment—those offered by a person he dislikes. A daily prayer before going to bed, for instance, takes on a significant value of protection and warmth if learned from a warm and accepting parent. It becomes something threatening and to be thrown off as soon as possible if it is a harshly enforced ritual or presented as a form of sacrifice to ward off the wrath of an angry god. Values related to acceptance or rejection of other human beings are significantly but still unconsciously formed at this time. A four-year-old caucasian child, who attended a nursery school in which all other children were black, came home to tell with delight that she and her friend had touched each other's hair, that their hair felt different, but that both were so soft and pretty. Both of those children had begun to incorporate the value of beauty in variety. They could do this without conflict because the adults in school and at home cherished this particular value. Frightened or bigoted adults may have conveyed a sense of inferiority or superiority to the children that would have distorted their natural appreciation for each other.

Value formation becomes far more conscious during early school age. At that time, children begin to raise questions, but are still comparatively easily persuaded by their elders. The injunctions or preferences of the adult world are, most of the time, accepted or followed. Yet, emotionally, on the inside, is the beginning of a reordering. It is a simplistic view of human nature that makes parents totally responsible for the thinking, feeling, or actions of their children. It assumes that if parents only told children what to do, the children invariably would accept the parents' value system. Such a view assumes that value formation is purely an intellectual learning process.

Boris Pasternak,[4] in his beautiful description of the coming of age of a girl, Zhenya, in Russia before the revolution, gives us a good insight into this interplay of emotion and value development in the young child. He talks about Zhenya's and her brother's early childhood years:

Sometimes Zhenya believed that she neither could nor should have things any better; she deserved nothing different because of her wickedness and impenitence. Meanwhile, though the children never became wholly aware of it, the behavior of their parents threw them into confusion and rebellion; their whole beings shivered when the grownups were in the house, when they returned—not *home,* but to the house.

Their father's rare jokes fell flat and sounded mostly out of place. He felt this and sensed that the children noticed it. A tinge of sorrowful confusion never left his face. When he was irritated, he became a complete stranger, from the instant he lost his self-control. One is not touched by a stranger. But the children took care never to answer him impudently.

The mother confused both children. She showered them with caresses and gifts and passed whole hours with them when they least desired it, when it oppressed their childish consciences because they felt that they did not deserve it.

And often, when an exceptional calm ruled their souls, when they did not feel like criminals, when everything mysterious that shies away from revelation, and is like the fever before the rash, had left their consciences, they saw their mother also as a stranger, who pushed them aside and became angry without reason.

At first they had sometimes cried; then, after a particularly violent outburst of anger on their mother's part, they became frightened. In the course of the years this fear turned into a concealed hostility which struck ever deeper roots in their hearts.

These circumstances molded the children. They never knew this, for even among grownups there are few who know and feel what shapes them, forms them and links them with one another.*

*From *The Adolescence of Zhenya Luvers,* by B. Pasternak. Copyright © 1961 by Citadel Press. Reprinted by permission.

Pasternak describes here with great sensitivity how the emotional relationship between parents and children defeat the parents' wish to transmit their own values to the children and how, in this authoritarian culture, not a reasoned questioning of values, but a hidden rebellion is born. Those who advocate education purely by precept and the use of punishment and reward forget that, early in life, the human being's value formation is related to both thinking and feeling. Only the person damaged very early may remain simply an imitator or pure reactor. . . .

To summarize, my theory of value formation is a developmental one. It assumes a continuing inquiry, but sees adolescence as the most significant period of value formation. It is based on a view of man as an inter-acting developing being, capable of making choices though part of powerful systems that may enhance or hinder this capacity. Value formation is an emotional-intellectual process influenced by human interaction.

Out of this theory, combined with a philosophy that accepts as basic values the dignity of each human being and the responsibility of men for each other, come guidelines for the educational process in its widest meaning:

1. The purely didactic and the punishment-award approaches not only contradict those basic values, but they work only in closed, authoritarian societies. They have no place in an open society dependent on the participation of people.

2. Children and young people must not only be exposed to a variety of value systems, but must be encouraged to discover them and to question themselves and others.

3. Young people must be helped to work through and think through value questions, and not to accept value pronouncements on a purely emotional basis.

4. Generations must meet in mutual honesty and openness, accepting value differences.

The consequence of such guidelines is an education for life with constant quest. It is a life that neither allows for total certainty nor for evasion of action because of uncertainty. This is hard. One of my favorite writers, Morris West,[5] describes the encounter of a man with his former teacher, a priest, whom he had not seen for many years. He says to this teacher:

> You taught me better than you know. . . . You left me with this itch to mend the world—but never taught me the art of living in it comfortably. . . .

No greater tribute could be paid to a teacher. Such education places the heavy burden of "realistic idealism" on all people. They must learn to see the world with its good and bad aspects. They cannot be Pollyannas, nor can they be pessimists who give up the struggle. They cannot afford the armor of denial or of cynicism. Their humanness is constantly exposed, yet it must be tough. The vulnerability brought about by despair is part of youth, because the young usually have not had much experience with their own strength and capacities. It is one of the major tasks of the older generation to afford them genuine opportunities to test their strength, to discover their capacities so that they have a "bank" of positive experiences to draw from at the times when defeats occur—and those times are inevitable. In *The Ladder of St. Augustine,* Longfellow expressed so well the continued tenacity that is needed if life is to be lived fully:

> We have not wings, we cannot soar;
> But we have feet to scale and climb
> By slow degrees, by more and more,
> The cloudy summits of our time.

## REFERENCES

1. Fairchild, H., ed. 1944. Dictionary of Sociology. Philosophical Library, New York. (p. 332)
2. Kant, I. Zum Ewigen Frieden. Inselverlag, Leipzig. (p. 16) *Translated by Gisela Konopka.*
3. Nelson, L. 1956. System of Ethics. Yale University Press, New Haven. (p. 25) *Translated by Norbert Guterman.*
4. Pasternak, B. 1961. The Adolescence of Zhenya Luvers. Citadel Press, New York. (pp. 10–11)
5. West, M. 1964. Backlash. Pocketbooks, New York. (p. 31)

# Moral Education and the Schools

## Diane Ravitch

The trustees of the Free School Society, a philanthropic organization that established tuition-free schools in the early 19th century for poor children in New York, knew perfectly well what to expect of their teachers: only to have "the most unblemished characters with regard to moral conduct," to be truthful, sincere, frank, open, self-controlled, firm, reasonable, loving, and kind. They were responsible, after all, for nothing less than "the habits and characters of the men and women of the next generation." There was no doubt in the minds of the Society's leaders that the "evil example" of parents and the neglect of a proper education were what caused children to become the "pests of society."

In the 19th century, the belief that schooling had a beneficial impact on character and morals was far more widely held than was the notion that it led to a higher income. Elementary readers often contained a set piece, of the kind which children were supposed to memorize and recite, with titles like "Knowledge Is Better Than Wealth," a point presumably worth stressing because of the popularity of the contrary view. Moral education was homiletic, stressing rote memorization of simplistic slogans, but there did seem to be broad agreement throughout American society on the importance of inculcating a moral code that stressed industry, honesty, bravery, piety, diligence, orderliness, punctuality, and frugality.

The relative simplicity of 19th-century moral strictures is interesting today for the contrast that it offers to our own muddled state. "Moral education" is hardly discussed any longer among American educators; if anything,

the phrase itself has become discredited, conjuring up as it does insincere posturing, empty and hypocritical lecturing. The issue is further complicated by disagreement over such traditionally moral questions as pornography, infidelity, abortion, drugs, euthanasia. Besides, certain behavior once generally considered anti-social now finds apologists; the defacing of public property, for example, now a common phenomenon, has been lauded in both the academic and the popular press as an ingenious expression of folk art. In fact, there is scarcely any form of individual behavior, regardless of its personal or social consequences, without its defenders, whether it is Eldridge Cleaver justifying rape, Yippies justifying "trashing," Watergaters justifying eavesdropping and burglary. A great many people, on both the Left and Right ends of the political spectrum, seem to have concluded that one can choose which laws to obey and which to ignore. Personal morality has become a matter of each doing his own "thing" and negotiating afterward for amnesty or immunity, as circumstances warrant.

Let us for the purposes of this essay consider moral education, as the Free School Society did in 1820, to mean that which influences the "habits and characters" of the rising generation, or, in John Dewey's phrase, "ideas of any sort whatsoever which take effect in conduct and improve it, make it better than it otherwise would be." In this sense, we are surrounded throughout our lives by moral educators, whose influence on our behavior, values, and attitudes may be good or bad. The family is the primary moral educator, offering daily lessons on how to act toward others; the law educates; the government educates; the media educate. The number of sources attempting to influence habits and character is large; obviously not all of them accomplish their ends, nor are all their ends salutary. In many instances, indeed, the educators follow curricula of which they themselves are not aware.

Moral education *in school* has a special importance because the school represents a planned and presumably controllable environment; the public school, moreover, as opposed to the private school, is a place to which presumably everyone in the community has access through a variety of representatives and on a variety of levels. Adults who are responsible for school policy can deliberate and choose among ways of creating a "proper" school environment. Yet today, people who think and write about education are divided, not only on how to go about creating a "proper" environment, but on the question of whether it is possible to do so, and even whether schools have the right to do so. There are basically three approaches to the question of moral education. First, there are those who believe that the school should not try to influence the development and attitudes of students at all. Second, there are those who believe that the school should implant specific attitudes in students. Last, there are those who believe that it is possible to educate within a framework of moral values without resorting to indoctrination.

The notion that schools should teach no values at all commands a diverse following. It is the view of "romantics" like A. S. Neill of Summerhill and of a portion of the contemporary "free school" movement; both groups are opposed to the imposition of adult authority and discipline, which they see as an attempt to squelch the freedom and individuality of the child. The teaching of values in public schools is also opposed by those groups whose values are threatened or offended by the majoritarian position. Thus, Catholics reject public-school nonsectarianism, militant blacks reject "pasteurized" approaches to black history, political radicals reject patriotic interpretations of American history; the list could be extended to include others who perceive that their rights and values are compromised in a public-school setting. Many such groups form their own schools, expressly to preserve and inculcate their own values.

Yet another version of the anti-value approach was stated last year in an article in the *Harvard Educational Review* by Carl Bereiter,* a professor at the University of Toronto who achieved some fame for his part in creating a highly structured reading program known as

* "Schools without Education," August 1972.

the Bereiter-Engelmann method. Bereiter argues that schools are not successful in influencing the way children turn out in later life and hence should not even try to do so. He maintains that only parents have a "clear-cut right" to educate their children and that schools should stick to providing child-care and skill-training.

At the opposite pole from the anti-value adherents are those who believe that the school must purposefully instill values and that indoctrination is a legitimate function of the school. This camp, too, includes a curious collection of bedfellows, among them the ideological extremes of American politics, religious groups, and old-fashioned moralists who would like to see the schools drill "proper" attitudes into the heads of their charges. (Of course, those deeply committed to a particular ideology never see its transmission as "indoctrination," but only as education in the true faith.)

Educational radicals are divided on the question of indoctrination. Some romantics, as I previously noted, oppose any attempt to press authority on children. But others on the Left believe that the school should transmit a radical perspective of American society, one which will expose its sickness and rapacity. The political Right, too, believes in indoctrination. Conservatives feel that the schools should insure conformity and obedience, as well as unquestioning acceptance of American institutions; in support of their views they undertake campaigns to remove controversial books from public-school lists or to fire nonconforming teachers.

The third path to moral education is the direction in which I would argue schools and teachers should aim. The reasons emerge from a consideration of the problems that arise when one decides either to teach no values at all or to indoctrinate.

All education implies the transmission of values. How a teacher acts toward children; how he resolves disputes among them; whether or not he requires children to be responsible for themselves and to act responsibly toward others—in short, every lesson he teaches, every decision he makes, every expectation he holds, has the potential of influencing his students' ideas about the world. In not giving children responsibility, in not expecting them to clean up after themselves, in not demanding that they cooperate with their fellows or requiring them to respect the rights of others, a teacher does not suspend the teaching of values but simply substitutes one set of values—a supremely selfish one—for another. Similarly, a teacher who will not teach a subject until his students ask to be taught, proceeding on the assumption that what children want is what is best for them and that he must not manipulate their growth, is in reality indulging in an elitist manipulation of another kind; by refusing to guide, inspire, prod, or challenge his students, by withholding choices and declining to impart skills and attitudes, he may be actively blocking the child's freedom and growth.

But suppose a teacher exposes his students to history and literature and the various academic disciplines while withholding judgment about good and evil, desirable and undesirable? This is what Professor Bereiter proposes in his article, "Schools without Education." Here too the teacher would merely be substituting one set of values, the values of moral relativism, for another. Perhaps, more to the point, it is difficult, if not impossible, to imagine what a school without education would look like. In such a school, dedicated solely to skills and custodial care, teachers would energetically refrain from any effort to influence the behavior, values, and convictions of their students. This may do for a good vocational training program, but how can one teach literature or history without a sense of the good? Can either physical or social sciences be taught without regard to their human and social consequences? Dewey wrote that the teaching of geography, for example, was pointless unless connected with social life, with questions of how and why people's lives were influenced by geographical facts. To learn facts without understanding their implications is nonsensical; yet implications, interpretations, and judgments mean values.

The teachers in a school without education would have to work very hard to avoid exposing their students to the great works of art, like Picasso's *Guernica* or Shakespeare's trage-

dies, which make moral judgments on history and comment on how a man should live and die. The works that would have to be excluded from the curriculum of the Bereiter school would fill an entire library. In addition, since children from such a school would have no guidelines by which to assess their own behavior or anyone else's, literature and history, stripped of judgments, could be taught only as an accumulation of sterile facts and dates.

The school environment is itself a prime focus for the continual exercise of moral choice. The everyday occurrences of a school life, as of life in general, require evaluation and decision. A teacher is often faced with the dilemma of choosing among the conflicting rights of individuals or between the rights of an individual and those of the community. How is a teacher to deal with cheating? What is he to say to the student who asks for advice about a moral problem not connected with school—for example, the knowledge that a classmate has committed a crime: should he report him or help to conceal the facts? Most children are taught informally to be good team players, and not to be squealers; does Watergate cast this in a different light? Is it wrong for such questions to be discussed in a classroom?

What children need to learn is not the right answer, but how to think about a problem; banishing the subject is too easy a solution. This is not to say, however, that the school must lend itself to indoctrination. A teacher indoctrinates if he teaches without giving evidence for his conclusions and evidence (or tools) for criticizing them; if he purveys his own point of view, or a particular ideology, as though it were established fact, intentionally disregarding differing views, or ideologies; if he presents only one side of a controversial issue; if he teaches what he knows to be false. The indoctrinated person tends to have pat answers for difficult questions; though he may defend his views with logic and proofs, he is likely to treat evidence in a slipshod fashion, reinterpreting facts to fit his ingrained faith.

If a teacher sets out to instill the belief that whites are evil, that whites are good, that blacks are inferior, that blacks are superior, that America is a sick society, that capitalism is the best economic system, then he is indoctrinating. Where the educator concentrates on teaching methods of inquiry, ways of assessing evidence and arriving at reasonable conclusions, the indoctrinator concentrates on implanting convictions. The educator succeeds when his students have learned enough to choose their own point of view, even if it challenges the teacher's; the indoctrinator succeeds when his students have absorbed his ideology.

In a new book, *Free the Children,*\* Allen Graubard chides those "free" schools that shy away from politicizing their students. He feels that many of these schools, though obviously part of the counter-culture, are unnecessarily fearful of the charge of indoctrination, and that they should forthrightly immerse their students in a radical perspective of politics and culture. Graubard advocates indoctrination because he believes that the radical analysis of American society is correct, just as others believe that their ideology, and only theirs, is correct. In this Graubard resembles indoctrinators of the opposite political persuasion. When I was going to high school in Houston, Texas in the 1950's, for example, we were taught that Senator Joseph McCarthy was the greatest living American and that those trying to do him in were Communists. Our class was compelled to sit through anti-Communist and anti-Socialist lectures and movies; books about Russia, its geography, its history, and its infamous economic system were carefully removed from the shelves of our high-school library. Teachers who did not agree with the orthodoxy of the times were watched closely by parents and "members of the community," who occasionally sat in on classes to check out suspected subversives.

The indoctrination program of the Houston public schools was not especially effective; in fact it was probably counter-productive, it being the general tendency of my silent generation to discount whatever we were told by our teachers. Perhaps it is the inevitable reaction of adolescents against their environment that explains why many students of the 60's who were schooled in a libertarian atmosphere subse-

\* Pantheon, 306 pp. $7.95.

quently chose highly authoritarian figures for their heroes. In any event, the mark of dogmatism is as clearly identifiable on the Left as on the Right. Writing in the *Harvard Educational Review,* Graubard quotes a statement by "the students" of a West Coast free school, giving their view of the public schools: " . . . after graduation from school the students go out into the world trained to fit into society. Our economic system must create men and women to fit its capitalistic needs. The system has to have men and women who have the same values, who feel free and independent but who will nevertheless do what is expected of them, people who can easily be controlled." This may have been easier to understand as the statement of an individual, rather than the collective voice of "the students." As it is, one wonders if there are divergent views at that school, whether the students have learned to criticize their own thinking and that of their teachers or are simply feeding back the ideology they are taught with no more independence of mind than those who learned morality by rote in the 19th century.

Where will these students go in order to avoid fitting the needs of a society they deplore? If they become reformers, they will help to ameliorate the ills of society and thus end up strengthening the system; if they engage is useful work, they will be perpetuating the status quo. Graubard is himself stumped on the question of how one lives in a society as "sick" as ours without contributing to the sickness; he proposes nothing more dramatic than that free-school people try to get elected to local school boards and press for government funds for their non-public schools in the form of a voucher plan.

Indoctrination, whether it takes place in an authoritarian or a libertarian context, is an inappropriate and coercive solution to the problem of moral education in a democratic society. But is there a middle ground between indoctrination and the abdication of all values? Lawrence Kohlberg of Harvard University has articulated a developmental approach to moral education which blends together Dewey and Jean Piaget and attempts to establish a theoretical rationalization of just such a middle ground.

On the evidence of crosscultural studies, Kohlberg believes that there are unmistakable stages of moral development which are common to all societies and all cultures. Morality does not consist of a predetermined list of values, force-fed into young children, nor is it the spontaneous unfolding of the individual's impulses and emotions. Morality, Kohlberg has written, is justice, "the reciprocity between the individual and others in his social environment." A commitment to justice implies a commitment to individual rights, to freedom, and to a society which embodies these principles. The language of justice is comprehensible across time and across national and cultural boundaries, whether it is spoken by a Socrates, a Gandhi, a Thoreau, a Solzhenitsyn, or a Martin Luther King.

Kohlberg's views echo those of John Dewey, who wrote that "apart from participating in social life, the school has no moral end nor aim." Those who would teach schoolchildren without exposing them to the principles of justice, without making them aware of their social responsibilities and without awakening them to genuine moral dilemmas, cannot be called educators. In contrast to the romantic (or value-free) educator, whose concern for the child's freedom makes him reluctant to direct the learning process, and the cultural transmitter (or indoctrinator), who sees education as an input-output process, Kohlberg's educator wants his students to think rationally and critically. Thus, he exposes his students to problematic situations, examples of social conflict among groups and individuals, which they must think about and participate in resolving. The goal of the teacher is not to find the "right" answer, but to encourage students to progress in their capacity to make moral judgments and to assess the consequences of their actions.

In order to teach justice, a school must itself be just; it must be committed to equality of educational opportunity, to respect for rationality, and to freedom of belief. These values necessarily preclude the use of indoctrination. Writes Kohlberg: "Not only are the rights of the child to be respected by the teacher, but the child's development is to be stimulated so that he may come to respect and defend his own

rights and the rights of others." If indoctrination has no place in Kohlberg's scheme, it is likewise clear that the school's responsibility to its students does not begin and end with skill-training, by standing back and seeing whether children develop their own sense of values. The school's responsibility is to enable the student to grow by training him both to follow and to lead; to impart his cultural heritage; to prepare him to be a full participant in the political process; and to cultivate the physical, intellectual, and emotional discipline which will enable him to do well in later life.

This, the classic liberal idea of moral education, may seem inappropriate, to say the least, at a time when almost all critics are agreed that we should lower, not raise, our expectations of what schools can do. These critics have a point, for many Americans have indeed come to believe that the schools and the schools alone will bring about a just and equal society, quite irrespective of the actions of other private and public agencies. Putting so much faith in the corrective power of schooling is a way of avoiding other kinds of social and economic reform.

Yet what is needed now is not lowered but changed expectations. True, schooling does not guarantee success, but lack of schooling does appear to guarantee lack of success. Undeniably there is much that is wrong with the schools, including their tendency to substitute indoctrination for moral education. But the schools are where the children are, and the importance of improving them cannot be slighted. To rescue the schools and the idea of education from both unreal expectations and from nihilistic assaults is an urgent task, for what we do or fail to do in this area will have a profound effect on the future of society as a whole.

Whatever we may think about the current state of moral education, moral education goes on. Whether it is to be planned around a core of values stressing what Kohlberg has called the universal ethical principles, or imposed by those with a single message to proclaim, or haphazardly conducted by whatever images and models may impinge on a child's consciousness, is a choice which we make, consciously or unconsciously. In this connection

Dewey's reflections in his *Moral Principles in Education* (1909) remain appropriate today:

> We need to see that moral principles are not arbitrary, that they are not "transcendental"; that the term "moral" does not designate a special region or portion of life. We need to translate the moral into the conditions and forces of our community life, and into the impulses and habits of the individual.

## SUGGESTIONS FOR FURTHER READING

Beech, R. P., & Schoeppe, A. Development of value systems in adolescents. *Developmental Psychology,* 1974, *10,* 644–656. In this study of the value systems of pupils in grades 5, 7, 9, and 11, the most striking finding was the relative stability of rankings over all grades, suggesting a core cultural pattern. The boys displayed a "more unitary theme of increasing achievement orientation, while girls exhibited a dual theme of achievement and the stereotyped feminine sex role."

Bender, N. J. Value systems in a changing culture. *Journal of Religion and Health,* 1973, *12,* 259–277. The author comments on two books by the sociologist P. A. Sorokin, *The Basic Trends of Our Times* and *The Crises of Our Age.* The basic theme is that a revolution exists in the United States relating to many areas of society including families, women's roles, and adolescents. Our culture is portrayed as sensate—obtaining truth through sensory perception—leading to materialism, relativism, and ultimately to nihilism and chaos.

Crosby, J. F. The effect of family life education on the values and attitudes of adolescents. *Family Coordinator,* 1971, *20,* 137–140. A program of family-life education proved effective in modifying adolescents' attitudes toward themselves and their families.

Emmerich, W. Developmental trends in evaluations of single traits. *Child Development,* 1974, *45,* 172–183. Developmental trends in value judgments and trait definitions were determined from questions submitted to 687 middle-class fourth- to eleventh-graders asking them to evaluate descriptions of hypothetical persons of their own sex.

Ermalinski, R., & Ruscelli, V. Incorporation of values by lower and middle socioeconomic class preschool boys. *Child Development,* 1971, *42,* 629–632. A comparison was made between groups of lower- and middle-class boys in the incorporation of five adult middle-class values.

Farnsworth, D. L. Dilemma of the adolescent in a changing society. *Psychiatric Annals,* 1973, *3*(5), 87–100. The view is expressed that present-day adolescents are no different from those of other years, but that something is nonetheless seriously wrong with them, as witnessed by their widespread use of drugs. Adolescents' problems are also discussed with regard to careers, sexual behaviors, changes in family structure, and the rise of a youth culture. It is concluded that developing values acceptable both to adults and to youth is a fundamental task of society.

Goodall, K. Shapers at work. *Psychology Today,* June 1972, pp. 53–62; 132–138. This report concerns the use of Skinnerian psychology to change children's behavior in mental hospitals, classrooms, prisons, reform schools, and mental-health centers. The techniques involved, which relate to behavior modification and shaping, are sometimes recommended for teaching children and for automatically inducting them into the values sanctioned by society.

Guilford, J. S. Maturation of values in young children. *Journal of Genetic Psychology,* 1974, *124,* 241–248. Differences in values according to age were determined for a sampling of first-, second-, third- and fourth-graders.

Hawkes, T. H. Ideals of upper elementary school children. *Psychology in the Schools,* 1973, *10,* 447–457. The investigation reported here concerns the types of ideals chosen by upper-elementary-school children and reasons given for those choices.

Kohlberg, L., & Kramer, R. Continuities and discontinuities in childhood and adult moral development. *Human Development,* 1969, *12,* 93–120. This discussion of longitudinal data, involving the same subjects from age 6 to 25 and their middle-age fathers, concerns moral development as an evolving process and variations of the process itself.

Maddock, J. W. Morality and individual development: A basis for value education. *Family Coordinator,* 1972, *21,* 291–302. A comprehensive theory of children's moral development is related to the dynamics of value acquisition and education.

McMahon, M. G. Celebrating human uniqueness: Second thoughts. *Phi Delta Kappan,* 1974, *55,* 618–621. The writer identifies potential social, psychological, and moral dangers accruing to the definition of children and youth in terms of uniqueness; and he stresses the need for developing identification with, and compassion for, others. He perceives the stress on human uniqueness as fostering alienation and unconcern for others.

Musgrove, P. W., & Reid, G. R. Some measures of children's values. *Social Science Information,* 1971, *10,* 137–153. An analysis was made of 11- and 12-year-olds' values on the basis of their reactions to mass media.

Thornburg, H. Behavior and values: Consistency or inconsistency. *Adolescence,* 1973, *8,* 513–520. Children's and adolescents' values are discussed in terms of consistency over the years and factors that determine them.

Thristelthwaite, D. L. Accentuation of differences in values and exposures to major fields of study. *Journal of Educational Psychology,* 1973, *65,* 279–293. A random sampling of college students was surveyed to test the contention that curricular specialization produces a polarization between scientific and humanistic cultures.

# 17

## Issues Concerning Work and Play

In recent years considerable interest has focused on work, play, and related issues. Even in the elementary grades, career education has gained a foothold, along with concern for the world of work. Smoker (1974) even goes so far as to discern a "strong possibility that career education is the major redirection of the entire educational system" (p. 72). Of course, society's regard for work is nothing new, although the emphasis on career education for children is. But for centuries, play was largely overlooked as inconsequential, or even time-wasting. Certainly it occupied a lower place in the hierarchy of virtues than its presumably character-building complement, work. Of late, however, play has come into its own, partly because of the increase in leisure time. Also, the materials of play have become big business, and advertisements maintain awareness of them. Most important of all, psychologists have discovered in play a mine of virtues.

## VALUES OF PLAY

Play, psychologists agree, has certain characteristics (Martinello, 1973). For one thing, it is voluntary; it is free. The individual himself decides whether he will or will not play. It is not imposed upon an individual as a moral duty. It is not a task that must willy-nilly be performed. Play involves a certain naturalness; to explore, to search one's environment, to find out about oneself. Play also has a certain fantasy quality whereby one can simply set aside one's real life. Not that play lacks seriousness. It can be very serious indeed (Martinello, 1973). One can lose oneself in it, bestowing on it one's complete concentration.

Play's virtues are many and varied; we will name only a few. In play a child extends the limits of his or her skills. Consider the infant who, having learned to hold an object, puts it in his or her mouth. The infant looks at the object, shakes it, bangs it, drops it, and fits it into every activity possible. Children determine how things work and what they can do. They take their toys apart simply to find out what makes them tick. Even the 6- to 8-month-old infant can manipulate a single object up to a half hour (Bruner, 1973).

In play, children develop feelings of mastery and competence, as they transcend the limits of their ordinary being (Martinello, 1973). They are not the passive victims of circumstance. Instead, they decide fate while testing their own cognitive and affective potential. In other words, they structure the world as they will. They fit things into new patterns and endow them with fresh meanings. Hence, they prefer materials that are not so realistic that they cannot fantasize their world (Sutton-Smith, 1971).

Play is also good for the emotions. In fantasy children can act out their problems and test solutions without fear of the consequences. They work through negative emotions and, in consequence, feel less aggressive (Singer, 1972). True, play produces tension, but not the sort that generates anxiety. Among monkeys, youngsters deprived of play develop more serious impairments than those deprived of mothering (Bower, 1972).

## CAREER EDUCATION

Oddly enough, concurrent with this emphasis on play is a concern for the world of work, in the form of career education. Such education has been variously defined. However, according to Weagraff (1974), "career education is best described as a systematic way to acquaint students with the world of work in their elementary and junior high school years, as well as to prepare them in high school and college to enter and advance in a career field chosen from among many" (p. 45). Educators subdivide public-school career education into four overlapping phases. Phase 1, elementary-school grades 1 to 6, is concerned with developing awareness of the world of work. This phase involves answering such questions as: What are occupations and who works in them? How do workers go about their jobs? Phase 2, embracing grades 7, 8, and 9, provides prevocational and exploratory experiences. Phase 3, at about grade 10, permits students to explore a single occupational cluster more deeply or to begin specialized training. Phase 4, embracing the last year of high school or post-secondary institutions, provides actual training for a career.

Various reasons are given to support the cause of career education, among them that 2½ million young people conclude their formal education without a career goal or any marketable skill (Marland, 1973). Another reason is to prevent the overcrowding of particular fields, and to suggest alternate routes and broader options. In any case, children need experience in exploring and developing the full range of their academic and nonacademic talents, in order to acquire personal competencies, self-confidence, and self-knowledge.

Programs of career education have assumed various forms. Some involve children's actually working in different lines of business. In one school, children explored careers in pollution control and related careers in the environmental sciences (Marland, 1973). In another, adolescents became short-term employees in large corporations and in small neighborhood stores. The basic design often revolves around career clusters, largely because of the great diversity of the American economy, with over 45,000 job titles. These jobs have been reduced to 16 clusters, including marketing, communications, personal service, and so forth.

## MAJOR ISSUES

Certain issues have arisen concerning both the foregoing topics—play and career education. Insistent questions are being asked about the worth of play, the quantity and types of play needed, and conditions most conducive to worthwhile play experience. Questions regarding career education also abound. Is there not danger of premature closure—that children will settle on a life goal too soon, developing a sort of tunnel vision that precludes scanning the broader horizon? Also, do not such programs focus children's attention too much on present work patterns, reducing their vision of the work world to come? Besides, may not relating occupations to all other aspects of curriculum create a disproportionate concern for work and undue deemphasis of humanistic, aesthetic, and abstract topics? In a society where work is becoming increasingly less important in relation to leisure-time activities, will a strong career orientation prove dysfunctional?

The topics of work and play are both so broad that no brief selections would be representative of the literature. Instead, the articles here are simply intended to be provocative of thought and discussion on these subjects. Many writers of late have told why they believe play is important. It would be worthwhile for the student to compare Bruno Bettelheim's views regarding play, as given in the first selection, with those of others', whose writings are cited in the Suggestions for Further Reading. In the second article, John Morris summarizes the major issues concerning career education. What is needed, but thus far lacking, is a body of literature and research that confronts the question: How can children be helped to develop balanced programs of work and play in their own lives? This question would also concern the values and attitudes attached to work and play and their function in an individual's total personality and life-style.

## REFERENCES

Bower, E. M. Play's the thing. In R. D. Strom and M. E. Bell (Eds.), *Elementary education today.* American Association of Elementary-Kindergarten-Nursery Educators, A National Affiliate of the National Education Association, 1972.

Bruner, J. S. Organization of early skilled action. *Child Development,* 1973, *44,* 1–11.

Marland, S. P., Jr. Career education: For and against. *School Review,* 1973, *82,* 57–66.

Martinello, M. L. Play-grounds for learning. *Elementary School Journal,* 1973, *74,* 106–114.

Singer, J. L. The imaginative dimension in child development. *New York State Psychologist,* 1972, *24*(2), 4–5.

Smoker, D. *Career education: Current trends in school policies and programs.* Arlington, Va.: National School Public Relations Association, 1974.

Sutton-Smith, B. Children's play—Very serious business. *Psychology Today,* July 1971, pp. 67–69; 87.

Weagraff, P. J. The cluster concept: Development of curricular materials for the public service occupations cluster. *Journal of Research and Development in Education,* 1974, *7*(3), 45–53.

# Play and Education

## Bruno Bettelheim

In this century, the importance of play in educating and socializing children has been recognized in theory, while greatly neglected in practice. The more we became consciously aware of the psychological significance of unstructured, spontaneous play, the more we curtailed the child's opportunity to engage in it. We supervise and direct his play, and we schedule his day with so many in and out activities that there is little time left for his own play. Freud noted that play is the means by which the child accomplishes his first great cultural and psychological achievements. Play is his language of expression and also, if we are ready to understand, of communication. Freud was impressed with how much and how well children express their ideas and emotions through play—particularly those thoughts and feelings they fear to acknowledge to themselves and to others. Through playing out feelings, children master emotions which would otherwise overwhelm them.

Adults are uncomfortable with and anxious about play. In our preschools and early grades, we press for precision and purpose in children's activities. As Harold Dunkel writes, "The child no longer plays ball; he is a member of the Little League. He does not make stinks or contraptions; he prepares a project for the Science Fair."[1] The need, nowadays, to systematize children's play—to organize and supervise it in order to give it what we adults view as purpose—stems from the fact that the adult world has become separated from the world of children. With the exception of a mother's homemaking tasks, children can no longer emulate significant adult pursuits in their play. Adult activities have become too removed from the place where the child's world unfolds, if not also from his comprehension. Conversely, it has become more difficult for adults to take children's play seriously. We are as reluctant to join the child in his play as equals as we are to let him participate in our adult activities.

But this separation of the world of children from the world of adults is a comparatively recent development. Until the eighteenth century (and even more recently in some parts of the world), the play and games of children were also the play and games of adults. There were understanding and empathy between adult and child as they shared an equally meaningful activity. Goethe tells us that one of his earliest memories is of throwing his mother's dishes out the window. He began by tossing his own newly acquired doll dishes onto the street. The appreciation and enjoyment of his behavior by the adults who were present encouraged him and urged him on. He extended his game to throwing out his mother's dishes as well. "My neighbors continued to signify their approval and I was delighted to have them amused." Freud recognized Goethe's game as an expression of his wish to get rid of his newborn sibling. It was the adult enjoyment of his play and their tacit understanding that permitted Goethe to substitute his personal distress ("I have been thrown away") for a new-found self-worth ("Adults approve of me, in spite of what I feel"). Of course, that was just the assurance Goethe needed at this critical moment in his life. But how many children would be given this support today by serious and educated adults? And how much have we all lost by it—children and adults alike?

The much-discussed generation gap is deeply rooted in this early child-adult world separation. While the generation gap is not a new phenomenon, the intensity of alienation between the generations is relatively recent. Conflict between the young and their parents is most acute during adolescence. Psychoanalysis could show that a deep ambivalence of this period—the great demands and the severe frustrations—is largely a revival of the earlier oedipal struggles of the 3–5-year-old. But the literature generally restricts itself to a discussion of sexual attachment and disappointments, ignoring

all other experiences characteristic of this early period of development, the "play age par excellence." Never again will imaginative play be as important as at nursery school age—that is, at the oedipal period. Flight into fantasy is also reactivated in adolescence—as evidenced by "playing" with problems, the belief in "magic" solutions to them, and, most dramatically, reliance by some on drugs. Were children permitted to engage freely and fully in "childish" fantasy during childhood, I am sure they would not feel compelled later to attempt to recover and reenact their lost childhood through drugs. The oedipal child's disappointment in adults who refused to take his child's play seriously is recreated as the adolescent blames adults for their indifference to what moves him now. In earlier times, when adults were partners in play with their children, no generation gap could be revived in adolescence simply because it had not previously existed in childhood.

If we gave children the opportunity to play, maybe some of them would not be driven to compensate for time lost in childhood by playing "revolution" or "cops and robbers" in their twenties. Bertrand Russell, borrowing from Freud, remarks, "It is biologically natural that (children) should, in imagination, live through the life of remote savage ancestors." Biological and emotional development does not permit skipping entire stages of growth. If children do not have sufficient chance in childhood, they must work through their "savage stage" as soon as they manage to free themselves from those who have inhibited them. They endeavor to make up in much more dangerous form as adults what they were forced to miss in fun as children.

## WHAT PLAY DOES FOR CHILDREN

Though the words "play" and "game" are often used interchangeably, each belongs to a different stage of development, with play coming first. Play refers to activities of the young child having no rules other than those he himself imposes and having no intended end result in external reality. But the child is serious in his play efforts, and they have deep impact on his inner life. In play, the child's fantasy dictates what is going to happen next. Games, on the other hand, are those activities characterized by agreed-upon and often externally imposed rules, and by a requirement to use the implements of the activity in the manner for which they are intended—not as fancy dictates. (There is, of course, a continuum from free play activity to well-structured games, and some activities partake of aspects of both). There is an important difference between a play activity in which a boy sends his toy automobile through the air, fantasizing its power as it annihilates tall buildings, and a board game, in which his toy automobile marks his every move, predetermined by an elaborate set of rules.

Play begins at the level of fantasy. When a child embarks on playing out fantasies as opposed to merely engaging in them—in playing war or a game in which he is ruler of a kingdom—he not only seeks the vicarious satisfaction of aggressive or megalomanic daydreams but, far more important, he also acts openly and within the context of his reality on the pressures of his unconscious, his wishful thinking. Then he can no longer compensate for his feelings of inadequacy by fantasizing himself in control of others, because, when he plays out this fantasy with others, the child begins to learn the limitations of reality. The other children will insist that he "obey" the laws he imposes on them. He learns that an absolute ruler remains sovereign only as long as he enjoys the good will of his subjects. By playing out his fantasies, the child inevitably subjects them to the test of reality. This forces him to submit his fantasies to conscious control. And so he uses play to become master of himself.

Every child must learn the limits reality imposes on the realization of those fantasies involving others as well as himself. If he is annoyed at a person, he may fantasize that he tears that person's head off—it does not matter in imagination, because the deed can be amended. But if the child translates his angry daydream into the reality of play—by tearing the head off his toy animal—he learns reality's limitations; the animal's head is not so easily

replaced. With such experiences, the vengeful fantasy, "I'll tear his head off," gradually diminishes to "I could wring his neck" (meaning, "I want to do it, but I won't because to do so would have irreversible consequences"). The desires of the unconscious have been tempered by submission to the test of a "play" reality. Respect for the demands and limitations of reality are first experienced and learned in play.

*Fantasy play*—as opposed to pure fantasy—builds a bridge between the unconscious world inside us and the external reality around us. Fantasy and reality temper each other: fantasy without reality is asocial and chaotic; reality free of fantasy is harsh and cold. Today many people suffer because in their lives the worlds of fantasy and reality remain isolated from each other. Without the experience that fantasy helps us to accomodate to reality, reality cannot be successfully assimilated—the child either sacrifices his inner life of fantasy or encapsulates it so that it remains untouched by reality and, hence, no longer can be of help in dealing with it. When these two worlds are not integrated, life may come to be experienced as grueling and unpleasant—as demanding but not also rewarding, as draining of emotional energy but not also generating it.

*Imaginative play* provides the next step of development. Through it the child learns more controlled self-mastery. Imaginative play can provide an opportunity for self-assertion. When a child builds a tower of blocks and subsequently knocks it down, it is not because his destructive drives suddenly overcome his constructive behavior. His conduct has deeper significance. In building, the child was subject to certain restrictions—limitations of the blocks, the laws of gravity, technicalities of balance and support. Even while he asserted his dominance over the blocks by making them fit his design, he had to make allowances for the nature of the material he was using. That is, he was subject to the demands placed by external reality upon his own imagination. The child revolts against these demands when he destroys the tower. By doing so he is not so much giving vent to his destructive tendencies as he is assuring his dominance over his environment. The experience mirrors a crucial and often misunderstood learning about the relation between inner and outer reality and their integrated mastery.

What the child learns through such an experience is that he can be supreme master, but only of a chaotic world. If he wants to retain some mastery in a structured and organized world, he must forego his "infantile" desire for total mastery and learn to compromise between his wishes and the exigencies of reality.

Slowly through the experience of his play, he learns that total mastery leads to chaos, as when he destroys the tower of blocks. If he wants to build a towering structure that does not topple, he must successfully take into account the limitations of his skills in shaping external reality. After repeated play, compromise between inner reality and external reality becomes habit. Only through such an experience can a child learn to restrict his inner demands in accordance with what he can do and what is feasible in the world. Such play is the process by which the child learns that wishes, ability, and reality must all be considered when striving to achieve a goal. Through such experiences, he learns to benefit himself and his world, while at the same time making peace with the legitimate demands of both inner and outer reality.

Children's walking rituals are exemplary of imaginative play. We all recall engaging in walking rituals as children. We walked along ledges, stepped only on certain squares of the pavement, walked as close to buildings as possible. Whatever the specifics, walking rituals are a spontaneous invention; while they may be subject to change from time to time, the essence of the activity is that the rules are self-chosen and self-imposed. The child will reject outside suggestions about how to conduct his play. If his pattern is to step on none of the cracks in the sidewalk, he will feel he is perverting his game if it is suggested to him that he step on all the cracks. The walking ritual is an experiment in and demonstration of self-mastery, a proof of one's capacity to command one's own activity. The child learns that he has some control, if not of the outside world, at least of his own actions within it. If the self-imposed character of the game were obscured, the child would merely be performing as others ordered, and no experiment in self-regulation would take place.

To a child, the "magical" dimension of the play is in suddenly becoming his own master—no longer is he subject to the restrictions of the adult world. He has not only defined his tasks, he has performed them, and with no outside help. What greater magic for a child than to use a simple device, meaningless to anyone else, and through that device to remove himself from a life of "bondage" to a life of "freedom"? The secret is all the more exciting because no one else knows or can even guess what he is really doing, especially those adults who think the play is only an avoidance of cracks. The feeling of potency the child can derive from this activity convinces him that he has mastered, not only his own fate, but also that of the "masters" who don't know what he is really doing. Hence, the rhyme, "Step on a crack, break your mother's back." What gives the child power over himself also gives him power over his parents.

That such play activities have been maligned and misunderstood is evident when we consider how they have been interpreted. Children who build towers of blocks and subsequently destroy them are generally considered to be motivated by a need to discharge aggression. While this is true of some children, it is not the underlying motive for all children who engage in such play. Similarly, walking rituals have been "explained" as compulsive efforts to bind anxiety. While it is true that some children develop all kinds of rituals because they feel they will then be protected from some danger, it is erroneous to conclude that such thinking is the rationale for all children who engage in repetitive activities subject to stringent inner rules. Practically all human activities can lend themselves to elaboration or misuse in the service of pathology; but the fact they do has little bearing on their true nature.

# REFERENCE

1. *Elementary School Journal* 68 (November 1967): 57.

# Issues in Career Education

## John E. Morris

Career education—". . . the total effort of public education and the community aimed at helping all individuals to become familiar with the values of a work-oriented society, to integrate these values into their personal value systems, and to implement these values into their lives in such a way that work becomes possible, meaningful, and satisfying to each individual"[1]—is one of the most recent additions to public education.

## PURPOSES OF ARTICLE

The purposes of this article are to give a brief summary of the present scope of career education, its role in the curriculum, and to raise several crucial issues. These issues are raised without any attempt at critical analysis or to derive possible alternatives or solutions, for this must be done by each local public school system contemplating the implementation of a career education program. These issues are not intended as negative reactions to a new curriculum concept or new directions for public education. Career education may be what is needed by many students but it may not be for *all* students from "womb to tomb." We should not be swept off our feet by a program which promises so much to so many for there have been other programs which have made similar promises. Instead, we must give serious consideration to the realities of public education as well as to the prospects and promises of career education. The extent to which career education becomes a major development instead of a fad depends primarily on the extent to which its supporters are able to deal effectively with

Reprinted from *Clearinghouse*, 1973, 48(1), 32–36. Copyright 1973 by Fairleigh Dickenson University. Reprinted by permission of the Helen Dwight Reid Educational Fund.

these issues. The basis for these issues is stated or clearly implied in much of the current career education literature.

## SCOPE OF CAREER EDUCATION

[The President] has placed the prestige of his office behind career education and major programs are already developing in such states as Wisconsin, Ohio, Michigan, Georgia, North and South Carolina, New Jersey, and Mississippi and in such major cities as Pontiac, Dallas, and Baltimore. Several state departments of education have already, or plan to do so in the near future, moved to make career education a part of the curriculum for K–12 and undergraduate teacher education programs. It has been endorsed by the National Education Association, the National Association of Chief State School Officers, the American Vocational Association, and the National Advisory Council on Vocational Education. Millions of dollars have already been spent by the U. S. Office of Education and state departments of education and many millions more have been committed.

Sidney P. Marland, Jr., U. S. Commissioner of Education, views career education as a major development necessitated by the failure of the general education curriculum which neither prepares a great majority of students for higher education or for a job.[2] To Commissioner Marland:

> The purpose of elementary and secondary education in the United States is to prepare all students as well-developed people to enter successfully either a job or some form of post-secondary education, whichever they choose, as soon as they leave the elementary-secondary education system.[3]

Most schools serve the needs of only a small part of their student body—the college bound. Marland states that in the 1970–71 school year ". . . there were 850,000 elementary and secondary school dropouts. There were 750,000 general education students who graduated from high school but who did not attend college and were not prepared for entering a job. There were 850,000 high school students who entered college (in 1967) but dropped out in 1970.''[4] These factors, coupled with the current economic conditions and high unemployment among high school and college graduates, account for much of the present emphasis on career education.

## ROLE OF CAREER EDUCATION IN THE CURRICULUM

Career education is viewed by its proponents as an all-encompassing curriculum concept. All educational experiences of all students, kindergarten through the college or university, should:

> . . . involve preparation for economic independence, personal fulfillment, and an appreciation for the dignity of work. It seeks to give meaning to all education by relating its content to the job world. Under career education, every student . . . should leave the school system with a salable skill—a minimum of an entry level job skill upon leaving at or before the end of high school or a more advanced skill if continuing his education in a technologically or academically oriented post-secondary institution.[5]*

It attempts to relate all learning and all academic areas to the many ways that adults live and earn their living. Career education attempts to make learning meaningful by relating it to the world of work. It would require that ''. . . every classroom teacher in every course at every level emphasize, where appropriate, the career implications of the substantive content he seeks to teach.''[6]

## CRUCIAL ISSUES

*First,* what are schools for? Is preparation for a job or for post-secondary education, as stated by Marland,[7] the only purpose of elementary and secondary education? If these

*From *Career Education: What It Is and How to Do It,* by K. B. Hoyt, et al. Copyright © 1972 by Olympus Publishing Company. This and all other quotes from this source reprinted by permission.

are the only purposes, would it be appropriate to consider schools in China or Cuba, or in many other countries for that matter, good examples of career education programs? The ''Fourth Annual Gallup Poll of Public Attitudes Toward Education''[8] provides some insight into parent's attitudes about the purposes of public education. The curriculum was cited as the area considered to be particularly good. While 44 per cent of those polled stated that the reason why they wanted their children to get an education was to get a better job, 43 per cent wanted their children to learn how to get along better with people at all levels of society.

When asked which educational programs should receive more attention at the elementary level, those polled listed skills of reading, writing, and arithmetic first, how to solve problems and think for themselves second, and vocational skills sixth. At the secondary level (grades 7–12) teaching students to respect law and authority ranked first, teaching students how to solve problems and think for themselves ranked second, and teaching vocational skills ranked third.

*Second,* in view of the issues raised above, is it reasonable to expect ''. . . every classroom teacher in every course at every level to emphasize, where appropriate, the career implications of the substantive content he seeks to teach,''[9] and also teach the many other things which are expected? One of the greatest problems of public education is the ''creeping,'' some would say ''galloping,'' curriculum. We are constantly *adding to* but seldom *taking from* the curriculum. Can the schools be all things to all people at all times?

*Third,* will work, as conceived by the promoters of career education, continue to be a value in our society? The task of predicting values becomes more and more difficult because of the rapid pace of change.[10] In the past values have changed so slowly that we expected each generation to be like the previous one. Values may now become obsolete within one's lifetime or less. To assume that a work ethic value will be necessary or even desirable for a large portion of society's members may be a mistake.

Is career education attempting to promote a value that now seems useful to the over-30 generation but already inappropriate for many of the under-30 generation? A recent study by Goodwin[11] suggests that this may already be happening, especially among white suburban teen-agers. Also, the present proposals for a permanent guaranteed annual income suggest, at least for a rather large segment of society, that a non-work ethic or life-style is possible.

*Fourth,* Hoyt states that: "Career education's goal is to make work possible, meaningful, and satisfactory to every individual, for the best measure of man is what he achieves and how he serves."[12] Is it realistic, possible, or even probable for a great post-industrial society like ours to have zero unemployment? Zero unemployment has never been a public goal of President Nixon's administration. Then, what about those who, for many reasons, cannot work? Goodwin[13] cites statistics from the government's Work Incentive Program (WIN) showing that of the 1.6 million welfare recipients eligible for training, only 10 per cent were deemed suitable. Is public education, by interlocking career education into the curriculum at every level, capable of achieving such a goal? If society comes to expect this of public education and the goal is not realized—like so many of those in the past—what will happen to the public's confidence in an institution which already has a rather serious credibility gap?

Is it possible to make work meaningful and satisfactory to every individual? The accounts of workers who are not satisfied with their jobs are more prevalent than those expressing job satisfaction. Faunce states that:

> The most persistent indictment of industrial society is that it has resulted in the alienation of industrial man. Loneliness in the midst of urban agglomeration; loss of social anchorage in mass society; the absence of a predictable life trajectory in an era of unprecedented social change; and the powerlessness of man within the complex social, economic, and political systems he has created are common themes in the social criticism of the industrial way of life. Concern with the alienated quality of existence is particularly widespread today. . . . However, alienation has been recognized and condemned as a product of industrialism almost from the time of the initial disruption of traditional ways during the Industrial Revolution.[14]

Can the schools, even with the widespread implementation of career education programs, be expected to reverse or erase such conditions? To many, education is supposed to reduce such social ills as crime, poverty, racism, prejudice, pollution, VD, and drug abuse. A look at recent movements—environmental education, Black studies, improvements in teaching of math and science—indicates that the schools have not been the initiator but have attempted to respond to the demand for some kind of action. The success in these endeavors has not been very good. In some cases failure is so obvious that schools are building a failure syndrome.

Few would argue that achievement is unimportant. Achievement or success has always been and continues to be a basic societal value. The problem arises in the way our society measures achievement. In the job market it is largely measured in terms of one's salary and position. In school it is measured in terms of grades, promotion to a higher grade, honors received, admission to a college, and scholarships received. Our schools and society accommodate everything but failure. An achievement oriented society tends to cause alienation and class differences. How does society measure a man who does not achieve—make passing grades, get a good job, make a good salary? Can career education deliver on such a goal?

*Fifth,* career education is supposed to be a part of all substantive content in the school curriculum. There is some evidence that at least in one area, social studies, this is not the case. *A Guide for Coordinated Vocational Academic Education (CVAE): Interlocking Procedures*[15] lists 26 activities for interlocking the academic curriculum with vocational education. In these activities social studies is mentioned in an incidental way in only three. In the interlocking activity "Dressmaking" the social studies class ". . . studied manners and good grooming, had a demonstration by a cosmetologist of proper use of makeup and hair care, and had a demonstration by a model of how to walk, sit, and stand." Is this "substantive content" appropriate for the social studies curriculum? An examination of current social studies literature does not support it.

Another example occurred in one workshop[16] designed to assist junior high teachers in designing activities for interlocking. No social studies teachers participated because they were told that: "Career education is not for social studies teachers."

*Sixth,* will career education be future oriented to the extent that it becomes more than a futile exercise in obsolescence? A fundamental problem with most vocational secondary programs and many Federally funded job training programs has been their inability to keep pace with rapidly changing job requirements. People have been trained with machines no longer used for jobs which no longer existed. Given the funding levels which seem to be realistically available to public education in the years ahead, is it possible to produce students who will have salable skills in the market place of the future?

Toffler, in describing the technological systems of tomorrow, states:

> . . . the most valued attributes of the industrial era become handicaps. The technology of tomorrow requires not millions of lightly lettered men ready to work in unison at endless repetitious jobs, it requires not men who take orders in unblinking fashion, aware that the price of bread is mechanical submission to authority, but men who can make critical judgments, who can weave their way through novel environments, who are quick to spot new relationships in the rapidly changing reality.[17]*

He then states that the kind of education system needed is one which will ". . . generate successive alternative images of the future—assumptions about the kinds of jobs, professions, and vocations that may be needed twenty to fifty years in the future. . . ."[18]

The emphasis of career education is on the present. It is largely concerned with existing jobs in a local community which provide "hands-on" experiences. Is it possible that students will find themselves not only trapped in careers which are not ". . . meaningful and satisfying . . ."[19] but also will they find that they have missed their opportunity to develop

the "cope-ability"[20] so necessary in the future?

*Seventh,* can the public schools, as presently structured, hope to adequately accommodate a curriculum concept so far-reaching as career education? Should career education even take place in the schools as they are now organized? Should it even be considered as a part of every course at every level of the curriculum? Since all learning does not and cannot take place within the school, is the world outside the school a more appropriate setting for career education?

Coleman lists several categories of skills which students should learn and suggests that schools are not responsible for all skills. He states that:

> Schools are prepared to do what they have done all along: teach young people intellectual things, both by giving them information and giving them intellectual tools, such as literacy, mathematics, and foreign languages. Schools are not prepared to teach these other skills— and the history of their attempts to change themselves so that they can do this shows only one thing: that these other activities—whether they are vocational education, driver training, consumer education, civics, home economics, or something else—have always played a secondary and subordinate role in schools, always in the shadow of academic performance. . . . all this means that they (schools) are destined to fail as educational institutions in areas other than teaching of intellectual skills.[21]

## CONCLUDING REMARKS

Career education's aim of revitalizing the work ethic in American society is an admirable one. The work ethic has and continues to play an important role, but the task of maintaining and even furthering this value has never rested with public education. The issues raised here, and there are others which could be added or substituted for some of those included, should be given serious consideration by all interested in public education. Can career education add relevance to the curriculum and help bring about a reorganization of education based on future needs of students and society? If so, it will certainly become a major development. If not, it will certainly be another educational fad which will soon fall by the wayside.

## REFERENCES

1. Kenneth B. Hoyt, *et al., Career Education: What It Is and How To Do It* (Salt Lake City, Utah: Olympus Publishing Co., 1972), p. 1.
2. Sidney P. Marland, Jr., "Career Education: Every Student Headed for a Goal," *American Vocational Journal,* 47:34–62, March, 1972.
3. *Ibid.,* p. 35.
4. *Ibid.,* p. 36.
5. Hoyt, *op. cit.,* p. 2.
6. *Ibid.,* p. 7.
7. For an in-depth examination of this question see: Robert L. Ebel, "What are Schools For?"; Joseph Junell, "The Limits of Social Education"; and Theodore Brameld, "Education as Self-Fulfilling Prophecy," *Phi Delta Kappan,* 54, September, 1972.
8. George H. Gallup, "Fourth Annual Gallup Poll of Public Attitudes Toward Education," *Phi Delta Kappan,* 54:33–46, September, 1972.
9. Hoyt, *op. cit.,* p. 7.
10. See, for example, Alvin Toffler's *Future Shock* (New York: Bantam Books, 1970).
11. Leonard Goodwin, "How Suburban Families View the Work Orientations of the Welfare Poor: Problems in Social Stratification and Social Policy," *Social Problems,* 19:337–348, Winter, 1972.
12. Hoyt, *op. cit.,* p. 4.
13. Goodwin, *op. cit.*
14. William A. Faunce, *Problems of An Industrial Society* (New York: McGraw-Hill Book Co., 1968), p. 84.
15. This guide was prepared by the Division of Vocational Education of the University of Georgia, 1970–71, under a grant from the Division of Vocational Education of the Georgia State Department of Education and the U. S. Office of Education.
16. I participated in three such workshops in Georgia during the Summer of 1972.
17. Toffler, *op. cit.,* pp. 402–403.
18. *Ibid.,* p. 403.
19. Hoyt, *op. cit.,* p. 1.
20. Toffler, *op. cit.,* p. 403.
21. James S. Coleman, "How Do the Young Become Adults," *Phi Delta Kappan,* 54:229, December, 1972.

## SUGGESTIONS FOR FURTHER READING

Call, J. D. Games babies play. *Psychology Today,* August 1970, pp. 34–37; 54. The games that infants and young children play are perceived as significant for emotional and cognitive development.

Caplan, F., & Caplan, T. *The power of play.* Garden City, N. Y.: Anchor Press-Doubleday, 1973. Play is interpreted as facilitating sound physical development, good family and social relations, healthy ego power, learning, and creativity.

Ellis, M. J. *Why people play.* Englewood Cliffs, N. J.: Prentice-Hall, 1973. Both classical and modern theories and issues about play are reviewed and criticized. Provocative suggestions are made relative to play at home, at school, and on the playground.

Fagot, B. I. Sex differences in toddlers' behavior and parental reaction. *Developmental Psychology,* 1974, *10,* 554–558. Toddler-age children and their parents were observed in their own homes while the children were at play in order to distinguish sex differences. In addition, comparisons were made between the parents' answers to a child-rearing questionnaire and the parents' observed behaviors toward their children.

Feitelson, D., & Ross, G. S. The neglected factor: Play. *Human Development,* 1973, *16,* 202–223. This study was designed to determine whether thematic play depends on modeling and whether the level of thematic play relates to performance on conventional creativity tests.

Fitzgerald, T. H. Career education: An error whose time has come. *School Review,* 1973, *82,* 91–105. Career education is portrayed as contrary to the best interests of the individual and to the basic purposes of education.

Friend, J. G. *Personal and vocational interplay in identity building: A longitudinal study.* Boston: Branden, 1973. This longitudinal study of 40 girls and women for the period of preadolescence through maturity focuses on the dynamics that define their work identities, their feelings of personal integration, and attitudes toward self as reflected in their occupational choice.

Halverson, P. M. Career development in the elementary school: A rationale. *Elementary School Journal,* 1974, *75,* 122–128. Certain questions are asked and propositions examined relative to career-development plans in the elementary school. Both the goals and content of career-education plans are examined in some detail, as is a pilot program for initiating them.

Holland, J. L. Vocational guidance for everyone. *Educational Researcher,* 1974, *3,* 9–15. Holland examines current practices in vocational guidance, debunks certain common notions on the topic, and suggests practical plans for making it effective.

Marland, S. P. Career education: For and against. *School Review,* 1973, *82,* 57–66. The Assistant Secretary for Health, Education, and Welfare discusses career education in terms of innovative approaches, curriculum materials, mini-models and future prospects.

Martinello, M. L. Playgrounds for learning. *Elementary School Journal,* 1973, *74,* 106–114. The concepts of play and leisure are treated in terms of their significance for education, the value of playgrounds, the nature of the games played there, and the significance of all of these for children's development.

Murphy, J. F. *Concepts of leisure: Philosophical implications.* Englewood Cliffs, N. J.: Prentice-Hall, 1974. Six basic concepts of leisure are discussed with regard to their dimensions and significance. The relationship between work and leisure is discussed with regard to the impact of work on the life of the individual in the American culture. The author also considers the impact of a work-leisure pattern of life in our postindustrialized society.

Nash, R. J., & Agne, R. M. Careers, education and work in the corporate state. *School Review,* 1973, *82,* 67–78. After stating the reasons that career education is encouraged as a revolution in American schools, the authors suggest ways that such education needs redirection.

Riley, S. S. Some reflections on the value of children's play. *Young Children,* 1973, *28,* 146–153. Aspects of play and work in the classroom are discussed, including various views on the subject. The concept of play is being made to fit respectably into the current preoccupation with academic achievement. The value of play is being reappraised as many are coming to recognize it as essential for normal child development.

Strom, R. Play and family development. *Elementary School Journal,* 1974, *74,* 359–368. The author describes how parents can teach their children through the uses of specially designed toys and the results obtained through this method.

# 18

## Children's Rights

One of the latest of the civil-rights movements to sweep the country concerns the welfare of children. Historically, societal rights have been limited to adults, and children have been subject to parents and other adult authorities (Worsfold, 1974). However, this concept is currently under fire. Sponsoring their cause have been numerous welfare groups and children's advocates, including lobbyists and lawyers (Children's Rights, 1974). And at least some children have come to perceive themselves as an oppressed minority. In one instance several children, aged 8 to 13, some of them already veterans of antiwar parades since the tender age of 4 or 5, picketed a ten-cent store that barred minors except when accompanied by an adult because of increasing rowdiness and shoplifting (Children's Rights, 1974).

## MAJOR ISSUES INVOLVED

Children's rights are of special concern in school, which they are compelled, willy-nilly, to attend. Matters of suspension, too, are coming under fire; and courts are increasingly defending children's rights to a hearing (Children's Rights, 1974). Evaluation practices, too, arouse ire, especially from minority groups. They argue that testing instruments are biased in favor of the white middle class, and they protest the use of test results to place children in particular tracks or programs. Tracking, or ability grouping, involves placing children in classes or groups according to intelligence-and aptitude-test scores. To adopt such plans, critics claim, is to limit the child's educational opportunities and the development of his or her potential. Such practices, asserts Mercer (1974), violate the child's right to be evaluated with "a culturally appropriate normative framework." Many educators have wrongly assumed that there is just one normal curve, and that this single distribution can be used to classify all children regardless of their cultural background. Besides, such practices deny the child's right to be treated as a multidimensional human being (Mercer, 1974). That is, a child has a right to be evaluated as one who plays many roles. A child may do poorly at school, for example, but adapt effectively elsewhere.

Another fight concerns school files which contain potentially damaging medical and psychological data about children (Children's Rights, 1974). The advent of computerized data banks is a potential threat to children's privacy. A spokesman for a legal defense fund cited a children's program where psychologists, teachers, and other "instant experts" put undesirable labels on students, choosing from a list of computer-code characterizations such as sex deviate or paranoid. Presumably such information was to be sorted in a data bank to help government agencies looking for ways to aid children. True, "only certain officials are supposed to see the reports. But the codes can be cracked, and the information is practically useless compared to the danger of its falling into the wrong hands. A [child] could be branded for life because a teacher thought he acted sort of weird back when he was seven years old'' (p. 44).* Questions are also being raised about common practices of giving pupils psychological tests and asking them personal questions about their family lives in order to determine which children might become drug abusers or delinquents. As a result of such abuses, a Congressional committee has approved laws to make confidential records available for inspection at the demand of parents and children above a certain age. They could challenge their contents at a hearing and prohibit their distribution to credit bureaus, prospective employers, and law enforcement officials.

Another subject of controversy, corporal punishment, is rapidly becoming a thing of the past. Nevertheless, the practice still varies a great deal from place to place. Austin, Texas, recently reinstated corporal punishment; however, at least three states forbid any such punishment of school children at all (Children's Rights, 1974). Some states simply forbid certain kinds of corporal punishment: in Nevada, for example, a child is not to be struck on the head.

Questions are being raised, too, about placing youngsters in special schools for the retarded or in slow classes. A San Francisco high school graduate made headlines by filing an educational malpractice suit demanding a million dollars from the school system for failure to teach him to read properly (Children's Rights, 1974).

Another issue concerns the censorship of what children see on television or in films, or what they read in textbooks or paperback books. The Supreme Court has ruled that state legislatures and local councils may restrict obscene materials if the rules followed are consistent with community standards. Even more controversial is the question of censoring children's textbooks because of presumably objectionable language or unfair treatment of minorities or females. According to Professor David Davis of the University of Wisconsin, the First Amendment should guarantee children's rights to read all kinds of literature with-

out any government restrictions (Blue, 1973).

Children are simply overwhelmed by too much ''guidance,'' according to some critics. Ronald A. Erickson, professor of education at the University of Chicago, calls upon the states to abandon their role as children's super-parents, dictating every detail of their lives. It is impossible to reconcile the nation's basic democratic principles with the state's role as super-parent. Instead, education should become a ''regulated open market,'' with modes of child rearing left unspecified and alternate life-styles respected. Within a framework of more freedom, ''we would seldom encounter examples, as we often do today, of potential Chopins who must leave their pianos to participate in what is for them an inane classroom discussion of baroque music, of Olympic skating champions whose high school graduation diplomas are held up for lack of physical education credits, and of many other children who could learn inestimably more of what is important and useful to them in settings that the law now makes generally inaccessible during the prolonged period of compulsory school attendance'' (Erickson, 1974, p. 414).

Parents' rights to practically supreme power over their children are also being questioned. Burt (1972) calls attention to ''the hallowed status'' of parent-child relationships and common abuses of parental authority (p. 96). Consider, for example, the involuntary institutionalization of mentally retarded or disturbed children. Some parents are claimed to use this means of getting rid of children who, for any reason, have become a burden. Parents may also deprive children of medical treatment, despite expert opinion that it is needed (Tucker, 1974). Where they are too young or uncomprehending to seek proper medical aid themselves, they should be represented by some advocate. Above all, children should be protected against parental abuse, either physical or psychological.

Indeed, children may require protection against even well-meaning adults. However, adults do not always fully understand children's interests. Nor are the child's interests always synonymous with those of their parents or guardians. It might serve the parents' needs to rely on grandmother as a babysitter; how-

*From ''Drive for the Rights of Children,'' *U. S. News and World Report,* August 5, 1974. Copyright 1974. Reprinted by permission.

ever, the grandmother might seriously over-protect the child. Hence, at the very minimum, children should be consulted about their wishes and aims. Such wishes, along with other information, should be weighed, the more heavily as the child becomes older. Overall, if we recognize the principles of children's rights, we automatically make adults more accountable concerning children.

Various bills of rights have been proposed for children—for example, Judge Lois Forer's proposal in the following article. In addition to such fundamental rights as those mentioned by Judge Forer, Thomas (1974) suggests that a child have these rights: to be involved in making decisions that affect his or her daily life; to live under a single system of rules and regulations; to know in advance what disciplinary actions will follow certain forms of misconduct; to appeal decisions having major impact on the child's life; to be disciplined by those who know the child best; to be rewarded in meaningful ways; and to grow through experimentation even if it involves trespassing certain rules.

## STATUS OF SITUATION

A certain amount of progress is being made on children's behalf. Increasingly, adults who abuse their children are being brought to court and sometimes convicted. Various assumptions about parents' legal authority over their children are being challenged—for example, regarding the custody of children in divorce cases. In certain localities, children may not be suspended from school without a hearing. Children or their parents may, in some states, be permitted to see school records upon request. Moreover, the very fact that various organizations have become concerned about children's rights is creating a more general awareness that their rights should be examined.

Nevertheless, this whole area will probably remain controversial, and many questions defy ready answers. How can one be sure that children's advocates know what is best for children? Perhaps more traditional ways of dealing with children are better simply because they have been tested by time. Suppose that courts be required to hear the child's own views: how can judges be sure that the child is not simply the mouthpiece for some adult who is using the child for his or her own ends? How can a proper balance be struck between the rights of children as humans and the need to protect them against their own ignorance and immaturity? To arrive at reasonable answers to these questions, a great deal of wisdom will be required. According to Paul Goodman (1971), all of us at all ages "must use and enjoy one another, and are likely to abuse and injure one another. This situation is not something to cope with polemically or to understand in terms of freedom, democracy, rights and power, like bringing lawyers into a family quarrel. It has to be solved by wise traditions in organic communities with considerable stability, with equity instead of law, and with love and compassion more than either" (p. 1).

As suggested in the foregoing, there are many views regarding children's rights. We find an interesting comparison of such views in the selections that follow, the first by Lois Forer and the second by Richard Farson. Their views do not conflict; rather, they complement and supplement each other.

## REFERENCES

Blue, R. Pupils' rights and the paper invasion. *Elementary School Journal*, 1973, *74*(1), 2–8.

Burt, R. A. Protecting children from their families and themselves: State laws and the constitution. *Journal of Youth and Adolescence*, 1972, *1*, 91–111.

Drive for the rights of children. *U. S. News and World Report*, Aug. 5, 1974, pp. 42–44.

Erickson, R. A. In States as "super-parents" of school children. *Intellect*, 1974, *102*(2357), 414.

Goldman, S. Children's rights. *Ms.*, Oct. 1973, p. 116.

Goodman, P. Introduction. In Paul Adams, et al., *Children's rights*. New York: Praeger, 1971.

Mercer, J. R. A policy statement on assessment procedures and the rights of children. *Harvard Educational Review*, 1974, *44*, 125–141.

Thomas, G. Children in institutions. *Children Today*, 1974, *3*(2), 34–35.

Tucker, Y. Y. The child within. *Ms.*, September 1974, p. 70.

Worsfold, V. L. A philosophical justification of children's rights. *Harvard Educational Review*, 1974, *44*, 142–157.

# The Rights of Children

## Lois Forer

I am delighted to have the opportunity to discuss the problems of the child and the law with those responsible for the education of young children. We have assumed that adults spoke for children, protected them, provided for them and disciplined them. If the system failed in any way, then the adults would take action. A child, in the words of the court, had "no right to liberty, only to custody." Even the word "custody" has a nonhuman connotation. The law defines custody as "the care or keeping of anything."

We know that simply the keeping of a child in a home or a classroom is not enough. We have been warehousing children in institutions (including schools) long enough. It is time to look at children as persons—individuals with rights, dignities, needs and separate individualities.

In considering this important area of the rights of children, educators, physicians and interested citizens often look to the lawyer in vain.

"What are the rights of children? What is the law?" These questions are being asked by nonlawyers with increasing frequency.

## WHAT LAW?

The lawyer who is asked this question may well reply, "What law?" It is an anomalous and incredible fact that there is very little case and statutory law setting forth the rights of

Reprinted by permission from *Young Children*, Vol. XXVII, No. 6. © 1972, National Association for the Education of Young Children, 1834 Connecticut Avenue, N. W., Washington, D. C. 20009.

Lois G. Forer is Judge, Court of Common Pleas, Philadelphia, Pa., author of *No One Will Lissen: How Our Legal System Brutalizes the Youthful Poor*, John Day Co., 1970, paperback, Grosset & Dunlap; *The Death of the Law*, David McKay, 1975.

children. Although the United States Supreme Court passes on some 2,500 cases a year and decides on the merits of approximately 400 cases a year, it was not until 177 years after the founding of this nation that the court ruled on a case raising the constitutional rights of a child. The much discussed *Gault* case (337 U.S. 1), which was decided the following year, 1967, was limited to four procedural points in delinquency hearings in juvenile court. Even these rulings are hedged with limitations. The decision did, however, signal a radical change in jurisprudential theory. Contrary to the prior state cases and the views of the many authorities on the juvenile court, the *Gault* decision indicates that children do have some constitutional rights. The extent and limits of those rights have not been clarified.

Thoughtful persons who deal with the minds and bodies of children are deeply disturbed by many difficult and sensitive decisions affecting the lives of children that they are required to make, and they seek legal guidance. There are few clear legal answers to their questions. To date the legal profession appears to be oblivious of the vast unchartered area of legal problems involving the lives of children.

It is interesting to speculate on the reasons for this legal vacuum. Almost half of all Americans are under the age of 21. In our highly structured, complex society, many agencies of government take actions affecting children's lives, often with drastic results. Yet there are few cases challenging such actions or alleging that the constitutional rights of the child have been infringed. Other issues of limited importance and involving comparatively few people have been before the courts again and again and have been the subjects of exhaustive scholarship.

Probably there are many psychological and sociological reasons for the law's neglect of the rights of children. In America's youth-oriented society, adults may have ambivalent feelings toward children. Today a child is an economic liability. He is no longer a source of cheap or unpaid labor on the farm or in the family business. Few parents can look forward to being supported by their children in old age. Campus unrest and the growing juvenile delinquency rate provokes cries of "Get tough!" Such conditions do not give rise to a concern for the rights of young people.

A simpler explanation for the scarcity of law involving the rights of children is the fact that very few children have been represented by counsel. Most of the children in institutions, whether for the delinquent, the neglected or the mentally ill, are indigent. Prior to the *Gault* decision, it was considered inappropriate, if not unauthorized, for counsel to appear in juvenile delinquency proceedings. Conferences are held on the subject, "What is the role of a lawyer in Juvenile Court?" There is still the subconscious assumption that a lawyer should not function like a lawyer in Juvenile Court. In innumerable other situations in which children's welfare and liberty are involved, there is no requirement that the matter be judicially determined or that children have counsel. In many proceedings affecting the lives of children, they are not now represented by counsel—for example, neglect and dependency cases which may result in the child being institutionalized. The battered baby has no one to speak for him while the parents or foster parents who have abused him are represented by counsel, often at public expense. No provision is made to furnish lawyers for these children. Without counsel, there are seldom appeals or written opinions that would form the basic materials for legal scholarship. Consequently, there is little research or analysis of these problems.

The principal legislation governing children is the Juvenile Court Act. Every state has by statute established a special court to handle cases of neglect, dependent and delinquent children. The primary purpose of such legislation and the principal activity of these courts is the processing of children whose behavior is disruptive to the community, the schools or their families. With minor variations these acts create courts with broad powers and loose procedures. Nowhere in the standard juvenile court law or the new Model Juvenile Court Act are there any specifications of the rights of a child or the procedures that he may invoke for his protection or to obtain redress for wrongs done to him. These wrongs may be mistreat-ment by parents or custodians, the school system, the police, the welfare department, or others. The laws governing the treatment of animals are more specific than those with respect to children.

## A BLANK SLATE IS AT LEAST A CLEAN SLATE

Since there is so little precedent, we are in the unusual position of being able to consider what the law ought to be. Social reformers often engage in Utopian speculations about restructuring society, the family or government. Lawyers frequently err in the other extreme by presenting a legislative package that deals with specific abuses but fails to consider basic injustices structured in the larger system. This paper tries to avoid both pitfalls. Although urging those concerned with the problem of children to give their attention to the wide range of legal issues involving the rights of minors, it seeks primarily to ask questions, explore concepts and suggest avenues of inquiry.

Legal rights do not exist separate and apart from daily life. Constitutional and statutory guarantees are meaningful only if they protect the individual from real hazards. If lawyers, courts and legislatures are to devise substantive and procedural laws to guarantee and implement the rights of children today, they will need factual information with respect to life as it is actually lived in the inner cities, in the affluent suburbs, in small towns and rural areas. They must put aside preconceived notions of childhood innocence, Biblical ideas of filial devotion, the ethic of hard work and frugality. They must examine reality, unpleasant and shocking though it may be. They must learn how such institutions as schools, reformatories, juvenile courts and hospital clinics actually function, not simply read the reports of statistics and goals. They must study the lives of America's children as they are lived day by day in the family, in school and on the streets. This is not a task for lawyers alone. It requires the *expertise* of many disciplines—especially the teachers who know the child and his needs, who see him meeting challenges, succeeding, failing, dropping out.

## DON'T ASK A LAWYER "WHO IS A CHILD?"

Perhaps the first inquiry should be to determine who is a child. At present there is no clear answer. One might say that under the law anyone who is not an adult is a child. But this reply is deceptively simple. A quick glance at the pertinent statutes reveals a patchwork of inconsistent, anomalous and conflicting age levels.

If the child, at whatever age, is denied full legal rights, then what duties of protection does society owe to him? Concepts of right develop imperceptibly, without scientific proof, technical argument or documentation. When the time is ripe, a declaration is made that certain rights, not heretofore formulated in law, are inalienable, inherent or self-evident. And society grudgingly concedes that such is the fact. Freedom from want, for example, is a peculiarly twentieth century notion. It is hard to think of another time in history when society would have recognized a right to sustenance on the part of the individual and a correlative obligation on the part of government to support the citizenry. Perhaps we are now ready to recognize that there are certain human rights which all children have and certain corresponding obligations on the part of society to implement those rights.

## FOUR RIGHTS ARE INHERENT IN ALL CHILDREN

I suggest that in formulating a juvenile jurisprudence there are four basic rights which the law should recognize as inherent in all children; i.e. (1) the right to life, (2) the right to a home, (3) the right to an education and (4) the right to liberty.

Liberty is the only one of these postulated rights that the courts have considered even indirectly. The decisions are fragmentary and based upon inexact analogies to the criminal law. They turn on due process questions of the procedures by which a child is institutionalized, but skirt the fundamental issue of the right of the state to deprive a child of his liberty under

circumstances in which an adult could not be removed from society. Children are deprived of liberty in our complex contemporary world for many reasons. Alleged delinquency is only one. A child may be removed from his home, immured and isolated from society and deprived of an education because he is mentally retarded, emotionally disturbed, nonconforming, difficult, refuses to attend school or perhaps is just unloved or unlovable. These are the majority of children whom the state places in institutions.

The emerging doctrine of right to treatment is an indirect and perhaps clumsy judicial attempt to mitigate the harshness of depriving the noncriminal person of his liberty. Significantly, the seminal cases involve adults, not children, although vastly larger numbers of children are placed in institutions.

The perplexing problem of what to do with these difficult children, who are often sloughed off on the state by their parents, should be considered in the context of the child's right to freedom. Legality of the commitment would then be the issue—not the procedures by which he was committed or the quantum of care that he receives or the existence of institutional peonage. These are inexact and difficult facts to prove and really peripheral to the question of whether the child (or adult) must be incarcerated to protect society or to save his own life.

## THE RIGHT TO LIFE IS SELF-EVIDENT

The right to life seems self-evident. I am not discussing abortion. But once an infant is born, it should be clear that no one has a legal right to take its life. In 1972, we would be shocked at the thought that a parent would be permitted to kill his child. We would also reject the notion that a parent has the right to maim or deform his child.

The parent who fails or refuses to provide medical care for his child may be little different from these other parents whose conduct shocks the contemporary American conscience. Natural parents, foster parents and institutions in which children are housed frequently fail to provide necessary medical care and treatment. Often the young infant is literally starved to death. It is not only infants who are denied care. Older children are equally at the mercy of adults with respect to obtaining medical care. Few children are able to consult a physician on their own. Parental consent is required for hospital treatment and perhaps for psychiatric care even when a teenager has money of his own and voluntarily seeks help.

There is little statutory law governing health care for children. Medical treatment is not yet a recognized constitutional right. Although the government does provide some free clinics and the law prescribes certain entitlements under aid to dependent children programs, there are few procedures by which a child may claim these benefits for himself. If medical treatment or surgery is necessary to save the life of a child, most courts will order that such treatment be provided irrespective of the wishes of the parent. These cases usually arise when a child is already in a hospital and the parent refuses to give consent to a blood transfusion or surgery. The cases of battered or abused children require much thought. Society simply ignores this problem though, of course, many teachers are certain that their pupils are mistreated—and the numbers are incredible. It is estimated that there are from 500,000 to 2,500,000 of these children each year in the United States. Often these children are denied necessary medical care because society will not pay for it. Children are put out of hospitals too soon because the hospital cannot afford to maintain such nonpaying patients. They are placed in foster homes because these are cheaper than hospitals, although the foster parents cannot provide the care which these very sick babies require. Medical care in public institutions for children is often deplorable.

There are many other situations, not life or death emergencies, but very serious illnesses, in which a child is denied medical care because of the ignorance, poverty or neglect of parents or guardians. Although few statistics are available with respect to the incidence of childhood illness as related to the economic status of the family, it is undoubtedly true that there is more preventable and curable illness among children of poor families than of middle-class and well-to-do families. The law fails to provide a structure by which these children can obtain necessary treatment and care. Unless a child is actually committed to a mental hospital or a correctional institution, the juvenile courts do not order medical treatment. Thus a child who is delinquent (criminal) may receive some treatment, whereas a child who is discharged (acquitted) will not receive any medical care unless it is voluntarily provided by his family.

Twenty years ago Medicare for the aged sounded improbable and visionary. Today it is a fact. Some system of financing medical care for the poor children in America is a necessity. The poor child may be physically crippled by accident or disease or mentally stunted by malnutrition. The right to life should include a structure by which medical care to cure and prevent such conditions is available and a legal mechanism to protect children from abuse.

The right of a child to have a home would appear to be self-evident to most Americans. In the United States, children are not permitted to sleep in the streets, on vacant lots or park benches. If there is no other place for a child without family or friends, he will be put in a detention center until some place can be found for him.

## HOMES FOR THE FRIENDLESS

No one believes that a child, if he is incapable of caring for himself or if he does not have a safe dwelling, should be permitted to roam the streets and forage for himself. Society must provide a home for him. In the nineteenth century, orphan asylums were a popular form of charity. They were indeed an improvement over the workhouse and the indenturing or apprenticing of orphans who had to work for their keep. The *de facto* orphan, the child who has a parent but no home, is a commonplace. Often a parent refuses to provide for his child. "You take him, Judge. I can't do nothin' with him," says the mother or father. Very few judges will compel an unwilling parent to care for his child. If the parent does not want him, the child will be sent to an institution even though he has not committed any crime.

The institutions in which such adolescents are placed have all the characteristics of a jail. A detention center is not a hotel or boarding school. The children may not leave. They are locked behind bars or walls. They cannot attend public school. They have none of the pleasures of life. In the United States today a child who is deprived of a home is also deprived of his liberty. Little thought is given to the critical need for nonpenal shelters for such children. It would cost less to provide boarding schools than jails. Both the right to a home and the right to liberty are violated when unfortunate noncriminal children and youths are held in detention. There have been few legal challenges to this common and deplorable practice.

## THE INVERSE OF AN OLD LAW

The right to an education is basic. It is really the inverse of an old law. For more than half a century, America has had compulsory school attendance statutes. If a child refuses to go to school, his parents can be fined and he can be sent to jail. In twentieth century America there is no place for functional illiterates. Thus, although the law requires the child to attend school, it seldom requires the school to educate him nor does it explicitly give the child a right to attend school. We are all familiar with the school dropout. But the pushout—the child put out of school—is an equally serious problem.

Compulsory school attendance laws operate like a penal sentence. They prescribe the number of hours, days and years a child must spend in school. When he has served his time, he is released regardless of his skills, or lack of them. Often the most ignorant are permitted to leave school early and are encouraged to drop out at or before legal school-leaving age. Possibly a different type of attendance law should be drafted, one that makes legal school leaving dependent upon skills rather than time served. If a child is functionally literate, reasonably well informed and employable at age 16, why must he remain in school another year if he prefers to get a job? Conversely, just because he is 17, should he be permitted to leave if he cannot read or function in the adult world?

Children are often excluded from the public schools because they are disruptive. Many of these children are not "bad" or delinquent. At age eight how bad can a child be? Whether one agrees with Skinner or Rousseau, we reject the notion of the bad seed. Children can be helped. Often they are made antisocial and hostile by their treatment in school. Undoubtedly, many of these boys and girls are difficult to manage in classes of 25 to 35 pupils. Consequently, brain-damaged, emotionally disturbed and nonconforming children are pushed out of the school system. Whether these children have a legal or possibly a constitutional right to attend school is unclear. Since most of the children who have been excluded from public school are too poor to afford to retain counsel, this question has not been litigated.

The law has largely ignored the rights of the child vis-à-vis the school system, except for cases on haircuts and discipline, and these generally involve the well-to-do suburban child. Again the few reported cases turn on procedural points adopted by analogy from administrative law—the right to a hearing and the right to counsel. While such aspects of due process are important, they are of relative insignificance if the child has no substantive right to attend school. The unresolved and largely unformulated question I would pose as follows: "Does every child have a right to elementary and secondary education suitable to his physical, intellectual and emotional needs at public expense?" And I urge you to make your community give an affirmative answer to this question.

It is obvious that some children, because of physical handicaps, severe mental retardation or emotional disturbance cannot function in a regular school program. There are also many normal children who are simply putting in time at school but not learning. They are being deprived of an education as surely as the child who is excluded from the classroom. Neither the educational bureaucracy nor the lawyers have faced the question of the rights and remedies of these pupils. In some communities special public schools have been established for the retarded, the emotionally disturbed, pregnant girls and those who want to drop out of the standard classroom program. Many of these are very successful. We need more of them.

I should like to mention briefly the question of freedom of choice in education. Certainly it should be the right of parents to provide forms of education for their children other than the public schools if they wish to do so, meet state standards and pay for it. These schools often provide experimentation that is useful and may become a model for the public schools. But the base of elementary and secondary education in America has been the public schools.

Today there are many proposals which, if effectuated, would not merely erode but destroy the public schools. One such program is the voucher plan which would give the parents a sum equivalent to the cost of maintaining a child in the public school and let him use it to purchase private education. In theory some believe that under this plan the poor child will have equal opportunity with the rich to have freedom of choice in attending a nonpublic school. However, there are not enough private schools to accept all these children. Few private schools will accept difficult, culturally deprived or academically untalented children. Private school fees are often higher than public expenditures per child. Few poor parents have the time or skills to establish and operate their own schools. The result will be again a public subsidy of the middle class and an impoverishment of the poor with a resultant loss in the quality and character of public education.

The public schools could, however, offer a freedom of choice to the student by operating different kinds of schools. They could have traditional schools, Montessori-type schools, English-type open classrooms and a wide variety of programs so that the parents could with the help of guidance counsellors and teachers choose the school best suited to the needs of the child. There are many possibilities and great opportunities with the help of federal and state monies to try newer and better ways of educating our children in these difficult and restless times.

We know that we must do better in all areas of life in America. We know that the rising demand among suppressed people all over the world—colonials, blacks, women—will impel change either peacefully or, if we resist necessary improvements, by force. Children are also a suppressed group. Children are demanding a place and a voice in the larger soci-

ety. A group of high school students in Philadelphia, for example, intends to sue for student representation on the school board.

We cannot wait for these problems to be resolved piecemeal in 51 different jurisdictions by the aleatory processes of litigation. More direct and speedy remedies are required. Lawyers and teachers, in cooperation with doctors and sociologists, must devise statutes, rules, regulations and government institutions to formulate and enforce the rights of American children.

Young people today are restless and impatient. They have little faith that the customary legal processes will solve their problems. Neither appeals to belief in law and order and the democratic way nor threats of repressive measures will quiet them. Society will either recognize now the rights of the young and the obligations of government to provide a decent environment, meaningful education and an opportunity to live a healthy, free life to every child, or it will have to provide jails and mental institutions later. The price of delay may be far greater than the cost of action.

# Birthrights

## Richard Farson

There is no way to have a liberated society until we have liberated our children. And right now our society is organized against them. The ideal child is cute (entertaining to adults), well-behaved (doesn't bother adults), and bright (capable of bringing home report cards the parents can be proud of). Efforts of parents

Reprinted with permission of Macmillan Publishing Co., Inc., from "Birthrights," by Richard Farson. *MS. Magazine*, March 1974, *11*(9), 66–67ff. Copyright © 1974 by Richard Farson.

to produce these traits have so inhibited children that neither adults nor children can always see the remarkable potentialities that lie beyond or outside them. Because we have become increasingly alert to the many forms of oppression in our society, we are now seeing, as we have not seen before, the predicament of children: they are powerless, dominated, ignored, invisible. We are beginning to see the necessity for children's liberation.

People are not liberated one by one. They must be liberated as a class. Liberating children, giving them equality and guaranteeing their civil rights, may seem to violate the fairly recent realizations that children are not simply miniature adults, and that childhood is a special time of life, with special qualities and problems. In fact, never before in history have parents and teachers had so much "understanding" of children, or at least of their physical and social development. But the "understanding" has led not to improved conditions for children, but simply to more control of them and consequently more burdensome responsibilities of supervision for parents. So that now the best things that happen between parent and child happen by accident or by surprise, very often breaking all rules in the process. Actually, anyone who isn't bewildered by child-rearing, who doesn't find it an extremely formidable and trying experience, probably has never lived with children.

Moreover, increased understanding and concern has not been coupled with increased rights. As a consequence, children's rights have actually diminished, for we have simply replaced ignorant domination with sophisticated domination. With increased attention to children has come resentment. Our efforts to shape children, to reform them, to fix them, to correct them, to discipline them, to educate them, have led to an obsession with the physical, moral and sexual problems of children; but they have not led to our liking them more, or realizing their potential.

By holding a limited and demeaned view of children and by segregating them almost completely from the adult world, we may be subverting their capacity for genius. It has been pointed out that we no longer have infant and child prodigies—or at least that they are now much rarer than before. In the past, when children were an integral part of the community, they sometimes did show great genius. By the age of 17 months, for example, Louis XIII played the violin. He played tennis when he still slept in a cradle. He was an archer, and played cards and chess, at six. Today we might worry a bit about precocity of that magnitude, but then, people took it for granted. One wonders whether we have sacrificed genius for homogeneity and conformity.

The nuclear family (two adults and their minor children), a completely self-contained unit, not dependent upon the community, is a relatively new development. Child care once was distributed among several adults in an extended family; now it falls entirely on the parent or parents. The children do little for the family, and almost nothing for each other or themselves. Overburdened parents feel an increasing sense of both responsibility and guilt as society's expectations of what families should offer their children rise—and yet the community spends less of its money and energy on aid of children or parents.

Though technically the law no longer regards them as chattels, children are still treated as the private property of their parents. The parent has both the right and the responsibility to control the life of the child.

It will take quite a revolution in our thinking to give some of this control back to the child. Nevertheless, the acceptance of the child's right to self-determination is fundamental. It is the right to a single standard of morals and behavior for children and adults, including behavior decisions close to home. From the earliest signs of competence, children might have, for example, the right to decide for themselves about eating, sleeping, playing, listening, reading, washing, and dressing; the freedom to choose their associates, to decide what life goals they wish to pursue.

Parents may argue that the right to self-determination will bring with it the risk of physical and psychological damage. No doubt some risks are involved. But under present conditions, many children are severely damaged—physically, socially, and emotionally.

Compared to the existing system, the risks of harming children by accepting their right to self-determination may be greatly over-rated. Impossible as it seems, it may be that the situations we try hardest to avoid for ourselves and for our children would be actually the most beneficial to us. One can make a good case for a calamity theory of growth—many of our most eminent people, for instance, have come from the most calamitous early childhood situations. Of course, we don't want calamities to happen to our children, but we can be a bit more relaxed about our protectiveness.

In any event, it's time to admit that no one knows how to grow people.

Since most concerns center on the problems of living with a self-determining child, our first thoughts focus on the home. While liberation cannot be truly accomplished at home—because the home is not separate from the rest of society—the situation illustrates in microcosm the dimensions of the problem as it might exist in society at large.

Take, for example, family mealtimes. No one should be expected to prepare a meal at a special time for children simply because they choose not to eat at the regular hour. However, most children could, with some special arrangement and training, prepare meals for themselves when necessary. Those children whose schedules demand special timetables would receive the same consideration afforded any adult member of the household in similar circumstances—but no more.

Loss of authority over a child in areas such as nutrition does not mean that the child cannot be influenced. In the absence of adult tyranny, adult judgment and information have to be the primary influence and are more likely to be accepted.

Bedtime is a case in point. Most parents know that children enjoy sleeping as much as adults do. Resistance to it comes largely from adult pressures. Because adults' sleeping habits are governed largely by the pressures to engage in productive activity during the daytime hours, we adhere to nighttime sleeping hours. Children, too, must follow daytime hours to fulfill their compulsory attendance in school.

If children came to these conclusions for themselves, by suffering the consequences, they would be capable in the long run of learning, as most adults have, that when we are too tired we pay for it the next day. This would make the ritual of going to bed less of a vehicle through which adults and children express their mutual antagonisms. Believe it or not, bedtime is not a big issue in some homes. Children either go to bed by themselves or they are simply covered up on the spot where they drop off to sleep.

What about other physical dangers, such as children playing where they might injure themselves? The first answer is that of course we cannot risk a child's death. Just as we would pull an adult out of the path of an onrushing car, we would do the same for a child. There is no double standard in an emergency situation.

In fact children are equally concerned about safety—their own and their parents'. They try, for example, to keep their parents from chain-smoking, drinking too much, getting too fat, driving dangerously, or working too hard. While they are seldom successful at this, the point is to recognize the concern and responsibility as mutual.

Life is inevitably risky and almost everyone agrees that it is important that children be given the opportunity to take risks in order to develop, to push their limits, to discover their potential. What we fail to realize is that most of the dangers that children face are "man-made" and that, not recognizing what we've done to ourselves, we've accepted the responsibility to protect our children, by constant supervision, from dangers we've created—backyard pools, electrical sockets, poisons under the sink, and speeding automobiles. Unlike man-made dangers, natural dangers like cliffs and crashing waves usually signal their own warning.

Most sports involve some physical risks, but children *do* climb trees even if falling might hurt them; they ride horses, take gymnastics, and engage in other athletics.

Of course, the elimination of all danger in our society is certainly not a realistic nor desirable goal, but we will have come a long way in making the world safer for children if we can solve the problem of the automobile—the Number One enemy of children. Besides creating a situation requiring constant supervision, automobiles have actually decreased the mobility of children while increasing the mobility of adults. This problem is one of social design, and its solution will require some difficult choices for us in city planning, and the utilization of financial resources. We must build cities with children in mind, and devise transportation systems that work for them. It means reducing our use of and reliance on the automobile. It means reorienting our work, play, family life, and commercial activities so that they are all close to each other, which would have the additional benefit of developing stronger communities, more interpersonal activity and greater involvement.

We must find ways of protecting children as best we can from the lethal dangers, where the first lesson is the last one. In our well-meaning protective attitude, however, we must not include the idea that it is our right to have children and to raise them as we see fit. The 1970 White House Conference on Children held that the rights of parents cannot infringe upon the rights of children, and all of us may soon come to the conclusion that the ability to conceive a child gives no one the right to dominate or to abuse her or him. The decisions about a child's home environment should not belong to the parents alone. Parents will have more responsibility than they have authority. They will have to depend more heavily on judgment, advice, and persuasion.

Given the fact that child-rearing practices differ widely from country to country, it is hard to pinpoint a parent's responsibilities and a child's needs. In some cultures children are wrapped tightly, in others they are always naked; some children have close ties with their father, some do not even know their father; some are exposed to the elements as a test of maturity, some are held and fondled almost constantly.

Despite this diversity, there are certain widely shared, if debatable, views of basic needs. Children need loving care as newborns and in early infancy. They need, for what we would call normal physical growth, certain nutritive elements. For their minds to develop they need stimulation and variation. And as children grow older they need to be with adults with whom they can identify. Despite current convention, however, none of these so-called basics justifies the nuclear family as the only model of family life.

Parenting in the nuclear family is difficult, demanding, restrictive, and expensive. Having children is unbelievably burdensome. It is not just the battered children who grow up in oppressive circumstances, but to some degree *all* children. The degrees of oppression vary, but one kind is universal: that children have no alternative but to live with their parents or be housed by the government in some jail-like alternative. Even when family life is delightful, the child should have other options.

Furthermore, the truth is that more than 60 percent of Americans live in domestic arrangements other than the nuclear family: single people with or without children, married people without children or with stepchildren, couples with grown children, homosexual couples or groups, elderly people living in nursing homes, convicts in prisons, students in residence halls, children living with one parent or in institutions, communal arrangements, and so forth.

Ignoring this reality, we persist in glorifying the nuclear family instead of exploring alternate living arrangements into which the child may fit just as well—or better.

One of the few well-known alternatives which honors the child's right to self-determination is A. S. Neill's Summerhill, an English residential school where the freedom and equality of children is of paramount concern and the children's participation in the government of the institution is fundamental to its operation.

Multiple parenting is the core concept of other alternatives now in practice. It means several adults share child-rearing responsibilities through community efforts.

In this country child-care arrangements for "normal" kids present a terrible financial burden, usually to the parent, whereas the state pays for all those incarcerated in reform schools and prisons and the 200,000 children in foster-care programs. The approximately $12,000 a year it costs the state to keep one child in an institution should certainly be enough to pay for many different kinds of state-supported institutions which are not prisons, but offer realistic placement options for those children in most serious difficulty at home.

People who want alternative living arrangements need thoughtfully designed programs which (1) place more choice in the hands of the child, (2) redistribute the costs so that neither the state nor the parents suffer the total burden, (3) make use of previously unused resources, including laypeople and paraprofessionals, teenagers, or retired people, and (4) provide a variety of arrangements for new home environments from which to choose.

Large numbers of people could be involved in a professionally managed membership network, a kind of nongeographic community to which participants pay regular dues. Alternative home environments for children which could be developed by such a network are primarily multifamily communes, child-exchange programs, and children's residences.

The multifamily commune could work if there were an organized network to help with problems of autocratic leadership, to establish standards of sexual behavior and fair distribution of maintenance and other responsibilities before the experiment begins and throughout its life. Obviously children would have to participate fully in all aspects of the communal life.

A second model is child exchange where families would swap children, much like today's foreign-exchange student programs. This program would accommodate children who have created a problem for their parents, or children who would like to have the chance to experience new situations.

The problem with child exchange presently is that it is informal, haphazard, and uncommon. But the need is there. (A man took a newspaper ad offering his child in exchange for another troublesome teenager, and within the first few days he received more than 70 responses.) Within a membership network the exchanges could be arranged at the option of

the children as well as the parents, and counseling and contracts would also be introduced to help safeguard the system.

A third possible alternative involves residences operated by the children. Organized by the network staff and similar to those now operated by and for the elderly, these would have adults in residence as consultants or in other capacities, but would be, by and large, managed by children functioning in self-determined and self-governing ways. One of the problems is that this plan might seriously reduce children's contact with adults (though the children themselves might be far less age-segregated than they are in schools now). Another is that the financing for children's residences would have to come largely from parents and government, and that might impose parent control. Finally, infant care would require adult legal responsibility. While these problems are challenging, they are not insurmountable.

Another model, not requiring a membership network, is the day-care or day-and-night care facility financed not only by parents but by government, business and industry, and society at large.

Then there are basic changes to be made in our current living facilities. Children are simply not considered important enough by those adults who design the environment. Only in places that are used exclusively by children—classrooms, playgrounds, and the like—do we find facilities built to children's scale.

Consider the daily experience of small children—taking a shower under an uncontrollable waterfall pouring down from several feet overhead, gripping the edges of a toilet seat that is far too high and too large, standing on tiptoe to reach a cabinet or a sink, trying to see in a mirror so high that it misses them completely. Then they must go out into the world to try to open doors too heavy for them, negotiate stairs too steep, reach food on tables and shelves that are too high, pass through turnstiles that hit them directly in the face, see a film almost totally obscured by the back of the auditorium seat in front of them, get a drink out of a fountain they can't reach, make a phone call from a pay telephone placed at adult height, bang into sharp corners just the height of their heads, and risk their safety in revolving doors. Having physical reminders that there are children in the world would help to make us more alert and attentive toward them, making their lives safer and more interesting. The real advance for children will come when adults recognize them as an integral part of the community, expecting them to be around, naturally looking out for them and scaling conveniences to their size.

We must also find a health-care solution that works—for all members of our society. A child must have the right to obtain medical treatment without parental consent. This doesn't mean that the physician is empowered to dictate the kind of treatment a child receives without having to explain it to the parent, but rather that the child is empowered to deal directly with the physician and to have some freedom and responsibility in the actions taken with respect to her or his own health. (In cases where the children are too young or uncomprehending to seek medical attention on their own they should of course be represented by a parent or advocate.) Minors should be given complete information on their condition and on the procedures that are suggested for their treatment, as well as information on a variety of health problems, notably those of birth control and venereal disease. Adopted children must also have the right to obtain their natural family's medical history.

In health, welfare, and education, a child's ignorance is a strong political ally of adult society, and adults have learned to rely heavily on it. Because children are excluded from almost every institution in our society, they don't know what to do to gain power over their own lives. They are separated from the adult world, barred from important conversations, kept out of the rooms where decisions are made, excluded from social gatherings, dinner parties, and business meetings, and denied access to information about society and themselves.

Students' school records provide a good example of this exclusion. Information—including IQ scores, teachers' or counselors' reports, personality data, and health records—is, in most cases, withheld from both parent and child. The secrecy of this system prohibits the careful evaluation of the information's accuracy. Neither parent nor child—but especially not the child—is usually permitted to challenge it. Even though we evolve and change, these records are cumulative and permanent and there is no practice of their systematic destruction at various points in a person's life. Teachers, police officers (who may be able to use the material against a child or parent), and other enforcers of society's rules have access to the file even if they cannot demonstrate a need for the information. The file is often available for medical or educational research purposes. All this may represent a tremendous threat to individual privacy and to the liberation of the child.

Students are labeled and categorized; the advantaged are secretly placed on tracks toward college or vocational training and others are damaged by derogatory material appearing on their permanent files as the result of temporary anger or prejudice of teachers. The serious flaws of all diagnostic measures recorded in these files, the questionable nature of psychological tests used, the fact that having certain knowledge and therefore certain expectations of children tends to be self-confirming, the way in which test scores prejudice teachers and administrators—all these factors combine to make the keeping of records a capricious and sometimes dangerous procedure.

Children are also systematically denied information in sexual matters. The average child sees literally thousands of filmed and televised murders, yet parents and the media strain to keep sex out of the child's thoughts.

The fact that children want information about sex does not mean that they should be able to invade adults' bedrooms. Adults and children alike should have control over their private lives. At this point, however, the privacy that needs protection is the child's. Adults think nothing of entering children's private space (if indeed they have private space); of opening their mail, going through their drawers, interrogating them about associates or activities. As a result, most children have little or no private life.

Subjecting children to such prohibitions

and deceptions ultimately threatens our democratic process; above all else, that process requires an independent and informed citizenry. The most potent weapon against tyranny is knowledge that is easily accessible to all. Whenever one group decides what is and what is not desirable for another to know, whenever a "we-they" condition exists, society becomes vulnerable to totalitarian controls. The acquisition of information by the child causes adults distress for exactly the same reasons; it empowers children, and makes it less easy to control and dominate them.

Our predisposition to ignore children's concerns, deal expeditiously with their questions, and deny them entry into the world of adults, is precisely the reason they tend to remain ignorant, dependent, and impotent. It's time to give up our adult privileges and make room for the autonomous child.

Individual action is vital, but it can never be sufficient. Only concerted action taken on many fronts can enable children to escape their prisons. Either we do this together—or it won't be done at all.

## SUGGESTIONS FOR FURTHER READING

Bereiter, C. The right to make mistakes. *Intellect,* 1973, *102,* 184–190. In this preview of the book *Must We Educate?* (Prentice-Hall, 1973), Bereiter considers children's rights, especially in the area of directing their own education.

Berg, L., Adams, P., Ollendorf, R., Neill, A. S., Berger, N., & Duane, M. *Children's rights.* New York: Praeger, 1971. This collection of papers covers wide-ranging issues relating to the rights of infants, children, and adolescents.

Blankenship, R. M. Civil rights of public school students. *Teachers College Record,* 1971, *72,* 495–503. School students' rights are discussed in terms of the concept of *in loco parentis,* free speech, privacy, and right to due process.

Blue, R. Pupils' rights and the paper invasion. *Elementary School Journal,* 1973, *74,* 2–8. This article concerns students' rights relating to school records, relevant court cases, and implications for school policy.

Burt, R. A. Protecting children from their families and themselves: State laws and the Constitution. *Journal of Youth and Adolescence,* 1972, *1,* 91–111. This article explores the rationale for court application, by constitutional mandate, of safeguards for a wide range of child protection laws.

Child advocacy. Articles in *American Journal of Orthopsychiatry,* 1971, *41,* 798–808. This section contains three brief articles relating to child advocacy as proposed by the Joint Commission on Mental Health of Children.

Holt, J. Stimulus response/Slave and superpet. *Psychology Today,* May 1974, pp. 38; 133–134. A critic of our schools makes a case for granting children the same responsibilities and rights that adults enjoy, including the right to vote, the right to enter into quasi-familial relationships outside their own immediate family, and the right to do in general what any adult may legally do.

An interview with Marian Wright Adelman. *Harvard Educational Review,* 1974, *44,* 53–73. An attorney for the civil-rights movement focuses on various issues involving student rights: excluding children from school, labeling and treating children with special needs, the child's right of privacy, the use of children in research, and other issues.

Kirp, D. Student classification, public policy, and the courts. *Harvard Educational Review,* 1974, *44,* 7–52. This article deals with student classification issues in terms of their constitutionality and possible infringement on human rights.

Levine, A., with Cary, E., & Divoky, D. *The rights of students: The basic ACLU guide to a student's rights.* New York: Discus Books, 1973. This book concerns civil liberties of students in the broadest sense, as well as corporal punishment, tracking, school records, and other areas having a bearing on student rights.

Polier, J. W. Myths and realities in the search for justice. *Harvard Educational Review,* 1974, *44,* 112–124. A juvenile-court judge discusses children's rights in terms of the right to due process, the right to privacy, the right to equal protection, and relevant recommendations.

Worsfold, V. L. A philosophical justification of children's rights. *Harvard Educational Review,* 1974, *44,* 142–157. The author discusses children's rights in terms of several philosophical conceptions of social justice.

Birthrights

**333**

# 19

## Ethical Issues Involved in Child Research

By tradition, the American concept of democracy imposes an obligation to protect the individual from undue manipulation by others. The problems of preserving this principle are apparent in such dilemmas as these: How much should the free dissemination of knowledge be restrained in the interest of national security? To what extent should confirmed criminals' rights be respected when the safety of the community is at stake? Is censorship of publication an infringement on individual liberties? Should parents with hereditary defects be allowed to have children? Is it the parents' right to keep children from being vaccinated, when they could acquire and spread communicable disease? Especially in recent years, such problems have come to the fore, given impetus by such factors as the civil-rights movement and the population explosion, which make society impinge more forcibly on the individual.

While all the foregoing factors have provided the climate for a conflict between private rights and behavioral research, more specific factors have precipitated concern in this particular area. For one thing, the proliferation of such research has made it more visible. Similarly, its very proliferation has caused it to involve more and more people, as additional and more representative subjects are sought. Moreover, psychologists are being employed to apply the products of their research to all major areas of industry, education and social institutions in general. The subsidization of behavioral research from public funds gives the public a right, even an obligation, to inquire about how it is being done.

Indeed, strong reasons may be given for a degree of coercion in order to obtain subjects for child research. Since every individual benefits from research on others, everyone correspondingly has some obligation in this area. Certainly the whole progress of humankind hinges on outcomes of research. Nor can research on adults provide all the answers needed for helping children. If parental consent becomes extremely difficult to obtain, subjects available for study may be too few or atypical to provide valid results.

Beyond such generalities, very difficult questions may arise. Perhaps the parent may object to the experimentation in question for personal, philosophical, or religious reasons. Or perhaps the researcher may feel so compelling a need to consummate his or her studies that a child is treated not as a person but as a subject. After all, a great many professionals in universities and medical centers must conduct research to insure their own advancement. They have many and subtle ways of insuring that children and their parents cooperate. Parents may be subtly led to feel that the child will not be accorded the utmost in care unless the child becomes a subject. On the other hand, parents may insist that a child be used as a subject for medical research, in the belief that none of the proven remedies can save the child. Does the doctor have an obligation in this case?

Other questions regarding child research abound: Might a parent forbid his child's being included in research that involves his entire class at school? What obligation does the medical researcher have with regard to patients who, unless voluntarily informed, may be unaware that they have become guinea pigs? Should the parent's consent be sufficient, or does a child have any say-so in such matters? Should facilities for treatment be more readily granted to children whose parents have consented to their being used in research?

Ethical questions arise in all areas of child psychology and psychiatry. In treating a child, should the child's own welfare or that of society take precedence? Suppose that test-tube babies with highly selected genes might have the best chance of living a happy, effective life. Should this factor be given precedence over a couple's personal desire to have children? At what age should a child's own wishes be given more concern than those of the parents? Such issues permeate every science and profession concerned with child welfare and research.

In the first article that follows, two child psychiatrists (Melvin Lewis and Herbert Schwartz), a pediatrician (Jerome Grunt), and a social worker (Audrey McCollum)—all of Yale University School of Medicine—consider the matter of informed consent in child research and offer certain recommendations. In the second selection, Arno Motulsky discusses ethical issues involved in current treatment and research regarding genetic diseases.

# Informed Consent in Pediatric Research

**Melvin Lewis**
**Audrey T. McCollum**
**A. Herbert Schwartz**
**Jerome A. Grunt**

In recent years, several exploratory studies of conflict between research and social values have been carried out. Some of these studies have been focused on behavioral research;[1-3] others, on certain nonbehavioral aspects of pediatric research.[4, 5] In pediatric research the principle that "informed consent" must be obtained from the parents of the child who is a research subject, and, where appropriate, from the child himself, has become accepted as an ethical necessity. The question, however, remains as to the *meaning* of informed consent in the context of pediatric research. Herein lie some difficult issues.

The purpose of pediatric research is to clarify problems in understanding normal and pathological processes and in the diagnosis and treatment of disease. Such research has the ultimate goal of benefiting individual children, even though the child who is a research subject may derive no benefit from it.

When and to what extent is subjecting a child to pain and anxiety justifiable? A simple guideline might be: When there is no possible benefit to the child, then any procedure that harms the child in any way is categorically unethical. What constitutes "benefit" and "harm" of course remains to be defined in the individual case. Moreover, this guideline leaves unresolved the question of the conditions under which the parent has the right to

Reprinted from *Children* (now *Children Today*), Children's Bureau, Office of Child Development, Office of Human Development, U. S. Department of Health, Education, and Welfare.

give consent for research to be performed on his child when the research cannot help the child but holds out promise of great good for many other children. The fact is, there is no simple guideline.

Some medical writers have approached this question in a general way by suggesting some preliminary considerations—such as the design and value of the research and whether, if it has been done before, it is worth repeating—to be followed by an evaluation of the physical and psychological risks for the child. Psychological hardship for the child, sometimes amounting to trauma, may be caused by many factors, such as the nature of the specific research procedures, the child's separation from his mother, changes in the child's environment, and possible shifts in family relationships or intensification of conflict in the parents' feelings about a defective child.[6]

The nature of "informed consent" has also been approached in a general way. For example, a declaration adopted by the Council of International Organizations for Medical Science states:

If at all possible, consistent with patient psychology, the doctor should obtain the patient's freely given consent after the patient has been given a full explanation . . . . However, the responsibility for clinical research always remains with the research worker; it never falls on the subject even after consent is obtained.[7]

And a report of the British Medical Research Council states:

By true consent is meant consent freely given with proper understanding of the nature and consequences of what is proposed. Assumed consent or consent obtained by undue influence is valueless and, in this latter respect, particular care is necessary when the volunteer stands in special relationship to the investigator, as in the case of a patient to his doctor, or a student to his teacher . . . . In general, the investigator should obtain the consent himself in the presence of another person.[8]

The value of such statements is limited by their lack of specificity. They also fail to mention a further general but important concept:

Truly informed consent cannot be confined to a single moment in time; it is a continuous process, subject to modification and even at times withdrawal, depending on changes in the conditions of the subject and the research.

## SOME RELEVANT ISSUES

### Investigator's Awareness

Several perplexing issues confront the investigator as he seeks to obtain informed consent from the subject.

1. Because advancement on a medical faculty today largely depends on demonstrated productivity in research, a sense of urgency may subtly influence the investigator's presentation of his proposed studies. An investigator needs a high level of self-awareness, as well as integrity, to determine the degree to which his studies serve the needs of children as distinct from his own needs for advancement.

2. Distinguishing the study aspects that might be expected to benefit the child directly from those that may only benefit other children in the future is often difficult. Because it is easier to discuss with a parent a research protocol that will result in direct benefit to the child involved, an investigator may perceive benefits in his research that may not so readily be perceived by physicians unconnected with the study.

3. When the research is concerned with a rare condition or a little-tried therapeutic agent, the basis for a complete assessment of physical risk may be inadequate. Assessment of psychological risk may offer even greater difficulty, since the investigator may have had little training in this work.

4. Effective communication with the child or his parent may not occur. Even the most conscientious and thorough presentation of the purpose of the research and the procedures and risks involved may be insufficient; the reactions of the child or his parents during the explanation must be understood. A careful interview technique is required for perceiving symptoms of an anxiety that may be preventing the subject from hearing, understanding, and

remembering the facts being explained to him. Training in such interviewing has seldom been a part of the investigator's preparation.

## Involving the Child

Can one ever have the truly informed consent of a child? Most investigators make a judgment as to how much information to convey to a child and how much consent to expect from a child. The factors that are usually weighed include the child's age and developmental stage, his level of anxiety, and the degree of emotional support he receives from his parents.

Schoolage children should in some instances be involved in the consent procedure. However, children, as well as adults, need time to comprehend and accommodate to a research plan and procedures. This means that much of the protocol and much of the consent must be broken down into assimilable parts, with the investigator making his judgments at many stages during the research.

## Parental Consent

The final responsibility for giving consent rests with the child's parents or guardian. However, many factors interfere with their capacity to give truly informed consent. Their lack of medical background limits the ability of many parents to understand the nature, aims, and methods of the proposed research, or the possible benefit to their child. Their anxiety about their child and their expectation that research implies "using" the child as a "guinea pig" may further limit their capacity to assimilate explanations. Moreover, they may see no alternatives to consent. For example, some parents regard the suggestion that their child be hospitalized as a research subject as confirmation that the child is seriously ill and may therefore feel that they will be doing the child a disservice if they do not comply. Some parents are prepared to give consent to a trial therapy but feel the therapy will only be made available if they consent to a broader research protocol.

The enticement of obtaining free medical care for the child because he will be participating in research may influence the parents' decision. Conversely, some parents feel less in control of the situation, and more anxious, when they are not required to pay a fee.

Parents are not always aware of the potential psychological stress the procedures may impose on their child. An occasional parent in consenting to the research may be acting out unconscious hostile wishes against the child or may be influenced by anxiety, guilt, and depression. Ethically, the child should not be regarded as the property of the parent to be used as a means to the parent's ends, but should be approached as an individual person with his own specific needs and anxieties.

A parent may ask himself, or may be requested to ask himself: "Are the research procedures that are being considered for my child the kind I would consent to have performed on myself as a child?" This question, however, does not provide a true test of informed consent for the following reasons: (1) neither the parents nor the physician may comprehend the psychological issues involved in consent for oneself; (2) the needs and anxieties of a child are different from those of an adult, and, in some instances, the child cannot speak meaningfully for himself, either about his anxieties or about the proposed research; (3) in considering only his own feelings about the procedures, the parent may be regarding the child as his property rather than as another human being with needs and feelings of his own.

Parental consent, therefore, cannot be regarded as "informed" until parents have had time and opportunity to understand the nature of the proposed research, their feelings and attitudes about it, its relevance to their child's medical needs, and its physical and psychological risks in relation to their child's stage of development and personality structure; and to consider alternative sources of appropriate medical care.

A few brief case examples will illustrate some of the complexities involved in the meaning of informed consent. They are presented with the parents' permission and, in one case, the adolescent child's.

## CHANGING MEANING

The following case illustrates how the meaning of informed consent can undergo changes when uncertainties about the risks of therapy create anxiety in both the patient and the parents, resulting in a weakened sense of trust in the investigator.

A 14-year-old girl who had a brain tumor partly removed at the age of 4 had been under the observation of a pediatric endocrinologist for 2 years. She and her parents became increasingly concerned because of her lack of adequate growth and sexual development. Her delayed development was producing serious psychological and social difficulties for her. Therefore, the parents urged the endocrinologist to consider treating the girl with growth hormone.

The endocrinologist pointed out that growth hormone was available for therapy only in research, thus necessitating the acceptance of a research regimen for the patient and that its use might be associated with some danger since the few data that were available indicated that it might enhance tumor growth. He explained that because of the risk of tumor growth, he was reluctant to institute the therapy until he could obtain more information from colleagues around the country. The parents had understood from the patient's pediatrician and neurosurgeon that the growth hormone therapy would be appropriate and would involve little risk. Therefore, the delay in instituting the studies engendered mounting anger and anxiety in the family.

When the endocrinologist felt assured that the risk of tumor growth was small, he again reviewed the plans for study with the patient and her parents, and arranged for her admission to a pediatric research center.

In this conference, the patient and parents had given formal consent. However, in the preadmission interview with the research center social worker, the parents showed evidence of a marked increase in anxiety. This was expressed in several ways. They seemed angry with and mistrustful of the endocrinologist, with whom they had previously had a good relationship. They complained of his style of communication, apparent reluctance to proceed, and lack of clarity about the procedures involved in the research. They indicated their inability to comprehend the protocol because of its highly technical language. They indirectly expressed fears that their child might die as a result of the treatment, and they reported personality changes in her that they thought reflected either a breakdown in her ability to cope with difficulties or brain changes associated with tumor regrowth. The mother feared that her own psychological integration might be compromised if things did not go well for her child.

At the request of the investigator the patient was examined by the child psychiatrist. She proved to be a bright, somewhat compulsive girl, who was able to express her feelings vividly. During her first week in the hospital, she described feelings of moderate bewilderment and said that she had "never felt so nervous" in her life. She was particularly afraid "for some unknown reason" of having a glucose tolerance test. Gradually the reason for this particular focus of her fear became known. The investigator had at one time expressed uncertainty as to whether the test would be performed. Now the patient wondered whether she was being made a guinea pig. This set off a chain of other fears. Would she get sick? Would the hormone make the tumor grow? Would she then die? How safe was she, and who would take care of her? Would her mother stay with her? Would the hormone help her? She doubted the good judgment of her parents because she knew they did not know exactly what to expect.

Afraid of the research, this patient was at the same time afraid that she would lose her friends because of her small size, lack of development, and disinterest in such feminine preoccupations as clothes. She also felt unable to meet her parents' academic aspirations for her. Her depression, fears, and anxiety not only made her unable to ask the investigator questions but also led to a helpless compliance.

Soon after the patient's admission to the hospital more data on the growth hormone became available, confirming the assumption that its use carried few risks. This information, plus the genuine concern demonstrated by the endocrinologist, helped the parents reestablish their previous trust in him and made for a much smoother hospital course for the girl.

In this case, the investigator's task of assuring that the consent to the research was made on a truly informed basis became difficult because the procedures contemplated involved risk but no guarantee of gain for the child, thus creating anxiety in both parents and child.

The meaning of the parents' consent underwent several changes that reflected an increase in anxiety and concomitant distortions in judgment. Although highly intelligent, the parents could not understand the protocol outlining the clinical procedures that would take place, primarily because of their anxiety.

The 14-year-old patient was capable of a great deal of understanding and clearly benefited from the psychiatrist's help. However, because of the suppressed anxiety she was experiencing, her initial consent was less meaningful than it appeared. When she was confronted by the reality of the procedures, increasing anxiety altered her perception of the research.

Thus, a succession of attitudes may occur. Initially, the child may feel anxious about the proposed research. However, before he has been confronted with any of the actual procedures, he may find it easier to deny his anxiety and so consent to the research. As the research approaches, his level of anxiety may rise, thus weakening his consent and perhaps leading to a wish to retract. Once the first procedures are completed, the patient's anxiety may abate, changing once more the meaning of his consent.

## THE CHILD'S INTERESTS

While the parents and investigator may have a contractual agreement based upon apparently informed consent, it does not follow that this consent is necessarily in the child's best interests. In some instances, psychiatric evaluation of a child's capacity to cope with the hospitalization may be indicated before admis-

sion. These points are illustrated in the following case.

Research procedures were suggested for a 7-year-old extremely obese, short girl to rule out the possibility of a brain tumor or other organic disease and to establish whether treatment with growth hormone was indicated. The parents gave their consent after the investigator had carefully gone over the complex technical research protocol with them. However, in the preadmission interview with the social worker, they showed signs of being seriously confused and anxious about the procedures. They feared that lethal air bubbles would result from the intravenous infusions or brain damage from the electroencephalogram. Their consent, obviously not "informed," seemed based on the expectation that if the child gained weight without growing she would become unable to move and would develop dangerous heart disease.

Because these parents described their child as enuretic and prone to night terrors and temper outbursts, suggesting that she might be overwhelmed psychologically by the studies, a child psychiatrist was asked to evaluate the child prior to admission. The social worker held several interviews with the parents to clarify their fears and misconceptions.

Their daughter, Alice, a child of above average intelligence, understood that the doctors "might" be able to find something to help her grow, but she definitely did not want to go into the hospital. However, she said that if there were not "too many needles" and if she did not feel them too much, she would go into the hospital for the 17 days required. She dealt with her anxiety through an obsessional accounting of the procedures to be followed in the hospital. She told the psychiatrist she wished her parents would stop talking about the hospitalization and would "hurry up and get it over with." On the whole, she showed good judgment and an ability to cope with stress.

Because the physician-investigator was concerned about the possibility of a brain tumor and because the family was under considerable stress, the psychiatrist recommended that the child be admitted to the hospital as soon as possible. A plan for collaborative supportive care between the social worker and the psychiatrist was carried out during and after hospitalization.

Here, the initial consent of these parents was meaningless because of their emotional disturbance, but the child was able to understand the nature of the research, and was further prepared for it by the child psychiatrist. This preparation was especially important because of the urgent medical indication for proceeding.

## SPECIAL ARRANGEMENTS

In some instances, it may be important to design a therapeutic nursing regimen before hospital admission to safeguard the child's psychological integrity, as in the following case.

A mother gave consent for hospitalizing her 7-month-old infant son, David, for study and surgery. The child had Cushing's disease, a serious endocrine disorder. The hospital regimen would include motor restraint on a metabolic mattress—a device for collecting feces and urine—thus subjecting the child to the risk of social isolation.

David had reached that developmental stage in which children are wary of strangers and so was particularly vulnerable to intense separation anxiety. However, his mother, who was attending school, maintained that she could make only brief evening visits to him a few times a week during the proposed 2-month hospitalization period. She had already turned most of the daily tasks of the child's care to her own mother. David's urgent need for medical treatment precluded any delay in hospitalization pending efforts to change his mother's attitudes.

Because this mother gave consent to the research without providing any safeguard for the child's psychological development, the pediatric investigator, social worker, nurse, and pediatric child development specialist collaborated in instituting a therapeutic regimen to meet the infant's developmental needs. This regimen consisted of: (1) encouraging the mother to be warmly attentive to her child during her visits and to give clear signals to him when she was about to leave; (2) assigning the same nurses to the child on each shift; and (3) providing the child with tactile, visual, verbal, and social stimulation through the provision of toys and caressing, massaging, and other forms of attention from staff members and other patients. David was also regularly moved from the metabolic mattress onto a potty in a carriage, thus allowing him more motor activity and changing his environment from a depressing, monotonous one to a more interesting one. David made appropriate developmental gains in the 2 months he was in the hospital.

## INTERRUPTION OF RESEARCH

In some instances, a child's responses to the stress of the research may require the studies to be terminated before completion, as it was in the following case.

Charles, a blind 7-year-old boy, was expected to die within the year from an inoperable brain tumor. Charles' mother gave consent for the boy to be hospitalized and subjected to endocrine studies that could not benefit him in any way. The justification for the studies was the possibility of their leading to earlier identification of brain tumors in other children.

The mother's motives in giving her consent for the studies were complex. She told the staff that she felt Charles' life would have been worthwhile if, through the studies, it led to knowledge that would benefit other children. This statement implied that her consent was partly a way of dealing with Charles' impending death (although Charles would die, the knowledge gained through him would live on) and partly a way of compensating for his loss (Charles would die so that other children might live). However, the statement also implied the existence of unconscious anger toward Charles, since it disregarded the severe stress to which the child would be subjected.

The psychological stress proved to be particularly severe since the medical procedure heightened the fears commonly experienced by a child at Charles' developmental stage—concern about body intactness and manipulation. Frequent venipunctures, necessary for the research, led to acute panic states in the child. Moreover, the usual means of dealing with such stress through play, visual, auditory, and tactile experiences, and motor activity were denied to Charles by his blindness and the imposed restraint necessary to the procedures.

When Charles was threatened with further restraint because reaching his difficult veins satisfactorily would require cutting through his skin, the investigator terminated the research.

In this case, recognition of the incomplete resolution of the mother's feelings about her child's impending death, developmental anxieties in the child, and the acute stress imposed by the procedures led the pediatric investigator to decide to discontinue research that could have no direct benefit to the child.

## RECOMMENDATIONS

In view of the difficulties involved in determining the meaning of informed consent, we suggest the following safeguards for children being considered for participation in medical research:

1. The nature of the research design and all risks to the child should be assessed by a review committee that includes pediatric investigators who are not involved in the research as well as the pediatric investigator who is to conduct the study. This will provide safeguards against the investigator's inevitable bias and gaps in knowledge.

2. The review committee should include a professional person especially equipped to assess the psychological risks to the child. This person would have to be aware of those areas of development especially vulnerable to impairment at the child's developmental stage, have the interviewing skill required for assessing the child's degree of vulnerability, and understand the kinds of stress likely to be provoked by the research procedures.

3. The investigator should have a series of personal interviews with the parents and at times with the child to build a relationship of trust, and establish an understanding of the research goals and methods and of the risks involved.

4. When the investigator lacks the skill or experience necessary for preparing the parents and the child for the research, correcting their misconceptions about it, and dealing with the child's reactions as the admission date approaches, a social worker and a psychiatrist may be called upon to help fulfill these functions, in supplementary preadmission interviews.

5. The investigator, research director, nurse, social worker, and psychiatrist should plan in advance for the child's care in the hospital since special arrangements may be required to prevent impaired development.

6. The research team should include a pediatrician, nurse, child psychiatrist, child psychologist, or social worker to provide a continuing evaluation of the psychological reactions of the child and his parents to the research procedures and to train research personnel in the early recognition of emotional stress and ways of dealing with it.

7. The activities of all the staff members of the research team should be coordinated in regularly held interdisciplinary conferences.

8. Followup care should be provided to deal with whatever reactions to the research procedures may occur after the child's discharge from the hospital.

9. Parents and staff members should have an understanding of what parts of the psychological information revealed during the research are to be shared with other members of the staff and what parts will remain in confidence; and all staff members should understand the need for discretion in divulging such information.

## REFERENCES

[1] Clark, K. E.: Privacy and behavioral research. Office of Science and Technology, Executive Office of the President, Washington, D. C. February 1967.

[2] Smith, M. B.: Conflicting values affecting behavioral research with children. *Children,* March–April 1967.

[3] Lewis, M.: Privacy, behavioral research and social values. *International Journal of Psychiatry,* June 1968.

[4] McCollum, A. T.: Mothers' preparation for their children's hospitalization. *Social Casework,* July 1967.

[5] McCollum, A. T.; Schwartz, A. H.: Pediatric research hospitalization: its meaning to parents. *Pediatric Research.* In press.

[6] Schwartz, A. H.; Landwirth, J. L.: Birth defects and the psychological development of the child: some implications for management. *Connecticut Medicine,* vol. 32, no. 6, 1968.

[7] Hersch, J.: Declaration of Helsinki. *Lancet,* October 14, 1967.

[8] Her Majesty's Stationery Office: Report of Medical Research Council, Cmnd, 2382. London, England. 1962–63.

# Brave New World?

## Arno G. Motulsky

The public media in the last few years have been full of articles about research in molecular biology and genetics. These fields have come to interest the educated layman; DNA has become a household word. While the stories presented often are quite accurate, they must be digested by readers whose background in biology is usually sketchy. Even those previously exposed to biology usually learned the subject in a conventional way that usually had little relevance to their gaining an understanding of human biology.

The media outdo each other in presenting lurid stories likely to titillate the jaded appetites of their clientele. The results often are a preoccupation with artificial fertilization, cloning, manprimate chimeras, creation of man to genetic specifications, and other far-fetched consequences of the new biology. It is sometimes implied that further advances in biology *must* lead to the universal application of these methods accompanied by an abandonment of conventional reproductive methods and a lowering of the value of human life in general. In his *Brave New World,* Huxley (*1*) described a future society which practiced cloning and artificial fertilization of individuals preassigned to castes stratified by intellectual ability. Orwell portrayed a totalitarian state in his *1984* (*2*). Thoughtful human beings rightfully become frightened when these developments are painted as the ways of the future.

Comparisons have been made between the current state of biology and the state of nuclear physics before the atomic bomb. It is hoped that by intensive discussions of the possible consequences of the new biology, mankind will be better prepared for the coming of the "biological age" than it was for the "nuclear age." Professionals outside of biology and medicine have become interested in these issues. Lawyers, sociologists, philosophers, and theologians have joined biologists, physicians, and geneticists to discuss the current scene and how to approach the future (*3*). A new field—bioethics—is being born (*4*). While there is no dearth of literature in this new field, much of it is somewhat unrealistic.

Research and methods of management of birth defects are intimately tied up with modern biological techniques which, according to the "gloom and doom" prognosticators (*5*) will lead to the Brave New World. Most researchers in the biomedical sciences and practitioners of medicine have been less pessimistic than many of our confreres in the humanities, social sciences, and theology. In general, those trained in biology and medicine have taken a more pragmatic, but possibly a more short-sighted view of these new developments. Problems of genetic counseling, intrauterine diagnosis, and screening are with us now and raise a variety of ethical issues quite different from the sensational ones drummed up by some of the mass media.

Reprinted from *Science,* 1974, *185*(4152), 653–663. Copyright 1974 by the American Association for the Advancement of Science. Reprinted by permission.

## BIOLOGIC ORIGINS OF ETHICS

Evidence for man having evolved from lower forms of life comes from many areas of biology, including protein chemistry—a field in which extensive studies have revealed similarities in the amino acid sequences of proteins from related species (6). While many details remain unknown, the grand design of biologic structure and function in plants and animals, including man, admits to no other explanation than that of evolution. Man therefore is another link in a chain which unites all life on this planet. Studies of proteins have indicated that man and his closest nonhuman relative—the chimpanzee—differ from each other by no more than do subspecies of mice or sibling species of fruit flies (7). Yet, man differs from all other animals, including the most intelligent chimpanzee, by his ability to use complicated oral and written languages and to conceptualize abstract thoughts. With these unique endowments, our species can create cultures and technologies. We can know our past and worry about our future. We no longer need be subject to blind external forces but can manipulate the environment and eventually may be able to manipulate our genes. Thus, unlike any other species, we may be able to interfere with our biologic evolution. It is most remarkable that the human brain had already reached this supreme position at the dawn of prehistory. The biological substrate that later created the philosophies of Plato and Spinoza, the religions of Jesus and Buddha, the poetry of Shakespeare, Molière, and Goethe, as well as modern science, may have been in existence about 50,000 years ago. There is little evidence that our brains have changed much during this period. Our ancestors some 2000 years ago were certainly similar to us (8).

The building of ethical systems by man may be considered a unique property of the human brain. No other species is known by us to have ethical systems. Just as the human brain gives man his unique language capacity, enabling him to learn to speak Chinese or English, so does the brain give man his "ethical capacity," allowing him to express his values in a variety of ethical systems. A biological substrate for cooperativity and altruism may have developed by natural selection (9). Lone hunters were less likely to survive than those who cooperated with each other. Thus, human "goodness" and behavior considered ethical by many societies probably are evolutionary acquisitions of man and require fostering. Alleviation of suffering, freedom from want, neighborly love, and peace are attributes practically all modern societies would aspire to. Unfortunately, man's altruistic instincts are often overpowered by his aggression. To curb this tendency without dogma and rigid rules is a difficult task facing present-day societies. The human brain is unlikely to change biologically in the foreseeable future. It is also unlikely that man will become extinct. Mass starvation and nuclear war may decimate human populations, but some men are likely to prevail and as long as records of cultural achievements remained in some libraries, high technological achievements would be possible in a few generations.

An ethical system that bases its premises on absolute pronouncements will not usually be acceptable to those who view human nature by evolutionary criteria. New knowledge and new ways of coping with nature offer new and different challenges which the past cannot necessarily help us with. Many persons feel that the consequences, immediate and remote, of a given act should be the sole criterion for judging whether the act is good or bad. Such an ethical system knows no absolutes, no black and white, no a priori do's and don't's, but must laboriously draw up a balance sheet of all the consequences of man's acts (10). Most of us are philosophic utilitarians; that is, we want to do the most good for the largest number. We want this goal achieved by consensus rather than by edict, and we value freedom of action. How free we really are, however, is not entirely clear. Data from such different fields as behavioral genetics and Skinnerian psychology (11) raise questions about our cherished beliefs of freedom of action, and until considerably more work has been done in human neurobiology, neurogenetics, and behavioral psychology, we will be unable to settle how open our choices really are.

Fried, a legal scholar with philosophical

inclinations, has pointed out that we need a "philosophical anthropology"—a new system that would attempt to harmonize the scientific view of man with existing or new codes of ethics (*12*). He states that existing ethical systems are inadequate and that a consequentialist, situational ethics would also be unsatisfactory. Yet, where is this "philosophical anthropology" to come from? Biology itself cannot provide it, and all philosophical systems are relative and not absolute. In a search for a unifying philosophy of man's existence, Monod (*13*) suggested an "ethic of knowledge" to replace existing beliefs; objective search after the truth and after the truth alone would be the cornerstone of this ethical system. This code would omit all emotional, poetic, and aesthetic human aspirations. It is unlikely that such an austere system would appeal to most people.

Where do we go from here? I fully agree with Sinsheimer (*14*), a molecular biologist, who said that the enormity of our ethical problems should not paralyze us into inaction. Our recent triumphs in using the brain to help us in our understanding of ourselves and of the universe should not be the terminus but the beginning of a new era of man's life on this planet and even elsewhere. Nevertheless, I urge caution in our applications of current technology. Modern science has been around for only 200 years in man's evolutionary history; biology has been revolutionized only during the last 20 years. We know relatively little about most of human biology, particularly human genetics. Thus the genetic regulation of human behavior and the genetic determinants of normal traits as well as of common diseases and birth defects are largely unknown (*15*). Intensive research on these topics must be conducted and the underlying basic phenomena must be discovered before we attempt to apply genetic knowledge on a grand scale. Yet paradoxical forces exist that tend to spur us to action. People clamor for the fruits of research to be brought from the laboratory into the public domain. Public funds are spent and, for financial support to continue, practical applications are expected in the near future. As a result, premature applications are likely to be attempted. The public wants cures and prevention of disease; yet, for some of the most serious problems the basic knowledge that would enable us to "deliver the goods" is lacking.

The task of human biologists and physicians is to understand the biology of man and to apply research in a humane and cautious way, with respect for the individual human being. It is likely that in so doing, boundaries will be crossed that were previously considered absolute. The nature of man is to explore and to experiment; to stop exploration and experimentation at this juncture would be to act against those attributes which make us most human. . . .

## GENETIC COUNSELING

Genetic counselors usually are physicians with training in medical genetics who first make an accurate diagnosis of the disease in question, and then provide their patients with information about the natural history of genetic diseases, about the risks of these diseases occurring in offspring, and about the available alternatives to bearing affected children. The aim of such counseling is to enable a couple or a person to make rational decisions about whether or not to reproduce. Although at least one follow-up study has suggested that those who have been counseled get a good grasp of the meaning of risk and avoid reproducing if the risks of their having affected children are high (*16*), some data (*17*) have indicated that the meaning of genetic risk may not always be well understood.

Most counselors consider their work to be little different from any other medical practice; they put the interests of the patient and his family before the interests of society and the state, and pursue medical, not eugenic, objectives. Untoward effects on society may be pointed out, but most counselors do not attempt to give advice based on considerations of the gene pool.

Genetic counseling has thus, traditionally, been nondirective. It is usually maintained that every family situation is different and that the meaning of a given risk varies from family to family, so that in some cases even high recurrence risks may justify a future pregnancy. Some critics (*18*) have suggested that families expect more definite advice than is often provided, saying that because a genetic counselor understands the total impact of the disease and the real meaning of risks better than does the family, he should advise what he or she thinks would be the best course of action. Until better studies have been made of these matters, it will be impossible to make any firm conclusions. In the meantime, depending on the assessment of the counseling problem, many experienced counselors are usually nondirective, but may occasionally alter their approach.

There are also some broad ethical issues associated with genetic counseling. The motivation of a couple who by their own initiative seek counseling is usually different from that of a couple referred to counseling by a physician or some other interested party. Those who seek genetic counseling may be better educated than those who do not and they may, consequently, obtain a better understanding of the risks for their future offspring. With an increasing availability of genetic services, more people who may be unaware that a genetic problem exists or who may not be motivated to seek advice, may nevertheless receive genetic counseling. Under such circumstances, the counseling may be "forced" upon persons. Provided that the information given them is nondirective, they will probably not object, but if a counselor advises reproductive restraint, for example, when such advice has not been asked for, the problem will be more difficult. In countries where private health insurance programs are the rule, it might be possible for the insurance companies involved to withhold benefits from a sick child born to parents who were advised not to reproduce. In countries where health insurance is nationalized, regulations for withholding benefits from certain patients with genetic disease would probably be difficult to administer, and might not be passed for this reason.

Although laws authorizing the sterilization of certain patients have existed in the United States for many years, most of them are no longer applied. The excesses of Nazi Germany in this regard are not many years behind us.

Recent newspaper reports of the sterilization of retarded black girls in the southern United States created much furor. Although a logical case can be made for the voluntary sterilization of persons who carry certain harmful genes, who should make the decision for those persons lacking the intellect to decide for themselves? Legal safeguards to prevent possible abuses of existing laws are absolutely necessary and no decision to sterilize a person should be made without the concurrence of representatives of that person's family, the legal and the medical professions, and public representation at large. Laws authorizing enforced sterilization for genetic reasons should be strongly rejected, largely because the rights of couples to make their own decisions, even if this decision might result in the birth of a defective child, must be defended. Improvements in education in human biology, and a greater availability of genetic counseling and related services, should go a long way toward enabling people to make rational decisions about reproduction and toward reducing the numbers of children born with genetically determined illness. The marked change in popular attitudes toward abortion in many societies is a good example of how attitudes regarding reproductive practices can alter rapidly.

Other ethical problems may arise when genetic counseling is extended to family investigations. Some genetic diseases may be delayed in the onset of symptoms and their carriers may not know that they are affected. Identification of a clinically affected patient allows the performance of diagnostic tests of the relatives at risk. Following diagnosis of a disease in its early stages life-saving treatment may be initiated. There is little question that case-finding among relatives is strongly indicated when treatment and prevention of the disease is possible, for example, in hereditary polyposis of the colon, Wilson's disease, and porphyria. How far should the physician or medical geneticist go in order to trace all persons at risk? Should health departments get involved to ensure case-finding among scattered families? Who should be responsible for checking that everyone at risk has been examined?

More problems arise if a disease is clearly genetic in origin but no definite treatment is available (for example, Huntington's chorea). Should one attempt to detect those who are affected before they are clinically ill? Would most persons want to know many years before symptoms develop that they will die prematurely of an incurable disease? If a person were told that he had a high probability of developing such a disease in his middle years, he might decide not to have children. What can be used as guidelines? The relatives may be completely unaware of the risks. The very communication of the problem might create anxiety in a person even if he or she decided not to pursue the matter. Should we insist that relatives at risk be given the relevant information? While no generally applicable rules can be made, many observers point out that some information is better than none, and that the relatives have a right to know. The withholding of information is considered a form of medical paternalism. Nevertheless, some physicians occasionally decide not to pursue investigations to detect a genetic disease in family members when nothing can be done to prevent or cure the disease. Often the patient and his immediate family can provide assistance or guidance concerning the potential interest of other relatives in genetic counseling. We need many more data on these matters.

## INTRAUTERINE DIAGNOSIS

The development of intrauterine diagnostic techniques, such as amniocentesis, for the detection of chromosomal errors, X-linked diseases, and certain inborn errors of metabolism, is revolutionizing genetic counseling (19). New sonographic and optical methods are being explored and may widen the scope of intrauterine diagnosis for other conditions. However, most problems requiring genetic counseling cannot yet be approached by intrauterine diagnosis. Researchers in this field foresee a time in the future when amniocentesis may be used routinely in the monitoring of most, if not all, pregnancies. Before this comes about, however, a variety of technical and logistical problems will have to be solved.

More diseases need to be diagnosed and the absolute safety of the mother and fetus will have to be ensured. While it is difficult to prophesy, wide use of this procedure appears more likely than some of the more futuristic biological schemes under discussion. Unless it is used for every pregnancy, intrauterine diagnosis will have little impact on the population frequency of most birth defects (20).

When a fetus is found by intrauterine techniques to be genetically defective, the parents usually choose to abort it. Abortion causes serious ethical problems to many people for religious or personal reasons, although, first in Japan and more recently in the United States, there has been a rapid change in public acceptance of this procedure. The abortion of a fetus affected with a devastating disease such as Tay-Sachs or mongolism is accepted by many individuals who would oppose abortion for reasons of family limitation or convenience. More difficult problems will arise, however, as milder genetic defects are diagnosed as an unexpected finding following amniocentesis for indications of more harmful diseases. Should an abortion be performed for Klinefelter's (XXY) or Turner's (XO) syndromes? What about cleft palate where a single operation would cure the affected child? Difficult decisions will have to be made about the normality or abnormality of a fetus, because any fetus not considered up to "standard" might be rejected. The problem would become particularly acute should intrauterine diagnosis and abortion become simplified and more widely available. If it becomes possible to diagnose, and thus to abort, defective fetuses at an earlier stage in development than is now possible, many people might choose abortions who would hesitate to undergo this procedure during the early portion of the second trimester of gestation as is now required.

Scenarios have been considered in which the state enforces abortions to save money that would otherwise be spent on the care of persons with severe birth defects. Such a step seems unlikely. It is more probable that most people would voluntarily seek this method of avoiding birth defects. Some observers have suggested that the widespread acceptance of intrauterine diagnosis by many couples might lead to public rejection of children with preventable birth defects who could have been aborted. This development is also improbable: attitudes of the public and of medical personnel toward patients with cancer of the lung, which could have been prevented by their not smoking, is no different from attitudes toward patients with cancer of the colon, which we do not know how to prevent.

Many physicians refuse amniocentesis to pregnant mothers who say that they will not undergo abortion in the event of the fetus being found defective. They say that for these mothers, the early diagnosis of untreatable disease in the fetus would be harmful psychologically and would serve no purpose. In opposition to this viewpoint, one can point out that most amniocenteses give normal results, and that the total happiness generated in families receiving such results outweighs the anguish of the rare couple who know that they will have an affected child but choose not to abort it. It is therefore difficult to establish absolute values regarding who should and who should not be given tests that are available.

The possible dysgenic consequences of selective abortion have been considered in detail elsewhere (29). While these practices will cause some increase in the numbers of deleterious genes, few serious long-term problems are likely to arise.

The most serious question concerning the ethics of widespread abortion to prevent the birth of genetically defective children is based on the following reasoning: Why go to all the trouble and expense of doing intrauterine tests that might harm the fetus if inspection of the infant and diagnostic tests at birth would be much easier? An infant with serious birth defects could be "terminated" at that time (21). Proponents of this viewpoint suggest that a newborn baby should not be considered legally "human" until certain standards of normality have been assured, pointing out that passive infanticide, that is, the withholding of treatment, has always been practiced with severe birth defects. There are awesome implications in these arguments. Most societies differentiate

between life in the womb and life after birth. Each month of pregnancy allows for the development of emotional bonds, particularly between the mother and her infant. Perhaps because of recognizing these bonds, most societies in the 20th century have rejected infanticide and place great value on human life after birth. To practice active infanticide for medical purposes to me appears regressive and loathsome, and in effect would officially sanction already existing trends toward the blunting of human sensitivity. The next step, logically, might be the extension of such practices to so-called "mercy killings" at all ages of life, starting with the aged and incurably ill. The experiences of Nazi Germany only 30 years ago show that such practices, which were followed by genocide of almost half of the world's Jewish population, can become a reality.

It is sometimes said that selective abortion after intrauterine diagnosis is an interim measure, and that in the future it will be possible to treat birth defects and genetic diseases either pre- or postnatally. This view is probably unrealistic. Efficacious treatment for a complex defect such as Down's syndrome and similar structural defects is difficult to imagine. Many types of existing and future postnatal therapies cause a certain amount of suffering in the child. Prenatal therapy applied to the fetus may be dangerous to the mother also. Therefore, even when effective treatments for more birth defects have been developed, many parents will probably prefer a safe abortion with the assurance that their next child will not be affected with the disorder for which selective abortion was performed. This means that abortion for genetic defects discovered by intrauterine diagnosis is here to stay for a long time.

The control of common recessive diseases, such as cystic fibrosis, is most likely to be achieved by detecting heterozygous carriers before or after marriage or mating and by developing methods that will enable physicians to differentiate between normal, heterozygous, and affected fetuses by intrauterine techniques. Carriers would be informed of the 25 percent probability of their offspring being affected if they mated with a carrier of the same disease, and diagnosis could be made in utero, with the mother having the choice of aborting an affected fetus.

Such an approach, if applied by a large fraction of the population, would reduce the numbers of children born with such recessive genetic diseases, and therefore might receive high priority in the allocation of funds for medical research. As a consequence, more basic investigations of this and similar diseases might be deemphasized, or abandoned, in favor of developments of methods leading to the intrauterine diagnostic approach. It is therefore conceivable that treatment of recessive diseases based on a fundamental causative understanding might not be developed because of lack of research efforts. While the discovery of good screening methods and intrauterine tests requires a certain amount of basic understanding, it is clear that the goal of intrauterine diagnosis is more limited and requires fewer total resources than more comprehensive research.

## SEX CHOICE

Determination of the sex of a fetus is already feasible with amniocentesis, and this makes possible sex choice by selective abortion. Since the procedures are somewhat novel, and since a second trimester abortion is required, this technique is rarely used except to detect and abort male fetuses affected with genetic diseases which are linked to the X chromosome, such as hemophilia and the Duchenne type of muscular dystrophy. The procedure is usually refused to couples who desire a child of a certain sex after they have had several children of one sex only. If prenatal amniocentesis becomes a routine procedure, however, sex choice will probably be practiced more often.

While abortion as a means of sex choice may be objectionable, other more acceptable procedures by which to choose the sex of a child may soon be discovered. For example, it might become possible to separate X from Y sperms, in which case sex choice by using the husband's X or Y sperms for insemination would be a simple way of having children of the desired sex. A sociologist has pointed out that if sex choice were widely practiced, more males would be selected than females, and, because of this, there would be significant long-term effects on society, such as an increase in homosexuality (22). The social effects of a preference for male children would be delayed for almost a generation, however, and it is of interest in this regard that the state of Alaska already has an excess of males, but has not encountered serious societal dislocations.

Significant changes in sex ratio could probably be avoided if the composition of the population were carefully monitored, so that any deviation from an acceptable ratio could be brought to the attention of the public. Widely disseminated discussions regarding possible untoward consequences might then change preferences in sex selection of children. The recent rapid change in styles of family size indicates that swift alterations in reproductive practices do occur. Thus, there is no indication that research on sex choice should be placed under rigid control. In fact, such research should be encouraged, since the discovery of a simple method for choosing the sex of children would allow ideal family planning.

## POPULATION SCREENING FOR GENETIC REASONS

Screening for diseases, such as PKU, which are potentially treatable or preventable by medical or surgical methods, raises fewer problems than screening for conditions for which patients require either conventional genetic counseling about recurrence risks or intrauterine diagnosis following genetic advice. There are several recessive diseases, such as sickle cell anemia, thalassemia major, Tay-Sachs disease, and cystic fibrosis, that are either very difficult to treat or cannot be treated effectively. Each of these conditions is relatively frequent in a certain ethnic group; the conditions range in frequency from 1 in 100 for sickle cell anemia in certain populations in Africa to 1 in 4000 for Tay-Sachs disease in Ashkenazi Jews. Such frequency figures indicate that a significant fraction (3 to 25 percent) of the respective populations are heterozygous carriers for the relevant genes. Tests for detecting carriers of these diseases already exist (except for cystic fibrosis). When carriers receive counseling, they are informed of the 25 percent chance of their children being affected if they marry a carrier of the same gene. In Tay-Sachs disease, intrauterine diagnosis and selective abortion of affected fetuses is already possible. To be most effective, testing procedures should be initiated prospectively, that is, before a child with the disease is ever born. Retrospective counseling following the birth of an affected child is not an effective means of disease prevention since only 12.5 to 25 percent of cases can be prevented in this way (21). Some geneticists believe that even in the absence of intrauterine diagnosis, population screening followed by genetic counseling of all carriers would cause a reduction in disease frequency because of reproductive restraint among married carriers or appropriate mating choice among those not yet married.

In practice, the widespread screening for sickling in the United States probably has had several untoward consequences (23). Many screening programs were set up without counseling components, and many carriers of the harmless sickle cell trait, because they were not informed otherwise, came to believe that they had a mild form of, or a tendency to, sickle cell anemia. Social stigmatization, occupational discrimination, uprating of insurance premiums, and psychologic invalidism of sickle cell trait carriers were among the results of these programs. In addition, there was a lessened choice of marriage partners for the many people who mistakenly believed that a sickle cell trait carrier was a less desirable mate. In some instances, when a child with a positive sickling was found to have two nonsickling parents, the illegitimacy thus detected became known to the legal father.

These well-meaning screening programs therefore produced serious problems because the social consequences to a person being identified as a carrier were not taken into consideration (24). Before anyone is asked to give consent for screening, they should be fully informed of all the possible social, as well as medical, consequences of being diagnosed as a carrier. Certainly, before programs for screening the total populations at risk are developed, there should be an extensive assessment of existing practices. Many, but not all, of the problems in sickle cell screening apply to the screening of other diseases of this type.

Much of the misunderstanding about sickle cell anemia and other recessive diseases would certainly be eliminated if the entire population at risk received special educational programs during their early years. Genetic counseling of trait carriers alone would not be satisfactory because the total population at risk needs to be informed.

A better long-term solution to the problem of sickle cell anemia and other hemoglobinopathies, in my view, would be the development of techniques for diagnosing them in utero as are already available for Tay-Sachs disease. The carrier status of a potential mate would then be less important since intrauterine tests could be offered to all couples where both partners were carriers, and affected fetuses could be aborted if desired by the parents. Although this approach has raised cries of "genocide" among some black leaders, programs of this kind for Tay-Sachs disease are in operation in some Jewish communities (25). The approach used in these programs is an attempt to make all members of the Jewish community aware of the disease and of its frequency in the Jewish population, and to encourage all members to be tested. An end result similar to that obtained by screening the total population at risk could be obtained if obstetricians tested all pregnant Jewish women (26) and arranged for the testing of husbands only if their wives showed positive tests. More medically oriented schemes of this type have the advantage of arriving at the same results without alarming the whole community. On the other hand, in the United States the community approach seems more practicable at this time than enlisting the cooperation of obstetricians and general practitioners who attend the pregnancies of Jewish women.

A program that omits community participation runs against the current trends that aim at maximum dialogue between experts and the public. Nevertheless, complex issues of this kind are understood with difficulty by many people and therefore will cause unnecessary anxiety. Physicians are not required to inform their patients about all possible medical risks of a given procedure, for if they did so, every simple intervention might cause much anxiety. In a recent court ruling, it was stated that untoward risks of a medical or surgical procedure that carry a risk of 1 percent or less need not be discussed with patients. An analogous rule for genetic diseases might be worked out. Thus, genetic diseases that affect fewer than a small fraction of the population might best be dealt with medically without extensive community involvement.

As soon as the absolute safety of intrauterine diagnosis is established, it would be prudent to initiate the screening of all pregnant women older than about 38 years for fetuses affected with Down's syndrome (mongolism). All physicians, regardless of their attitudes toward abortion, should know about the procedures and should fully inform appropriate patients about the possibility of their giving birth to affected children and about the alternatives available. Fortunately, with more effective and widespread family planning, there will be fewer pregnancies among women of relatively advanced maternal age, and consequently fewer cases of Down's syndrome.

## PROBLEMS IN EARLY DETECTION OF GENETIC DISEASE OF LATE ONSET

In the future it might be possible to detect early in life, even at birth, a variety of diseases that may cause medical problems later in life. In this category are the hyperlipoproteinemias which predispose affected persons to myocardial infarction in middle age (27). Although we have no proof yet that drugs and dietary manipulations defer the onset of coronary disease if instituted early, such an outcome is likely. We should, therefore, consider some of the problems that might have to be faced in the future.

For example, what would be the reaction of parents who were told that their hyperlipidemic child had a 50 percent chance of having a heart attack at age 50 years? Would this be enough of a risk to make them change the family diet, or administer a drug all through childhood? Would they be willing to educate the child to a life style that would reduce the probability of his having a heart attack? Would it be child neglect if the parents refused to use a medical or dietary regimen that would help the child 50 years later? Would society be able to ensure in some manner that children would be provided with the environment their genotype required for optimum health?

Particularly difficult problems would be encountered if it became possible to identify future psychiatric disease. We already know that a person with an XXY chromosomal constitution (Klinefelter's syndrome) has an increased risk of suffering mental retardation and of minor sociopathy, but we know of no way to reduce these risks. What should the parents of an XXY child be told? If amniocentesis were to be applied universally, the identification of XXY would probably lead to abortion of many such fetuses. The data regarding the XYY chromosome pattern are still too confused (28) to be certain about the risks of criminal or antisocial behavior. It is certain, however, that many parents would choose abortion of an XYY fetus if the risk of its showing such behavior were significantly increased over that of the general population.

The detection of individuals predisposed to schizophrenia could create serious problems if we did not also find a way to prevent the manifestations of the disease. Would it not be tragic for parents to know that their newborn child would develop a serious crippling mental disease at age 20 years? While research on the genetics of schizophrenia and on the effects of the environment on the manifestation of the disease is proceeding, many families participating in this research may obtain information about their children that they probably would rather not know. If a major gene for schizophrenia could be identified, it is likely that tests for this gene could be done in utero and many parents might decide to abort an affected fetus. Thus, it is clear from developments in many genetic diseases that intrauterine diagnosis followed by selective abortion will have wide applicability.

## ARTIFICIAL INSEMINATION

Artificial insemination with donor sperm (AID) in cases of male infertility has been practiced for many years. The practice is handled by a few physicians who usually select donors to match the husband's general appearance and background. Genetic investigation of the donors by history or laboratory tests is not usually done, and the legal status of children born after AID has not been well defined. The use of donor sperm if both members of a couple carry the same recessive gene can prevent the birth of a defective child. This practice, however, is not often selected in genetic counseling as an alternative method of reproduction.

In recent years, sperm banks have been formed in several cities of the United States to make it possible for men to leave a specimen at a bank before undergoing vasectomy, so that they can have children if for any reason they choose to do so. While the short-term storage of sperm appears to be safe, the effects of long-term storage have not been fully tested, and research in this area raises problems concerning human experimentation. There are many questions that have not been satisfactorily answered by existing sperm banks and none of the banks, as far as I know, have been licensed by any federal or state agency.

Sperm banks could be used to widen considerably the selection of potential donors for AID, particularly if all donors were subjected to genetic investigations. Such a development would bring us close to Huxley's *Brave New World,* except that the donors would be chosen by the physician in consultation with the couple, rather than by the state. The usual practice of the donor remaining anonymous to the couple receiving AID would probably be continued because it prevents undue psychological attachment by the mother to the donor. Sperm banks could also be used for the storage of sperm by young men who might want to have children later in life, but who want to reduce the risk of mutations that occur at a higher frequency in the sperm of older persons. Persons receiving exposure to radiation or mutagenic chemicals could avoid potential problems by depositing their sperm in a bank before exposure. The use of sperm from outstanding human individuals has been recommended by Muller (*29*) as a method of upgrading the genetic constitution of man. He recommended that the sperm be stored until the "candidate" had died so that there could be general agreement about his social worth. Such a scheme is unlikely to be adopted by most women. Furthermore, we know too little about the genetics of desirable human qualities to be able to forecast the outcome of such a practice.

## FERTILIZATION IN VITRO

There has been much discussion about the problems that would arise if it became possible to produce human "test-tube babies" *(30).* In this procedure, human ova would be removed from a woman and would be fertilized in vitro. After some cell divisions the resulting blastocyst would then be reimplanted in the uterus (*31*) where development would proceed as in normal pregnancies. Such "test-tube babies" can be produced in lower species and only a variety of technical, rather than conceptual, obstacles prevent the application of the procedures to man. In its simplest application, a woman with a blocked fallopian tube could thus become pregnant with her own ova fertilized by her husband's sperm. The ova and sperm could, however, be from any human source, and any woman could serve as the "baby carrier."

Fears have been expressed that a government might use these techniques in schemes to breed its citizens. However, in the absence of knowledge of the genetics and the gene-environment interaction of most normal human traits, directed human breeding is not possible; the results would be no more predictable than they are now when a couple has a child in the conventional way. A moratorium on research in this area, as suggested by the American Medical Association (32), would serve no useful purpose because prohibition on research in one country can easily be circumvented by such research being conducted elsewhere. Only a moratorium declared by an international commission would be likely to have results. Pointing out the possible dangers of misuse in a wide variety of forums may be the most effective means of preventing abuse.

The achievement of human fertilization in vitro will raise many problems concerning the safety of the procedure. For example, how could a couple give consent to a procedure that might lead to their child being born with a birth defect? This problem is analogous to many earlier situations where women have used birth control pills or antifertility drugs that might have harmed the fetus. Experimentation with long-stored sperm raises similar difficulties. The prohibition of experimentation of this kind with human beings would effectively stop a wide variety of studies. For example, all work on intrauterine diagnosis would have to stop because we cannot yet be absolutely certain that a fetus subjected to amniocentesis is not harmed in some subtle way. If the use of fertilization in vitro for human beings were preceded by thorough studies of the process in subhuman primates, some of the risks involved might be reduced. Fortunately, the early period of embryonic development appears particularly resistant to birth defects in experimental animals, so that some observers feel that experimentation with nonhuman primates could be dispensed with. Furthermore, any pregnancies in women brought about by fertilization in vitro could be very carefully monitored by chromosomal and other inspection techniques. Even with these precautions, however, some defects might not be discovered and a defective baby might be born. In this context it should be recalled that at least 2 percent of all infants born following conventional pregnancy have severe birth defects.

Provided that the decision to use fertilization in vitro is made voluntarily by the couple wanting a child and, ideally, provided that physicians other than the investigators make the couple fully aware of all the potential dangers, there should be no reason to prevent such a couple from participating in this kind of human research. Sufficient experience might be gained in this manner to ensure its safety. Because a couple who would otherwise be sterile could, by fertilization in vitro, be given a chance of having a normal child of their own, it is difficult to agree with those who suggest that normal procreation is human and fertilization in vitro is inhuman (30). I consider novel reproductive technologies as a more human activity than making babies in the usual way. Thus, reproduction by intercourse in man differs little from sexual reproduction in most animal species. Nevertheless, it is clear that unlike the prevention and treatment of relatively rare genetic diseases which may be considered as medical problems, the various social and ethical issues raised by fertilization in vitro deserve wide discussion.

## EMBRYO RESEARCH

If we are to acquire new insights into the biology of man and his birth defects, studies of developmental biology must include research on human embryos. A large number of embryos are aborted in the United States, Japan, and the Scandinavian countries. Some of these embryos, or at least parts of them, are used for studies aimed at understanding mechanisms of development. Since most of the embryos are dead within minutes of being aborted, and since autopsy is a medical tradition, these studies raise few ethical problems. Difficulties arise when embryos removed by abortion procedures are kept alive for research purposes. The use of living embryos facilitates studies of human development and of the effects of physical, chemical, and infectious agents on the embryo. While many individuals might not object to a fetus being kept alive for several hours, they might seriously object to a fetus being kept alive for the purpose of an experiment that might take days or even weeks to complete. Informed consent should undoubtedly be obtained before an embryo is kept alive for research purposes. Presumably, the mother who is to be aborted would be the most appropriate person to give such consent.

There are no compelling medical reasons to attempt ectogenesis, that is, fetal development entirely outside the body. However, a large amount of information that might eventually be of great value in finding methods for the prevention and treatment of birth defects could be gleaned from prolonged studies of fetal development in vitro, particularly if early embryos were used. While many biologists and medical investigators do not consider such studies to be unethical, there is sufficient public criticism of this work that any study of this sort needs the most meticulous scrutiny. However, the outright condemnation of such investigations must be deplored.

## CLONING

Cloning of man would involve the creation of a human being who was genetically identical to the donor of a somatic cell nucleus implanted in an enucleated egg. Cloning has been accomplished in amphibians and has been discussed as a possibility for mammals (33, 34). Huxley anticipated the process by the Bokhanovski procedure in his *Brave New World*. If cloning of man ever became possible, there is no reason to believe that it would be widely used, even for medical purposes. Cloning as a means of dealing with genetic disease by duplicating either the mother's or the father's genotype is unlikely to be utilized.

The creation of groups of cloned military scientists or brute soldiers in the service of a state bent to conquer the world is a remote possibility. If such an event were to occur, one might presume that other countries would respond by cloning similar groups of individuals. However, simpler ways of subjugating people would probably be more attractive to politicians than cloning, because clones would take as long to develop as any normal human being. Extensive discussions of cloning can be found elsewhere (42, 43). Since so many ethical problems of immediate urgency are with us now,

problems associated with cloning can be dealt with in due course—if they ever arise.

## GENE THERAPY: GENETIC ENGINEERING

Recent developments in molecular biology allow the synthesis of genes, and the possibility of introducing genes into cells by viral transduction has been raised. As a result, much recent discussion has been devoted to gene therapy (35). More generally, even the possibility of creating human beings to genetic specifications has been raised. Unfortunately, too much has been promised in this field. First of all, only defects in Mendelian traits whose biochemistry is understood (or possibly polygenic traits to which a major gene contributes) could be approached with gene therapy. We know next to nothing about the control mechanisms of mammalian cells. While a gene whose messenger RNA can be isolated can now be manufactured relatively easily, its safe introduction into the nucleus of a specialized cell followed by normal function remains exceedingly problematical. Moreover, each genetic disease presents different problems of gene therapy. While gene therapy of somatic cells appears far away, gene therapy of eggs or sperm, or of gonads, with ultimate genetic cure may never be achieved (36). A group of scientists interested in gene therapy have disclaimed an interest in that aspect of gene therapy which would preserve detrimental genes or maintain them in the population [see (37)].

Clinical investigations of gene therapy by means of viral transduction will raise serious ethical problems because of the possibility of untoward consequences such as cancer. Initially, gene therapy could be tried only for the most severe and lethal diseases, and only after very careful animal experimentation. However, most genetic diseases which are conceptually amenable to gene therapy are individually rare. The more common genetic diseases and birth defects are multifactorial and would not respond to gene therapy unless a major manipulatable gene could be identified. Most normal traits are polygenic, so that the manufacture of a man according to genetic specifications must remain in the realm of science fiction. The genetic manipulation of viruses for the prevention of viral diseases, possibly including cancer, is more likely to be achieved than is the management of genetic diseases by gene therapy. Similarly, genetic engineering of plants to provide more food for hungry man is another exciting possibility. In general, it has become clear that the techniques of intrauterine diagnosis and abortion of defective fetuses will be of much greater importance in the control of birth defects than will gene therapy.

## SUMMARY

Recent developments in biology and medicine are raising new problems in the prevention and treatment of birth defects, and in research on these diseases. The problems include immediate issues such as genetic counseling, abortion for birth defects, the withholding of complex treatments from individuals in some situations, screening for genetic and other diseases, artificial insemination, and fertilization in vitro. Other problems, such as the dysgenic effects of modern medicine and the possibilities of cloning and gene therapy, are more remote. Each of these issues should be considered on its own merits and by its immediate and remote consequences rather than by a priori absolute criteria. Ways must be found to deal with these issues in a manner acceptable to most human beings. Open discussions and freedom from coercion are the best guarantees for ultimate success. The ethical human brain is the highest accomplishment of biologic evolution. By harmonizing our scientific, cultural, and ethical capabilities, the potentially achievable results can place us at the threshold of a new era of better health and less human suffering.

## REFERENCES

1. A. Huxley, *Brave New World* (Harper & Row, New York, 1932).
2. G. Orwell, *1984* (Harcourt, New York, 1949).
3. M. Hamilton, Ed., *The New Genetics and the Future of Man* (Eerdmans, Grand Rapids, Mich., 1972); B. Hilton, D. Callahan, M. Harris, P. Condliffe, B. Berkley, Eds., *Ethical Issues in Human Genetics* (Plenum, New York, 1973).
4. D. Callahan, *Hastings Cent. Stud. No. 1* (1973), p. 66.
5. J. R. Maddox, *The Doomsday Syndrome* (McGraw-Hill, New York, 1972).
6. M. O. Dayhoff, Ed., *Atlas of Protein Sequence and Structure* (National Biomedical Research Foundation, Washington, D. C., 1972), vol. 5.
7. M. C. King and A. C. Wilson, *Genetics* **74,** s140 (1973).
8. G. S. Omenn and A. G. Motulsky, in *Genetics, Environment, and Behavior,* L. Ehrman, G. S. Omenn, E. Caspari, Eds. (Academic Press, New York, 1972), chap. 7, p. 131.
9. C. H. Waddington, *The Ethical Animal* (Atheneum, New York, 1961).
10. J. Fletcher, *N. Engl. J. Med.* **285,** 776 (1971); in *The New Genetics and the Future of Man,* M. Hamilton, Ed. (Eerdmans, Grand Rapids, Mich., 1972), chap. 3, p. 78.
11. B. F. Skinner, *Beyond Freedom and Dignity* (Knopf, New York, 1971).
12. C. Fried, in *Ethical Issues in Human Genetics,* B. Hilton, D. Callahan, M. Harris, P. Condliffe, B. Berkley, Eds. (Plenum, New York, 1973), p. 261.
13. J. Monod, *Chance and Necessity* (Random House, New York, 1971).
14. R. L. Sinsheimer, in *Ethical Issues in Human Genetics,* B. Hilton, D. Callahan, M. Harris, P. Condliffe, B. Berkley, Eds. (Plenum, New York, 1973), p. 341.
15. For a discussion of the current state of medical genetics, see A. G. Motulsky, *Am. J. Hum. Genet.* **23,** 107 (1971).
16. C. O. Carter, K. A. Evans, J. A. F. Roberts, A. R. Buck, *Lancet* **1971-I,** 281 (1971).
17. C. O. Leonard, G. A. Chase, B. Childs, *N. Engl. J. Med.* **287,** 433 (1972).
18. B. Childs, personal communication.
19. A. Milunsky, *The Prenatal Diagnosis of Hereditary Disorders* (Thomas, Springfield, Ill., 1973).
20. A. G. Motulsky, G. R. Fraser, J. Falsenstein, *Natl. Found. March Dimes Birth Defects Orig. Art. Ser.* **7** (No. 5), 22 (1971).
21. F. Crick, cited in *Nature (Lond.)* **220,** 429 (1968).
22. A. Etzioni, *Science* **161,** 1107 (1968).

23. A. G. Motulsky, *Israel J. Med. Sci.* **9**, 1341 (1973).

24. G. Stamatoyannopoulos, in *Proceedings of the Fourth International Conference on Birth Defects,* Vienna, Austria, September 1973, in press.

25. M. M. Kaback and J. S. O'Brien, in *Medical Genetics,* V. McKusick and R. Claiborne, Eds. (HP Publishing, New York, 1973).

26. Testing for Tay-Sachs carrier status requires an assay of hexosaminidase A. The level of this enzyme in the plasma increases during normal pregnancy. However, white cells can still be used to discriminate between normal and carrier pregnant women. Carrier testing during pregnancy, therefore, would be technically more difficult but probably could be worked out logistically.

27. J. L. Goldstein, H. G. Schrott, W. R. Hazzard, E. L. Bierman, A. G. Motulsky, *J. Clin. Invest.* **52**, 1544 (1973).

28. E. B. Hook, *Science* **179**, 139 (1973).

29. H. Muller, *Perspect. Biol. Med.* **3**, 1 (1959).

30. L. R. Kass, *N. Engl. J. Med.* **285**, 1174 (1971).

31. R. G. Edwards, in *The Biological Revolution: Social Good or Social Evil?* W. Fuller, Ed. (Doubleday, New York, 1972), chap. 9, p. 128; in *Proceedings of the Fourth International Conference on Birth Defects,* Vienna, Austria, September 1973, in press.

32. Editorial, *J. Am. Med. Assoc.* **220** (No. 5), 721 (1972).

33. J. Lederberg, in *Challenging Biological Problems,* J. A. Behnke, Ed. (Oxford Univ. Press, New York, 1972), chap. 1, p. 7; *Am. Nat.* **100**, 519 (1966).

34. B. D. Davis, *Science* **170**, 1279 (1970); P. Ramsey, *Fabricated Man* (Yale Univ. Press, New Haven, Conn., 1970).

35. T. Friedmann and R. Roblin, *Science* **175**, 949 (1972).

36. E. Freese, Ed., *The Prospects of Gene Therapy* [Fogarty International Center Conference Report, Department of Health, Education, and Welfare, Publ. No. (NIH) 72-61, 1972].

37. Supported in part by PHS grant GM-15253.

## SUGGESTIONS FOR FURTHER READING

Barber, B. Research on human subjects: Problems of access to a powerful profession. *Social Problems,* 1973, *21,* 103–112. Reasons are given for the criticism aimed at sociological research concerning minorities. Constraints within the field that either facilitate or hinder obtaining hitherto excluded knowledge concerning minorities are discussed.

Bersoff, D. N. The ethical practice of school psychology: A rebuttal and suggested model. *Professional Psychology,* 1973, *4,* 305–312. A model is offered for ethical practice in school psychology. Suggestions are made for ethical practice, including the involvement of both parents and child in assessing processes to be used and the sharing of assessment impressions immediately following treatment sessions. Also recommended are opportunities to clarify or disagree with evaluations made by the psychologist.

Blumfeld, A. Ethical problems in child guidance. *British Journal of Medical Psychology,* 1974, *47,* 17–26. A case of a 13-year-old boy in a child-guidance clinic is described. The boy's difficulties resulted in a conflict between the parent and the clinic staff over the manner in which his problems should be treated. Questions are raised about conceptual and practical confusions between staff and clients.

Duff, R. S., & Campbell, A. G. Moral and ethical dilemmas in the special-care nursery. *New England Journal of Medicine,* 1973, *289,* 890–894. Problems are discussed relative to a large special-care nursery where medical technology can prolong life for infants with poor prognoses, and where parents can affect management decisions concerning their infants. Also discussed are the finality of such decisions, the possible error in prognoses, and issues that influence the kinds of decisions that are made.

Etzioni, A. Stimulus/response: Doctors know more than they're telling you about genetic defects. *Psychology Today,* June 1973, pp. 26–36; 137. Since doctors make judgments about whether expectant parents should be told about possible genetic abnormalities of the fetus, a counsel of "wise people" should be instituted to deal with such new technologies. Such a procedure would take the decisions about how to use such new methods away from individual professionals and, instead, place it in the hands of the public.

Garbin, J. P. Professional values vs. personal beliefs in drug abuse. *Social Work,* 1974, *19,* 333–337. This article concerns the professional social worker in the area of drug abuse whose personal beliefs may conflict with his or her professional responsibilities. Also discussed are the stresses that workers may experience in dealing with drug addiction, influences of a professional code of ethics, and legal considerations.

Gergen, K. J. The codification of research ethics: Views of a Doubting Thomas. *American Psychologist*, 1973, *28*, 907–912. The current code of ethical standards for research in psychology is critically examined. Certain research procedures that are perceived as violating the code of ethics have not been empirically tested; and the establishment of such codes without any empirical justifications seems to be unwise. It is suggested that in place of ethical codes, empirically based advisory statements should be required. A codification of ethics that determines or defines research parameters solely from the standpoint of the subject population is seen to obscure the interpretation of experimental results.

Glass, B. Evolution in human hands. *Phi Delta Kappan*, 1969, *50*, 506–510. Glass examines factors that bring about genetic changes in populations and discusses possibilities for controlling evolution for the betterment of the species.

Plaus, F. X. Privacy: Right, privilege, responsibility, and control. *Ontario Psychologist*, 1973, *5*(4), 4–10. The individual's right to privacy is discussed, along with the need for professionals to respect such privacy. The ethics of privileged communication and the professional's responsibility for matters of privacy are also considered.

Robinson, D. N. Harm, offense, and nuisance: Some first steps in the establishment of an ethics of treatment. *American Psychologist*, 1974, *29*, 233–238. This discussion of ethical issues relates to the involuntary treatment of individuals who have not consented to such treatment or who are unable rationally to give their consent. Court decisions involving First-Amendment rights are discussed, along with their implications for the state's right to involve individuals in involuntary therapy or hospitalization.

Seeman, J. Deception in psychological research. *American Psychologist*, 1969, *24*, 1025–1028. This article focuses on deception in research and various aspects of this problem.

Shaw, A. Dilemmas of "informed consent" in children. *New England Journal of Medicine*, 1973, *289*, 885–890. The question is considered whether parents have the right to give consent regarding surgery on minor children and whether this means that they also have the right to deny consent when such denial can mean death for the child. Certain ethical, moral, and legal questions about the rights and obligations of physicians, hospital staff, parents, and society are also discussed.

# Glossary

acculturation: the process by which an individual learns the attitudes, modes of thinking, and behaviors characteristic of the larger social group or culture.

affective: pertaining to feeling or emotion.

age-specific: characteristic of a particular age.

alternative family: any of the family living styles other than that of the traditional two-parent nuclear family.

alternative school: any form of schooling other than that which is currently typical in the public schools of the country.

amniocentesis: perforation or tapping, as by a needle, of the innermost membrane of the sac enclosing the embryo.

anoxia: a physiological condition caused by an insufficient supply of oxygen.

antihemophilic globulin: a sterile preparation that contains a small amount of human plasma capable of reducing the usual clotting time of bleeding, used in the treatment of hemophilia (see definition).

apgar ratings: the condition of the newborn based on certain criteria including, among others, color, heart rate, muscle tone, and respiration.

aptitude: a natural ability in some particular skill or area of learning.

autism: the condition of being completely dominated by subjective, self-centered trends of thoughts and behavior.

autoerotic: pertaining to the gratification of sex feeling by one's own acts or thoughts without participation by anyone else.

behavior genetics: that area of genetics concerned with the study of hereditary factors in behavior.

behaviorist: one who treats objective, observable manifestations as critical for understanding human behavior. Subjective consciousness and feeling are dismissed as unessential or considered as mediating processes between stimulus and response.

bioethic standards: conduct and moral judgment pertaining to the study and treatment of living organisms.

catharsis (drive reduction): a cleansing or purgation. In Freudian terms, the patient purges the mind of repressed material by telling whatever comes into the mind (free association).

child psychology: the division of psychology concerned with child behaviors, both normal and abnormal.

chimeras: impossible or foolish fancies.

cloning: the process of asexual reproduction in which the progeny have a single parent and identical heredity.

cognitive: relating to processes of awareness, knowing, and thinking.

cognitive style: the characteristic way an individual organizes his or her approach to mental tasks, including specific ways of relating to the problem at hand.

commune: a close-knit community of people who share common interests and activities, as in the area of child rearing.

compensatory education: schooling especially designed to expedite the academic progress of children who suffer some sociocultural or economic disadvantage.

conditioning: a training process designed to establish a predictable response. In its classical sense, when two stimuli—an adequate one and an inadequate one—are presented simultaneously to an organism on successive occasions, the inadequate stimulus acquires the potential of evoking a response similar to that normally aroused by the adequate stimulus.

constancy hypothesis: the theory that if a stimulus produces a particular sensation or perception on one occasion, the same stimulus will bring about the same response, even in other environments, provided that the condition of the organism remains unchanged.

*counterculture:* a culture, or way of life, that develops within a larger culture and has no real substance of its own; its only function is to criticize the major culture, and its activities reflect reactions to that culture.

*critical period:* time during which particular experiences may have especially profound and enduring effects.

*cryoprecipitate:* a precipitate that forms when soluble material is very cold.

*cultural pluralism:* conceptualization of a culture as composed of more than one relatively distinct subculture, each with its own characteristic lifestyle and ways of behaving.

*cultural relativism:* the theory that criteria of judgment are dependent on the particular culture (way of life of a people) involved.

*defense mechanism:* a reaction intended to maintain the individual's feelings of adequacy and worth.

*deprivation:* a condition characterized by deficiency of material and/or nonmaterial benefits normally enjoyed by members of a given society, especially because of poverty or membership in a minority group.

*developmental permutations:* variations from the normal course of development.

*developmental psychology:* the branch of psychology concerned with characteristic behaviors at successive stages of development and the processes involved in moving from one stage to another.

*developmental quotient:* a measure of a child's overall rate of development, as compared with that of other children the same age.

*dialysis:* separation; dissolution; in chemistry, the separation of crystalloids from colloids in solution by means of the more rapid diffusion of crystalloids through a moist membrane.

*disadvantaged:* persons who, because of some characteristic of the group to which they belong—for example, its social class, race, or religion—are denied the advantages normally enjoyed by members of the society.

*dizygotic (DZ) twins:* twins that develop from two separate fertilized cells (zygotes) and that are no more alike than other siblings. They may be either of the same or of the opposite sex. Also called fraternal twins.

*DNA (deoxyribonucleic acid) and RNA (ribonucleic acid):* two key chemicals in the genes that deter-

mine whether substances causing particular characteristics (for example, blue or brown eyes) will be produced. DNA is believed to contain the chemical blueprint for the cells.

*Down's syndrome:* mongolism; a condition usually characterized by a final mental age between 4 and 7, a small brain, a docile disposition, and a short life span.

*dyad:* a two-person combination.

*dysgenic:* opposite of eugenic; producing a deterioration of hereditary qualities.

*egosyntonic:* possessing a personality in harmony with the environment.

*empirical:* based on observation and experimentation.

*empiricist:* (1) one who uses methods of experiment and observation; (2) one who disregards or is ignorant of scientific principles and relies solely on practical experience.

*environmentalist:* one who stresses the role of environment, as compared with heredity, in the development of the organism.

*ethics:* the code or system of morals of a particular group.

*etiology:* the study of origins and causes.

*eugenic:* relating to the study and arrangement of conditions conducive to the improvement of future generations' mental and physical characteristics.

*Fabry's disease:* a disease characterized by abnormal accumulations in various tissues and resulting in serious symptoms, including edema of the legs and paresthesias of the extremities. The condition may lead to uremia, hypertension, or even death.

*field dependent:* incapable of isolating an object from compelling background forces.

*field independent:* capable of isolating an object from compelling background forces.

*fraternal twins:* dizygotic twins; twins developed from two eggs.

*free schools:* schools that emphasize unusual freedom for teachers and pupils with regard to curricular and extracurricular activities.

*gene:* an inferred submicroscopic structure within the chromosome that constitutes the ultimate physical unit of heredity and that is transmitted in the germ cell from parent to offspring.

*genocide:* the systematic extermination or killing of a people.

*hemophilia:* a hereditary condition in which the blood fails to clot properly so that uncontrollable bleeding may occur. It occurs in males and is transmitted by females.

*hereditarian:* one who emphasizes the role of heredity, as opposed to environment, in the development of the organism.

*heredity:* a term denoting the totality of factors transmitted to an individual from his ancestors, as well as the process by which an organism produces comparable organisms—including mechanical details of transmission of such characters through factors in the gene plasm.

*heterozygous:* having one or more recessive characteristics and, therefore, not breeding true to type; hybrid.

*hippies:* a contemporary version of the Bohemian who believe in liberty, living for the moment, and completely free self-expression.

*homeostatic:* pertaining to the maintenance of balance or constancy in the bodily processes.

*homeostatic adjustment:* the establishment of balance within the bodily processes.

*humanist:* one who is philosophically concerned with the ideas and ideals of human beings.

*Huntington's chorea:* a rare form of psychosis involving rapid neurological deterioration and finally death.

*hyperkinetic:* characterized by excessive muscular activity observed in many disordered psychical and physical states.

*hypermotility:* characterized by excessive movement.

*hypothesis:* an admittedly tentative explanation of a body of data.

*identical twins:* monozygotic twins; twins developed from one egg.

*identification:* the process of merging one's goals with those of another or modeling after another.

*ideology:* the doctrines, opinions, or way of thinking of an individual or group.

*imprinting:* form of learning in very young animals that determines the course an instinctive behavior will take; for example, a gosling learns to follow whatever moving object it sees during some specific, relatively brief period.

*infanticide:* the murder of a baby.

*innate:* inborn; congenital.

*instinct:* an enduring tendency to act in an organized way that is innate, complex, relatively unvarying,.and common to the species. Recently the term has been more loosely defined as behavior that is the product of maturation rather than learning.

*intellectualization:* a defense mechanism that consists in analyzing a problem in intellectual terms in order to avoid confronting one's own emotions.

*intuitive:* having knowledge of something without the conscious use of reason.

*in vitro:* observable in a test tube.

*IQ:* intelligence quotient, a score derived from an intelligence test indicating how the individual's demonstrated mental ability compares with that of others at the same developmental stage.

*kibbutz:* a collective farm settlement in Israel.

*Klinefelter's syndrome:* a pattern of medical symptoms that includes excessive development of the male mammary glands, involvement of gonads, and urinary secretion.

*longitudinal research:* research involving repeated observations of or measurements on the same individuals over a span of time.

*matrix:* that within which something exists or occurs, giving it meaning.

*maturation:* developmental changes based on heredity, in contrast to those deriving from environmental conditions.

*megalomanic:* characterized by having delusions of greatness.

*memory trace:* a presumed change within the nervous system that persists between the time that something is learned and the time it is consciously recalled.

*menarche:* the establishment or beginning of the menstrual function.

*microcosm:* a miniature universe; any locality or situation that might be regarded as a miniature of the world.

*monozygotic (MZ) twins:* identical twins; twins derived from splitting of a single fertilized egg, or zygote.

*moral relativism:* the theory that the basis of morality is relative, differing according to time, place, circumstance, and persons involved.

*mother-surrogate:* any person or object acting as a substitute for the mother.

*motor abreaction:* a process of working off a disagreeable experience or feelings through muscular or motor expression.

*multifactorial:* relating to, or involving, more than one factor.

*mutant gene:* a gene in which an abrupt variation in character has occurred that henceforth duplicates itself in the new form.

*neonate:* the newly born.

*neuropsychiatric:* involving both nervous and psychological upset.

*neurosis:* see psychoneurosis.

*nuclear family:* the family composed only of the father, mother, and children, as distinct from the extended family, which includes all the descendants of a common grandparent and all their relatives.

*nurturance:* an attitude on the part of the parent,

usually the mother, of warmth and assistance toward the child.

*nurturant-supportive:* involving warmth and involvement (personal love and compassion).

*obsessive-compulsive:* characterized by disturbing and persistent thoughts (obsession) and repetition of ritualistic and irrational behaviors.

*Oedipal:* having a repressed desire for sex relations with the parent of the opposite sex.

*Oedipal theory:* a complex of beliefs associated with the idea that the boy identifies with his father and loves his mother.

*Oneida community:* a settlement of communists at Oneida, Madison County, New York, founded in the mid-19th century. The marriage system was complex, with no ceremony or permanent ties between couples, and the community assumed responsibility for the education of the children. This marriage system was abandoned in 1879; and community of property was displaced by a system of cooperative privileges.

*organismic:* pertaining to an organism, or any living creature capable of maintaining itself.

*pathological:* pertaining to a diseased or abnormal condition of the organism or its parts.

*perinatal:* occurring at, or pertaining to, the time of birth.

*phenylketonuria* (PKU): a type of congenitally faulty metabolism often associated with mental defects.

*pluralistic society:* a group of persons forming a single community overall, composed of more than one relatively distinct subculture.

*polygenic:* having more than one source or origin.

*prosocial:* approved by, or favorable to, society in general.

*provincialism:* narrowness of outlook.

*psychoanalysis:* a body of doctrine associated with Freud and modified by his followers; a special technique for discovering hidden motivation.

*psychoneurosis:* a somewhat poorly defined class of mental disorder, less serious than psychosis, and leaving the personality relatively intact.

*psychosis:* the scientific name for severe mental disturbances; commonly called insanity.

*pyloric stenosis:* a condition characterized by a narrowing or stricture of a duct or canal through which the stomach contents enter the duodenum.

*retinoblastoma:* a tumor having its origin in retinal germ cells.

*retrospective study:* research based on recollection of such past experiences as may have been relevant to the subject of investigation.

*schemata:* basic elements in cognitive organization, or mental life.

*schizophrenia:* a group of psychotic reactions characterized by distortions of reality and by extreme intellectual, emotional, and behavioral disturbances.

*self-actualization:* the process of moving through sequentially higher stages of motivation and organization to adequate achievement of one's potential.

*sensory threshold:* the minimum intensity at which a stimulus becomes effective, or apparent to the sense.

*sex role:* the pattern of behaviors characteristic of male or female in a particular society.

*sex-role biculturalism:* participation in the way of life traditionally associated with both sexes.

*sharpening:* a process of carefully distinguishing differences in perceived objects.

*socialization:* the process by which an individual learns to behave like, and to get along with, others in the society and culture.

*sociocentric:* having primary focus on the group.

*sociopathy:* a condition characterized by hostility toward society.

*sonographic:* pertaining to mechanical recording of sound.

*stress:* a condition created by abnormal tension, especially when no ready solution is available for a crucial problem.

*superego:* conscience; the aspect of the psyche that holds the id (primitive impulses) in check.

*tabula rasa:* (1) blank slate; (2) the mind before impressions are recorded on it.

*trait:* an enduring or persistent characteristic that distinguishes one individual from another.

*transcendental:* supernatural; in Kantian philosophy, transcending human experience but not knowledge; pertaining to a metaphysical system that seeks the essence of reality through investigating processes of thought rather than the content of experience.

*transduction:* transmission of power from one system to another.

*traumatic:* productive of psychological or physical shock to the organism.

*triage:* the sorting out and classification of wounded persons who have been brought for treatment to a hospital.

*Turner's syndrome:* a pattern of symptoms that includes retarded growth and sexual development, webbing of neck, and low posterior hairline margin.

*value:* in the ethical sense, the worth an individual ascribes to various activities, ideas, and objects.

*vasectomy:* surgical removal of the vas deferens, or duct that conveys sperm from the testicle to the ejaculatory duct of the penis.

*vernacular:* the everyday language of the ordinary people in a particular locality.

*vestibular stimulation:* the application to receptors within the semicircular canals of the inner ear of an appropriate form of physical energy.

*vicarious:* experienced by someone through imagined, instead of actual, participation in an experience.

*viral transduction:* the process of transmitting a virus from one location to another.

*yippie:* a relatively aggressive, fun-loving, hippie-type person.

*Zionist:* an individual supportive of the movement for establishing, lately of advancing, the Jewish national state in Palestine.

*zygote:* a cell formed by the union of two gametes, or reproductive cells.

# Index

J